Collins

CW00552816

KS3 SCIENCE NOW

LEARN AND PRACTICE BOOK

TRACEY BAXTER, AMANDA CLEGG, KAREN COLLINS AND ED WALSH

William Collins' dream of knowledge for all began with the publication of his first book in 1819.
A self-educated mill worker, he not only enriched millions of lives, but also founded a flourishing publishing house. Today, staying true to this spirit, Collins books are packed with inspiration, innovation and practical expertise. They place you at the centre of a world of possibility and give you exactly what you need to explore it.

Collins. Freedom to teach.

Published by Collins
An imprint of HarperCollins*Publishers*
The News Building, 1 London Bridge Street, London, SE1 9GF, UK

HarperCollins*Publishers*
1st Floor, Watermarque Building, Ringsend Road, Dublin 4, Ireland

Browse the complete Collins catalogue at
collins.co.uk

10 9 8 7 6 5 4 3 2 1

ISBN 978-0-00-853152-2

British Library Cataloguing-in-Publication Data
A catalogue record for this publication is available from the British Library.

Authors: Tracey Baxter, Amanda Clegg, Karen Collins and Ed Walsh
Publisher: Katie Sergeant
Product manager: Joanna Ramsay
Product developer: Holly Woolnough
Development editors: Jessica Ashdale, Gillian Lindsey, Julie Thornton
Copyeditor: Aidan Gill
Proofreader: Julie Gorman
Answer checker: Life Lines Editorial Services
Illustrator: Ann Paganuzzi
Cover designer: Happy Designers
Internal designer: Ken Vail Graphic Design
Typesetter: Jouve and 2Hoots
Production controller: Alhady Ali
Printed and bound by Martins the Printers

This book has been endorsed by The WISE Campaign for gender balance in Science, Technology, Engineering and Maths (STEM) - WiseCampaign.org.uk

MIX
Paper | Supporting responsible forestry
FSC™ C007454
FSC
www.fsc.org

This book is produced from independently certified FSC™ paper to ensure responsible forest management.

For more information visit: www.harpercollins.co.uk/green

Contents

1 Cells and organisation road map

Where are you in your learning journey and where are you aiming to be?

1.3 Studying cells

- identify microscope parts
- describe observing cells
- interpret evidence

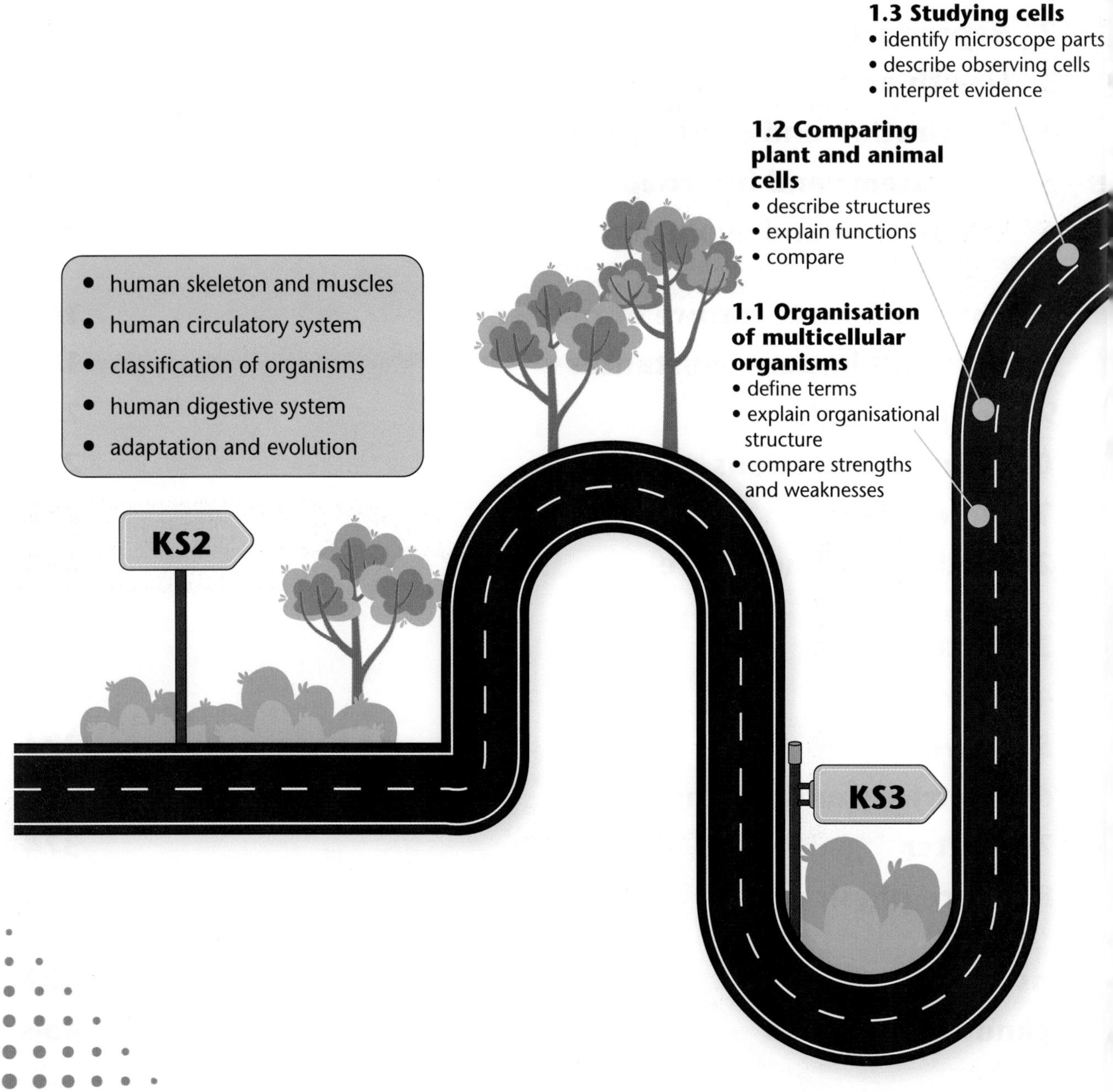

1.4 Unicellular organisms
- recognise organisms
- describe differences
- compare adaptations

1.5 Specialised cells
- classify specialised cells
- describe examples
- explain link between structure and function

1.6 Movement in and out of cells: diffusion
- define processes
- describe examples
- explain factors affecting diffusion

- eukaryotes and prokaryotes
- animal and plant cells
- cell specialisation
- microscopy

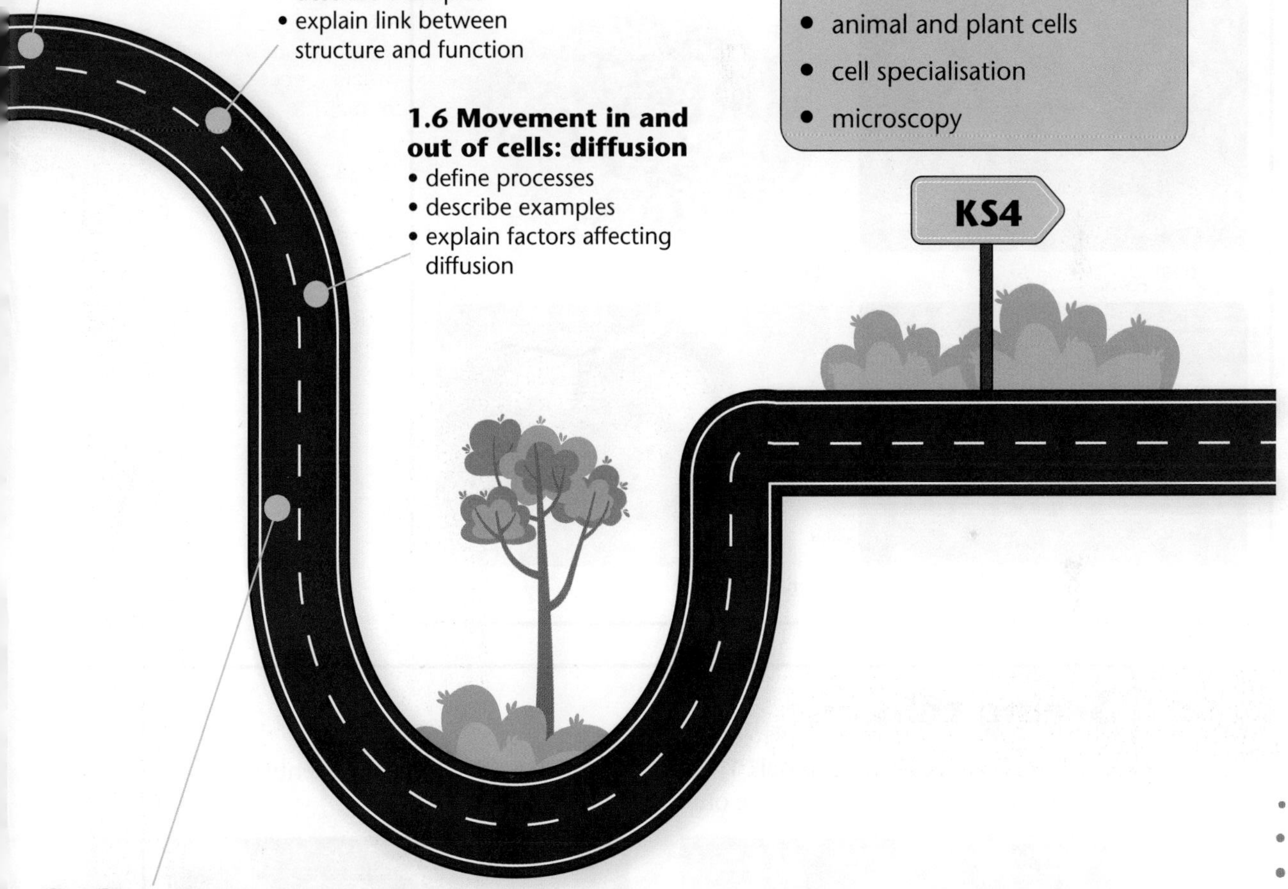

Maths and practical skills

- describing the development of scientific methods and theories over time, including publishing results and peer review
- carrying out scientific enquiries to test predictions
- observing and measuring, including the evaluation of repeatability
- interpreting observations and data
- presenting reasoned explanations
- using SI units and chemical names
- deriving and using simple equations

1 Cells and organisation

All living organisms are made of cells – they are the building blocks of life. Cells cannot be seen except under a microscope; this is why it took so long to discover them. Some organisms are made of only one cell; most are made of millions of cells working together.

How many cells?

Look at these living organisms. Do you think they are made from one cell or more? Which do you think are the most complex?

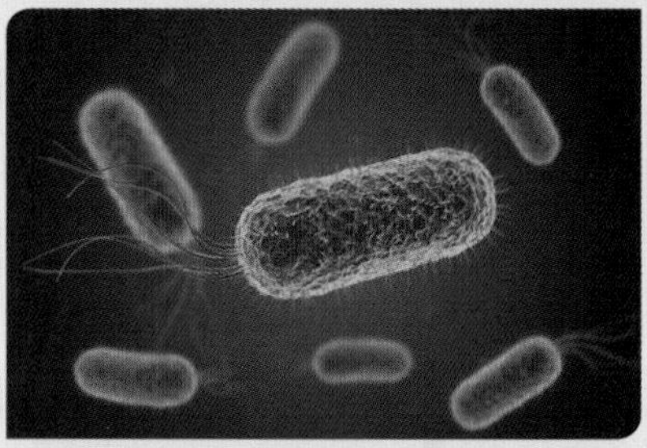

bacterium

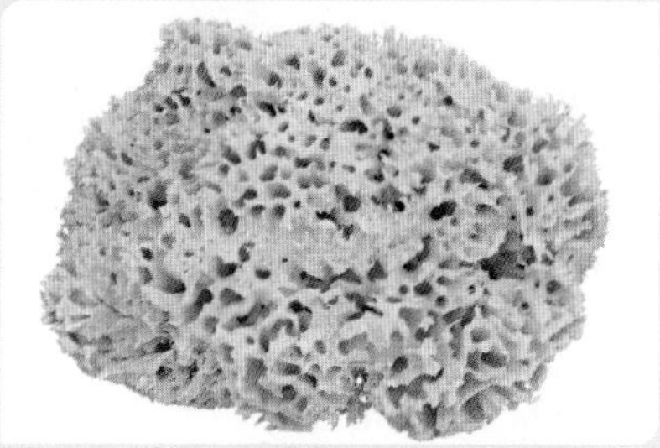

sponge

moss

human

Seeing cells

Have you ever been to hospital? Think about the ways doctors and scientists can explore what is happening inside our bodies.

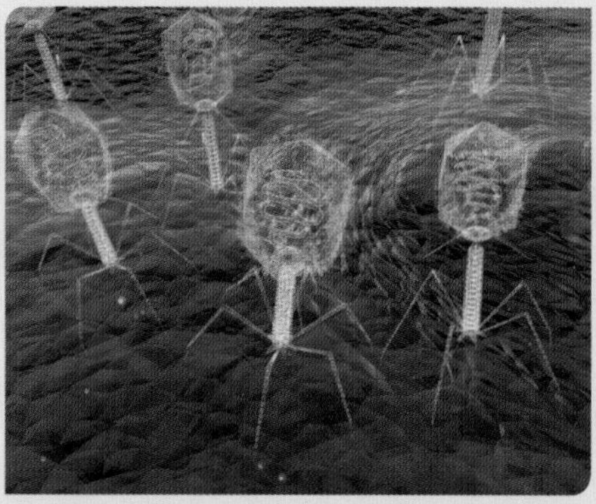

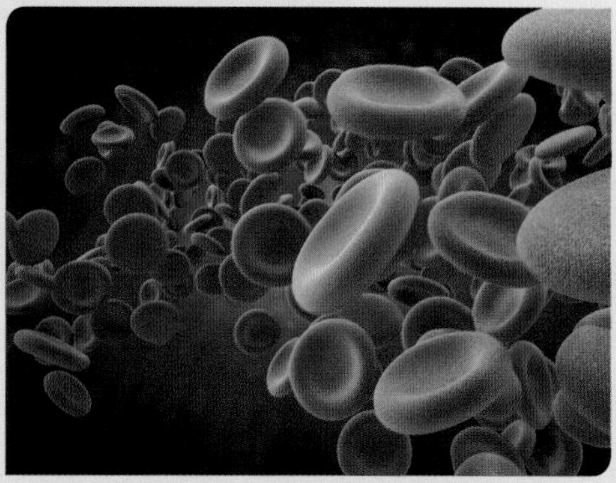

Micrographs of viruses (left) and red blood cells (right)

The development of microscopes has meant that we can see individual cells. The most powerful microscopes can even see viruses. What differences would it make to our lives if we did not have this technology?

Using your science skills

Could you be a pathologist?

You make accurate decisions while being thorough because your advice could save lives. Doctors, nurses and surgeons rely on your judgements and advice in treating patients with cancer and other diseases. Strength and resilience are needed because there will be times when, sadly, the team cannot cure the patient.

Being a pathologist means working with the latest technology to study cells, tissues and diseases. This means that you need to recognise what a wide range of cells and their parts should look like so that you can identify quickly and reliably when things are not normal. You also need to be able to link cell structure to function to help with making a diagnosis. You are part of a team of dedicated professionals, all working to improve the lives of patients. Pathologists also play a critical role in researching and developing more accurate diagnoses and treatments, improving lives not only now but also in the future.

Microbiologists study microorganisms such as bacteria, viruses and fungi. Some study diseases caused by microbes while others study how we can use microbes to help us. They work all around the world studying how microbes help us in medicine and food production.

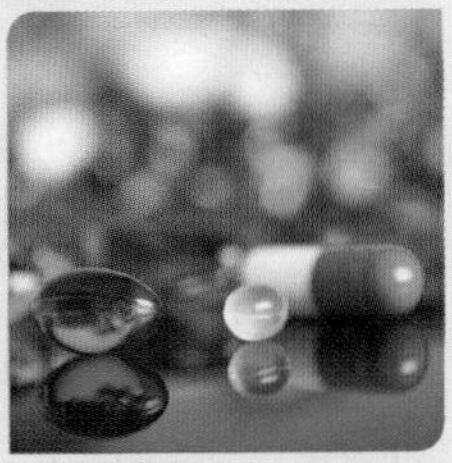

Pharmaceutical researchers study the effects of drugs on cells and organisms. Researchers need to understand how well drugs diffuse in and out of cells as this affects how well they work as medicines. This research is a hugely important step in the process of licensing medicines for human use.

Zoologists study animals, their behaviour and their interactions with their surroundings. This allows us to understand how animals are adapted to their environment, which is key to wildlife conservation. This helps us to learn how organisms have adapted to their environment. Some zoologists work in the outdoors, all over the world, whereas others work in a laboratory or a zoo.

Botanists are plant biologists. Some study plant structures to try and find useful chemicals produced by plants. Lots of medicines originally came from plants, such as aspirin and morphine. Others may study plant genetics and development to improve crop yield and agriculture.

Fertility scientists may study sperm cells to try and help people who would like to have a baby. Microscopes are used to check whether enough sperm cells are produced, and to look at the sperm cells in detail to observe any abnormalities.

Ophthalmic laboratory technicians make lenses for glasses and contact lenses and also for equipment such as microscopes and telescopes. Microscopes are vital to allow us to study cells and microorganisms. Laboratory technicians usually learn these skills on the job as they use very precise and high-technology machinery in their work.

Knowledge organiser

'Multi' means many; 'uni' means one.

Multicellular organisms contain many cells; **unicellular** organisms are made of only one or a single cell.

Organelles are parts of cells that have specific functions (jobs).

↓

Cells are the building blocks of living things.

↓

Groups of similar cells form a **tissue**.

↓

Different tissues work together to make up an **organ**.

↓

Organs work together to make an **organ system**.

↓

Organ systems work together to form **organisms**.

A **light microscope** is used to **magnify** objects that are too small to see with the unaided eye. With a light microscope, we can observe microscopic organisms, such as bacteria, and inside cells to see the cell parts and organelles.

Electron microscopes allow much greater magnification than light microscopes. They are bigger and more expensive than light microscopes. They use a beam of electrons to form a very detailed image of a sample.

Organisms can be classed into two groups based on how their genetic material is stored.

Prokaryotes:

- thought to be the first organisms on Earth
- all are unicellular
- don't have a nucleus
- have very few organelles
- example: bacteria.

Eukaryotes:

- usually bigger and more complex than prokaryotes
- some are unicellular, most are multicellular
- genetic material is stored in a nucleus
- have other organelles, such as mitochondria
- examples: animals, plants, fungi, amoeba.

Unicellular organisms are simply a cell with organelles working together. Unicellular organisms are adapted in different ways. Examples are:

- **bacteria** – there are many types of bacteria but all have no nucleus
- **algae** – these are plant-like and contain chloroplasts to make their own food
- **yeasts** – these are fungus-like and absorb nutrients from their surroundings.

Bacterium

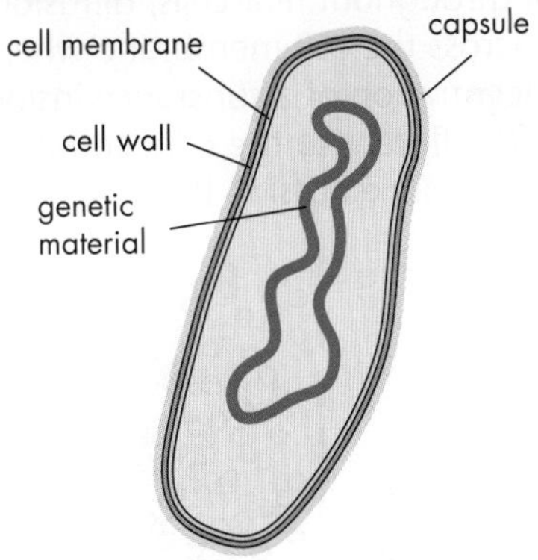

Animal cells and plant cells have some cell parts or organelles in common but some differences too. This is because the cells have different functions.

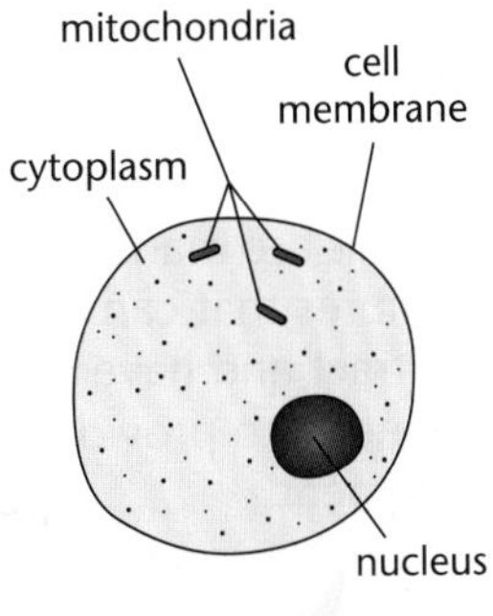

Animal cell

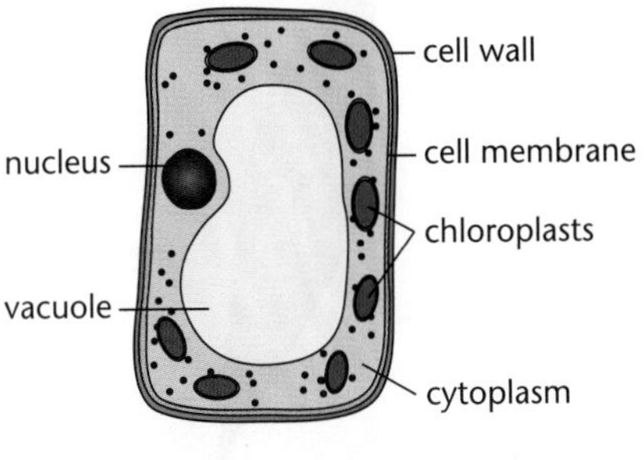

Plant cell

Key vocabulary	
algae	a unicellular organism that has a nucleus and contains chloroplasts for photosynthesis
bacterium	a simple unicellular organism; some bacteria can cause illness
capsule	structure that covers the outer layer of the cell wall of a bacterium
cell	the 'building block' that all living things are made from
cell membrane	the layer around a cell that controls substances entering and leaving the cell
cell wall	the tough outer layer of a plant cell
chloroplast	a structure in plant cells where photosynthesis takes place
cytoplasm	the main component of a cell; the place where reactions take place
electron microscope	an instrument that produces a magnified, detailed image of a sample using a beam of electrons
eukaryote	an organism whose cells store genetic material in a nucleus
genetic material	material that transmits information from one generation to the next during reproduction
light microscope	an optical device used to see magnified images of tiny objects and structures
magnify	to make something look bigger
mitochondria	the structures in a cell that produce energy (by respiration)
multicellular	made of many cells
nucleus	the part of a cell that contains the genetic material
organ	a collection of tissues that work together to perform a function
organelle	a structure in a cell with a specific function (job)
organism	a living thing
organ system	organs that coordinate with one another in body processes
prokaryote	a unicellular organism that has no nucleus
tissue	a collection of body cells that work together to carry out a task
unicellular	made of one cell
vacuole	a bubble of water and nutrients in a plant cell
yeast	a unicellular fungus

Cells in any organism start out exactly the same: these are called **stem cells**. These cells then grow and change their structure to adapt to a certain function. We say the cells become **adapted** and **specialised**.

Movement of substances in and out of cells:

- controlled by the cell membrane
- substances such as glucose and oxygen pass into cells
- waste products such as carbon dioxide and urea pass out of cells
- only some substances allowed through the cell membrane, so it is a **semi-permeable membrane**.

How quickly diffusion happens depends on several factors or **variables**:

- temperature – the higher the temperature, the faster the rate of diffusion
- concentration of particles – the greater the difference in concentration between the two sides of the cell membrane, the faster the rate of diffusion
- **surface area**-to-**volume** ratio – the higher the ratio for a cell, the faster the rate of diffusion.

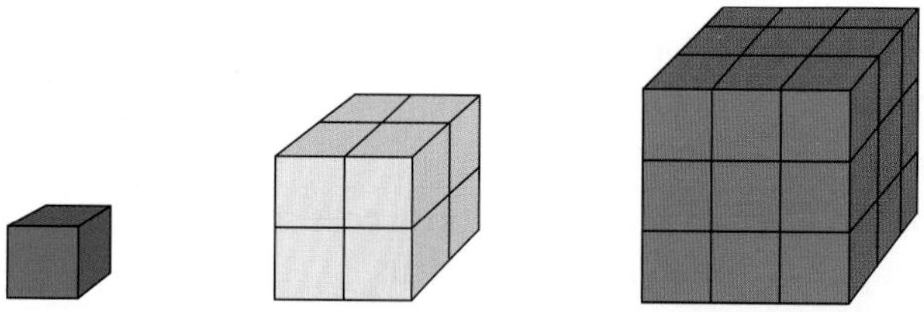

The smaller cube has the highest surface area-to-volume ratio; this means that diffusion can happen at a faster rate across smaller cells than larger cells.

surface area of a cube = area of one side × number of faces

volume of a cube = length × breadth × height

surface area-to-volume ratio = surface area ÷ volume

Diffusion is the movement of substances (in the form of liquid or gas particles) from an area of high **concentration** to an area of lower concentration, until the concentration is equal throughout. For cells, diffusion occurs across the cell membrane when the concentration of a substance inside the cell is different to the concentration of that substance outside the cell.

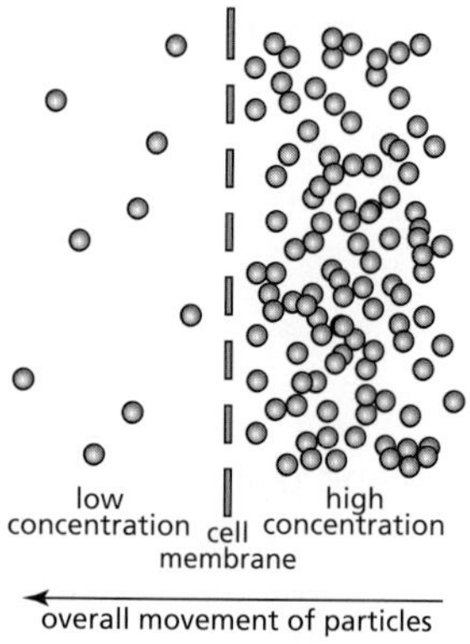

Specialised animal cells include **sperm cells**, **muscle cells**, **nerve cells**, **red blood cells** and **egg cells**. All these cells have a nucleus, cell membrane and cytoplasm, but they look very different.

Sperm cells have a tail to move them and a large head containing a nucleus (this contains the genetic material).

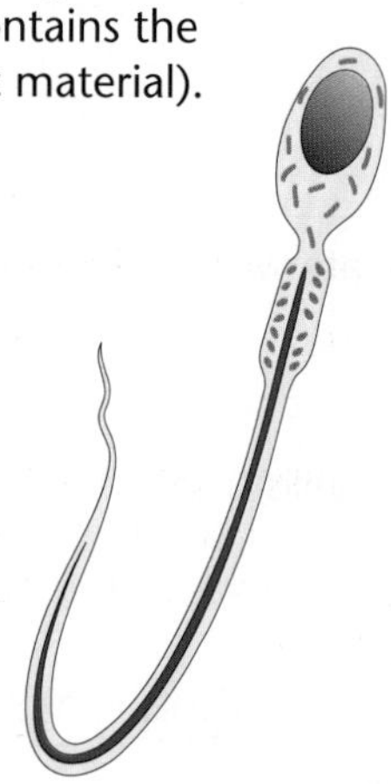

Nerve cells have long extensions of cytoplasm that allow them to transmit impulses around the whole body.

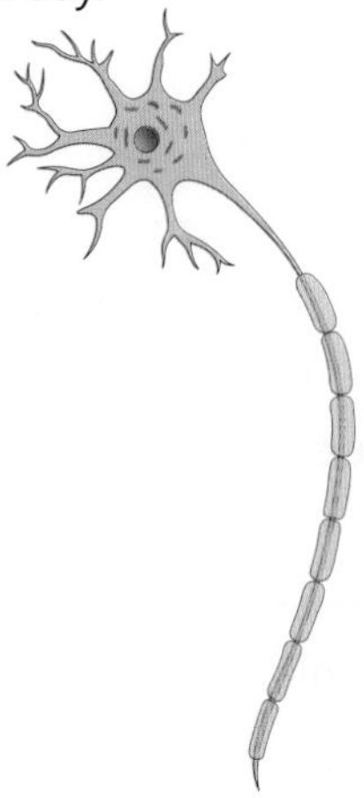

Muscle cells are made of protein fibres that can expand and contract and have lots of mitochondria to provide energy for movement.

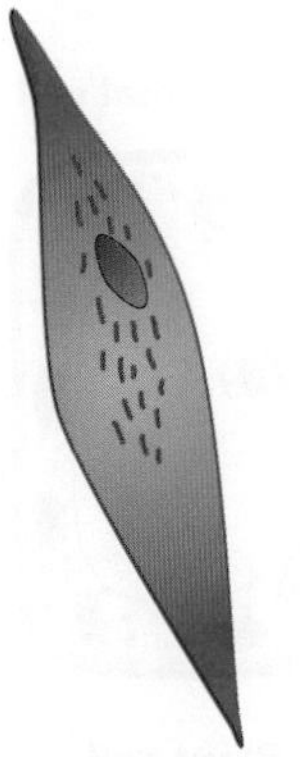

Specialised plant cells include upper **leaf cells**, **root hair cells** and **guard cells**.
Each is adapted to its function (job).

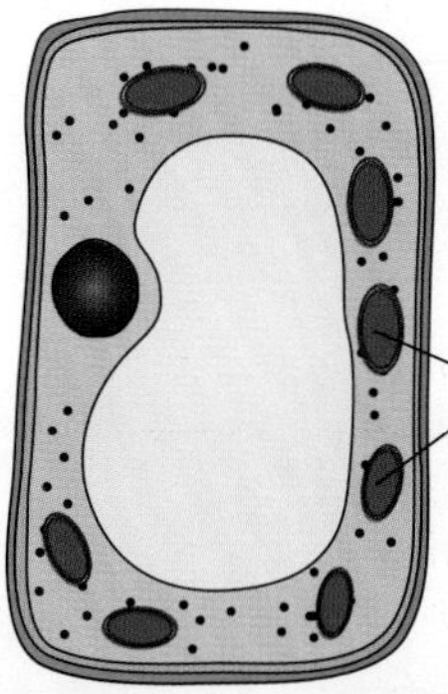

Leaf cells contain chloroplasts to absorb energy transferred from sunlight for photosynthesis.

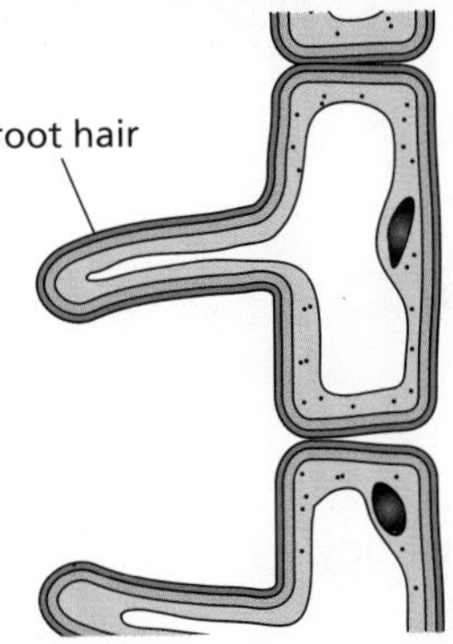

Root hair cells have long extensions, called root hairs, that absorb water into the roots. They do not have chloroplasts, because chloroplasts are needed to absorb energy transferred from sunlight and these cells are not exposed to sunlight.

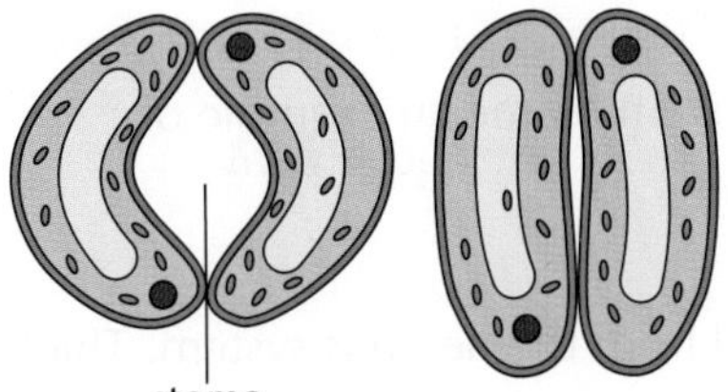

Guard cells can change shape to open a space to allow gas to pass into and out of the leaf.

Key vocabulary	
adapted	having special features that help with a specific function (job)
concentration	the amount of something per unit volume, for example, sugar dissolved in water
diffusion	particle movement that causes particles in a liquid or gas to spread out
egg cell	the female sex cell in animals
guard cell	a specialised leaf cell, found on either side of a stoma (pore), that controls the opening and closing of the stoma
leaf cell	a specialised cell within a leaf; some are specialised for photosynthesis, for example
muscle cell	a specialised body cell that makes up muscle tissue
nerve cell	a specialised body cell that transmits information around the body in the nervous system
red blood cell	a specialised cell in the blood that carries oxygen
root hair cell	a specialised plant cell found on plant roots
semi-permeable membrane	a membrane that allows some, but not all, particles to pass through
specialised cell	a cell that has features that help with a specific function (job)
sperm cell	the male reproductive cell of an animal
stem cell	an unspecialised body cell that can develop into another, specialised cell
stoma	the pores on the underside of a leaf, surrounded by guard cells
surface area	area of the outer surface of an object
variable	something that increases or decreases over time or has a different value in different situations
volume	amount of space an object takes up

1.1 Organisation of multicellular organisms

You are learning to:
- define the terms cell, tissue, organ, organ system and organism
- explain the organisational structure in multicellular organisms
- compare the strengths and weaknesses of unicellular and multicellular organisms.

1. Name the building blocks that all organisms are made from.
2. A group of similar specialised cells working together are called ______________________.
3. What is the name given to a group of different tissues working together?
4. Match each organ to the system it is part of.

heart	digestive system
brain	nervous system
stomach	breathing (respiratory) system
lungs	circulatory system

5. Match each organ to its function.

heart	controls many functions of the body
brain	pumps blood around the body
kidneys	transfer gases between the blood and air
stomach	filter waste from the blood
lungs	digests some foods

6. **a** Describe what 'unicellular' means as in 'a bacterium is a unicellular organism'.
   b Apart from bacteria, name **two** other examples of unicellular organisms.

Worked example

Using the nervous system as an example of a human organ system, name an example of:

a a cell **b** a tissue **c** an organ

that form part of that system.

This is asking for one example of each type of structure and all from the nervous system. Think about what makes up the nervous system.

a brain cells **b** brain tissue **c** brain

The nervous system includes the brain; the brain is made of brain tissue; brain tissue is made of brain cells.

7 Using the human circulatory system as an example, name **one** example of **each** of the following involved with this system:

a a cell

b a tissue

c an organ

d an organ system

e an organism.

8 Unicellular organisms are very successful and make up most life on Earth. Suggest why they are so successful.

Worked example

Multicellular organisms have organs such as a brain and heart. Explain why unicellular organisms do not have organ systems.

This question asks you to **explain**. The first step when answering an explain question is to **state** a fact.

Unicellular organisms are made of only one cell.

Then **explain** why that fact means that unicellular organisms do not have organ systems.

Therefore, cells do not work together as tissues, there are no tissues to form an organ and no organs to form an organ system.

9 Multicellular organisms are able to carry out more complex processes than unicellular organisms. Explain why.

10 The earliest organisms were unicellular. Some of these gradually evolved into multicellular organisms, with tissues and organs. Describe how this may have happened.

Worked example

Yeast is a unicellular organism used in making bread. Bakers need to allow time for the yeast cells to reproduce during the process. Yeast can multiply every 90 minutes.

How long does it take for the number of yeast cells to increase to 8 times the original number?

Assume you are starting with one yeast cell, and calculate how many cells would exist after each 90 minutes.

1 to 2 cells after 90 minutes

2 to 4 cells after 180 minutes (90 + 90)

4 to 8 cells after 270 minutes (90 + 90 + 90)

Therefore, after 270 minutes, there are 8 times as many yeast cells.

11 Some bacteria can reproduce as rapidly as every 20 minutes. Starting from one single bacterium, calculate how many bacteria would exist after 2 hours.

1.2 Comparing plant and animal cells

You are learning to:
- describe the structures found in plant and animal cells
- explain the functions of structures in plant and animal cells
- compare plant and animal cells.

1. To observe cells in a classroom, we need to use a piece of equipment called a ____________________________.

2. Choose **three** parts of a cell that are found in both animal cells and plant cells:
   cell wall
   cell membrane
   nucleus
   chloroplast
   cytoplasm

3. On the diagram below of an animal cell, choose from the words to identify the labels **a**, **b** and **c**:

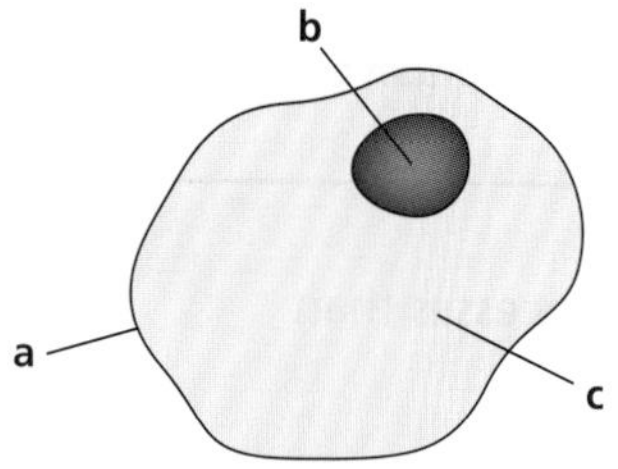

cytoplasm

nucleus

cell membrane

4. On the diagram below of a plant cell, identify the labels **a**, **b**, **c**, **d** and **e**.

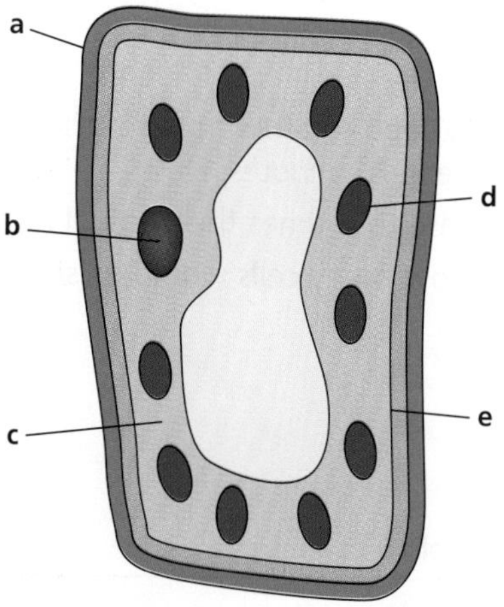

5. Describe the function of each of these parts of a cell:
   a nucleus
   b cell membrane
   c chloroplast.

6 All cells contain cytoplasm. Explain why.

7 This light microscope image shows cells from inside the cheek of an animal.

a Identify the cell parts **i**, **ii** and **iii**.

b Name another organelle present in these cells that we cannot see in this image because it is too small.

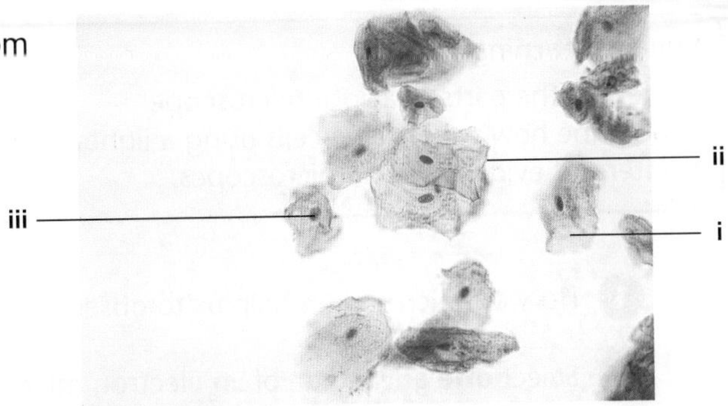

8 Describe the key difference between red blood cells and other animal cells.

Worked example

Charlotte and Abel are trying to decide what type of cell they are looking at.

Charlotte says this must be an animal cell because it doesn't have any chloroplasts and animal cells do not have chloroplasts.

Abel says it must be a plant cell because it has a cell wall and a cell membrane.

Suggest who is correct and explain why.

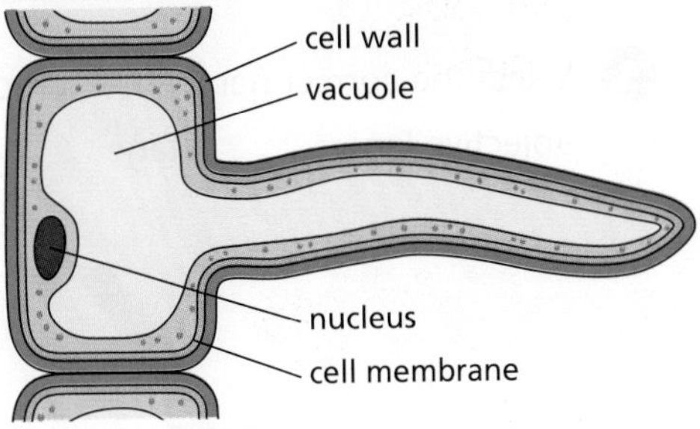

It is important in questions where two or more opinions are given, that you explore each statement thoroughly. There is not usually a completely correct or completely incorrect opinion.

Abel is correct that this is a plant cell as it has a cell wall.

However, both plant and animal cells have cell membranes, so this feature does not help us to decide.

Charlotte is correct that animal cells do not have chloroplasts.

However, some plant cells do not contain chloroplasts either: only those cells where photosynthesis takes place contain chloroplasts (as these contain chlorophyll).

9 Dev says that plant cells hold their shape because of their cell wall. Kristi says that it is the vacuole that supports the plant cell, and the cell wall controls what moves in and out of the cell. Suggest who is correct and explain why.

10 In a condition called anaemia, patients have a lack of red blood cells. Doctors take blood samples and the 'red blood cell count' is measured.

The normal range for a red blood cell count is between 4.1 and 5.5 million/microlitre. The graph shows the red blood cell count for a patient being treated for a low red blood cell count.

Use the graph to calculate:

a the red blood cell count at the start of the treatment

b how long after treatment began that the patient reached the normal range for red blood cell count.

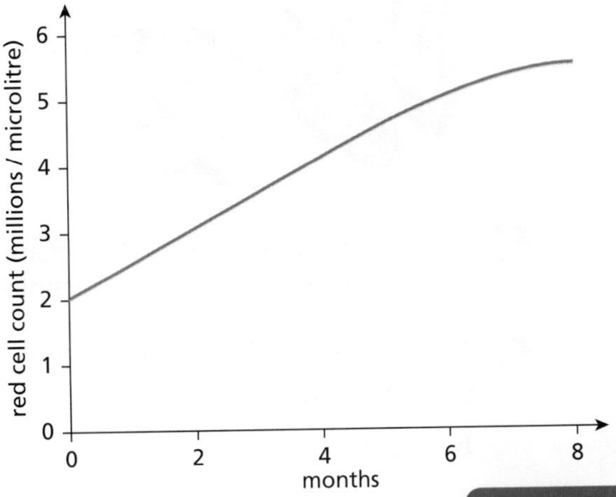

1.3 Studying cells

You are learning to:
- identify the parts of a light microscope
- describe how we observe cells using a light microscope
- interpret evidence from microscopes.

1 How do microscopes help us to observe cells?

2 Select **one** advantage of an electron microscope over a light microscope.

a An electron microscope is cheaper than a light microscope.

b An electron microscope is more portable than a light microscope.

c An electron microscope allows us to see smaller objects.

d An electron microscope is easier to use.

3 Select the correct name for each part of the microscope labelled **a**, **b**, **c** and **d**.

objective lens   stage   focusing wheel   eyepiece lens

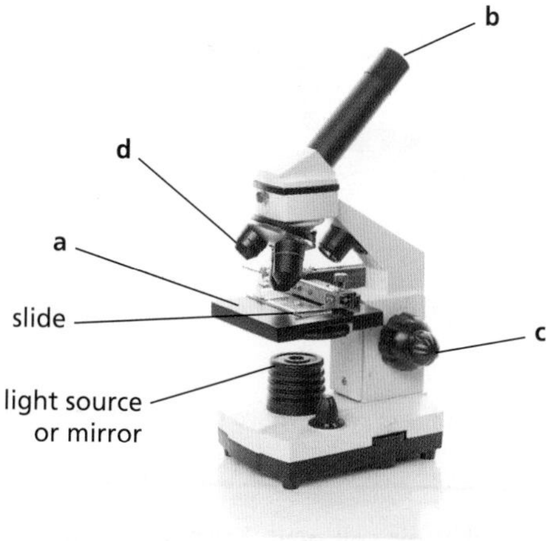

4 The image below shows a bacterium as seen with an electron microscope. Explain why we can see more detail than when a bacterium is observed with a light microscope.

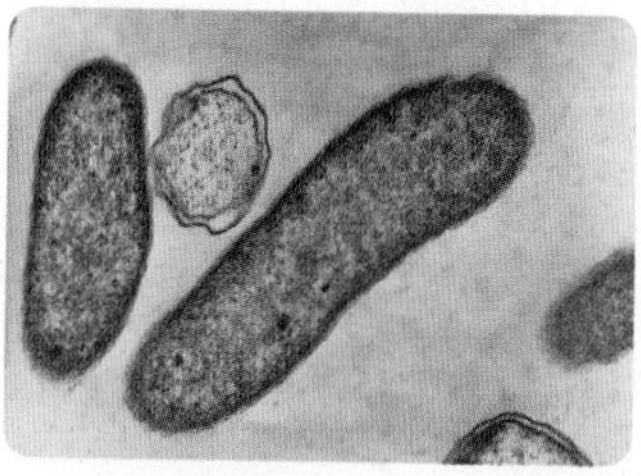

5 A hospital laboratory technician examines cells under the microscope to screen for cervical cancer. Why does the technician add a stain to the sample on the slide?

6 Explain the functions of the following parts of a light microscope:

a bulb or mirror

b stage.

7 Sami and Aya are learning to use a light microscope. They are looking at samples at different magnifications.

The total magnification of a microscope is calculated using the equation:

total magnification = magnification of eyepiece lens × magnification of objective lens

Calculate the missing numbers **a**, **b** and **c** in the table below.

Magnification of eyepiece lens	Magnification of objective lens	Total magnification
×10	×4	**a**
×10	×10	**b**
×10	×40	**c**

8 A scientist studied how well plant cells survived at different temperatures. They heated cell samples to different temperatures: 30 °C, 40 °C, 50 °C, 60 °C and 70 °C, and then observed them under a microscope. They concluded that the cells looked normal at 40 °C but were destroyed at 50 °C.

a How could the scientist test whether these results are repeatable?

b How could the scientist get a more accurate result of the exact temperature at which the cells are destroyed?

9 Keesha observed onion cells under the microscope and made a drawing in pen as shown in the image.

a Suggest **three** improvements to make the drawing more scientifically accurate.

b Identify **three** cell structures that Keesha could label.

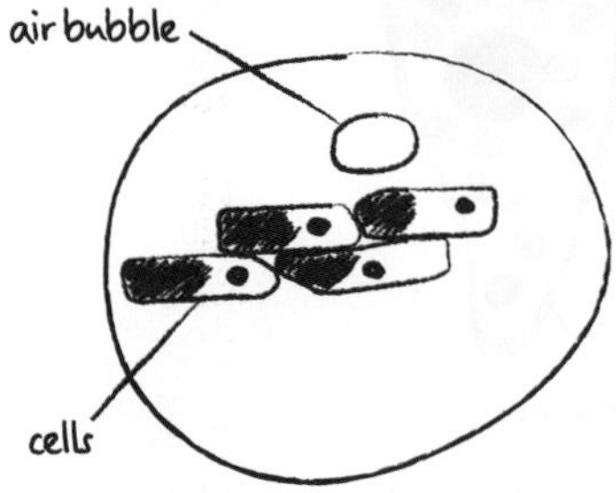

Worked example

There are 1000 μm in 1 mm.

Convert the values in mm into μm.

mm	μm
1	(1 × 1000) = 1000
10	(10 × 1000) = 10 000
250	(250 × 1000) = 250 000
0.1	(0.1 × 1000) = 100

10 **a** How many times smaller than a mm is a μm?

b An animal cell has a diameter of 10 μm. Write this diameter in mm.

c A bacterial cell is $\frac{1}{10}$ the size of the animal cell. What size is the bacterial cell in:

i μm **ii** mm?

1.4 Unicellular organisms

You are learning to:
- recognise different types of unicellular organisms
- describe differences in a range of unicellular organisms
- compare adaptations of unicellular organisms.

1. Name **one** characteristic that *all* unicellular organisms have in common.

2. Identify which of these organisms are unicellular:

   bacterium   cactus   seahorse   yeast

3. Unicellular organisms vary a lot in their size and structure but can be classed as either prokaryotic or eukaryotic. Which class is believed to have existed on Earth first?

4. One key difference between prokaryotic and eukaryotic organisms is how they store their genetic material. Describe how each stores its genetic material.

5. Of the two unicellular organisms shown below, suggest which one existed first. Justify your answer.

a

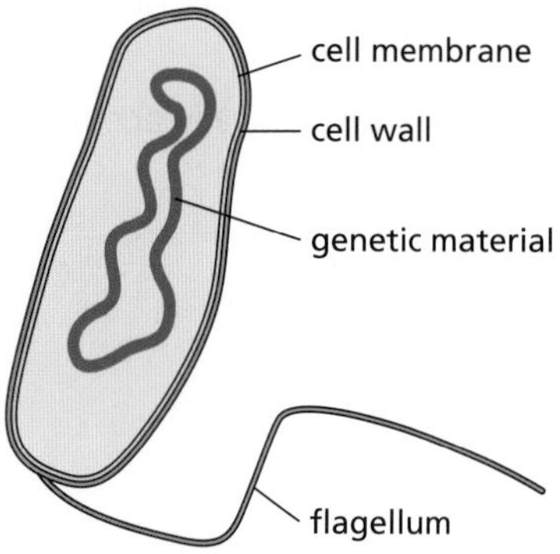

b

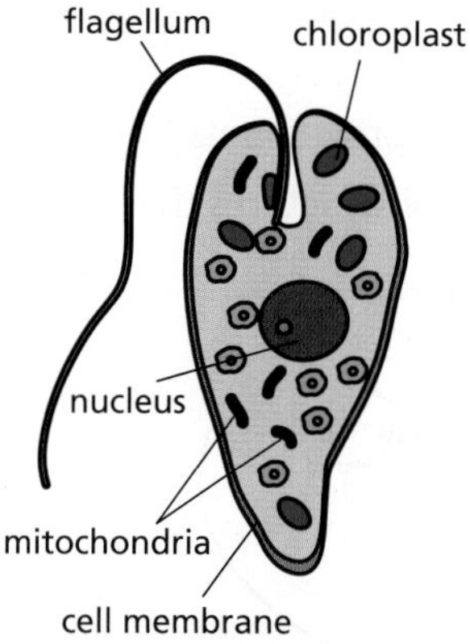

6. A microbiologist (a scientist who studies microorganisms) has discovered a type of bacterium that lives in hot springs close to volcanoes, up to temperatures of 90 °C.

   Why might the microbiologist not be concerned about getting infected by the bacterium?

7. The diagram shows a paramecium, which is a eukaryotic unicellular organism.

   Explain how cilia are important in feeding for this organism.

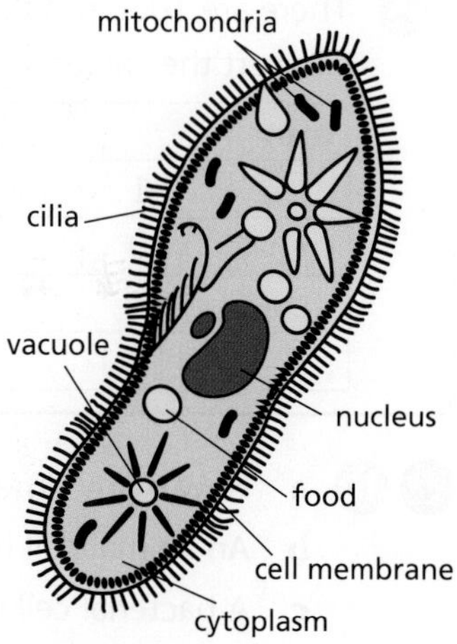

8 The image shows a newly discovered unicellular organism. One scientist describes it as having plant-like features. Another says that it also has animal-like features. Choose **one** feature that makes this organism:

a plant-like

b animal-like.

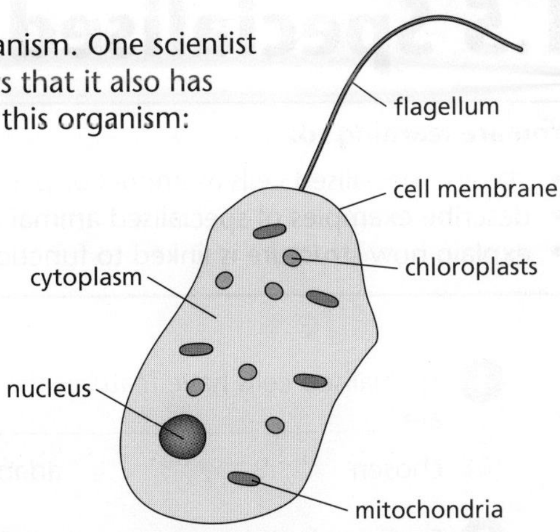

Worked example

Two students are studying images of cells. One cell has no nucleus or other organelles.

Tom says that this must be a bacterial cell as they don't have a nucleus. Oran says that this cannot be a bacterial cell because bacterial cells contain chloroplasts.

Discuss which student is correct and why.

In questions where students are giving their opinion, each opinion must be considered carefully. It is often the case that although there is one best answer, the other ideas are partly correct.

Bacterial cells do not contain a nucleus, so Tom is correct.

However, Oran is correct that some bacterial cells do contain chloroplasts, although not all do.

9 Two students are learning about the variety of life on Earth. Ben says that all unicellular organisms are very simple. Layla disagrees and says that some unicellular organisms are complex.

a Explain why Layla is correct.

b Suggest why Ben might assume that all unicellular organisms are simple.

10 Compare the structures of these unicellular organisms and suggest what their structures tell us about how they live.

a

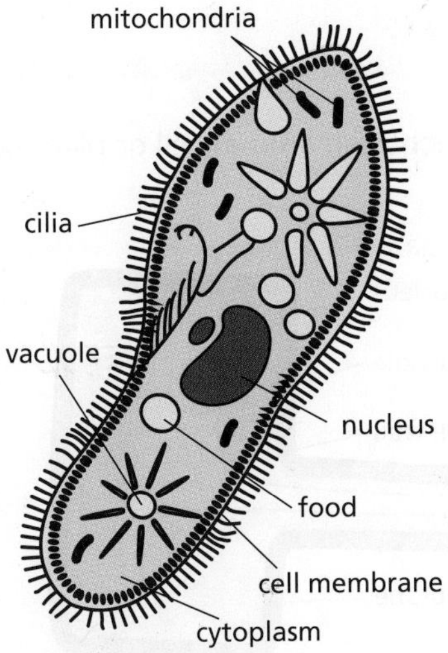

b

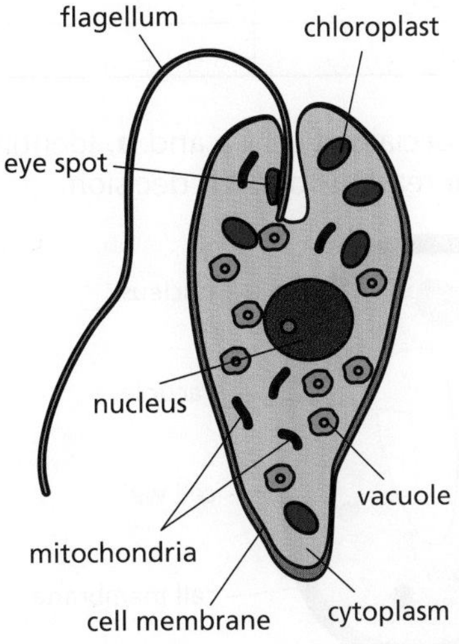

1.5 Specialised cells

You are learning to:

- classify specialised cells as animal or plant cells
- describe examples of specialised animal and plant cells
- explain how structure is linked to function in specialised cells.

1 Specialised cells have features that help them to carry out a certain function. We say that cells are ______________________________ to the function. Choose the missing word.

chosen adapted forced created

2 Explain why it is important that all living things have specialised cells.

3 All new cells start out as stem cells. What is a stem cell? Select the best definition.

a A specialised plant cell.

b A cell that can develop into any specialised cell.

c A specialised cell in an animal.

d A nerve cell.

4 Match each of the specialised cells in the images to its name.

a

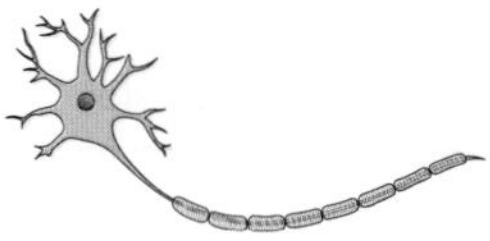

b

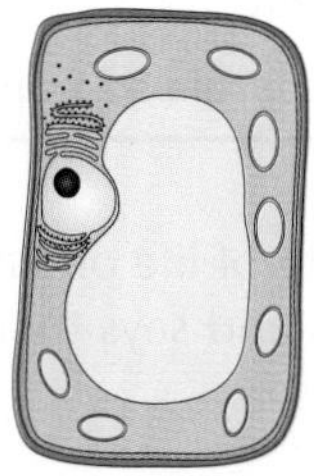

c

d

Name of cell	Image
red blood cell	
nerve cell	
muscle cell	
leaf cell	

5 Look at specialised cells **a** and **b**. Identify whether each is an animal cell or plant cell. Give at least **two** reasons for each decision.

a

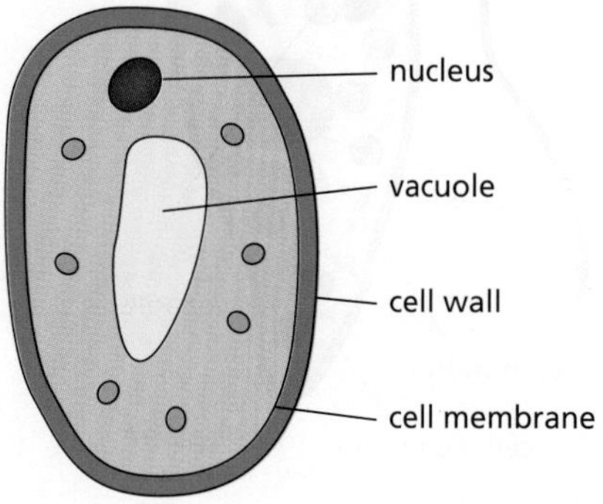

b

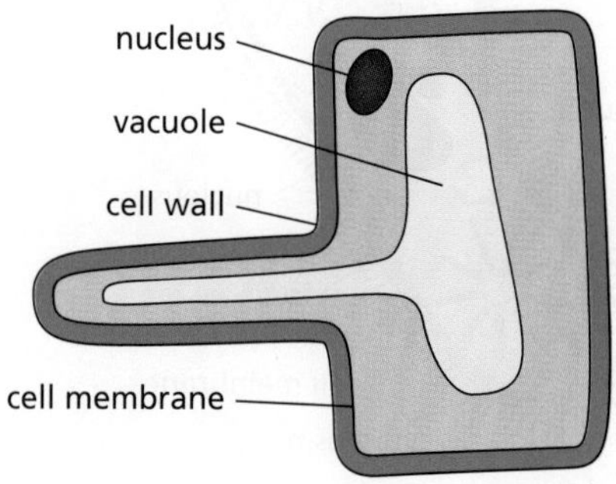

6 For each of the specialised cells in the table, describe its function and explain **one** way it is adapted to its function.

Name of cell	Function of cell	One way the cell is adapted to its function
red blood cell		
nerve cell		
muscle cell		
leaf cell		

Worked example

Smooth muscle is found in many parts of the body, such as blood vessels and organs.

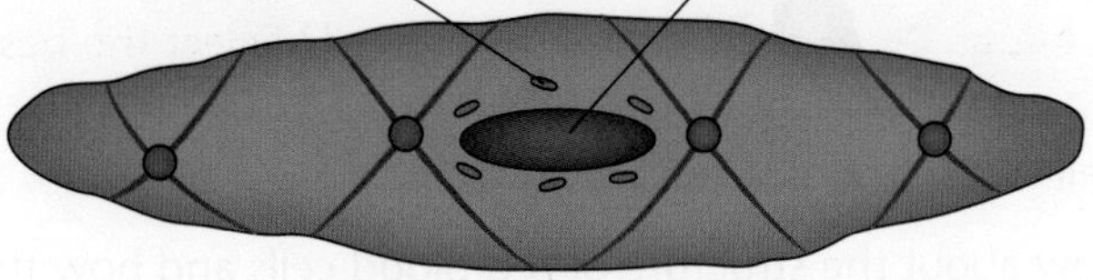

smooth muscle is made of protein fibres

Explain how the structure of these muscle cells helps with the functions of:

a contracting to create movement

b releasing energy.

This question asks you to 'explain'. The first step when answering an explain question is to **state** a fact.

a The muscle cells are made from protein fibres.

Then **explain** why that fact is useful.

This allows the cells to rapidly expand and contract to create movement.

b The muscle cells contain lots of mitochondria. Energy is released in mitochondria.

7 Sperm cells are specialised cells adapted to carry genetic material to the egg cell.

For each of the adaptations of sperm cells listed, explain how the adaptation helps the sperm cell to perform a specific function:

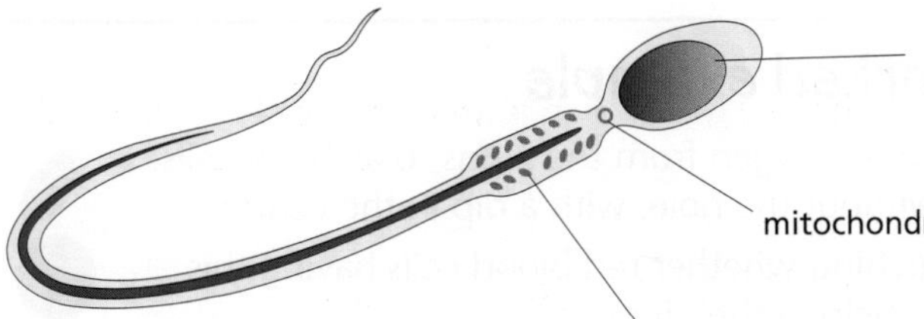

a tail

b large head

c lots of mitochondria.

8 Anaemia is a deficiency disease that affects the *number* of heathy red blood cells. Sickle cell disease is an inherited condition that affects the *quality* of the red blood cells.

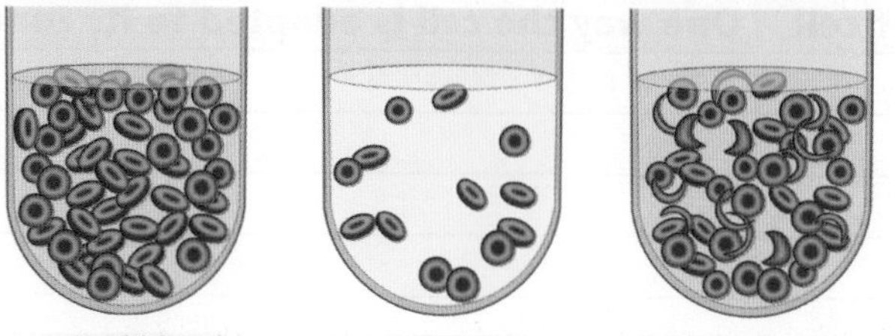
normal blood
anaemia
sickle cell disease

With sickle cell disease, some of the red blood cells have a different shape to the usual disc shape.

normal red blood cell
sickle cell disease

Use what you know about the structure of red blood cells and how they are adapted to their function to answer these questions.

a Explain why a patient with anaemia might feel tired.

b Suggest whether a patient with sickle cell disease is likely to feel tired. Explain your answer.

9 These images both show muscle cells but from different parts of the human body.

a Compare the structures of the two cells.

b Describe the function of each part of the cells: cell membrane, cytoplasm, nucleus and mitochondria.

c Which of these images do you think shows heart muscle? Explain your answer.

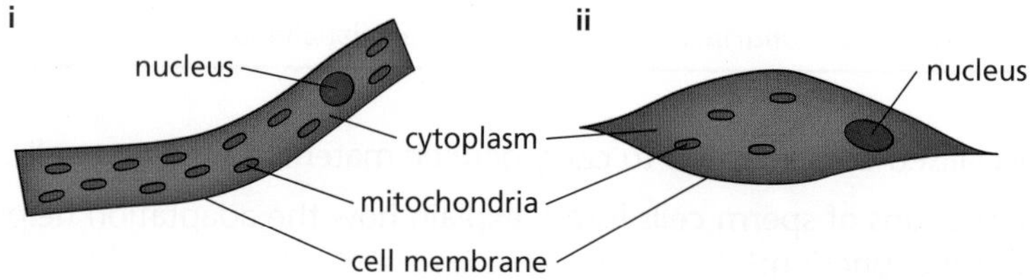

Worked example

Red blood cells have the function of carrying oxygen from the lungs to all body cells. They have a shape like a doughnut but without the hole, with a dip in the centre.

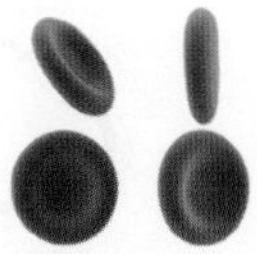

A haematologist (blood scientist) is researching whether red blood cells having this shape, rather than being spherical, might help in their function.

The haematologist's estimates of the surface area and volume of the two shapes are shown in Table 1.

	Surface area	Volume	Surface area-to-volume ratio
dipped shape	136	90	
spherical shape	120	150	

a Calculate the surface area-to-volume ratio for each shape of cell.

Dipped shape: surface area-to-volume ratio = $\frac{136}{90}$ = 1.5

(This can also be written as a ratio 1.5 : 1)

Spherical shape: surface area-to-volume ratio = $\frac{120}{150}$ = 0.8

(This can also be written as a ratio 0.8 : 1)

b Suggest whether the dipped shape of a red blood cell makes it better adapted to its function than a spherical cell.

The dipped shape of a red blood cell does make it better adapted for carrying oxygen as it has a larger surface area-to-volume ratio than a spherical shape. This means that it can carry more oxygen per cell.

10 Root hair cells are specialised cells adapted to absorb water and minerals from the soil. Many other plant cells are adapted to carry out photosynthesis.

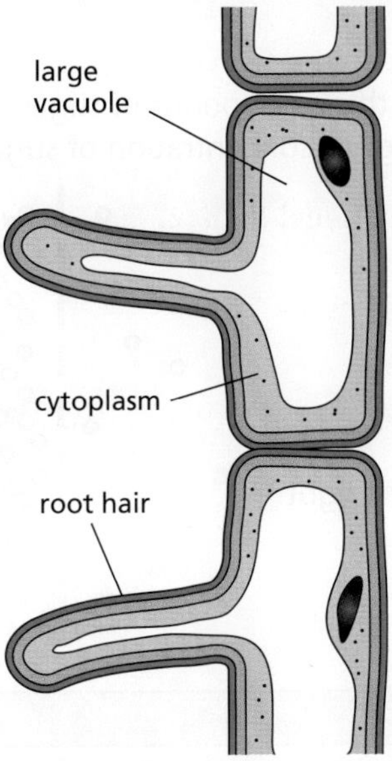

a Describe how the cytoplasm and vacuole of a root hair cell are adapted to absorb water but not to carry out photosynthesis.

b Botanists (plant scientists) need to decide which of three types of plant will best survive in dry soil. They have calculated the surface area and volume of a sample of 20 root hairs from each plant and calculated a mean for each.

	Mean surface area of a root hair (mm^2)	Mean volume of a root hair (mm^3)	Surface area-to-volume ratio
Plant 1	12	12	
Plant 2	12	18	
Plant 3	24	48	

i Suggest why the botanists measured 20 root hairs and calculated a mean.

ii Complete the table to show the surface area-to-volume ratio for each of the plants.

iii Suggest which plant is most likely to absorb more water and will be best suited to the dry soil.

1.6 Movement in and out of cells: diffusion

You are learning to:
- define the process of diffusion
- describe examples of diffusion in living things
- explain how different factors affect the rate of diffusion.

1 Complete the sentence using the words below:

higher particles lower

Diffusion is the spreading of ________________ from where there is a ________________ concentration to where there is a ________________ concentration.

2 Which type of substances can diffusion occur in? Select all that apply.

solids liquids gases

3 Maryam adds two teaspoons of sugar to her tea. Lydia adds three teaspoons of sugar to her tea. If they have the same volume of tea, who has the higher concentration of sugar solution, Maryam or Lydia?

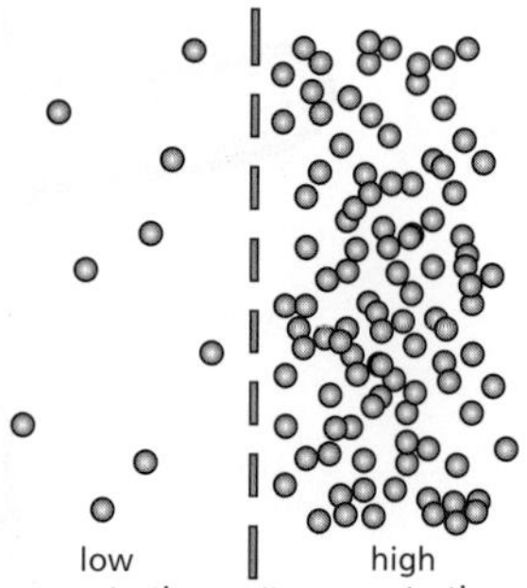

4 Choose the correct statement about the diagram.

a particles move from right to left

b particles move from left to right

c no particles move

d equal numbers of particles move from left to right as from right to left.

5 Which substances diffuse into a single-celled animal, such as an amoeba cell, and which diffuse out?

Substance	In or out?
carbon dioxide	
nutrients	
urea	
oxygen	

6 Hakim is investigating diffusion in different liquids. Part of his method is:

- Add 5 ml of coloured liquid to a well in the centre of an agar jelly plate.
- Start the timer.
- Measure the distance travelled by the coloured liquid every 30 s for 4 min.
- Repeat using other coloured liquids.

a Suggest why the liquid needs to be coloured.

b Hakim selects from a range of measuring cylinders to measure the liquid (10 ml, 100 ml and 250 ml). He chooses the 10 ml measuring cylinder. What did Hakim improve by choosing the 10 ml measuring cylinder rather than one of the larger ones? Choose from the words below:

repeatability prediction accuracy control

7 We can use an everyday example of diffusion as a model to help us to understand how diffusion happens inside living things.

Carmine sprays an air freshener at one end of a room.

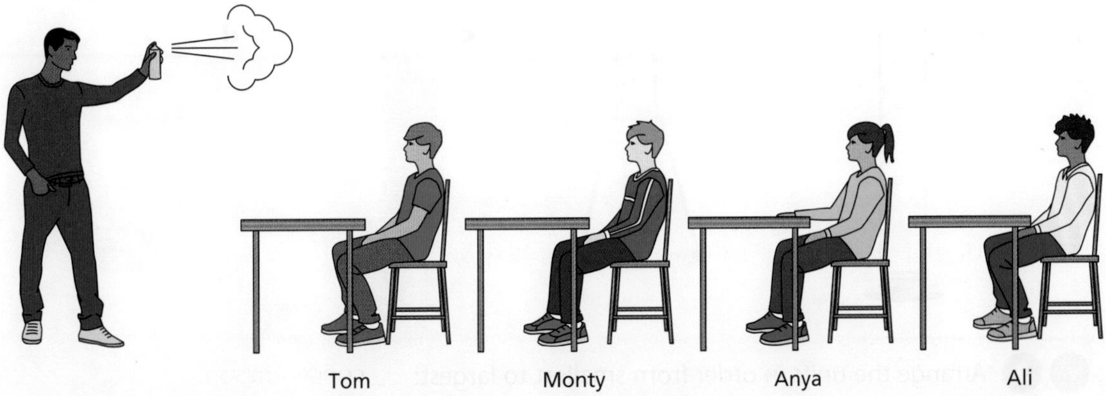

a Carmine asks each student to raise their hand when they can smell the air freshener. Suggest the order you would expect them to raise their hands.

b Explain why everyone in the room smells the air freshener eventually.

c Considering this model, suggest **one** way it is similar to oxygen diffusing into a cell and **one** way it is different.

8 Cells of bigger volume need more substances to pass in and out of the cell than smaller cells. As substances move and in and out by diffusion, the size of a cell is important. Using a model of cells as cubes, we can compare how effective diffusion might be.

a Calculate the surface area, volume and surface area-to-volume ratio for each cube in the table.

Length, breadth, height of cube (cm)	Surface area (cm^2)	Volume (cm^3)	Surface area-to-volume ratio
1, 1, 1			
2, 2, 2			
3, 3, 3			

b If each of these cubes were a cell, such as an amoeba, which would have the biggest challenge in ensuring it transported enough oxygen and nutrients into the cell? Explain your answer.

9 Some unicellular organisms make food by photosynthesis; others feed by taking in nutrients from the environment. All unicellular organisms rely on diffusion to survive.

a Explain why diffusion is so important to these organisms.

b Most unicellular organisms are microscopic so can only be seen with a microscope. Considering the way that they feed, suggest why it is beneficial for unicellular organisms to be small, rather than increasing to the size of a multicellular organism.

Maths and practical skills

1 Choose the most appropriate piece of equipment to measure a volume of 10 ml.

a

b

c

d

2 Arrange the units in order from smallest to largest:

metres (m) millimetres (mm) micrometres (μm) kilometres (km)

3 Identify the parts **a**, **b**, **c** and **d** of the light microscope using the words provided.

light source objective lens stage eyepiece lens

Worked example

Yua investigates whether temperature affects the number of stomata (pores) that are open on the underside of a leaf.

She keeps plants at different temperatures for a fixed time and then counts the number of open stomata in a fixed area of leaf for each plant. She repeats this three times.

Explain why she repeats the observations.

When carrying out investigations, we often repeat our measurements two or three times. Think about what it tells you if all three repeat readings are similar; what if one is very different?

Carrying out repeat measurements checks the repeatability of the measuring method. If the results are similar each time, Yua can trust them. If any of the results are not similar, Yua can choose to repeat that reading again or ignore it.

4 Jed compares the number of chloroplasts in different plant cells. Using a microscope, he estimates the number of chloroplasts in one palisade (upper leaf) cell, one guard (lower leaf) cell and one root hair cell. He concludes that palisade cells contain the most chloroplasts.

a Suggest how Jed could improve the repeatability of his experiment.

b Explain why Jed is probably correct that there are more chloroplasts in palisade cells than the other cells.

5 Charlotte is looking at skin cells under a microscope. She uses the method below:

- Place the skin sample on a slide and add a drop of dye.
- Cover the sample with a glass cover slip.
- Place the sample on the microscope stage.
- Focus the microscope to see the cells.

Explain why:

a dye is added to the sample

b a glass cover slip is placed over the sample.

6 **a** Complete the table by converting the units.

m	mm	μm
0.1	100	**i**
2.6	**ii**	2600 000
iii	24 000	24 000 000

b An even smaller unit of measurement is the nanometre. 1 μm = 1000 nm. How many nm are there in:

i 1 mm

ii 1 m?

7 Chen is investigating the effect of temperature on diffusion. He follows the method below:

- Remove a small disc from the centre of the agar plate.
- Measure 50 ml of water and heat until it reaches 50 °C.
- Add this to a bowl and place the agar plate in the bowl for 5 minutes.
- Use another pipette and fill the hole in the agar with undiluted food colouring.
- Measure and record how far the food colouring spreads in 30 seconds.
- Repeat at a range of other temperatures.

a In this investigation, identify:

i the independent variable

ii the dependent variable.

b Chen next decides to change the independent variable to concentration of food colouring. Write the question that Chen is investigating.

Worked example

A student is asked a question by their teacher: *Do plant cells get bigger when the plant is given more water?* Design an investigation to answer the question.

The question asked gives you clues as to what will change and what will be measured in an investigation.

You can see from the question that the factor that changes is the volume of water. This is the independent variable.

Also from the question, you can see that what is being measured is the size of the plant cells. This is the dependent variable.

Then consider any factors that may need to be controlled; these are called the 'control variables'.

So that they can compare cells, the student will need to use the same type of plant. This is one control variable.

When designing a method, there is often not just one correct answer, many methods could be valid.

One suggested answer is:

Water plants of the same type with different volumes of water, for example: 50 ml, 100 ml, 150 ml, 200 ml, 250 ml, 300 ml.

Leave each plant for the same length of time.

Using a microscope, observe cells from three samples of each plant. Prepare samples from the same part of each plant, for example, the leaf.

Take measurements of the leaf size plus any observations of how they might be different.

8 Sally notices that when she eats salt and vinegar crisps, her lips feel wrinkly. She wonders whether the salt or the vinegar in the crisps is affecting her cells. Her teacher gives her a cotton bud to collect cells from inside her cheek and a light microscope.

Design an investigation for Sally to answer the question: *Does salt or vinegar affect the cells in my mouth?*

9 Stelios observes a water flea under a microscope using an eyepiece lens of ×10 and an objective lens of ×10.

a Calculate the total magnification of the microscope.

b Use the equation:

image size = actual size × magnification

to calculate the actual size of the flea if the image is 20 mm.

c Express this answer in μm.

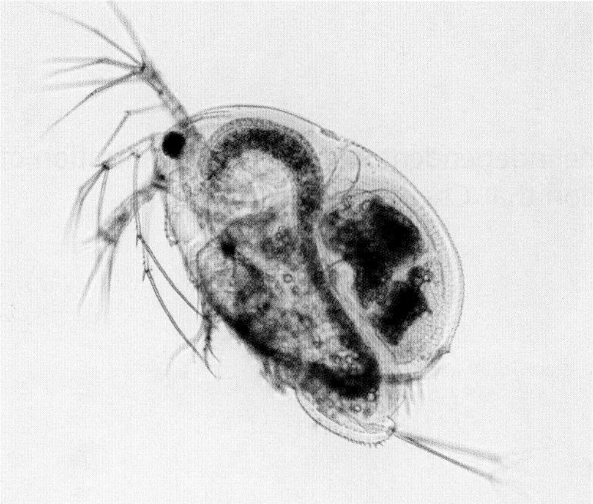

10 Peter investigated the effect of changing concentration on the rate of diffusion. He used a range of concentrations of glucose solution and timed how long it took for the solution to travel through an agar block.

a Peter added a dye to the glucose solution. Suggest why.

His results are shown in the table.

Concentration of glucose solution (g/l)	Time taken to travel through the agar (s)	Rate of diffusion = 1/time (1/s)
0.5	10.0	0.10
1.0	**i**	0.25
1.5	5.0	0.20
2.0	**ii**	0.50
2.5	1.6	0.62
3.0	1.4	0.69

b Two results have been deleted from Peter's results table. Rate is calculated by 1/time, where the time is measured in seconds. Using the rate value, calculate the time taken to travel through the agar at a concentration of 1.0 g/l and 2.0 g/l (**i** and **ii** in the table).

The graph of Peter's results is below.

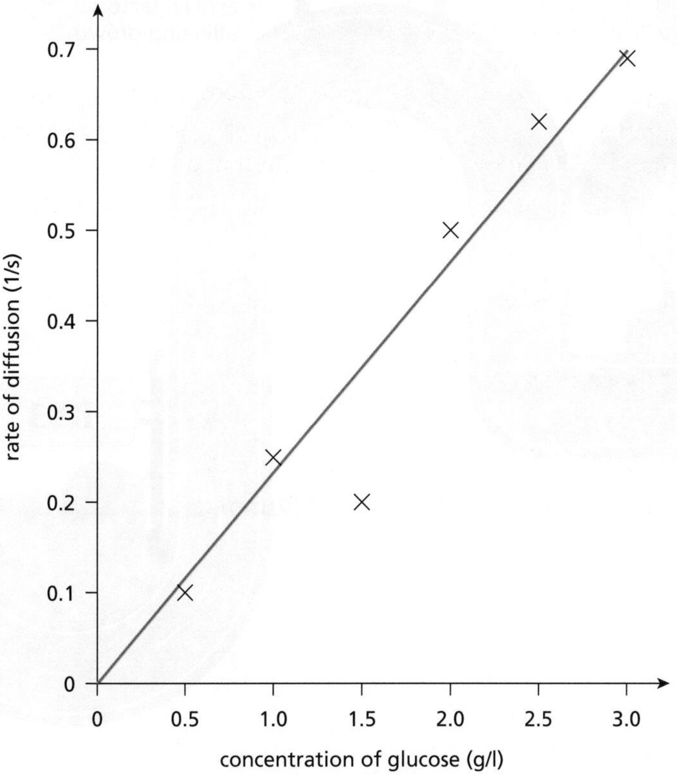

c State which of the results (which concentration of glucose) is anomalous (doesn't fit the pattern).

d Write a conclusion for Peter.

2 Reproduction road map

Where are you in your learning journey and where are you aiming to be?

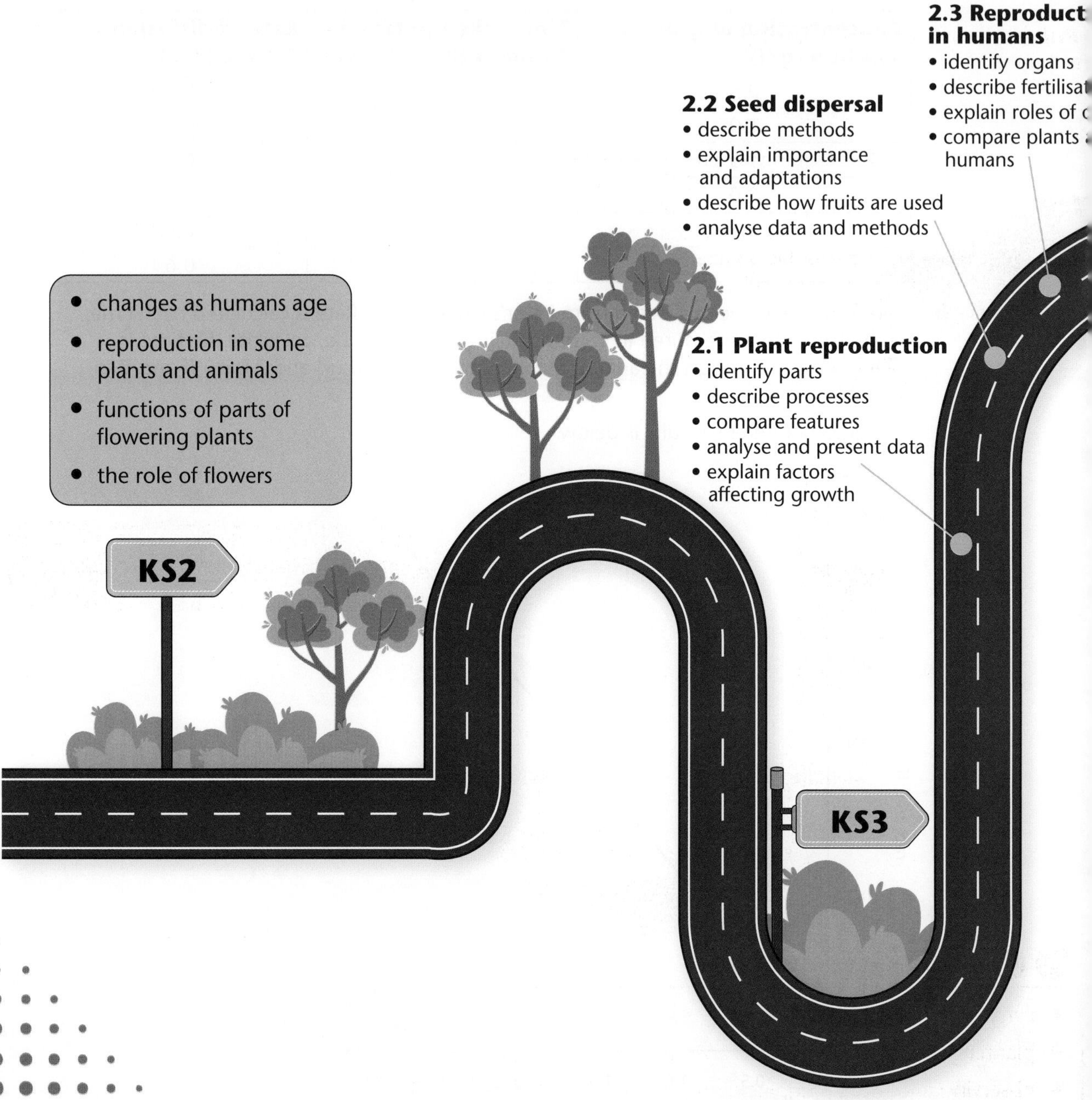

Puberty and the menstrual cycle
escribe and explain changes
escribe the menstrual cycle
pply the menstrual cycle to infertility

2.5 Development of a foetus and the effect of lifestyle
- describe foetus development
- explain role of the mother
- discuss factors affecting development

- hormones in human reproduction
- contraception
- use of hormones to treat infertility
- sexual and asexual reproduction
- advantages and disadvantages of sexual and asexual reproduction
- meiosis

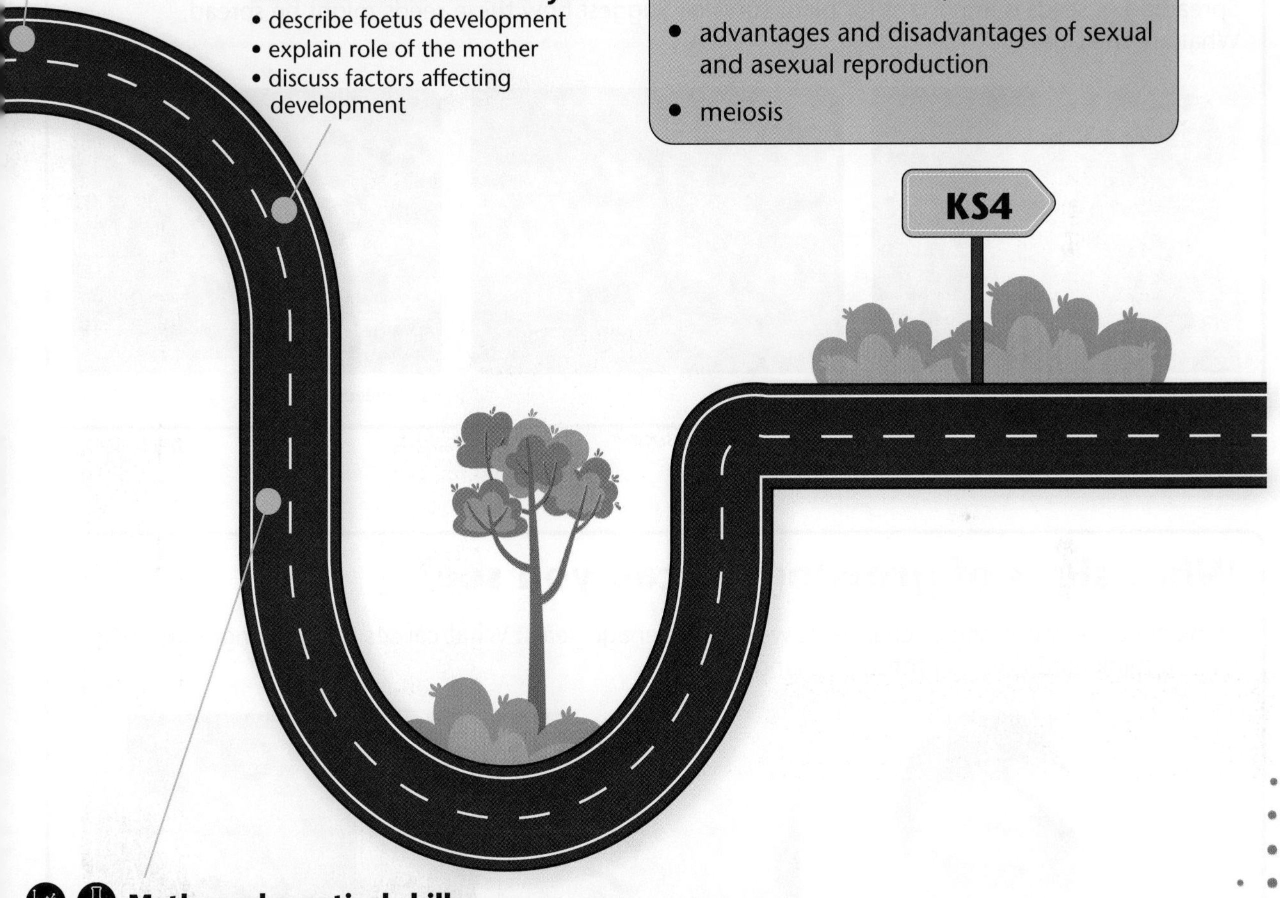

Maths and practical skills

- carrying out scientific enquiries to test predictions
- planning an investigation, identifying and managing the variables
- observing and measuring, including the evaluation of repeatability
- interpreting observations and data
- suggesting improvements to practical work
- calculating results and converting between different units
- presenting reasoned explanations
- writing scientific questions

2 Reproduction

Without reproduction, no new organisms would exist. Animals and plants both have to grow and mature to be able to reproduce. There are similarities and differences in how reproduction happens in animals and plants. For example, both animals and plants need male sex cells and female sex cells to produce new offspring. However, a lot of animals move to find a mate, whereas flowering plants reproduce without moving.

Do you recognise any of these seeds?

Spreading of seeds is important for plant survival. Suggest how these seeds might be spread. What are the clues?

dandelion

tomato

catchweed

What signs of growing up can you see?

Think about how our bodies change as we reach teenage years. What causes these changes and why do you think our bodies go through changes?

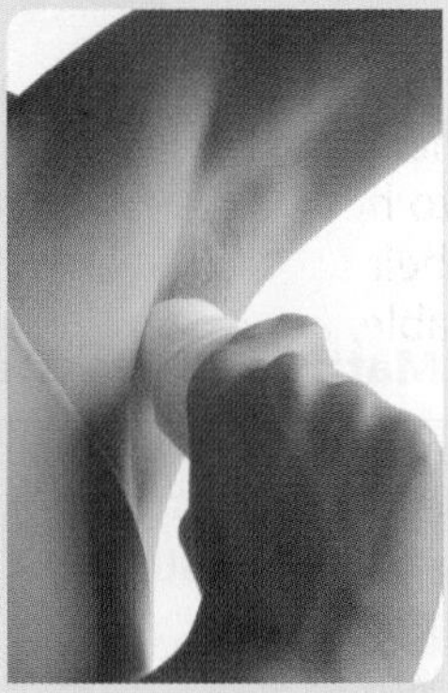

Using your science skills

Could you be a horticulturist?

You grow and sell plants for food or for display. You are an expert in how plants reproduce and how to maximise growth to avoid food scarcity, for example by knowing the best conditions for wind and insect pollination. You need patience to experiment with growing unusual or exotic plants and to see the results of breeding techniques. Resilience is needed: some growth factors are out of your control, such as pests or the weather. You may sell directly to the public, for example at markets, or to shops and restaurants, so you need a business brain to follow market trends and to make a profit.

Imagine how rewarding it would be to grow the food that ends up on our tables in a restaurant.

Midwives support women and their families through pregnancy and when their babies are young. They need to be experts in healthy pregnancy and how a foetus develops so they can spot the signs when development is not progressing as it should. These health professionals are compassionate and caring as they support families through very personal and important times.

Conservation zoologists ensure animals do not become extinct. They may work with animals in captivity or in the wild. They understand how the animals reproduce and develop and help to make sure offspring are produced. They tend to focus on one species because they need to have deep knowledge.

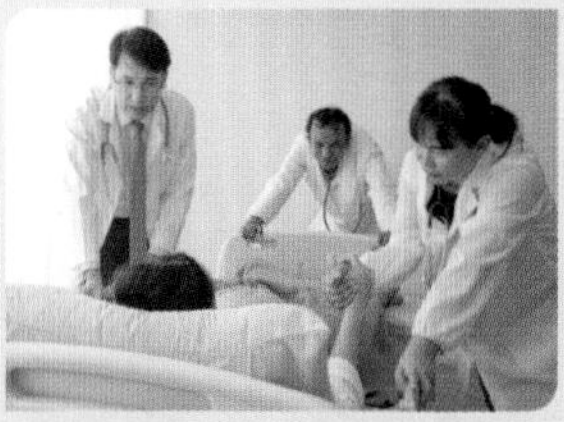

Fertility nurses (or reproductive nurses) work with couples and individuals who have problems getting pregnant. These patients may be undergoing treatment to help them to get pregnant or may need to have counselling to help them to cope with their problems. Fertility nurses need to be adaptable, approachable and knowledgeable.

Gardeners carry out a wide range of activities. A skilled gardener produces plants from seeds and ensures the best conditions are created to support pollination by wind and insects. They have a love of the outdoors and for providing the best natural environment within the gardens they care for.

Animal breeders produce animals for a range of purposes, for example for shows, sport or pets. They need good knowledge of the animals they work with and how they reproduce. They must ensure the health and safety of the breeding animals before and during pregnancy, and monitor the health of the offspring during pregnancy and after birth.

Fertility counsellors work with individuals or families who are having difficulty getting pregnant to allow them to explore their emotions and to help them to cope better. They could help people to decide whether to have treatments or to come to terms with not having children, for example.

Knowledge organiser

Reproduction is the production of offspring.

In sexual reproduction, the male sex cells fertilise the female sex cells. Sex cells are also called **gametes**.

In flowering plants, the male gamete is a pollen cell and the female gamete is an ovule.

In humans, the male sex cell is a sperm and the female gamete is an ovum.

Fertilisation is the joining of the nucleus of a male gamete and the nucleus of a female gamete.

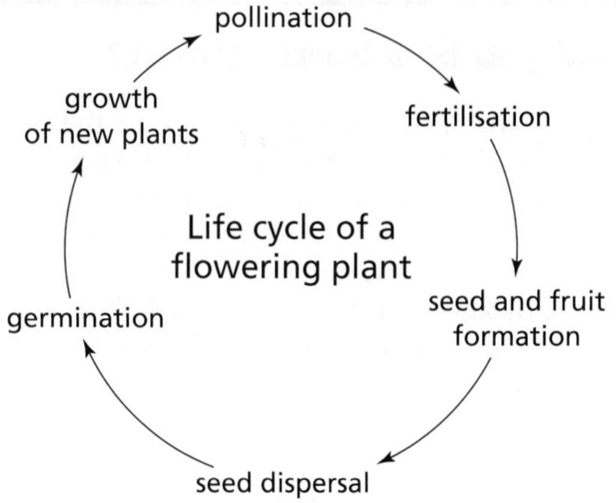

Most flowers have male and female parts.

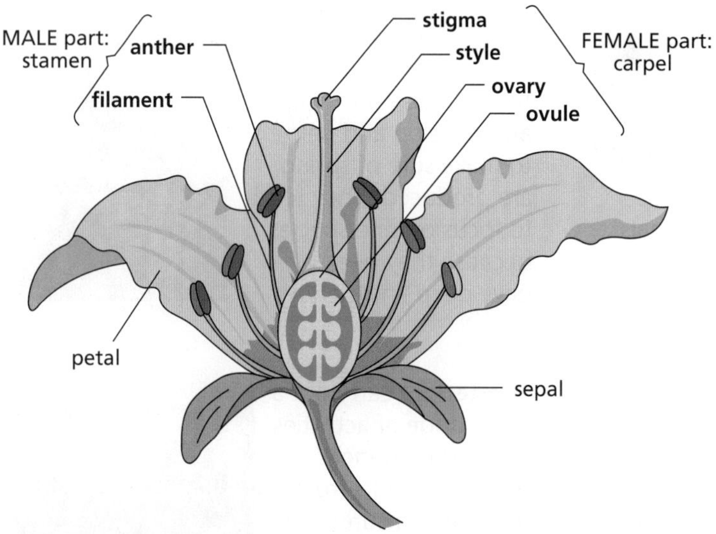

Methods of seed dispersal can be investigated and compared. For example, the distance travelled by seeds dispersed by different methods can be measured. Here, the independent variable is the method of dispersal; the dependent variable is the distance travelled.

Following fertilisation, each fertilised ovule becomes a **seed**, and the ovary develops into a **fruit**. The fruit protects the seeds until they are ripe and ready to form a new plant.

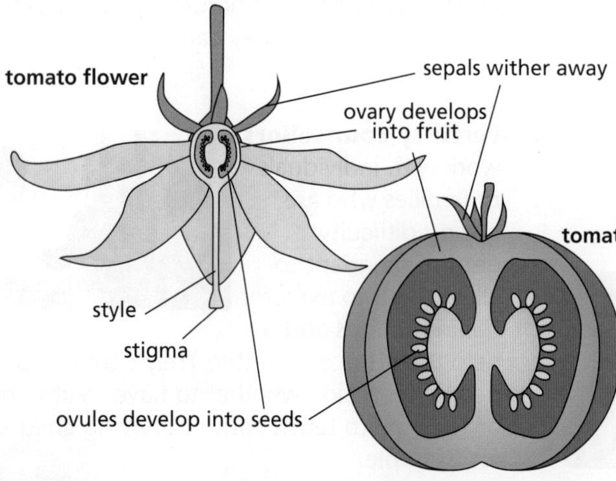

Seed dispersal can happen by:

- wind

- explosion – pods explode on touch
- water

- animals – they eat the fruit and carry the seeds inside them.

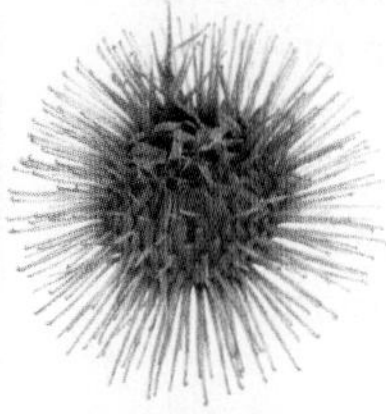

Pollination is when pollen produced in the anther is transferred to the stigma of a different plant of the same type. Pollen can be transferred by wind or insects.

Insect-pollinated plants	Wind-pollinated plants
have brightly coloured flowers to attract insects	have long anthers that hang outside the flowers, so pollen is caught on the wind
have sweet smells to attract insects	produce huge amounts of pollen to increase chances of pollination
produce nectar inside the flower to attract insects inside or near the pollen	have long, feathery stigmas that hang outside flowers so pollen can stick to them
produce sticky or spiky pollen to stick to insects	often have no scent or bright colours as don't need to attract insects

Following pollination, the nucleus of the male pollen cell moves to the ovary, where it joins with the nucleus of the ovule. This is called fertilisation.

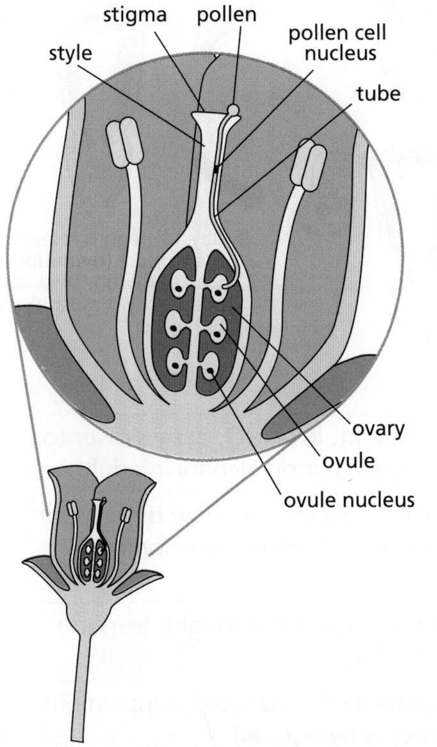

Key vocabulary	
anther	the pollen-producing part of the stamen of a flower
carpel	the female part of a flower
fertilisation	the joining of the nucleus of a male sex cell with the nucleus of a female sex cell
filament	the 'stalk' of the stamen that supports the anther
fruit	the ovary of a plant after fertilisation; the fruit contains the seeds
gametes	sex cells
germination	the stage when a seed begins to grow into a plant
insect pollination	pollination caused by insects carrying and transferring the pollen
ovary	the organ in female plants that contains ovules, and in animals that makes egg cells
ovule	the female sex cell (egg) of a plant
pollination	the process of transferring pollen from the anther of a flower to the stigma of a flower on another plant of the same type
reproduction	the production of offspring
seed	the ovule of a plant after fertilisation
seed dispersal	the spreading of seeds from a plant to a new area
stamen	the male part of a flower
stigma	the pollen-receiving part of a flower
style	the female part of a flower through which pollen travels to fertilise an ovule
wind pollination	pollination caused by wind carrying and transferring the pollen

Structure and function of the male human **reproductive system**:

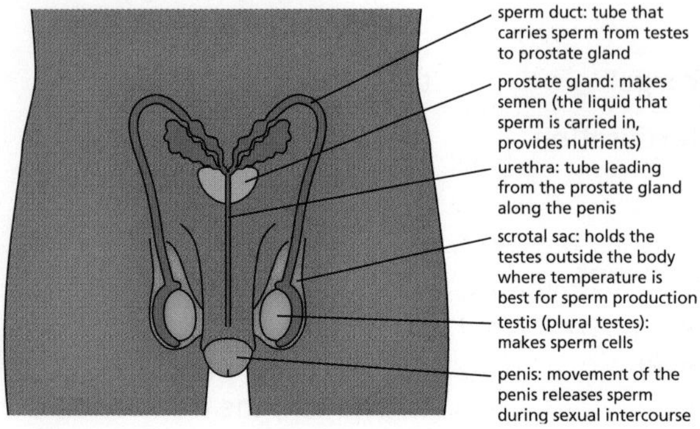

Structure and function of the female human reproductive system:

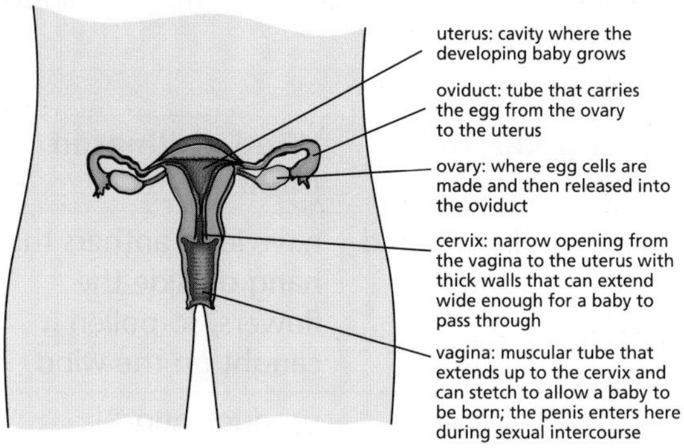

Puberty is the period of physical changes that enable a person to reproduce. In humans, puberty takes place between 8 and 16 years old. It is controlled by **hormones**.

Changes at puberty for girls	Changes at puberty for boys
widening of the hips	shoulders broaden
menstrual cycle begins	voice deepens
breasts become bigger	penis and testes grow
	sperm is produced
height spurt	
hair develops in armpits and around reproductive organs	

The **menstrual cycle** in females lasts for about 28 days. Exact timings of each stage vary between individuals.

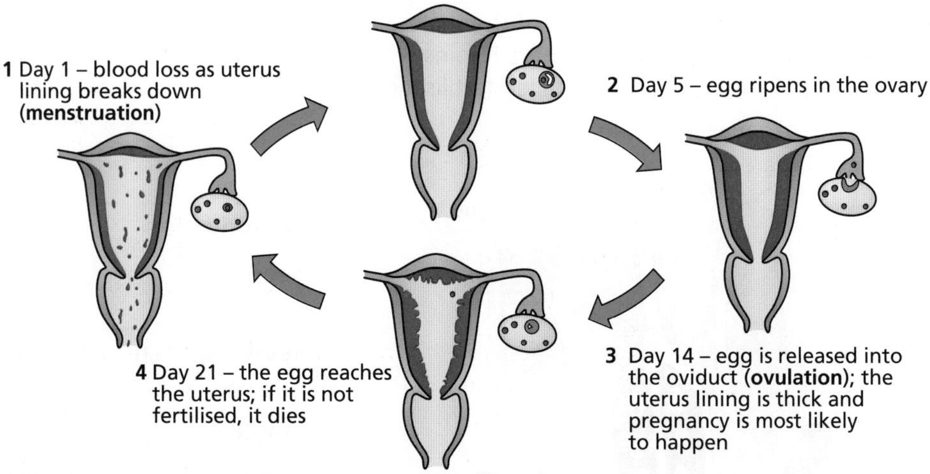

Alcohol	Higher rate of stillbirth, lower birth weight, lower IQ; baby slower to move and think, more likely to be dependent on alcohol in adulthood.
Smoking – nicotine and carbon monoxide	Much higher risk of stillbirth, premature delivery and low birth weight resulting in poor development; greater likelihood of developing asthma.
Drugs – marijuana, cocaine	Higher rate of stillbirth, premature birth, low birth weight, learning difficulties and likely addiction to the drug.
Nutrition – folic acid	Good for the development of the brain and spinal cord; supplements should be taken as soon as pregnancy is recognised.

Sexual intercourse transfers the male sex cells (sperm) into the female body. The penis is inserted into the vagina and its movement stimulates release of sperm. The sperm cells then travel to the uterus, where they might meet an egg and fertilisation can take place.

The ability to reproduce is called **fertility**. People who cannot reproduce are said to be infertile. There are many reasons for **infertility**, such as problems with the menstrual cycle in females or lack of healthy sperm production in males.

Following fertilisation of an egg cell, **cell division** takes place.

- The cell divides to two cells, these cells then divide to make four cells, and so on to form a ball of cells.
- Within the first few weeks, these cells are **stem cells**, so they are not yet specialised.
- Once the ball of cells is big enough, the cells begin to differentiate and become specialised. At this stage, the ball of cells is then called an **embryo**.
- At approximately 8 weeks when most of the organs are formed, the embryo becomes a **foetus**.

A human foetus develops for about 38 weeks during pregnancy. Pregnancy is also known as **gestation**. During this time, the foetus is supported by the following:

- **placenta**
- **umbilical cord**
- **amniotic fluid**.

At the end of the pregnancy, the baby is born. This is called **birth**.

Key vocabulary

amniotic fluid	the liquid that surrounds the foetus to protect it
birth	the process of a baby leaving the mother's body naturally through the vagina
cell division	the process of a cell dividing
cervix	the opening between the uterus and the vagina
embryo	young foetus before its main organs are formed
fertility	the ability to reproduce
foetus	the developing baby during pregnancy
gestation	the process where the foetus develops in the uterus, also known as pregnancy
hormones	chemicals made in the body and carried in the blood as chemical messengers to help to control organs and processes
infertility	being unable to reproduce
menstrual cycle	the cycle in which the lining of the uterus is prepared for pregnancy, but if no fertilised egg is implanted the lining is shed (menstruation)
menstruation	the monthly breakdown of the uterus lining leading to bleeding from the vagina (a period)
ovary	the female organ where egg cells are made
oviduct	the tube in a female animal that carries the egg cell from the ovary to the uterus and where fertilisation happens
ovulation	the release of an egg cell from the ovary during the menstrual cycle
penis	the sex organ of a male animal which carries sperm out of the body
placenta	the organ that provides the foetus with oxygen and nutrients and removes waste substances
pregnancy	the process where the foetus develops in the female uterus, also known as gestation
prostate gland	the gland where semen is made and added to sperm
puberty	changes that occur in boys and girls as they become human adults
reproductive system	the organs in a male or female organism involved in reproduction
scrotal sac	the sac that contains the testes, outside the body for temperature control
sperm duct	the tube through which sperm travels from the testes
stem cells	unspecialised body cells that can develop into other, specialised cells
testis	the organ of a male animal where sperm are made
umbilical cord	the tissue that attaches the foetus to the mother's placenta
urethra	in a male, the tube in the penis through which sperm travels
uterus	the part of the woman's body where a foetus develops
vagina	the part of the female body where the penis enters during sexual intercourse and that stretches during birth

2.1 Plant reproduction

You are learning to:
- identify the parts of a flowering plant involved in reproduction
- describe the process of reproduction in flowering plants
- compare the features of insect-pollinated and wind-pollinated plants
- analyse and present data on the growth of pollen tubes
- explain factors that affect the growth of pollen tubes.

1 Identify the parts of a flowering plant, choosing from the words provided.

ovule stigma ovary
anther filament style

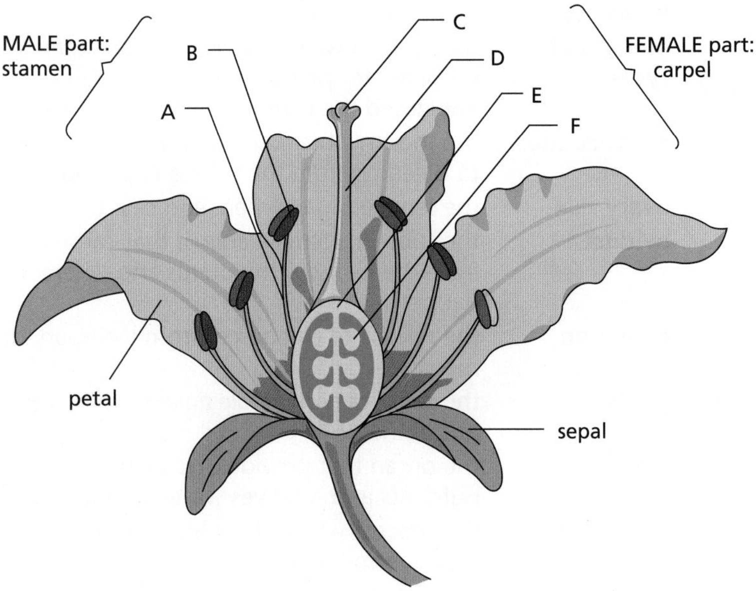

2 Match each of the words with its definition.

a male sex cells landing on the stigma	fertilisation
b the nucleus of the male sex cell joining with the nucleus of the female sex cell	pollination
c spreading of pollen, for example by wind or insects	dispersal

3 **a** Name the male sex cells of a flowering plant.

b Name the part of the plant that contains the female sex cells.

4 Match each flowering plant part to its function.

Function	Part
a produces pollen	stigma
b sticky to collect pollen from the wind or insects	anther
c contains the ovules which grow into seeds	filament
d colourful to attract insects	ovary
e supports the anther	petal

5 Some flowering plants produce nectar deep inside the flower. Explain how this helps with pollination.

6 Describe the role of pollen tubes in plant reproduction.

7 Explain why in some plants the stigma produces a chemical to prevent pollen tube growth if its own pollen grain lands on it.

8 Antonia says that the main stage of plant reproduction is pollination.

Akeeb says that fertilisation is more important than pollination.

Comment on these statements and explain why both pollination and fertilisation are needed for plant reproduction.

9 Image **a** shows a flowering plant that has long styles.

Image **b** shows a flowering plant with long, feathery stigmas.

a

b

i Identify which of these is the wind-pollinated plant and which is the insect-pollinated plant.

ii Explain how the design of the stigma and style benefits each type of plant.

iii Using the images, compare **two** other features that would help to identify how each plant is pollinated.

Worked example

For pollination to lead to fertilisation, a pollen tube grows from the pollen through the style. A student believes that the growth of these pollen tubes may be affected by the temperature of the surroundings.

a The student carries out the investigation by adding sugar solutions of different temperatures to pollen grains and measuring how long each grows in 6 hours.

For this investigation, identify:

i the independent variable

ii the dependent variable

iii **two** control variables.

The independent variable is what is changed in an investigation.

The dependent variable is what you measure in an investigation.

The control variables are factors that could affect the outcome that you try to control or keep the same during an investigation.

a i temperature

ii length of pollen tubes

iii type of pollen (same plant); concentration of sugar solution.

b Write a title for the investigation.

An investigation title should include the independent variable and dependent variable, e.g. 'An investigation into the effect of the independent variable on the dependent variable'.

b Investigation into the effect of temperature on growth of pollen tubes.

c One factor that was kept the same during the investigation was concentration of the sugar solution.

i What type of variable is sugar concentration?

The sugar concentration used was 40 g sugar per 100 ml of distilled water. This is also represented as 40%.

ii The technician only has 20 g of sugar. Explain how a 40% sugar solution can be made using 20 g of sugar.

Remember the control variable definition from above.

'%' or 'per cent' means 'per 100'.

So, 40 g of sugar in 100 ml would be the same as 80 g in 200 ml. Think about the proportions of each substance when you work out your answer.

c i control variable

ii 20 g sugar and 50 ml water

10 Following pollination, the stigma releases a substance that includes sugar, and this causes a pollen tube to grow from the pollen grain. Thomas wants to investigate the effect of the concentration of sugar on how long a pollen tube grows.

a For this investigation, identify:

i the independent variable

ii the dependent variable

iii **two** control variables.

b Thomas repeats his experiment three times. The average results are shown below.

Concentration of sugar (%)	0	5	10	15	20	25
Average length of pollen tube (mm)	0	25	32	42	27	22

i Suggest what Thomas should do next to find the optimum (best) glucose concentration for growth of pollen tubes for this pollen.

ii Suggest why Thomas calculated an average length of pollen tube for each concentration.

iii Concentration is shown here as %, meaning g/100 ml. If Thomas wanted to use a solution of 30%, what mass of glucose and volume of water should be used?

c Thomas uses a light microscope to observe and measure the pollen tubes, with an eyepiece lens magnification of ×4 and an objective lens magnification of ×40.

i What is the total magnification of the microscope?

ii He measures the image as 32 mm. Calculate the actual (real) length of the pollen tube. Show your answer as μm.

A bee pollinating a lily flower

Lily pollen tubes

2.2 Seed dispersal

You are learning to:
- describe different methods of seed dispersal
- explain why seed dispersal is important and how seeds are adapted to different methods of dispersal
- describe how fruits are used in seed dispersal
- analyse experimental data and methods for seed dispersal mechanisms.

1 Following fertilisation, changes take place in each part of the flower. Choose from the phrases to complete each sentence (use each phrase either once/more than once/not at all):

Plant part	**Choose from:** … falls off. … becomes a seed. … becomes a fruit.
a The fertilised ovule …	
b The ovary …	
c Each petal …	
d Each sepal …	

2 State **three** ways in which seeds may be dispersed (spread out).

Worked example

Seeds released from exploding pods, such as witch hazel, do not travel far from the parent plant. Seeds carried by water, such as coconut, travel much further.

In one investigation, witch hazel seeds travelled 8 m and coconut seeds travelled 120 km.

How many times further than the witch hazel did the coconut seed travel?

Witch hazel seeds travelled 8 m.

Coconut travelled 120 km = 120 000 m.

The coconut travelled $\frac{120\,000}{8} = 15\,000$ times further.

3 The distance travelled by different seeds was recorded. The table below shows how far some seeds dispersed from the parent plant.

Seed	**Average distance travelled by seeds (m)**	**Average distance travelled by seeds (km)**
dandelion	100 000	
maple	4000	

a Show the distance travelled for each seed in km.

b The measurements were repeated with seeds dispersed during a storm. Suggest how the distance travelled by the seeds would change in a storm.

4 Complete the paragraph using the words below.

grow temperature nutrients germination

Seeds are packed with ___________________.

These help the new plant to ___________________.

Once the conditions such as water and ___________________ are suitable, the seed grows into a new plant.

This process of a seed growing into a new plant is called ___________________.

5 Dispersal of seeds means that new plants grow far away from the parent plants. Explain why this is helpful for growth of new plants.

6 Describe the stages involved from a pollen cell fertilising an egg cell in another tomato plant to new tomato plants growing.

7 Pea pods and courgettes are often classed as vegetables, not fruits.

a Define 'fruit'.

b Explain why pea pods and courgettes are both actually fruits rather than vegetables.

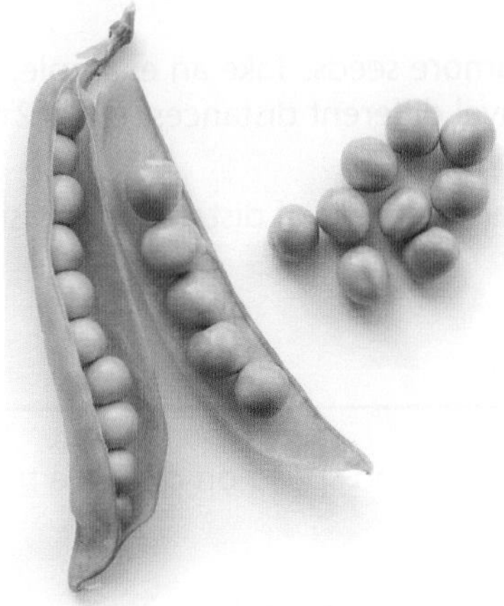

pea pod

courgette

8 The images show a coconut, dispersed by water, and sycamore seeds, dispersed by wind.

coconut

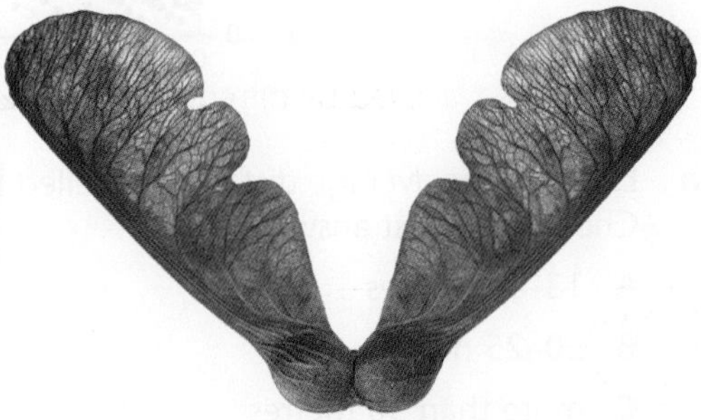

sycamore seeds

Explain how the coconut is adapted to travel by water and how the sycamore seed is adapted to travel by wind.

Worked example

An investigation was carried out to investigate the effect of wind speed on distance travelled by sycamore seeds. The graph below shows the results.

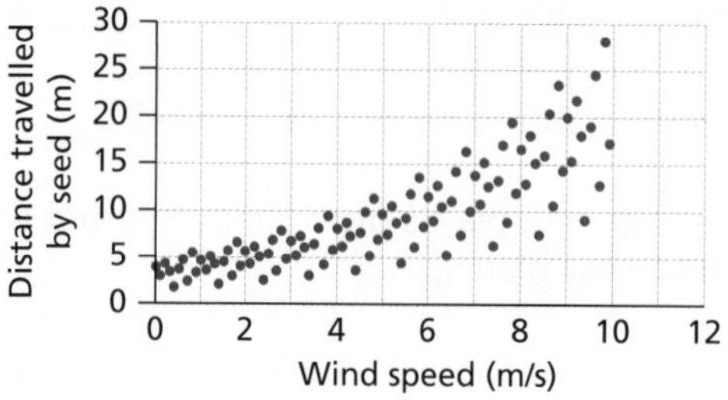

Which of these statements is true? Choose **two** answers.

A For any wind speed, the distance travelled by a sycamore seed may vary.

B The trend is, the stronger the wind, the larger the distance that sycamore seeds travel.

C If a sycamore seed lands 5 metres from the tree, the wind speed was approximately 6 m/s.

D Sycamore seeds always behave in the same way.

The dots on the graph show the results for individual sycamore seeds. Take an example, such as a wind speed of 8 m/s: at this speed, different seeds travel different distances, e.g. 12 m and 20 m.

The graph also shows a trend: consider whether the overall picture is of distance increasing as wind speed increases.

Check each statement carefully.

A and B

9 An investigation was carried out to investigate the effect of wind speed on distance travelled by sycamore seeds. The graph below shows the results.

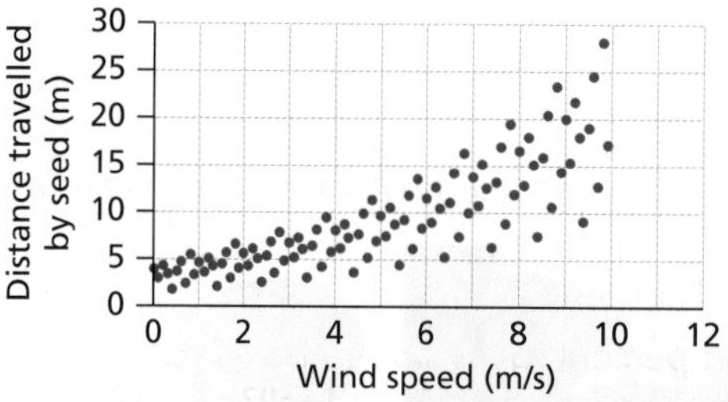

a Estimate the average distance travelled by a sycamore seed when the wind speed is 8 m/s. Choose the best answer.

A 13–16 metres

B 20–25 metres

C more than 30 metres

D less than 10 metres

b Identify the independent variable and the dependent variable in this investigation.

c Write a conclusion about the effect of wind speed on distance travelled by the seeds.

10 Garden centres must be certain that the seeds they sell are likely to germinate and produce new plants for their customers.

To be certain of selling the best seeds, botanists can calculate the 'germination percentage'.

$$\text{germination percentage} = \frac{\text{seeds germinated}}{\text{total number of seeds}} \times 100$$

A botanist uses the following method.

- Count out 200 seeds from seed sample **A** and place on an absorbent material inside a tray.
- Carefully saturate the absorbent material.
- For each of 10 days, check to see that the absorbent material remains moist.
- After 10 days, count the number of germinated seeds.
- Repeat the procedure another two times for seed sample **A**.
- Repeat the whole procedure for seed sample **B**.

The table below shows the results for two different seed samples.

Seed sample	Number of germinated seeds after 10 days			Average number of germinated seeds	Germination percentage
	1	2	3		
A	160	176	156		
B	184	179	189		

a Suggest why the absorbent material was kept moist during the experiment.

b Calculate the average number of germinated seeds for both samples, **A** and **B**.

c Calculate the germination percentage for both samples, **A** and **B**.

d A good germination percentage is said to be 80%. Which of these seed samples would you recommend that the botanist should sell?

e The botanist wonders whether they could sell more seeds if they can advertise that the seeds germinate just as well in less than 10 days. Suggest how they could test whether the seeds reach a germination rate of 80% in less than 10 days.

2.3 Reproduction in humans

You are learning to:

- identify the organs of the male and female reproductive systems
- describe fertilisation in humans
- explain the roles of each of the organs in reproduction
- compare reproduction in flowering plants and humans.

1. Complete the sentences using the words below.

   sperm   reproductive   eggs

   The job of the human ________________ system is to produce offspring.

   The male system makes ________________ and the female system makes ________________.

2. Fertilisation is an essential part of reproduction. Define what fertilisation in humans is.

3. Identify the parts of the female human reproductive system by choosing from the words below.

   cervix   vagina   uterus   ovary   oviduct

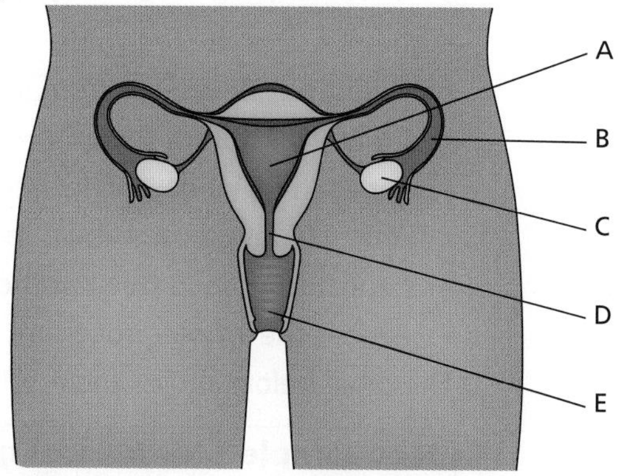

4. Identify the parts of the male human reproductive system by choosing from the words below.

   prostate gland   sperm duct   urethra
   testis   scrotal sac   penis

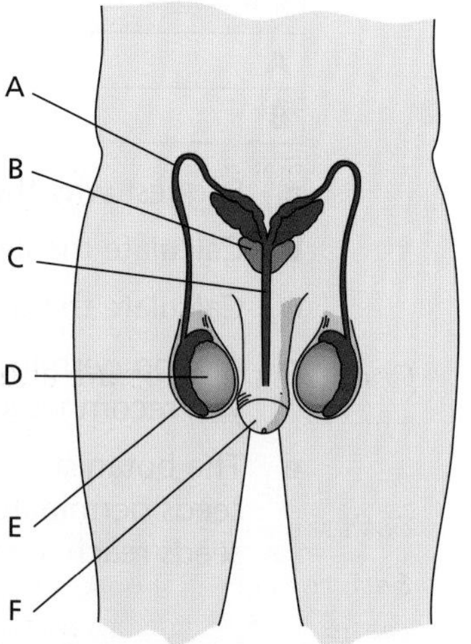

5. What role does semen play in reproduction? Choose **one** answer.

   a produces sperm
   b provides sperm with nutrients
   c guides sperm to the vagina
   d warms sperm up

6. Match each part of the male reproductive system to its role.

Part
a sperm duct
b testis
c scrotal sac
d penis

Role
producing sperm
passing sperm to the prostate gland
passing sperm into the vagina
controlling the temperature of the testes

7 Explain the function of each of the following parts of the female human reproductive system:

a oviduct
b ovary
c vagina
d uterus.

8 Explain why an egg moves from where it is made to the uterus.

9 For each of the parts of the human reproductive system below, identify what performs the same role in flowering plants:

a sperm
b egg
c testis
d ovary.

10 A fertility laboratory technician is analysing samples to check the quality and quantity of sperm cells in patient samples.

a Name the piece of equipment that the technician would use to observe and count the sperm cell samples.

The sperm cell count is measured for three patients.

Patient	Sperm cell count (per ml)
A	15 million
B	8 million
C	200 million

Remember: there are 1000 μl in 1 ml.

b Convert the sperm count for each patient into μl.

A count below 12 million cells per ml is said to be a low sperm count.

c Another patient shares his results as 9400 sperm per μl.

i Show this result as per ml.

ii Would this patient be diagnosed as having a low sperm count?

d If a patient does not have a low sperm count, suggest **one** problem their sperm may have that could cause the patient to be infertile.

11 **a** Explain what is meant by 'ovulation'.

b Describe the stages of human reproduction from ovulation to fertilisation. Structure your answer in a logical order.

Worked example

Compare the structure and function of a human egg cell and sperm cell.

When comparing, both the similarities and differences should be described, with both the egg cell and sperm cell mentioned for each feature.

Both the egg cell and the sperm cell contain a nucleus, containing genetic material.

Both the egg cell and the sperm cell move; the egg from the ovary to the uterus, and the sperm from the testis to the prostate gland (and to the vagina via the penis during intercourse).

However, whereas the sperm cell can move itself with its tail, the egg cell cannot move itself but is moved along by hairs in the oviduct.

An egg cell is larger than a sperm cell (as it contains a food source).

More sperm are produced than eggs. Only one egg is released from the ovary each month, whereas millions of sperm cells are released via the penis during ejaculation.

12 Compare reproduction and the reproductive systems in humans and flowering plants.

2.4 Puberty and the menstrual cycle

You are learning to:
- describe and explain some of the changes in the male and female body during puberty
- describe the process and function of the menstrual cycle
- apply the menstrual cycle to causes of infertility.

1 Fill the gaps using the words below.

hormones reproduce puberty

Between the ages of 8 and 16 years, human bodies change. This period of time is called ___________.

The physical changes happen to allow a person to ______________.

These changes are controlled by chemicals called ______________.

2 Between which ages does puberty usually happen?

A between 4 and 12 years
B between 8 and 16 years
C between 16 and 24 years
D between 20 and 28 years

3 For each of the changes during puberty listed below, identify whether they take place in **males**, **females** or **both**:

a testes grow
b hips widen
c height growth spurt
d menstruation starts.

4 How long is the menstrual cycle on average?

a 8–15 days
b 24–35 days
c 34–42 days
d 50–60 days

5 Blood is lost during menstruation. Where does this blood originate from?

vagina ovary uterus egg

6 Choose **one** possible reason for infertility:

a releasing two eggs in one menstrual cycle
b having a menstrual cycle lasting for less than 28 days
c not releasing any eggs during the menstrual cycle
d slow breakdown of the uterus lining

7 The age for the start of menstruation ranges by five years.

a If the youngest age to start menstruation is approximately 10.5 years, what is the approximate oldest age to start?

b If a girl has her first menstrual period at age 14 years, at what age could she become pregnant?

8 Explain the reason for each of the changes caused by puberty:

a hips widen in girls
b breasts become bigger in girls
c penis grows in boys
d sperm is produced in boys.

9 Some changes in puberty are not directly linked to the physical process of reproduction. Other changes in males include broadening of the shoulders, deepening of the voice and growth of facial hair. Explain how these changes in males may help to support reproduction in humans.

10 Match the approximate days in the diagram to each stage of the menstrual cycle:

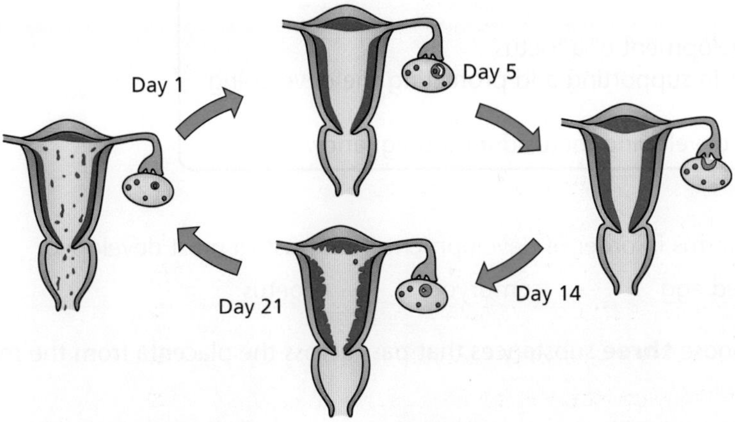

Approximate day
1
5
14
21

Stage
a The lining of the uterus begins to build up and an egg ripens in the ovary.
b The egg is released by the ovary. The uterus lining is ready to receive a fertilised egg.
c The period (menstrual bleeding begins).
d The egg passes into the uterus. If it is unfertilised, it will die.

11 Dora and Karla are discussing pregnancy. Dora says that menstruation continues during pregnancy. Karla says that periods stop when you are pregnant. State who is correct and explain your answer.

12 **a** Describe the sequence from an egg ripening to it being fertilised. Link each step to days in the menstrual cycle, assuming a cycle of 28 days.

b Explain why we can only estimate the date that an egg is fertilised.

c For a female who starts her periods on her 15th birthday, estimate how many eggs she has released by the time she becomes pregnant at age 23 if her cycle is usually 28 days.

13 **a** A fertility consultant is working with a patient who has been trying to become pregnant without success. For each of the following medical issues the consultant speaks to the patient about, suggest how they could cause infertility:

i lack of ovulation

ii blockage in the oviduct

iii cysts growing around the ovary (endometriosis).

b Some fertility drugs increase the number of eggs that are produced each month.

i Suggest what type of chemical these drugs contain.

ii Suggest which of the conditions in part **a** could be treated with these drugs. Explain your answer.

2.5 Development of a foetus and the effect of lifestyle

You are learning to:
- describe the stages in the development of a foetus
- explain the role of the mother in supporting and protecting the developing foetus
- discuss the factors affecting a developing foetus during pregnancy.

1 Arrange the following terms in order of development from least to most developed:

baby fertilised egg embryo foetus

2 From the list below, choose **three** substances that pass across the placenta from the mother to the foetus:

carbon dioxide oxygen glucose urea vitamins

3 What is so special about stem cells? Choose the best statement.

a They are the first cells to develop after fertilisation.

b They can develop into any specialised cells.

c They are larger than normal cells.

d They can perform special tasks.

4 Identify the parts using the labels below.

amniotic fluid
placenta
vagina
umbilical cord
uterus wall

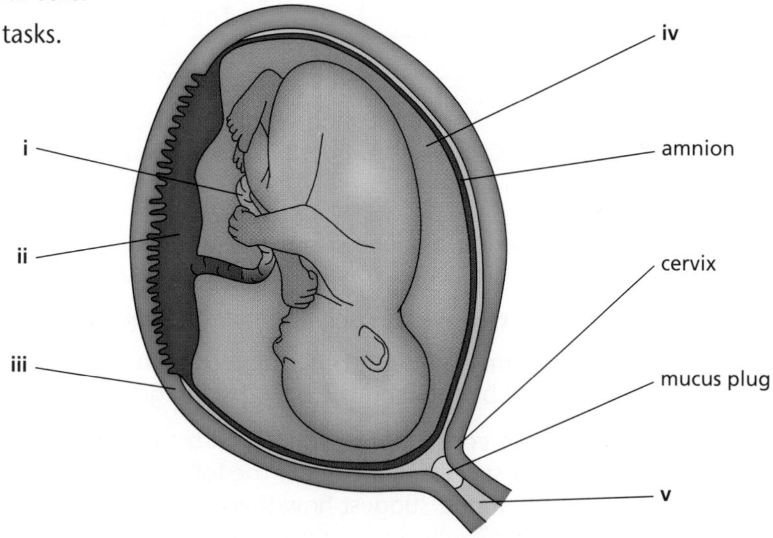

5 A pregnant woman is having a scan of her developing foetus.

Gestation (weeks)	8	12	16	20	24	28	32	36	40
Size (length) of foetus (mm)	40	100	140	190	230	270	300	340	380

a The foetus measures 150 mm. What is the likely number of weeks of gestation? Give your answer as a range.

b Suggest why we can only estimate the gestation of a foetus.

c Suggest **one** factor that might cause the foetus to be smaller than average.

6 Match each of the structures supporting the developing foetus with its role:

Structure
a umbilical cord
b placenta
c mucus plug
d amniotic fluid

Role
i where nutrients, oxygen and waste products exchange between the mother's blood and the foetus's blood
ii attaches the foetus to the placenta and contains blood vessels
iii protects the foetus from infections, bumps and knocks
iv prevents infections reaching the uterus

7 Explain how nicotine in a cigarette reaches the developing foetus of a mother as she smokes. Give your answer as a logical sequence.

8 Summarise the advantages and disadvantages of the placenta allowing some substances to pass across it.

9 In vitro fertilisation (IVF) can be used to help couples with fertility issues to have a baby. During IVF, eggs may be collected from the female and mixed with sperm in a laboratory. The fertilised eggs are grown in the laboratory for 6 days before being transferred into the uterus of the female.

On average, cell division takes 18 hours.

a Why do we say 'on average' rather than an exact length of time?

b Estimate how many cells are present 6 days after the single egg is fertilised.

10 A study was carried out to investigate the effect of smoking on the birth weight of babies. Data was collected from 32 pregnant women, some non-smokers and some smokers.

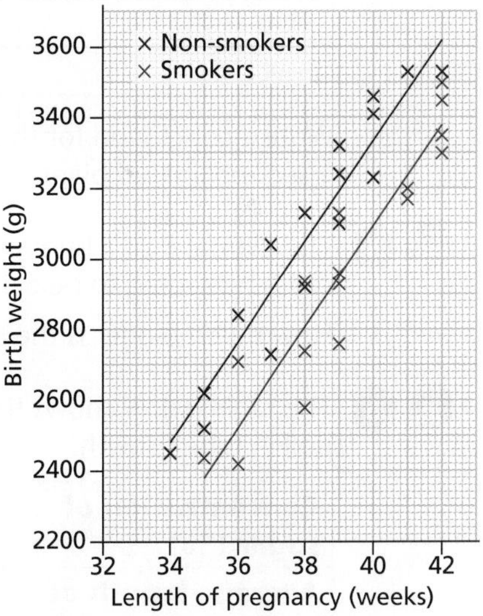

a Decide whether each of these statements is 'true', 'false' or 'needs more information'.

i For both smoking and non-smoking mothers, the general trend is that the longer the pregnancy, the higher the baby's birth weight.

ii This study shows that women who do not smoke have babies with higher birth weights than the babies of women that do smoke.

iii In this study, the baby with the highest birth weight was born at 40 weeks.

iv Mothers who smoke a lot have a greater effect on birth weight than mothers who only smoke a little.

v For any length of pregnancy, non-smoking mothers always have babies with higher birth weights than the babies of smoking mothers.

b Using the graph, comment on whether this data supports medical advice about smoking while pregnant.

c Suggest **one** way that this research could be improved:

i to increase repeatability

ii to explore whether how much a pregnant mother smokes affects the birth weight.

Maths and practical skills

1 Aki has made a paper model of a seed dispersed by the wind. He measures how long the model stays in the air for. Select the unit he should use for time taken:

minutes days hours seconds

2 Match each word linked with practical investigations to its definition.

a This is a statement about what you think will happen.	validity
b This means that the investigation is designed to collect evidence that can answer the question.	prediction
c We can improve this by repeating our experiment or by using a bigger sample size.	repeatability

3 A sonographer is carrying out an ultrasound scan of a foetus. The image on the screen measures 27 cm. The magnification is ×3.

What is the actual size of the foetus? Show your answer in mm.

4 The table below shows data for the volume and number of pollen grains produced by wind-pollinated and insect-pollinated plants.

Type of pollination	Average volume of pollen grains (μm^3)	Average number of pollen grains per flower
wind	490	14 000
insect	675	7000

Write a conclusion for this investigation about the pollen produced by wind-pollinated and insect-pollinated plants.

5 The diameter of a human egg cell is measured to be 0.1 mm. The diameter of a human sperm cell is measured to be 5.1 µm.

How much bigger is the egg cell than the sperm cell?

6 The table below shows the results of an investigation into the effect of sugar concentration on pollen tube growth.

Concentration of sugar (%)	0	5	10	15	20	25
Average length of pollen tube (mm)	0	25	32	42	27	22

a Write a question that this investigation is designed to answer. Start the question with: 'Does changing…'.

b Identify the range of sugar concentrations used in this investigation.

c The experiment at 0% concentration used pure water. Explain why this sample was included in the investigation.

7 A team of researchers want to study the effect of age on amount of sperm produced. They want to make sure that the investigation is valid.

a What does 'valid' mean?

b What data should they collect to ensure that the evidence is valid?

c In this investigation, name:

i the independent variable

ii the dependent variable.

8 James and Lia carry out an investigation into the effect of the mass of a seed on how far it travels. They make model seeds as shown in the diagram below:

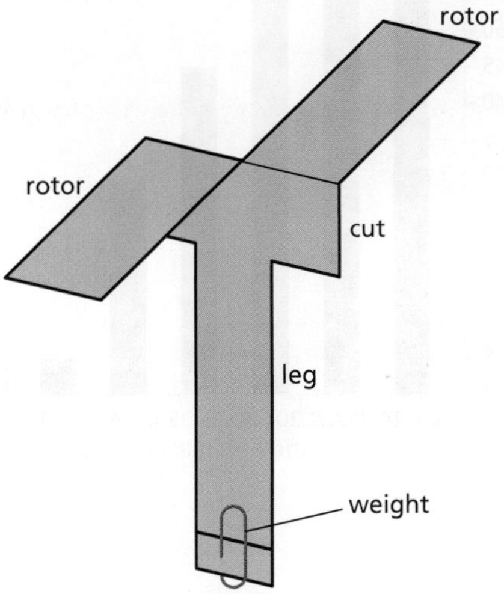

a Identify:

i the independent variable

ii the dependent variable.

b Suggest how James and Lia could change the mass of their model seeds.

c Suggest suitable units in this investigation to measure:

i mass

ii distance.

d Part way through their experiment, James got hot and opened a window. Suggest why this might affect the validity of their results.

e James and Lia predict that as the mass of the seeds is increased they will not travel as far. Sketch a graph to show the trend that they might see in their results if their prediction is correct.

Worked example

The graph below shows the effect of female age on the chance of becoming pregnant.

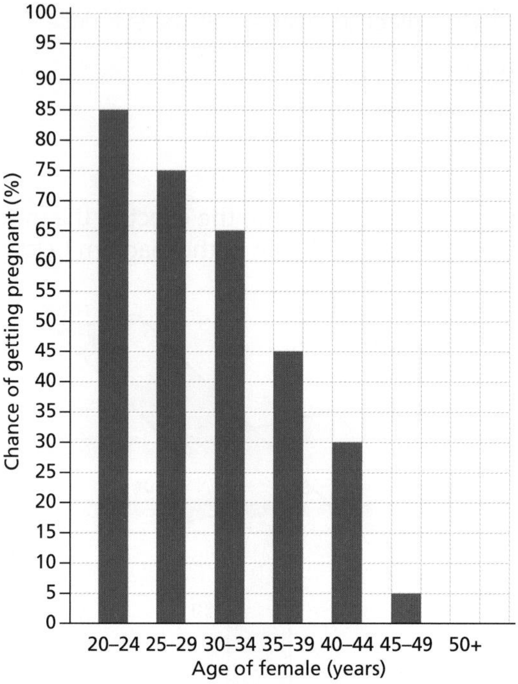

a In this investigation, identify:

i the independent variable

ii the dependent variable.

The independent variable is what we change.

The dependent variable is what we measure.

i *age of female*

ii *chance of getting pregnant*

b **i** Write a conclusion for this investigation.

ii Identify whether there are any anomalous results.

The conclusion must be linked to the title or aim of the investigation. Remember that this question is about the effect of age on chances of getting pregnant. What is the trend shown in the graph?

Do all the results fit the same pattern?

i **As age increases, the chance of getting pregnant decreases.**

ii **There are no anomalous results, all fit the same pattern.**

c Explain why it is important that a large sample was used in this investigation.

Think about whether all females are the same; would it be likely that all 20–24 year olds had the same chance of getting pregnant?

Females within any age group will vary; by investigating a large sample it makes it more likely that the result represents the average.

9 A study was carried out to investigate the effect of smoking on fertility in men. The following chart shows the results.

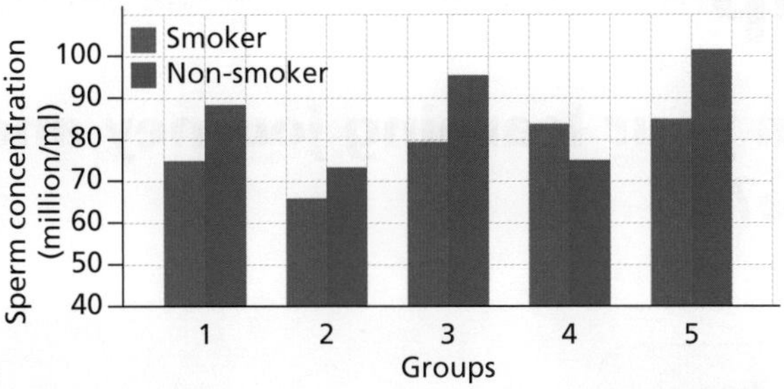

a In this investigation, identify:

i the independent variable

ii the dependent variable.

b Controlling other factors can be challenging when working with humans, but suggest **one** factor that you might want to keep the same between all the men studied.

c Explain why several (five) groups of men were studied.

d **i** Identify which group had an anomalous result.

ii Describe how an anomalous result should be treated when making conclusions.

e Write a conclusion for this investigation based on the data.

10 The histogram shows birth weight data for 188 babies.

115 were born to mothers who smoked and 73 to mothers who did not smoke.

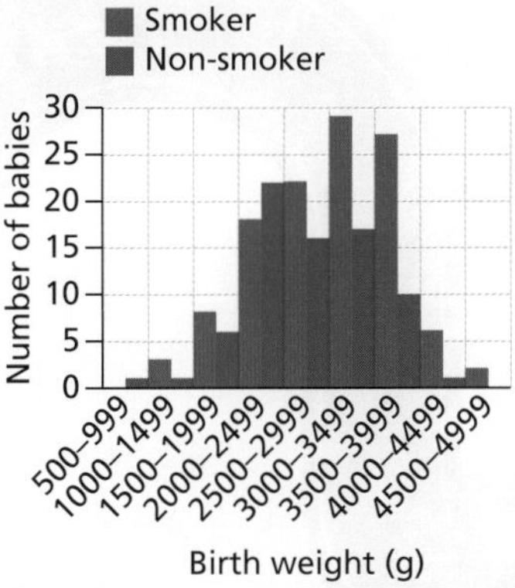

a The researcher who collected the data predicted that the babies of non-smokers would have higher birth weights than the babies of smokers.

i Provide **two** pieces of evidence from the graph that suggest the prediction was **incorrect.**

ii Provide **two** pieces of evidence from the graph that suggest that smoking does cause lower birth weight of babies.

b The researcher decides to collect further data and increases the sample size. Explain how this will affect the repeatability of the data.

c In many investigations that we carry out, we control some variables.

i Explain why this is not possible in a study of this kind.

ii Apart from smoking, suggest **one** other factor that may affect the birth weight of babies in this sample.

3 Health and human systems road map

Where are you in your learning journey and where are you aiming to be?

- how animals get nutrition from what they eat
- basic parts of the human digestive system
- types of human teeth and their functions
- how water and nutrients are transported within animals
- the functions of the skeleton and muscles
- the impact of diet, exercise, drugs and lifestyle on the human body

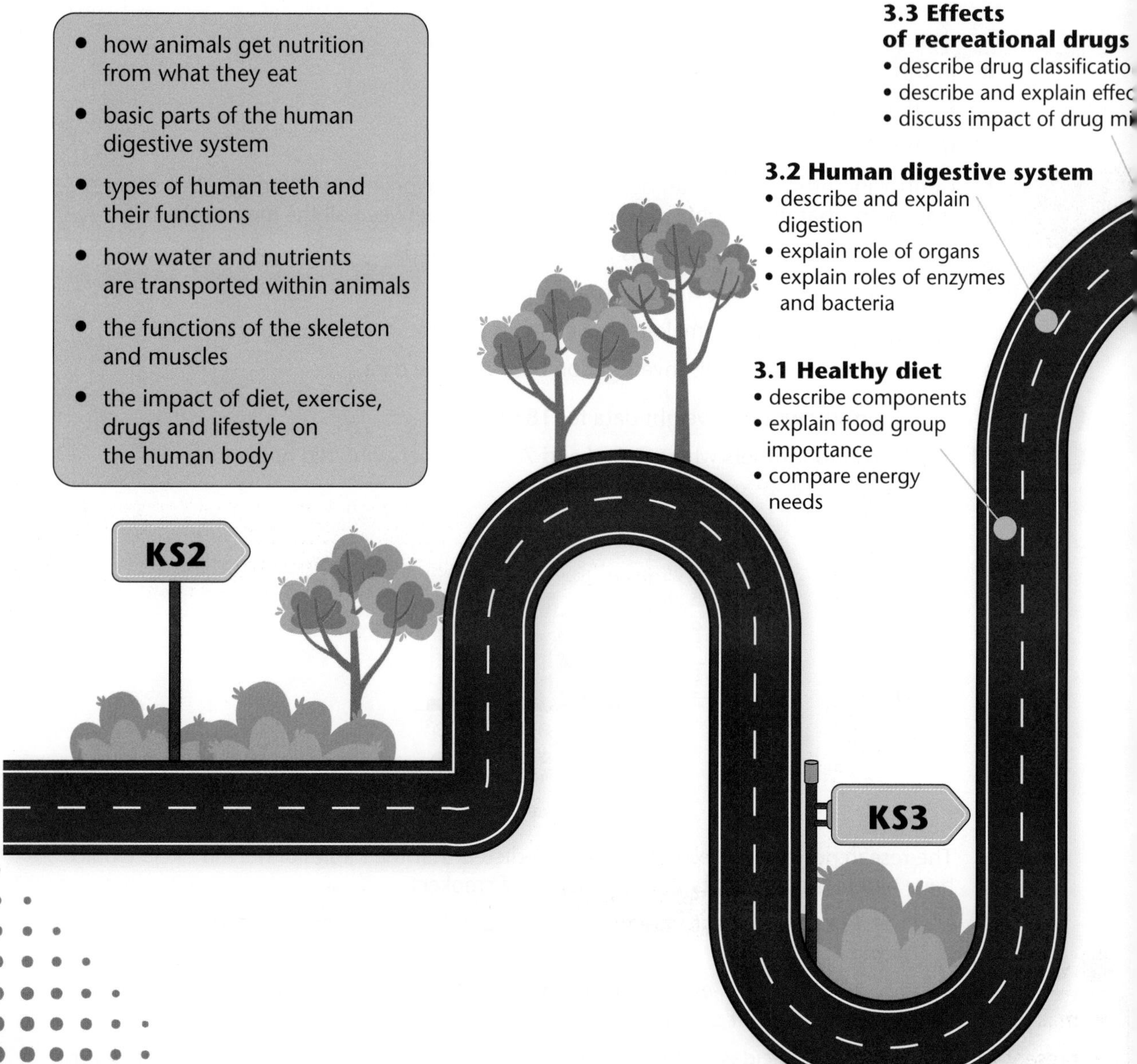

- the human digestive system
- metabolism
- health issues
- the effect of lifestyle on some non-communicable diseases
- infection and response
- respiration
- the heart and blood vessels
- response to exercise

3.4 Human skeleton, joints and muscles
- identify bones
- describe and explain functions
- describe the role of joints
- explain antagonistic muscles
- state forces exerted by muscles

3.5 Human breathing system
- identify parts
- explain breathing in humans
- explain adaptations for gas exchange
- explain importance of air pressure
- describe lung volume measurement
- describe and explain impact of disease and lifestyle

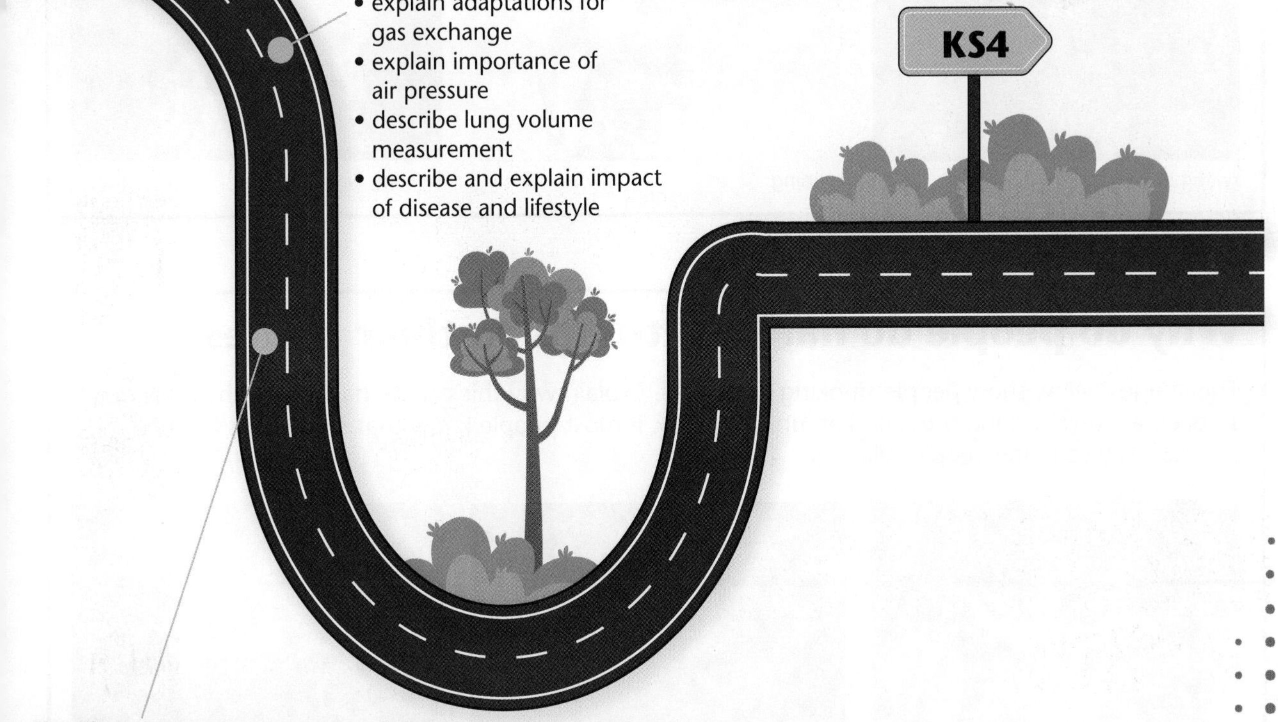

Maths and practical skills

- making scientific predictions
- present reasoned explanations
- planning an investigation, identifying and managing the variables
- calculating results and converting between different units
- presenting data using tables and graphs
- analysing data and identifying anomalous results
- using equations to calculate answers

3 Health and human systems

The human body carries out a large number of processes without us even thinking about them, such as moving, breathing and digesting our food. Maintaining a healthy lifestyle, for example through eating a healthy diet and avoiding recreational drugs, is essential to support these systems to work effectively.

Why is what we eat important?

Each of the people below is using energy in different ways. Energy comes from the food we eat. Suggest why an athlete, such as the swimmer, might have to strictly control their diet. List some healthy foods that they might eat.

swimming

running

keeping warm

Why do people do harmful things to their bodies?

The images below show people smoking cigarettes. Explain why this can be harmful to the individual smoker, a crowd around them and an unborn baby. If most people know that smoking is harmful, suggest why so many people still do it.

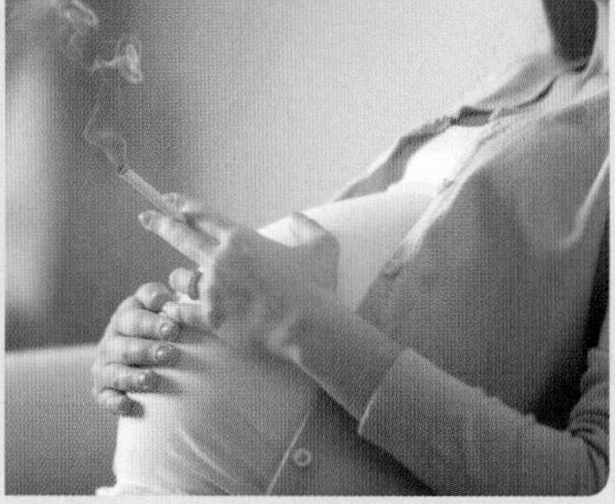

Using your science skills

Could you be a sports scientist?

You use your extensive knowledge of how the human body works to help people improve their sporting ability. You work with individuals or whole sports teams, so have good people skills and can support and motivate others. Your understanding of body systems, such as the skeletal system, muscles and the breathing system, ensures maximum strength and efficient movement. You understand good nutrition and how best to meet energy needs during different activities. You solve problems, for example determining the best way to recover from injuries, and are willing to learn about new sports and their demands.

As a sports scientist, you work as part of a team, for example with coaches, dieticians and doctors, as well as athletes, all with the same goal of maximising performance safely.

Dieticians study information about food and nutrition and provide practical advice and guidance on a suitable diet for their patients. This could be to treat health problems or to prevent disease.

Physiotherapists treat patients with injury or illness that affects their movement. They use manual therapy of the body and also advise on exercise to improve mobility and to manage pain of the patient.

Personal trainers develop exercise routines to increase the fitness, strength and mobility of clients. They ensure that exercises are suited to the individual and are carried out using correct techniques to minimise the risk of injury.

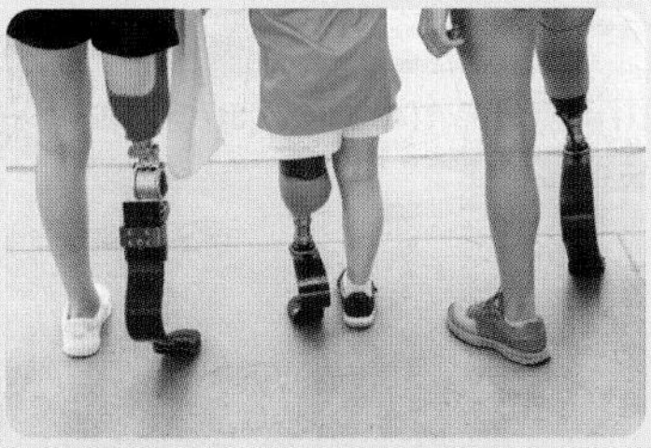

Prosthetists design and fit prosthetic limbs to patients, following guidance from doctors. They must understand the specific need of each patient and what will support their movement best, for example matching to the real limb or being designed for a particular sport.

Occupational therapists support patients who struggle to carry out activities that they previously managed, for example due to old age or illness leading to decreased mobility. They ensure that appropriate support equipment is provided, such as walking frames and rails, and that equipment is used safely.

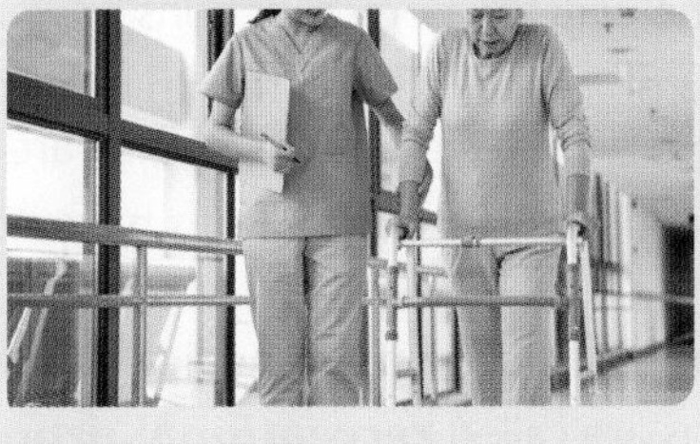

Sports engineers design equipment for the sports industry. This is a wide-ranging role that involves research and development of improved technologies, for example, exercise bikes, running shoes or technology to improve the measurement of lung capacity.

Knowledge organiser

Food provides us with **nutrients** and energy. Food contains chemical energy. We need energy:

- to grow
- to move
- to repair
- to keep warm.

Food labels tell us about ingredients and energy. These help us to make informed choices about what we eat.

Energy in food is usually measured in **kilojoules** (kJ) but is sometimes shown as **calories** (cal). The amount of energy we need varies.

A healthy human diet (balanced diet) contains seven food groups:

Food group	Uses in the body
carbohydrates	Two types: starches and sugars. Provide energy.
proteins	Important for growth and repair.
lipids (fats and oils)	Stored as a reserve energy supply. A layer of fat under the skin provides insulation against cold.
minerals	e.g. iron for red blood cells and calcium for bones.
vitamins	e.g. vitamin C for repair of the skin and vitamin D for taking up calcium.
dietary fibre	Needed to keep the large intestine working well.
water	Needed to stop a person becoming dehydrated.

The human digestive system contains many organs of the body. **Physical digestion** and **chemical digestion** take place here.

0 hours

Food enters the mouth where it is chewed by the teeth, rolled into a ball by the tongue and moistened by **saliva** ready for swallowing.

1 hour

Food is swallowed and passes into the **oesophagus** which carries the food to the **stomach**.

2 hours

The stomach breaks down food physically by muscle contraction and chemically by **enzymes**. The acid conditions kill bacteria and help the enzymes to work.

6 hours

The **small intestine** digests the food further using different enzymes and absorbs it into the blood.

10 hours

In the **large intestine** water is absorbed to make the waste (faeces) more solid.

16–24 hours

The **faeces** are passed out through the **anus**.

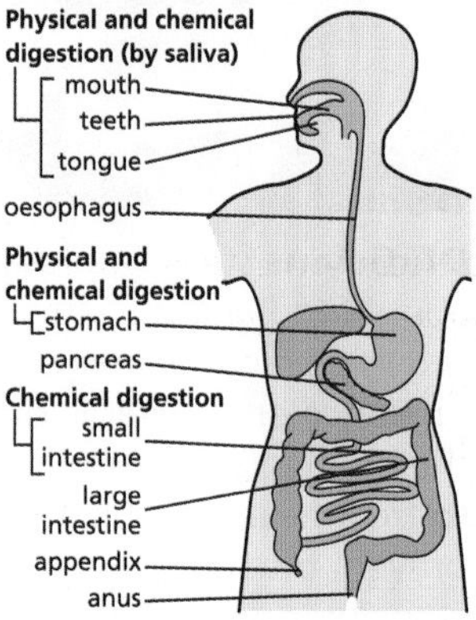

Condition	starvation	obesity	deficiency diseases
Cause	not taking in enough energy from food over a long period	taking in too much energy from food over a long period	lack of certain nutrients in the diet, such as vitamins and minerals
Possible problems	weight loss, muscle loss, dry hair and skin, fatigue, death	heart disease, joint problems, diabetes	lack of vitamin C – scurvy lack of vitamin D – deformities such as rickets lack of iron – anaemia (pale, severe exhaustion)

A **drug** is any substance that affects the way the body functions.

Some drugs can be bought legally at a pharmacy (e.g. caffeine, nicotine, alcohol, paracetamol). Legal drugs have been tested to check they are safe.

Other drugs are illegal (e.g. cannabis and heroin). Illegal drugs have not usually been checked for safety.

Prescription drugs are prescribed by a doctor to treat medical conditions.

Any drugs not used for medical reasons are called **recreational drugs**.

Use of recreational drugs can lead to **addiction**. This means that a person finds it very difficult to stop using it. Examples of addictive drugs are nicotine, alcohol, cocaine and heroin.

Organ	How it is adapted to its function
oesophagus	Contains rings of muscle that contract behind the bolus to move the food along.
stomach	Contains muscles to squeeze the food. Secretes acid to kill bacteria. Contains an enzyme to digest protein.
pancreas	Releases enzymes that digest carbohydrates, protein and fats.
small intestine	Contains muscles to move the food along the tube and enzymes to complete digestion. Has thin walls and a good blood supply to help absorption of nutrients into blood.

Enzymes are 'biological catalysts': they speed up reactions without being used up themselves.

Food group	Carbohydrate (starch)	Proteins	Fats
Product of digestion	glucose	amino acids	fatty acids + glycerol
Enzyme involved	amylase	protease	lipase
Where the enzyme is found	mouth and small intestine	stomach and small intestine	small intestine

Key vocabulary	
addiction	physical or psychological dependence on a substance
anus	the opening at the end of the digestive tract, where faeces leave the body
calories	the unit of energy in food, shown on food packaging labels
carbohydrates	the food group that includes starches and sugars
chemical digestion	the breakdown of food by enzymes
deficiency disease	an illness caused by a lack of a certain nutrient
dietary fibre	the food group needed to move food along the large intestine
digestion	the breakdown of food from larger to smaller molecules (to use to release energy)
drug	any chemical that affects the way that the body works
enzyme	a substance that speeds up reactions in the body; biological catalyst
faeces	the solid waste released through the anus
kilojoule (kJ)	a unit of energy, 1000 joules
large intestine	the organ of the digestive system where water is absorbed into the body
lipids (fats)	the food group that is important for energy stores
minerals	elements such as iron and calcium needed in the diet
nutrient	a substance in food that we need to eat to stay healthy
obesity	a medical condition in which the amount of body fat is so high that it harms health
oesophagus	the tube within the digestive system from the mouth to the stomach
pancreas	the organ of the digestive system that produces enzymes
physical digestion	mechanical digestion of food
proteins	the food group important for growth and repair
recreational drug	any drug, legal or illegal, used for its effects rather than any medical reason
saliva	the liquid produced in the mouth that helps swallowing and digestion
small intestine	the organ of the digestive system where food is digested and molecules absorbed into the blood
stomach	the organ of the digestive system where most food breakdown takes place
vitamins	important nutrients needed in very small quantities in our diet

The human **skeleton** has four main roles:

- it supports the body
- it protects the organs (e.g. cranium protects the brain)
- it allows movement (at joints)
- it produces blood cells (in **bone marrow**).

Joints occur where bones meet.

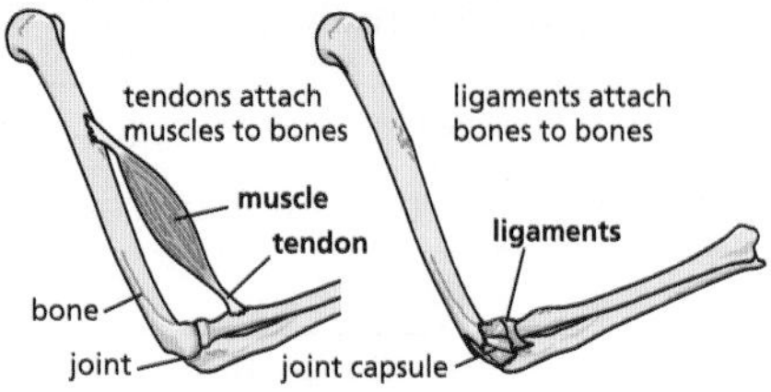

The human skeleton is made of 206 bones. Some are very small.

Vertebrate animals have a backbone; the scientific name for the bones in the back is vertebrae.

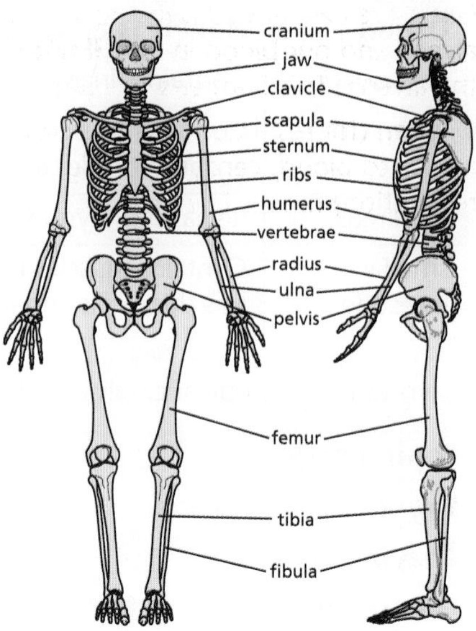

The human breathing system is within the chest cavity.

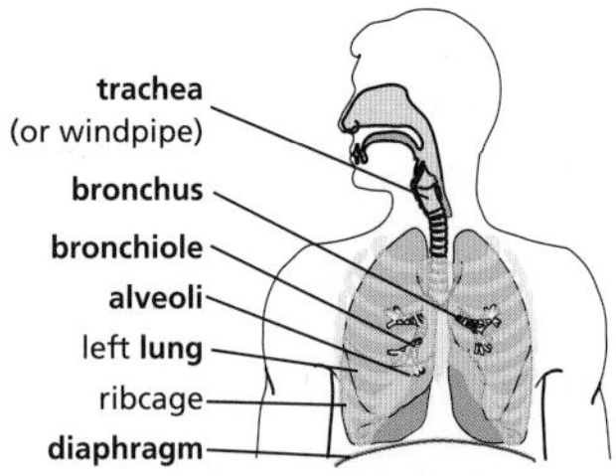

Breathing is brought about by movements of the ribcage and diaphragm.

There are four types of joint in the human skeleton:

1. ball and socket joint, as in the hip
2. hinge joint, as in the elbow
3. pivot joint, as in the neck
4. fixed joint, such as those in the cranium, do not allow movement

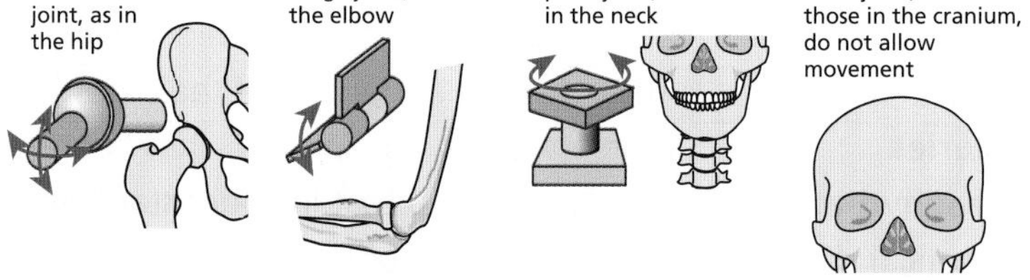

Skeletal muscles can only **contract** (pull), they cannot push.

When a muscle pulls (contracts), it gets shorter; when it **relaxes**, it returns to its original length.

Most muscles work as **antagonistic pairs**: when one of the pair contracts, the other relaxes.

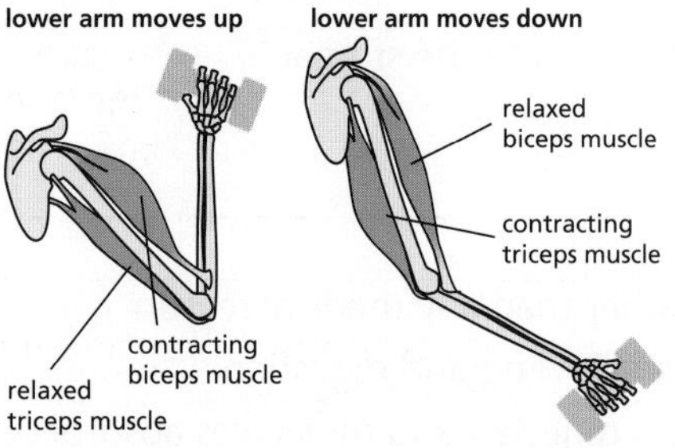

Exercising muscles makes them stronger. The strength of muscles can be measured in newtons, N.

Changes in volume in the chest space during breathing in and breathing out causes changes in pressure in the lungs.

- When the chest volume is high, the air pressure inside the chest space is low.
- When the chest volume is low, the air pressure inside the chest space is high.
- Just before breathing in, pressure in the lungs *falls below* **atmospheric pressure**, so air rushes *into* the lungs.
- Just before breathing out, pressure in the lungs *rises above* atmospheric pressure, so air rushes *out of* the lungs.

Pressure is measured in **pascals**, Pa.

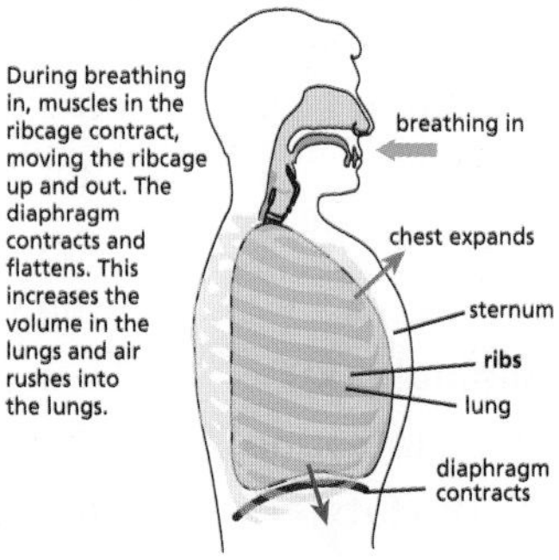

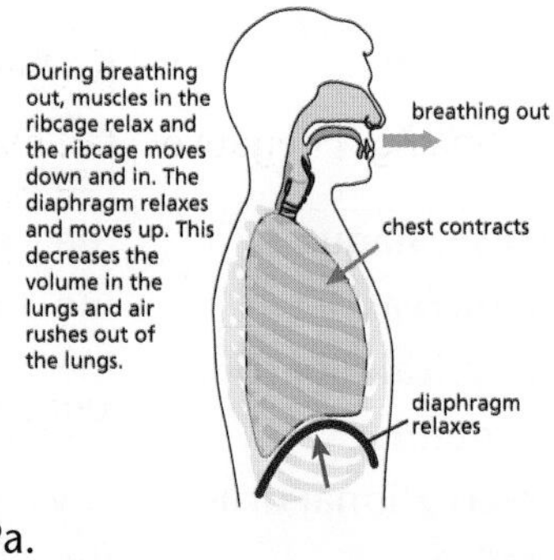

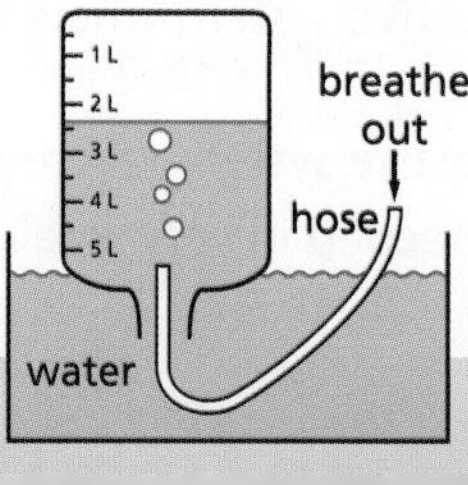

Lung volume can be measured in the classroom by displacing water. As you breathe out strongly through the tube, water is displaced. The volume of water displaced is equal to your lung volume.

Gases are exchanged between air inside the alveoli and our blood in **capillaries** outside the alveoli. This happens by diffusion.

Oxygen (for respiration) moves from the alveoli to blood; carbon dioxide (from respiration) moves from the blood to alveoli.

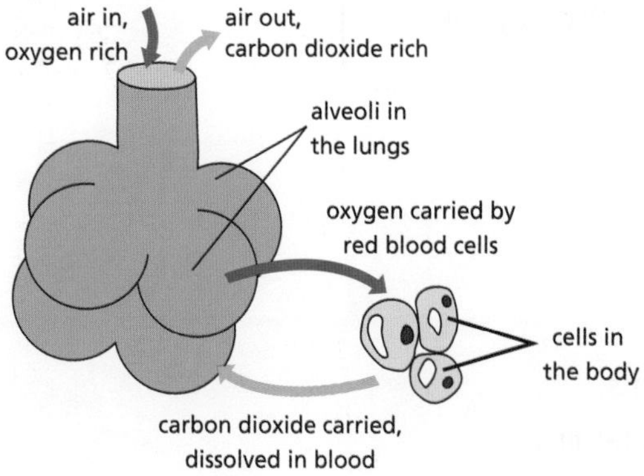

Alveoli are adapted to their function by having:

- a large surface area for gases to pass across
- a thin lining
- a good supply of capillaries to bring and take away blood.

Some behaviours and diseases can affect our breathing system:

Factor	Impact	Effect
exercise	positive	increases lung volume as the muscles in between the ribs are strengthened
asthma	negative	decreases volume of air moved in and out of lungs due to narrowing of bronchioles as they become inflamed
smoking	negative	tar: may cause lung cancer; damages tiny hairs in bronchioles meaning smoke and dirt can enter the lungs, causes smokers' cough carbon monoxide: decreases the amount of oxygen that blood can carry

Key vocabulary	
alveoli (singular alveolus)	where gas exchange happens in the lungs
antagonistic pair (of muscles)	pair of muscles that work together to move bones at a joint; as one contracts, the other relaxes
atmospheric pressure	the pressure exerted by the surrounding air
biceps	the muscle in the front of the upper arm
bone marrow	a soft substance at the centre of large bones, where blood cells are made
bronchioles	passageways that carry air from the bronchus to the alveoli
bronchus	the tube that carries air between the trachea and the lungs
capillary	a small blood vessel
contract	to become shorter; when a muscle shortens in makes a pulling motion
diaphragm	the muscular layer at the base of the chest cavity
joint	the place where two bones meet; allows movement
ligament	connects one bone to another bone; made of stretchy fibres
lung	one of two bag-like organs that are the main breathing structures
lung volume	the volume of air that can be breathed out following a big breath in
muscle	a tissue of the body that can contract and relax to produce motion; consists of long cells
pascal (Pa)	unit of pressure
relax	lengthening of a muscle, to return to its original length
skeleton	the framework made of bone that supports the soft tissues of the body and protects the internal organs
tendon	connects muscle to bone; made of stretchy fibres
trachea (or windpipe)	the tube that connects the mouth to the bronchi in the lungs
triceps	the muscle in the back of the upper arm
vertebrate	an organism having a backbone

3.1 Healthy diet

You are learning to:

- describe the components of a healthy diet
- explain the importance of each food group within the body and some of the deficiencies caused by a lack of specific nutrients
- compare energy needs of different people and suggest healthy ways of meeting these needs.

1 Choose the correct sentence ending.

A healthy diet is a diet that:

a does not contain any fat.

b contains the same amount of fat and protein.

c contains all the food groups in different amounts.

d contains carbohydrate, protein, minerals and vitamins.

2 A healthy diet contains seven food groups. Complete the list using the first letter given for each group:

carbohydrates

fats and oils

water

a p________

b v________

c m________

d f________

3 Match the use in the body to the correct food group.

a enables growth and repair	**i** water
b stores energy	**ii** carbohydrate
c keeps the body hydrated, which is important for many body processes	**iii** protein
d provides energy	**iv** fat

4 Find the best match between each food group and a food that supplies it.

a protein	**i** pasta
b fibre	**ii** vegetables
c water	**iii** fish
d carbohydrate	**iv** herbal tea

5 Three patients have each been diagnosed with a different deficiency disease, but their notes have been mixed up.

a Identify which of the patients is likely to have anaemia, rickets or scurvy.

Patient	Deficiency detected	Disease
i	iron	____________
ii	vitamin D	____________
iii	vitamin C	____________

b For each condition, suggest **one** symptom that the patient may have:

i rickets

ii scurvy.

c The medical notes for one patient say that they should eat lots of spinach, liver, beans and pulses. Suggest which condition this patient has.

Worked example

A student has been given two samples of food and asked to decide which is milk powder and which is fruit juice. He tests each for protein. The table below shows the test for protein.

Food group	Chemical used to test	Positive result
protein	biuret solution	colour change from blue to mauve

The results are:

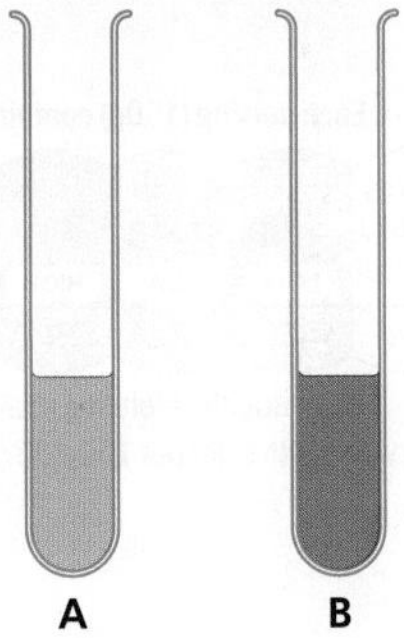

a Which of the sample(s) contains protein?

b Which of the samples is likely to be milk powder? Explain your answer.

c Name a food group that the fruit juice contains that could be tested for.

a B

b B, because milk contains protein and fruit juice does not.

c sugar (carbohydrate)

6 Food tests are used to work out the food types that food samples contain. The table below shows the tests for two carbohydrates: starch and sugar.

Food group	Chemical used in test	Positive result
starch	iodine	colour change from orange to blue/black
sugar	Benedict's solution	colour change from blue to orange

The diagrams show the results for two food samples for each test.

Test for starch

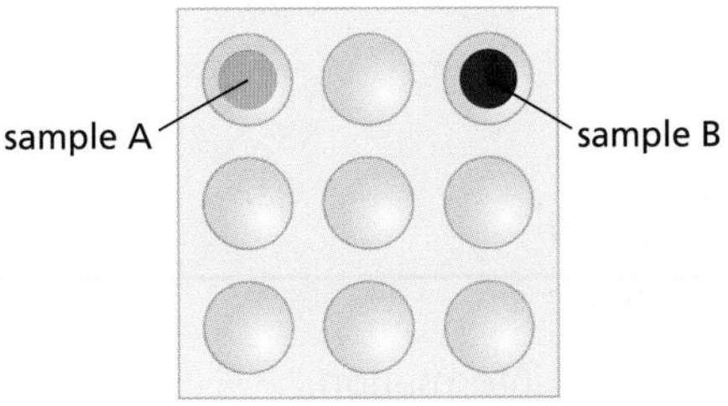

Test for sugar

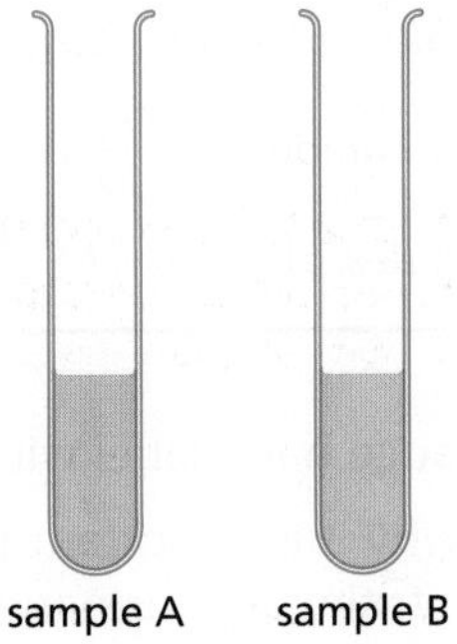

a Write a conclusion for each sample.

b One of the samples was bread and the other was honey. Suggest which was **A** and which was **B**.

7 **a** Some people believe a Mediterranean diet is linked to good health and a lowered risk of heart disease. It includes fats from healthy sources.

Choose **one** of the fats that you would recommend to someone wanting to eat a Mediterranean diet.

i olive oil

ii butter

iii fried chicken

iv chocolate bar

b A TV programme gives the message that to be healthy you need to remove fats from your diet. Explain why this message is **incorrect** and why it is often believed that fat is not good for us.

Worked example

The image shows the nutritional information on a food label.

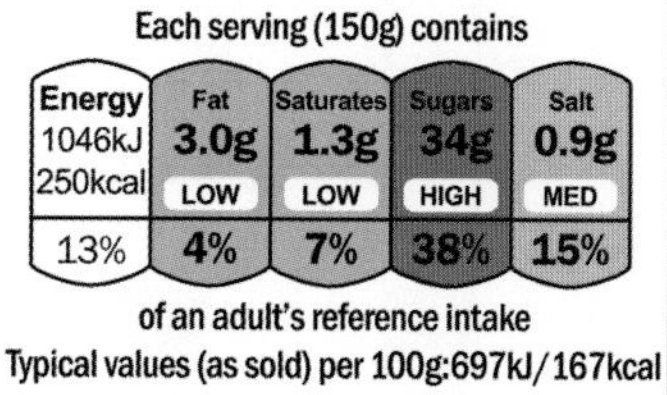

a Name the **two** units of energy shown in this label.

These are listed under the 'energy' headings.

kilojoules and kilocalories

The traffic light system indicates whether foods contain low, medium or high amounts of any of the food groups, compared to the recommended daily amount.

b Name which food type this food contains in:

i high amounts __________

ii low amounts __________.

Red shows 'high' and green shows 'low.'

i *sugars*

ii *fat (or saturated fat)*

One portion of this food contains 0.9 g of salt. This is 15% of the daily recommended amount.

c Calculate the total daily recommended amount of salt.

If 0.9 g is 15%, what would 100% be?

15% of the daily recommended amount = 0.9 g

1% of the daily recommended amount = $\frac{0.9}{15}$ *g*

100% of the daily recommended amount = $\left(\frac{0.9}{15}\right) \times 100 = 6$ *g*

8 A tin of pasta in tomato sauce has a label with nutritional information.

a Explain **two** reasons why it is important that foods are labelled accurately with both the ingredients and the nutritional information.

b The energy in the food is shown in calories. A portion contains 180 calories and the tin contains three portions. Calculate how many calories there are in this whole tin.

c In a portion of this food, there are 1210 mg of sodium. Convert this to show how many grams one portion contains.

d A portion contains 15 mg of cholesterol, which is 5% of the daily recommended amount. Calculate the total daily recommended amount of cholesterol.

9 A dietician is advising a patient on how to eat more healthily. The image shows an 'eat well plate', designed to help people to eat the different food types in the recommended proportions.

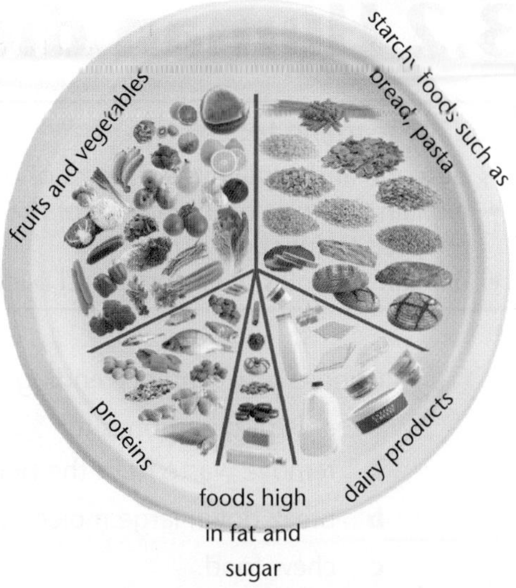

a Using the 'eat well plate', list the food types in order of the relative amounts that should make up an average meal for the patient, from most to least.

b Based on the 'eat well plate', approximately what fraction of a meal should be made up of dairy products? Choose from the fractions below:

$\frac{1}{2}$ $\quad \frac{1}{4}$ $\quad \frac{1}{6}$ $\quad \frac{1}{10}$

c For each food named below, name **two** of the food groups that each fits into:

i cheese

ii butter

iii doughnut

d The guidance for the 'eat well plate' states that 'this shows the proportion of each type of food that should be included in an average meal.' Suggest why the word 'average' is used.

10 Daniel and Tamara are both obese and are seeking advice to help them to lose weight. The average man is thought to need approximately 10 500 kJ of energy per day. The average woman is thought to need approximately 8400 kJ of energy per day.

a Describe **three** ways that losing weight might benefit Daniel and Tamara.

b Explain why the energy needs per day for a man and woman are described as 'average'.

BREAD Nutrition

Typical values	1 100g contains	2 Each slice (typically 44g contains)	% RI*
Energy	985kJ 235kcal	435kJ 105kcal	 5%
Fat	1.5g	0.7g	1%
of which saturates	0.3g	0.1g	1%
Carbohydrate	45.5g	20.0g	
of which sugars	3.8g	1.7g	2%
Fibre	2.8g	.2g	
Protein	7.7g	3.4g	
Salt	1.0g	0.4g	7%

BUTTER Nutrition Facts

Serving size 1 Tbsp (14 g)
Servings per container 32

Amount per serving	
Calories 100	kJ 420kJ
% Daily values	
Total Fat 11g	**17%**
Saturated Fat 7g	**35%**
Trans Fat 0g	
Cholesterol 30mg	**10%**
Sodium 0mg	**0%**
Total Carbohydrate 0g	**0%**
Protein 0g	**0%**

Vitamin A 8%
Not a significant source of dietary fibre, sugars, vitamin C, calcium and iron.

The food labels on the right show the nutrition information labels from bread and butter.

c **i** Tamara loves buttered toast and is quite fussy about other foods. Calculate how many slices of buttered toast Tamara could eat per day to stay within her 8400 kJ target.

ii Tamara decides that she can eat just toast and lose weight by staying under her 8400 kJ target.

Provide advice to Tamara explaining why she should not just eat buttered toast. Suggest some other food groups that would be good to introduce into her diet, and explain why.

Some food labels show the energy content of food in calories as well as, or instead of, kilojoules.

1 calorie = 4.2 kJ

d Calculate the energy needs per day in calories of:

i an average man

ii an average woman.

3.2 Human digestive system

You are learning to:
- describe and explain the process of digestion
- explain the roles of the organs of the digestive system and how they are adapted to function
- explain the roles of enzymes and bacteria in digestion.

1 Choose **one** sentence ending.

The role of digestion is to:

a remove waste from the body.

b break down large molecules into smaller ones.

c chew food.

d make us feel full by eating.

2 Name the organ of the digestive system where digestion is completed.

3 Choose the type of energy stored in food.

chemical light sound heat

4 Identify the organ that is involved in digestion but the food does **not** pass through it.

small intestine stomach oesophagus pancreas

5 On the diagram, identify the part where:

i waste leaves the body

ii products of digestion are absorbed into the bloodstream

iii waste (faeces) becomes more solid

iv food is churned and acid is produced.

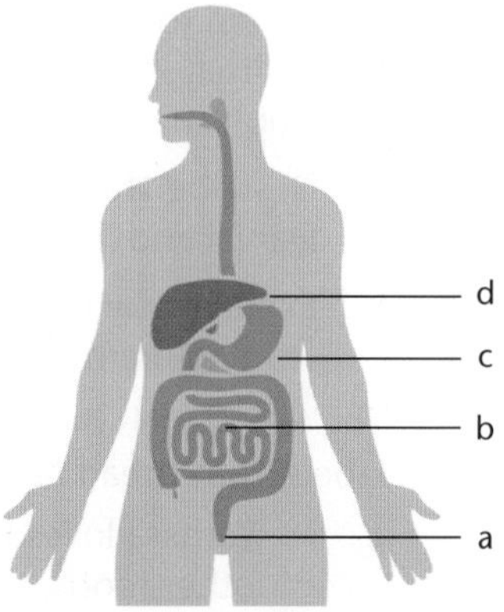

6 Probiotic yogurts contain live microorganisms. They are recommended as a way of supporting digestion. Suggest why.

7 An enzyme that digests proteins is being investigated. Protein solution is mixed with the enzyme solution at different pHs and the amount of digestion compared.

Results show that the enzyme can only digest proteins when in an acidic solution, and not in a neutral or alkaline solution.

a Identify the independent variable in this investigation.

b Describe **two** control variables.

c Suggest which part of the digestive system this enzyme works in naturally. Explain your answer.

8 **a** Explain what is meant by:

i physical digestion **ii** chemical digestion.

b Name a part of the digestive system where:

i only chemical digestion takes place

ii both chemical and physical digestion takes place.

c Do bacteria support us with physical or chemical digestion?

9 Digestion of food is completed in the small intestine. The small intestine has several adaptations.

a The wall of the small intestine contains muscle. Explain why.

Digested food molecules move through the walls of the small intestine into the bloodstream.

b Food molecules move from where there is a higher concentration (in the small intestine) to where there is a lower concentration (in the bloodstream). What is the name of this process?

c Explain how the adaptations labelled **i, ii** and **iii** on the diagram of the wall of the small intestine help the movement of food molecules.

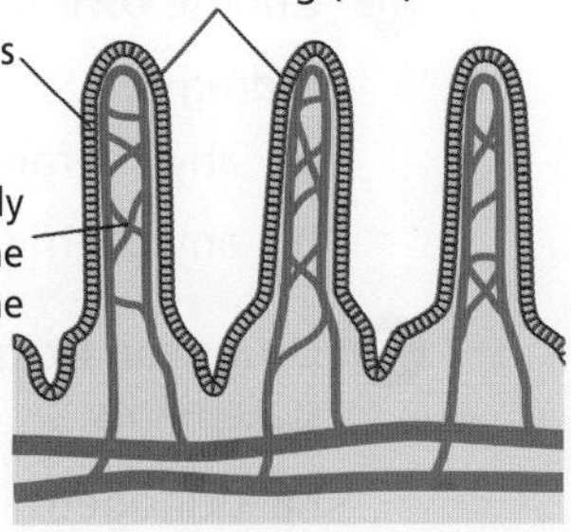

d Digestion is complete by the time the food has passed through the small intestine, but the waste still then passes through the large intestine and the anus. Explain the purpose of the:

i large intestine **ii** anus.

Worked example

a Name **two** food groups found in steak.

protein and fats

The diagram below shows how proteins are digested.

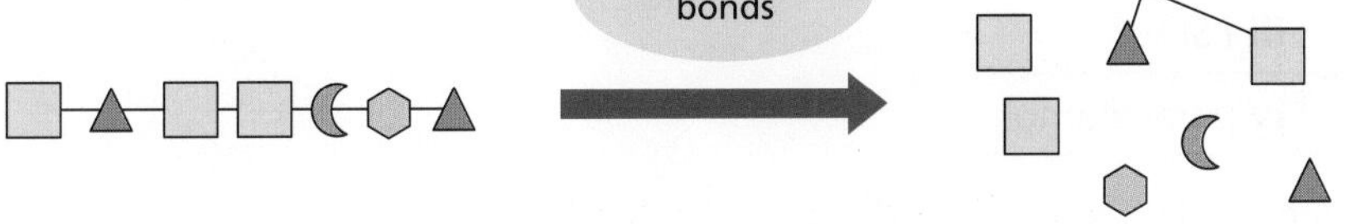

b Name the enzyme that breaks down the protein.

protease

c Name **two** parts of the digestive system where the protein in the steak could be digested.

stomach and small intestine

d Enzymes are 'catalysts'. What does this mean?

Enzymes speed up reactions.

e Lipase enzyme breaks down fats. Explain why mixing lipase enzyme with protein does **not** result in an increase in amino acids.

First, try to explain why lipase enzymes can break down fats. What is it about enzymes that means they could not break down a different food?

Enzymes are 'specific'. This means that they can only catalyse one type of reaction. This is due to the shape of the enzyme and the molecules that they break down.

10 A boy eats a meal of pasta.

a Identify the main food group of pasta.

Enzymes will help to digest the pasta.

b Explain why the pasta needs to be digested.

c Name the enzyme that will digest the pasta and the products of digestion.

d Enzymes are 'specific'. What does this mean?

e The boy has a rare condition where his body does not make enough enzyme to digest the food molecules in pasta. Suggest why this might lead to him feeling tired.

3.3 Effects of recreational drugs

You are learning to:

- describe how we can classify drugs and give examples
- describe and explain the effects of some recreational drugs
- discuss the impact of drug misuse on health and behaviour.

1 Choose **one** sentence ending.

A drug is:

a any chemical that causes harm.

b any chemical that cures disease.

c any chemical that affects the way the body works.

d any chemical that you can become addicted to.

2 Drugs can be grouped into similar types. Use the words given below to complete the statements.

hallucinogens   stimulants   painkillers   depressants

a _________ relieve pain.

b _________ speed up body systems.

c _________ slow down body systems.

d _________ cause us to see things that do not exist.

3 Match the drug types to the examples.

a painkiller	**i** alcohol
b stimulant	**ii** nicotine
c depressant	**iii** LSD
d hallucinogen	**iv** paracetamol

4 **a** Explain what is meant by 'recreational drugs'.

b Why might people take recreational drugs?

5 Drugs affect systems of the body both positively and negatively. The drugs below can all be addictive. For each of the drugs below, select the effect it may have on the body.

a codeine	**i** brain activity and alertness increased, temporary energy increased
b heroin	**ii** nervous system slowed down, relaxed feelings
c cocaine	**iii** brain chemicals affected, see or believe things that are not real
d psilocybin mushrooms	**iv** pain messages are blocked, feel less or no pain

e Explain why drugs having the effects of both **ii** and **iv** might be used when someone is having an operation.

6 Drugs such as tranquillisers (sleeping tablets) can lead to addiction over time and can cause harmful side-effects.

Explain why drugs such as these are prescribed, despite having harmful side-effects.

7 Most drugs cause side-effects.

a Explain what is meant by 'side-effect'.

b Painkillers are used to help treat the painful condition of the joints called arthritis. Painkillers can cause problems in the gut, such as nausea, vomiting and constipation. Why do doctors still prescribe these painkillers with the risk of causing these gut problems?

c A group of university students are studying for exams and decide to drink lots of strong coffee to help them to stay awake to revise.

i Name the drug that coffee contains that could keep them awake.

ii Describe and explain the side-effects of the drug to the students, to persuade them that it would not be a good idea to continue this for a long time.

8 A research scientist is investigating the potential side-effects of a new energy drink. They ask volunteers to drink a small amount every day for 2 weeks and to record any effects that they experience from a list, e.g. headache, more energy, increased hunger.

a Explain why it is important to include a large sample size.

b Which of the following does increasing the sample size improve?

i repeatability **ii** accuracy **iii** precision **iv** range

c The trial also includes a group of volunteers who do not sample the drink at all. Explain the purpose of this group.

An improvement is suggested to include 'blind trials.' This means that some volunteers would drink the energy drink whereas others would drink a different drink. None of the volunteers would know which drink they had.

d Suggest why this would be a good improvement to the investigation.

9 Cannabis is illegal in the UK. It is used as a recreational drug by smoking it.

In some parts of the world, it is legal to use cannabis. Some patients with conditions that cause long-term pain claim that cannabis eases their pain.

Cannabis falls into two drug categories: depressant and hallucinogen.

a Explain the possible side-effects of cannabis.

Some people believe that cannabis should be legalised and so be freely available. Others believe that it should not be legalised.

b Evaluate the advantages and disadvantages of using cannabis and of making cannabis available legally.

10 **a** Long-term recreational drug use can lead to addiction. For example, heroin use may lead to heroin addiction. Discuss how this heroin addiction can be damaging to:

i the drug user's health **ii** the drug user's family **iii** society more widely.

b Like heroin, alcohol is also a depressant drug that is addictive. Some people argue that alcohol is damaging to the health of more people than heroin. Suggest why they might think this.

11 The data below shows the number of deaths caused by drugs in 2011 in England.

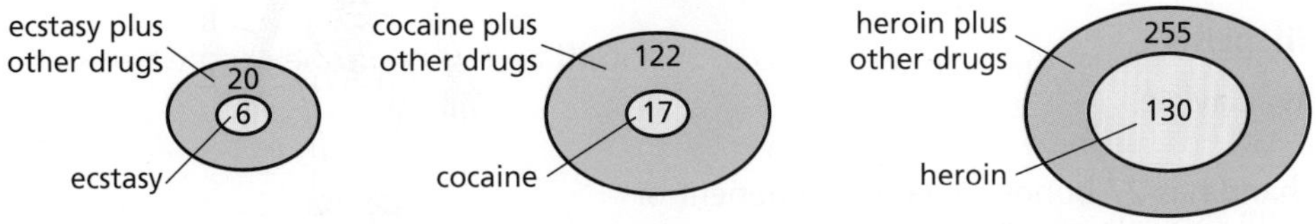

a **Using evidence from the data**, write a conclusion about which drug causes the most deaths by itself.

b **Using evidence from the data**, comment on the risk of death from taking more than one drug.

c The cost of all three of these drugs has decreased since 2011. Suggest what effect this might have on the numbers of deaths.

3.4 Human skeleton, joints and muscles

You are learning to:
- identify bones of the human skeleton
- describe and explain the function of the human skeleton and muscles
- describe the role of joints and the movement that each allows
- explain how antagonistic muscles work together to bring about movement at joints
- state that the force exerted by muscles can be measured.

1. The skeleton supports the body and produces blood cells. Choose **two** other functions from this list:
   a allows movement
   b makes the body rigid
   c protects the organs
   d produces egg cells.

2. How can you increase the strength of your muscles?
   a eat more protein
   b rest the muscles
   c exercise the muscles
   d eat less fat

3. Name the part of the body that each part of the skeleton protects.

a cranium	**i** reproductive organs
b ribs	**ii** spinal cord
c pelvis	**iii** brain
d backbone	**iv** lungs

4. Match the names of the bones to the labels, **A–D**:
   i fibula
   ii radius
   iii pelvis
   iv clavicle.

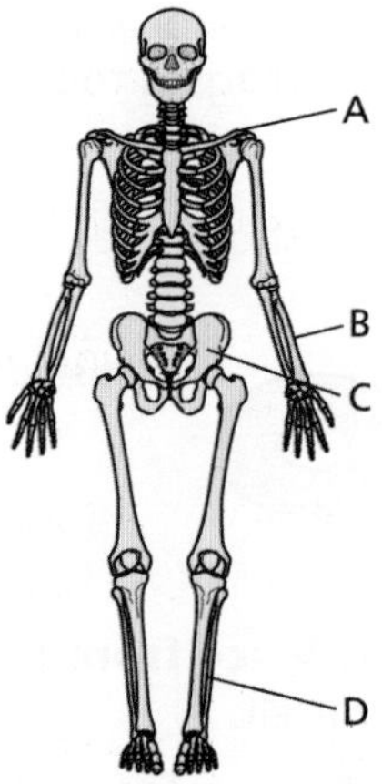

5. The hand has 27 bones. What is the benefit of having so many bones?
   a to make it strong
   b so that there is less chance of breaking a bone
   c to allow us to rotate our fingers
   d to increase flexibility

6 Match the scientific name to the common name of each bone.

a sternum	**i** thigh bone
b humerus	**ii** skull
c femur	**iii** breast bone
d cranium	**iv** upper arm bone

7 Bones are made of different substances, as shown in the diagram.

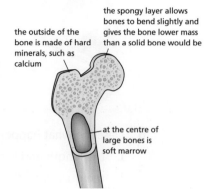

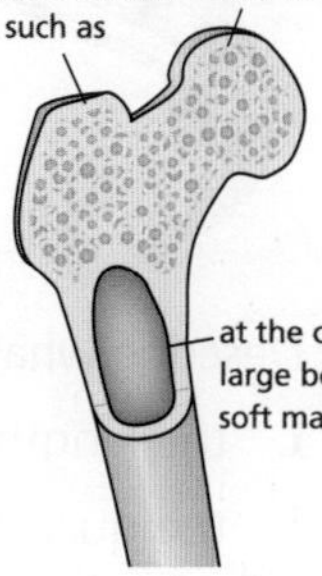

a Why is it important for the outside of bones to be hard?

b **i** Why is it helpful for the spongy layer to allow the bones to bend slightly?

ii How does the lower mass affect how well we move?

c What is made in the bone marrow?

d Many bird bones have a larger proportion of spongy layer than human bones. Suggest why.

8 In the human skeleton, joints are either fixed or moveable. We have three types of moveable joint: hinge, pivot, and ball and socket.

a Define a 'joint' in the skeleton.

b Which type of joint is each of the following?:

i cranium

ii hip

iii elbow

iv neck

c Explain why it is important to have:

i fixed joints

ii different types of moveable joints.

9 Human bone remains can be used to find out information about the person that they came from.

The length of a femur can be used to predict the height of the person, using the equation:

$$\text{height (cm)} = (\text{length of femur (cm)} \times 2.6) + 0.65$$

a A human femur is found at an archaeological dig. The femur is 43.5 cm long.

i Predict the height of the person rounded to the nearest cm.

ii Show your answer in m.

b Other evidence suggests that the remains are most likely of a teenage boy. Explain why the estimate of height may not be accurate.

10 Most muscles work in pairs, in which case they are called antagonistic muscles.

a Explain what is meant by 'antagonistic muscles'.

To lift the upper leg up, the quadriceps (thigh) muscle contracts.

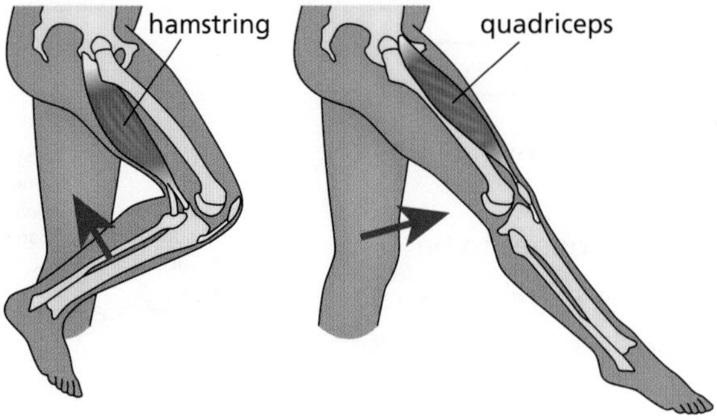

b Describe what happens to the following when the quadriceps contracts:

i the length and breadth of the quadriceps

ii the quadriceps' antagonistic muscle (the hamstring).

c Once the upper leg is lifted (as in 10a), describe and explain how the upper leg then lowers again, using the following words in your answer:

quadriceps hamstring contracts relaxes shortens and fattens

Worked example

An investigation was carried out to find out whether a person's mass affects the strength of their leg muscles.

The mass of weights that could be pushed with the legs was measured for 6 males and a force calculated for each. The results are shown below.

Mass of male (kg)	Force exerted by leg muscles (N)
59	290
72	440
76	80
64	380
88	600
82	520

a Redraw the results table in a way that makes it easier to draw conclusions about how mass affects the force exerted by muscles.

Sometimes, reordering the results makes it easier to look for a pattern. As this investigation focuses on the effect of mass, we should order the masses logically.

Mass of male (kg)	Force exerted by leg muscles (N)
59	290
64	380
72	440
76	80
82	520
88	600

b **i** Identify the anomalous result in the data.

ii When analysing these results to make a conclusion, what would you do about this anomalous result?

Spotting an anomalous result is important. Just as important is deciding how to treat anomalous results.

It is worth considering whether you think there may have been an error in taking the reading.

b i The result for the 76 kg man.

ii Either repeat the reading in case there was an error or ignore that result when making a conclusion.

c What conclusion can you make from this investigation?

As the mass of a male increases, the force exerted by the leg muscles increases.

11 A group of scientists collect data about muscle strength in people of different ages.

For each age, they test 10 people and then calculate the average upper body strength. The table below shows the results.

Gender	Age	Force exerted by upper body (N)
Female child	10	14
Female child	15	26
Female	30	38
Female	45	26
Male child	10	17
Male child	15	30
Male	32	68
Male	45	68

a What does 'N' represent in the final column?

b **i** Explain why the average force of 10 people is shown rather than just the result from one person.

ii Within the 10 repeat readings from one age group, describe what the tester should do if one result is anomalous (doesn't fit with the other results).

c Decide which **two** are supported by the data.

i Children have less upper body strength than adults.

ii As adult males age, they lose upper body strength.

iii Males have greater upper body strength than females.

iv As adult females age, they lose upper body strength.

3.5 Human breathing system

You are learning to:
- identify the parts of the human breathing system
- explain how breathing takes place in humans
- explain how the breathing system is adapted for gas exchange
- explain the importance of air pressure in bringing about breathing
- describe how lung volume can be measured
- describe and explain the impact of disease and lifestyle on the breathing system.

1 Choose the correct sequence to describe the movement of air into the body.

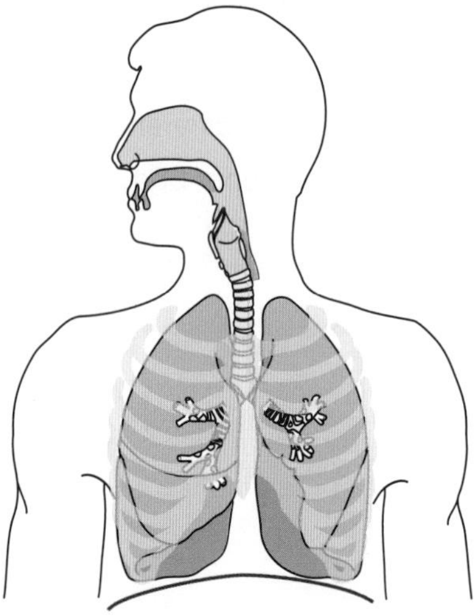

a trachea; bronchus; bronchioles; alveoli; blood
b trachea; bronchioles; bronchus; alveoli; blood
c trachea; bronchioles; alveoli; bronchus; blood
d bronchus; trachea; bronchioles; alveoli; blood

2 Which of the following has a positive effect on breathing?

a cancer
b exercise
c asthma
d smoking

3 Arrange the following in order of estimated lung size, from smallest to biggest.

A adult male
B adult female
C baby
D 10-year-old child

4 Complete the sentences to show how we breathe in.

a The ribs move ________ (up and out / down and in).
b The diaphragm moves ________ (up / down).
c The volume of the chest ________ (increases / decreases).
d Air rushes ________ (into / out of) the lungs.

5 Name the process by which gases move between the alveoli and blood.

a breathing

b respiration

c excretion

d diffusion

6 The diagram shows a model of the breathing system.

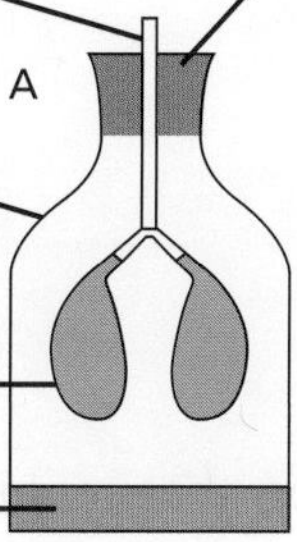

a In this model, what represents:

i the lungs?

ii the diaphragm?

iii the trachea?

b When thinking how breathing takes place, this model does **not** represent the ribcage well. Suggest **one** reason why.

7 **a** Match each change in volume to the effect on pressure by choosing the correct word in each statement.

i Increased volume in the lungs leads to (increased/decreased) pressure.

ii Decreased volume in the lungs leads to (increased/decreased) pressure.

b What is the unit of measurement for atmospheric pressure?

8 An investigation was carried out to compare the lung volumes of men of different ages. The results are shown in the table below.

Age (years)	25	30	35	40
Lung volume 1 (l)	6.0	5.7	6.3	6.2
Lung volume 2 (l)	5.6	5.8	6.1	6.0
Lung volume 3 (l)	5.8	5.6	6.5	3.4
Average lung volume (l)	**A**	**B**	**C**	(see part **b**)

a Calculate the missing values **A**, **B** and **C**.

b In the results for the male aged 40 years, one of the results is anomalous.

i State which result is anomalous.

ii Calculate the average lung volume result for the male aged 40 years (decide what to do with the anomalous result).

c Suggest **one** other factor about these men that may have affected their lung volume.

Worked example

The effect of smoking on fitness was investigated. Fitness levels of people who had smoked for different lengths of time were compared.

Volunteers were grouped as below:

- smoked 0–2 years
- smoked 2–5 years
- smoked 6–10 years
- smoked more than 10 years

A control group was also created.

a In the investigation, identify:

i the independent variable

length of time as a smoker

ii the dependent variable.

fitness level

b i Apart from length of time smoking, name **three** other factors that could affect results.

Any three factors from: age; gender; current physical activity; number of cigarettes smoked per day.

ii Suggest how you could ensure that any **one** of the factors does not affect the investigation.

If there are other factors that could vary within a group and could affect the results you should try to control them (note this is **not** always keeping them the same).

For example, choose volunteers who have:

similar ages

same gender

similar levels of activity in everyday life

similar numbers of cigarettes smoked per day

c Suggest what the control group should contain.

A control group is included as a way of ensuring that any differences measured are due to the factor being investigated.

The control group should contain non-smokers.

9 **a** What is meant by 'lung volume'?

b When measuring lung volume, explain why you should take a deep breath in before the breath out.

c Researchers carried out a long-term investigation into the effect of exercise on lung volume. Lung volume was measured at the start of the investigation and then every 3 months, for each of two groups of people.

- Group 1 carried out regular aerobic exercise (such as running) over a year.
- Group 2 carried out no additional exercise.

i Explain why it was important that this investigation was carried out over a long time (one year).

ii Why was lung volume measured at the start of the investigation for Group 1?

iii Group 2 is a 'control group'. Explain why it is important to include a control group in this investigation.

Average results showed that Group 1 increased lung volume whereas Group 2 did not.

iv Write a conclusion for this investigation.

v Explain what changes occur in the breathing system with regular exercise that increases lung volume.

10 Once air enters into alveoli, oxygen passes across into the bloodstream. Alveoli have adaptations.

a Explain how each adaptation supports gas exchange:

i large surface area

ii thin surface

iii surrounded by many blood capillaries.

b The diagram shows the 'bumpy' surface produced by the alveoli. If the surface was smooth instead, which of the adaptations listed in part **a** (**i**, **ii** or **iii**) would be affected?

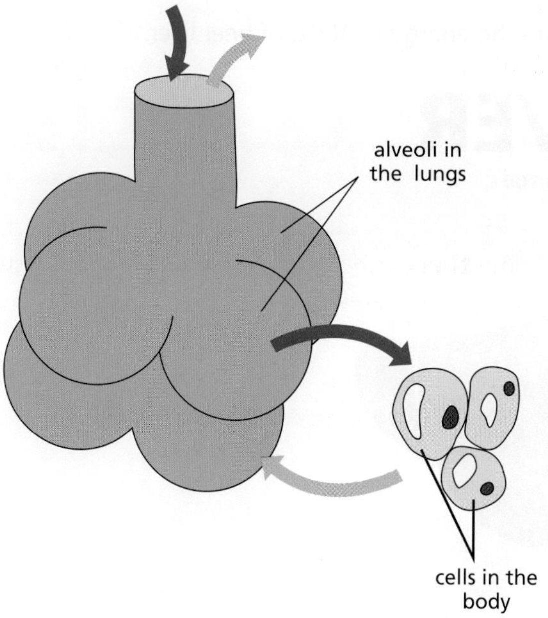

c **i** Name the gas that passes from the blood into the alveoli.

ii What is the name of the process that uses the oxygen and produces the carbon dioxide?

11 Breathing is brought about by differences between the pressure of the air in the lungs and the pressure of the air around us (atmospheric pressure). Change of pressure in the lungs is caused by a change in volume of the lungs.

a Explain what happens to the following just before we breathe in:

i the volume of the lungs

ii the pressure inside the lungs

iii the pressure inside the lungs compared to the pressure of the air around us

iv the movement of air in or out of the lungs.

b The pressure in the lungs for one man is recorded as a minimum of 3.8 kPa and a maximum of 9.5 kPa.

i Calculate the overall change in pressure during breathing in and out for this man. Show your answer in Pa.

ii Which of these two values would occur just before the man breathes out?

c Predict the overall movement of air if the pressure inside the chest is equal to atmospheric pressure.

Maths and practical skills

1 What is a lung volume of 3.9 l in ml?

a 0.0039 ml

b 39 ml

c 390 ml

d 3900 ml

2 Using the food label below, calculate the energy in 300 g of beef liver.

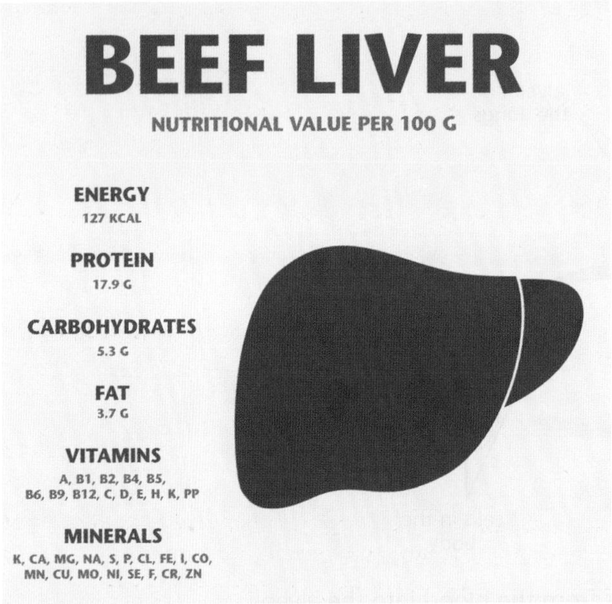

3 In an investigation into the effect of temperature on the time taken for an enzyme reaction, which two units of measurement would be used?

a N and s

b °C and ml

c g and ml

d °C and s

4 The graph shows the rate at which an enzyme works at different temperatures. At what temperature does this enzyme work best?

a 12 °C

b 20 °C

c 37 °C

d 60 °C

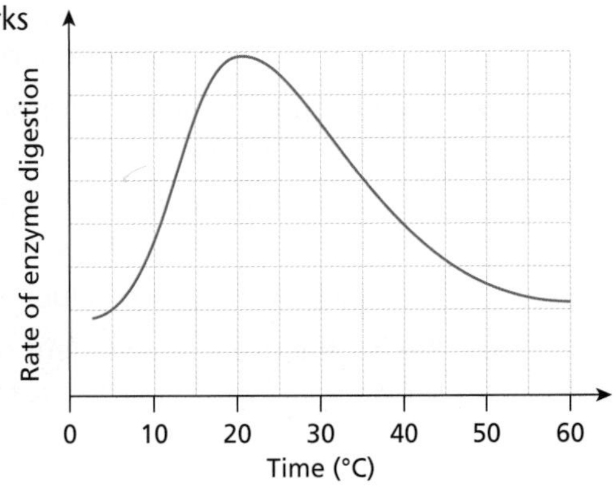

Worked example

Some students are investigating the effect of temperature on enzyme activity. They mix an enzyme solution with full-fat milk and measure the time taken for the fats to be broken down.

a What is the name of the enzyme used in this reaction?

lipase

b In the investigation, identify:

i the independent variable

The independent variable is what is changed.

temperature

ii the dependent variable

The dependent variable is what is measured.

time taken

iii two control variables.

Control variables are those that you monitor or try to keep the same as they could affect the results.

concentration of enzyme solution; volume of milk

5 In an investigation to study the effect of different types of exercise on breathing rate, identify:

a the independent variable

b the dependent variable.

6 A girl uses the apparatus below to measure her lung volume.

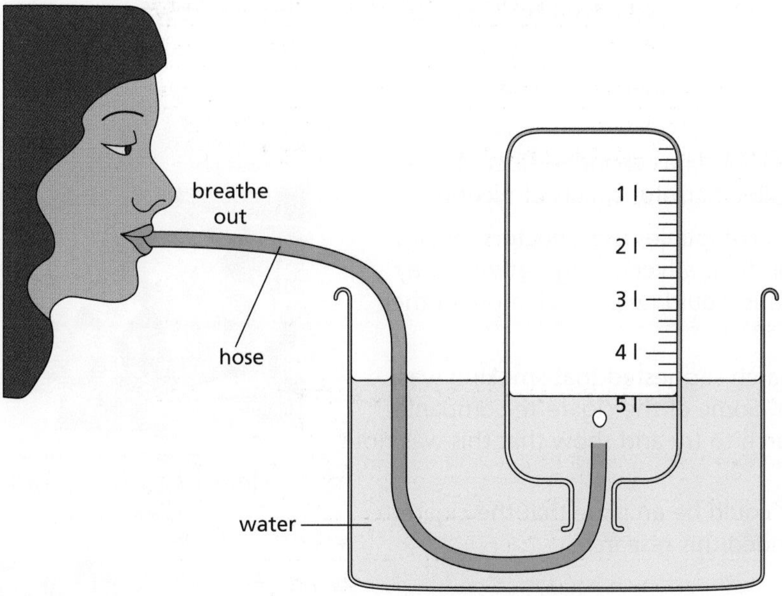

a What is the lung volume of the girl?

b How would the result be affected if the girl took a bigger breath in before repeating the measurement?

7 Foods are being tested to determine which food groups they contain. The following shows the positive test results to look for:

starch – iodine changes from orange to blue/black

sugar – Benedict's solution changes from blue to orange

protein – Biuret solution changes from blue to mauve

The table below shows the results for some unknown samples.

Food sample	Starch test observation	Sugar test observation	Protein test observation
A	blue/black	blue	blue
B	orange	orange	blue
C	orange	blue	mauve

a List the food groups contained within samples **A**, **B** and **C**.

b Identify which of the samples is most likely to be:

i honey

ii egg white

iii pasta.

c Ethanol is used to test for fat. Why is a water bath needed to heat the solution?

i ethanol is an irritant

ii ethanol is flammable

iii ethanol is poisonous

iv ethanol needs to be diluted

8 The image below shows an old advert for cigarettes. When this advert was made, the dangers of cigarettes were not understood.

a Cigarettes contain nicotine. What type of drug is nicotine?

b Explain how thinking has changed since this advert about the possible harmful effects of nicotine.

c Many cigarette companies used doctors, nurses and dentists on their adverts. Suggest why they believed that this would help to sell more of their cigarettes.

In the 1950s, research suggested that smoking was linked with cancer. Some of the cigarette companies then funded research to try and show that this was not true.

d Explain why it could be an issue that the cigarette companies funded this research.

Camels Cigarettes, 1946

9 A class is using a model to investigate how oxygen passes from the alveoli in the lungs into the bloodstream by diffusion.

They soaked a piece of agar gel (jelly-like solid) in red food colouring. They put the piece of agar gel into a beaker of water and observed it every 5 minutes for 20 minutes.

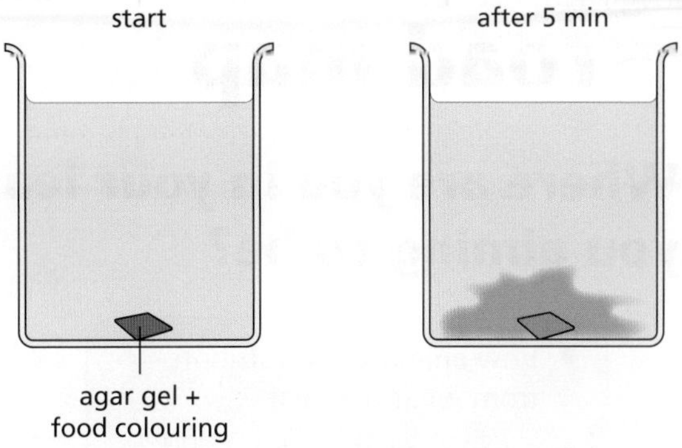

a In this model, what represents:

i the alveoli?

ii oxygen?

iii blood?

b Predict what the students would see after 15 minutes.

c Explain why the red food colouring diffused into the water. Use the word 'concentration' in your answer.

10 Students were shown a model of digestion in the small intestine. The starch represents food that we eat.

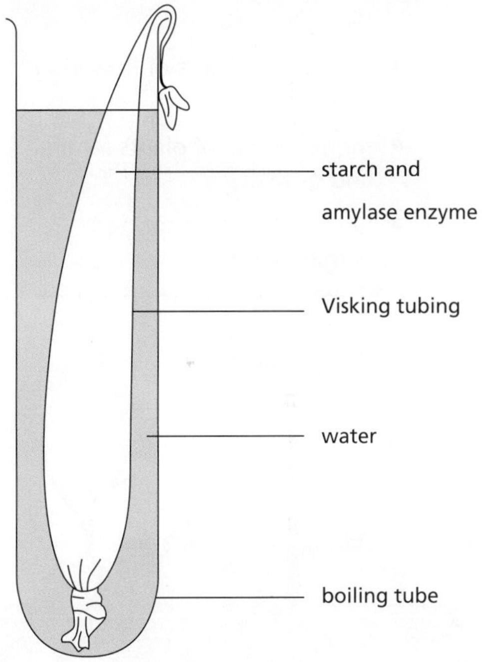

a What is represented by:

i the Visking tubing?

ii the water?

As soon as the starch and amylase were mixed, the tube was incubated at 30 °C for 30 minutes. After 30 minutes, glucose was detected in the liquid inside the tubing and the water around the tubing.

b **i** Explain why glucose was present inside the tubing after 30 minutes.

ii Why did the water around the Visking tubing also contain glucose after 30 minutes?

iii Starch was not present in the water surrounding the tubing. Explain why.

The students want to investigate whether glucose would be detected after incubating at different temperatures: 20 °C, 30 °C, 40 °C, 50 °C, 60 °C.

c For this investigation, identify:

i the independent variable

ii the dependent variable

iii **two** control variables

iv the range of values of temperature.

4 Respiration and photosynthesis road map

Where are you in your learning journey and where are you aiming to be?

- how animals get nutrition from what they eat
- basic parts of the human circulatory system
- how water and nutrients are transported within animals
- basic parts of the human digestive system
- functions of parts of flowering plants
- requirements of plants for life and growth
- how water is transported within plants

4.1 Aerobic respiration
- recall and describe the equation
- describe where it takes place
- explain mitochondria adaptations
- describe and explain evidence

4.2 Anaerobic respiration
- recall and describe the equation
- explain oxygen debt
- describe organism examples
- describe fermentation
- explain uses of fermentation

4.3 The importance of respira
- compare aerobic and anaerobic
- describe links with plants and anima
- explain animal and plant dependen

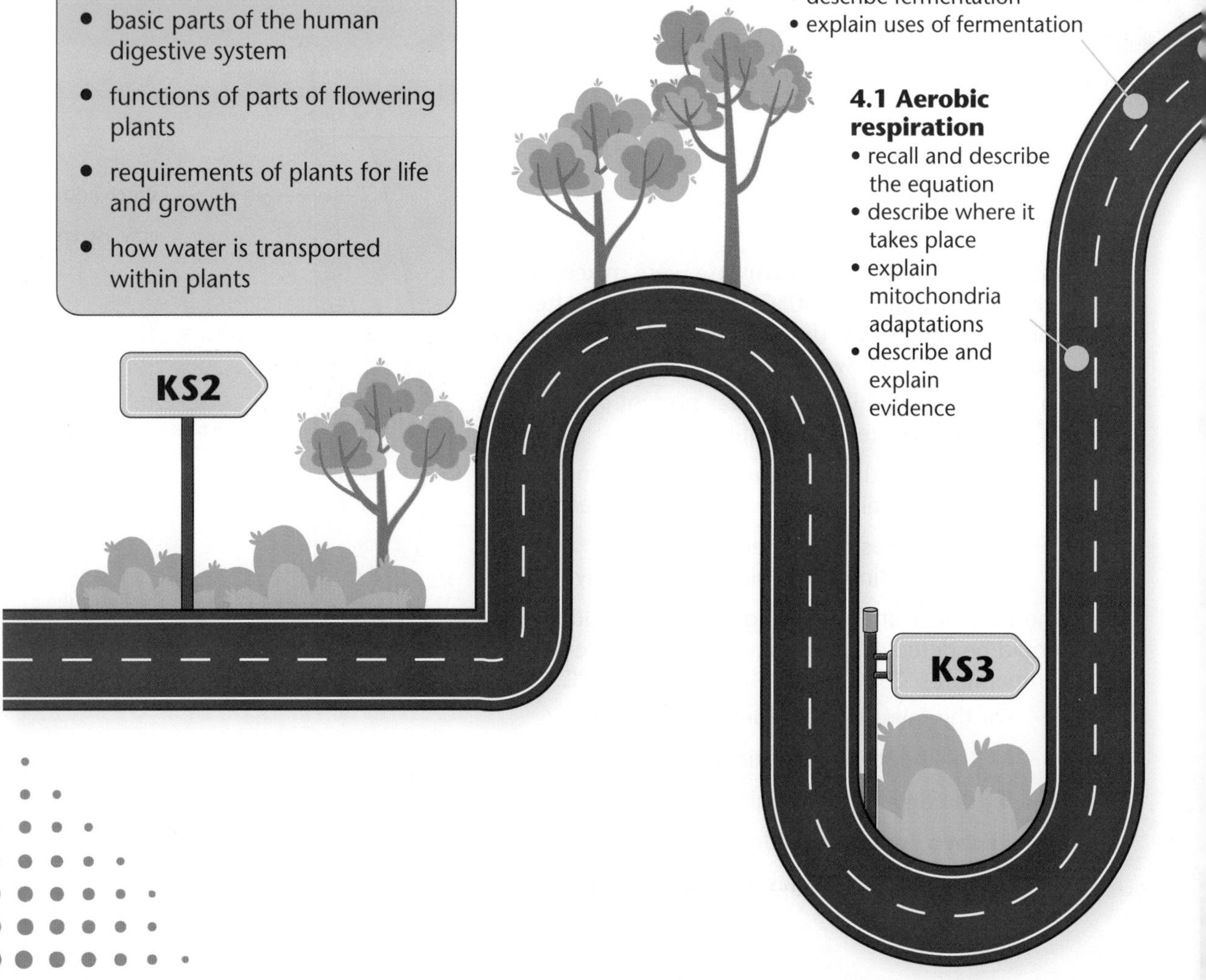

4.4 Photosynthesis
- explain importance
- recall the equation
- identify affecting factors
- interpret data

4.5 Adaptations of plants for photosynthesis
- describe leaf adaptations
- explain gas exchange
- explain water and mineral movement
- describe importance of minerals

- respiration
- animal and plant cells
- transport in cells
- photosynthesis

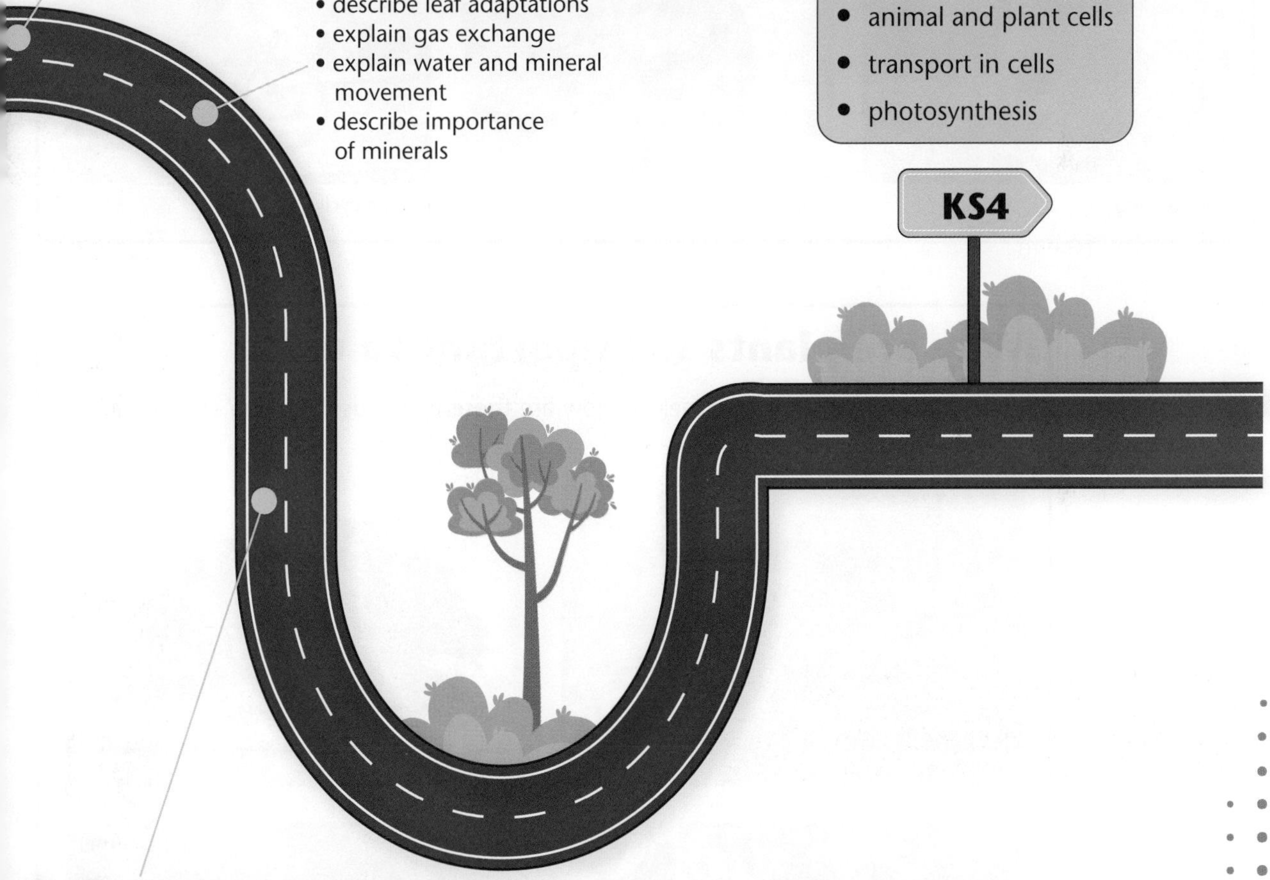

Maths and practical skills

- observing and measuring, including the evaluation of repeatability and accuracy
- making scientific predictions
- carrying out scientific enquiries to test predictions
- carrying out practical work safely
- calculating results and converting between different units
- presenting data using tables and graphs
- analysing data and identifying anomalous results
- presenting reasoned explanations

4 Respiration and photosynthesis

Animals and plants need energy to grow, repair tissues and reproduce; animals also need energy to move. This energy is released from glucose by a chemical reaction in all living cells called **respiration.**

In animals, that glucose comes from digestion of the food they eat. Plants, however, need to make their own glucose by a chemical reaction in some plant cells called **photosynthesis**.

What links breathing and digestion?

We know that digestion and breathing are essential processes. But why are they so important for the activities shown below?

dog running

human hurdling

human cycling

Why are plants so important to us?

Look at the images of plants below. How are these plants useful to us? (Some have several uses.)

Now think back to the previous question about digestion and breathing. How can plants help us to get the energy that we need?

Using your science skills

Could you be a bakery food technologist?

You modify recipes and baking methods for existing bakery products to make sure that they are safe and that customers like them. You also develop new products by trialling new recipes and new ways of baking.

You split your time between a bakery and a science lab, carrying out research and then scaling up and putting your ideas into practice. You have excellent knowledge of the chemical reactions that occur when baking and use this to, for example, tweak ingredients, baking techniques and temperatures. You have a good understanding of food nutrition and how to reduce calories, reduce additives, etc.

As a bakery technologist, you work alongside other bakers and a wider manufacturing team that relies on you to make exciting but sensible suggestions that will sell. You have roles as both scientist and baker, and use your creativity to make delicious products.

Forestry technicians maintain forests, grasslands and even mountain environments. They use knowledge of the conditions and nutrients that plants need to ensure that the plant species continue to grow.

Winemakers oversee the entire wine production process from grape harvesting to grape crushing, fermentation and bottling. They use their scientific understanding of fermentation to alter a wine's composition and taste.

Technical brewers oversee the brewing process, including monitoring and tweaking the ingredients and the conditions for making beer. They understand the chemical reactions taking place in brewing and use their creativity with this knowledge to develop new products.

Exercise physiologists investigate how clients respond and adapt to muscle activity. They work with a whole range of people, from athletes to hospital patients. They use extensive knowledge of respiration, breathing, the circulatory system, the nervous system and the skeletal system to improve performance and fitness or to help prevent disease or illness.

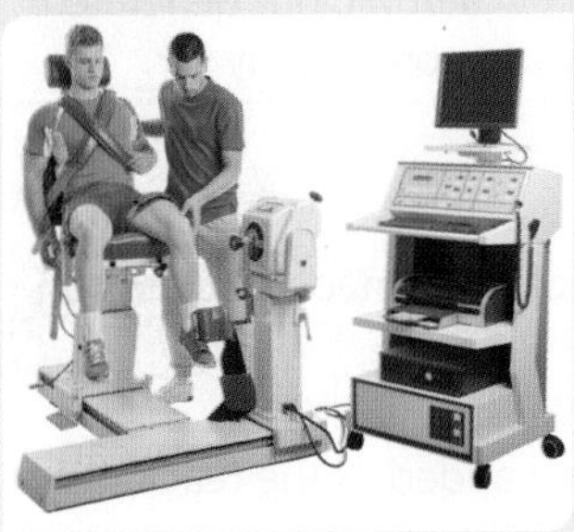

Mitochondria research scientists carry out research into one or more of the many conditions that affect mitochondria. Symptoms of mitochondrial diseases are extremely wide ranging, and include tiredness, seizures, diabetes, learning difficulties and hearing and vision problems. Researchers work to understand what causes the issues and to develop treatments to prevent, cure or treat some of these diseases.

Knowledge organiser

Respiration happens in every living cell. It is the chemical reaction that releases energy from **glucose**. All living things – animals, plants and microbes (microorganisms) – need energy. Some uses are given on the right.

Animals need energy:	Plants need energy:
to grow and repair tissues	to grow and repair tissues
to reproduce	to reproduce
to keep the body at a suitable and fairly constant temperature	to transport water
to contract muscles in order to move	to absorb nutrients

Aerobic respiration uses oxygen:

glucose + oxygen → carbon dioxide + water (+ energy)

glucose	oxygen	carbon dioxide + water	(+ energy)
Animals get glucose from digestion of food. Glucose is carried by the blood from the small intestine to all cells of the body.	Animals get oxygen from breathing. Oxygen is carried by the blood from the alveoli in the lungs to all cells of the body.	In animals, the waste carbon dioxide and water are carried by the blood from the cells to the lungs, where it is breathed out.	The energy released is needed for many life processes in animals and plants.
Plants make glucose by the process of photosynthesis.	Plants get oxygen by diffusion from the air *or* by photosynthesis.	In plants, the waste carbon dioxide and water diffuse from the leaves into the air *or* are used in photosynthesis.	

Anaerobic respiration takes place when there is not enough oxygen for aerobic respiration or when energy is needed to be released quickly. In animals, for example, **aerobic respiration** (in mitochondria) switches to anaerobic respiration (in the cytoplasm) during vigorous exercise. Even while there is still some oxygen left in your body, anaerobic respiration may begin, as it releases energy quickly.

The process differs in animals and plants and microbes.

In animals:	glucose	⟶	lactic acid (+ energy)		oxygen needed to get rid of the **lactic acid** is the '**oxygen debt**'
In plants and microbes:	glucose	⟶	ethanol + carbon dioxide	(+ energy)	this is called **fermentation**

Comparing aerobic and anaerobic respiration:

	Location	Reactants	Products	Energy generated
aerobic respiration	mitochondria	glucose and oxygen	carbon dioxide and water	more energy than anaerobic but not generated as quickly
anaerobic respiration	cytoplasm	glucose	animals – lactic acid plants and microbes (fermentation) – ethanol and carbon dioxide	less energy than aerobic but generated more quickly

Fermentation (anaerobic respiration) by yeast is useful to humans.

- **brewing** – in beer and wine making, **ethanol** is the useful product. The type of drink made depends on the source of sugar, for example, grapes for wine, hops and barley for beer.
- **baking** – in bread making, carbon dioxide is the useful product as it causes the bread to rise.

In brewing and baking, water is first added to dried yeast to activate it. Sugar is then added as the reactant for respiration.

Glucose and oxygen are the **reactants**.
Carbon dioxide and water are the **products**.

Aerobic respiration takes place in cell organelles called **mitochondria**. These are sausage-shaped and found in most animal and plant cells. Their structure is adapted to carry out their function.

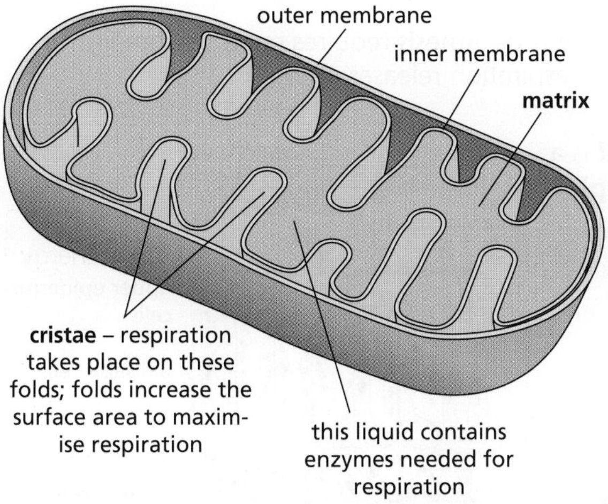

We can use experiments to show that animals and plants produce water and carbon dioxide, the products of respiration.

- Water – when we breathe onto a cold mirror or window, water vapour condenses onto the cold surface. If a plant is grown in a plastic bag, water vapour condenses inside the bag.
- Carbon dioxide – in the set-up below, **soda lime** absorbs carbon dioxide, **limewater** tests for carbon dioxide. B stays clear showing no carbon dioxide; D turns cloudy showing carbon dioxide has been produced.

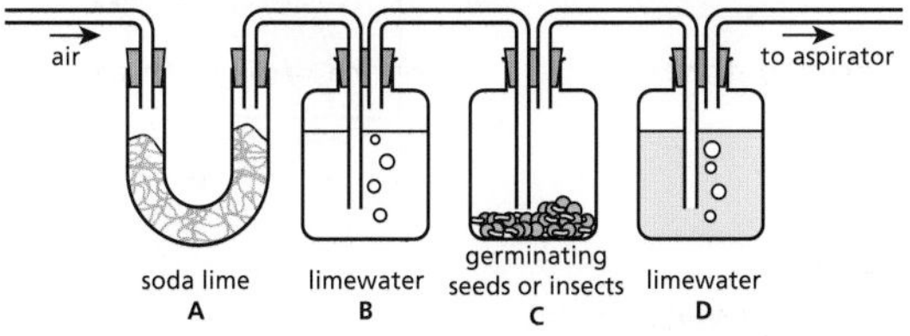

Glucose can be stored in organisms. It can then be used to release energy as and when needed.

In the animal and human body, glucose is stored:

- as **glycogen** in muscles and the liver
- as fat.

In plants, glucose is stored as starch.

Key vocabulary	
aerobic respiration	respiration involving oxygen
anaerobic respiration	respiration without using oxygen
baking	cooking with dry heat, for example, in an oven as is done with bread and pastries
brewing	the production of beer using fermentation
cristae	the folds of the inner membrane of a mitochondrion where respiration takes place
ethanol	an alcohol produced during anaerobic respiration in plants and microbes
fermentation	a type of anaerobic respiration taking place in plants and some microbes
glucose	a simple organic sugar molecule, used in respiration
glycogen	organic glucose molecules linked in a long chain; a storage molecule
lactic acid	the substance produced in anaerobic respiration in animals
limewater	a solution used to test for the presence of carbon dioxide
matrix	the liquid inside a mitochondrion which contains the enzymes needed for respiration
mitochondria	an organelle found in most animal and plant cells where respiration is carried out
oxygen debt	the oxygen needed to break down lactic acid produced as a result of vigorous exercise
products	substances that are produced by a chemical process or reaction
reactants	substances that react in a chemical process
respiration	the process in living things in which energy is released from glucose
soda lime	a chemical that absorbs carbon dioxide

Life on Earth and human activities are dependent on plants for many reasons:

- food (green plants are at the start of all feeding relationships)
- raw materials for fabrics and building
- fuel
- medicines
- decorating homes, gardens, parks
- green plants help to maintain the balance of carbon dioxide and oxygen in the atmosphere.

Comparing photosynthesis and respiration.

- Photosynthesis takes place in green plants; respiration takes place in both plants and animals.
- The products of photosynthesis (glucose and oxygen) are the reactants of aerobic respiration.
- The products of aerobic respiration (carbon dioxide and water) are the reactants of photosynthesis.
- Photosynthesis requires energy (from light); respiration releases energy.

Photosynthesis takes place in green leaves. **Chlorophyll** is a green pigment and is found in organelles called **chloroplasts** in some plant cells. Leaves are adapted for photosynthesis.

Adaptation	Function
waxy and waterproof **cuticle**	prevents water loss
transparent layer below cuticle	allows light through
palisade cells packed with chloroplasts	increase photosynthesis
stomata on underside	open and close to control gas exchange
air spaces	allow gases to move inside the leaf

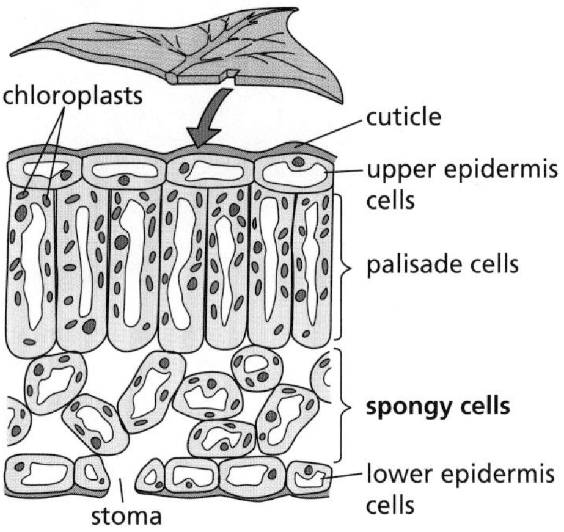

Photosynthesis is the reaction used by green plants to make the carbohydrate glucose using light energy.

$$\text{carbon dioxide} + \text{water} \xrightarrow{\text{light}} \text{glucose} + \text{oxygen}$$

reactants → *products*

Stomata are opened and closed by specialised **guard cells**. Through the stomata:

- gas exchange happens – gases pass in and out of the leaf
- water can be lost.

Stomata close when water levels are low and at night (as there is no sunlight for photosynthesis).

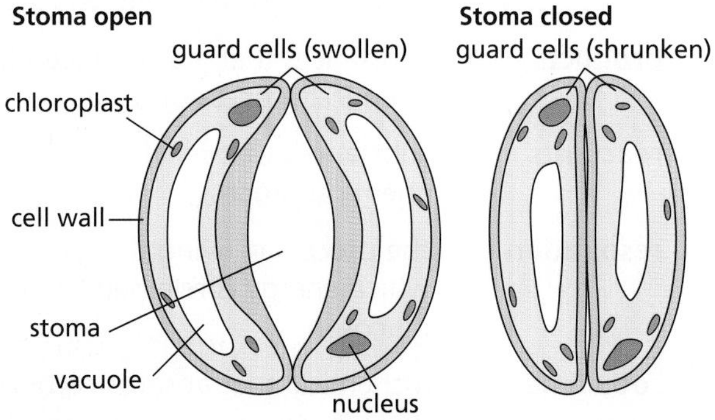

Glucose from photosynthesis is stored as starch. Testing leaves for starch with **iodine** shows whether or not a plant has been photosynthesising. The experimental steps are shown below.

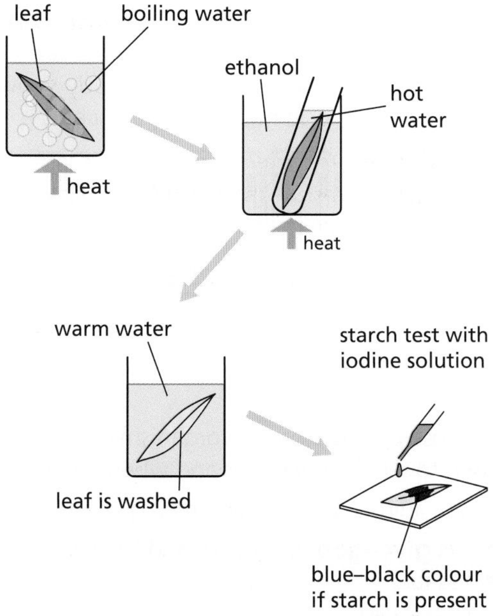

Water and **minerals** move into a plant through the roots from the soil. **Root hair cells** do not contain chloroplasts because they are not exposed to light. The cells are adapted to their function by having extensions called root hairs, to increase the surface area for absorption.

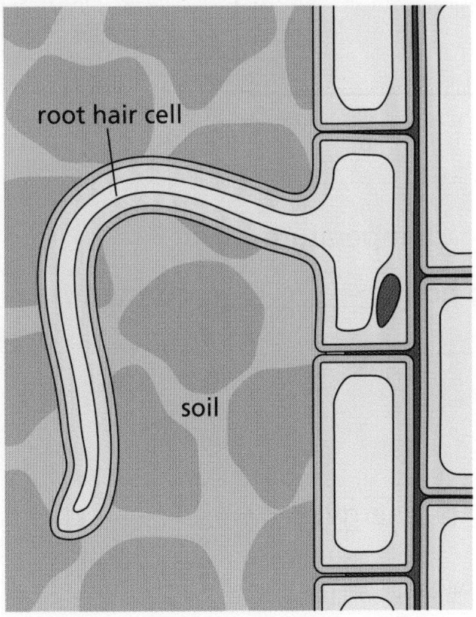

Some minerals are essential nutrients to keep plants healthy. If they are missing or deficient the plant's health is affected.

Mineral	Effect of deficiency
nitrates (contain nitrogen)	poor growth and yellow leaves
magnesium	cannot make chlorophyll
phosphates (contain phosphorus)	poor root growth

Plants have tissues that are specialised to transport substances.

1 Water moves up the plant from the roots to the leaves through **xylem**.

2 Glucose made by photosynthesis moves from the leaves and around the plant through **phloem**.

Transpiration is the loss of water from a leaf. Most water is lost in hot, dry, windy conditions. Leaves can be adapted to reduce water loss by:

- having a thick waxy cuticle
- having narrow, curled or folded leaves to reduce their surface area
- closing their stomata.

Key vocabulary	
chlorophyll	the green pigment in plants that traps sunlight for photosynthesis
chloroplasts	organelles within some plant cells that contain chlorophyll
cuticle	the waxy, waterproof outer layer of a leaf
guard cells	cells that open and close the stomata
iodine	a chemical used to test for the presence of starch
minerals	elements such as iron and calcium needed to keep living things healthy
palisade cell	a plant leaf cell that is long and narrow and packed with chloroplasts
phloem	a tissue made up of long tubes that transport glucose made in the leaves to other parts of the plant
photosynthesis	a process carried out by green plants; light energy, carbon dioxide and water react to produce glucose and oxygen
rate of photosynthesis	the measure of how much photosynthesis takes place in a set time
spongy cells	plant leaf cells that have large spaces around them to allow gas exchange
starch	a large molecule made by plants as a way to store food (glucose)
stomata (singular: stoma)	a minute pore in the lower surface of a leaf
root hair cell	a specialised cell in roots of plants, hair-like extensions that provide a large surface area
transpiration	the movement of water in plants as it is taken up through the roots and released from the leaves as water vapour
xylem	a tissue made of cells that form a long tube through the plant to transport water and minerals from the roots

4.1 Aerobic respiration

You are learning to:
- recall the aerobic respiration equation and describe what it shows
- describe where respiration takes place in cells
- explain how mitochondria are adapted for respiration
- describe and explain experimental evidence for respiration.

1 Fill in the gaps using the words below.

muscles oxygen energy temperature

We need energy to contract ____________ and to keep body ____________ constant.
The main purpose of respiration is to release ____________.
Aerobic respiration uses ____________.

2 Complete the equation for aerobic respiration.

________ + oxygen ⟶ carbon dioxide + ________ (+ energy)

3 What are the products of respiration? Choose **two** answers.

a energy
b carbon dioxide
c oxygen
d water

4 Where in the cell does aerobic respiration take place? Choose **one** answer.

a cell wall
b cell membrane
c chloroplast
d mitochondria

5 Match each word with its definition.

a	aerobic respiration	**i**	released in plant and animal cells by respiration
b	breathing	**ii**	inhaling oxygen and exhaling carbon dioxide
c	energy	**iii**	chemical process that uses oxygen and glucose to release energy
d	glucose	**iv**	one reactant of respiration

6 Why do marathon runners eat carbohydrate-rich meals, such as pasta, to prepare for a race? Choose **one** answer.

a Carbohydrate chains in pasta are broken down into glucose for respiration.
b The race takes a long time and they will not be able to have a meal.
c Carbohydrates in pasta can be built into protein chains.
d Carbohydrate chains in pasta are broken down into energy.

7 Mitochondria are adapted for aerobic respiration. The image below shows a human mitochondrion.

a Label it using these words:

cristae inner membrane outer membrane matrix

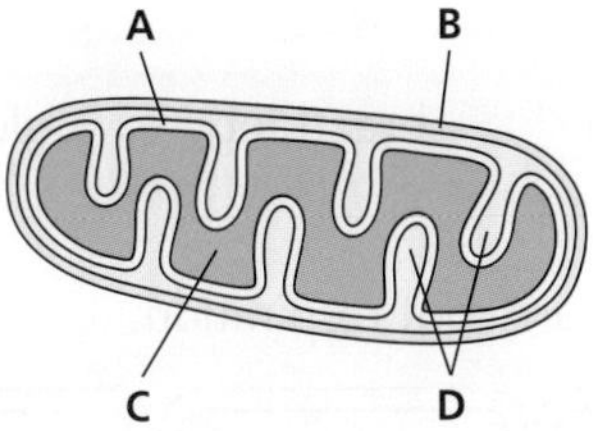

b Explain how each of these parts is adapted for respiration:

i the inner membrane

ii the matrix.

c Within the same human, mitochondria like the one below were also seen.

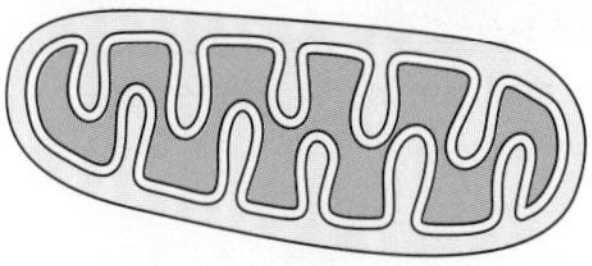

Compare how much respiration could take place in this mitochondrion and the one shown in part **a** above. Explain your answer.

Worked example

Carbon dioxide is made during respiration.

Use your knowledge of respiration and breathing to explain how carbon dioxide is made and removed from the body.

Give your answer in a logical sequence.

When asked to give an answer in a logical sequence, you need to provide a step-by-step answer in the order that things happen. You can use bullet points. (A good tip is to write the different steps on sticky notes so that you can then arrange into the correct sequence.)

Glucose and oxygen react in respiration.

Carbon dioxide and water are produced.

Carbon dioxide is transported in the bloodstream from body cells to the lungs.

Carbon dioxide moves from the bloodstream into the lungs.

The carbon dioxide is breathed out.

8 Breathing and respiration both involve oxygen but are not the same thing. Explain the role of oxygen in both breathing and respiration, and how the processes are different.

9 A boy eats a breakfast of brown toast and honey.

Describe the sequence of events in his body from eating the breakfast to the food providing him with the energy he needs for his PE lesson.

Give your answer in a logical sequence.

In your explanation, include the following key words:

digestion starch enzymes bloodstream breathing glucose oxygen mitochondria

10 The apparatus looks for evidence that insects and seeds carry out respiration.

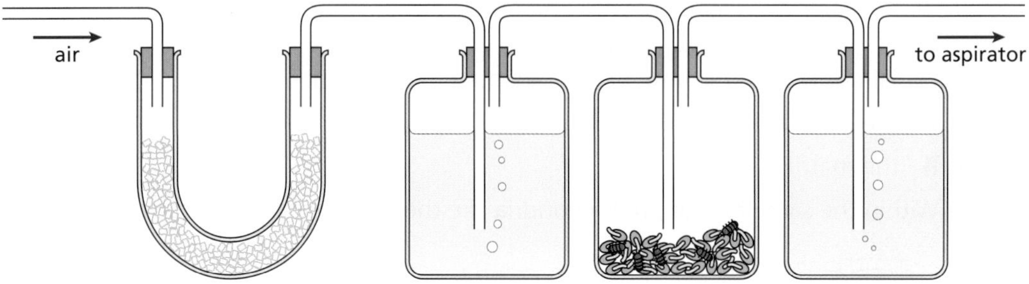

a What does limewater test for?

b What is the purpose of the soda lime?

c Flask B is a control. Explain why it is used in this investigation.

d The diagram shows the apparatus at the start of the experiment. Describe what would be seen in flask D after 30 minutes. Explain why.

e One student suggests that the soda lime is in the wrong position and connects flask A between C and D. Predict what will be seen in Flask D after 30 minutes. Explain your answer.

Worked example

A scientist studies the rate of respiration of germinating seeds at different temperatures. The results are shown below.

Temperature (°C)	Rate of respiration (bubbles of carbon dioxide per minute)
20	5
30	20
40	35
50	48
60	29
70	10

a What is the independent variable in this investigation?

The independent variable is what we change.

temperature

b Which type of graph should be used to display these results?

When the independent variable has a whole range of values that could be continuous, we use a line graph. For example, a graph to show how height varies as age increases.

When the independent variable has distinct values, or categories, we use a bar chart. For example, a graph to show how many people have blue, green and brown eyes.

line graph

c Draw a sketch graph of the results.

A sketch graph shows the shape of a graph but doesn't plot the actual points. The axes should be labelled and units included.

similar graph to below, axes labelled, including units, but points not plotted, shape of graph shown

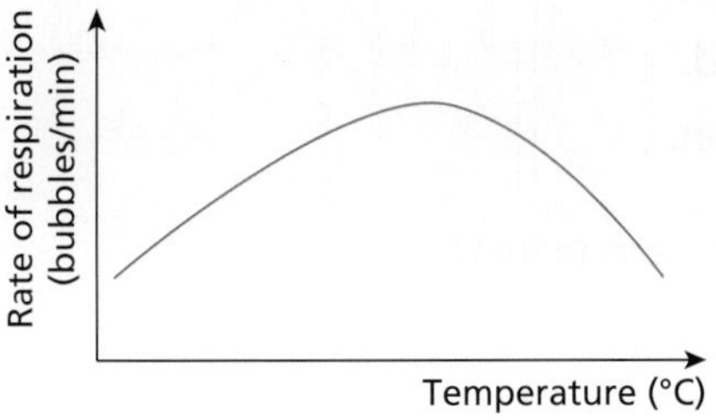

The scientists then compare the rate of respiration in different types of seeds, including broad been seeds, pumpkin seeds, sunflower seeds and poppy seeds.

d What is the independent variable in this investigation?

type of seed

e Which type of graph should the scientist use to display these results? Explain your answer.

bar chart, as the independent variable has discrete categories

11 A cell biologist looks at cell images and compares the number of mitochondria in different human cells. The results are shown below.

Type of cell	Estimated number of mitochondria per cell
skin	800
muscle	5500
liver	4200
brain	1800
kidney	3900

a Suggest why the number of mitochondria is 'estimated'.

b Which type of graph would be the best to use to represent this data?

c Sketch a graph of these results.

d Arrange these cell types in order from those needing the least energy to those needing the most energy.

Scientists predict that mitochondria take up 15% of the volume of a muscle cell.

e Calculate the volume of the mitochondria in a muscle cell of volume 3500 μm^3.

4.2 Anaerobic respiration

You are learning to:

- recall the anaerobic respiration equation and describe what it shows
- explain what is meant by 'oxygen debt'
- describe examples of organisms that carry out anaerobic respiration
- describe what is meant by 'fermentation'
- explain some uses of fermentation.

1 Select 'true' or 'false' for each statement.

a Plants and animals can carry out anaerobic respiration.

b Anaerobic respiration means 'without oxygen'.

c In anaerobic respiration, no energy is released.

d Fermentation is a type of anaerobic respiration.

2 What are the **two** products of anaerobic respiration in plants?

a lactic acid

b ethanol

c carbon dioxide

d water

3 Match each keyword to its explanation.

a fermentation	**i** product of anaerobic respiration in animals
b ethanol	**ii** reactant in anaerobic respiration in plants
c glucose	**iii** product of anaerobic respiration in plants
d lactic acid	**iv** anaerobic respiration in plants

4 Which **two** of these does yeast need to grow and respire?

a water

b oxygen

c sugar

d carbon dioxide

5 Fermentation is used in industry. Match the reactants to the products.

a yeast and grapes	**i** bread
b yeast and flour	**ii** wine
c yeast and hops	**iii** cheese and yoghurt
d milk	**iv** beer

6 Students investigated the effect of temperature on fermentation. The apparatus used is shown below.

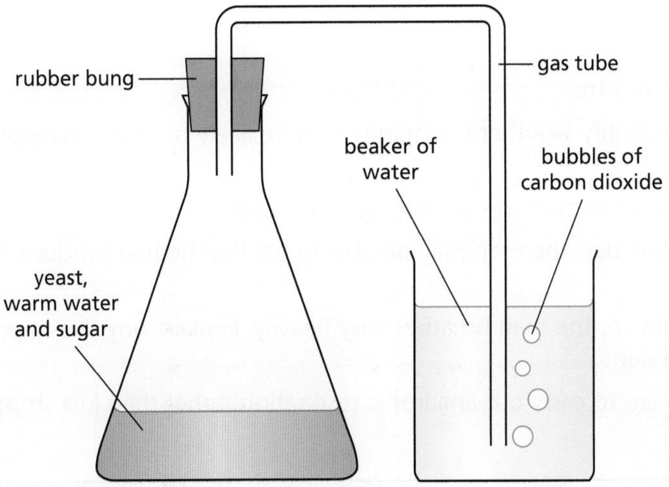

Explain the purpose of each substance and each item of apparatus:

a warm water

b sugar

c rubber bung and gas tube

d beaker of water.

7 Below is the word equation for fermentation:

glucose → ethanol + carbon dioxide

a Of the organisms below, select which **two** can carry out fermentation:

i animals

ii plants

iii microbes.

b Fermentation is used for both brewing and baking. For each of these processes, identify the most useful product of fermentation:

i brewing

ii baking.

c What causes each of these features in bread and beer?

i air pockets in bread

ii froth on top of beer

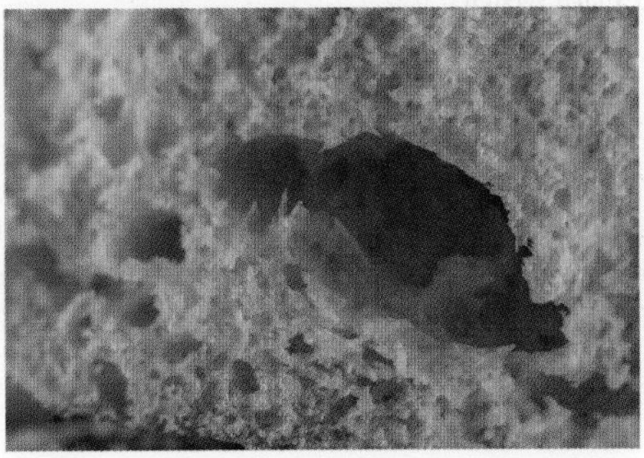

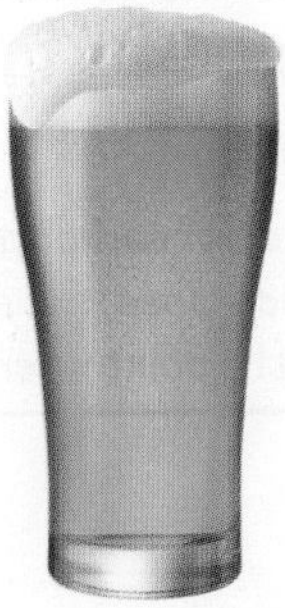

8 Consider these stages of a man's exercise routine:

1 gentle walk to warm up for 100 m

2 slow jog for 200 m

3 fast sprint for 50 m

4 slow jog to cool down for 50 m.

a For each of the stages, identify whether the man was more likely to be using aerobic or anaerobic respiration.

b Identify the stage(s) when the man was producing lactic acid.

c Describe how, on the next day, the man may be able to tell that he had produced lactic acid.

d At the start of his cool down, the man breathes very heavily. Explain why this happens, using the term 'oxygen debt'.

e Why is it useful to the man to carry out anaerobic respiration rather than just stopping altogether?

Worked example

The graph below shows a sketch graph of an investigation into the effect of the mass of carbohydrate eaten on the speed of a runner.

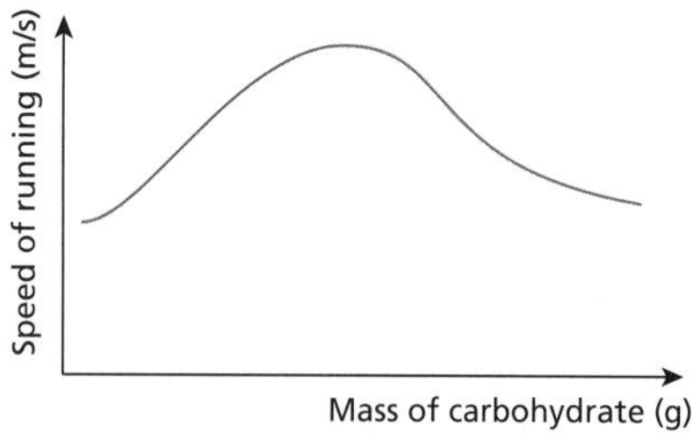

a Identify:

i the independent variable

ii the dependent variable.

b Describe the relationship between the mass of carbohydrate and the speed of running shown by the graph.

A graph tells a story and shows the relationship between two variables. We describe this relationship using the sentence structure below:

As (independent variable) (increases/decreases), the (dependent variable) (increases/decreases).

Sometimes, graphs have more than one part; any answer must tell the whole story.

This is also sometimes asked as 'write a conclusion'.

a i mass of carbohydrate

ii speed of running

b Initially, as the mass of carbohydrate increases, the speed of running increases, but then as the mass of carbohydrate increases, the speed decreases (back to a similar speed as at the start). Using the graph, we can see the point where the mass of carbohydrate provides maximum speed of running.

9 Three students investigated the effect of temperature on the number of bubbles of carbon dioxide produced per minute by yeast cells. The table shows the data they collected.

Temperature (°C)		0	5	15	25	35	45	55	65	75	85
Bubbles released per minute	Student 1	0	3	16	30	23	1	0	0	0	0
	Student 2	0	4	18	32	27	5	1	0	0	0
	Student 3	0	2	15	27	25	1	0	0	0	0

a Write a conclusion for the investigation.

b Draw a sketch graph of the results.

c The three students separately carried out the same investigation in the same way. Explain why this is better than collecting the results only once.

d **i** What is the range of temperature values used in this investigation?

ii The students want to carry out another experiment to find the exact temperature at which the most carbon dioxide is produced. Suggest what range of temperatures they should use in this new experiment.

10 A student wants to investigate whether the type of sugar affects the rate of fermentation. They mix yeast with warm water and sugar and collect the carbon dioxide bubbles. The number of carbon dioxide bubbles are counted for 30 seconds. The student then repeats the same method with other types of sugar.

a For this investigation, identify:

i the independent variable

ii the dependent variable

iii **two** control variables.

The table below shows the results.

Type of sugar	Number of bubbles in 30 s			Average number of bubbles in 30 s
	Trial 1	Trial 2	Trial 3	
glucose	20	24	22	**A**
sucrose	12	2	14	**B**
sweetener	6	7	8	**C**

b **i** Identify **one** anomalous result.

ii Explain what should be done with the anomalous result when calculating average results.

iii Calculate the average number of bubbles for each sugar (**A**, **B** and **C**).

c What type of graph should be used to display these results? Explain your answer.

4.3 The importance of respiration

You are learning to:
- compare aerobic and anaerobic respiration
- describe some plant and animal systems that are linked with respiration
- explain how animal and plant systems are dependent on respiration.

1 Fill in the gaps using the words below.

breathing circulatory digestive skeletal

In humans, glucose for respiration is provided by the __________ system.

Oxygen for aerobic respiration is brought into the body by the __________ system.

Both glucose and oxygen are carried to cells by the __________ system.

The energy released by respiration is then useful to the __________ system to allow muscles to contract and move joints.

2 Where is carbon dioxide transported from and to by the circulatory system in animals? Choose **two** answers.

a from lungs to body cells
b from body cells to lungs
c from muscle cells to lungs
d from lungs to muscle cells

3 In which part of the cell do the following processes take place?

a aerobic respiration
b anaerobic respiration

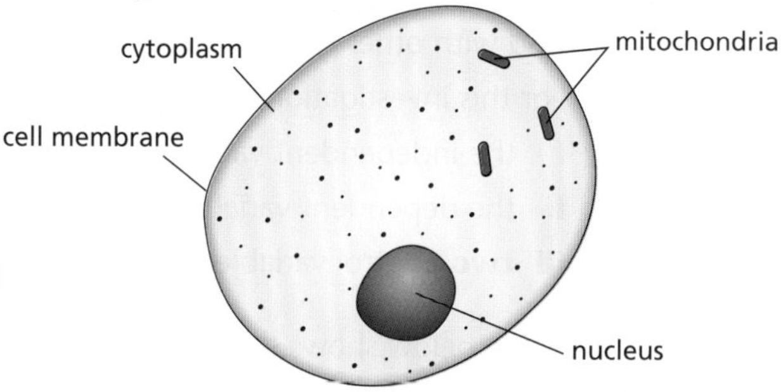

4 What happens to carbon dioxide produced during aerobic respiration in plants? Choose **two** answers.

a moves out of the plant through the leaves
b moves out of the plant through the roots
c is used in photosynthesis
d is used to make water

5 **a** Look at the images below. For each one decide whether aerobic or anaerobic respiration is most likely to take place.

i

ii

b Select the **two** situations where aerobic respiration may switch to anaerobic respiration in humans:

i when there is no oxygen available
ii when there is no carbon dioxide available
iii when energy is needed to be released quickly
iv when energy is no longer needed

6 Complete the table to compare aerobic and anaerobic respiration in animals.

	Reactants	Products	Amount of energy (more/less)
Aerobic respiration			
Anaerobic respiration			

7 Each of the problems below would reduce the amount of respiration, but for different reasons. Link each problem to the way it reduces respiration.

a bronchitis (blockage in the bronchi)	**i** too little oxygen transported around the body
b poor carbohydrate digestion	**ii** too little glucose available for respiration
c heart failure (weak heart)	**iii** too little oxygen brought into the body

8 Enzymes are needed for both aerobic and anaerobic respiration. Glucose is broken down in respiration to release energy.

a What effect do enzymes have on reactions?

b If a piece of toast is eaten, which enzyme breaks down the starch in the bread into glucose for respiration?

c Suggest which uses more enzymes: aerobic or anaerobic respiration. Explain your answer.

9 Glucose can be stored in the body of animals in different ways.

a Explain why it is helpful for animals to be able to store glucose.

b **i** Describe **two** parts of the body that store glucose as glycogen.

ii Name **one** other way that glucose is stored in the body of animals.

10 A problem with the digestive, breathing or circulatory systems has a negative impact on respiration.

a Explain the importance of respiration. Give at least **two** examples.

b Explain why a problem in each of the systems causes a decrease in the amount of respiration:

i digestive system

ii breathing system.

c Suggest why a decrease in respiration affects breathing and digestion.

11 Mitochondrial disease is a group of disorders, all affecting how well the mitochondria work. Around 1 in 5000 people have mitochondrial disease.

a **i** In a population of 67 million people, calculate the estimated number having mitochondrial disease.

ii Explain why this is only an estimate.

b Mitochondrial disease has the greatest impact on the heart and muscles. Suggest why.

c Explain why mitochondrial disease causes each of the following outcomes:

i slow growth

ii poor digestion, particularly in the intestines and stomach.

4.4 Photosynthesis

You are learning to:

- explain the importance of photosynthetic plants to life on Earth
- recall the photosynthesis equation and describe what it shows
- identify factors that affect the rate of photosynthesis
- interpret data from photosynthesis investigations.

1 Complete the equation for photosynthesis, choosing from the words below.

nitrogen   oxygen   starch   water

carbon dioxide + ___________ → glucose + ___________

2 Plants produce glucose by photosynthesis. Which process uses glucose in plants?

a transpiration

b digestion

c respiration

d combustion

3 How do the mass of soil and the mass of the plant change as a plant grows in a pot? Choose **one** correct statement.

a Mass of the soil and plant both increase.

b Mass of the soil and plant both stay the same.

c Mass of the soil stays the same and mass of the plant increases.

d Mass of the soil increases and mass of the plant stays the same.

4 Match each plant to an example of its use.

a tomato	**i** building
b cotton	**ii** medicine
c oak tree	**iii** food
d opium poppy	**iv** fabric

5 What is the source of energy for photosynthesis?

6 **a** For each of the times below, decide whether photosynthesis, respiration or both take place in plants:

i day time

ii night time.

b At which time (day or night) would the concentration of carbon dioxide be the highest? Explain your answer.

7 A teacher wanted to find the best temperature to grow his green bean plants. They measured the rate of photosynthesis at different temperatures. The graph shows the results.

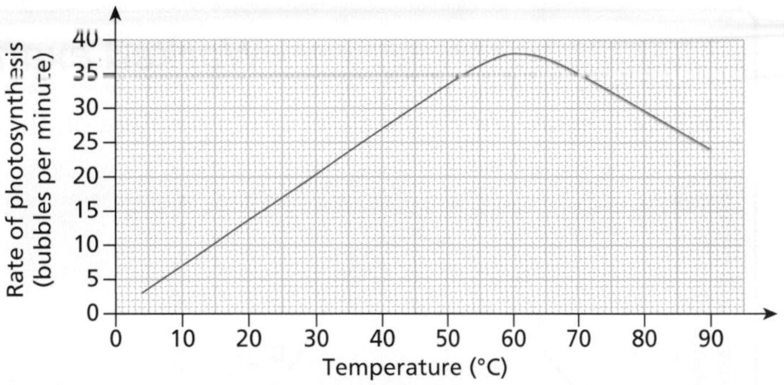

a For this investigation, identify:

i the independent variable

ii the dependent variable

iii **one** control variable.

b What temperature would you suggest the green beans are grown at?

Worked example

a A student is testing a leaf for starch. Match each step in the process with its purpose.

A place the leaf in boiling water	**i** removes the chlorophyll
B put the leaf in hot ethanol	**ii** kills the cells and removes the waxy layer
C add iodine	**iii** blue/black shows starch present
D look for colour change	**iv** tests for starch

Think back to food tests: iodine was used to test for starch.

A – ii; B – i; C – iv; D – iii

b A plant was kept in the dark for 6 days.

i Would this plant be carrying out respiration, photosynthesis or both?

Think about what each process requires and how the dark would affect each process.

only respiration as photosynthesis needs light energy

ii Would this leaf contain starch?

no starch as no photosynthesis

Remember, glucose is stored as starch in plants.

iii What colour would iodine be after testing this leaf for starch?

orange

8 A student investigated the need of a plant for air. The air was removed from a container and a green plant was placed inside and the container kept sealed for 3 days.

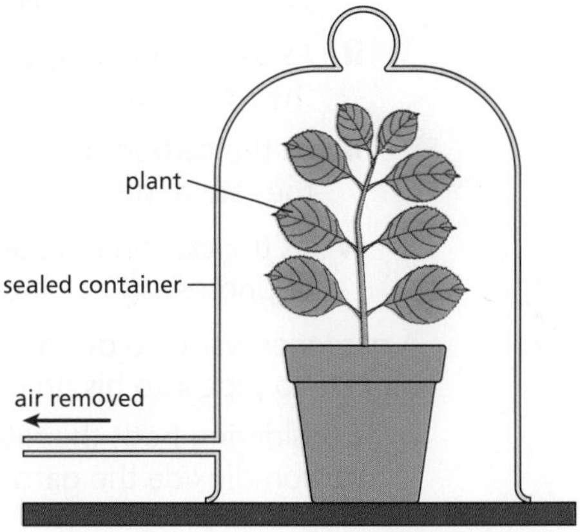

a Would photosynthesis take place in this plant? Explain your answer.

b After 3 days, one of the leaves was removed and tested for starch using iodine. What would the colour of the iodine be? Explain your answer.

Carbon dioxide was then pumped into the container. After 2 days, the air inside the container was tested and found to contain oxygen.

c Explain why the container contained oxygen.

Worked example

The graph below shows the effect of temperature on the rate of photosynthesis.

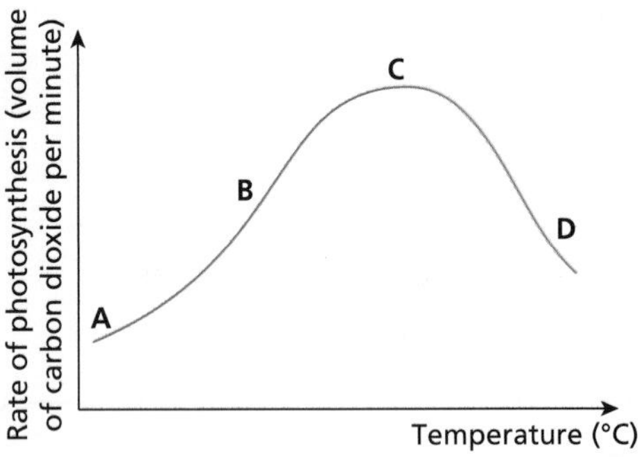

When you look at a graph, you can sometimes break it into parts, as in A, B, C and D on this graph.

a Where on the graph is the rate of photosynthesis at its maximum?

Where is rate at its highest? (Where is the peak/highest point of the graph?)

C

b Where on the graph is the rate at its lowest but slowly increasing?

As temperature increases, rate increases slowly. (Where is the slope/gradient the least steep but slowly getting steeper?)

A

c Where on the graph is the rate of photosynthesis increasing quickly?

The graph is steepest where there is a small change in temperature but a big change in rate.

B

d Where on the graph is the rate of photosynthesis decreasing?

The slope is going in the opposite direction (downwards).

D

9 The graph shows the effect of carbon dioxide concentration on the rate of photosynthesis.

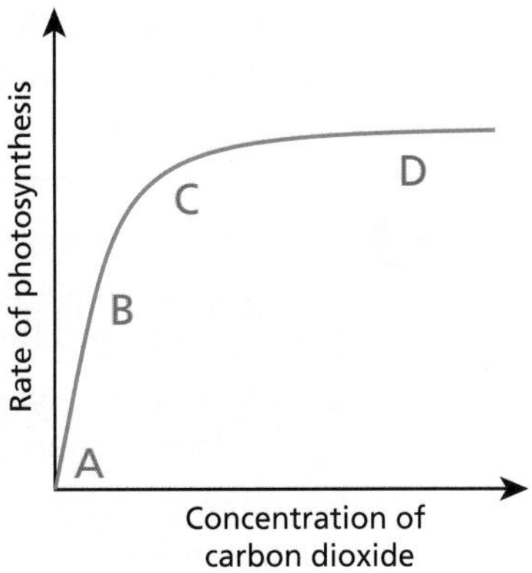

a Match each description to the correct letter on the graph.

i With a carbon dioxide concentration of zero, the rate of photosynthesis is zero.

ii As the carbon dioxide concentration increases further, the rate of photosynthesis remains constant.

iii As the carbon dioxide concentration increases further, the rate of photosynthesis increases only slowly.

iv As the carbon dioxide concentration increases, the rate of photosynthesis increases quickly.

A gardener wants to decide which concentration of carbon dioxide to pipe into his greenhouse.

b Considering both the rate of photosynthesis and cost, explain which concentration of carbon dioxide the gardener should choose (that is, shown at **A**, **B**, **C** or **D**).

10 **a** **i** State whether oxygen is a reactant or product of photosynthesis.

ii State whether oxygen is a reactant or product of respiration.

b Explain how the concentration of oxygen in the air above a corn field changes between sunrise and sunset.

c Choosing between sunrise and sunset, when will the oxygen concentration be at its:

i highest concentration?

ii lowest concentration?

11 The apparatus below was used to investigate the effect of light on photosynthesis. The number of bubbles per minute was counted as a measure of the rate of photosynthesis.

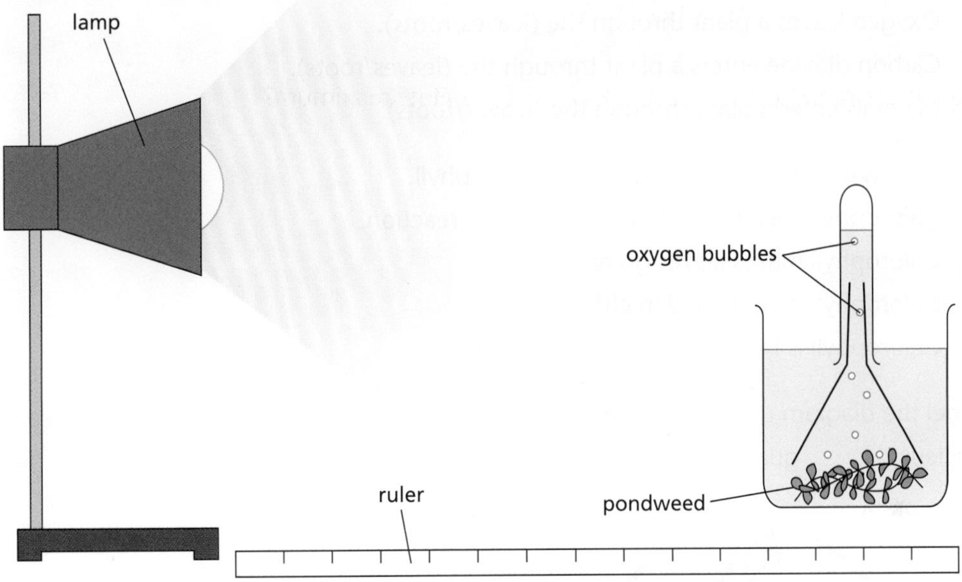

A student considers a number of different changes that they could make to the set-up.

a Predict and explain the effect of each of the changes below on the number of bubbles counted per minute.

i Increase intensity of the light bulb.

ii Increase the distance between the light and pondweed.

iii Increase the volume of water.

b After the initial investigation, the student repeats it, but without the pondweed. Explain why it was a good idea to do this test.

Reading **A** was recorded as 72 bubbles per minute. Reading **B** was recorded as 1 bubble every 2 seconds.

c Predict which was closer to the lamp, **A** or **B**. Explain your answer.

4.5 Adaptations of plants for photosynthesis

You are learning to:

- describe how leaves are adapted for photosynthesis
- explain how stomata control gas exchange in leaves
- explain how water and minerals move through a plant
- describe the importance of minerals to plant growth.

1 Choose the correct words in brackets to complete each sentence.

a Water enters a plant through the (leaves/roots).

b Oxygen leaves a plant through the (leaves/roots).

c Carbon dioxide enters a plant through the (leaves/roots).

d Minerals enter a plant through the (leaves/roots).

2 Choose **two** correct statements about chlorophyll.

a Chlorophyll speeds up the photosynthesis reaction.

b Chlorophyll makes leaves green.

c Chlorophyll is contained in chloroplasts.

d Chlorophyll is in all parts of plants.

3 Label the diagram using the words below.

nucleus guard cell stoma

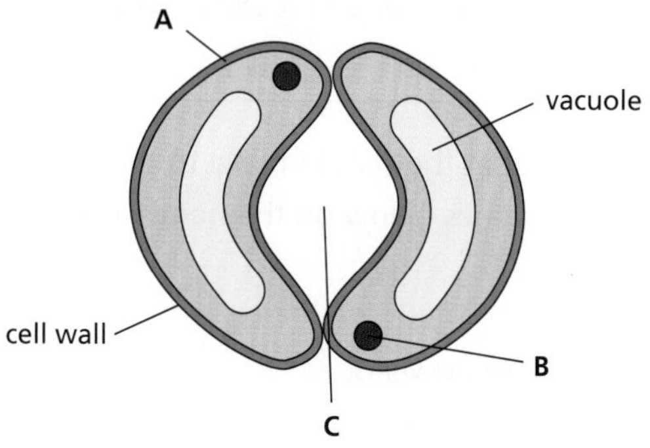

4 Match the descriptions to the type of leaf cell.

a	transparent cells at the top of the leaf	**i**	palisade cells
b	long narrow cells packed with chloroplasts	**ii**	spongy cells
c	cells with large air spaces between them	**iii**	lower epidermis cells
d	cells found on the lower layer of the leaf	**iv**	upper epidermis cells

5 How are the leaves of the water lily adapted for photosynthesis? Choose **two** answers.

a They have a large surface area to trap sunlight.
b They float.
c They contain chlorophyll to trap sunlight.
d They have brightly coloured flowers.

6 Transpiration is the loss of water from a plant. Plants need water for photosynthesis and for support.

a Describe the role of the following in providing plants with water:
  i roots
  ii xylem.

b Of the following conditions, choose the **three** that will increase transpiration:

wet dry windy still hot cold

7 The image below shows guard cells and stomata viewed through a microscope.

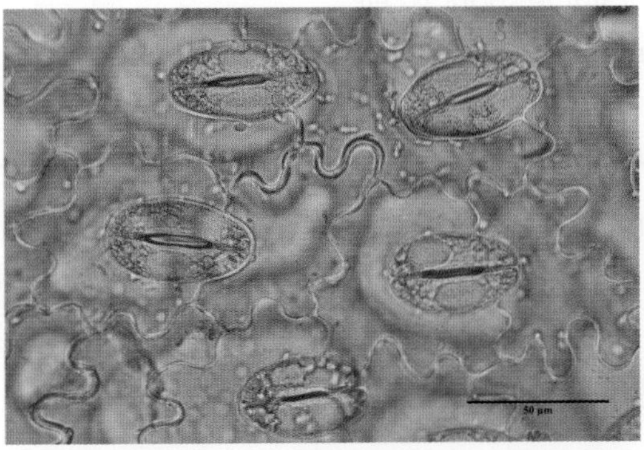

The image is measured as 7.5 mm long when magnified ×150.

a **i** Calculate the actual length of the guard cells using the equation below:
image size = actual (real) size × magnification
  ii Show your answer in µm.

b The stomata in this image are closed. What effect will this have on:
  i water loss from the plant?
  ii movement of carbon dioxide into the plant?

8 The image below shows a view of mint plants from above. New leaves form at the top of the plant.

a Mint plants grow in shady areas. Explain why it is important that the leaves are well adapted to absorb sunlight.

b Suggest how each of the features below helps the plant to carry out photosynthesis.

i As new leaves grow, they grow at a different angle to the leaves underneath, rather than directly over the leaf beneath.

ii The leaves at the top of the plant are smaller than those underneath.

Worked example

Investigations were carried out to estimate how many chloroplasts were present in palisade cells and spongy cells.

A student estimates that there are 615 chloroplasts in a single palisade cell. The student reads that palisade cells contain four times the number of chloroplasts as spongy cells.

a Suggest why there are more chloroplasts in palisade cells than spongy cells.

Palisade cells are closer to the top of the leaf, closer to light, so have more chloroplasts to absorb light for photosynthesis.

b Estimate how many chloroplasts there are in a single spongy cell.

Remember that this will need to be a whole number.

154 rounded up ($\frac{615}{4} = 153.75$)

9 **a** Explain what moves in and out of stomata.

The number of stomata was counted on leaves from different environments. The results are shown in the table.

Leaf sample	Concentration of stomata
A	20 per cm^2
B	12 per cm^2
C	63 per cm^2
D	31 per cm^2

b Predict where each leaf sample was taken by matching it to one of the environments described below.

i high levels of carbon dioxide in the air

ii medium levels of carbon dioxide in the air

iii low levels of carbon dioxide in the air

iv extremely low levels of carbon dioxide in the air

c Leaf sample **C** was found to have a total surface area of 10.4 cm^2. Estimate the total number of stomata on this leaf.

d Choose which type of graph you would use to display these results (environment versus concentration of stomata). Explain your answer.

Worked example

a Describe the function of plant roots.

Remember that there may be more than one function and you should include them all.

Plant roots take in water and minerals from the soil so that they can pass up the plant to the leaves. Plant roots also anchor the plant into the ground.

b Explain how roots are adapted to each function.

Make sure that each function is considered.

Roots need to reach water and minerals throughout the soil. Therefore, they are long and can spread deep and wide. They also have root hair cells that have hair-like projections; these increase the surface area of roots to allow more absorption. Roots spread deep or wide to ensure that the plant is held securely.

10 There are several types of leaf cell. Each is adapted to its own function and to support photosynthesis.

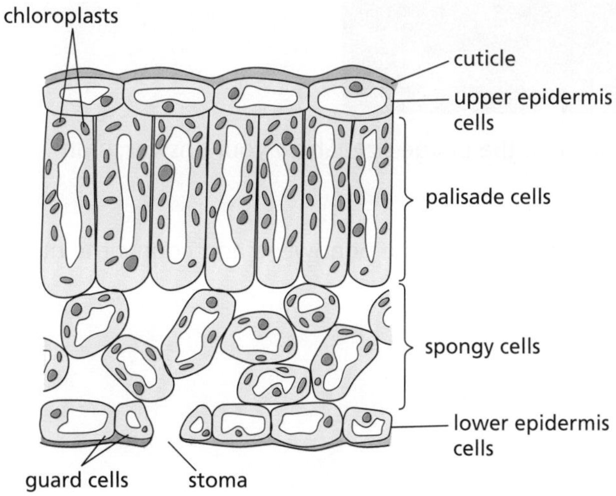

a For each of the cells below, explain how the adaptations support photosynthesis:

i upper epidermis cells are transparent

ii palisade cells are long and narrow and contain chloroplasts, particularly at the top of the cell

iii spongy cells have gaps between them and contain chloroplasts

iv guard cells surround a stoma and cause it to open and close.

b Explain why:

i palisade cells are near the top surface of the leaf

ii guard cells are near the bottom surface of the leaf.

Maths and practical skills

1 A student uses a microscope to measure leaf cells. Choose the best unit for this measurement.

a km

b m

c μm

d s

2 The guard cells on the image below measure 30 μm.

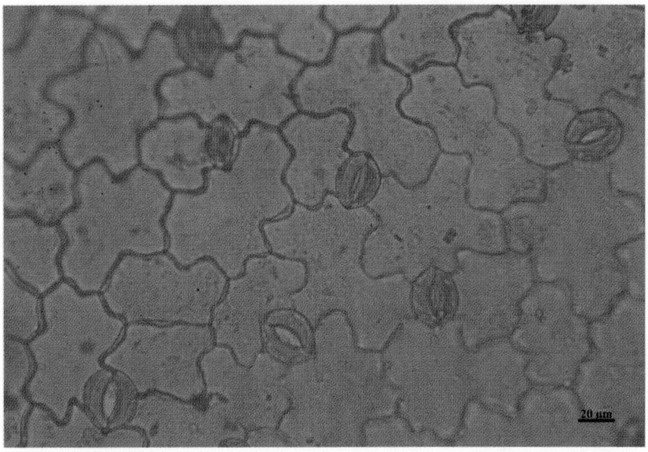

a If they are magnified ×300, calculate the image size. Show your answer in μm.

b Show your answer in mm.

3 A student changes the distance of the lamp from the pondweed and counts the number of bubbles per minute.

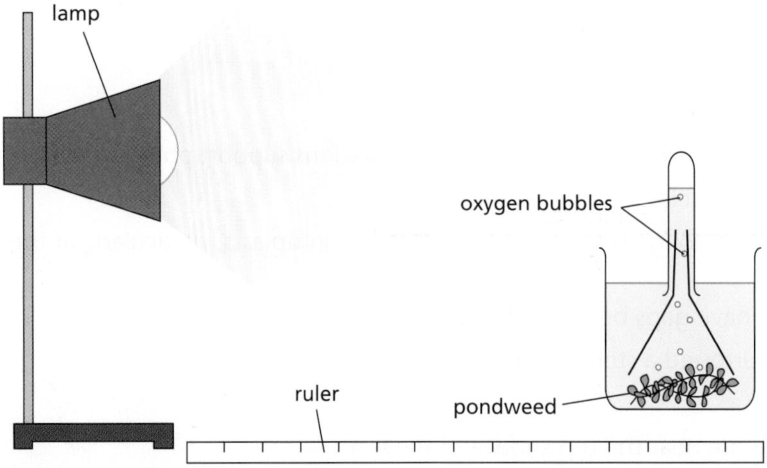

In this investigation, identify:

a the dependent variable

b the independent variable.

4 Ashton and Naga are investigating water loss from a plant in different conditions.

Ashton says that he thinks more water will be lost in windy conditions than still conditions.

Select what type of statement this is from the words below:

a prediction

b conclusion

c explanation

d evaluation.

5 A student blows out into limewater.

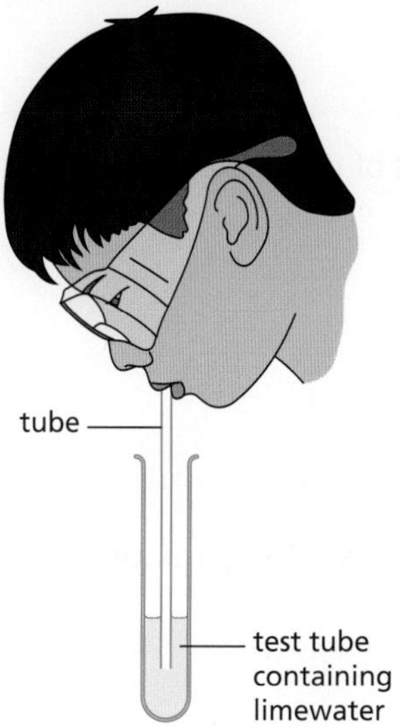

a Which gas does limewater test for?

b How would the limewater change if the result is positive?

6 A new runner does a workout as follows:

walk	5 minutes
gentle jog	3 minutes
sprint	1 minute
gentle jog	2 minutes
sprint	2 minutes
walk	2 minutes

a Calculate the percentage of the exercise for which the runner was most likely respiring anaerobically.

b Explain why the runner breathes heavily after respiring anaerobically.

7 The image shows an animal body cell.

a Which letter shows the site of aerobic respiration?

b Which letter shows the site of anaerobic respiration?

c Describe how a muscle cell would compare in terms of the structure identified in part **a**.

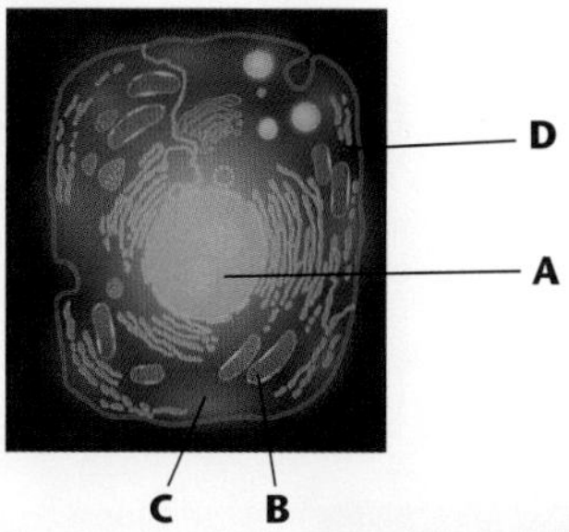

8 A group of students is investigating fermentation. They set up the apparatus as below.

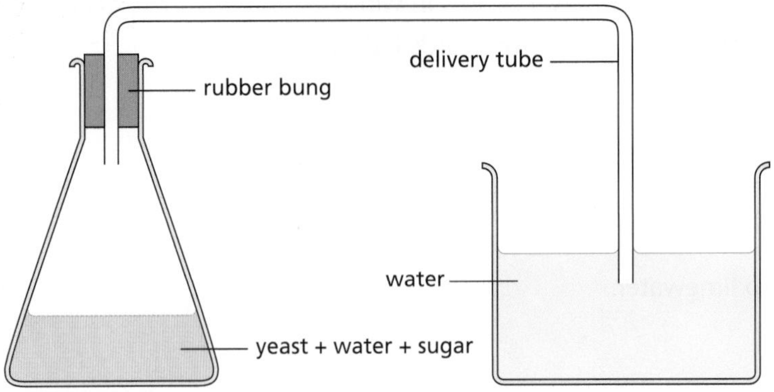

They added water to yeast in the conical flask.

They then added sugar to the flask and counted the bubbles of gas released into the beaker of water.

a What is the purpose of each of the steps below?

i adding water to the yeast

ii adding sugar to the solution

iii attaching the delivery tube

b Which gas was given off as bubbles?

The students want to investigate whether changing the mass of sugar added produces more bubbles of gas.

c Identify:

i the independent variable

ii the dependent variable

iii **two** control variables.

9 A leaf from the plant shown in the photograph is tested to see whether the plant has been carrying out photosynthesis.

The student carries out the following steps:

A boil the leaf in ethanol

B rinse the leaf in warm water

C add iodine

a Explain the purpose of:

i boiling in ethanol

ii adding iodine to the leaf.

The result of adding iodine to the leaf is shown in the diagram.

b Explain what the result tells us about:

i where starch is present in the leaf

ii where photosynthesis has taken place.

10 The rate of photosynthesis was measured at different temperatures.

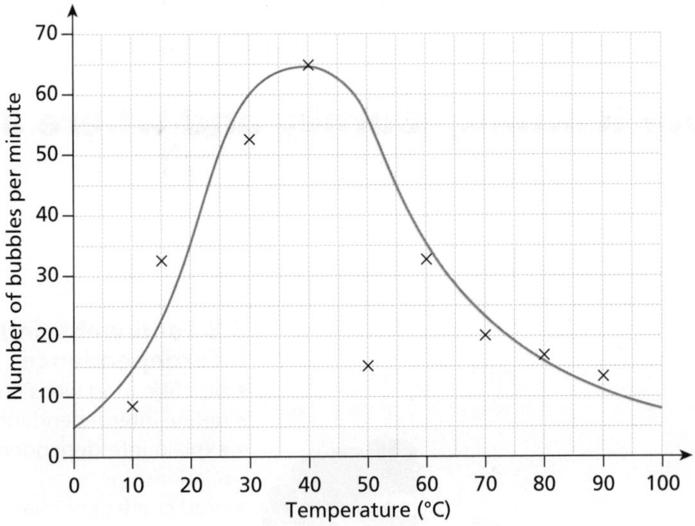

a Using the graph, identify:

i the dependent variable

ii the independent variable.

b What is the optimum temperature for this reaction?

c **i** Identify the anomalous result on the graph.

ii Suggest a reason for this anomaly.

The student wanted to find the optimum temperature more accurately. They repeated the investigation focusing on temperatures between 30 °C and 60 °C.

The results are shown below.

Temperature (°C)	Number of bubbles per minute			Average number of bubbles per minute
	Trial 1	Trial 2	Trial 3	
30	50	54	51	
40	62	58	60	
50	44	45	46	
60	32	60	34	

d **i** Identify an anomaly in the results table.

ii The student realises they used the incorrect temperature for this anomalous result. Predict whether the temperature they used was higher or lower than 60 °C. Explain your answer.

iii Decide how to treat the anomaly, and calculate the average for each temperature. Give your answers to one decimal place.

5 Ecosystems and interdependence road map

Where are you in your learning journey and where are you aiming to be?

5.1 Food webs and interdependence
- describe food webs and chains
- define interdependence
- explain interdependent relationships
- predict effect of changing populations

- construct and use food chains
- the role of flowers
- how environments can change and affect living things

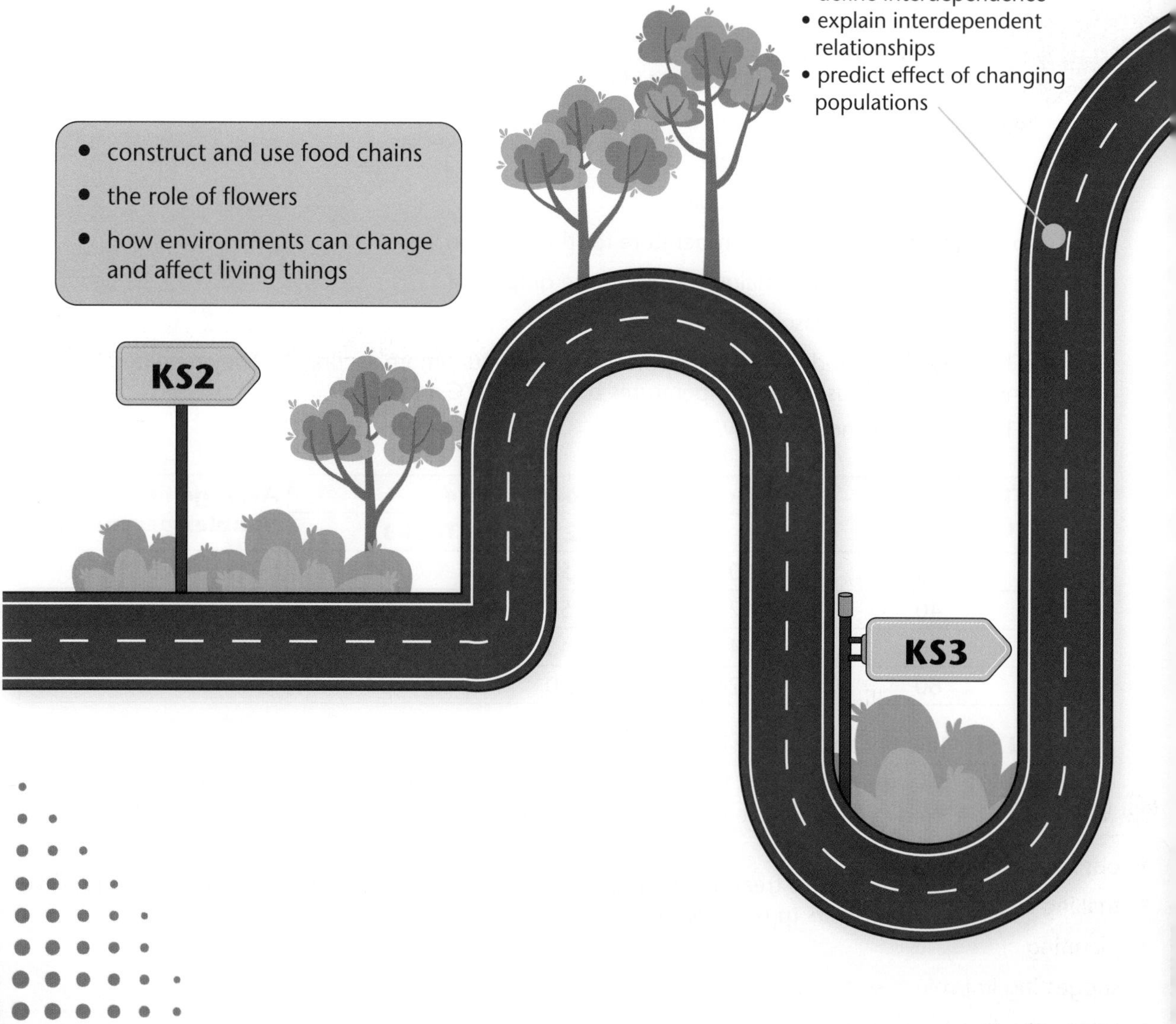

The importance of insects
ain importance of insects
cribe food security
uss food security risks

5.3 Impact of organisms on their environment
- describe effects of humans
- describe how toxins enter food chains
- explain how toxins accumulate
- apply sampling techniques

- adaptations, interdependence and competition
- organisation of an ecosystem
- trophic levels in an ecosystem
- food production
- extinction
- biodiversity and the effect of human interaction on ecosystems

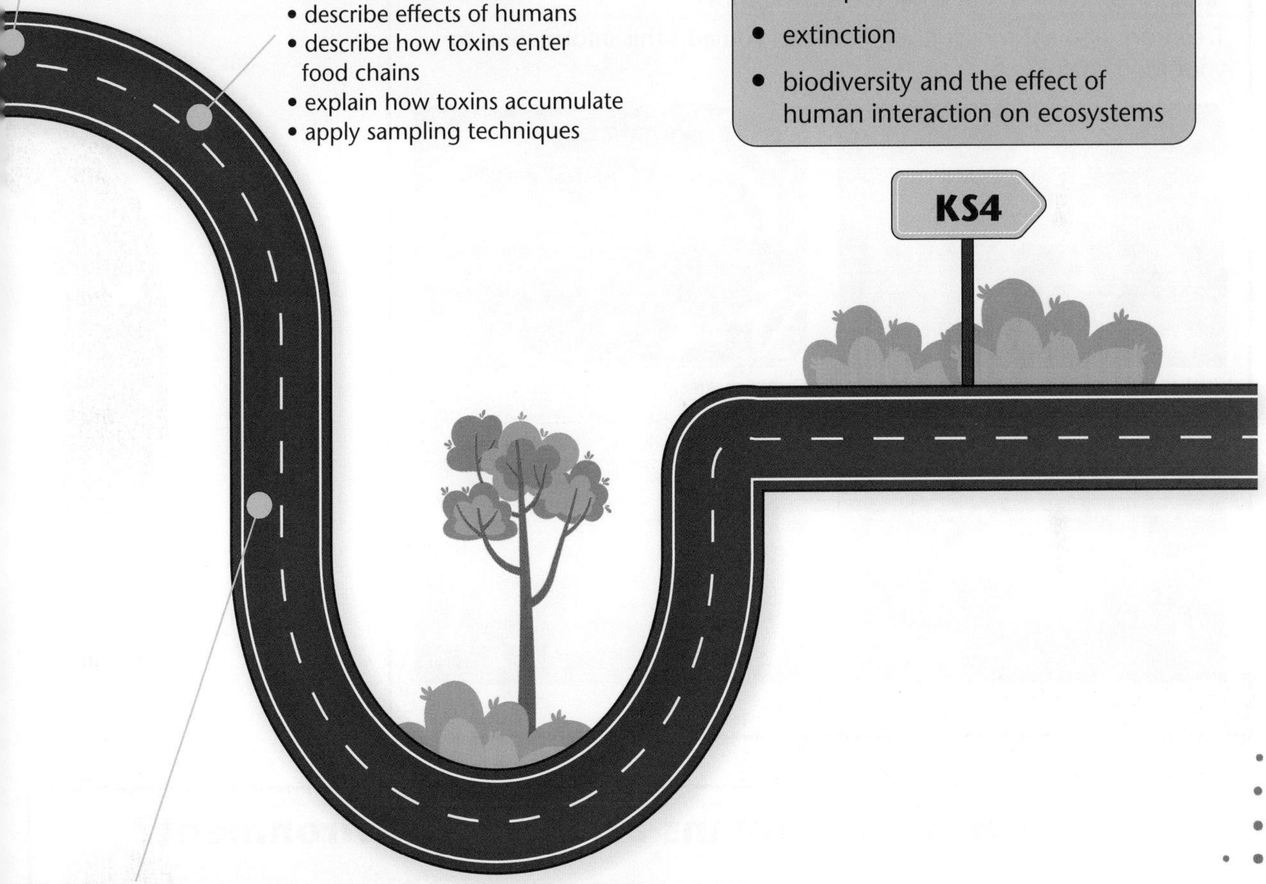

Maths and practical skills

- observing and measuring, including the evaluation of repeatability
- making scientific predictions
- planning an investigation, identifying and managing the variables
- suggesting improvements to practical work
- using sampling techniques
- analysing data and identifying anomalous results
- presenting reasoned explanations

5 Ecosystems and interdependence

Organisms are not isolated in their environment. They interact with other individuals of their own species, with other species and with their physical environment. The study of organisms and their environment is called ecology.

What eats what?

Can you draw a food chain to show the feeding relationships of these organisms? Think about what the arrows show.

Tree frogs also eat mosquitoes; how can you add this information to your food chain?

Cricket

Garter snake

North American tree frog

Grass

How do humans affect the environment?

Look at this waterside environment.

Which organisms might be found here?

What actions might humans take that would impact on this environment? For each action, think about how it would affect the organisms living there.

Using your science skills

Could you be an environmental toxicologist?

You study the effects that chemicals have on people, animals, plants and the environment. You analyse the benefits and risks of using these chemicals.

You might work in a variety of industries: you could be researching the effects of pesticides, waste products from farming, or waste from food or toiletries factories. You might also do some detective work to try and work out why wildlife has been harmed and then suggest how the problems could be reversed. Your work could involve using computer models, carrying out laboratory experiments and undertaking fieldwork.

You will work with scientists researching other areas, so you must be able to communicate your results thoroughly and clearly through writing and public speaking.

Your work could influence whether chemicals are manufactured, altered or banned from use, so your decisions help to ensure that environments are safe to maintain a range of life.

Beekeeping is about so much more than just honey. Bees can be used for crop pollination, wax production or collecting pollen. **Bee keepers (apiarists)** raise and care for bees using a variety of skills such as woodwork, honey extraction, disease and parasite control and queen rearing, and use their knowledge of the fascinating cycles and interactions that occur within a colony of bees to maintain the health of hives.

Wildlife population modellers use data captured in the wild to predict future changes in population sizes and to predict the effect of changes, such as introducing a new predator. They have knowledge and experience of techniques used to sample populations, as well as computer skills to analyse data.

Nature conservation officers protect environments and the living things in them, for example, in woodlands, coastal areas or grasslands. Part of the role is to encourage the community to use the areas and to educate people about the need for conservation. They also put plans in place to maintain the range of living things in the environment.

Organic farmers produce food without using harmful chemicals and pollutants, using natural fertilisers and thinking about how the farm affects local wildlife. Organic farming incorporates high standards of animal care and is a complete system designed to care for the soil, plants, animals, natural environment and climate.

Rare breed farmers ensure that rare breed animals do not become endangered or extinct. They ensure the animals are healthy by managing the farmland to provide a suitable environment and food. These farmers must be knowledgeable about the animals and the methods for breeding them.

Veterinary epidemiologists respond to and prevent outbreaks of disease in animals. They may research how diseases spread in different animals, or monitor data and make predictions about disease spread. They will then provide advice on how to reduce the spread, for example, by developing vaccination programmes.

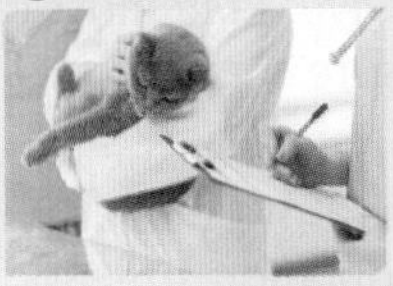

Knowledge organiser

The biological material that makes up the organisms in a **population** is known as **biomass**. This biomass contains chemical energy.

Some of the biomass is transferred between populations when organisms are eaten. Energy is then released. We say energy flows from one organism to another when it is eaten.

The amount of energy available at each step decreases as organisms use energy to move and grow.

An **ecosystem** is made up of the **community** of organisms and the physical environment. The organisms interact with each other and the physical environment.

The feeding relationships within a community of organisms can be modelled using **food chains**. Food chains show how biomass (and energy) transfers or flows from one organism to another and between populations.

grass → rabbit → fox

A simple food chain – the arrows show the transfer of biomass

Each population of organisms in a food web can affect the others. For example, in the food web on the right:

- a decrease in the amount of grass seed means less food for the mice, and so their numbers may decrease
- fewer mice means less food for the owls
- the owls may then eat more shrews, and the number of shrews may decrease
- the number of worms may then increase, as fewer are eaten by shrews.

Each organism can also be affected by the physical **environment**.

Predator–prey relationships can be shown on a graph.

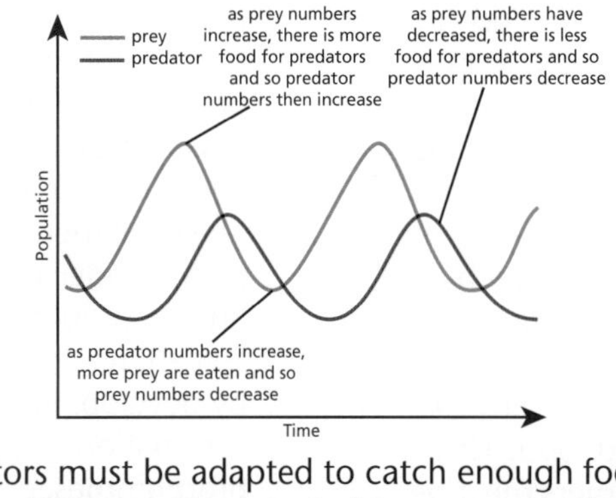

Predators must be adapted to catch enough food to survive. Prey must be adapted to escape predators to ensure survival.

A change in the prey population size affects the predator population size. This then affects the prey population size, and so on.

All food chains start with **producers** and include one or more **consumer**.

- Producers make their own food and are the source of biomass for food chains. They are green plants, so they make their food by photosynthesis using light energy.
- **Primary consumers** eat producers.
- **Secondary consumers** eat primary consumers.
- **Tertiary consumers** eat secondary consumers.

The levels in a food chain or web are called **trophic levels**. They show the position of an organism in the chain.

Food chains connect to form **food webs**. In the food web, we can see more relationships than the food chain. For example, the fox feeds on mice as well as rabbits, and mice also feed on the grass.

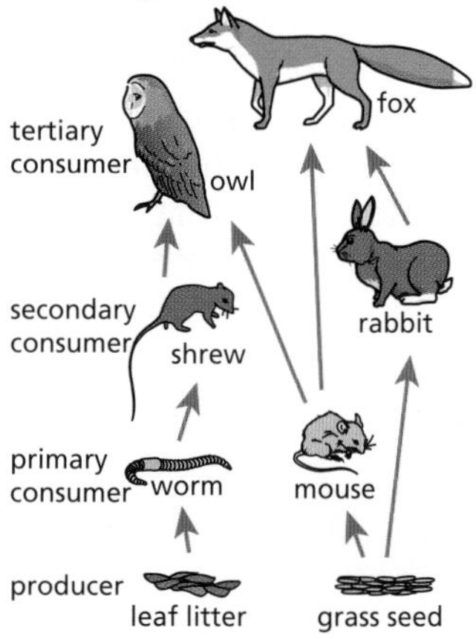

A simple food web

Different organisms in an ecosystem can affect each other in many ways.

Competition – organisms within an ecosystem compete for resources when they are in short supply. For example, plants may compete for water, animals may compete for food.

Predator–prey relationships – **predators** prey on other animals for food; **prey** are eaten by predators (for example, foxes prey on rabbits).

Symbiosis – a close, long-term relationship between different organisms. There are several types of symbiosis.

Insects are essential for the pollination of some plants, including some food crops (plants for food). For example, bees are extremely important to human food production, as they pollinate many types of fruit and vegetable crops.

Insect populations can be negatively affected by:

- increased predator populations
- disease
- adverse weather and changes in climate – this may mean that plants flower earlier, before insects are able to pollinate them, or for shorter periods
- pesticides
- a decrease in insect-pollinated plants, for example, when wild flowering plants are removed to grow crops.

Food security means that all people, at all times, have access to enough safe and nutritious food for an active and healthy life. Any factor that reduces insect populations is a risk to food security.

Monoculture is an intensive form of farming where single crops are grown over large areas. This reduces insect populations as there is not enough variety of food and there may not be enough nutrients for insect health.

A decrease in insect populations due to over use of **pesticides** (for example, a decrease in wild bees has led to farmers in China needing to hand pollinate fruit and vegetable crops as a way to increase food security)

Key vocabulary	
biomass	the mass of living organisms; contains chemical energy
commensalism	the type of symbiosis where one organism benefits but the other does not
community	populations of two or more different species occupying the same geographical area at the same time
competition	the struggle between organisms for resources or survival (for example, food)
consumer	an animal that eats other animals or plants
ecosystem	the living things and their non-living environment in a given area
environment	the surroundings, such as air, water, soil, climate and food sources, where an organism lives
food chain	part of a food web, starting with a producer and ending with a top predator
food security	when all people, at all times, have access to enough safe and nutritious food for an active and healthy life
food web	more than one food chain interconnected
monoculture	a single crop grown in a large space
mutualism	the type of symbiosis where both organisms benefit
parasitism	the type of symbiosis where one organism benefits and the other is harmed
pesticide	a chemical applied to crops to destroy pests
population	a group of the same type of organism living in the same area
predator	an animal that preys on other animals
prey	an animal that is hunted and killed by other animals (predators)
primary consumer	an organism that eats a producer
producer	the plant at the start of a food chain that makes its own food (typically a green plant)
secondary consumer	an organism that eats a primary consumer
symbiosis	a relationship between two different types of organism
tertiary consumer	an organism that eats a secondary consumer
trophic level	the position of an organism in a food chain
yield	the amount of useful product obtained

All organism populations in an ecosystem can affect other organism populations, for example, through competition or predation. These associations between living things are called **biotic factors**.

Within an ecosystem, physical factors such as temperature, availability of water, nutrients and light, carbon dioxide concentration and pH of soil, also affect populations. These physical factors are called **abiotic factors**.

The role that an organism plays within a community, including all the biotic and abiotic factors, is its **niche**.

Humans are a major factor in causing changes to the environment. As medical treatment has improved, humans are living longer. As the human population increases, the impact on the environment increases:

- habitats are lost as more land is needed for farming and building
- pollution increases as we have more factories and vehicles and we generate more rubbish
- animals are hunted for food, sport, medicines, their fur and horns, etc.

The impact of these actions is a decrease in the number and number of types of plants and animals. This reduces **biodiversity**.

Ecology is the study of the interactions between organisms and the environment. We study populations of plants and animals by **sampling**. Sampling is a scientific survey: the observations are used to make estimates about whole populations. Random sampling means we choose areas to sample at random rather than selecting them. This removes **bias**.

Quadrats are used to sample plants or slow-moving animals. A quadrat is a square frame (commonly 50 cm × 50 cm).

The quadrat can be used to sample in different ways:

- to count the number of a single species, for example, the number of barnacles
- to count the number of different species; this is a measure of biodiversity
- to estimate the percentage of the quadrat filled by any one species, for example, grass.

Global warming has a large impact on the environment. It is caused by **greenhouse gases**, such as carbon dioxide and methane, trapping too much heat around the Earth.

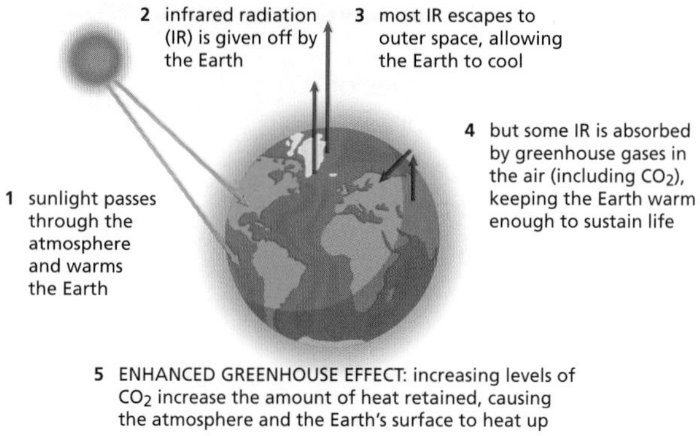

Several human activities add to these greenhouse gases:

- burning fossil fuels (coal, oil, gas) – releases carbon dioxide
- deforestation – fewer trees to take in carbon dioxide
- landfill waste – waste decomposes releasing methane.

The effects of global warming are wide-ranging and can lead to loss of **habitats** for many organisms, including humans:

- increasing land and ocean temperatures
- **climate change** (for example, more frequent **droughts**, storms, heat waves)
- melting glaciers
- rising sea levels.

Here is an example of using a quadrat to estimate the population size of daisies in a field.

1. Place the quadrat randomly within the area being studied.
2. Count how many daisies are within the quadrat.
3. Repeat the procedure 10 times within the field. Choose samples randomly, for example, by drawing the entire area as a grid and then choosing coordinates at random, as shown below.

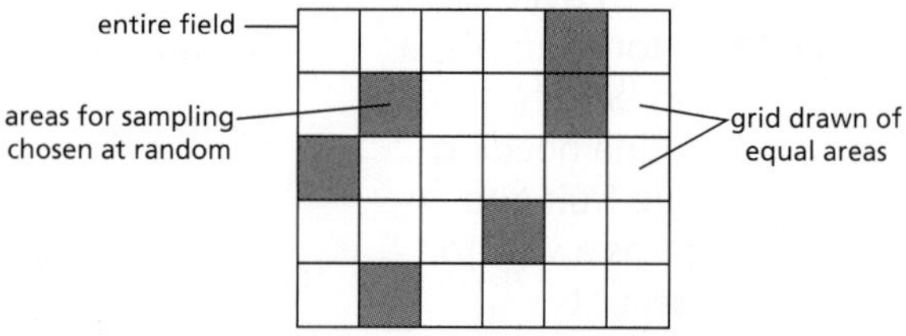

Ensure all squares are of equal size.

4. Calculate the average number of daisies.
5. Multiply the result to estimate the population size for the entire area (for example, if the area sampled makes up 20% of the entire field, multiply the average number by 5).

Critically **endangered** organisms are at risk of becoming **extinct**. A series of categories are used to describe how at risk a species is:

critically endangered
endangered
vulnerable
not threatened

Some species are extinct in the wild and exist only in captivity.

This scimitar-horned oryx is an example.

Rainforests are an example of a habitat affected by human activity. Nearly half of all animal species live in rainforests. Loss of habitat is the biggest threat to rainforests and the organisms living there.

- Primary consumers eat plants containing toxins; secondary consumers eat the primary consumer; and so on up the food chain.
- Organisms at the lower end of a food chain may take up only small concentrations of toxin.
- If these organisms are then eaten by organisms in the next trophic level, the toxin gets passed on.
- Organisms generally get bigger along a food chain, and eat more than one of the organisms in the previous trophic level. This means that the toxin becomes more concentrated as it passes through the food chain. This is known as **bioaccumulation**.

DDT is a pesticide that was used in the 1960s. It entered rivers and contaminated plants. The plants then entered the food chain. Otters at the top of the food chain were killed due to bioaccumulation.

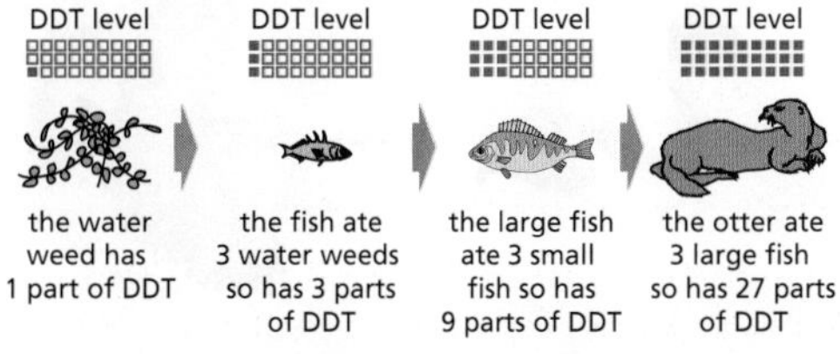
DDT level
DDT level
DDT level
DDT level
the water weed has 1 part of DDT
the fish ate 3 water weeds so has 3 parts of DDT
the large fish ate 3 small fish so has 9 parts of DDT
the otter ate 3 large fish so has 27 parts of DDT

Key vocabulary	
abiotic factors	physical factors within an environment
bias	a tendency to favour one thing or another, rather than being objective
bioaccumulation	the increase in the concentration of a chemical as it is passed from one organism to another along a food chain
biodiversity	the variety of different organisms within an ecosystem
biotic factor	a factor associated with the living things in an environment
captive breeding	the breeding of animals away from the wild, for example, in zoos or wildlife reserves, to conserve the species
climate change	the change in climate patterns, such as temperature and rainfall
conservation	the protection of the Earth's natural resources, including organisms and the physical environment
DDT	a pesticide used in the 1960s
drought	a prolonged period of abnormally low rainfall, leading to a shortage of water
ecology	the study of the interactions between organisms and the environment
endangered	when there are so few of a species left that it could become extinct
extinct	when a species dies out and no more individuals remain
fertiliser	a chemical put on the soil to increase its fertility and support crop growth
global warming	the gradual increase in the overall temperature of the Earth's atmosphere, caused by greenhouse gases such as carbon dioxide
greenhouse gas	gases such as carbon dioxide and methane that trap heat around the Earth
habitat	the natural home or environment of an organism
insecticide	a chemical applied to crops to kill insects that damage the crops
niche	the role of an organism within its ecosystem
quadrat	a square frame used in ecology to sample populations
rainforest	dense forest rich in biodiversity, typically found in tropical areas with consistently heavy rainfall
sampling	the study of part of a population to then infer a conclusion about a whole population
toxin	a substance that damages a living organism
vulnerable	when the number of a species drops but not so low that it is endangered

5.1 Food webs and interdependence

You are learning to:
- describe how food webs are made up of a number of food chains
- define examples of interdependence
- explain how different interdependent relationships affect each organism
- predict the effect of changing numbers of populations in a food web.

1 What is always at the start of a food chain?

a producer

b primary consumer

c secondary consumer

d tertiary consumer

2 Where does energy first come from in a food chain?

a food

b plants

c sunlight

d air

3 Fill the gaps using the words below.

web chain energy biomass

The biological material that makes up an organism is also known as the ___________.

A food __________ shows which organisms eat which other organisms in a habitat; more than one of these linked together is a food __________.

Organisms need to make or take in food so that they can release __________ from it.

4 Grasshoppers eats grass. Rats eat grasshoppers. Choose the correct food chain.

a grass → grasshopper → rat

b grasshopper → grass → rat

c rat → grasshopper → grass

d grass → rat → grasshopper

5 Of the organisms labelled **i–iii** in the food chain, identify which is:

a the predator **b** the prey **c** the producer.

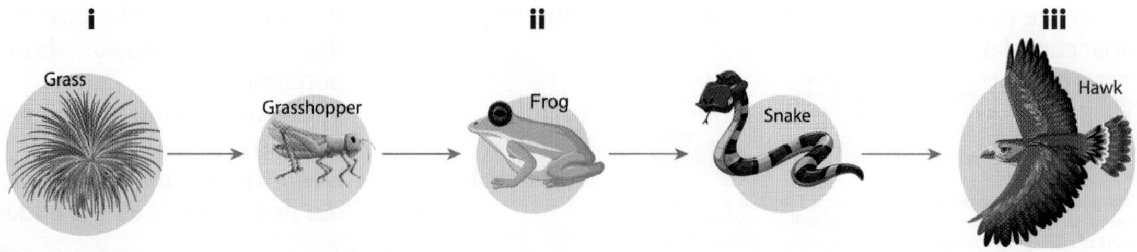

6 For each of the relationships described below, identify the type of interdependence:

a a flea feeding on the blood of a hedgehog

b a suckerfish attaching itself to a shark so that it can be transported and the suckerfish removing parasites from the shark

c cattle egrets (birds) resting near cattle; when the cattle stir up the grass as they move, they flush out insects, which the birds eat.

Worked example

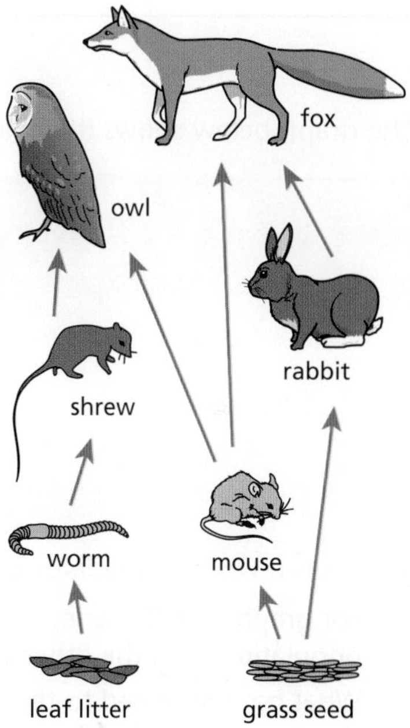

Using the food web, predict the effect of each of:

a **i** decreasing the rabbit population on the fox population

Think about the relationship between the rabbits and the foxes.

ii decreasing the rabbit population on the grass seed population.

Think about the relationship between the rabbits and the grass seed.

a **i** *fox population will decrease as fewer rabbits to eat*

ii *the grass seed population will increase as less of it will be eaten*

b Explain these two possible effects on the mouse population of decreasing the rabbit population.

i Why might the mouse population increase?

ii Why might the mouse population decrease?

You can track through the food chains within a web and think of the effect, step by step, for each organism.

Remember that within a food web, there are more relationships and so there are more possible effects.

Start with 'As rabbits decrease …' and then consider step-by-step how that might affect the foxes and then the grass seed.

b **i** *As rabbits decrease, less grass seed is eaten, so the grass seed increases. This provides more food for mice, so the mouse population will increase.*

ii *As rabbits decrease, there are fewer for the foxes to eat, so the foxes may then eat more mice, and the mouse population will decrease.*

7 A fish farmer needs to increase the number of trout in an ecosystem. The food web is shown in the diagram.

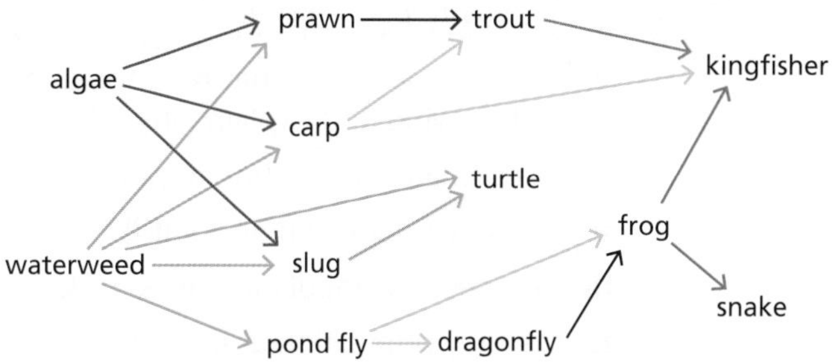

a Predict the effect on the number of trout if the farmer changed the following. Explain each answer:

i increases the number of prawns

ii decreases the number of kingfishers

iii decreases the number of frogs.

b How many trophic levels are there in the longest food chain within this web?

8 Consider a simple food chain of shrews eating worms and worms eating leaf litter.

a Draw a food chain to show the feeding relationship.

b **i** Describe what happens to the amount of energy available to the animals as you go along the food chain.

ii Explain why.

c Where does the energy in a food chain come from initially?

d Food chains usually have only four or five trophic levels. Suggest why, in terms of energy.

Worked example

The graph below shows the changes in population size of a predator and prey.

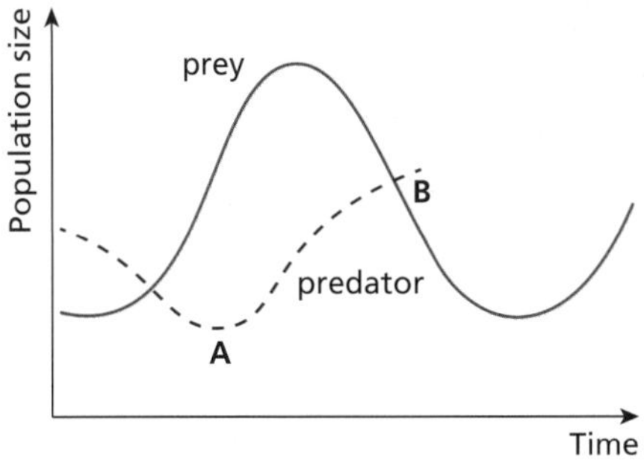

a Explain why the predator population decreases towards point A.

For graphs like this one, always consider the predator population in relation to the prey population (and the other way around).

What has happened to the prey population immediately before the predator population decreased at point **A**?

Previously, the prey population was low and so there was less food for the predators to eat; therefore, the predator population decreased.

b Predict whether the predator population will increase or decrease after point **B**. Explain your answer.

Again, consider what has happened to the prey population immediately before the time of point **B**.

The prey population has started to decrease and so there will be less food for the predators to eat; therefore, the predator population is likely to decrease after point B.

9 The graph shows the relationship between predator and prey.

a By referring to both the predator and prey populations, describe what is happening to each of the following and explain why it is happening:

i the predator population at point **A**

ii the prey population at point **B**

iii the predator population at point **C**

iv the prey population at point **D**.

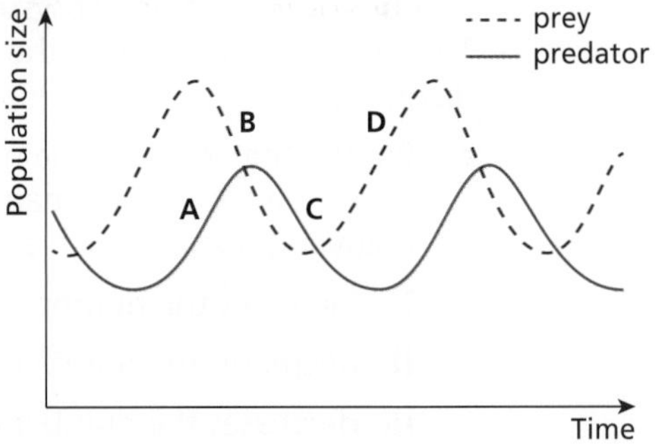

b Another predator species is introduced into the ecosystem. Predict the effect on:

i the prey species

ii the original predator species.

c What is the name of the relationship between the two predator species, both feeding on the same prey?

10 **a** From the food web below, identify:

i a producer

ii a predator of the harvester ant

iii a prey of the mongoose.

b Predict the following.

i What the harvester ant might eat if the star grass is decreased.

ii What would happen to the numbers of pangolin if both red oat grass and star grass were reduced. Explain your answer.

c Explain why food webs form, instead of organisms only forming food chains.

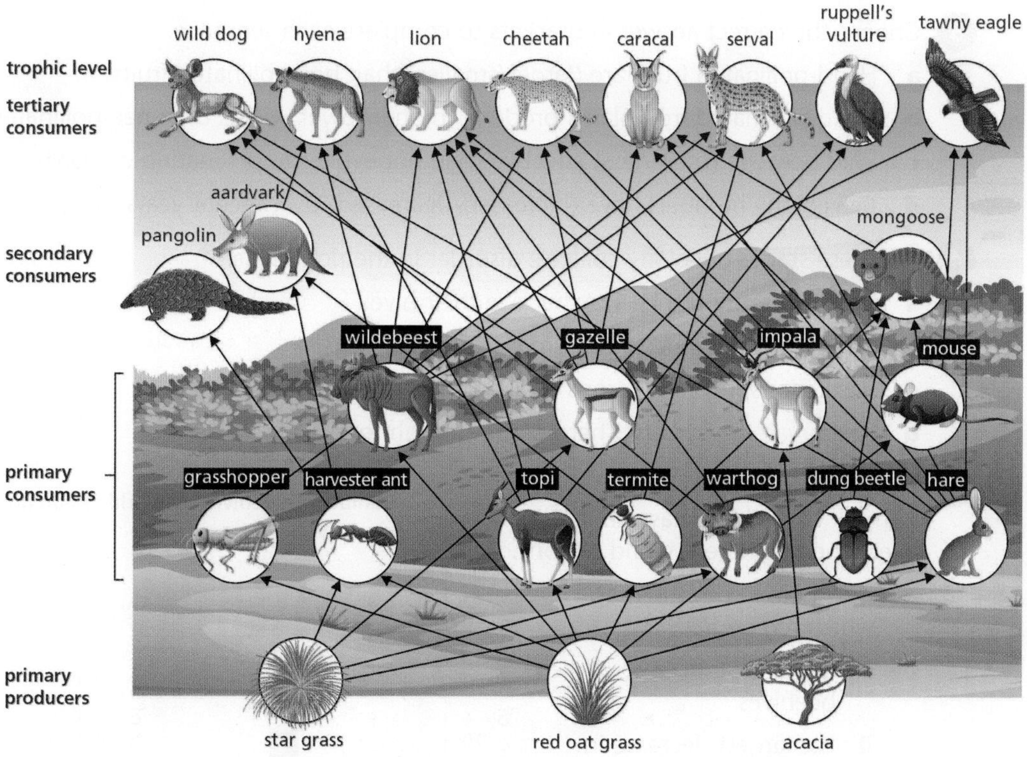

5.2 The importance of insects

You are learning to:
- explain why insects such as bees are so important in crop production
- describe what is meant by 'food security'
- discuss the risks to food security.

1 What is the name of the process that transfers pollen from the male part of a plant to the female part of a plant?

a fertilisation **b** reproduction **c** food security **d** pollination

2 What is monoculture?

a growing of single crops in a field
b growing of plants within a laboratory
c growing of all crops by only one farmer
d growing crops without pesticides

3 Choose the correct answer in brackets to complete each sentence.

a Hand-pollinated fruits are (larger/smaller) than bee-pollinated fruits.
b Hand-pollinated fruit plants produce (higher/lower) yields than bee-pollinated fruit plants.
c Wild bees are (more/less) effective than honeybees at pollinating orchards.
d Bee colony numbers have (increased/decreased) over recent years.

4 Put these stages of colony collapse disorder in the right order.

a Bees cannot find their way back to their hive.
b The colony becomes much smaller or disappears.
c Pesticides sprayed on crops weaken bees.
d Bee larvae die because there is not enough food.

5 The graphs show how the number of beehives has changed over time in different world regions.

a Using data from the graph, which region has had:
  i the largest increase in beehives
  ii the largest decrease in beehives?

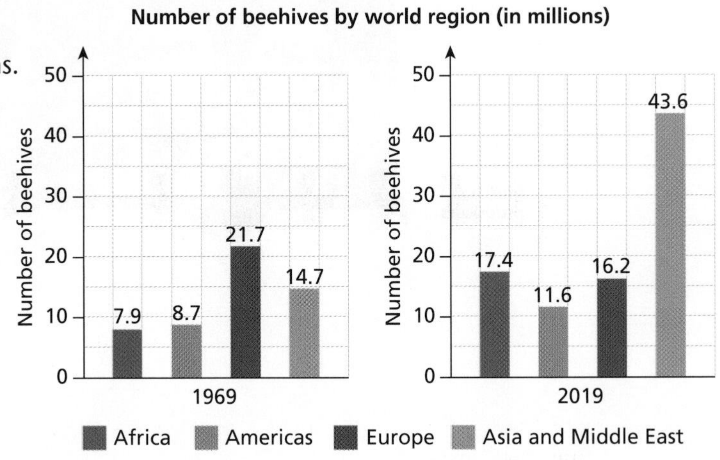

Some research suggests that the costs of keeping beehives has increased in some areas so that costs outweigh the income that can be generated.

b Suggest **one** area where this seems likely.

6 A fruit grower is comparing their crop yield for the previous two years.

The table shows the yields in 2020.

Fruit	Yield 2020
apples	1500 kg
pears	1200 kg
tomatoes	22 kg
cucumbers	44 kg

a All of the fruit crops are bee pollinated. Suggest **two** reasons why there might be a reduction in bee pollination from the previous year.

b The fruit grower had predicted a reduction of 50% in crop yields in 2021 compared with 2020. Calculate the predicted 2021 yields for each fruit.

c When the fruit grower calculated the actual yield of pears, they found that they had harvested 840 kg of pears. What percentage of the 2020 yield was this?

7 Food security data for the UK is shown below.

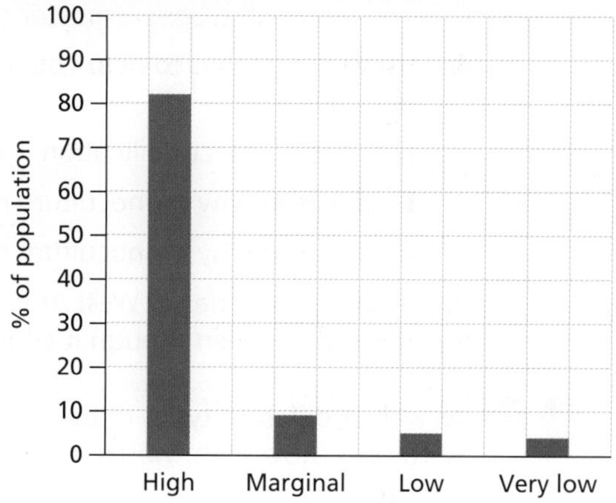

a **i** What percentage of the population were experiencing some form of food insecurity in 2018 (represented by marginal, low or very low)?

ii How might people judge whether they have low food security?

The data compares food imports (food brought into the country) and exports (food taken out of the country) for the UK in 2019.

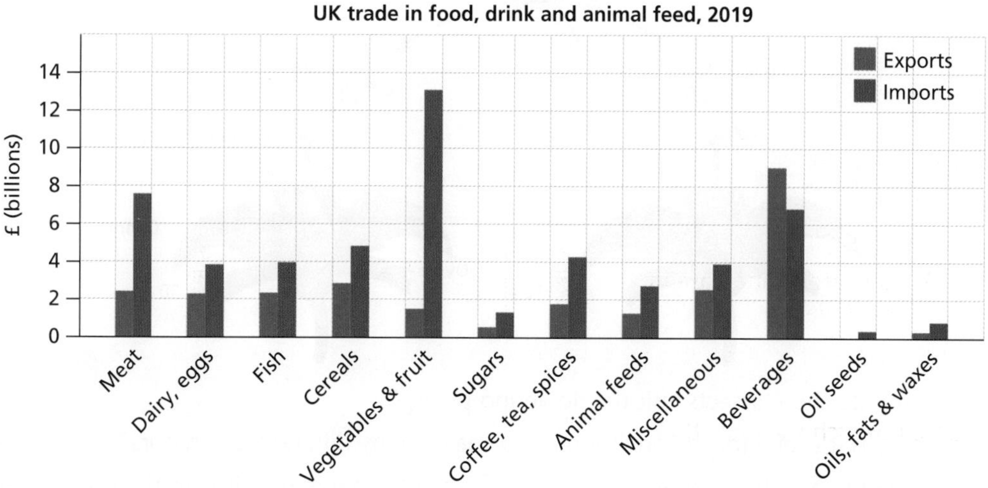

Some experts believe that to have high food security, a country should be able to export more than they import.

b Using this belief, for which food(s) did the UK show high security in 2019?

8 Monoculture can be a barrier to food security.

a Describe what is meant by 'food security'.

The images below show the farming methods of monoculture and polyculture.

Monoculture

Polyculture

b Using the images to help you, describe the difference between monoculture and polyculture.

c In terms of insect pollination, give:

i a reason why monoculture might lead to reduced populations of insects

ii a reason why monoculture might lead to decreased health of insects.

d In some countries of West Africa, cocoa plants are grown as monoculture. Suggest why this is done even though it could affect food security.

9 As well as different types of bees, there are many other pollinators in the UK, for example butterflies, hoverflies, wasps, moths and some beetles.

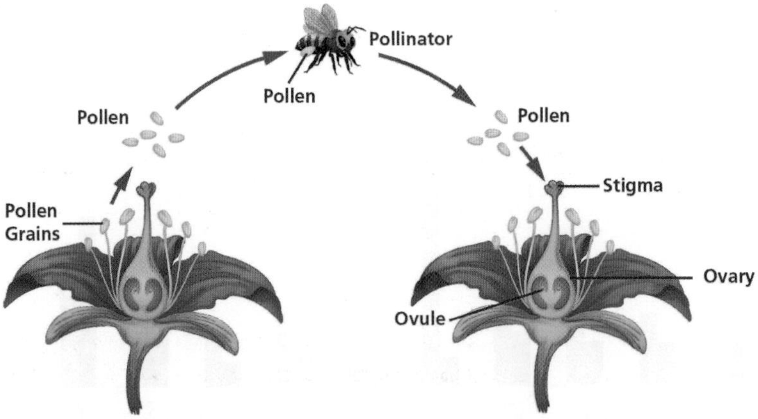

a Why do these insects visit the flowering plants?

b Why is it useful for the environment to have many different pollinators?

A team of scientists observes a meadow and counts how many visits to the flowers each type of insect makes.

c **i** What is the independent variable in this investigation?

ii What is the dependent variable?

iii Explain why counting the number of visits to a flowering plant may not give a true indication of how much pollination has taken place.

Worked example

A scientist investigated whether temperature affects how much pollination bees carry out. They observed how many visits bees made to flowering plants every 15 minutes at different temperatures. Their results are shown below.

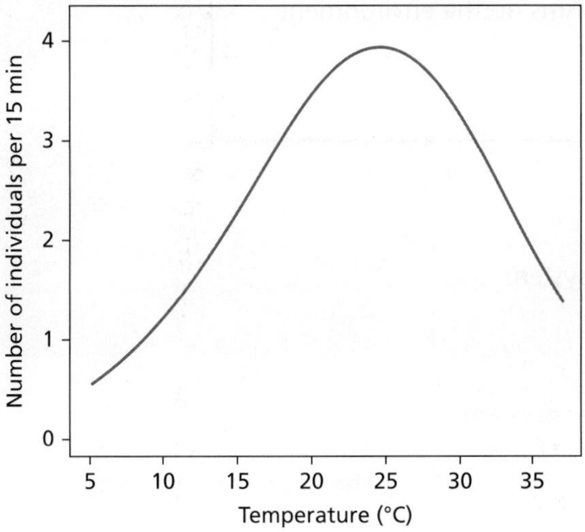

a What is the most effective temperature for bees to visit the plants?

25 °C

The scientist now wants to narrow down the best temperature for pollination to be successful.

b Describe the range that the scientist should focus on in a follow-up investigation.

Which temperatures should they focus around to find the most effective temperature? Remember, in science, you need to give both the lowest and the highest values.

20–30 °C

10 Scientists investigated whether the time of day affects the effectiveness of pollination. They measured what proportion of visits to the plant by a bumblebee resulted in pollination at different times of the day. The results are shown in the graph.

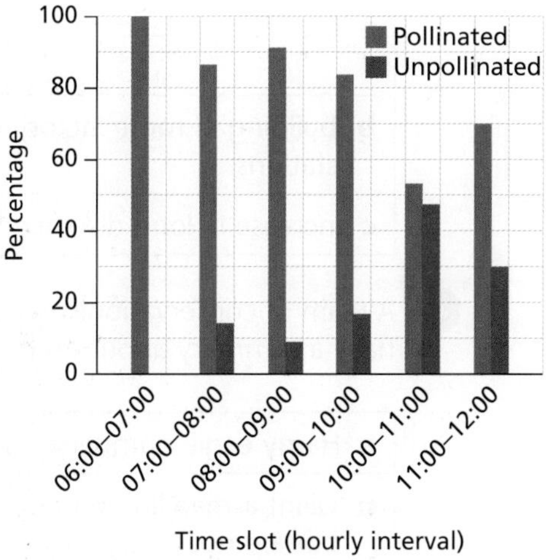

a Which is the **most** effective time of day for pollination of these plants by bumblebees?

b Which is the **least** effective time of day for pollination of these plants by bumblebees?

c Describe how the scientists could increase the repeatability of these observations.

The scientists now want to narrow down the best time for pollination to be successful.

d Describe the range of time that they should focus on in this follow-up investigation.

e When repeating the observations, suggest **two** factors that the scientists should try to ensure are similar to the first investigation.

5.3 Impact of organisms on their environment

You are learning to:
- describe the effects of humans and other organisms on the environment
- describe how toxins enter food chains
- explain how toxins accumulate in food chains
- apply sampling techniques.

1 What is meant by 'biodiversity'?

a the number of one species in an ecosystem

b identification of habitats

c the species that are endangered

d the variety of living organisms in an ecosystem

2 Nearly half of all animal species live in rainforests. What is the biggest threat to animals living in rainforests?

a loss of habitat

b change in temperature

c introduction of more animals

d parasites

3 As the human population increases, strain is put on the environment. Match each development to the risk that it causes.

a use of more land for farming	**i** plant and animal species moved away from their natural habitat
b building of more factories and power stations	**ii** natural habitats are lost
c increase in long distance travel	**iii** increase in pollution

4 A team of conservationists is carrying out a survey of different species in South America. They have a summary about each species. Match the summaries to the categories.

a Harpy eagle numbers are large compared to other areas.	**i** vulnerable
b Giant armadillo numbers have decreased slightly since the last survey but are not a major concern.	**ii** not threatened
c Candango mouse is no longer found here.	**iii** endangered
d Hyacinth macaw has so few numbers that it is at risk of becoming extinct.	**iv** extinct

5 What is meant by 'bioaccumulation'?

a breakdown of toxins by animals
b diversity of organisms in a food chain
c build-up of toxins as you go up a food chain
d run-off of toxins from fertilisers on crops

6 Why do most modern farmers not use manure as fertiliser?

a manure does not work as a fertiliser
b most crop farmers do not keep animals as well
c farmers do not like the smell
d manure contains insecticides

7 Global warming contributes to climate change.

a What is meant by 'global warming'?
b Explain how each of these activities contributes to global warming:
  i burning fossil fuels (coal, oil and gas)
  ii increasing landfill waste
  iii deforestation.

8 **a** How can toxins enter a food chain? Choose **two** answers.
  i Animals can make toxins such as DDT inside their bodies.
  ii Fertilisers run off fields and contaminate water.
  iii Pesticides are eaten by insects.
  iv Chemicals randomly change to become poisonous.

A toxic pesticide has been found to have entered the food chain shown below.

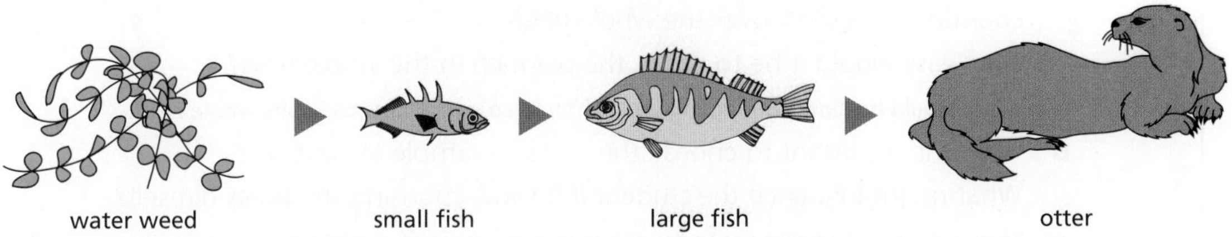

Chemists have analysed how much of the toxin is in each organism in the food chain. Their data is shown in the table below.

Organism	Concentration of toxin
A	10 parts per million
B	10 000 parts per million
C	50 parts per million
D	2500 parts per million

b Identify each organism **A**, **B**, **C** and **D**.
c Explain why the otter may die even though the toxin entered the water weed.

9 A group of conservationists wants to maintain the biodiversity in part of a forest.

a What is meant by 'biodiversity' in this forest?

The conservationists have observed bird species over time and have found that the hyacinth macaw is vulnerable and the toucan is endangered.

Hyacinth macaw

Toucan

b Which of the two species is most at risk of extinction?

The team is putting together a plan of how to ensure that these species do not become extinct.

c Suggest **two** different strategies that the team could use to ensure that these birds do not become extinct. Explain how each suggestion would help.

Worked example

A student is investigating the population of plantain plants on a field. He draws a plan of the field and draws grids on it to choose the areas to sample. He chooses numbers at random to decide the co-ordinates of the selected areas and shades them as below:

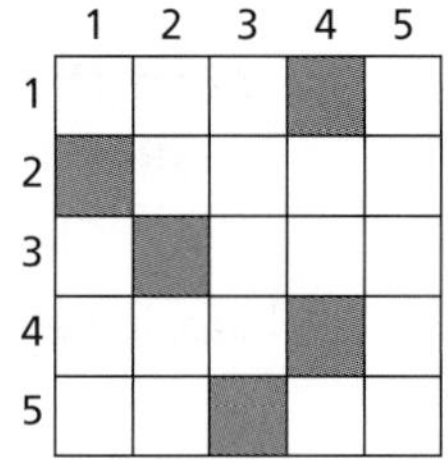

a Why has the student selected areas to sample, rather than counting the plants over the whole field?

How easy would it be to count the plantain in the whole field?

a It would be time consuming and difficult to count plants in the whole field.

b Why is it important to choose the areas to sample at random?

What might influence the student if he was choosing the areas himself?

To avoid bias, choosing areas for a particular reason (for example, choosing sunny spots or shady spots).

The results are shown in the table below.

Number of plantain plants per quadrat sample				
1	**2**	**3**	**4**	**5**
22	10	12	18	14

c Estimate the total number of plantain plants in the field.

Consider the number counted in the sample. Then consider what proportion of the field was sampled.

Total number of plantain plants in the sample = 76

5 squares out of a total of 25 for the field were sampled. This is $\frac{1}{5}$ (or 20%).

Therefore, total in the field = 76 × 5 = 380 plantain

10 A group of students investigated whether the amount of sunlight affected the growth of dandelions on their school field.

Using a quadrat, the students sampled 6 areas in full sunlight and 6 areas in partial shade. The results are shown below.

Amount of sunlight	**Number of dandelions per quadrat sample**						
	1	**2**	**3**	**4**	**5**	**6**	**Mean**
full sunlight	12	14	10	18	12	11	**i**
partial shade	6	4	2	2	3	7	**ii**

a Calculate the mean values shown by **i** and **ii** in the table **to one decimal place**.

b In this investigation, identify:

i the independent variable

ii the dependent variable.

c Write a conclusion for this investigation.

d **i** The quadrat is 0.5 m × 0.5 m. Calculate the area of the quadrat.

ii The total area of the field that is in full sunlight is 10 m × 6 m. Estimate the total number of dandelions in the field in full sunlight.

11 An aquatic food chain is shown below.

Insecticides containing mercury are used near the water where the phytoplankton grow and small traces enter the phytoplankton. Mercury is a toxin that affects the nervous system and reproductive system of animals.

Food chain	**How many does it eat?**	**Concentration of mercury (ppm)**
phytoplankton	–	0.5
↓		
zooplankton	100 phytoplankton	**i**
↓		
herring	50 zooplankton	**ii**
↓		
salmon	8 herring	**iii**
↓		
orca whale	10 salmon	**iv**

a What is a toxin?

b Animals with high levels of mercury can become confused, numb and make twitchy movements. Explain why.

The table shows how much each organism eats. The table also shows that the phytoplankton have a concentration of 0.5 parts per million (ppm).

c Calculate the concentration of mercury in each of the other organisms shown as **i–iv** in the table.

d State which organism is most likely to die from mercury poisoning. Explain your answer.

The salmon sources another food and starts to eat crayfish as well as herring.

e **i** Explain the effect this will have on the concentration of mercury in the salmon.

ii Explain the effect this will have on the concentration of mercury in the herring.

Maths and practical skills

1 What is the scientific name of the apparatus used in sampling, shown in the image below?

a square **b** frame **c** quadrat **d** sampler

2 The number of a species has been counted for 20% of an area. What should the result be multiplied by to estimate the total population size?

a ×2 **b** ×5 **c** ×10 **d** ×20

3 Workers in southwest China are hand pollinating plants in a crop field of area 60 m^2. Each worker can cover an area of 5 m^2. How many workers will be needed to cover the whole crop field?

a 55 **b** 12 **c** 300 **d** 10

4 The graph below shows population sizes for a predator and its prey.

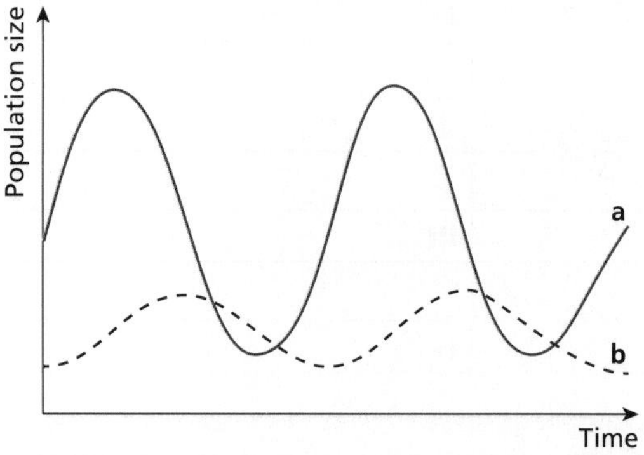

Which of the lines on the graph represents the prey?

5 Sequence the steps to show how you could estimate the size of a population of daisies in a field.

a Count the number of the daisies inside the quadrat.

b Choose sections of the field to sample at random.

c Place the quadrat on the chosen areas.

d Multiply the number of daisies counted to estimate how many would be in the whole field.

Worked example

The graph below shows data on loss of primary forest in parts of a rainforest.

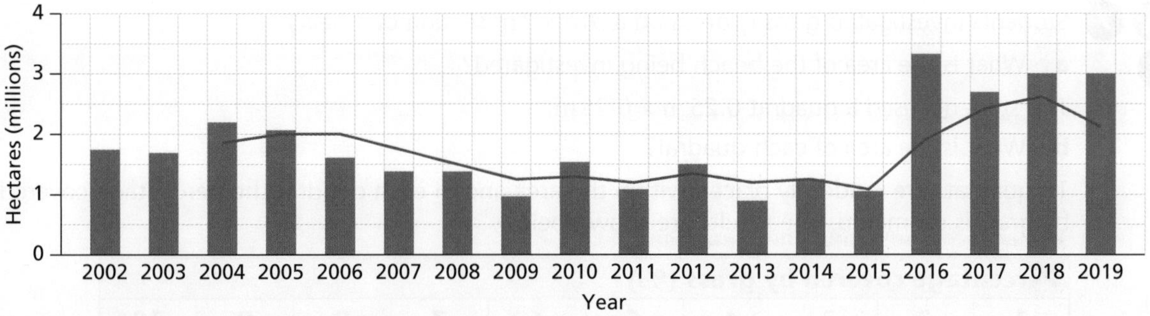

a **i** Which year had the smallest forest loss?

2013

ii Which year had the greatest forest loss?

2016

b What was the loss in both 2018 and 2019?

Read carefully from the graph and remember to include units. Even if the units are unfamiliar, just use them as they are given on the graph.

3 000 000 hectares

c Describe the trend in the data from 2002 to 2019.

When describing a trend, focus on the start and end points (2002 and 2019 here) and describe what has happened overall, rather than focusing on every slight increase or decrease.

forest loss has increased over time (with variation in loss and gain over time)

6 The graph below shows how the loss of trees in the rainforest has changed over time.

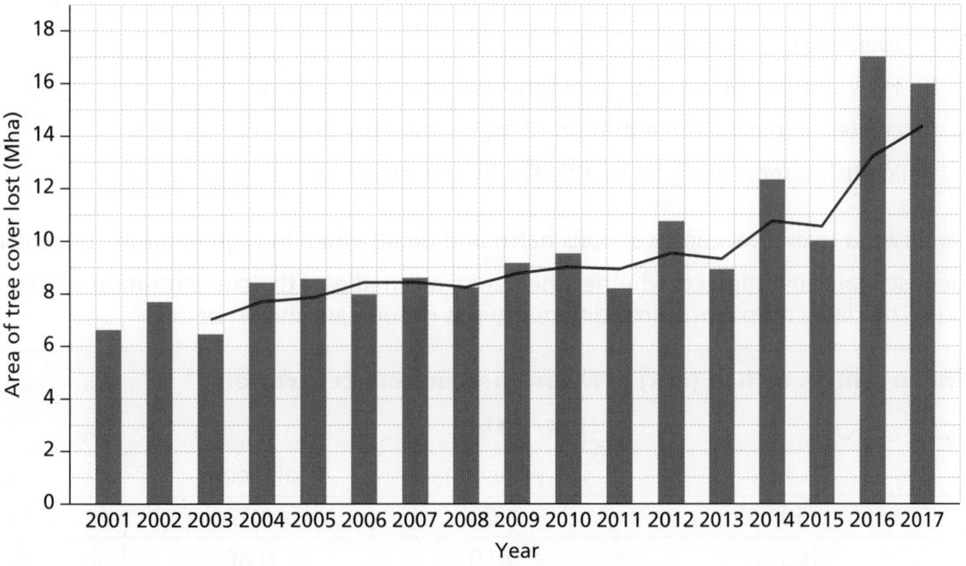

a Between which years was the biggest increase seen?

i 2003–2004

ii 2011–2012

iii 2014–2015

iv 2015–2016

One scientist predicted that the tree cover loss in 2018 would be the same as in 2017.

b What is the scientist's predicted tree cover loss in 2018?

c Describe the general trend of the data.

7 Students investigated grass growth on a 3 m × 3 m section of a beach.

a What is the area of the beach being investigated?

The students used a quadrat 0.25 m × 0.25 m.

b What is the area of each quadrat?

10 quadrats are randomly placed within the area and in each quadrat the percentage covered by grass is estimated. The results are shown below.

Percentage covered by grass (%)									
1	**2**	**3**	**4**	**5**	**6**	**7**	**8**	**9**	**10**
25	20	10	10	25	35	40	10	20	25

c Estimate the percentage covered by grass in this area of beach.

8 Methylmercury is a toxin that can enter food chains and is extremely harmful in high concentrations.

The data below shows the concentration of methylmercury found in three different types of tuna.

Tuna species	Concentration of methylmercury (mg/kg) Sample number								Mean concentration (mg/kg)
	1	**2**	**3**	**4**	**5**	**6**	**7**	**8**	
yellowfin	0.21	0.19	0.21	0.30	0.19	0.18	0.17	0.21	
albacore	0.20	0.24	0.02	0.31	0.35	0.22	0.25	0.34	
bigeye	0.35	0.42	0.47	0.41	0.45	0.52	0.48	0.46	

a **i** Identify the anomalous result in the data.

ii How should you treat an anomaly when calculating a mean?

b Calculate the mean concentration of methylmercury in each of the fish.

c Which fish is most likely to be affected by the toxin? Explain your answer.

9 Mercury is a toxin that causes serious harm and death when in high enough concentration.

Scientists have investigated whether the size of a fish affects the concentration of toxin in its body. The data comparing three different types of tuna are shown below.

Mean length of fish (cm)	Mean mercury concentration (mg/kg)		
	yellowfin	albacore	bigeye
50	0.05	0.10	0.15
100	0.10	0.30	0.45
150	0.30	0.55	0.95

a **i** Describe the trend in the mercury concentration as length increases for yellowfin tuna.

ii Is the trend the same for albacore and bigeye?

b Which type of tuna would give the greatest risk if eaten? Explain your answer.

Data was then collected about the depth that each tuna feeds at. The data is given in the table below.

Tuna species	Mean feeding depth (m)
yellowfin	100
albacore	150
bigeye	300

c Scientists believe that mercury levels in water vary based on the depth of the water.

Using both sets of data, can you conclude that mercury levels are more of a risk in water at 100, 150 or 300 m depth?

10 A student is investigating a population of snails on a seashore. They have decided on an area of 3 m × 3 m, and have drawn a grid of the area, as shown below.

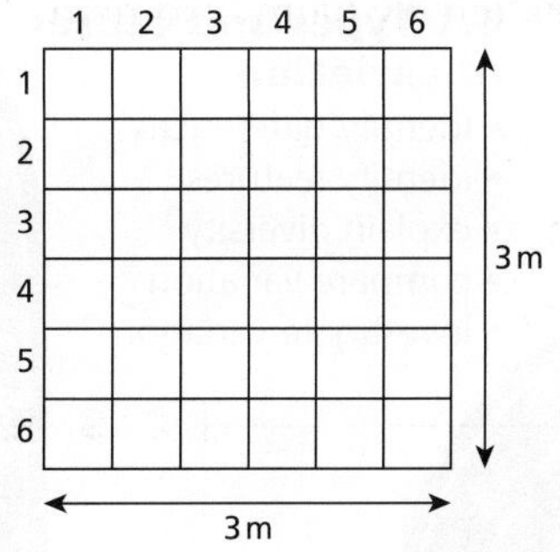

The student uses a die to identify the areas to sample. They roll the die twice to decide the coordinates to use. The results of the die rolling are shown below.

Sample	Top coordinate	Side coordinate
1	3	2
2	2	1
3	3	1
4	4	6
5	4	5
6	5	4

a Sketch the grid and shade the areas that the student will sample.

b Explain why the student selected the areas in this way rather than choosing where to place the quadrat.

c Using the grid, calculate the length of each side of the quadrat.

d The student counted 18 of the snails in the 6 areas sampled.

i What fraction of the whole area was sampled?

ii Estimate the size of the whole population in the area of the beach.

e The student believes that this species of snail may be reducing in number in this area. How could they check whether this is true?

6 Inheritance and evolution road map

Where are you in your learning journey and where are you aiming to be?

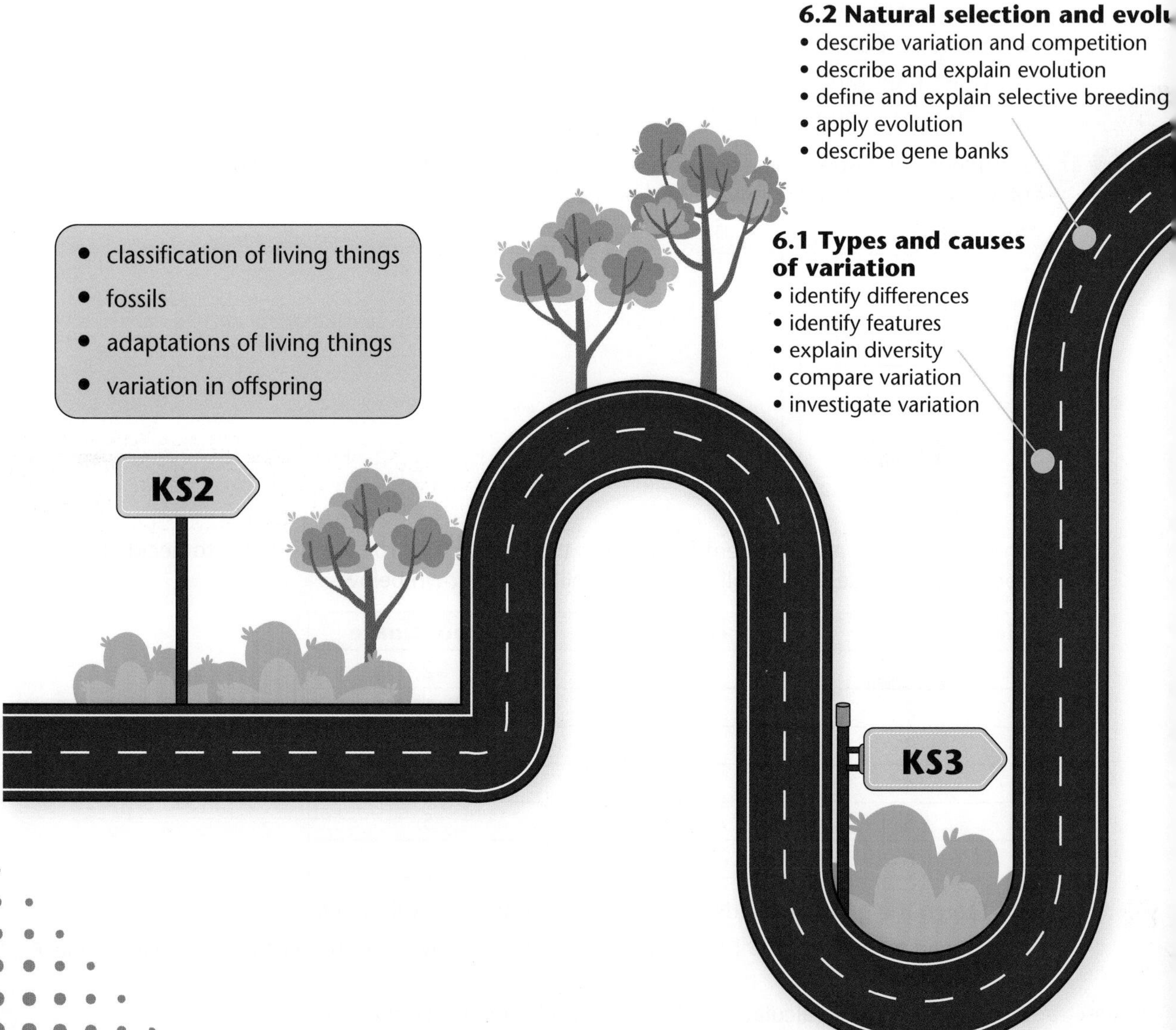

6.3 The role of chromosomes, genes and DNA in heredity
- describe relationships
- explain roles
- describe the DNA structure model
- explain extracting DNA
- explain some genetic disorders

6.4 Explaining inheritance
- explain inherited differences
- explain identical twin formation
- apply a model

- reproduction
- classification of living organisms
- variation and evolution
- the development of understanding of genetics and evolution

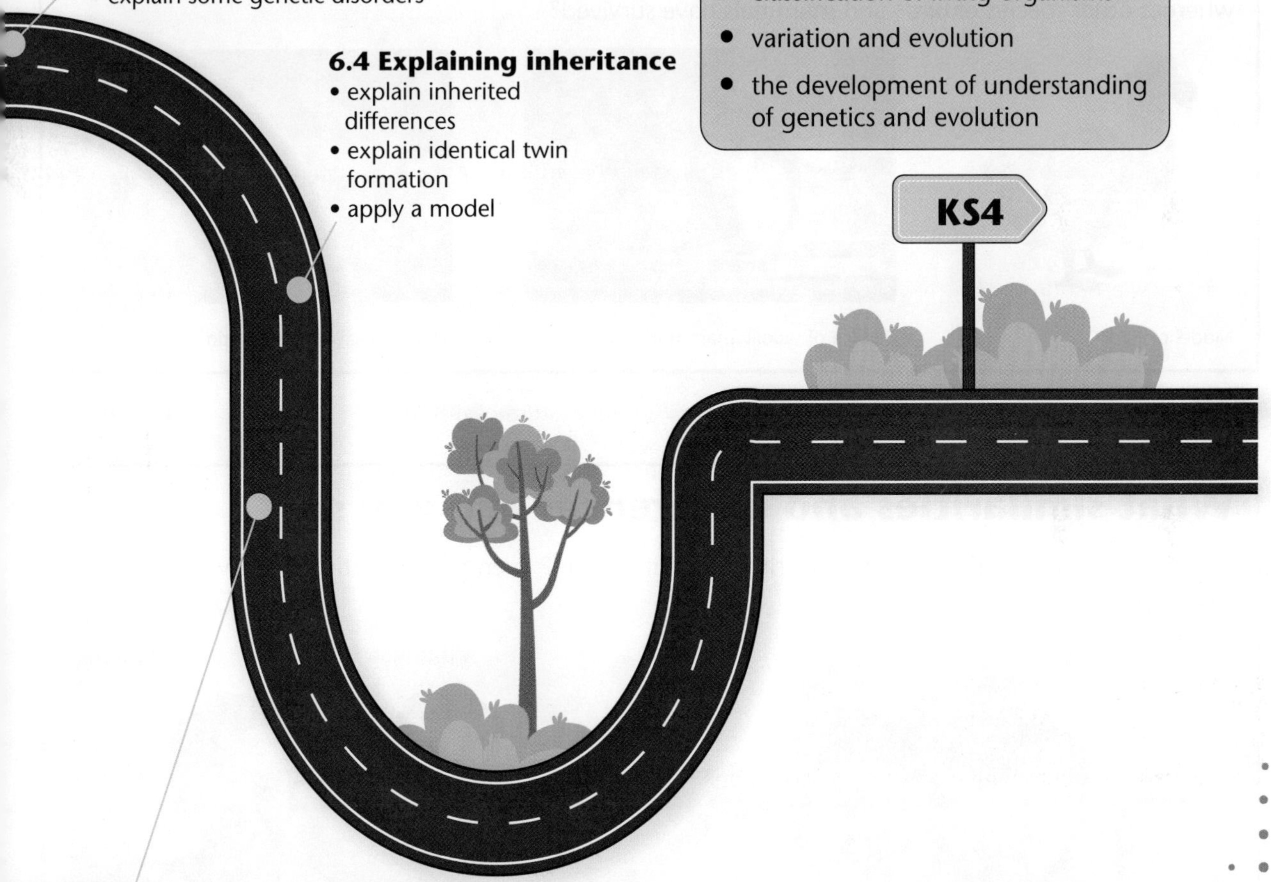

Maths and practical skills

- observing and measuring, including the evaluation of reproducibility
- describing the development of scientific methods and theories over time
- making scientific predictions
- planning an investigation, identifying and managing the variables
- calculating results and converting between different units
- presenting data using tables and graphs
- interpreting observations and data
- analysing data

6 Inheritance and evolution

Scientists have identified over 1.7 million species with different features and adaptations. Even within a species, there are lots of differences: think about how different humans look from one another. These variations are important for the survival of species.

Which of these do you recognise?

None of the animals below exist now. They are extinct. Why might these animals have become extinct whereas other species of birds and mammals have survived?

Model of dodo

Replica of woolly mammoth

Model of sabre-toothed tiger

What similarities and differences can you see?

Why do brothers and sisters have similarities and differences? Even these identical twins vary. How can that happen?

Brother and sister

Identical twins

Using your science skills

Could you be a forensic scientist?

You examine crime scenes for traces of genetic evidence, for example in blood and hair, so will need to cope with difficult situations and upsetting scenes. You may work long and unusual hours as samples will need to be collected and analysed quickly.

You will carry out scientific tests on the materials you find, so will be confident undertaking laboratory work. You will liaise with police teams to share your findings and may also attend court to present evidence and answer questions. You need to be thorough and extremely careful to ensure evidence is accurate.

The work is unlikely to be as glamorous as it sometimes seems in films, but is hugely important and is essential in criminal investigations as it could make the difference between a person being found innocent or guilty of a crime.

Museum curators bring together collections based on a specific theme, such as changes in living things over time or extinct animals. They find relevant objects, research the background to the collection and present the information in an accessible way for visitors to the museum. The role gives the opportunity to research many different fields and to communicate with, and educate, the public.

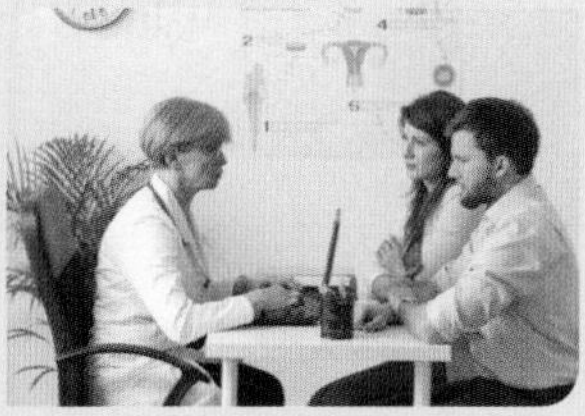

Genetic counsellors analyse and interpret genetic information to advise patients and families about their condition. They present information about inheritance patterns that helps patients to make decisions about having a family, for example. They need to be experts in genetic medicine but also have counselling skills.

DNA analysts are technicians working within a laboratory to analyse samples such as saliva, blood and semen. They carry out scientific tests to extract the DNA and try to determine who the samples belong to. This could be as part of criminal investigations or in determining whether people are likely to be part of the same family.

Biostatisticians collect and study numerical data to make predictions. For example, they use data to predict how long a person may live or the sequence of symptoms of a genetic condition. Aside from number crunching, they need to ensure that data collected is repeatable and without bias, and so they need a very good understanding of how to plan and carry out valid investigations.

Crop plant breeders improve the quality and quantity of food produced by crops and create new crop plants. They base their work on the fact that plants show natural genetic variation. Parent plants with desirable features are selected, such as those that produce large quantities of crops or those that are naturally resistant to disease, and new plants are bred. Breeders must be patient to see the results of their work and ensure that what they breed is useful to farmers.

Knowledge organiser

A **classification system** shows the **species** name (using Latin names) but is also used to show which other organisms are closely related. Carl Linnaeus developed the modern classification system.

Biodiversity is the variety of living things in an ecosystem. An ecosystem with high biodiversity is more likely to survive changes.

High biodiversity is linked with large variation.

Individuals of the same species have characteristics in common and can reproduce and produce **fertile** offspring.

The range of characteristics in a group is called **variation**. Variation *between* species is always greater than variation *within* species.

Variation can be described as **continuous variation** or **discontinuous variation**.

Type of variation	continuous	discontinuous
Description	feature has a whole range of values	feature has a limited number of discrete values
Graph plotted	histogram (**normal distribution** often shown as a bell-shaped curve). The most common value is the **mode** (150–154 cm in this graph) 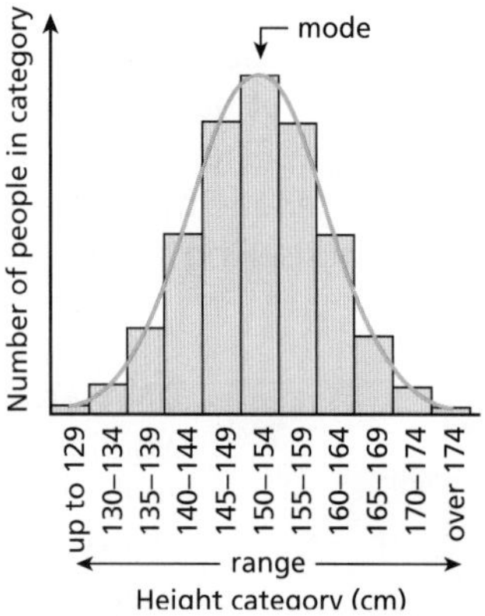	bar chart 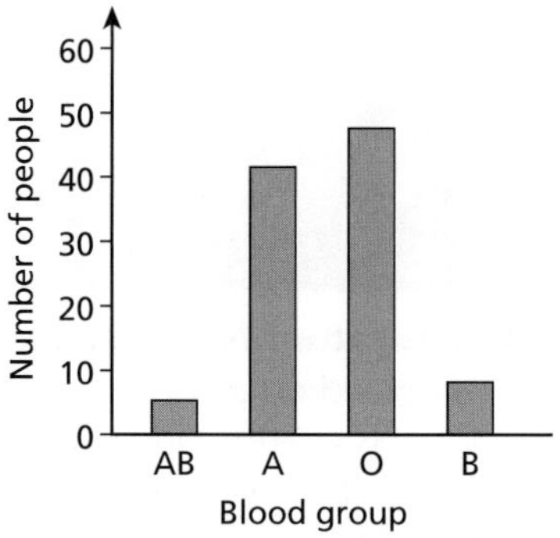
Examples	height, mass, intelligence	eye colour, blood group, tongue rolling

Genetic or **inherited** variation is caused by what is inherited from parents.

Environmental variation is caused by the environment around the organism.

Cause of variation	**Example of feature**
genetics	eye colour, blood group, natural hair colour
environment	scars, tattoos
both genetics and environment	height, mass, skin colour

Most features are affected by both genetics and the environment.

Evolution is a change in a species over many generations. Natural selection can happen quite quickly; evolution takes many generations. Through natural selection, some organisms are more likely to survive to reproduce and pass on their genetic information. Their offspring that inherit the selective advantage are more likely to survive to reproduce and pass on their genetic information. Over many generations, this can lead to an evolutionary change in the species.

Over many generations, the necks of giraffes have become longer because a long neck is an advantage for feeding

Selective breeding is used to produce plants and animals with desirable features. Examples in farming and horticulture are: crops that are resistant to disease; fruit trees that produce more fruit; chickens that produce more eggs; cows that produce more milk; cattle that produce lower-fat meat.

The process of **selective breeding** follows these steps.

1 Parent plants or animals are chosen that have desirable features (for example, a fruit tree producing large fruits and a fruit tree producing lots of fruit).
2 These are bred together.
3 The offspring showing the desirable features are selected (the offspring producing lots of large fruit).
4 These offspring are bred together.
5 The process is repeated over many generations.

The disadvantages of selective breeding are that it decreases variation and can cause deformities in organisms. Breeding of closely related individuals is called **inbreeding**.

In an environment where any resource is limited, such as food, shelter or mates, individuals of the same species compete with each other, as well as with individuals of different species.

Variation within a species or between species means that some individuals may be better adapted to compete in that environment than others.

The individuals that are better adapted are more likely to survive. This is **natural selection**: *nature selects the individuals that survive*. This is also known as **survival of the fittest**.

Extinction can be caused by too little variation in a population. If the environment changes and none of the individuals are adapted to the change, none of the species may survive.

Mass extinction is the extinction of a large number of species at the same time. This is very rare. It can be caused by natural events, such as climate heating and cooling, asteroids or disease.

Gene banks preserve genetic material by freezing, such as sperm and eggs in animals and seeds in plants. The aim is to stop species becoming extinct.

Key vocabulary	
biodiversity	the variety of living things in an ecosystem
classification system	a system that allows scientists to group organisms; for example, into a genus or species
continuous variation	variation that is distributed along a continuum, with a whole range of values, such as weight and height
correlation	how well sets of data are linked; a high correlation shows a strong link between the sets of data
discontinuous variation	variation that is distributed in discrete (separate) categories, for example, eye colour and blood group
environmental	linked to environmental factors
evolution	the change in a species over a very long period of time
extinction	the process of a species dying out
fertile	able to reproduce
gene bank	a store of genetic material that can be used in future to grow more organisms
genetic	linked with genes or heredity
inbreeding	breeding between close genetic relatives
inherited	passed on through genetic material
mass extinction	the extinction of a large number of species at the same time
natural selection	the process by which characteristics that can be passed on genetically become more common because they provide an advantage for survival
normal distribution	a spread of values usually linked with continuous variation; produces a bell-shaped curve
scatter graph	a graph of plotted points to show the relationship between two sets of data
selective breeding	the mating of two individuals chosen because of their characteristics, in an attempt to produce offspring with desired characteristics
species	a group of organisms that can interbreed and produce fertile offspring
survival advantage	having a characteristic that means that an individual is better adapted, and more likely to survive to reproduce, than other individuals
survival of the fittest	the existence of individuals that are better adapted to an environment, meaning that they are more likely to survive to reproduce and pass on their genetic material
variation	the range of characteristics across individuals of the same group or between groups

Genetic material is found inside the nucleus of a cell. Genetic variation is due to differences in the genes we inherit.

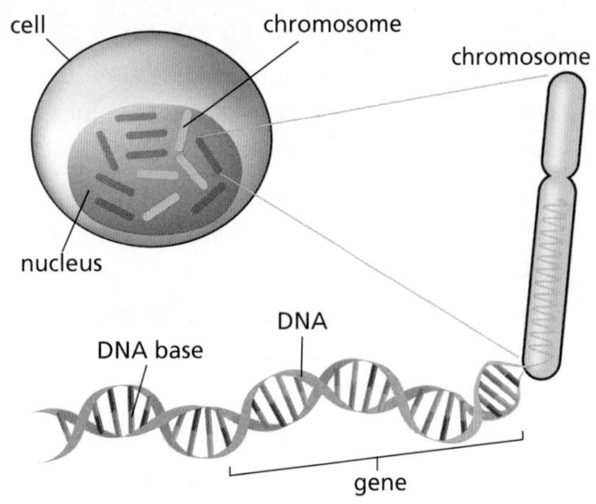

chromosomes	Genetic material is arranged into these thread-like structures, which are made of wound-up DNA.
DNA	Each DNA molecule contains two strands arranged as a **double helix**. Each strand is made up of four chemical **bases**: A, C, G and T. The two strands are held together by bonds between bases.
genes	Regions of the DNA that control the development of characteristics, such as eye colour and blood group. Each gene is made up of a different pattern of the four bases: Each chromosome contains hundreds to thousands of genes.

The discovery of the DNA model was achieved through the contributions of several scientists.

Scientists	Maurice Wilkins	Rosalind Franklin	Erwin Chargaff	James Watson and Francis Crick
Contribution to the discovery	Studied DNA using X-ray crystallography.	Produced the clearest image of DNA using X-ray crystallography.	Discovered that A pairs with T, and C pairs with G.	Used a modelling technique to build a large-scale model of DNA. They were awarded a Nobel Prize for their work.

A set of chromosomes in an organism is called a **karyotype**.

Chromosomes are arranged in pairs, as we inherit one chromosome of each pair from our mother and one chromosome of each pair from our father.

Humans have 46 chromosomes in each cell, that is 23 pairs.

Each of the chromosomes in a pair is the same size and carries genes for the same characteristic.

One pair of chromosomes determines whether an organism is male or female. These are the **sex chromosomes**. Males have one X and one Y chromosome (XY); females have two XX chromosomes (XX).

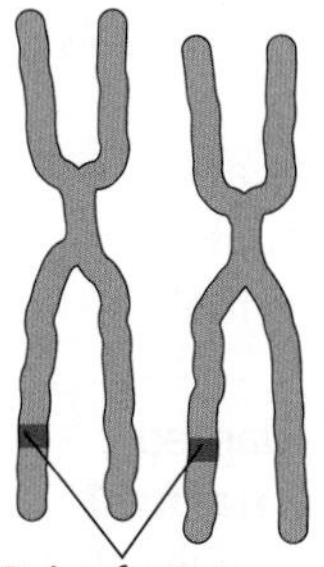

Chromosomes in a pair contain genes for the same characteristic in the same position

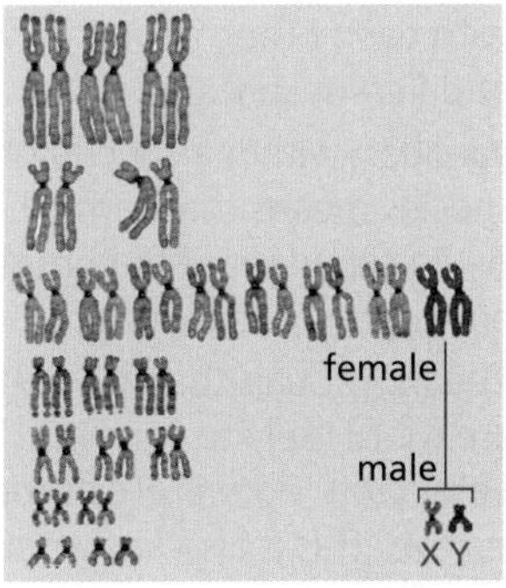

A female human karyotype

DNA can be extracted from many cells to allow scientists to study its structure.

Uses of extracted DNA include **forensic science**; medicine (to detect **genetic disorders**) and families (to find out whether people are related).

cells broken open by grinding → fat and protein in cell membranes broken down with salt solution → DNA solidified using ethanol → DNA separated by spinning

DNA extraction

We have two copies of every gene, one on each chromosome of a pair. Different versions of each gene are called **alleles**; e.g. there is an allele for blue eyes and an allele for brown eyes.

- The **dominant allele** controls the characteristic whether one or two copies of it are present; e.g. allele for brown eyes or red flower colour.
- The **recessive allele** only controls the characteristic when there are two copies present, e.g. allele for blue eyes.

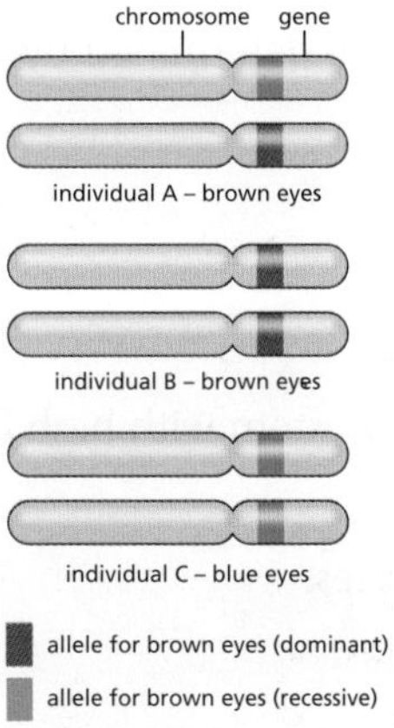

Genetic variation is caused by random mixing of genetic material. This passing on of traits is known as inheritance or **heredity**.

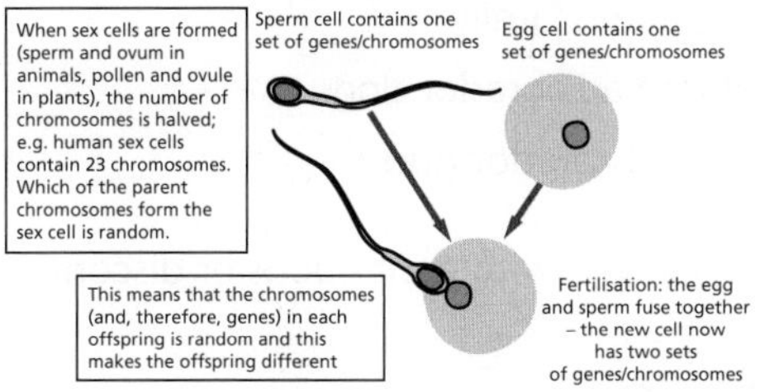

Identical twins are formed when a fertilised egg splits into two. Each twin is formed from the same sperm and egg and so they have identical genetic material.

Traits that are affected by the environment, such as weight and height, may show variation even between identical twins.

We can model inheritance using a **genetic diagram**. It helps us to predict the **probability** of characteristics.

1 identify the allele in each gamete

2 identify the offspring allele combinations

3 identify the characteristic of each offspring.

Possible gametes of parents	B	b
B	BB Brown eyes	Bb Brown eyes
b	Bb Brown eyes	bb Blue eyes

Possible combination of alleles in offspring. The probability of blue eyes is 1 in 4 or 25% or 1:3; the probability of brown eyes is 3 in 4 or 75% or 3:1.

We can show probability in different ways. For example, if we have four possible offspring we can express this as '*x* in 4', or as a percentage, or as a ratio.

Key vocabulary

allele	a version of a gene; can be recessive or dominant
base	a chemical that is a component of DNA: A, C, G and T
chromosome	a thread-like strand of DNA
DNA	deoxyribonucleic acid; the molecule that genes are made of
dominant allele	a version of a gene that controls the characteristic whether there are one or two copies of it
double helix	two strands that wind around each other like a twisted ladder; DNA has a double helix structure
forensic science	the science of collecting and examining physical evidence
gene	a region of DNA that controls an inherited characteristic
genetic diagram	a model used to predict the outcomes of a genetic cross
genetic disorder	a disorder caused by a fault in the genes or chromosomes
heredity	inheritance, the passing on of traits from parent to offspring
identical twins	twins developed from the splitting of a single fertilised egg; they share identical genetic information
karyotype	the number and appearance of all the chromosomes in a single nucleus
mutation	a change in the genetic composition of a cell
probability	the chance of something occurring
recessive allele	a version of a gene that controls the characteristic only when there are two copies of it
sex chromosomes	chromosomes that determine the sex of an organism; X and Y chromosomes in humans
trait	a characteristic
trisomy	a chromosomal disorder where there is an extra chromosome

6.1 Types and causes of variation

You are learning to:

- identify differences between species
- identify features that are inherited and features that are determined by the environment
- explain the importance of diversity
- compare continuous and discontinuous variation
- investigate variation within a species.

1 Choose the **two** true statements about an ecosystem with high biodiversity.

a It will be more able to survive changes.

b It will have a smaller variety of animal species.

c It will have a greater variety of plant species.

d It will be less able to survive changes.

2 Which **two** of the following statements are correct?

a A Siamese cat and a Labrador dog belong to the same species.

b A Sumatran tiger and a Siamese cat belong to the same family.

c There is a lot of variation between a Siamese cat and a Labrador dog.

d There is little variation between a Siamese cat and a Labrador dog.

3 For each of the examples below, identify whether it is linked with continuous or discontinuous variation.

a length of a dog's tail

b height in humans

c eye colour in animals

d colour of a cat's coat

4 Match each sentence to its correct ending.

a An example of a feature that is entirely inherited is …	**i** genetic variation.
b An example of a feature that is affected by the environment is …	**ii** environmental variation.
c The cause of gradual changes in a species over hundreds of years is …	**iii** natural hair colour.
d The cause of changes in an individual animal that do not affect the survival of the species as a whole is …	**iv** the appearance of the skin.

5 **a** Give an example of a characteristic where its variation is caused by:

i genetics (inherited) only

ii the environment only

iii both genetics and the environment

b Which causes most variation?

i genetics

ii environment

iii a mixture of both genetics and environment

6 Relationships between two sets of data are correlations. Identify the type of correlation between each set of data below. Choose from either positive, negative or no correlation for each one.

a age and height of children

b gender and intelligence

c height and foot size

d age and eye colour

Worked example

Data was collected on eye colour in a group of children. The graph of the data is shown below.

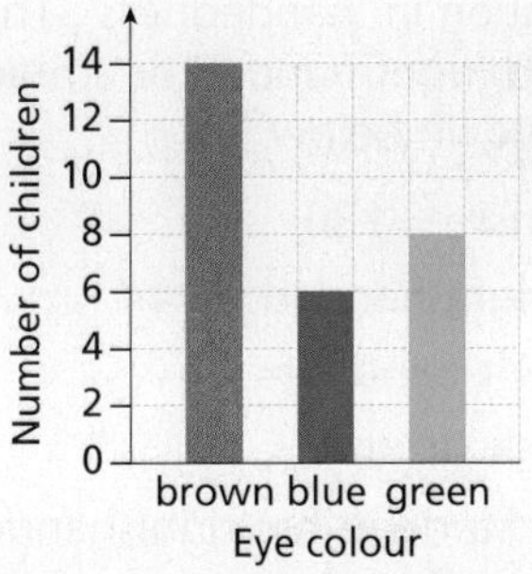

a Which type of variation does this show? Explain your answer.

Consider continuous and discontinuous variation – think about which type has discrete values rather than a range of values.

Discontinuous because eye colour has discrete values rather than a whole range of possible values.

b Select which type of graph this is.

i bar chart

ii histogram

iii scatter graph

It might help to think of a bar chart as looking like bars on a cell window; they have gaps between them.

i

c The height of children in the same group was then measured. Draw a sketch graph to show the likely shape of the graph.

Height shows continuous variation. Think about what shape you see with continuous variation.

line graph with a bell curve:

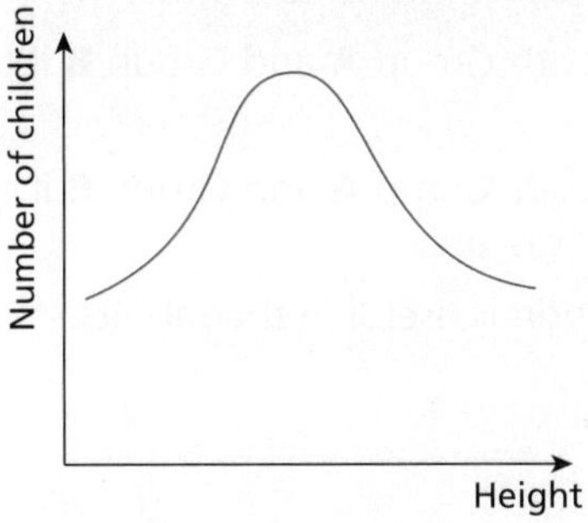

7 Students investigated variation in hair colour of the pupils in class. The results are shown below.

Hair colour	Number of pupils
brown	12
black	6
blond	8
red	2

a Does hair colour show continuous or discontinuous variation? Explain your answer.

b Draw a graph to show these results.

8 Students are investigating variation in 'handedness'. They are collecting data from students in the school on being left-handed, right-handed or ambidextrous (use both hands equally as well). Some of the results are shown below.

- Number of pupils in the sample = 180
- Number of pupils who are right-handed = 144
- Number of pupils who are left-handed = 27

a How many pupils are ambidextrous?

b **i** What percentage of the students are right-handed?

ii What percentage of the students are left-handed?

Another student repeats the data collection from their class of 30 pupils. They find that their results do not match the initial investigation.

c Why should the students make conclusions from the school data rather than the class data?

9 Viruses cause the illnesses myxomatosis and haemorrhagic disease in rabbits which can kill them.

The rabbits in Group **A** are resistant to the virus that causes myxomatosis.

The rabbits in Group **B** are resistant to the virus that causes haemorrhagic disease.

Group A

Group B

a What does it mean to be 'resistant' to a virus?

b Predict the effect on both Group **A** and Group **B** if they come into contact with the virus causing myxomatosis.

c Predict the effect on both Group **A** and Group **B** if they come into contact with the virus causing haemorrhagic disease.

d Explain why this variation is useful in the rabbits.

Worked example

Students investigated whether there was any correlation between the height of fruit trees and the number of fruit produced. They predicted that as height increases the number of fruit increases.

a Draw a sketch graph of the results if the prediction is correct.

A sketch graph shows the general shape of a graph, without plotting actual numbers.

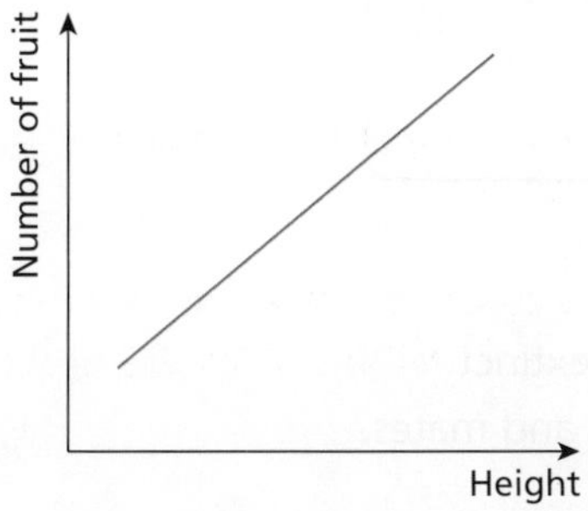

b Which type of correlation does this show?

Consider whether this is positive correlation, negative correlation or no correlation.

positive

10 One scientific theory says that holly leaves have spikes to prevent animals on the ground from eating the leaves.

Students are exploring whether there is a correlation between the height of the leaves on a holly plant and the number of spikes on the leaves.

a In this investigation, identify the type of variable for each of the following:

i the height of the leaves

ii the number of spikes per leaf

iii level of sun and shade for each plant.

b Assuming the students believe that the scientific theory is correct, write a prediction for the investigation.

c The students find there is a negative correlation between the height of the leaves and the number of spikes per leaf. Draw a sketch line graph of the results.

6.2 Natural selection and evolution

You are learning to:

- describe how variation causes competition and explain how this can lead to natural selection
- describe and explain the theory of evolution
- describe and explain how selective breeding can be used to produce offspring with desirable characteristics
- apply the theory of evolution to explain extinction
- describe the use of gene banks to preserve hereditary material.

1 Fill the gaps using the words below.

variation   adapted   compete   extinct

Organisms ________________ for resources such as food and mates.

Individuals differ, this is called ________________.

The individuals that are better ________________ are more likely to survive.

If all individuals were the same and none of them were adapted to a change, the species could become ________________.

2 Place the sentences in the correct order to describe the selective breeding process.

a Offspring with most of the desired characteristic are selected.

b Selected parents are bred.

c Repeated over many generations.

d Male and female with desirable features are selected.

3 Match the answers to the questions.

a Places where seeds are stored, so that new plants can be grown if the species is threatened or extinct.	**i** What are mass extinctions?
b Stores of frozen genetic material from animals that could be cloned in the future.	**ii** What is an endangered species?
c Abnormally large numbers of animals die in a very short time period or at the same time.	**iii** What are seed banks?
d Organisms at risk of extinction.	**iv** What are gene banks?

4 Match each organism with a feature selectively bred by farmers and horticulturists.

a beef cattle	**i** bred for disease resistance
b sheep	**ii** bred for larger flowers
c wheat	**iii** bred for lower fat content of meat
d roses	**iv** bred for thicker fleeces

5 Complete each sentence using the words provided.

a Charles Darwin proposed the theory of ____________ of the fittest.	**i** adaptations
b Darwin's theory explained that offspring with the best ____________ survive to breed and pass on these features.	**ii** offspring
c The theory of acquired characteristics explained that giraffes stretch their necks to reach leaves higher up on the tree, then pass their longer necks on to their ____________.	**iii** survival

6 Which **two** of these statements best describe natural selection?

a Organisms with the best adaptations are able to use more resources.

b Organisms with the best adaptations to their environment survive.

c Organisms with the best features pass these on to their offspring.

d Organisms with the best features live a long time.

7 Wild cheetahs are at risk of extinction. This is partly because there is very little variation in the population.

Cheetah in the wild

a What is extinction of a species?

b Using the example of a virus entering cheetah populations, explain how a lack of variation could lead to extinction.

c Describe the difference between 'extinction' and 'mass extinction'.

8 In New Mexico, both white mice and dark mice are found. The numbers of each type of mouse were monitored. The results are shown in the graph.

a **i** Describe the trend in the numbers of dark mice from 2006 to 2010.

ii Describe the trend in the numbers of white mice from 2006 to 2010.

b The sand where the mice are found became darker. How would this affect how well mice could be hunted by other animals?

c When the sand became darker, the number of dark mice started to increase and the number of white mice started to decrease. Using the data, predict which year the sand became darker.

Mouse population in New Mexico

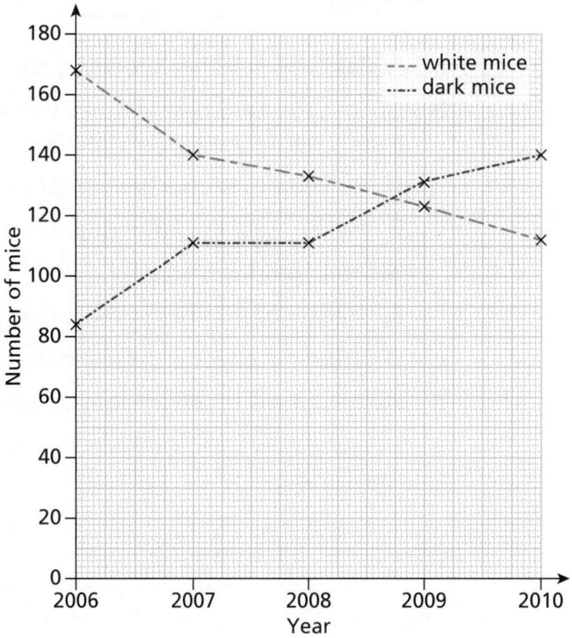

9 The image below shows two variations of a moth species: a pale, peppered colour, and a dark, black colour. Moths are eaten by birds.

a In the feeding relationship between the moth and the bird, identify:

i the predator

ii the prey.

b **i** On a pale surface, which moth has a selective advantage? Explain why.

ii On a dark surface, which moth has a selective advantage? Explain why.

Before the industrial revolution in the UK, trees were pale as there was little pollution. Then, during the industrial revolution, many trees were black due to pollution.

c Describe and explain how the number of each variety of moth changed from before to during the industrial revolution using the sentence starters below.

Before the industrial revolution, there were more __________________ moths. This is because …

During the industrial revolution, the number of __________________ moths decreased and the number of __________________ moths increased. This is because …

10 **a** Explain why selective breeding is used in farming.

b Choose the **two** best features that could be looked for in the parents selected to improve a dairy herd by selective breeding.

i Bull comes from a heifer that produces creamy milk.

ii Heifer produces large quantities of milk.

iii Male produces creamy milk.

iv Heifer comes from parents that produce lean meat.

c Describe the effect of selective breeding on the variation in a population.

d Describe **two** disadvantages of selective breeding in animals.

e Describe how selective breeding may be used to increase the size of flowers produced by a rose bush.

Worked example

One cause of a species becoming endangered is too little genetic variation in the population, which may then lead to extinction. Explain how a change in the environment of a population like this can lead to extinction.

Write your answer as step-by-step bullet points; you can then change the order if needed. Start from what genetic variation is and why too little can be a problem.

- *Genetic variation within a species gives individuals different adaptations.*
- *If there is little genetic variation, individuals are similar and adapted in similar ways.*
- *A change in the environment occurs, such as a change in prey available or in conditions such as temperature.*
- *As all individuals are similar, there could be very few individuals that are adapted to the change.*
- *Fewer organisms will survive to reproduce.*
- *The number of individuals will decrease and could reach zero; the species is then extinct.*

11 Over generations, peacocks (male) have evolved to have colourful tail feathers. It is believed that colourful feathers are more attractive to peahens (female).

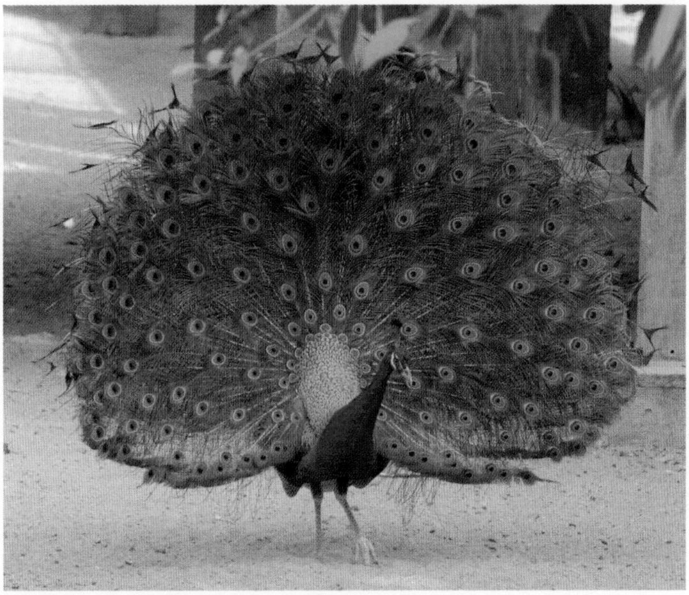

Peacock

Many generations ago, populations of peacocks were mixed with some peacocks having dull tail feathers and others having brightly coloured tail feathers.

Explain how, over many generations, populations of peacocks now have brightly coloured tail feathers.

In your explanation, include the following words and terms:

competition selective advantage natural selection reproduce evolution

6.3 The role of chromosomes, genes and DNA in heredity

You are learning to:
- describe the relationship between nuclei, chromosomes, DNA and genes
- explain the role of chromosomes, DNA and genes in heredity
- describe how the DNA structure model was developed, including the importance of collaboration
- explain the importance of extracting DNA, giving examples
- explain how some genetic disorders arise.

1 Choose **two** reasons why DNA is extracted from cells by scientists.

a to make a double helix

b to detect genetic disorders

c to solve crimes

d to find differences between identical twins

2 Fill in the gaps using the words below.

hair nucleus DNA chromosomes genes

Genetic material is found in the ________________ of a cell.

This material is arranged into thread like strands called ________________.

These strands are made of a chemical called ________________.

Along these strands are regions called ________________ which control development of features such as eye colour and ________________ colour.

3 DNA is made up of a series of chemicals that make a 'pattern'. What are these chemicals called?

a bases

b cell

c chromosomes

d nucleus

4 Match the stages in the discovery of the structure of DNA to the scientists involved.

a Started to use X-ray crystallography.	**i** Watson and Crick
b Took the clearest X-ray crystallography picture of DNA showing its helical structure.	**ii** Erwin Chargaff
c Used a molecular insert modelling technique to create a large model of DNA.	**iii** Maurice Wilkins
d Discovered the DNA base pairings.	**iv** Rosalind Franklin

5 Which **two** statements are correct?

a DNA is made up of a single chemical.

b Each gene is a pattern of four bases.

c DNA has two strands that form a helix.

d The sides of the DNA molecule are held by rungs made of sugar.

6 Choose **true** or **false** for each of the statements below. *Hint: read the statements carefully.*

a Chromosomes are made of genes.

b Chromosomes come in fours.

c Humans have 46 pairs of chromosomes.

d Genes control characteristics.

7 Chromosomes are made of DNA. Regions of the DNA are genes.

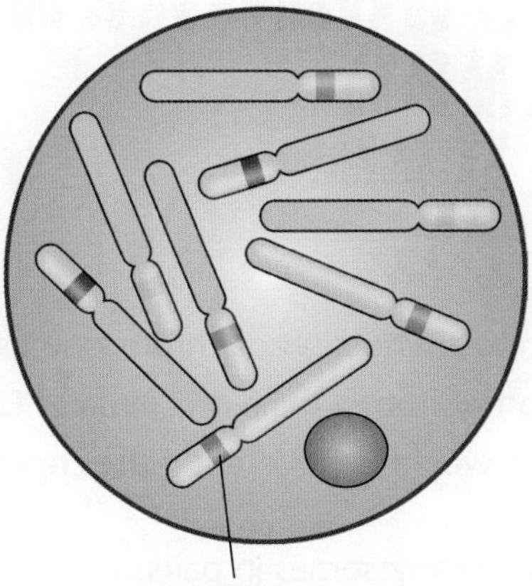

a In which part of the cell are chromosomes found?

b Explain the role of a gene.

c A student wants to observe human chromosomes. Explain why they should not use red blood cells for their investigation.

8 In forensic science, DNA is extracted from substances found at a crime scene. The DNA profile is then used to see if it matches the profile of people.

a Give **three** examples of substances that DNA can be extracted from in forensics.

b Explain how DNA analysis of substances at a scene helps police to convict a criminal.

c Cattle are worth a lot of money. DNA profiling has been used by police to prove that cattle were stolen from a herd on a farm. Explain how this can be proven.

d Explain why DNA profiling may not be useful to show that an item such as a picture was stolen.

9 Body cells in a gorilla have 24 pairs of chromosomes.

a What are the sex cells called in the following?

i female gorillas

ii male gorillas

b How many chromosomes will be in the gorillas' sex cells?

c African hedgehogs have 90 chromosomes in their body cells. Which **two** of these statements are true?

i There are 45 identical chromosome pairs.

ii The sex cells have 22 chromosomes.

iii The sex cells have 45 chromosomes.

iv The fertilised egg has 88 chromosomes.

10 The image below shows the chromosomes of a human from a cheek cell.

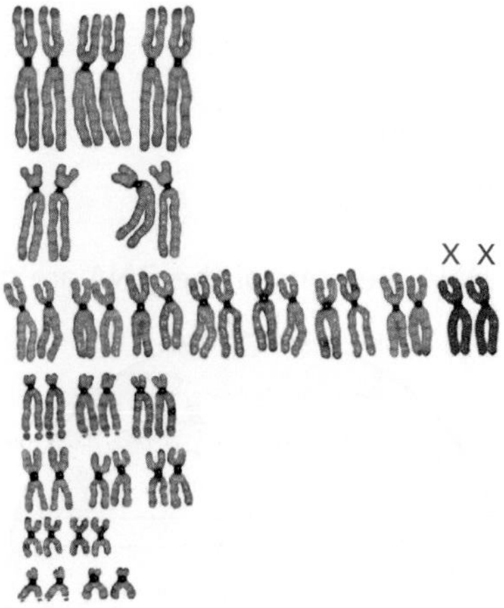

a What is the name given to a whole set of chromosomes?

b Are these the chromosomes from a male or a female? Explain your answer.

c Describe how this image would be different if the chromosomes were taken from a sex cell.

d Explain why we arrange chromosomes in pairs.

e This image shows that there are 46 chromosomes. In a person with a disorder called trisomy 21, how many chromosomes would be seen?

f Rose pollen contains 7 chromosomes. When leaf cells are observed under the microscope, how many chromosomes should be expected?

Worked example

A DNA molecule is made of two strands wound around each other.

a The shape of a DNA molecule is described as a 'twisted ladder'. What is the name given to this shape?

Consider how many strands a DNA molecule has. What shape do these strands form?

double helix

These two strands are held together by bonds between chemicals in each strand. There are four types of these chemicals, given the letters A, C, G and T.

b i What is the general name for these chemicals?

bases

ii What pairs do these chemicals form?

The four chemicals form two pairs.

A–T and C–G

c The sequence of part of one strand is shown below. Write the sequence of the opposite strand.

T	C	C	A	T	G

Remember to use the rules of the base pairings.

AGGTAC

11 The diagram shows the sequence of part of one strand of human DNA.

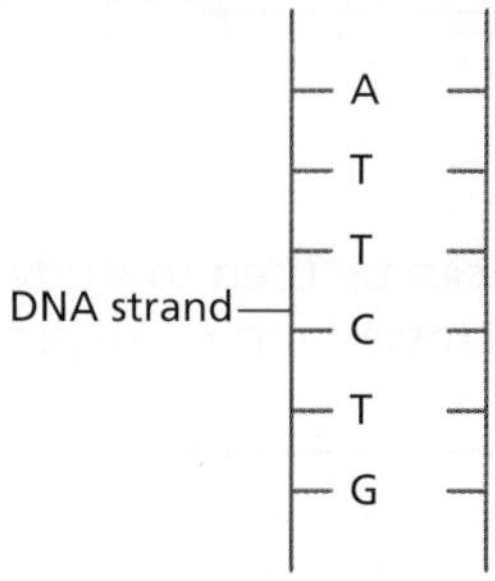

a What is the name of the chemicals shown by the letters?

b Write the sequence of the opposite strand (from top to bottom).

In another person, the sequence was found to be ATCCTG.

c What is the name of this type of change in the DNA sequence?

d What type of molecules are made from this DNA sequence?

e State whether or not each of the conditions below is caused by a change in a DNA sequence.

i Down's syndrome

ii chicken pox

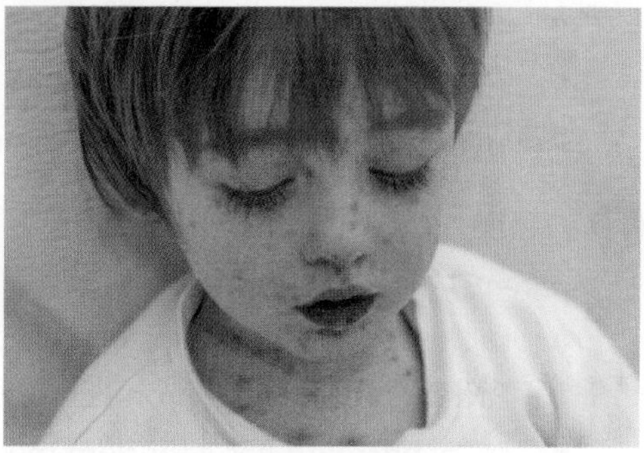

iii cystic fibrosis

iv polydactyly

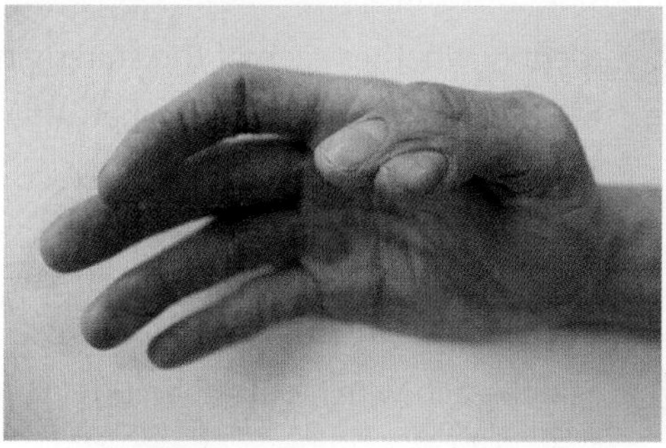

6.4 Explaining inheritance

You are learning to:
- explain how inherited differences arise by combination of genetic material from both parents
- explain how identical twin information can be used to study heredity
- apply a model to demonstrate genetic crosses and make predictions about offspring.

1 Choose **two** entirely genetic traits.

a height

b eye colour

c blood group

d hair length

2 Which **two** of these statements are true?

a All offspring inherit half of their genetic material from their mother and half from their father.

b Boys inherit most of their genetic material from their father.

c Girls inherit most of their genetic material from their mother.

d Identical twins inherit the same genetic material.

3 Fill the gaps using the words below.

parents'   different   father's   mother's

a Each sperm cell contains one chromosome from every pair of the _____ cells.

b Each egg cell contains one chromosome from every pair of the _____ cells.

c Every offspring has a random mix of their _____ genetic information.

d Each chromosome in a pair contains ______ genetic information.

4 Identify whether each of the statements is **true** or **false**.

a Identical twins happen when a fertilised egg split into two.

b Identical twins may not be exactly the same.

c Identical twins are only as similar as other brothers and sisters.

d When a fertilised egg splits, but not completely into two, conjoined twins occur.

5 Match each word to its definition.

a gene	**i** controls the characteristic whether there are one or two copies of the gene present
b allele	**ii** regions of the DNA that code for characteristics, such as eye colour
c dominant allele	**iii** versions of genes that code for characteristics such as blue or brown eyes
d recessive allele	**iv** controls the characteristic only when two copies of the gene are present

6 The image below shows the chromosomes in a pollen and an egg cell.

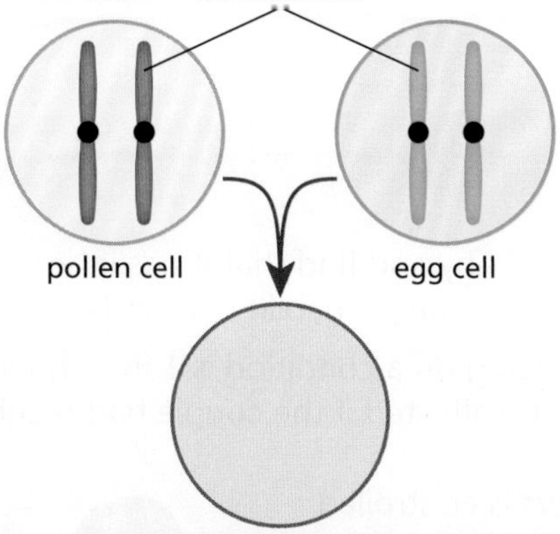

a How many chromosomes will be in the fertilised egg cell?

b Why might this plant have some features in common with both parent plants?

7 **a** Describe how identical twins are formed.

b Explain why identical twins have features in common, such as eye colour and natural hair colour.

c If one identical twin has the blood group AB, will the other identical twin definitely also have the blood group AB? Explain your answer.

d Identical twins do not have identical fingerprints. What does this tell you about what controls the development of our fingerprints?

Worked example

There is an equal chance of a couple having a baby boy as a baby girl.

a Choose **two** ways of expressing the probability of having a boy.

i 1 in 2

ii 1:2

iii 50%

iv 100%

Consider each possible answer in turn.

i and iii

b If the couple has two children, can they be sure of having one boy and one girl? Explain your answer.

Probability shows the **chance** of something happening rather than a prediction of what will definitely happen.

No, probability is the chance of a baby being a boy or a girl, but as chromosomes are mixed randomly, we cannot predict what the sex will be

c The couple had a baby boy and are now expecting another baby. What is the probability of them having another boy?

Probabilities are calculated based on the chromosomes that organisms have and pass on. Consider whether having a baby boy changes the chromosomes and the chances of sharing.

1 in 2 or 50% or 1:1

8 **a** A couple are told that there is a 1 in 4 probability of having a baby with a genetic condition. What is the probability shown as a percentage?

i 1%

ii 4%

iii 25%

iv 75%

b The couple then have a baby and find that it has inherited the genetic condition. If they have another baby, what is the probability of this baby having the genetic condition?

c If the probability of passing on a condition is 1 in 2, how many children would be expected to be affected if the couple had 6 children?

9 Colour in sweet pea flowers is controlled by genes. There are two alleles, one for red colour and one for white colour.

The allele for red is the dominant allele.

The allele for white is the recessive allele.

A botanist crosses plants with red flowers and white flowers by taking pollen from the red flower and pollinating the white flower. They are hoping to produce pink flowers.

Red flowers

White flowers

The red flowers have the alleles RR.

The white flowers have the alleles rr.

a **i** Name the allele in the red flower pollen cells.

ii Name the allele in the white flower egg cells.

iii Write the allele combination in all of the offspring.

iv What colour will the offspring be?

b Explain why the flowers produced were not pink.

Worked example

Earlobes are either 'attached' directly to the side of the head or are 'not attached' and have an earlobe that hangs slightly. Whether earlobes are attached or not is controlled by a particular gene, with two versions of the gene.

The allele for not attached, E, is dominant.

The allele for attached, e, is recessive.

Two parents both have the combination of alleles, Ee.

a Do these parents have attached or not attached earlobes?

Consider which is the dominant allele.

not attached

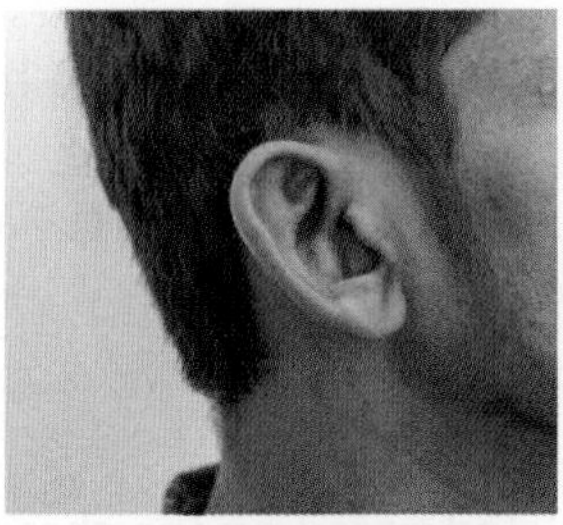

Earlobes not attached

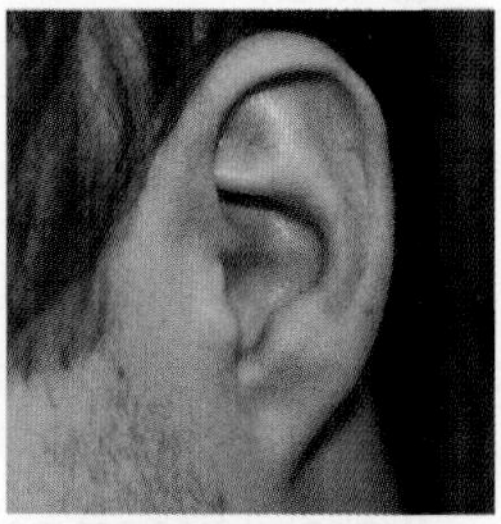

Ear lobes attached

The genetic diagram shows the possible offspring from these parents.

Possible sex cells of parents	E	e
E	(i)	(ii)
e	(iii)	(iv)

b Identify the allele combinations for each offspring, i, ii, iii and iv.

Each offspring inherits one allele from each parent.

i EE

ii E*e*

iii E*e*

iv *ee*

c Which one combination will lead to attached ear lobes?

For each offspring, work out whether their earlobes will be attached or not attached.

ee

d What is the probability of attached earlobes?

Write this as __ in 4.

1 in 4, 25% or 1:3

10 Eye colour is inherited. It is controlled by two alleles, one for brown eyes, B, and one for blue eyes, b.

a Considering the symbol for each allele, which allele is likely to be dominant?

The diagram below shows the possible offspring from a father with alleles Bb and a mother with alleles bb.

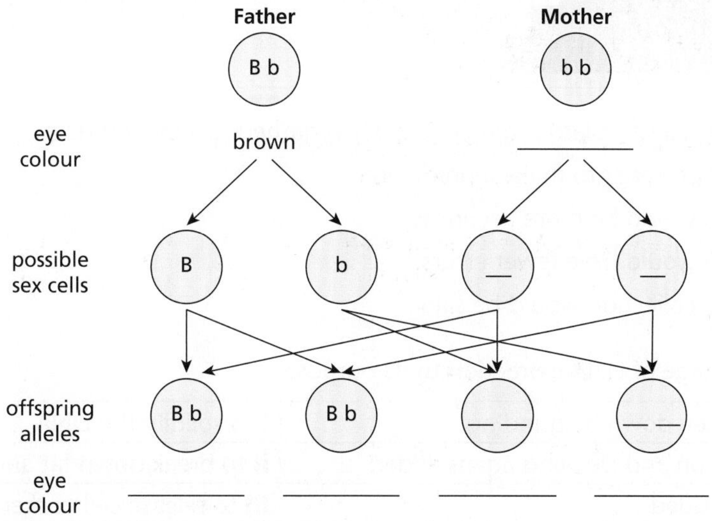

b Identify the eye colour of the mother.

c Identify the alleles in the possible sex cells of the mother.

d Identify the missing possible combination of alleles of the offspring.

e Identify the eye colour for each offspring.

f What is the probability of the couple having a child with blue eyes?

Maths and practical skills

1 The results of an investigation are shown in the graph on the right. What is the total sample size in the investigation?

a 18 **b** 8 **c** 10 **d** 26

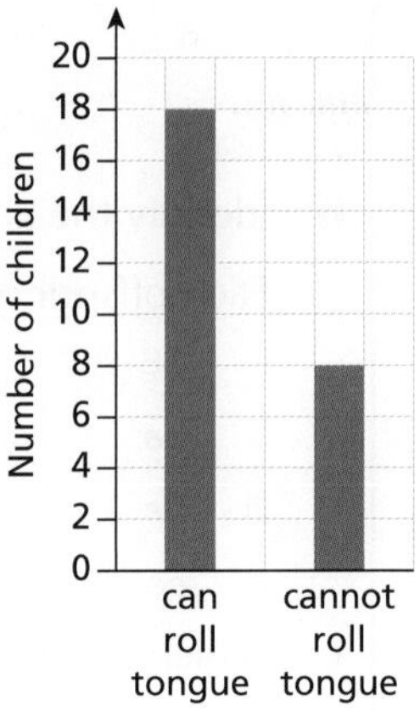

2 Match each example graph to the correct name.

A 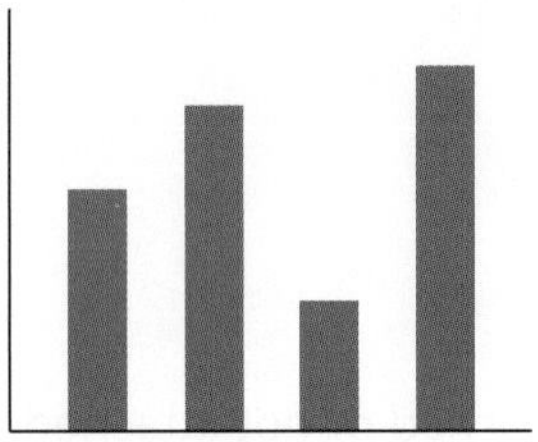	**i** scatter graph
B 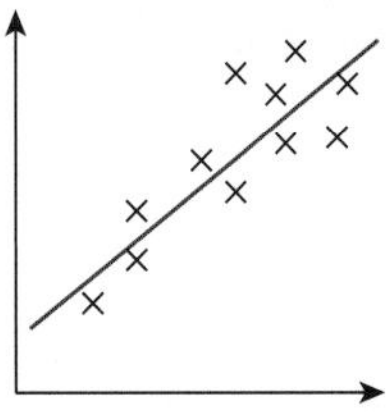	**ii** bar chart
C 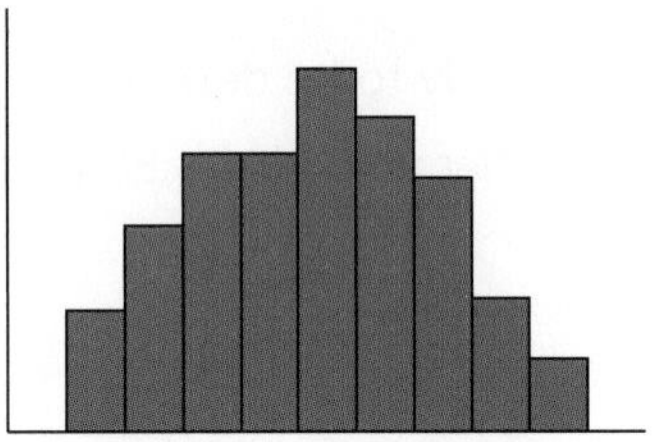	**iii** histogram

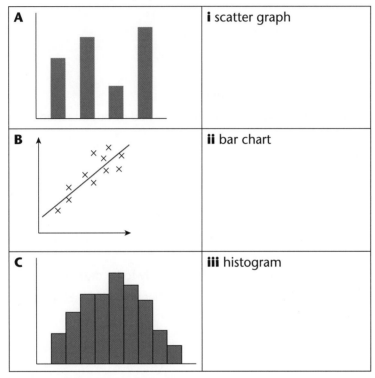

3 Why should you use a large sample size when gathering variation data?

a It would be easier to make a prediction.

b The data would be more accurate.

c The data would have fewer errors.

d The data collection would be safer.

4 Match the stage of DNA extraction to its purpose.

a cells broken down by grinding	**i** to solidify the DNA
b salt solution and cleaning agent added	**ii** to break down fat and protein
c ethanol added	**iii** to release cell contents

5 The probability of a couple passing on a genetic condition is 1 in 2. Choose **two** statements that mean the same thing.

a chance of 50%

b more likely to pass on the condition than not pass on the condition

c probability of 1:2

d if they have 4 children, predict 2 children affected

6 To create a DNA profile from a crime scene sample, approximately 0.001 g of DNA is needed. How many μg is this?

a 0.000001 **b** 1.0 **c** 1000 **d** 0.1

7 The graph below shows the variation in height of human males.

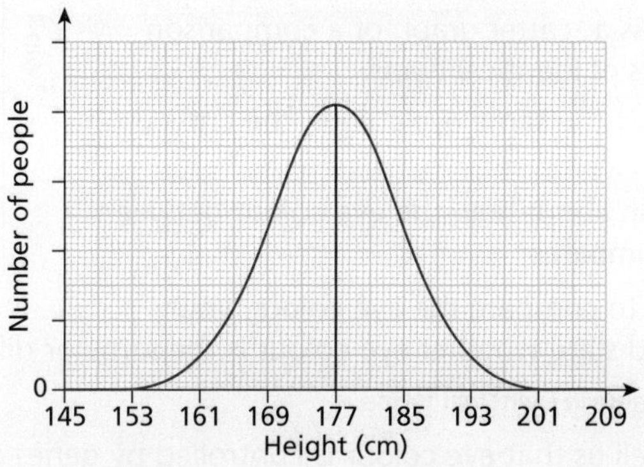

a Does this graph suggest that height has continuous or discontinuous variation?

b What is the mode value?

The relationship between height and lung volume was then investigated.

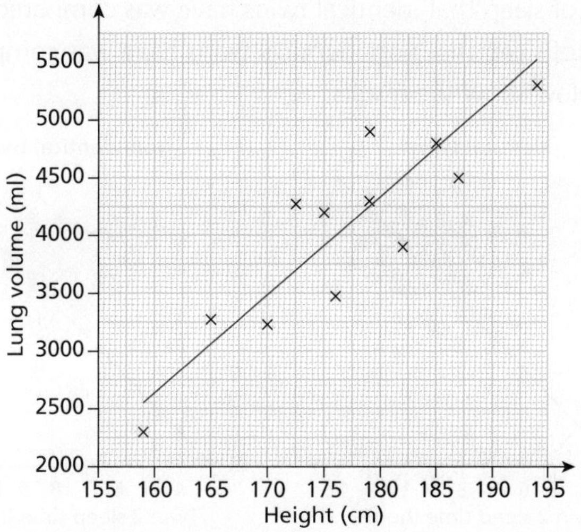

c **i** Describe what the scatter graph shows about the link between height and lung volume.

ii What type of correlation (positive, negative or no correlation) does this graph show?

8 The graph on the right shows the height of a population of pine trees in a forest.

a What type of variation is shown in this feature in the fir trees?

b How many trees are between 24 and 27 m tall?

c What is the total population size of these trees?

d What is the mode value?

e What is the range of the results?

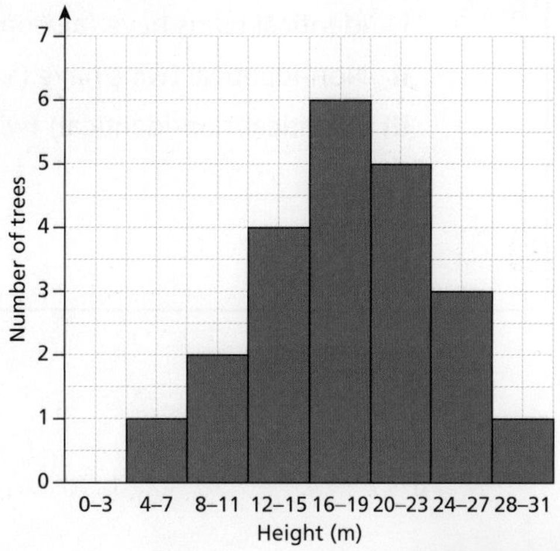

Worked example

Identical twin studies are really helpful in understanding which differences are caused by genes and which are caused by the environment.

The graph on the right is a scatter graph of a comparison between the eye colours of identical twins.

Where twins have exactly the same eye colour, the cross is on the dotted line.

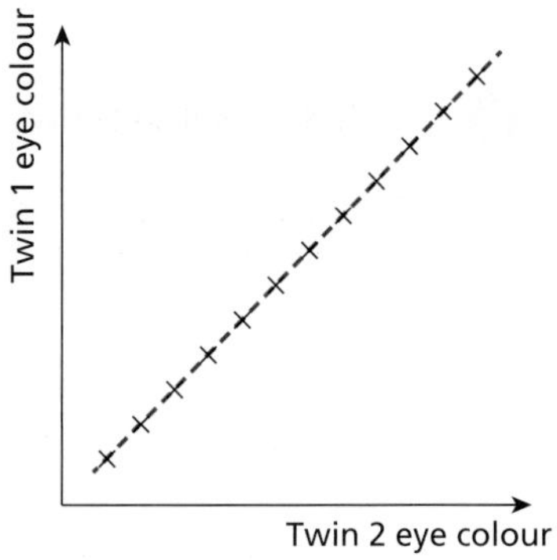

a **i** Make a conclusion about how the eye colour between identical twins compares.

As the study was to compare the eye colour, your conclusion should state whether eye colour is the same or different in identical twins.

Eye colour is the same in identical twins.

ii Does this study tell us that eye colour is controlled by genes or the environment?

genes

A study was carried out to try to find out whether the amount of sleep that we have is controlled by our genes or the environment.

The number of hours of sleep that identical twins have was compared.

The number of hours of sleep that non-identical twins have was compared.

The scatter graphs below show the results.

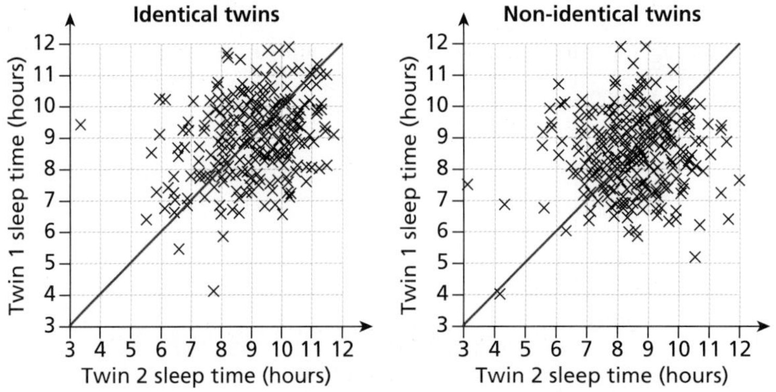

Where twins have exactly the same number of hours of sleep, the dot is on the dotted line.

b Choose the correct answer from the brackets for each statement.

i Identical twins have (all/some) of their genes in common.

ii Non-identical twins have (some/none) of the same genes.

iii (Identical/non-identical) twins are more likely to be similar.

i all

ii some

iii identical

c **i** Comment on whether many of the twins had the same number of hours of sleep.

Remember, when the twins have the same number of hours of sleep the cross sits on the dotted line.

Not many had the same number of hours of sleep (as not many crosses are on the line)

ii Does this study suggest that sleep is controlled only by genes or that the environment also has an effect?

If this was controlled by genes, would you expect more similarities between identical twins?

environment also has an effect

9 A study compared the intelligence between identical twins and then compared the intelligence between non-identical twins.

The graphs below show the results.

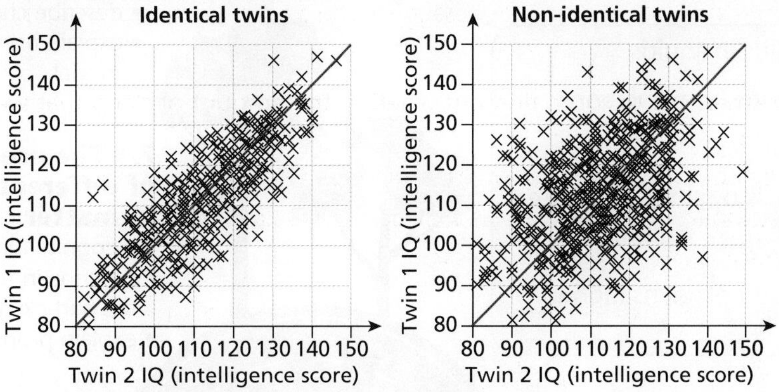

a Explain why identical twins are usually so similar.

b Compared to identical twins, do non-identical twins share more, less or the same number of genes?

Where twins have exactly the same intelligence, the dot is on the dotted line.

c **i** Which twins have the most similar intelligence, identical or non-identical twins?

ii Does this study suggest that intelligence is affected by genes?

10 The height of pea plants is controlled by genes.

Some plants are tall and some are short. There are two alleles, T for tall and t for short.

a Both parent plants have the combination of alleles Tt. This means that their sex cells contain T or t.

i What is the probability of the sex cells containing the T allele?

ii What is the probability of the sex cells containing the t allele?

The diagram below shows the genetic cross.

Possible sex cells of parents	T	t
T	TT	Tt
t	Tt	tt

Pea plants

b **i** What is the probability of the offspring having two of the same allele?

ii What is the probability of short plants being produced?

c In a crop of 120 offspring from these parent plants, how many do you predict would be tall?

dissolving solids in liquids

7 The particulate nature of matter road map

Where are you in your learning journey and where are you aiming to be?

7.3 Atoms, elements and compounds

- understand terms
• evaporation and condensation in the water cycle
- recognise differences
- use simple models

7.2 Changes of state

- recognise reversible changes
- describe changes of state
- explain using the particle model

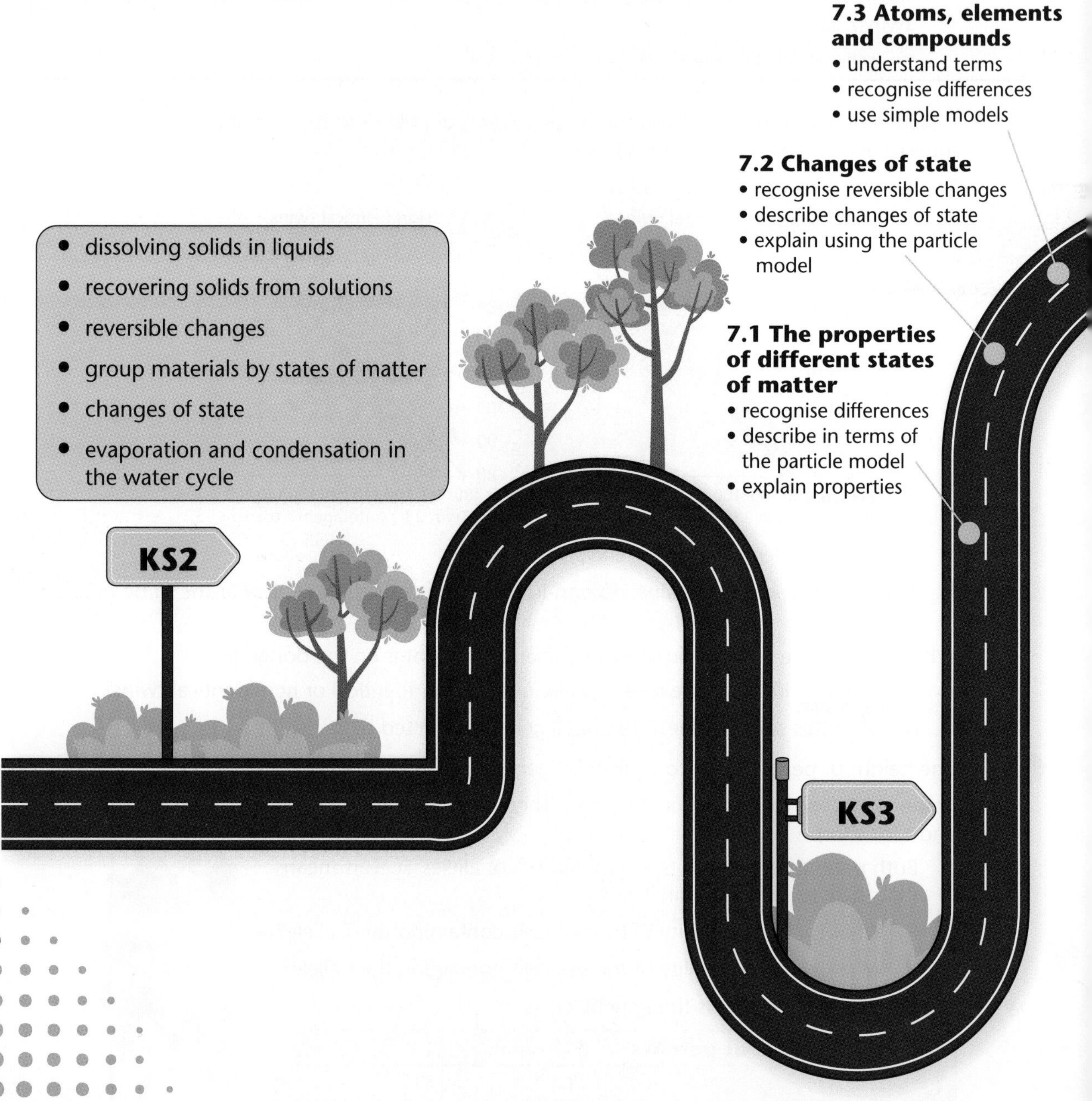

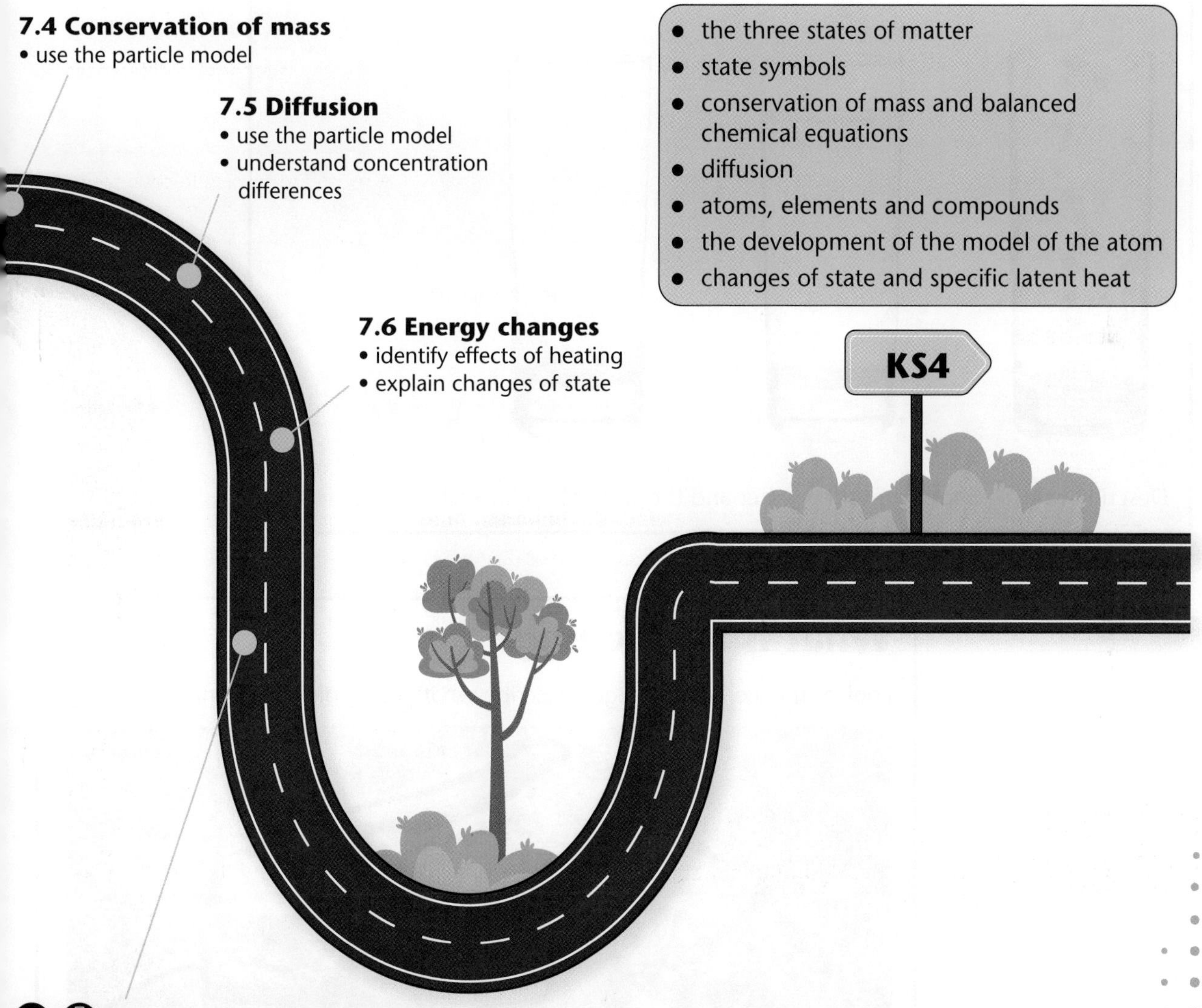

- the three states of matter
- state symbols
- conservation of mass and balanced chemical equations
- diffusion
- atoms, elements and compounds
- the development of the model of the atom
- changes of state and specific latent heat

Maths and practical skills

- analysing data
- calculating results and converting between different units
- interpreting observations and data
- planning an investigation, identifying and managing the variables
- observing and measuring, including the evaluation of repeatability, reproducibility, accuracy and precision
- using SI units and chemical names and symbols

7 The particulate nature of matter

We can explain the world around us using the particle model. Particles can be atoms or molecules. They behave differently in solids, liquids and gases. We can use the particle model to explain why water flows, why smells spread from one place to another and how ice melts.

Where did it go?

Describe what's happening to the water and the state it's in, in each photo.

What is happening?

Look at the ice in the image. Describe what you think is happening and why.

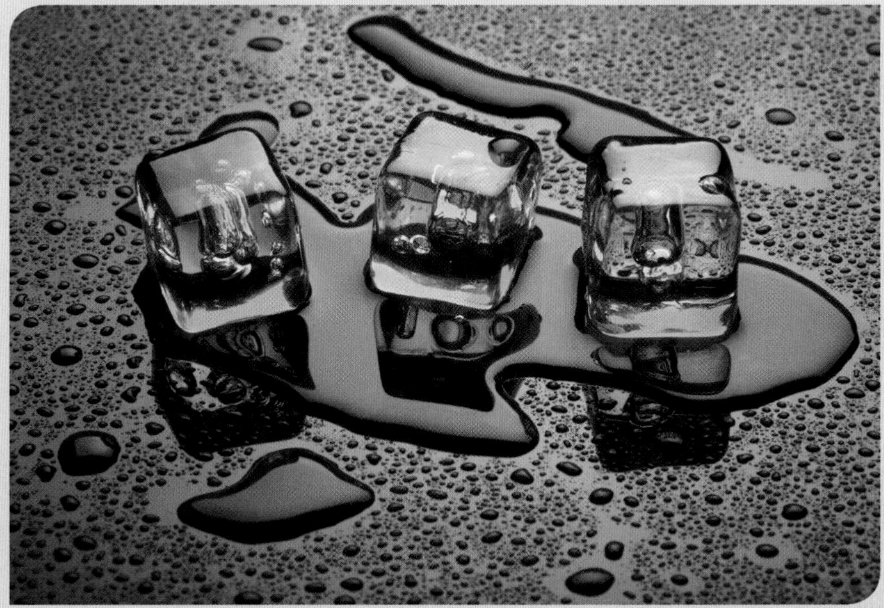

What do you think is happening to the mass of the ice cubes?

Using your science skills

Could you be an ice core analyst?

Could you analyse ice cores? You would normally work in Antarctica or Greenland and use a drill to remove a long column of ice; some ice cores have been drilled to over 3 km in depth. The ice cores are cut into short sections which are analysed in a lab.

Ice cores are made by drilling into the layers of snow that have built up on the ground. This is like pushing a metal straw into a layered cake. Each layer represents half a year. We can count the layers, like tree rings, to work out how far back in time the snow fell in each layer.

Working with ice cores tells us about the history of the Earth, including which gases were in the atmosphere hundreds of thousands of years ago. The ice core in the picture is from Iceland. It contains layers of black ash from volcanic eruptions over the centuries.

Ice cores contain bubbles of trapped gases. This is how we know what the carbon dioxide levels in the atmosphere were thousands of years ago. We can analyse the gas in the air bubble, and then count back the layers to work out when the air bubble was trapped.

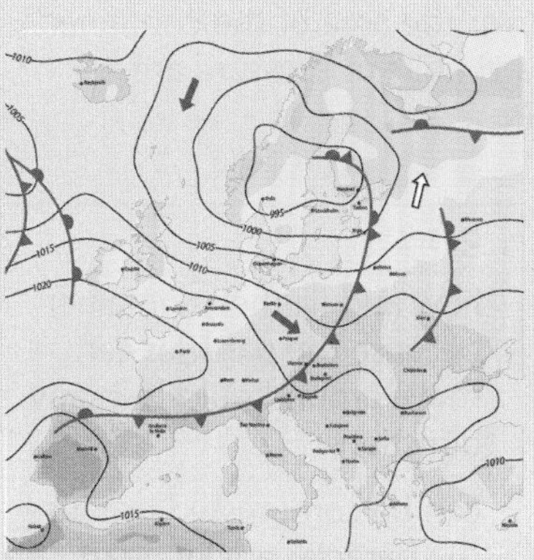

Weather forecasters use their understanding of air pressure to monitor the weather and predict what it will be like in the future. Air moves from an area of high pressure to an area of low pressure; we feel this as wind. Weather forecasters can predict the strength and direction of winds based on maps of air pressure measurements.

Food technologists are scientists and engineers working in the food industry. They develop new food products and make sure that the food we buy has the right flavour and texture. When manufacturing coffee, food technologists add volatile chemicals to coffee granules. These evaporate quickly when a new jar of dried coffee is opened and gives the coffee the freshly opened jar smell. A key part of their role is to ensure that the right processes are followed to make sure the food is safe for consumption and legal for sale, as well as tasty.

Nanotechnologists are helping to treat illnesses such as Alzheimer's disease and Parkinson's disease by finding new ways to deliver drugs to the brain. The brain is protected by a blood–brain barrier, preventing harmful substances from diffusing across from the blood to the brain. This barrier can also stop some helpful drugs from diffusing through to where they are needed. Nanotechnologists are using tiny nanoparticles to help solve this problem.

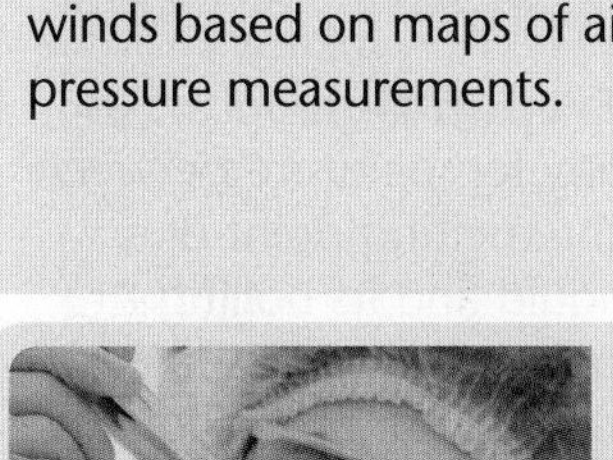

An **analytical chemist** analyses chemical compounds to work out which elements they contain, and their structures and properties. This is an important role in drug development and healthcare.

Knowledge organiser

All **matter** is made from **particles**, which are arranged in the different **states of matter**.

- In solids, the particles vibrate in their fixed positions.
- In liquids, the particles move randomly from their positions, but are always in contact with other particles.
- In gases, the particles move about randomly and very quickly, widely separated but colliding with other particles.

Temperature affects how quickly the particles move. At higher temperatures, particles in a solid vibrate faster, while in liquids and gases particles move around faster.

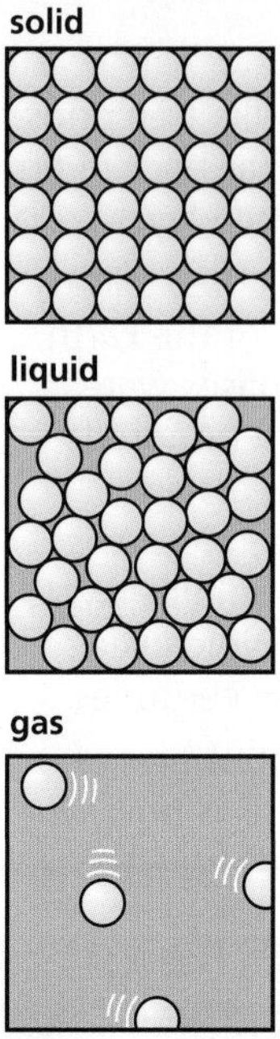

The particles in a solid have very strong, attractive forces between them, which hold the particles in their positions.

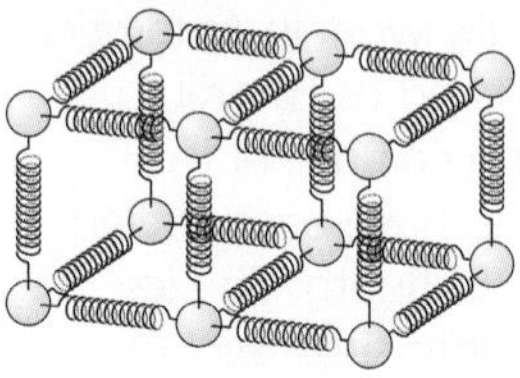

The forces between the particles in liquids are still strong, but not as strong as in solids. Gases have the weakest forces between particles.

When gas particles or liquid particles move, they collide with other particles and also with the sides of the container they are in. **Pressure** is a measure of the average force of these collisions over the area of the container's sides. The standard units of pressure are **kilopascals (kPa)**.

State of matter	solids	liquids	gases
Shape	fixed shape and cannot flow because the particles cannot move from their fixed positions	flow and take the shape of their container because the particles can move past each other	flow and fill their container because the particles can move around quickly in any direction
Compression	cannot be **compressed** as the particles are close together in a fixed position	cannot be compressed because their particles are close together and there are no spaces for them to move into	can be compressed because the particles are far apart with space between them for particles to move into

The change from a solid to a liquid or a gas, and from a liquid to a gas, are reversible changes. They are called **physical changes**. When materials are heated or cooled, they may change from one state to another. Water freezes to become ice at 0 °C and boils to become a gas at 100 °C.

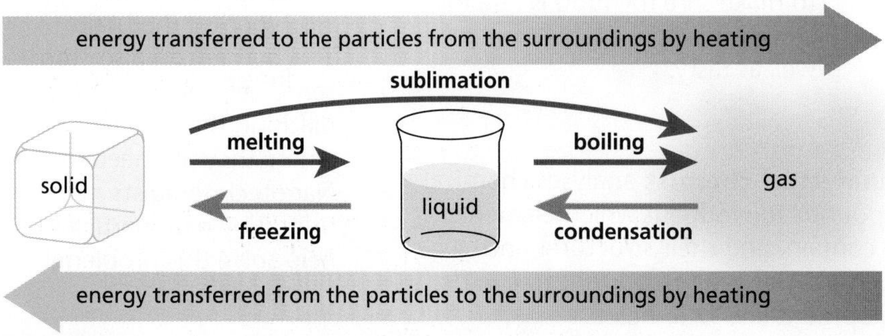

Boiling only happens at the **boiling point**, and the whole liquid turns into a gas. The particles gain enough energy to leave the liquid.

Evaporation occurs at any temperature between the melting point of a liquid and its boiling point. It only happens at the surface of the liquid. Some of the particles gain enough energy to leave the surrounding particles and become a vapour.

Atoms are the smallest parts of all substances. We can represent an atom by writing its element name, writing a symbol, or drawing a simple circular particle. John Dalton was the first person to propose using particles to represent atoms.

calcium, Ca oxygen, O chlorine, Cl

Some atoms can chemically bond together to form **molecules**. Here is a molecule of hydrogen and a molecule of oxygen.

Elements contain only one type of atom. Most elements are metals. Each element is identified by a unique symbol, which always begins with a capital letter.

Compounds are made from the atoms of more than one element, chemically bonded together. Compounds have different properties from the original elements.

We use the chemical symbols of the elements to write the **chemical formula** of the compound, which represents the **ratio** of atoms in each unit of the compound.

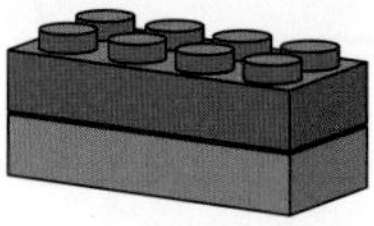

1 red brick and 1 blue brick, the ratio is 1:1

This model could represent one unit of the compound copper oxide, CuO

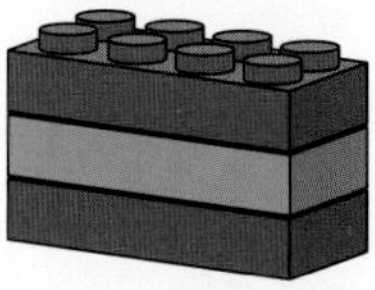

2 red bricks and 1 green brick, the ratio is 2:1

This model could represent one molecule of the compound carbon dioxide, CO_2

Key vocabulary

atom	the basic 'building block' of an element; it cannot be chemically broken down
boiling	the process that happens when a liquid changes state and turns into a gas, by reaching its boiling point
boiling point	the temperature at which a liquid changes state to a gas (or at which a gaseous substance condenses)
chemical formula	chemical symbols and numbers that show which elements, and how many atoms of each, a compound is made up of
collision	when objects hit each other with force
compound	atoms of more than one element chemically bonded together
compress	to make smaller by squashing or pushing together
condensation	the process that happens when a gas changes into a liquid when the temperature drops to the boiling point; for example, when water vapour condenses to form liquid water
element	a substance made of only one type of atom
evaporation	the process that happens when a liquid changes to a gas at the surface of the liquid; for example, when water evaporates to form water vapour
freezing	the process in which a liquid turns into a solid by being cooled to its melting point; for example, when water freezes to form ice
kilopascal (kPa)	unit of pressure
matter	anything that takes up space and has mass
melting	the process in which a solid turns into a liquid by being heated to its melting point; for example, when ice melts to form water
molecule	two or more atoms held together by strong chemical bonds
particle	a very small part of a material, such as an atom or a molecule
particle model	a scientific model in which all matter is made of a large number of very small particles; used to explain the properties of solids, liquids and gases
physical change	physical changes are reversible and include dissolving and changes from one state (solid, liquid or gas) to another
pressure	the average force on a certain area
ratio	a link between two values; for example, if the first value is twice the second value, the ratio is 2:1
state of matter	solid, liquid or gas
sublimation	the process that happens when a solid turns into a gas when heated, without becoming a liquid first
temperature	a measure of how hot an object is; the unit is normally degrees Celsius (°C)
viscosity	the resistance to flow

The law of **conservation of mass** means that matter cannot be destroyed or created, only transformed. This means that when a reaction takes place, the mass of the reactants always equals the mass of the products. This is also true when substances change state, when solutions are mixed together, or if a solute is dissolved in a solvent to form a solution.

Sometimes there appears to be a change in mass during a physical or **chemical change**. This change in mass can usually be explained because one of the reactants or products is a gas.

In a chemical reaction, the mass of the products may be less than expected because one of the products is a gas that has escaped into the surrounding air. If the mass of the products is more than expected, then one of the reactants is a gas. The gas atoms have chemically bonded to one of the other reactants.

When alcohol and water are mixed the volume is less, but the mass stays the same. This is because there are the same number of particles, but the mixture takes up less room

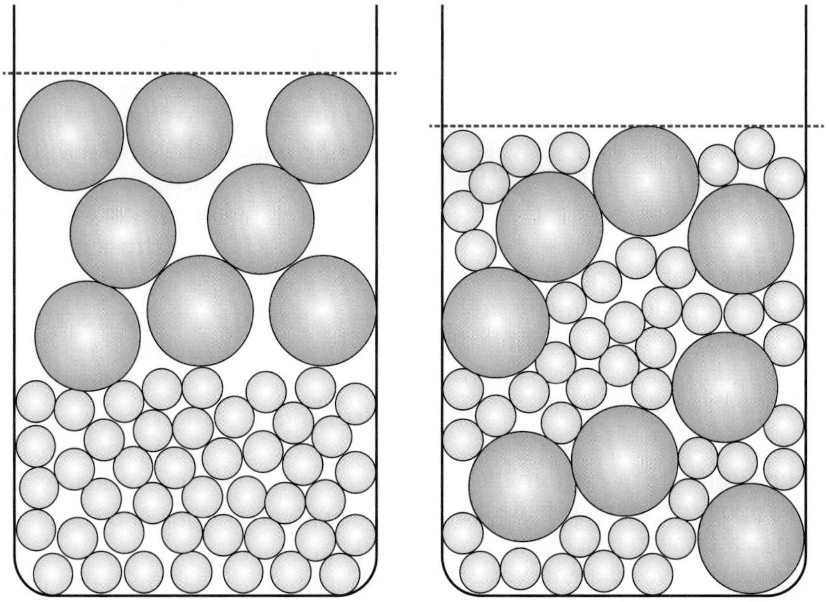

When a solid is heated, its temperature increases until it reaches its **melting point**. At the melting point, all the **energy transferred** by heating is used to overcome the forces between the particles, until the solid changes state. The temperature remains constant until all the solid has changed state. This 'extra heat' needed for the change of state is called **latent heat**.

This graph shows what happens to the temperature as an ice cube is heated. At the melting point, 0 °C, the temperature remains constant until all the substance has changed state from a solid to a liquid. The temperature also remains constant at the boiling point of 100 °C, until all the water has changed state from a liquid to a gas.

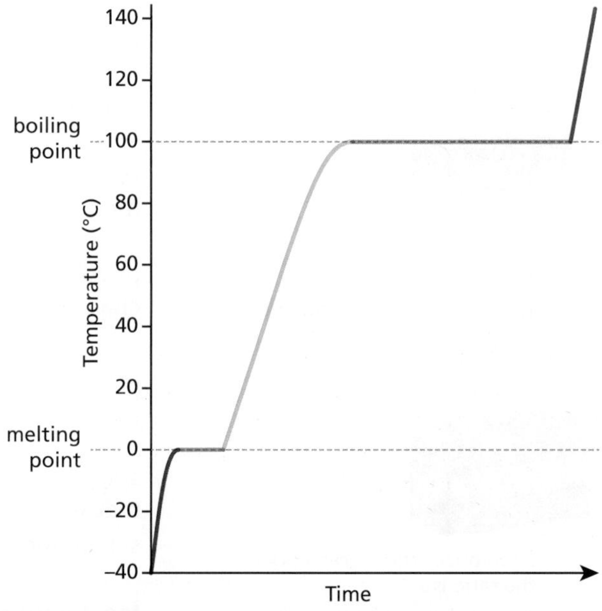

Heating causes solids, liquids and gases to **expand**. This is called **thermal expansion**. It means they take up more space when they are hot compared to when they are cold. Gases expand more than solids and liquids.

Diffusion is the movement of particles from an area of high **concentration** to an area of low concentration, until the concentration is equal throughout.

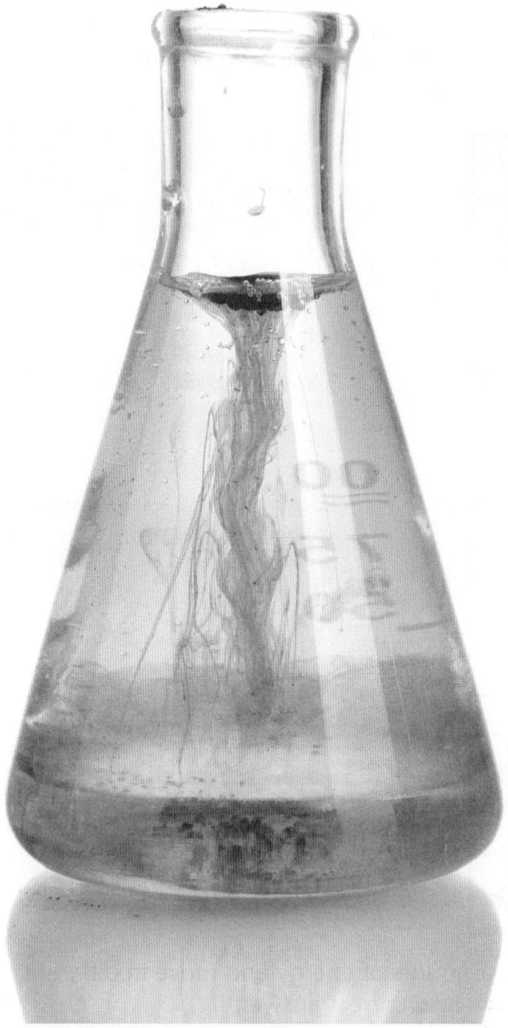

Diffusion happens because of the movement of particles in a gas or a liquid. There is hardly any diffusion in solids because the particles cannot move freely. Gas particles move faster and further than liquid particles, so diffusion in gases occurs faster than in liquids.

Key vocabulary

accurate	an accurate measurement is one that Is close to the true value
chemical change	an irreversible change caused when one substance combines with another to form a new substance, or one substance breaks down to form two or more others
concentration	a measure of the number of particles in a certain volume or space
concentration gradient	the difference in concentration between two areas
conservation of mass	matter cannot be destroyed or created, only transformed; this means the total mass does not change during physical changes or chemical reactions
diffusion	the movement of particles from a higher concentration to a lower concentration
energy transfer	the passing on of energy from one energy store to another
expand	get bigger
latent heat	the heat needed to change the state of a substance
melting point	the temperature at which a solid changes state to a liquid (or a liquid substance freezes)
precise	measurements are precise if they are clustered together around the mean
repeatable	measurements are repeatable when the same person carries out the same experiment under the same conditions and gets similar results
thermal expansion	when particles in a solid or liquid gain enough energy to occupy more space
true value	the actual value that a measurement should be

7.1 The properties of different states of matter

You are learning to:
- recognise the differences between solids, liquids and gases
- describe liquids and gases in terms of the particle model
- explain the properties of solids, liquids and gases, including gas pressure, in terms of the particle model.

1 The particle model can be used to show how particles behave in solids, liquids and gases. Match the particle model diagram to the state of matter.

a Solid

i) 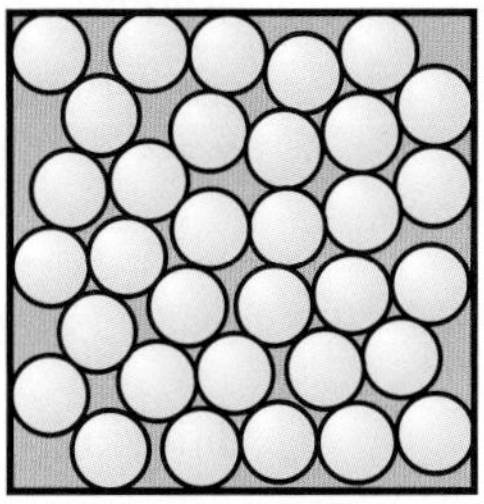

b Liquid

ii) 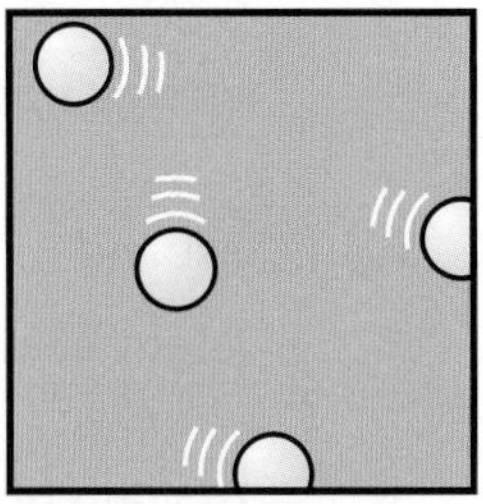

c Gas

iii) 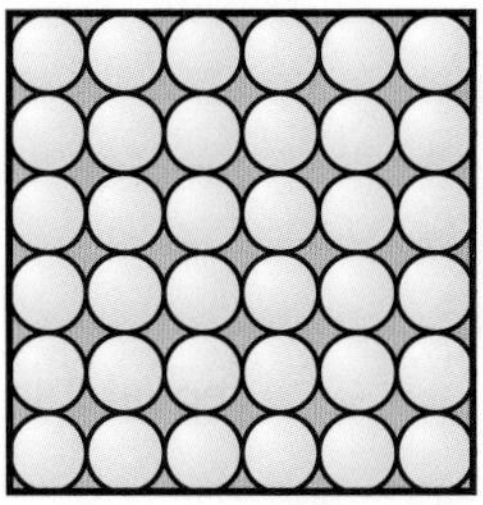

2 Particles in solids, liquids and gases have different amounts of energy and move in different ways. How do the particles move in a solid? Choose **one** correct answer.

a move about very fast

b vibrate in fixed positions

c move slowly past each other

3 There are forces between the particles in solids, liquids and gases. These forces cause the particles to be attracted towards each other. Are these forces strongest in solids, liquids or gases?

4 Some substances can be squashed or compressed into a smaller space. Can solids be compressed?

5 Use the particle model to explain why liquids can flow and solids cannot.

6 A teacher filled a syringe with air, then placed their finger over the end of the syringe so no air could escape. When they pushed the plunger of the syringe down, the air inside compressed into a smaller space.

- **a** Explain why the teacher was able to compress the air in the syringe.
- **b** What happens to the pressure inside the syringe as the air is compressed?
- **c** How does the arrangement of gas particles inside the compressed syringe differ from outside?
- **d** Explain why the mass of the gas inside the syringe stayed the same when it was compressed.

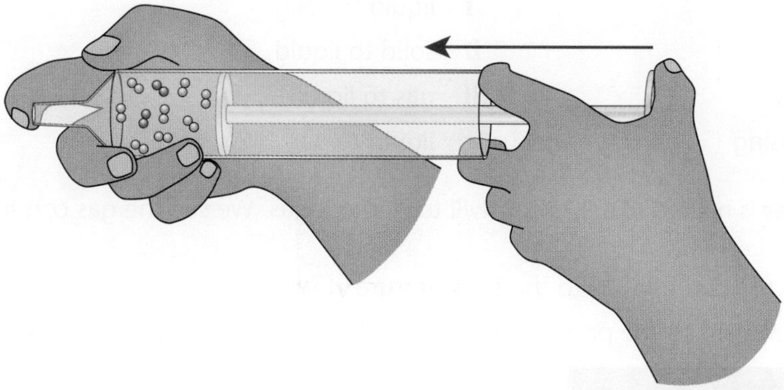

7 Use the particle model to describe the differences between liquids and gases. Your answer should link the particle model to the properties of liquids and gases. Include ideas about energy, forces and space between particles to explain the different properties of liquids and gases.

8 Explain how a sponge can be solid **and** can be compressed.

9 A cyclist used a pump to inflate the tyre on their bicycle.

- **a** Explain how adding air to a tyre increases the pressure.
- **b** The tyre was pumped up on a very cold day. What would happen to the pressure inside the tyre on a hot day?
- **c** Explain your answer to part **b** in terms of the movement of the gas particles.

10 Viscosity is the resistance to flow. Some liquids are more viscous than others. A liquid with a higher viscosity does not flow as easily as a less viscous liquid. Oil is more viscous than water, which means that it flows less easily than water. Use your knowledge of the forces between particles to explain this.

11 A student filled some 250 cm^3 measuring cylinders with different liquids. They dropped a marble into the first measuring cylinder of liquid and timed how long it took to reach the bottom. They repeated their experiment with the other liquids. Here is a table of their results.

- **a** Suggest which **two** liquids are the most viscous.
- **b** Which **two** liquids probably contain mostly water?

Liquid	**Time taken for the marble to fall (s)**
water	1
A	24
B	1
C	4
D	3
E	25
F	1

7.2 Changes of state

You are learning to:
- recognise changes of state as being reversible changes
- describe changes of state using scientific terminology
- explain changes of state using the particle model.

1 Match the following descriptions to the correct change in state.

a	melting	**i**	liquid to solid
b	boiling	**ii**	solid to liquid
c	freezing	**iii**	gas to liquid
d	condensing	**iv**	liquid to gas

2 If pure water is heated to 100 °C, it will turn into a gas. We see the gas coming out of a kettle as steam.

a What is the name given to the temperature at which a liquid becomes a gas?

b What happens to the particles in water as it turns from a liquid to a gas?

3 The melting point of a substance is the temperature at which the substance melts. What is the melting point of pure water?

4 A teacher used some dry ice to demonstrate sublimation. Dry ice is solid carbon dioxide. What change in state occurs during the sublimation of dry ice?

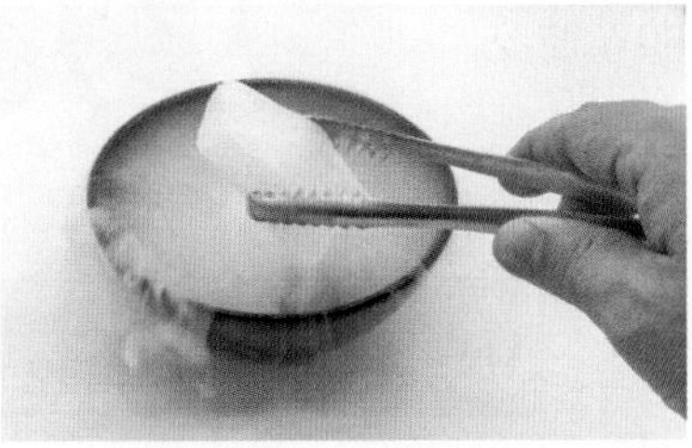

5 An ice cube is left out in the sun and begins to melt.

a Describe how the movement of the particles changes as the ice melts.

b Draw a particle diagram to show how the arrangement of particles changes as the ice cube melts.

c How can you show that melting ice is a reversible change?

6 A puddle of water evaporates from a road. Is the water boiling? Explain your answer.

7 As a gas is cooled, the particles lose speed and the thermal store of energy decreases. What would eventually happen to a gas if energy was continually removed from it?

Worked example

Propane gas can be bought in bottles to be used in some barbeques. Propane has a boiling point of –42 °C and a melting point of –188 °C. What state of matter is propane in at –92 °C?

The easiest way to start answering this type of question is to draw a number line and label it with the melting point and boiling point of the substance. Then add the temperature from the question.

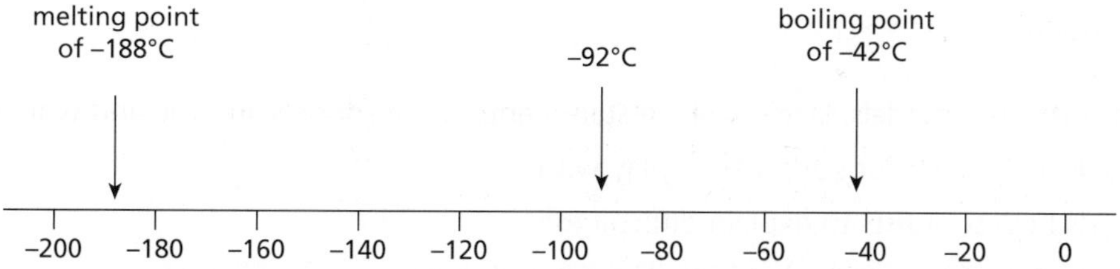

–92°C is between the melting point and the boiling point. This means the propane has melted to form a liquid, but has not boiled to form a gas.

liquid

8 Chlorine has a boiling point of –34 °C and a melting point of –102 °C. What state of matter is chlorine in at –26°C? Explain your answer.

9 Metals have different melting points. The melting point is the temperature at which the substance melts. Gold has a melting point of 2800 °C, whereas zinc has a melting point of 910°C. Explain why some metals have much higher melting points than others.

7.3 Atoms, elements and compounds

You are learning to:
- understand what is meant by 'element' and 'atom'
- recognise the difference between an element and a compound
- use a simple model to show differences between atoms, elements and compounds.

1 Look at this model of an oxygen molecule. Is oxygen an element or a compound?

2 Which statement best describes an atom?

a the smallest part of all substances

b more than one element chemically joined together

c anything that takes up space and has mass

d a unit of mass

3 Match the diagrams to the correct term. Each diagram can be used more than once.

a Atom

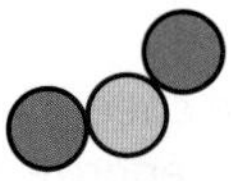

i)

b Molecule

c Element

ii)

d Compound

4 Scientists often use models. Decide which statements about models are true and which are false.

a Models are objects for scientists to play with.

b Models help scientists to explain difficult ideas.

c Models do not have to look exactly like the real thing.

d All ideas in science need models to explain them.

5 Which of the following substances are compounds?

carbon dioxide (CO_2)   oxygen (O_2)   copper (Cu)   ammonia (NH_3)

6 Explain the difference between an atom and an element.

7 Which **one** of these ideas about atoms is true?

a All atoms in a compound are identical.

b All matter is made of atoms.

c Atoms can be made in a chemical reaction.

8 Two students were discussing the differences between elements and compounds. During their discussion they made the following statements:

Student A: 'I think water is an element.'

Student B: 'Air is a compound. It contains more than one element.'

Explain why **both** students are wrong.

9 The particle model is a useful tool to represent atoms and molecules of elements and compounds. Explain why we use models to represent atoms.

Worked example

Silicon dioxide is a compound used in the chemical industry to make glues and sealants. It has the chemical formula SiO_2

How many elements are there in silicon dioxide, SiO_2?

Each element has a unique symbol that starts with a capital letter. Some elements will have a symbol with two letters: the first letter is always a capital letter, the second letter is always a lower-case letter.

In the formula SiO_2, Si is the symbol for one element (silicon) and O is the symbol for another element (oxygen). The '2' after the oxygen tells us that there are two oxygen atoms for every one silicon atom. The ratio is 1:2, one silicon atom for every two oxygen atoms.

two

10 A teacher demonstrated how to produce copper sulfate crystals from copper sulfate solution. Copper sulfate is a compound with the chemical formula $CuSO_4$. How many elements are there in copper sulfate, $CuSO_4$?

11 The chemical formula for sulfuric acid is H_2SO_4.

a How many atoms of oxygen (O) are there in the formula?

b What is the ratio of hydrogen (H) to sulfur (S) to oxygen (O) in the formula?

12 What is the ratio of hydrogen to oxygen in this water molecule? Use this ratio to write the formula for water.

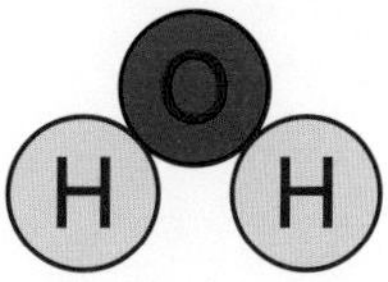

7.4 Conservation of mass

You are learning to:

- use the particle model to explain the law of conservation of mass in physical changes.

1 Which of the following is **not** an example of a physical change?

a melting ice

b dissolving sugar in water

c oxygen reacting with hydrogen

2 Which of the following statements about matter is true?

a It is possible to make new matter.

b Matter cannot be destroyed or created.

c Matter is the same as energy.

3 50 g of ice is melted in an empty bowl. What mass of water would be in the bowl once all the ice has melted?

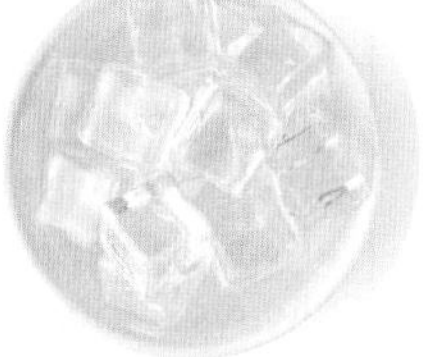

4 A beaker containing 50 g of warm water is placed on a balance. 2 g of salt is added to the water. The salt dissolves in the water. What would the reading on the balance be now?

a 50 g

b 48 g

c 52 g

5 A student heated 100 g of water in a beaker until all of it had turned to steam. What mass of steam would be made?

6 A teacher added water to a beaker at the start of an experiment. They measured the mass of the beaker and water before and after the water was boiled. The mass of the beaker and water at the start of the experiment was 200 g. The mass of the beaker and water at the end of the experiment was 180 g. Why does boiling appear to show a change in mass?

7 A student filled a balloon with air. They measured the mass of the balloon and then they placed the balloon into a freezer. The volume of the balloon decreased as the air inside the balloon cooled. What would have happened to the mass of the balloon of air as it cooled?

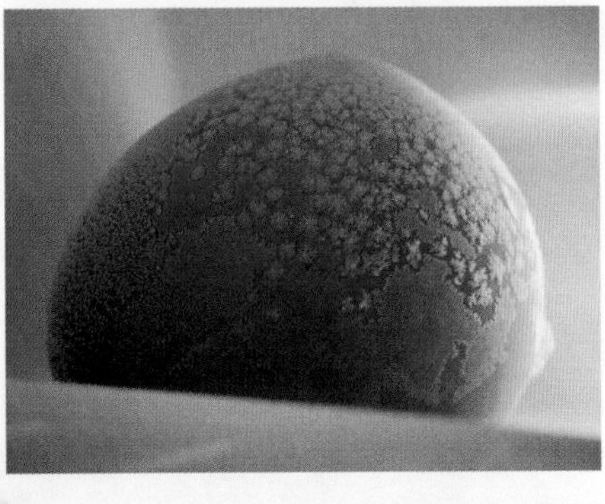

8 An experiment was carried out on a set of scales like the ones in the image.

Two beakers were placed on each side of the set of scales, one containing 50 g of water and one containing 2 g of salt. The scales were balanced. On the left side of the scales, the salt was poured into the beaker of water and stirred. The empty beaker was placed back on the scale. Which statement describes what happens next?

a The left side of the scales would move up.

b The right side of the scales would move up.

c The position of the scales would not change.

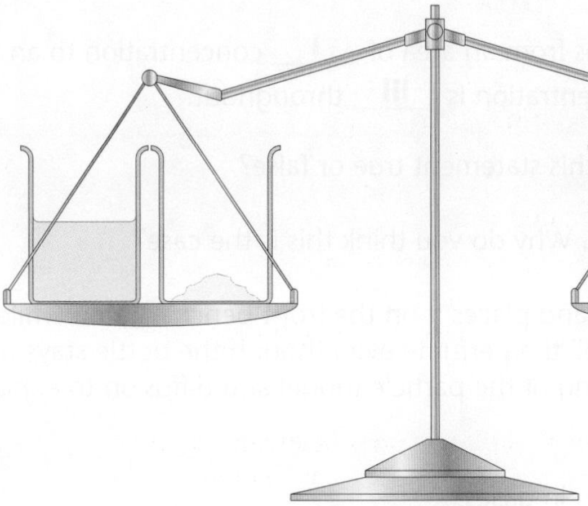

9 Mass is always conserved. When an indigestion tablet is added to water it begins to fizz. Explain why the mass of the tablet and water decreases when the tablet fizzes.

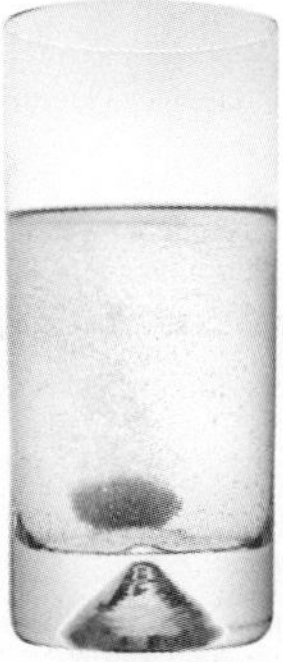

10 When magnesium is burned, the ash formed has a higher mass than the magnesium at the start. Why do you think this is the case?

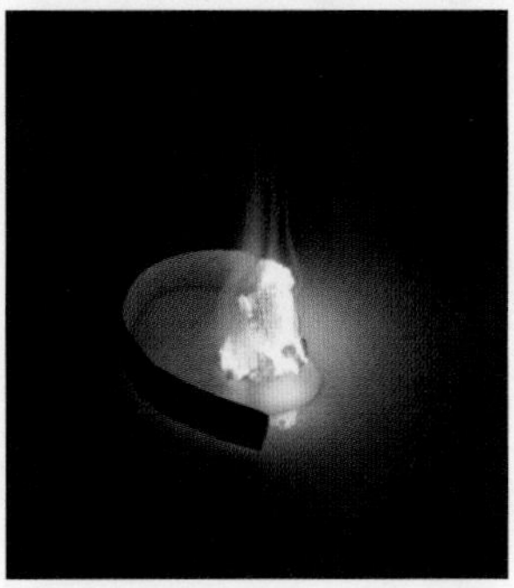

7.5 Diffusion

You are learning to:
- use the particle model to explain observations involving diffusion
- understand the role of concentration differences in diffusion

1 Use the words to complete the definition of diffusion.

high **low** **equal** **zero** **unequal**

Diffusion is the movement of particles from an area of ___**i**___ concentration to an area of ___**ii**___ concentration, until the concentration is ___**iii**___ throughout.

2 'Diffusion only happens in gases.' Is this statement true or false?

3 There is hardly any diffusion in solids. Why do you think this is the case?

4 A teacher opens a bottle of perfume and places it on the front bench. After a while, students at the back of the classroom can smell the perfume even though the bottle stays on the teacher's desk. Use your understanding of the particle model and diffusion to explain what is happening.

5 Why is diffusion in liquids slower than in gases?

6 The concentration of a solution is a measure of how many particles there are in a certain volume. The more particles there are, the higher the concentration. In diffusion, what do we call the difference between an area containing a lot of particles and an area containing fewer particles?

a the diffusion

b the concentration gradient

c a collision

d the surface area

7 How does temperature affect the rate of diffusion? Explain your answer.

8 A student investigated factors that affect how quickly water evaporates from different materials. They took pieces of three different materials (cotton, denim and polyester), soaked them in water and then pegged them onto a washing line.

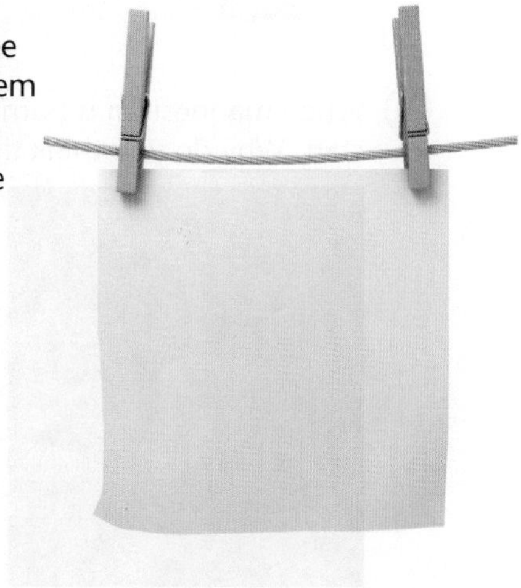

a What would speed up the evaporation of water from the materials? Suggest **two** factors.

b Name **two** variables the student will need to control during this experiment.

c Suggest how the student could measure how much evaporation has taken place from each material.

Worked example

Diffusion happens in the body. Dissolved gases can diffuse between cells and their surroundings. Look at the diagram of a simple animal cell. Will the gas move in or out of the cell? Explain your answer.

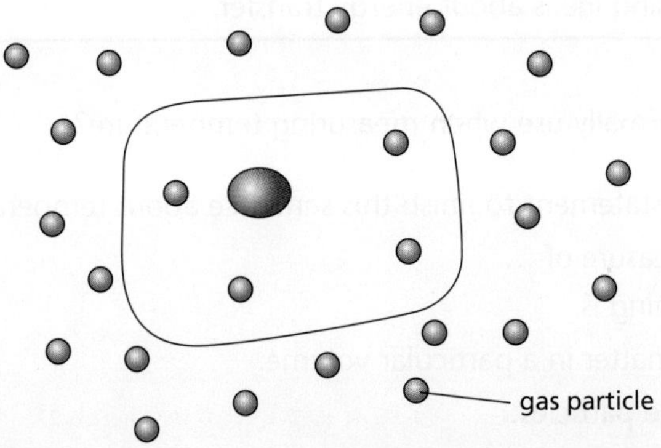

To answer this question we need to look at the number of particles inside and outside the cell to compare the concentrations. There are more gas particles outside the cell, this means the concentration of gas outside the cell is higher than inside. The gas will diffuse down the concentration gradient from outside the cell into the cell.

The answer needs to start with the fact.

Gas will diffuse into the cell.

Followed by an explanation. This needs to say why the gas moves into the cell.

This will happen because there is a higher concentration of gas outside the cell. Gas will diffuse down the concentration gradient into the cell.

9 Look at the following cell. Will the gas move into or out of the cell? Explain your answer.

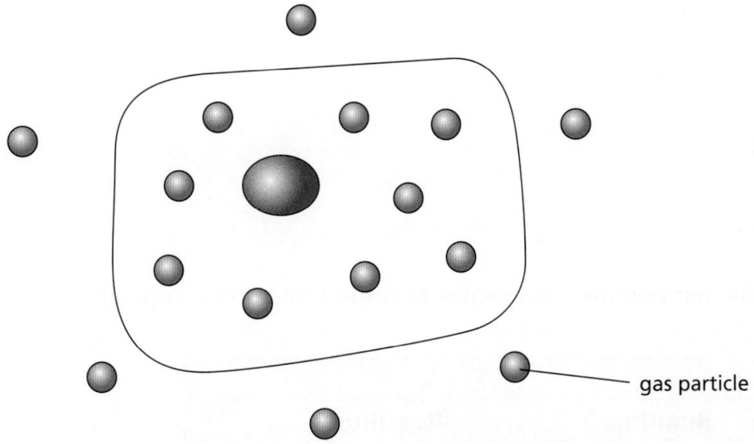

10 Larger particles are often heavier than smaller particles. They also take up more space and need more energy to move than smaller particles. Suggest how particle size might affect diffusion.

7.6 Energy changes

You are learning to:
- identify how heating affects the arrangement and movement of particles
- explain changes of state using ideas about energy transfer.

1. What unit do we normally use when measuring temperature?

2. Choose the correct statement to finish this sentence about temperature.
   Temperature is a measure of …
   a how hot something is.
   b the amount of matter in a particular volume.
   c the energy of the particles.
   d the physical state of something.

3. Which of these statements about what happens when solids, liquids and gases are heated is true?
   a Solids do not expand.
   b Liquids cannot expand without changing state.
   c Gases expand more than liquids and solids.

4. A beaker of water was heated using a Bunsen burner. Describe what happens to the movement of the particles as the water is heated.

5. A student measured the temperature of a beaker of water three times. Look at their data.

Temperature (°C)		
Reading 1	**Reading 2**	**Reading 3**
23.5	23.3	23.4

   a Calculate the mean temperature of the water.
   b Is the data repeatable?
   c Explain your answer to part **b**.

6. During an experiment, a teacher explained the importance of accuracy and precision when evaluating data. Explain the difference between accuracy and precision.

7. What happens to the temperature when a pure substance changes state?

8 Look at this graph showing how the temperature of ice changes as it is heated.

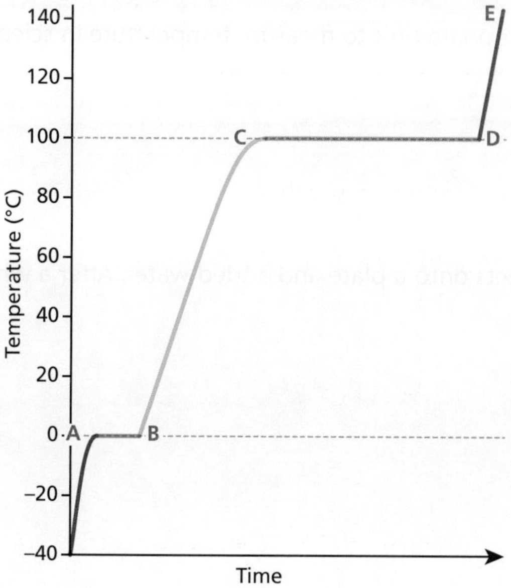

a Which letter on the graph shows when the ice begins to change state from a solid to a liquid?

b What is happening between points C and D on the graph?

9 A beaker containing 50 g of crushed ice was heated until it all melted. A student measured the temperature of the ice as it was being heated.

a The temperature of the ice stayed at 0 °C as the ice melted, even though it was still being heated. Explain why. Refer to particles in your answer.

b After all the ice had melted, the temperature increased again. Explain why. Refer to particles in your answer.

c What mass of water would be in the beaker once all the ice has melted?

10 At 700 °C, aluminium is a liquid, copper is a solid and water is a gas. Which **two** of the following statements are true?

a Water has weaker forces between its particles than copper and aluminium.

b At room temperature, water is a gas, aluminium is a solid and copper is a solid.

c Copper has a lower melting point than aluminium.

d Copper has stronger forces between its particles than aluminium and water.

11 Stearic acid is solid at room temperature (20 °C) and melts to form a liquid when heated. A test tube of stearic acid was placed into a beaker of hot water. The temperature of the stearic acid was measured as it cooled. The temperature data was used to draw a cooling curve for stearic acid, which is shown on the right. What is the melting point for stearic acid? Explain your answer.

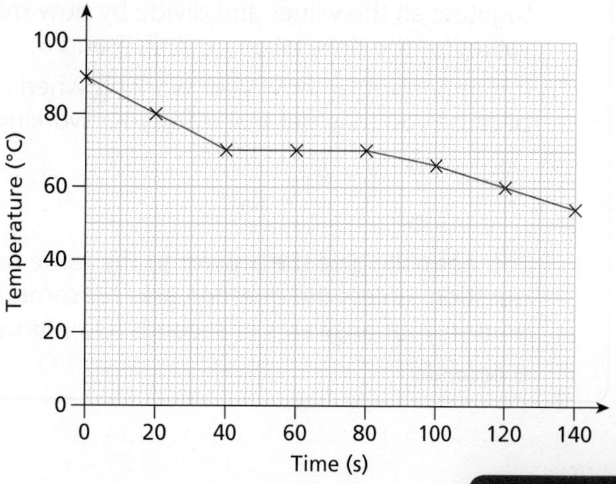

Maths and practical skills

1 Which of the following is the most appropriate unit to measure temperature in science?

a degrees Fahrenheit

b degrees Celsius

c joules

d degrees

2 A teacher placed different coloured sweets onto a plate and added water. After a while the plate looked like this.

What is the name of the process that has caused this to happen?

Worked example

A student timed how long it took a marble to drop through a large cylinder of liquid. They repeated their experiment five times. Calculate a mean time for their results.

Time taken (s)				
Test 1	**Test 2**	**Test 3**	**Test 4**	**Test 5**
6	7	7	5	6

One way to find the average is to calculate a **mean**. To calculate a mean, you need to add together all the values and divide by how many values there are. In this example you have 5 values for the time taken: 6, 7, 7, 5 and 6.

It is important to show your working when carrying out maths questions in science. This is because you may get marks for your working out, even if your final answer is wrong.

$$\frac{(6 + 7 + 7 + 5 + 6)}{5} = 6.2$$

You normally give the answer to the same number of decimal places as the numbers in the question, unless the question asks for something different. It is also important to include the units in your answer, s or seconds. Do not use 'secs' to represent seconds.

6 seconds

3 A student timed how long it took some crystals to dissolve and diffuse through a liquid. They repeated their experiment three times. Calculate a mean for their results.

Time taken (s)		
Test 1	Test 2	Test 3
65	72	57

4 A teacher heated an aluminium can containing a small amount of water, using a Bunsen burner. When they could see steam coming out of the hole at the top, they stopped heating. Using tongs, they turned the can upside down and put it into a bowl of cold water. There was a bang as the can crushed.

a Name the change in state taking place inside the can as it is heated.

b Why did the teacher use tongs to hold the can upside down in the cold water?

c When all the water evaporates, the can is filled with steam. What happens to the steam when the can is placed in the cold water?

d What happens to the pressure inside the can when it is placed in the cold water? Explain your answer.

e Why do you think the can crushed? Use ideas about gas pressure inside and outside the can in your answer.

5 Here is a table of melting and boiling points for three different elements.

Element	Melting point (°C)	Boiling point (°C)
nitrogen	–210	–196
sodium	98	883
aluminium	660	2467

a At what temperature does sodium become a gas?

b What is the physical state of nitrogen at 20 °C?

c Which element is a liquid over the biggest temperature range?

d Between which **two** temperatures will both sodium **and** aluminium be liquids?

6 A teacher placed a glass bottle into a bowl of hot water. They put a boiled egg on top, with the pointed end in the mouth of the bottle. The hole in the top of the bottle was too small for the egg to pass through.

They took the bottle out of the hot water and placed it in a bowl of cold water. The egg moved through the hole into the bottle. Suggest why this happened. Use your ideas about gas pressure and the particle model in your answer.

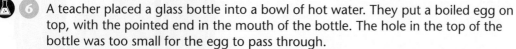

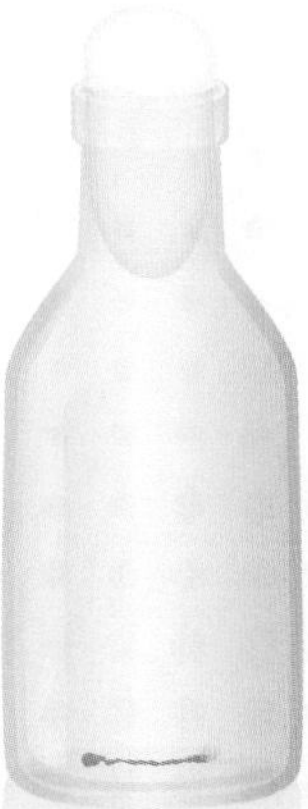

8 Pure and impure substances road map

Where are you in your learning journey and where are you aiming to be?

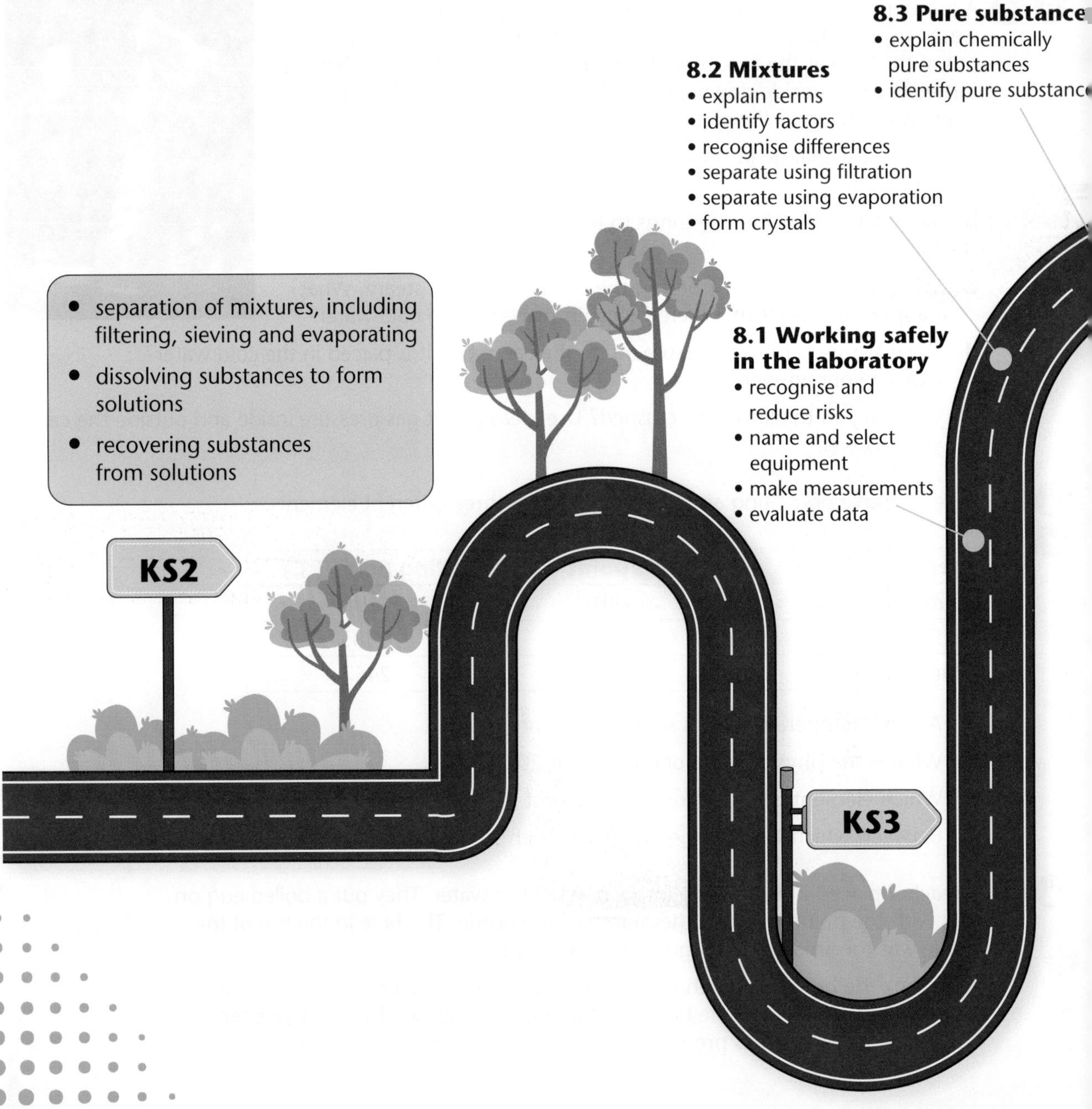

8.4 Distillation
- use distillation
- explain distillation

- pure substances
- chromatography
- mixtures
- fractional distillation and petrochemicals
- potable water

8.5 Chromatography
- separate dyes
- identify unknown substances

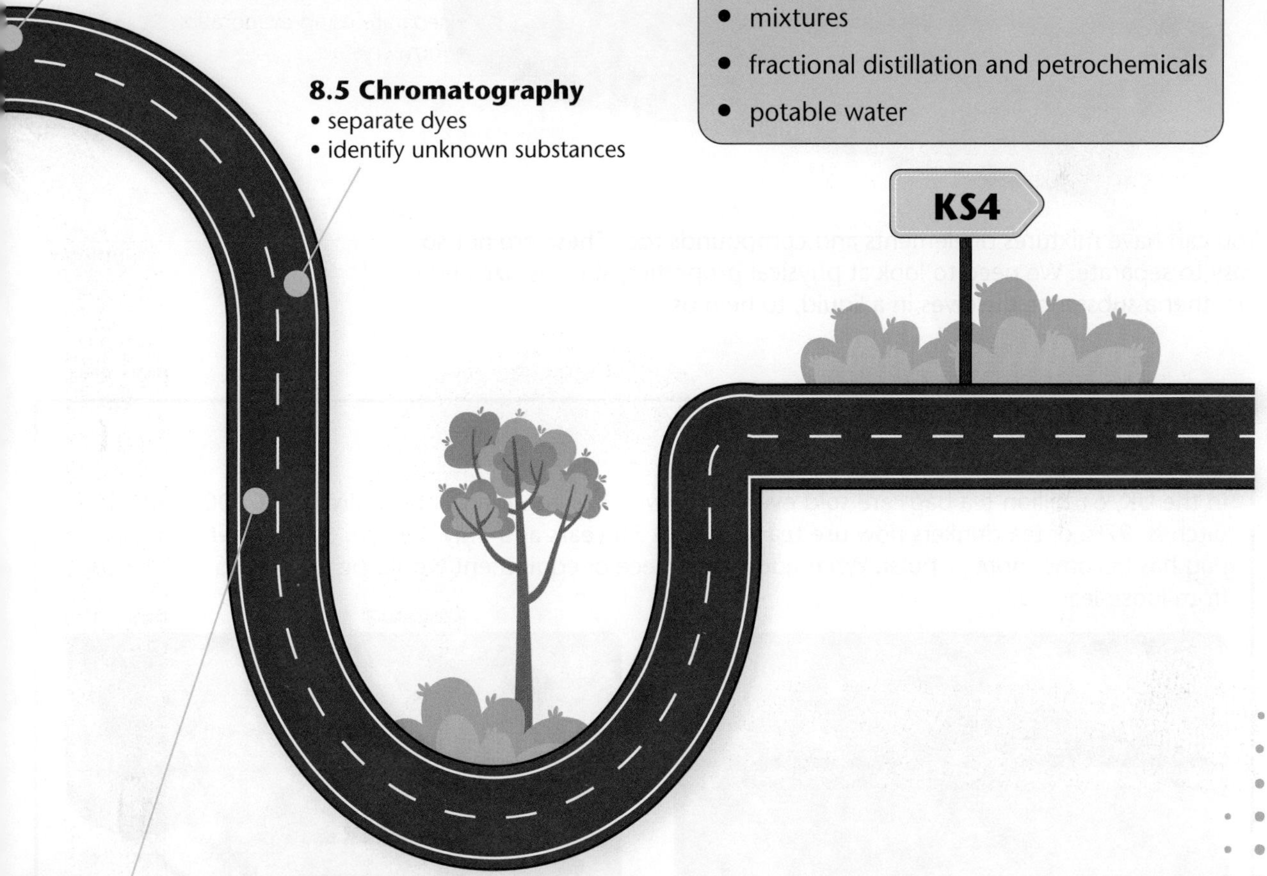

Maths and practical skills

- carrying out practical work safely
- presenting data using tables and graphs
- interpreting observations and data
- suggesting improvements to practical work
- evaluating data, including being aware of possible errors

8 Pure and impure substances

This pencil case contains a mixture of items. If the ruler is removed, then it has been separated from the mixture.

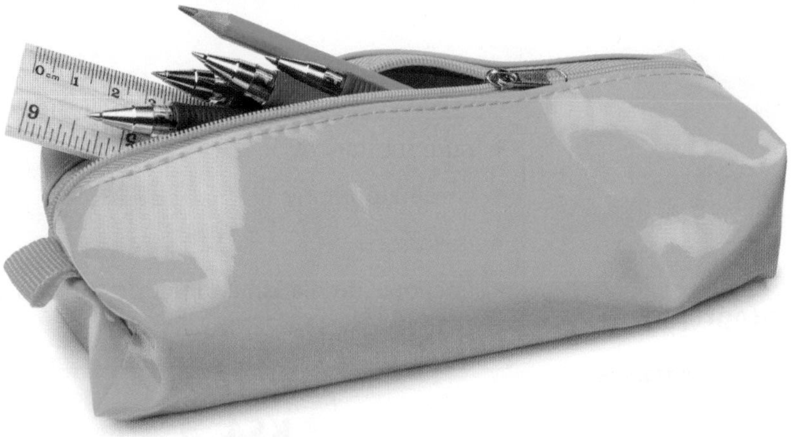

You can have mixtures of elements and compounds too. These are not so easy to separate. We need to look at physical properties, such as size and whether a substance dissolves in a liquid, to help us.

Anyone for tea?

In the UK, 61 billion tea bags are sold every year, which is enough to cover almost 31 000 football pitches. 97% of tea drinkers now use tea bags, but 50 years ago only 3% did. Suggest why the tea bag has become more popular. What additional piece of equipment would be needed to make a cup from loose-leaf tea?

loose-leaf tea

tea bag

Why does the water turn brown when a tea bag is placed into it?

Using your science skills

Could you be a forensic technician?

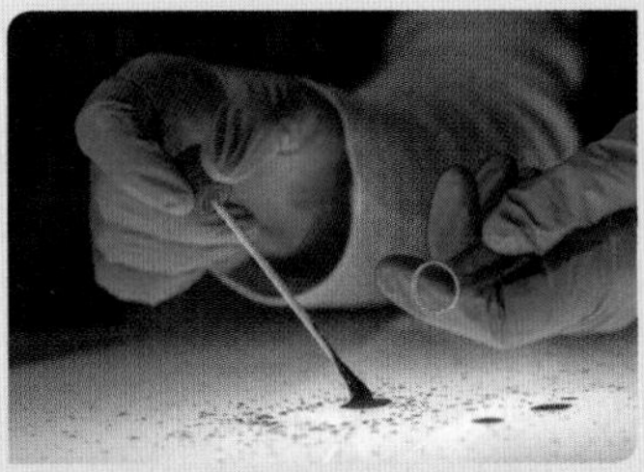

Many everyday substances are mixtures and sometimes the parts of a mixture can tell us something about a crime scene. Your job as a forensic technician would be to analyse and identify different parts of important mixtures using specialist equipment and techniques. There are many different areas of forensics. Your work could be connected with crimes against property, where a forensic technician collects and analyses evidence, such as paint or chemicals. You could also be involved in testing for banned drugs in athletes, examining samples for detecting poisons and analysing blood or urine samples for alcohol in drink-driving offences. Your reports would often be used as evidence in court.

Everyone needs clean and safe water to drink. **Water treatment operators** collect and test water samples to make sure the quality is high, and monitor online data to ensure water is safe to go into the water supply. They also ensure that the wastewater from drains and sewers is converted into a form that is safe to release back into the environment, and harmful substances are removed.

Health and safety managers have responsibility for developing and implementing safe working practices in every area of business, including construction sites, concert arenas, hospitals and schools. They ensure that risk assessments are carried out and that unsafe working practices are stopped. They also provide training and carry out proactive safety inspections.

Perfume chemists must understand how to separate fragrant oils from plants, purify them and then mix them with other substances to make a perfume. They need to understand the components in the perfume to ensure the smell is easily spread, lasts for a while, and is safe for human skin.

Medical scientists conduct research aimed at improving overall human health. They prepare and analyse medical samples, which often contain a complex mixture of substances. They use their findings to better understand the causes of different diseases and how they can be treated.

Knowledge organiser

We work with many different types of substances in chemistry. Some of these are **hazardous**. There are also many other hazards in a laboratory, including glass equipment, hot objects, or even bags on the floor. We need to identify these hazards, assess the **risk** and then try to reduce the risk. For example, we can reduce the risk of a chemical going into your eye by wearing safety goggles. Using a **Bunsen burner** can be hazardous. A yellow flame should be used when the Bunsen burner is not in use, so that it can be seen easily. The process of reducing the chance of someone being harmed is called a risk assessment.

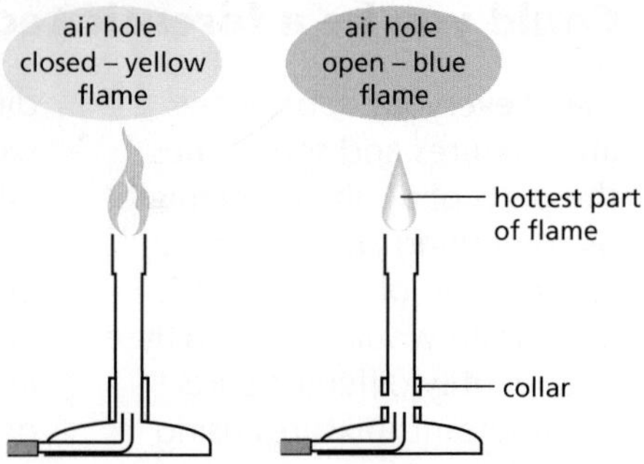

	The substance is hazardous to the environment
	The substance is hazardous to health
	The substance is corrosive
	The substance is flammable

Scientists across the world use the same **hazard symbols** to highlight the risks of using chemicals such as solvents.

To measure the volume of a solution, it is important to choose **apparatus** with the most appropriate scale and read it correctly using the level of the **meniscus**.

When a solid solute is added to a solvent, the total volume of the solution is usually less than the volume of the two substances separately. This is because the solute particles occupy spaces between the water molecules.

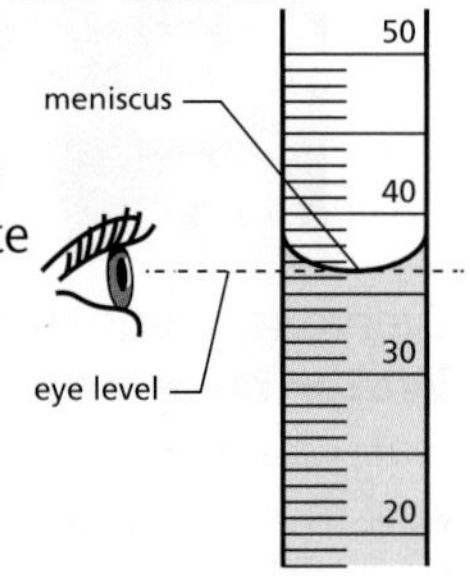

If you stir sugar into a cup of tea or coffee the sugar crystals disappear – they **dissolve**. The water is called the **solvent** and the mixture is called a **solution**. Substances that dissolve are described as **soluble**, and they are called **solutes**. If you stir sugar into water, sugar is the solute and water is the solvent.

Substances dissolve more in hotter solvents. This is because the solvent molecules have more energy and move faster. They can separate the solute particles more quickly.

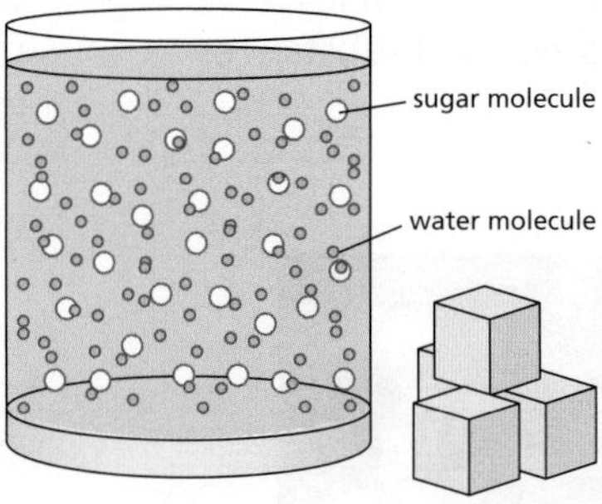

Some of the substances we work with in chemistry are **pure** substances. A pure substance contains only one type of element or **compound**. Chemically pure water only contains H_2O molecules. Bottled spring water is not the same as pure water. It also contains other substances known as minerals. It is a **mixture**.

Mixtures can be separated by making use of differences between substances. For example, magnets can be used to remove magnetic metals (cobalt, iron or nickel) from mixtures. Physical methods are used to **separate** mixtures. The method used depends on the physical properties of each component in the mixture.

Filtration can be used to separate a mixture of soluble and **insoluble** substances. A **filter** has microscopic holes that allow some substances to pass through but not others. For example, it can remove suspended solids from a liquid, such as sand from sea water. Larger items such as gravel and stones can be removed using a sieve.

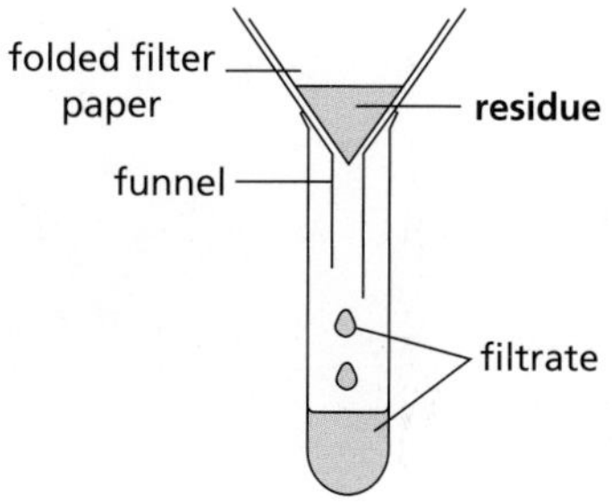

Soluble substances can be separated from their solutions by **evaporation**. When liquids are heated, they evaporate, turning into a vapour (gas). The solvent evaporates to leave behind the solid solute. If evaporation is fast, small crystals will form, but if evaporation takes a long time, then much larger crystals will be observed. **Volatile** liquids, like alcohol in perfumes, easily change to their vapour state.

Immiscible liquids like oil and water do not mix. They can be separated using a separating funnel.

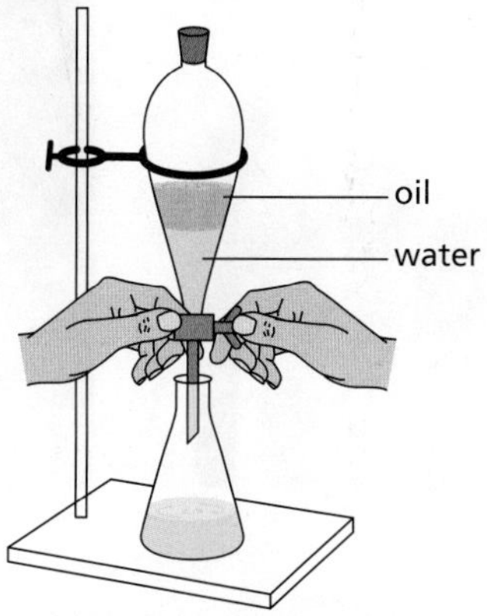

Key vocabulary	
apparatus	equipment used in a scientific experiment
Bunsen burner	a controllable gas flame used to heat substances
compound	two or more elements that are chemically joined together, such as water (H_2O)
crystallisation	when a solvent evaporates to leave crystals of solid
dissolve	when particles of a solute are mixed with particles of a solvent to form a solution
evaporation	the process of changing state from a liquid to a gas
filter	a material with microscopic holes used to remove insoluble solids from liquids
filtration	the separation of an insoluble solid from a liquid using a filter
hazard	something that can cause harm
hazard symbol	a standard symbol that warns of a particular type of hazard
immiscible	liquids that do not mix, but form separate layers
impure	an impure substance contains more than one type of element or compound
insoluble	unable to dissolve in a solvent
meniscus	the curved surface of a liquid in a container
miscible	miscible liquids will mix together
mixture	two or more elements or compounds mixed together, but not chemically joined
pure	a substance containing only one type of element or compound
residue	the solid left after evaporation has occurred
risk	the likelihood of a hazard causing harm
saturated (solution)	when no more solute will dissolve
separate	to divide a mixture into its components
solubility	the mass of solute that dissolves in a solvent at a particular temperature
soluble	able to dissolve in a liquid
solute	a solid that dissolves in a solvent
solution	the mixture formed when a solid dissolves in a liquid
solvent	a liquid in which a substance dissolves
volatile	a liquid which evaporates quickly

Different liquids boil at different temperatures. This information can be used to help separate mixtures of liquids by a process called **distillation**. A piece of apparatus called a **Liebig condenser** is used in distillation; it is a double glass tube. The outer tube is connected to a water tap, and cold water flows through it.

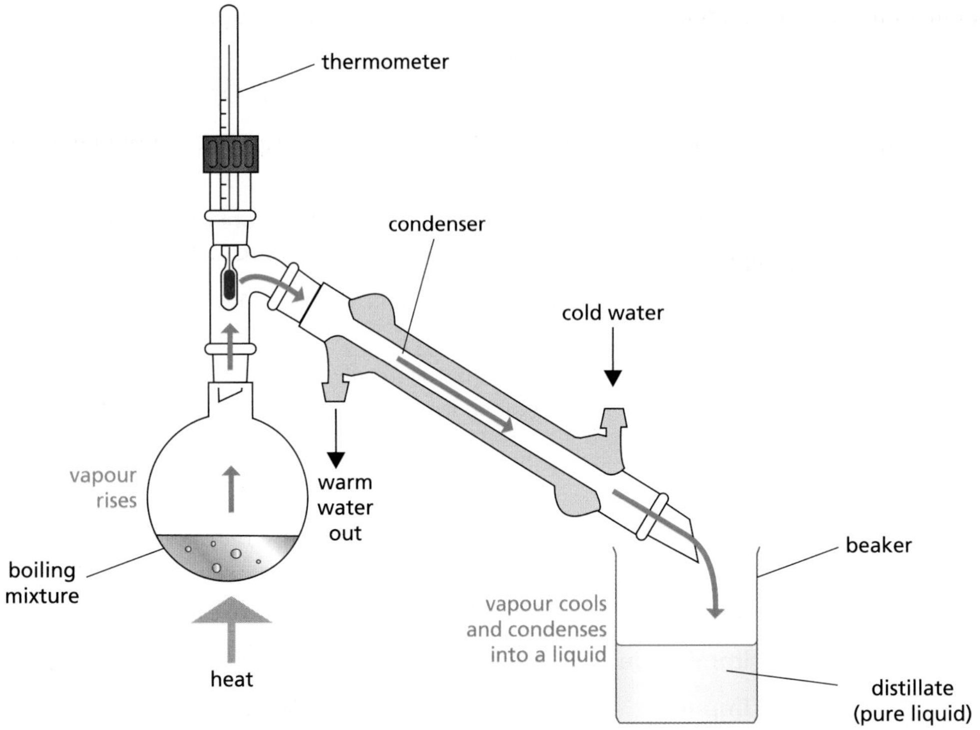

During distillation, a liquid mixture is heated. The liquid with the lowest boiling point changes into a vapour and rises. It flows through the inner tube of the Liebig condenser and is cooled by the water in the outer tube. The vapour **condenses** to a liquid, which flows into a collecting beaker. The collected liquid is known as the **distillate**.

Chromatography is another separating technique. It can be used to separate and identify unknown substances in a mixture. It is used by scientists to detect drugs, banned chemicals and explosives, and to identify dyes and paints.

An example of chromatography is the separation of black ink into different colours. Black ink is actually a mixture of different coloured inks. Filter paper and water can be used to separate them. This method of separation is called **paper chromatography**. It works because some of the inks are more soluble in water than others.

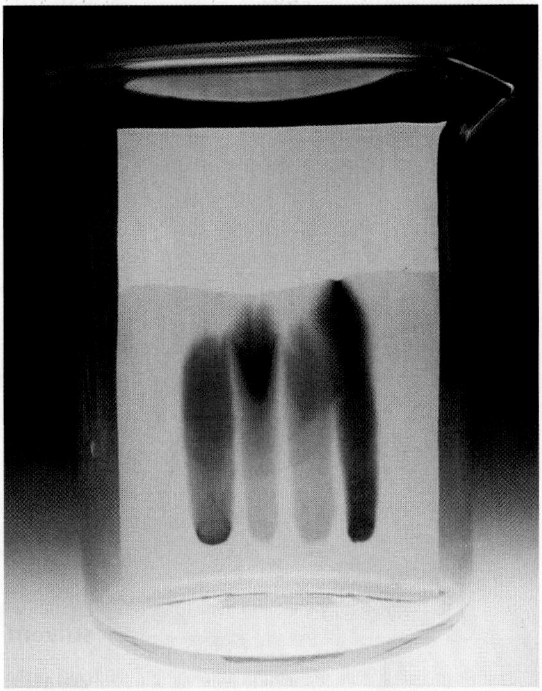

During chromatography, soluble substances travel up the filter paper when the end is dipped into a solvent such as water. Substances that are the most soluble travel the furthest. If a substance is not soluble in the solvent then it will not travel.

If the same conditions are used, the distance that a soluble substance travels up the paper is always the same. This allows substances to be identified. The **retardation factor** (R_f) is used to do this. It is calculated using the equation:

$$R_f = \frac{\textbf{Distance travelled by dye}}{\textbf{Distance travelled by solvent}}$$

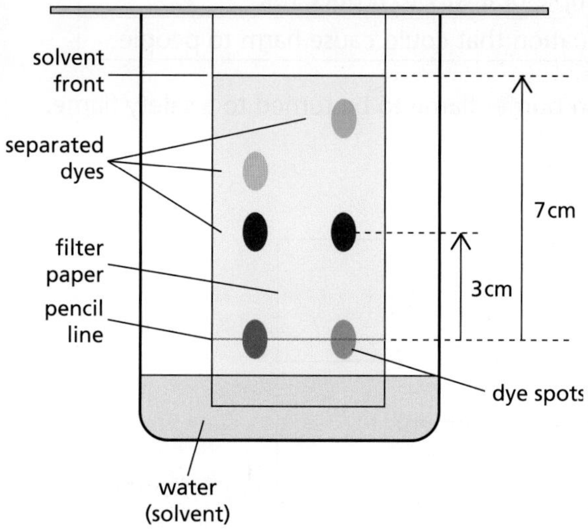

In all experiments, we gather data that needs to be evaluated. To evaluate data, we need to look at the **repeatability**, **reproducibility**, **accuracy** and **precision**. We also need to spot sources of error.

Random errors are caused by factors that can be difficult to control, such as a change in air temperature while taking readings. These errors are not predictable. Taking several measurements and calculating a mean can be used to reduce the effect of a random error.

Systematic errors cause readings to be consistently higher or lower than the true value. Carrying out many repeats will not deal with this type of error. A balance that reads 0.2 g more than the true value will do this every time it is used. It can be corrected by a process known as recalibration.

Key vocabulary	
accurate	very close to the true value
chromatogram	pattern of results obtained in chromatography
chromatography	a process used to separate a mixture of soluble substances
condense	the process of turning from a gas into a liquid
distillate	the pure liquid collected at the end of distillation
distillation	a process for separating liquids using heating and cooling
evidence	information gathered in a scientific way that supports or contradicts a conclusion
Liebig condenser	apparatus used for distillation
paper chromatography	a simple method of separating different inks or dyes
precise	when repeated readings of the same measurement give similar values
precision	how close together, or spread out, repeated measurements are
purify	make a substance pure or near to pure
random error	an error caused by changes that are difficult to control, such as a change in room temperature
repeatable	when the same person carries out repeat tests and the results are very similar
reproducible	when the experiment is carried out by a different person and they get similar results
retardation factor (Rf)	the distance a substance has travelled divided by the distance the solvent has travelled (in chromatography)
systematic error	an error caused by an inaccuracy with the measurement system; the error will be the same for every reading

8.1 Working safely in the laboratory

You are learning to:
- recognise and reduce risks when working in the laboratory
- name and be able to select appropriate equipment
- make and record accurate measurements
- evaluate data.

1 Link each key term to its meaning.

a hazard
b risk
c control measure
d safety goggles

i how likely something is to be harmful
ii how to reduce a risk
iii example of a way to reduce risk
iv a situation that could cause harm to people

2 The method in an experiment asks for a Bunsen burner flame to be turned to a safety flame. What colour would the safety flame be?

3 Match each hazard symbol to the risk it warns people of.

a 
b 
c 
d 

i corrosive
ii hazardous to the environment
iii health hazard
iv flammable

4 A student heats a solution using a Bunsen burner. He is wearing a lab coat and safety goggles.

a What are the potential hazards you can identify from this photograph?

b What can be done to reduce the risk of harm?

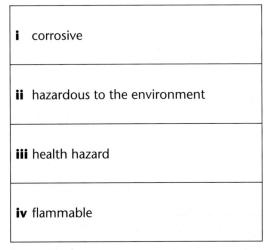

5 Complete the paragraph below about selecting an appropriate measuring cylinder for an experiment.

Measuring cylinders come in different sizes. You should select the size of measuring cylinder which is closest to the volume you will be measuring. This is because it allows the volume to be measured more __________.

Worked example

A student measured the water temperature in an experiment. They recorded their results in a table. How could the design of the student's results table be improved? Draw out your improved results table.

Water temperature	Time
50	1 min 30 secs
87	60 secs
100	0 secs

The top line in a results table should always include the heading and unit. The one in this table has no units. You should add these, using degrees Celsius (°C) for temperature and seconds (s) for time. The table also gives time in both minutes and seconds. Units should not be mixed like this, so you should convert all of the data to seconds. You can then remove the units from the lines of data in the table, as the unit will be shown on the top line instead. The independent variable should also be on the left of the table. In this example, the independent variable is time. Lastly, it would be better to measure the temperature of the water at regular time intervals, such as every 30 seconds. The student did not record a value at 30 seconds, so you will not show a data value for this time.

Here is an improved results table for the experiment:

Time (s)	Water temperature (°C)
0	100
30	
60	87
90	50

6 A student plans to measure the water temperature in a water bath during an experiment. They will record the temperature every 20 seconds for 2 minutes. The water temperature at the start of the experiment is 22 °C. Design a suitable results table.

7 A student plans an experiment to find out how quickly coffee powder dissolves in water.

a Name **three** pieces of measuring equipment that the student will need.

b The student extends their investigation to change the temperature of the water. What additional piece of measuring equipment will be needed?

c What will the student need to control in the experiment to find out which water temperature coffee powder dissolves fastest in?

8 In an experiment, two chemicals reacted to make a gas. A student tested whether changing the amount of one reactant would affect how long it took to collect 25 cm^3 of gas. Their results are shown below.

Amount of reactant (g)	Time to collect 25 cm^3 of gas (minutes)			
	Test 1	Test 2	Test 3	Test 4
1.0	2.0	2.3	2.1	
1.5	3.0	4.7	2.5	2.8

a Use the table of data to evaluate the quality of the data collected for 1.5 g of reactant. In your answer, think about precision, identify any anomalies and calculate a mean.

b The student used a timer to measure how long it took to collect the gas. The timer was stopped when the student noticed that 25 cm^3 of gas had been collected. Is this method likely to be a source of random or systematic error? Explain your answer.

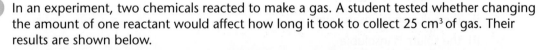

8.2 Mixtures

You are learning to:
- explain the terms solvent, solution, solute and soluble
- identify factors that affect dissolving
- recognise the differences between substances and use these differences to separate them
- separate an insoluble substance from a liquid using filtration
- separate a soluble substance from water using evaporation
- form crystals from solutions.

1 Name **three** pieces of equipment which would be needed to separate sand from sea water.

2 A student adds a vitamin C tablet to a glass of water. The solution goes cloudy at the start but then it becomes clear. What is happening?

a The vitamin tablet has reacted with the water.

b The vitamin tablet has dissolved.

c The vitamin tablet has disappeared.

3 Choose **two** statements that explain what happens during dissolving.

a The solvent reacts chemically with the solute to make a solution.

b The total mass of the solution is less than the total mass of the separate solute and solvent, because the solute has disappeared during dissolving.

c The solvent particles collide with the solute particles, which break up and spread throughout the solution.

d The total mass of the separate solute and solvent is the same as the total mass of the solution after dissolving.

4 A student measured out 2 g of blue copper sulfate crystals and added them to a beaker of water. The copper sulfate dissolved.

a How did the student know that the copper sulfate had dissolved?

b The student measured another 2 g of copper sulfate crystals and added them to the same beaker. The student noticed that not all the copper sulfate crystals dissolved this time. Which of the following describes this observation?

i the solution is saturated

ii the solution is unsaturated

iii the solute is insoluble

iv the solvent is insoluble

c What could the student do to increase the amount of copper sulfate that will dissolve?

5 Water goes through a multi-step treatment process before it can be used for drinking water. Insoluble particles are removed first. What process is used to do this?

a chlorination

b distillation

c evaporation

d filtration

6 A student rinsed their cup under the tap and left it to dry on a work surface. When the student moved the dry cup the next day, they noticed a white ring on the work surface.

a What happened to the water on the cup?

b Where did the white substance left on the work surface come from?

7 Iron and sulfur are mixed together.

a Why is it easy to separate iron and sulfur?

b After heating the mixture, iron sulfide is produced. Why is it difficult to separate iron and sulfur now?

8 A person used water to try and remove a stain from a carpet. This was unsuccessful. Ethanol was used instead and this worked. Explain why the stain was removed using ethanol but not with water.

9 The solubility curve shows the solubility of three substances in water at different temperatures. Use the solubility curve to answer the questions.

a How much sodium nitrate is dissolved in 100 g of water at 80 °C?

b A student is making a saturated solution of sodium nitrate. The water bath is set to 30 °C. How much sodium nitrate will the student need to add to 100 g of water?

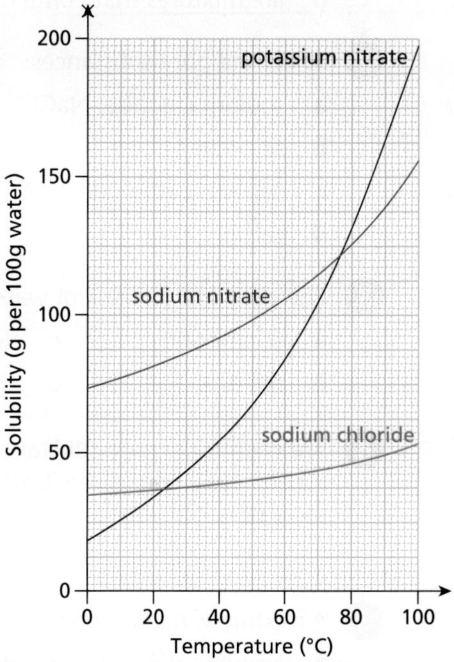

10 A student investigated the differences between substances. They wrapped three thermometers in cotton wool. The cotton wool for thermometer **A** was soaked in water. The cotton wool for thermometer **B** was soaked in ethanol. Thermometer **C** was set up as a control experiment. The readings on the thermometers were recorded for 10 minutes.

Time (minutes)	Temperature (°C)		
	A – water	B – ethanol	C – control
0	22	22	22
2	21	19	22
4	20	17	22
6	20	13	22
8	20	13	22
10	20	15	22

a What was the air temperature at the time of the experiment?

b Suggest what the control **C** for this experiment might be.

c Why did the temperatures reduce for thermometers **A** and **B**?

8.3 Pure substances

You are learning to:
- explain what is meant by a chemically pure substance
- identify pure substances.

1 Which statement correctly completes this sentence about pure substances?

Substances that are described as pure in chemistry…

a contain elements but not compounds.

b contain a single element or compound.

c are mixtures that have no impurities.

d are mixtures that contain only molecules.

2 Select the pure substances:

a sodium chloride, NaCl

b sea water

c calcium carbonate, $CaCO_3$

d carbon, C

3 The chemical formula of water is H_2O. Which key word describes water?

a compound **c** element

b mixture **d** alloy

4 Are chemically pure substances (such as zinc) and naturally pure substances (such as the juice squeezed from a fresh orange) the same? Explain your answer.

5 A mixture is made from more than one element or compound. It can also be described as:

a impure **c** distillate

b pure **d** residue

6 Pure ethanol has a boiling point of 78 °C.

At what temperature will ethanol start to boil when it is heated?

a approximately 75 °C **c** 78 °C

b over 78 °C **d** approximately 72 °C

7 Pure aluminium has a melting point of 660 °C. If molten (liquid) aluminium is allowed to cool it will become a solid. At what temperature does molten aluminium become a solid when it cools?

a 650 °C **c** 690 °C

b 660 °C **d** 25 °C (room temperature)

8 What information would you need to know to find out if a chemically pure substance is made from an element or a compound? Choose **one** answer and explain how it would show whether the substance was an element or compound.

a the mass of the substance

b the density of the substance

c the chemical formula of the substance

d the melting point of the substance

9 It is expected from secondary data that a particular liquid will boil at 76 °C, but during an experiment it is found to boil at 79 °C. Give a reason why this might occur.

Worked example

Gold can be mixed with other metals such as copper or silver to form a mixture called an alloy. This is easier to work with and less expensive than pure gold. It is used to make jewellery. The purity of the gold is measured in karats. Pure gold is 24 karats.

The percentage of gold in jewellery can be found from this equation:

percentage of gold = (number of karats ÷ karats in pure gold) × 100

What percentage of gold is present in a 22 karat gold bracelet? Give your answer to 2 decimal places.

You are told that 24 karat gold is pure, so it is 100% gold. Anything less than 24 karat gold is a mixture and impure. You can use the equation to calculate the percentage of gold present in the 22 karat gold bracelet:

percentage of gold = (22 ÷ 24) × 100 = 91.6666....

You have been asked to give your answer to two decimal places, so the correct answer is 91.67%

(22 ÷ 24) × 100 = 91.67% (to 2 decimal places)

10 Complete the table to show the percentage of gold present in 18 karat and 9 karat gold.

karat	Amount of gold present (%)
24	100
22	91.67
18	
9	

11 The finest silver is known in industry as pure silver. It contains 99.9% silver and is used to make bullion bars. It is too soft to use in jewellery. Sterling silver is often used instead. This is an alloy made from 92.5% silver plus other metals. Sterling silver jewellery is stamped 925. Scandinavian silver is also an alloy. It is given the stamp 830.

a Is the silver used in bullion bars a pure substance? Explain your answer.

b Suggest the percentage of silver and other metals in Scandinavian silver. Compare its purity with sterling silver.

8.4 Distillation

You are learning to:

- use distillation to separate substances
- explain why distillation can purify substances.

1 Choose **two** correct words from the list below to complete this sentence.

heating **cooling** **freezing** **melting**

Distillation involves two processes: ___________ and ____________.

2 Decide on the correct word to complete the paragraph.

Spectacles often steam up when a person enters a warm room. This is because water vapour has ______________ on the glass.

3 The diagram shows the distillation of sea water.

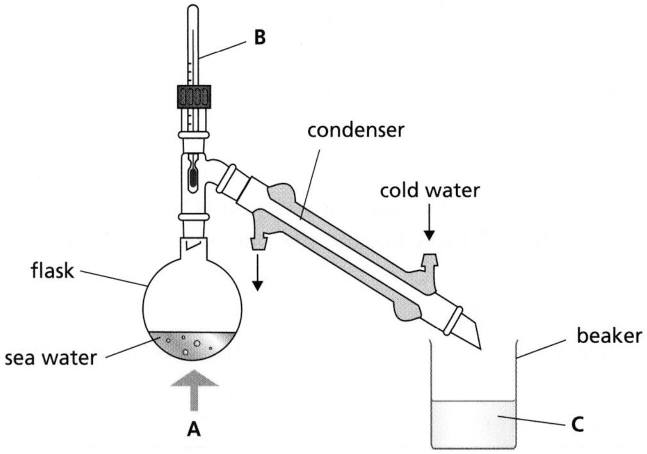

a Complete the labels **A–C** on the diagram of the distillation apparatus.

b Describe the function that part **B** performs in distillation.

c Which is the correct order of the processes that occur in the distillation of sea water?

i melting, boiling, condensing

ii boiling, condensation, evaporation

iii boiling, evaporation, condensation

iv melting, evaporation, condensation

4 A teacher set up a distillation experiment with some water and dark blue water-soluble ink. The ink has a higher boiling point than water.

a What colour is the distillate?

b Give the name of the pure liquid distillate.

c What test could you do to prove your answer to **b**?

d The teacher removed the heat from the round-bottomed flask before all the distillate had been collected. Why?

5 Our clothes can become stained with different substances. Not all stains are soluble in water. Dry cleaners use solvents other than water to wash clothes. Clothes are washed in the liquid solvent at 30 °C. They are then tumble dried at 60 °C.

a Suggest how the solvent is removed from the clothing during the dry-cleaning process.

b The solvents used in dry cleaning can be toxic. How could the solvent be collected after tumble drying so it is not released into the atmosphere?

6 Wine is a mixture that contains about 12% alcohol. The rest is mostly water. The alcohol in wine is called ethanol. It has a boiling point of 78 °C.

a Why is it **not** possible to boil wine to reduce the amount of water present and increase the alcohol content by evaporation?

b What method could be used to increase the alcohol content of wine?

7 The diagram represents particles in a gas, a solid and a liquid. The letters represent a change in state.

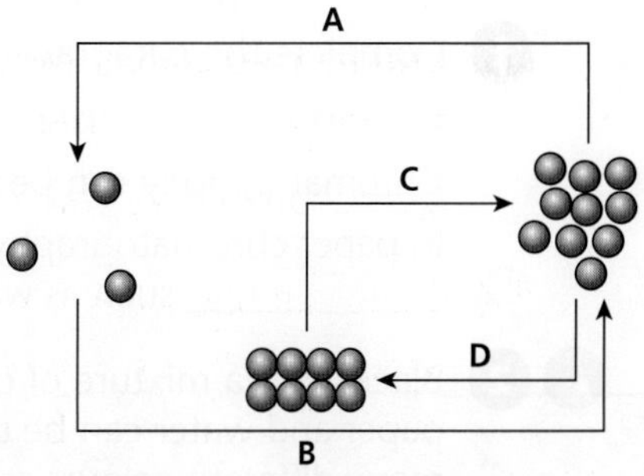

a Which process of changing state is represented by each letter?

b During distillation, which letter would occur in the round-bottomed flask? Use the diagram in question 3 to help you.

c During distillation, which letter would occur in the condenser? Use the diagram in question 3 to help you.

8 The following apparatus was used to obtain pure water from sea water.

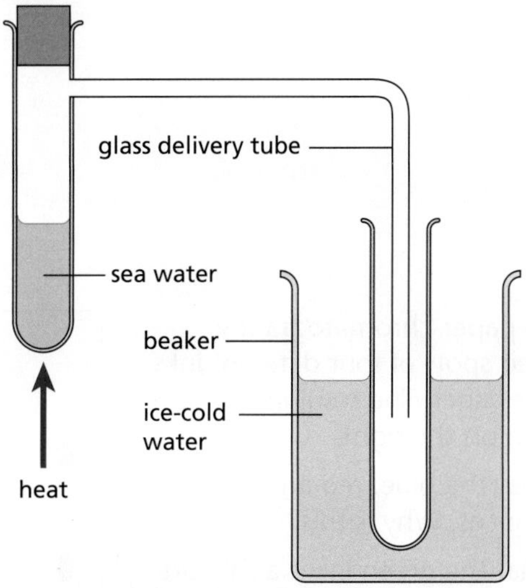

a Why was the beaker filled with ice cold water?

b Explain how this method works.

c What is this technique called?

d What might occur if hot water was used in the beaker instead of ice-cold water?

9 Use the diagram in question 3 to help answer this question.

a Which diagram below represents a cross-section through the condenser? Explain your choice.

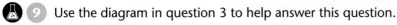

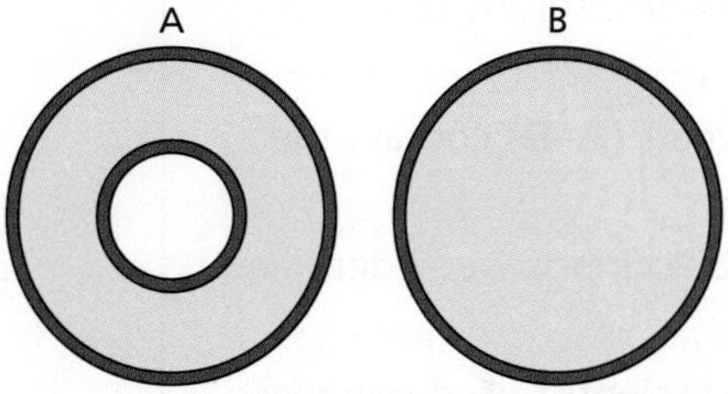

b What might happen if cold water entered the condenser at the top of the tube instead of the bottom?

8.5 Chromatography

You are learning to:
- use chromatography to separate dyes
- use chromatography to identify unknown substances.

1 Complete the paragraph using words from the list below.

insoluble **soluble** **solute** **solvent** **solution**

Chromatography can be used to separate the substances in a mixture.

In paper chromatography, __________ substances are carried up filter paper by a ____________ such as water.

2 Black ink is a mixture of colours. The diagram shows how filter paper and water can be used to separate these colours. How many different colours are found in this ink?

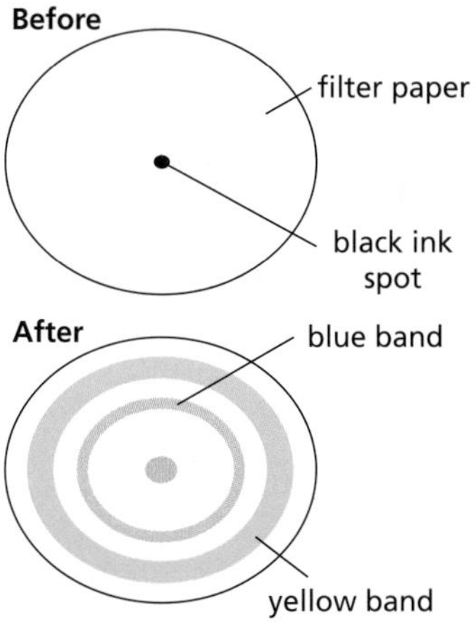

3 A student carried out a paper chromatography experiment. They placed spots of four different inks on a pencil line on filter paper. The resulting chromatogram is shown on the right.

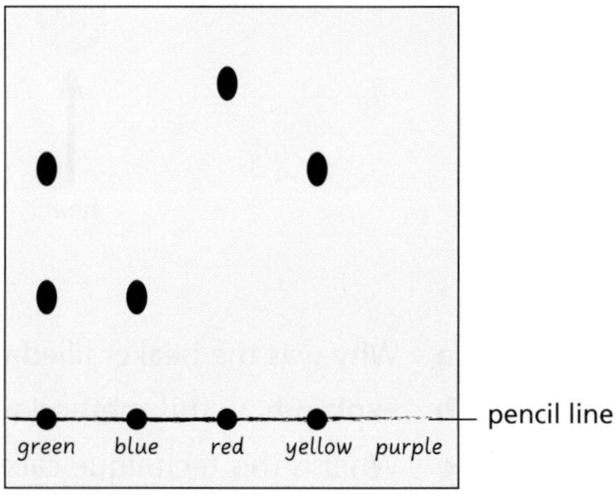

a The results show that the blue, red and yellow inks are pure substances. Why is this?

b The results show that the green ink is a mixture of other colours. Which **two** colours does the green ink contain?

c The student has a purple ink that contains a dissolved mixture of red and blue dye. Complete the chromatogram to predict the result for the purple ink.

d Why was the line on the filter paper drawn in pencil?

4 A food scientist uses chromatography to test several brands of sweets for a banned food colouring. A diagram of their results is shown on the right.

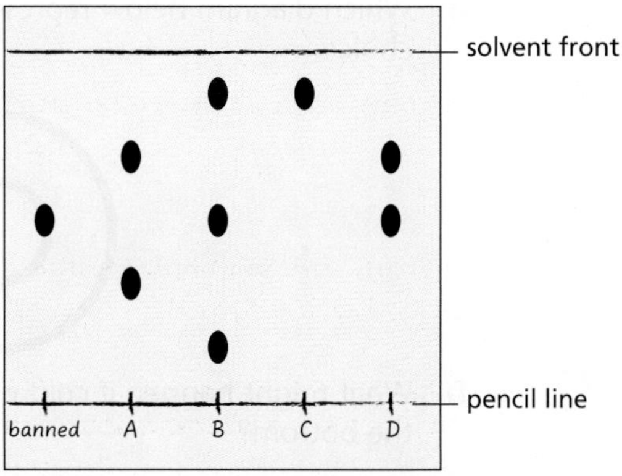

a Which brand(s) of sweets (**A**–**D**) contain the banned substance?

b How many different colourings were identified in the sweets?

c Suggest why the food scientist used one piece of filter paper for all the sweets rather than do each one separately.

5 The results of a chromatography experiment are shown below.

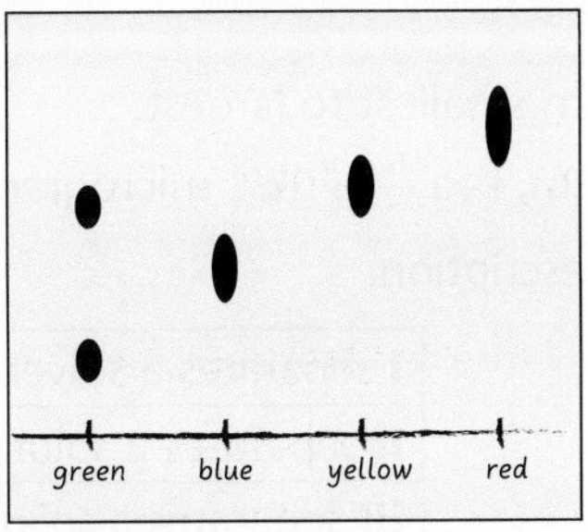

Complete the sentences.

The ____**i**____ colour is a mixture of dyes.

All of the other colours are ____**ii**____ substances.

The ____**iii**____ colour was the most soluble in the solvent used.

Worked example

Use the equation provided to calculate the retardation factor (R_f) for the blue dye in this chromatogram.

$$R_f = \frac{\textbf{Distance travelled by dye}}{\textbf{Distance travelled by solvent}}$$

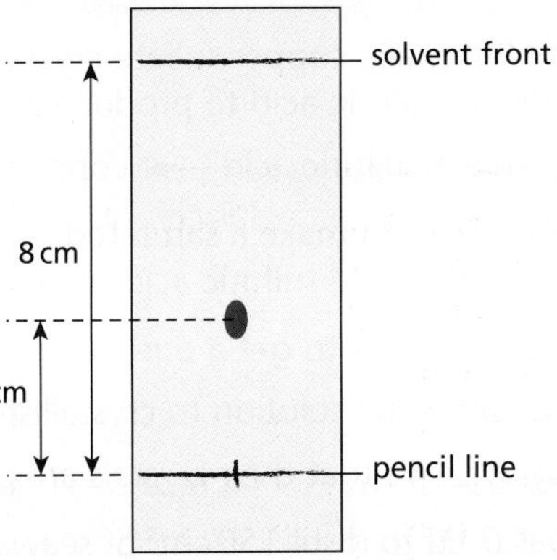

The distance moved by the blue dye from the pencil line where the spot was added, to the centre of the spot obtained after the solvent has run up the filter paper, is 3 cm. The distance the solvent front has travelled from the pencil line to the top of the solvent front is 8 cm. Use the equation provided to calculate the R_f value.

$R_f = 3 \div 8 = 0.375$

6 A red dye is separated into blue and purple dyes using paper chromatography. The blue dye travels 43 mm up the filter paper and the purple dye travels 26 mm. The solvent front is 53 mm. Calculate the retardation factor (R_f) for:

a the blue dye **b** the purple dye.

7 A scientist set up a chromatography experiment to identify the different pigments in a species of plant. The pigments did not travel up the filter paper. Explain why this occurred and suggest a change that the scientist could make.

8 Some of the solvents used in chromatography can be volatile and flammable. Volatile chemicals can be hazardous if they are inhaled. Suggest how the hazards from these solvents can be reduced when carrying out chromatography.

Maths and practical skills

1 Arrange the units in order from smallest to largest.

a gram, g **b** milligram, mg **c** microgram, µg **d** kilogram, kg

2 Match each key word to its description.

a filtration
b crystallisation
c distillation
d chromatography

i separates a solvent from a solution
ii separates a soluble solid from a solution
iii separates a solid from a liquid
iv separates different substances dissolved in a liquid

3 **a** Label the apparatus used to separate an insoluble solid from a liquid using the words provided.

filter paper **filter funnel** **boiling tube** **residue** **filtrate**

b Describe how to place item **A** into item **C**.

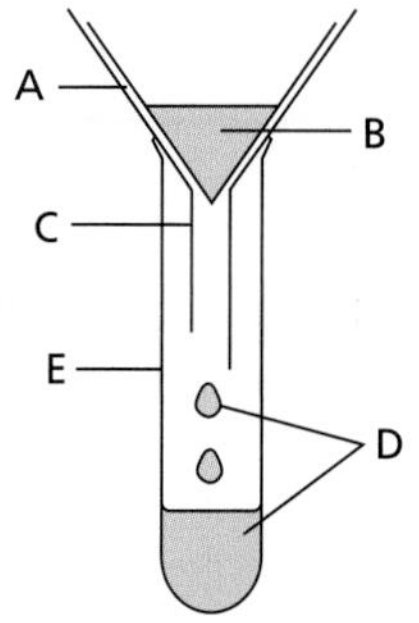

4 A student plans a method to make copper sulfate crystals. They know that black copper oxide powder will react with dilute sulfuric acid to produce a clear blue copper sulfate solution.

copper oxide + sulfuric acid ⟶ copper sulfate + water

The student's teacher tells them to make a saturated solution, so the student plans to add black copper oxide powder to dilute sulfuric acid until no more will react.

a What must the student do next to get a pure solution of clear blue copper sulfate?

b The student wants to allow the solution to crystallise slowly. How should they do this?

c How could the student prove that their crystals are pure?

5 The apparatus below was used to distil 150 cm^3 of seawater.

The cold water entered the condenser at 12 °C from the tap. The water leaves the condenser at point X.

a Predict the temperature at X. Choose from the list below:

i 12 °C **iii** 5 °C

ii 100 °C **iv** 45 °C

b Explain your answer to part **a**.

c What is the temperature reading on the thermometer when the sea water is boiling?

d Describe **two** ways the water vapour entering the condenser will be different from when it leaves the condenser.

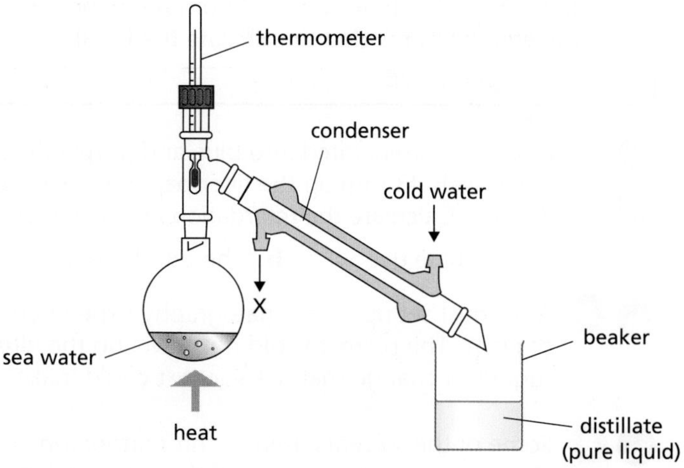

Worked example

A student uses chromatography to separate the pigments in a solution. Four pigments are seen on the chromatogram. The student calculates the R_f values using the equation below.

$$R_f = \frac{\textbf{Distance travelled by dye}}{\textbf{Distance travelled by solvent}}$$

The student records their results in a table, but they forget to note down how far the pigment travelled. Use the equation to work out the distance travelled by pigment **X**.

Pigment	R_f value	Distance travelled by the solvent (cm)	Distance travelled by the pigment (cm)
X	0.2	10.0	

To find the distance travelled by the pigment, you must rearrange the equation given. To do this you multiply both sides of the equation by the distance travelled by the solvent. That gives you this equation:

distance travelled by the dye = R_f × distance travelled by the solvent front

Now you need to substitute the values from the table into the equation.

distance travelled by dye = 0.2 × 10 = 2.0 cm

2.0 cm

6 Daffodil petals contain coloured pigments. A student wanted to investigate how many different pigments were present in one species of daffodil plant. The student ground a handful of fresh petals with some sand to form a paste. A solvent was added to the petal and sand paste.

a Which separating technique should the student use to separate the solution of pigments from the petal and sand paste?

b Use the equation for R_f to find the distance travelled by the three pigments in the table below.

Pigment	R_f value	Distance travelled by the solvent (cm)	Distance travelled by the dye (cm)
A	0.8	12.0	
B	0.75	9.2	
C	0.4	9.6	

c The student finds a trusted resource that lists the names of plant pigments along with their R_f values. The solvent used to find these R_f values is not the same as the solvent used by the student. Can the student use the resource to name the pigments in their experiment? Explain your answer.

9 Periodic Table road map

Where are you in your learning journey and where are you aiming to be?

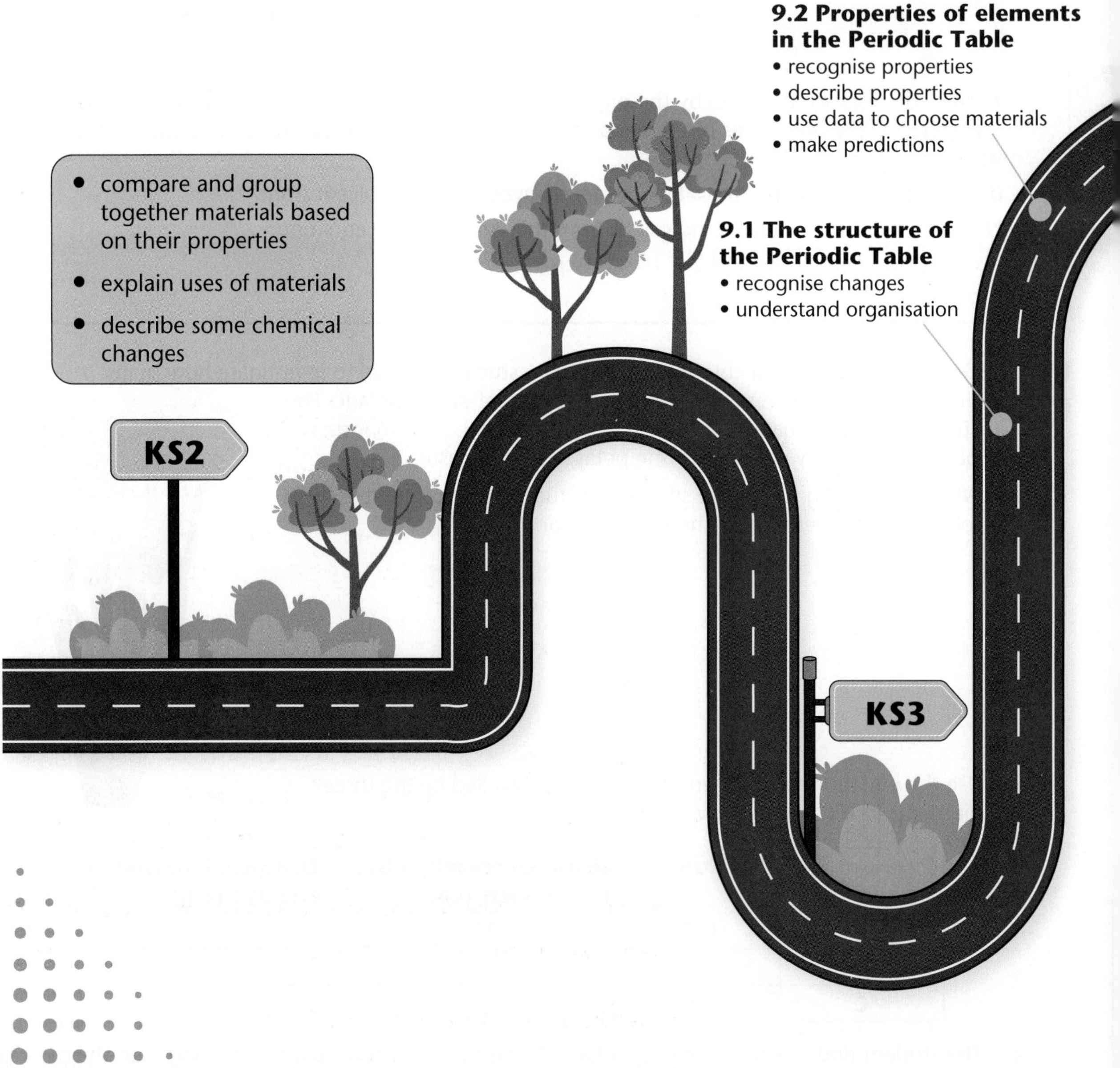

9.3 Reactions of elements and compounds

- recognise and represent elements and compounds
- understand conservation of mass
- interpret ratios
- balance equations

9.4 Using the Periodic Table

- understand reactions
- understand patterns
- recognise symbols and formulas

- development of the Periodic Table
- the Periodic Table
- metals and non-metals
- Group 0
- Group 1
- Group 7
- chemical bonds
- conservation of mass and balanced chemical equations

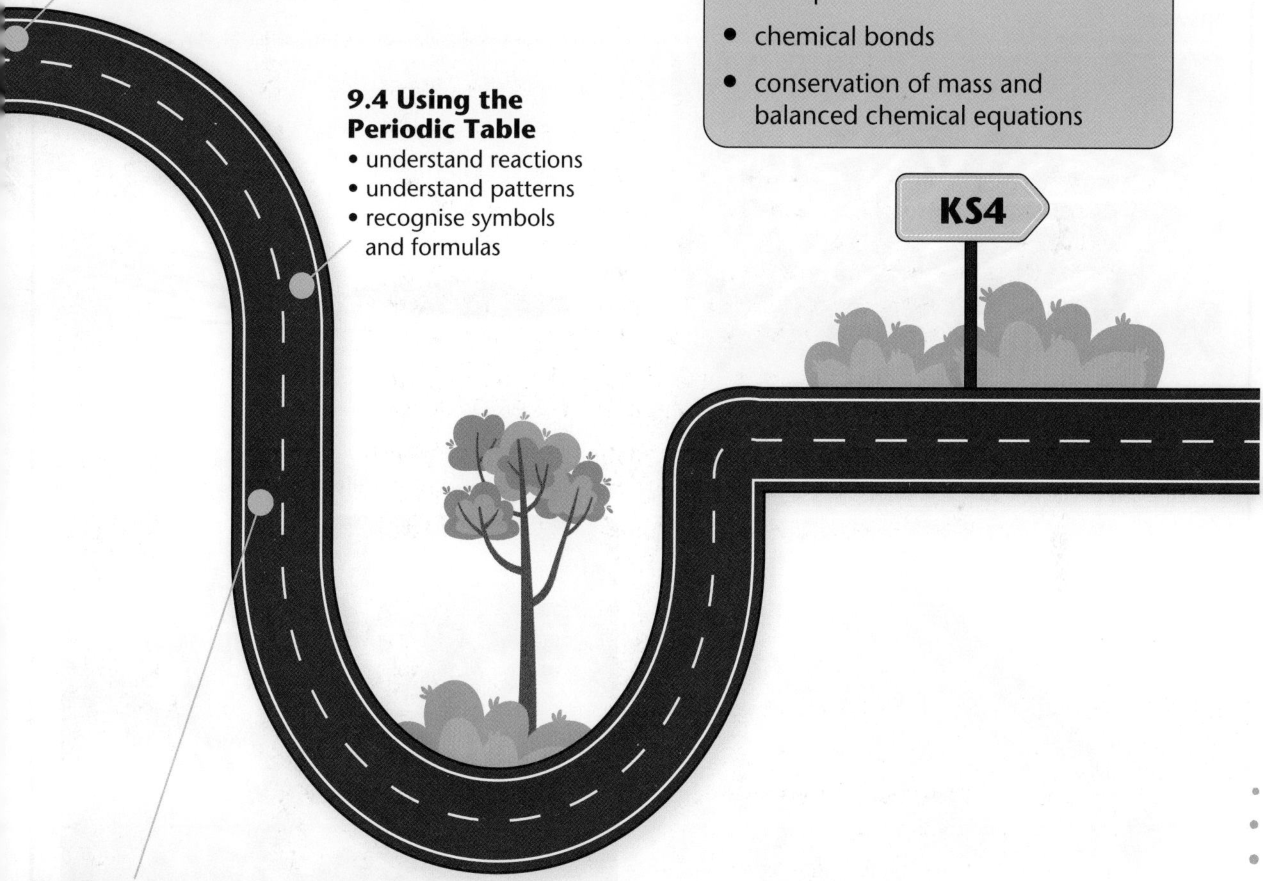

Maths and practical skills

- describing the development of scientific methods and theories over time
- interpreting observations and data
- using SI units and chemical names and symbols
- making scientific predictions

9 Periodic Table

Elements are the building blocks of every substance we know. Elements can be solids, liquids or gases. They can be metals, non-metals or have characteristics which are in between. Each element is unique, with its own properties. The Periodic Table is a way of organising all the known chemical elements so that similar elements are grouped together. This can help us predict the chemical reactions of elements. Elements can join together in many ways to produce an amazing range of different substances.

Look at the following materials. Which of these do you think will stick to a magnet? Explain your answer.

iron nail

graphite pencil

aluminium foil

nickel beads

Which of these materials can conduct electricity?

Using your science skills

Could you be a physical metallurgist?

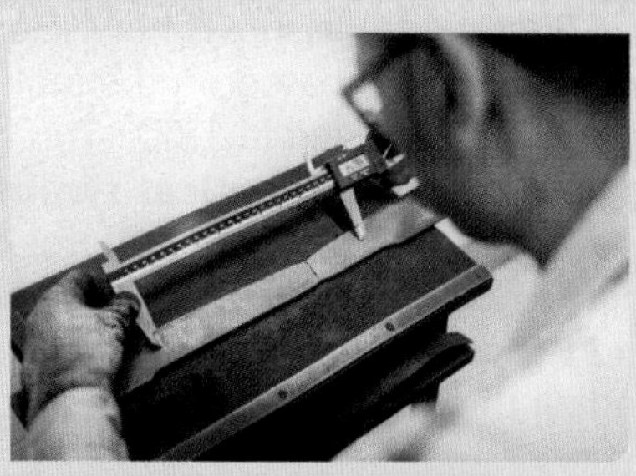

As a **physical metallurgist** you monitor the behaviour of metals in different conditions and as they encounter changes to help choose an appropriate metal for a specific function. You might investigate accidents where it is suspected the cause may be related to a failure in the structure of the metal, for example, in car crashes.

You might have a very important role in the design of structures such as buildings and bridges. When metals are heated, they expand, when cooled they contract. This means that a bridge containing metal will increase and decrease in size during the day or during different seasons of the year. It is important that the bridge can withstand these differences in temperature, so that it does not crack, buckle or break.

Electrical engineers design, build and maintain power systems, electronics and communication equipment. They need to understand materials and their ability to conduct electricity. They work in various locations, such as production plants, workshops, offices, laboratories and factories. They develop and test models, estimate costs and timescales, and research suitable solutions to problems such as increasing the use of renewable energy sources. Electrical engineers research suitable, efficient and sustainable technologies to enhance the overall performance of the designed electrical system.

Automotive engineers use their knowledge of metals and their structure and properties to design attractive, functional cars. By using lightweight metals such as aluminium, automotive engineers can reduce the amount of fuel used by the car when driving.

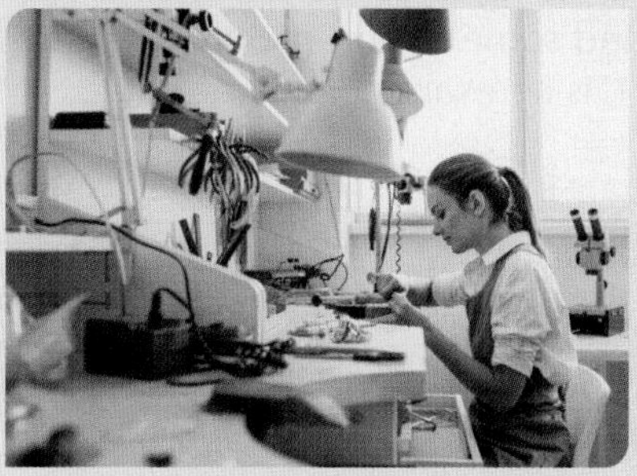

Jewellery designers use their knowledge of metals to design and make jewellery. They make use of non-toxic metals such as gold, silver and platinum and precious stones or enamel decorations. They produce designs for mass production or bespoke designs for an individual client.

A **geochemist** needs to have a detailed understanding of the Periodic Table. They investigate the amount and distribution of chemical elements in rocks and minerals and study the movement of these elements into soil and water systems. The research carried out by geochemists can help companies to find sources of oil and useful minerals, improve water quality and clean up toxic waste sites.

Knowledge organiser

The Periodic Table shows how scientific ideas develop over time. The modern Periodic Table is based on the table first published by Dmitri Mendeleev in 1869 and refined in 1871. This contained 64 known elements, each represented by a **chemical symbol**. Mendeleev put the elements in order of atomic mass and used patterns in their chemical properties to arrange them into rows and columns. He was sure that there were missing elements and left gaps for them. The modern Periodic Table contains 118 elements, and all the gaps in Mendeleev's table have been filled.

Reihen	Gruppo I. — R^{2}O	Gruppo II. — RO	Gruppo III. — R^{2}O^3	Gruppe IV. RH^4 RO^2	Gruppe V. RH^3 R^{2}O^5	Gruppe VI. RH^2 RO^3	Gruppe VII. RH R^{2}O^7	Gruppo VIII. — RO^4
1	H=1							
2	Li=7	Be=9,4	B=11	C=12	N=14	O=16	F=19	
3	Na=23	Mg=24	Al=27,3	Si=28	P=31	S=32	Cl=35,5	
4	K=39	Ca=40	—=44	Ti=48	V=51	Cr=52	Mn=55	Fe=56, Co=59, Ni=59, Cu=63.
5	(Cu=63)	Zn=65	—=68	—=72	As=75	Se=78	Br=80	
6	Rb=85	Sr=87	?Yt=88	Zr=90	Nb=94	Mo=96	—=100	Ru=104, Rh=104, Pd=106, Ag=108.
7	(Ag=108)	Cd=112	In=113	Sn=118	Sb=122	Te=125	J=127	
8	Cs=133	Ba=137	?Di=138	?Ce=140	—	—	—	— — — —
9	(—)	—	—	—	—	—	—	
10	—	—	?Er=178	?La=180	Ta=182	W=184	—	Os=195, Ir=197, Pt=198, Au=199.
11	(Au=199)	Hg=200	Tl=204	Pb=207	Bi=208	—	—	
12	—	—	—	Th=231	—	U=240	—	— — — —

Each element in the Periodic Table has a unique number, called its **atomic number**. This number increases from left to right across each period. Each element also has an **atomic mass**.

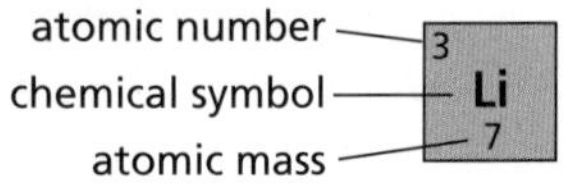

Elements are represented by their chemical symbols. The symbols can be obvious. For example, H represents hydrogen. Sometimes the symbols can be misleading, such as Cu for copper.

The Periodic Table is arranged in rows called **periods** and columns called **groups**. Groups are families of elements with similar physical and chemical properties. **Metals** are found on the left of the table and **non-metals** (except hydrogen, H) on the right. Some elements are **metalloids**. These are elements that have some properties of metals and some of non-metals. They are found between metals and non-metals in the Periodic Table; silicon, Si, is an example of a metalloid.

Key

- reactive metals
- transition metals
- poor metals
- metalloids
- non-metals
- noble gases

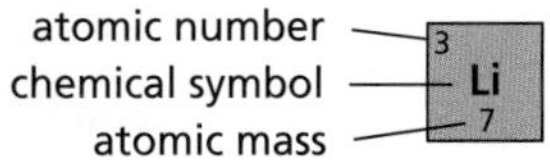

group number

period number	1	2											3	4	5	6	7	0
1	1 H 1																	2 He 4
2	3 Li 7	4 Be 9											5 B 11	6 C 12	7 N 14	8 O 16	9 F 19	10 Ne 20
3	11 Na 23	12 Mg 24											13 Al 27	14 Si 28	15 P 31	16 S 32	17 Cl 35.5	18 Ar 40
4	19 K 39	20 Ca 40	21 Sc 45	22 Ti 48	23 V 51	24 Cr 52	25 Mn 55	26 Fe 56	27 Co 59	28 Ni 59	29 Cu 64	30 Zn 65	31 Ga 70	32 Ge 73	33 As 75	34 Se 79	35 Br 80	36 Kr 84
5	37 Rb 85.5	38 Sr 88	39 Y 89	40 Zr 91	41 Nb 93	42 Mo 96	43 Tc 98	44 Ru 101	45 Rh 103	46 Pd 106	47 Ag 108	48 Cd 112	49 In 115	50 Sn 119	51 Sb 122	52 Te 128	53 I 127	54 Xe 131
6	55 Cs 133	56 Ba 137		72 Hf 178.5	73 Ta 181	74 W 184	75 Re 186	76 Os 190	77 Ir 192	78 Pt 195	79 Au 197	80 Hg 201	81 Tl 204	82 Pb 207	83 Bi 209	84 Po 209	85 At 210	86 Rn 222
7	87 Fr 223	88 Ra 226		104 Rf 265	105 Db 268	106 Sg 271	107 Bh 267	108 Hs 277	109 Mt 276	110 Ds 281	111 Rg 280	112 Cn 285	113 Uut 284	114 Fl 289	115 Uup 288	116 Lv 293	117 Uus 294	118 Uuo 294

57 La 139	58 Ce 140	59 Pr 141	60 Nd 144	61 Pm 145	62 Sm 150	63 Eu 152	64 Gd 157	65 Tb 159	66 Dy 162	67 Ho 165	68 Er 167	69 Tm 169	70 Yb 173	71 Lu 175
89 Ac 227	90 Th 232	91 Pa 231	92 U 238	93 Np 237	94 Pu 244	95 Am 244	96 Cm 247	97 Bk 247	98 Cf 251	99 Es 252	100 Fm 257	101 Md 258	102 No 259	103 Lr 262

- the elements in Group 0 are all unreactive gases
- the elements in Group 1 are all reactive metals and must be stored under oil to keep air and water away from them; they become more reactive further down the group
- the elements in Group 7 are all non-metals; they become more reactive further up the group; some are used to kill bacteria due to their chemical properties.

Metals have many useful physical properties. They are usually strong, shiny, good conductors of heat and electricity, and have high melting points. Iron, nickel and cobalt are the only metals that are **magnetic**.

a Metals are **ductile**, which means they can be stretched into wires

b Metals are **malleable**, which means they can be bent, rolled, hammered and shaped without them breaking

c Most metals are **sonorous**, which means they making a ringing sound when hit and can be used in musical instruments

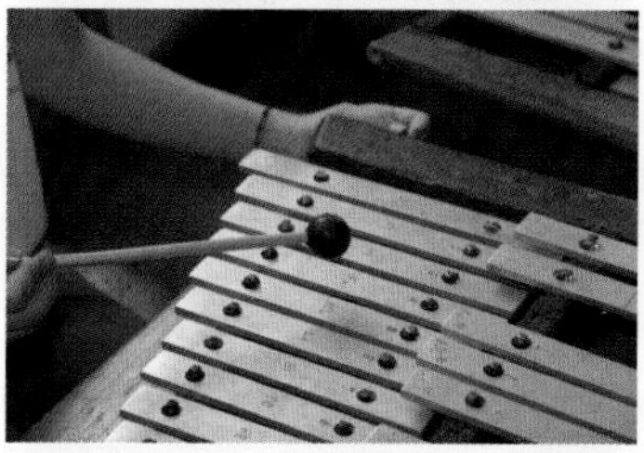

Non-metals are not shiny or strong. Most are unreactive and are gases at room temperature. They are very poor conductors of heat and electricity, and have lower **densities** than metals.

Some elements can be **toxic,** for example, mercury. Some elements are very reactive, for example sodium, so are unsuitable for some uses, such as, jewellery. Some elements are **radioactive**, for example, polonium and uranium, which means they emit nuclear radiation that can cause damage to living cells; however, they can be used to produce energy in nuclear power stations and to identify and treat cancer.

Key vocabulary	
atomic mass	the mass of one atom of an element
atomic number	the number of an element in the Periodic Table
chemical symbol	an abbreviation used to represent an element
density	the mass of a material per unit volume
ductile	can be stretched out into a thin wire
element	a substance made of only one type of atom
group	a vertical column of elements in the Periodic Table with similar chemical and physical properties
halogen	a non-metal in Group 7 of the Periodic Table
magnetic	produces a magnetic field
malleable	can be bent without breaking
metal	an element that can conduct electricity and heat; usually shiny and strong
metalloid	an element that has properties of metals and non-metals
noble gas	an unreactive gas in Group 0 of the Periodic Table
non-metal	an element that does not conduct electricity or heat; usually dull in solid form, but are often gases at room temperature
period	a row in the Periodic Table
Periodic Table	a table of all the elements in the universe arranged in order of atomic number
radioactive	emits nuclear radiation
sonorous	makes a ringing sound when hit
toxic	poisonous
transition metal	a metal element in the middle of the Periodic Table
trend	the general direction of data, such as an overall increase or decrease

When different elements combine, they form new substances called **compounds**. Elements and compounds can take part in **chemical reactions**, in which new substances are made.

Sodium is a metal that can react with the non-metal chlorine to make a new substance called sodium chloride. Sodium chloride is the chemical name for table salt. Sodium and chlorine are elements and sodium chloride is a compound. This chemical reaction can be represented using a word **equation**:

sodium + chlorine → sodium chloride
REACTANTS PRODUCT

The **reactants** are the substances that you start with and the new substances that are made are called the **products**. The products often look very different from the reactants, although this is not always the case.

Sodium **reactant**	Chlorine **reactant**	Sodium chloride **product**
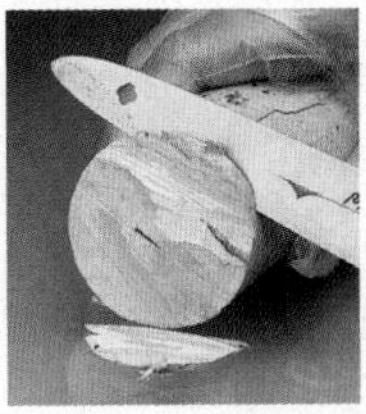		

A chemical reaction involves atoms being rearranged and chemically joined to each other. We can represent atoms as circles in diagrams or by using chemical symbols and **chemical formulae**. For example, carbon and oxygen are two non-metal elements that react to make carbon dioxide.

carbon + oxygen ⟶ carbon dioxide

$C + O_2 \longrightarrow CO_2$

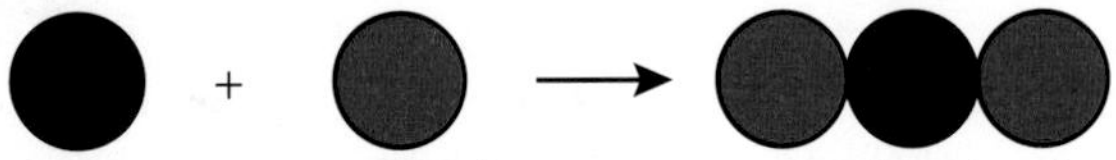

1 atom of carbon + 1 molecule of oxygen ⟶ 1 molecule of carbon dioxide

The name of a chemical compound can sometimes help us to interpret the formula. The prefix 'mono-' means 'one' and 'di-' means 'two'. 'Carbon dioxide' means that there are two oxygen atoms for every carbon atom. We do not put the number one in chemical formulae, so the chemical formula of carbon dioxide is CO_2.

Non-metals react with oxygen to form oxides that are **acidic**. Sulfur and nitrogen are non-metals and react with oxygen to produce sulfur dioxide and nitrogen oxides. These are often released into the atmosphere as waste from industrial processes. Sulfur dioxide and nitrogen oxides dissolve in rainwater to form **acid rain**, which causes problems such as damage to forests, lakes and buildings.

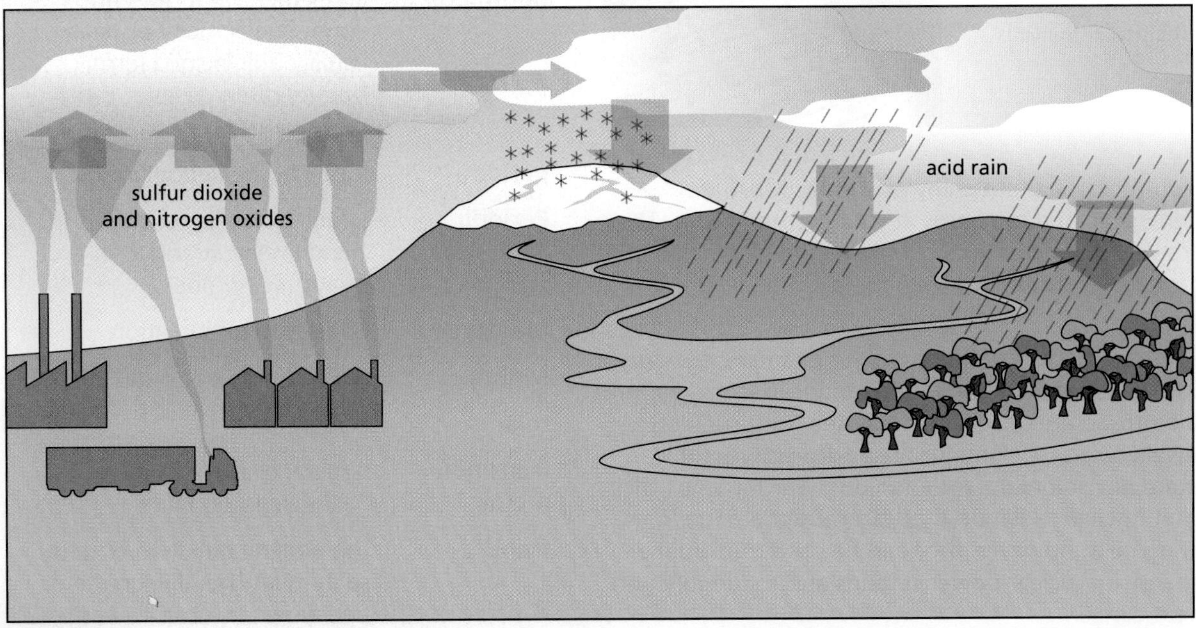

No atoms are lost or made in a chemical reaction. Two atoms of copper react with two atoms of oxygen to make two units of copper oxide. The number of atoms of each element must be the same on both sides of an equation – this is called a balanced equation.

$2Cu + O_2 \rightarrow 2CuO$

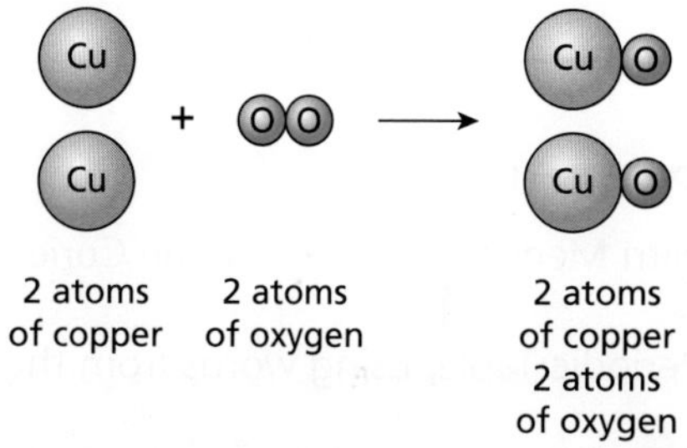

When the numbers of atoms are balanced on each side of an equation then the mass will also be balanced. The law of **conservation of mass** states that mass is never lost or gained during a chemical reaction. Zinc and oxygen react to make zinc oxide. The total mass of the reactants is exactly the same as the mass of the new products.

zinc	+	oxygen	→	zinc oxide
64g	+	16 g	→	64 + 16 = 80g

Reactants 80g — Product 80g

Patterns in the reactions and properties of elements allow us to predict how other elements will behave if we know something about them, such as their location in the Periodic Table, or whether they are a metal or non-metal.

Most metals react with oxygen to form a **base**. A base is a substance that neutralises an acid to produce a salt and water. Bases are usually **metal oxides**, metal hydroxides or metal carbonates.

Copper will react with oxygen to form copper oxide. Copper oxide is a metal base which is insoluble in water. A base that can dissolve in water is known as an **alkali**. Sodium hydroxide is soluble in water. It is a base and an alkali. Sodium hydroxide is used to make soap, paper and dyes, and is used in household products to clear drains and clean ovens. Alkalis (including sodium hydroxide) can be very corrosive and can cause burns.

Key vocabulary

acid	a substance that has a pH lower than 7
acid rain	rainwater that is made acidic by pollutant gases such as sulfur dioxide
alkali	a base that is soluble in water; has a pH above 7
base	a substance that will neutralise an acid
chemical formula	chemical symbols and numbers that show how many atoms of which elements are found in a molecule of an element or compound
chemical reaction	a process in which one or more substances are changed into others, by the rearrangement of their atoms
compound	atoms of more than one element chemically bonded together
conservation of mass	the total mass does not change during physical changes or chemical reactions
equation (chemical)	a chemical reaction written in terms of its reactants and products
indicator	a chemical that is a different colour in an alkali and in an acid; used to identify whether an unknown solution is acidic or alkaline
metal oxide	the product of a reaction between a metal and oxygen, for example, copper oxide; it is a base
non-metal oxide	the product of a reaction between a non-metal and oxygen; it is an acid e.g. carbon dioxide
pH	a scale that shows how acidic or alkaline a substance is, using numbers from 1 to 14
product	(of a chemical reaction) a substance made in a chemical reaction
reactant	a starting substance in a chemical reaction

9.1 The structure of the Periodic Table

You are learning to:
- recognise that the Periodic Table has changed over time
- understand how the modern Periodic Table is organised.

1 Which scientist developed the basis of the modern Periodic Table?

a Charles Darwin **b** Albert Einstein **c** Dmitri Mendeleev **d** Marie Curie

2 Complete this sentence about the structure of the Periodic Table, using words from the following list.

lines **elements** **periods** **groups**

In the Periodic Table, rows are called ___**i**___ and columns are called ___**ii**___.

3 Why is water not listed on the Periodic Table?

4 How is the modern Periodic Table arranged?

a by increasing atomic mass

b by increasing atomic number

c by increasing size of atoms

d in alphabetical order

group number

Key: reactive metals; transition metals; poor metals; metalloids; non-metals; noble gases

atomic number — 3; chemical symbol — Li; atomic mass — 7

period number	1	2											3	4	5	6	7	0
1	1 H 1																	2 He 4
2	3 Li 7	4 Be 9											5 B 11	6 C 12	7 N 14	8 O 16	9 F 19	10 Ne 20
3	11 Na 23	12 Mg 24											13 Al 27	14 Si 28	15 P 31	16 S 32	17 Cl 35.5	18 Ar 40
4	19 K 39	20 Ca 40	21 Sc 45	22 Ti 48	23 V 51	24 Cr 52	25 Mn 55	26 Fe 56	27 Co 59	28 Ni 59	29 Cu 64	30 Zn 65	31 Ga 70	32 Ge 73	33 As 75	34 Se 79	35 Br 80	36 Kr 84
5	37 Rb 85.5	38 Sr 88	39 Y 89	40 Zr 91	41 Nb 93	42 Mo 96	43 Tc 98	44 Ru 101	45 Rh 103	46 Pd 106	47 Ag 108	48 Cd 112	49 In 115	50 Sn 119	51 Sb 122	52 Te 128	53 I 127	54 Xe 131
6	55 Cs 133	56 Ba 137		72 Hf 178.5	73 Ta 181	74 W 184	75 Re 186	76 Os 190	77 Ir 192	78 Pt 195	79 Au 197	80 Hg 201	81 Tl 204	82 Pb 207	83 Bi 209	84 Po 209	85 At 210	86 Rn 222
7	87 Fr 223	88 Ra 226		104 Rf 265	105 Db 268	106 Sg 271	107 Bh 267	108 Hs 277	109 Mt 276	110 Ds 281	111 Rg 280	112 Cn 285	113 Uut 284	114 Fl 289	115 Uup 288	116 Lv 293	117 Uus 294	118 Uuo 294

57 La 139	58 Ce 140	59 Pr 141	60 Nd 144	61 Pm 145	62 Sm 150	63 Eu 152	64 Gd 157	65 Tb 159	66 Dy 162	67 Ho 165	68 Er 167	69 Tm 169	70 Yb 173	71 Lu 175
89 Ac 227	90 Th 232	91 Pa 231	92 U 238	93 Np 237	94 Pu 244	95 Am 244	96 Cm 247	97 Bk 247	98 Cf 251	99 Es 252	100 Fm 257	101 Md 258	102 No 259	103 Lr 262

Use the Periodic Table to help answer the questions below.

5 **a** How many elements can be found in Period 1 of the Periodic Table?

b 'Most elements in the Periodic Table are non-metals.' Is this statement true or false?

6 The table shows elements from the Periodic Table. Some elements are in the wrong places. Which row is correct?

	Metal	Non-metal
a	Na	Cu
b	Cl	Fe
c	Se	B
d	Mg	O

7 **a** Which of these elements is found in Group 1?

i helium, He **ii** francium, Fr

b Which element is in Group 6 and Period 5?

c What do elements in the same group of the Periodic Table have in common?

8 The diagram shows an outline of the Periodic Table. Five elements have been given the labels **A** to **E**.

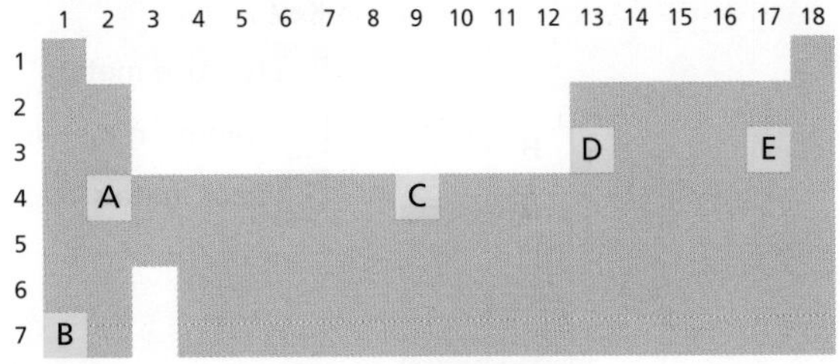

a Place the elements in order of their atomic number, starting with the lowest.

b Explain how you decided upon this answer.

c Which element is a non-metal?

9 The table shows the approximate time in history when some elements were discovered.

Element	Approximate time of discovery
gold, silver, copper, sulfur	early history
zinc	pre-1600
aluminium, sodium, magnesium, potassium	1800s

Suggest a reason why gold and silver were among the first to be discovered by humans.

10 In 1803, an English chemist called John Dalton wrote an article in which he assigned one atom of hydrogen, H, a mass of 1. This was then used to give **atomic masses** to every other known element. Carbon, C, has an atomic mass of 12, which means that 1 atom of carbon has 12 times more mass than 1 atom of hydrogen. Mendeleev used atomic masses in his version of the Periodic Table. Elements were not given **atomic numbers** until later, after the discovery of electrons and protons.

a Complete the table to show the atomic mass and atomic number for each element. Use the Periodic Table to help you.

Element symbol	Atomic mass	Atomic number
Li		
N		
O		
S		

b Which element has an atomic mass that is 20 times greater than that of hydrogen? Use the Periodic Table to help you.

c How did the article by John Dalton help Dmitri Mendeleev to produce his initial Periodic Table?

d Describe **three** ways in which the modern Periodic Table is different to the one produced by Dmitri Mendeleev.

9.2 Properties of elements in the Periodic Table

You are learning to:

- recognise the properties and uses of metals and non-metals
- describe the properties of non-metals and identify some uses
- use data and the properties of elements to choose materials suited to particular uses
- make predictions about the position of an element in the Periodic Table based on its physical and chemical properties.

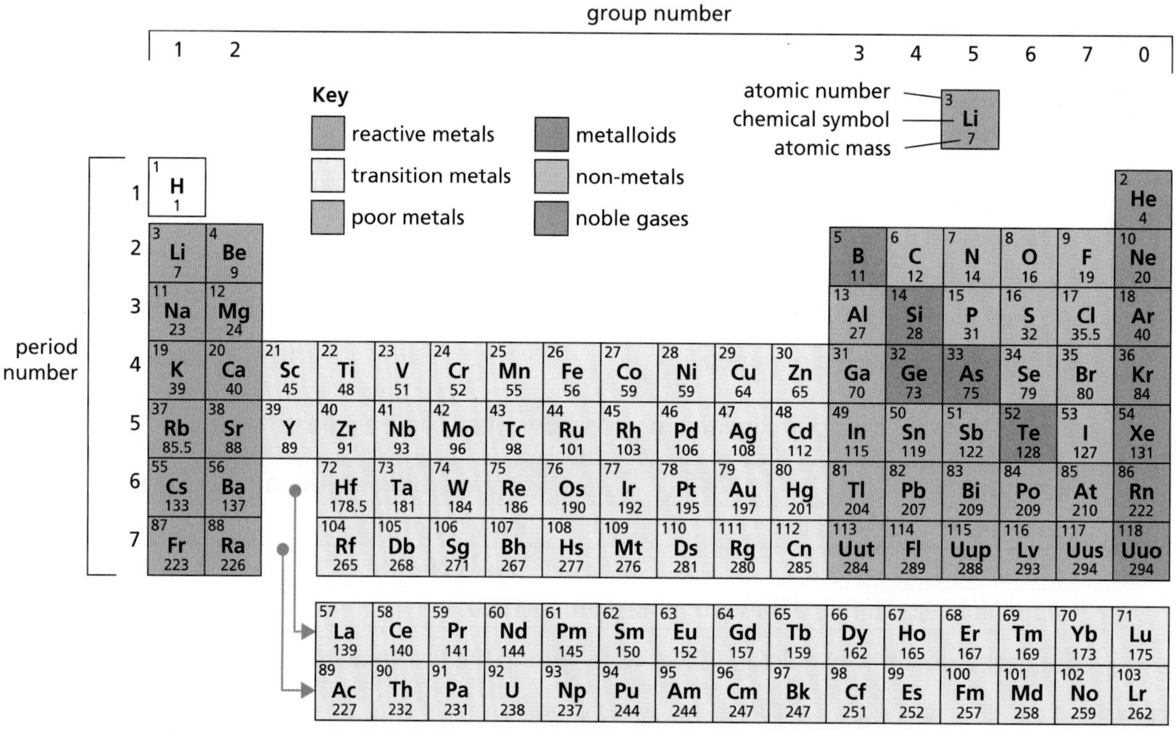

Use the Periodic Table to help you answer the questions below.

1 Place these properties of metals and non-metals in the most appropriate column in the table:

a shiny
b good conductor of heat
c poor conductor of electricity
d found on the right of the Periodic Table
e dense

Metals	Non-metals

2 Complete the sentence about elements in the Periodic Table.

Elements in the same ________ of the Periodic Table undergo similar chemical reactions.

3 The table lists some elements from the Periodic Table and their chemical symbols.

a Which of these elements could be malleable?
b Which of these elements is magnetic?
c Which of these elements is very unreactive?

Element	Chemical symbol
iron	Fe
copper	Cu
chlorine	Cl
oxygen	O
neon	Ne

4 Hydrogen is a non-metal element that is a gas at room temperature. A rigid airship filled with hydrogen carried passengers for the first time in 1936.

a Which of these properties of hydrogen would have made it a good choice to fill an airship?

i colourless **ii** no smell

iii low density **iv** non-toxic

b Are the properties listed in part **a** chemical or physical properties?

c Rigid airships are now filled with helium instead of hydrogen. Which of these properties of helium makes it a **better** choice than hydrogen for an airship?

i Helium has a higher density than hydrogen.

ii Helium is less flammable than hydrogen.

iii Helium is a gas at room temperature.

5 The diagram shows an outline of the Periodic Table. Five elements have been given the labels **A** to **E**.

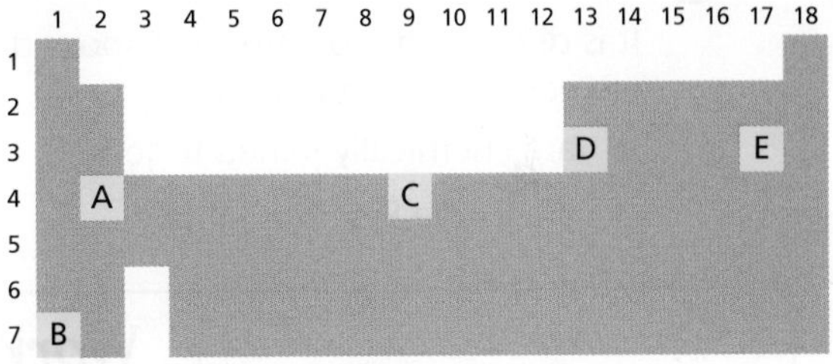

a Which elements would be able to conduct electricity?

b Which element would react very violently with water?

c Which element would be useful in treating harmful bacteria in drinking water?

6 A student plans to set up an experiment to find out if an unknown element is a metal or a non-metal. The element is a solid. They will use the equipment listed below.

bulb, wires, crocodile clips, power supply

Describe how the student could use this equipment to find out if the element is a metal or a non-metal. Your answer should include:

a a labelled diagram of the student's experiment

b a description of the results that would be obtained if the element is a metal and if the element is a non-metal.

7 The table below shows data for the melting points, boiling points and densities of several elements and water. Use the table and your own knowledge to answer the questions.

Element	Density (g/cm^3)	Melting point (°C)	Boiling point (°C)	State at room temperature
S	0.002	–219	–188	gas
T	0.0008	–248	–246	gas
U	0.003	–101	–34	?
V	3.1	–7.2	58.8	liquid
water	1.00	0	100	liquid

a Will element **U** be a solid, a liquid or a gas at room temperature?

b Which element will **not** float on water?

c Three elements are in the same group of the Periodic Table. Element **S** has the lowest melting and boiling points of the group. Suggest which element is **not** part of this group.

9.3 Reactions of elements and compounds

You are learning to:

- recognise and represent elements and compounds using formulae and symbols
- understand that mass is conserved during a chemical reaction
- interpret the ratio of atoms and the formulae of simple compounds
- be able to balance simple chemical equations.

1 'A chemical reaction involves the formation of one or more new substances.'

Is this statement true or false?

2 Which statement correctly completes the following paragraph about compounds?

It is difficult to separate a compound into the elements it is made of. This is because the elements in a compound...

a are chemically joined together.　　**b** cannot change state.

c are in the Periodic Table.

Worked example

What is the name of the compound formed in this reaction?

lithium + chlorine → __________ __________

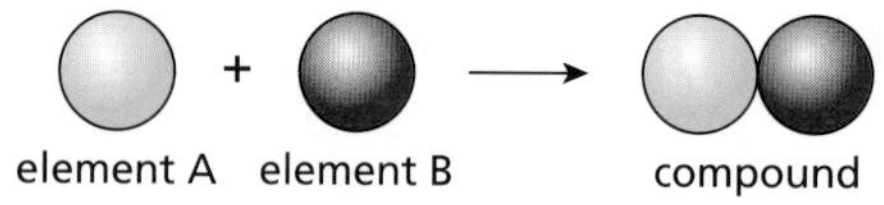

In a chemical reaction, atoms are rearranged and then join together differently to make new compounds.

The first part of the compound name comes from the element which is closest to the left-hand side of the Periodic Table (usually a metal). The second part of the name comes from the other element. If there are only two elements involved in the reaction, the last part ends in '-ide'. Lithium is a metal, so the first part of the compound name is 'lithium'

The second element is chlorine, so the second part of the compound name is 'chloride'.

The name of the compound is lithium chloride.

3 Name the compound formed when copper metal reacts with oxygen gas.

Worked example

Write this word equation as a sentence:

sodium + bromine → sodium bromide

Start on the left-hand side of the arrow and mention both elements or compounds that are reacting together. The arrow symbol means 'reacts to form'. Then name the compound(s) formed as the product of the reaction.

Sodium and bromine react together to form the product sodium bromide.

4 **a** Write this word equation as a sentence:

potassium + oxygen → potassium oxide

b Write a word equation from the following sentence: hydrochloric acid and calcium react together to produce calcium chloride and hydrogen.

5 Complete the particle diagram for the reaction below, so that the equation has the same number of atoms on both sides.

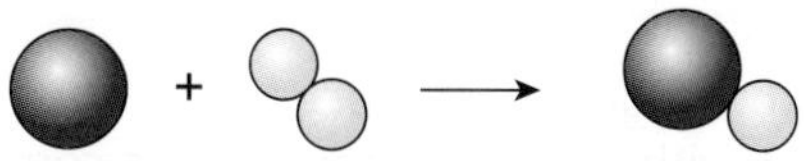

magnesium + oxygen → magnesium oxide

6 A student measured out the reactants for an experiment in two beakers on a digital balance.

The balance read 256.7 g. The student added the zinc granules to the hydrochloric acid.

There was a chemical reaction and hydrogen gas was released.

a The student noticed that the reading on the digital balance decreased. Explain why.

b 'Mass is conserved in a chemical reaction.' What does this statement mean?

c What additional equipment could the student use to show more accurately that mass was conserved in this reaction? Explain your choice.

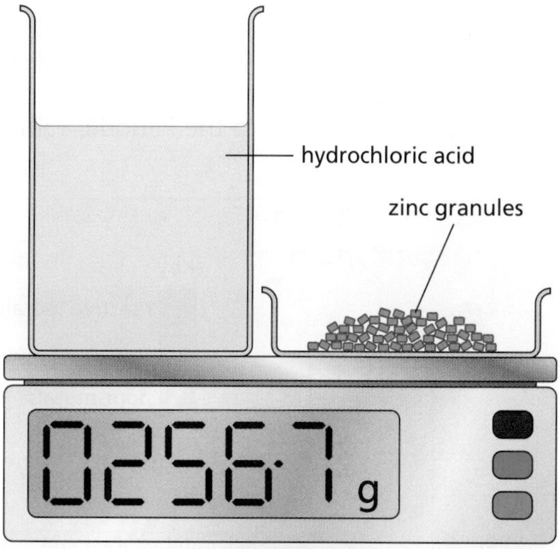

7 Magnetite is a type of iron ore. Iron can be extracted from magnetite through a chemical reaction with carbon monoxide.

magnetite + carbon monoxide → iron + carbon dioxide

The chemical formula of each substance in the reaction is shown in the table.

Substance	Chemical formula
magnetite	Fe_3O_4
carbon monoxide	CO
iron	Fe
carbon dioxide	CO_2

a Complete the following sentences about the chemical formulae in the table.

In carbon monoxide, there is one carbon, C, atom for every __**i**__ oxygen, O, atom.

In carbon dioxide, there is one carbon atom for every __**ii**__ oxygen atoms.

In magnetite, there are three iron, Fe, atoms for every __**iii**__ oxygen atoms.

b The symbol equation for the same reaction is shown below. This equation is not yet balanced.

$Fe_3O_4 + \_\_CO \rightarrow \_\_\_ Fe + 4CO_2$

The number of atoms on each side of the equation must be the same. Finish the table to show how many atoms of each element are currently shown on each side of the equation.

Element	Number of atoms on the left of the equation	Number of atoms on the right of the equation
iron (Fe)		
oxygen (O)		
carbon (C)		

c Which option shows the correct values needed to balance the equation?

$Fe_3O_4 + \_\_CO \rightarrow \_\_\_ Fe + 4CO_2$

i 4CO, 4Fe **ii** 4CO, 3Fe **iii** 2CO, 3Fe **iv** 3CO, 4Fe

9.4 Using the Periodic Table

You are learning to:

- understand that metals react with oxygen to produce bases
- understand that non-metals react with oxygen to form acidic compounds
- understand how patterns in reactions can be predicted using the Periodic Table
- recognise chemical symbols and simple formulae.

You may need to refer to the Periodic Table to help answer some of the questions.

Key: reactive metals; transition metals; poor metals; metalloids; non-metals; noble gases

atomic number / chemical symbol / atomic mass (e.g. 3 Li 7)

period number \ group number	1	2											3	4	5	6	7	0
1	1 H 1																	2 He 4
2	3 Li 7	4 Be 9											5 B 11	6 C 12	7 N 14	8 O 16	9 F 19	10 Ne 20
3	11 Na 23	12 Mg 24											13 Al 27	14 Si 28	15 P 31	16 S 32	17 Cl 35.5	18 Ar 40
4	19 K 39	20 Ca 40	21 Sc 45	22 Ti 48	23 V 51	24 Cr 52	25 Mn 55	26 Fe 56	27 Co 59	28 Ni 59	29 Cu 64	30 Zn 65	31 Ga 70	32 Ge 73	33 As 75	34 Se 79	35 Br 80	36 Kr 84
5	37 Rb 85.5	38 Sr 88	39 Y 89	40 Zr 91	41 Nb 93	42 Mo 96	43 Tc 98	44 Ru 101	45 Rh 103	46 Pd 106	47 Ag 108	48 Cd 112	49 In 115	50 Sn 119	51 Sb 122	52 Te 128	53 I 127	54 Xe 131
6	55 Cs 133	56 Ba 137		72 Hf 178.5	73 Ta 181	74 W 184	75 Re 186	76 Os 190	77 Ir 192	78 Pt 195	79 Au 197	80 Hg 201	81 Tl 204	82 Pb 207	83 Bi 209	84 Po 209	85 At 210	86 Rn 222
7	87 Fr 223	88 Ra 226		104 Rf 265	105 Db 268	106 Sg 271	107 Bh 267	108 Hs 277	109 Mt 276	110 Ds 281	111 Rg 280	112 Cn 285	113 Uut 284	114 Fl 289	115 Uup 288	116 Lv 293	117 Uus 294	118 Uuo 294

57 La 139	58 Ce 140	59 Pr 141	60 Nd 144	61 Pm 145	62 Sm 150	63 Eu 152	64 Gd 157	65 Tb 159	66 Dy 162	67 Ho 165	68 Er 167	69 Tm 169	70 Yb 173	71 Lu 175
89 Ac 227	90 Th 232	91 Pa 231	92 U 238	93 Np 237	94 Pu 244	95 Am 244	96 Cm 247	97 Bk 247	98 Cf 251	99 Es 252	100 Fm 257	101 Md 258	102 No 259	103 Lr 262

1 Choose the correct terms from the list to complete the sentence below.

acid **alkali** **oxygen** **a non-metal** **oxide** **carbonate**

A metal reacts with **i** ________ to form a metal **ii** _______, which is a base.

2 **a** What is the difference between a base and an alkali?

b Are all alkalis also classed as bases?

3 Titanium is a metal element.

a What compound is formed when titanium reacts with oxygen?

b Is this compound acidic or basic?

4 The following compounds are oxides:

sulfur dioxide, SO_2 **magnesium oxide, MgO**

a Which compound is basic?

b Which compound is acidic?

5 Iron, Fe, reacts with oxygen in damp conditions to produce iron oxide; this is also known as rust. Is rust an acidic or a basic oxide?

6 A section of the Periodic Table is shown on the right. Which element would you predict to have similar chemical properties to boron, B?

5 **B** 11	6 **C** 12	7 **N** 14	8 **O** 16	9 **F** 19
13 **Al** 27	14 **Si** 28	15 **P** 31	16 **S** 32	17 **Cl** 35.5

7 The pH scale measures how acid or how alkaline a substance is.

pH	1	2	3	4	5	6	7	8	9	10	11	12	13	14

A student reacted four unnamed elements (**A–D**) with oxygen to make metal oxides. They tested the pH of each metal oxide and recorded their results.

a Which elements are metals?

b Justify your choice.

Element	pH of metal oxide
A	4
B	8
C	11
D	2

8 The diagram shows an outline of the Periodic Table. Seven elements are labelled **A** to **G**.

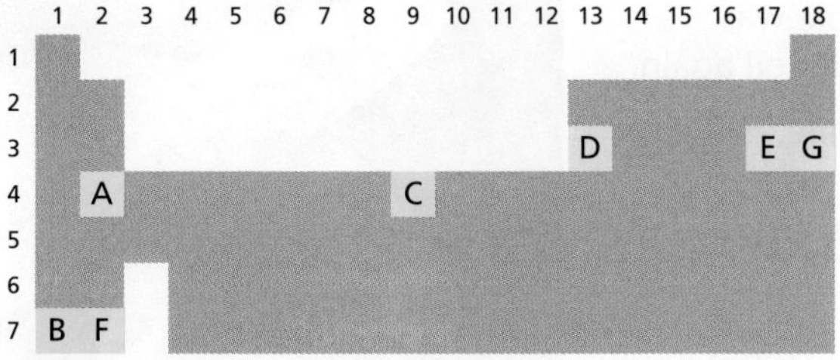

a Which of the elements **A** to **G** are in Period 3?

b Which elements will have similar chemical properties? Choose from the list below:

i D, E, G **ii** A, C **iii** B, F **iv** A, F

c Which elements will combine with oxygen to form a basic oxide?

d A student predicts that **one** of the elements will not react with oxygen at all. Give the letter of the element and explain why you chose this element.

9 Indicators are substances that can be used to identify if a substance is acidic or alkaline. Litmus is an example of an indicator. Litmus solution turns red in acid and blue in alkali. Red litmus paper stays red in acid and turns blue in an alkali. Blue litmus paper stays blue in an alkali and turns red in an acid.

A student tested solutions of some metal and non-metal oxides with litmus paper. Complete the table to show what colour the litmus paper would be when solutions of the oxides were tested.

Oxide	Colour of blue litmus paper	Colour of red litmus paper
magnesium oxide, MgO		
sulfur dioxide, SO_2		
sodium oxide, Na_2O		

Maths and practical skills

You may need to refer to the Periodic Table in the knowledge organiser to help answer some of the questions.

1 Aluminium, Al, has an atomic mass of 27. How many times greater is the mass of an atom of aluminium than an atom of hydrogen, H?

2 A student tested the conductivity of four elements using an electrical circuit. Each element was placed in a complete circuit with a bulb. Complete the table to classify the elements tested.

Element	Did the bulb light?	Metal, non-metal or metalloid?
hydrogen, H	no	
sulfur, S	no	
scandium, Sc	yes, brightly	
tellurium, Te	yes, dimly	

3 The elements in Group 1 of the Periodic Table are metals. They are stored in oil. A teacher removed a sample of a Group 1 metal from oil and cut a piece off using a knife. It was shiny on the exposed surface but soon turned a dull grey. The metal sample was returned to its container and stored under oil again.

a Group 1 metals can be cut with a knife. Is this an example of a physical or a chemical property?

b Why did the shiny metal quickly become dull when left exposed to the air?

c Suggest why the Group 1 metals are stored in oil.

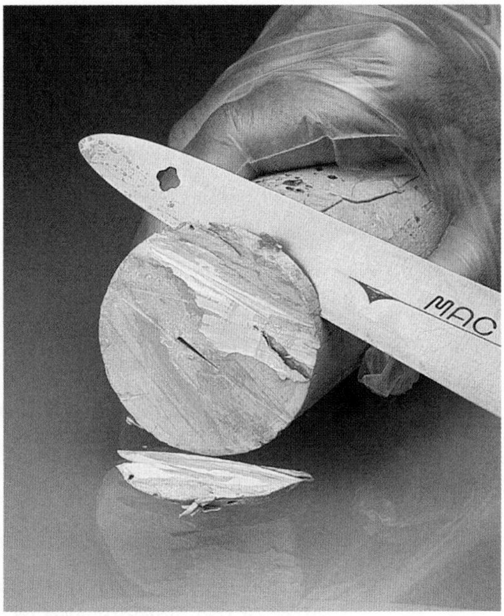

4 The table shows the elements in Period 2 of the Periodic Table.

Element	Li	Be	B	C	N	O	F	Ne
State at room temperature	solid	solid	solid	solid	gas	gas	gas	gas

a Use the table to decide which of the elements below has the highest melting point.

i beryllium, Be **ii** neon, Ne **iii** fluorine, F

b Explain your answer to part **a**.

c Will elements in the **same period** have the same physical properties?

5 The units that scientists use all over the world are standardised in the Système Internationale d'Unités (SI units). The base unit for temperature across the world is kelvin (K). Many scientists also use the unit degrees Celsius (°C) for temperature, so it is important to be able to convert °C into K and vice versa.

0 °C is equivalent to 273.15 K

Worked example

Convert 10 °C into K

To convert a temperature written in °C to K, add 273.15 to the temperature.

A temperature of 10°C would be 10 + 273.15 = 283.15 K

The table shows the melting points of a group of elements **E** to **H** in both °C and in K. Use the information in the table to calculate the melting point of elements **F** and **G** in kelvin (K).

Element	**E**	**F**	**G**	**H**
Melting point (°C)	180	98	63.5	39.3
Melting point (K)	453.15	**i**	**ii**	312.45

6 A gas burns in oxygen to produce carbon dioxide and water. A student writes the equation for this reaction:

$C_3H_8 + 4O_2 \rightarrow 3CO_2 + 4H_2O$

a Complete the table below to show how many atoms of each element are in the reactants and products.

Element	**Number of atoms in the reactants**	**Number of atoms in the products**
carbon, C		
hydrogen, H		
oxygen, O		

b Is the equation balanced? Justify your answer.

7 The graph shows the boiling points of elements in Group 7 of the Periodic Table. These elements are also known as the halogens.

a Underline the elements that are gases at room temperature.

fluorine **chlorine** **bromine** **astatine**

b Describe the trend for boiling point in the elements of Group 7.

c Iodine, I, is a black solid which is often used in photography and in medicine. It has an atomic mass of 127 and a boiling point of 184 °C. Plot the boiling point of iodine on the graph.

d Dmitri Mendeleev first organised elements in terms of increasing atomic mass.

Tellurium, Te, is a semi-solid grey powder. It has a boiling point of 988 °C and an atomic mass of 28. Mendeleev initially placed iodine in Group 6 and tellurium in Group 7, but then swapped them around. Further evidence has since shown Mendeleev's decision to be correct. Suggest **one** reason why Mendeleev decided to swap iodine to Group 7 and tellurium to Group 6.

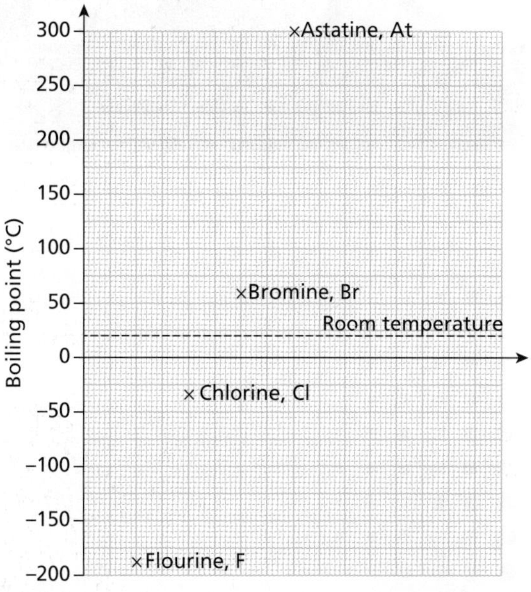

10 Chemical reactions road map

Where are you in your learning journey and where are you aiming to be?

10.3 Thermal decomposition

- state the meaning of thermal decomposition
- describe thermal decomposition
- use evidence
• describe combustion
- represent reactions
• describe how solutions are formed
• describe how to recover a substance from a solution

10.4 Oxidation

- state the meaning of oxidation
- describe oxidatio
- describe reductio
- represent reactio

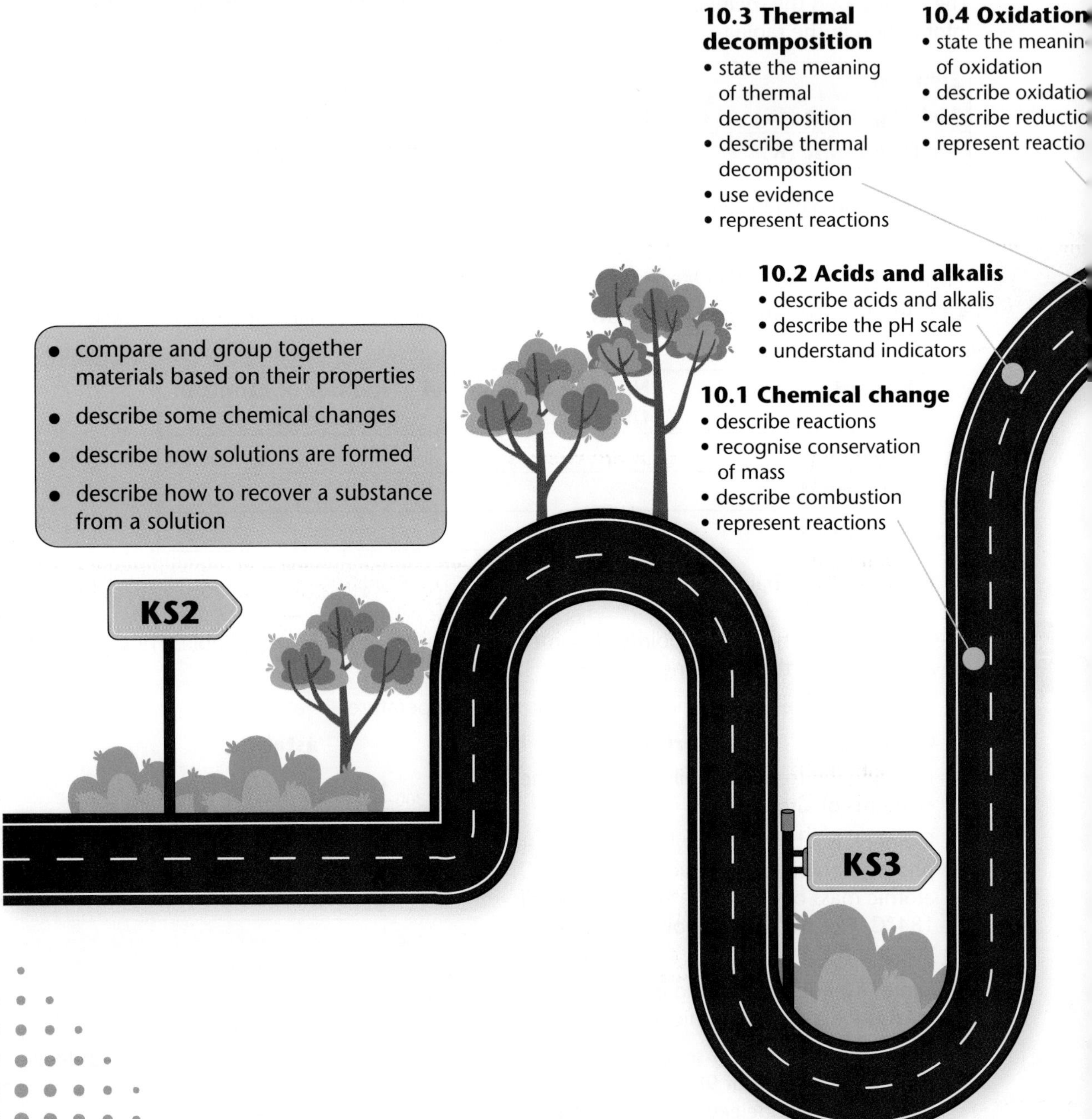

10.5 Neutralisation
- recall the neutralisation reaction equation
- explain how water is made
- apply models
- represent reactions

10.6 Reactions of acids and alkalis
- describe reactions
- predict reactants
- represent reactions

10.7 Displacement reactions
- represent and explain reactions
- make inferences about reactivity
- represent reactions

10.8 Energetics
- describe examples
- describe catalysts
- explain energy changes
- represent reactions

- conservation of mass and balanced chemical equations
- atoms, elements and compounds
- energy transfer during exothermic and endothermic reactions
- reaction profiles
- metal oxides; Group 7
- the pH scale and neutralisation
- reactions of acids with metals; neutralisation of acids and salt production
- catalysts

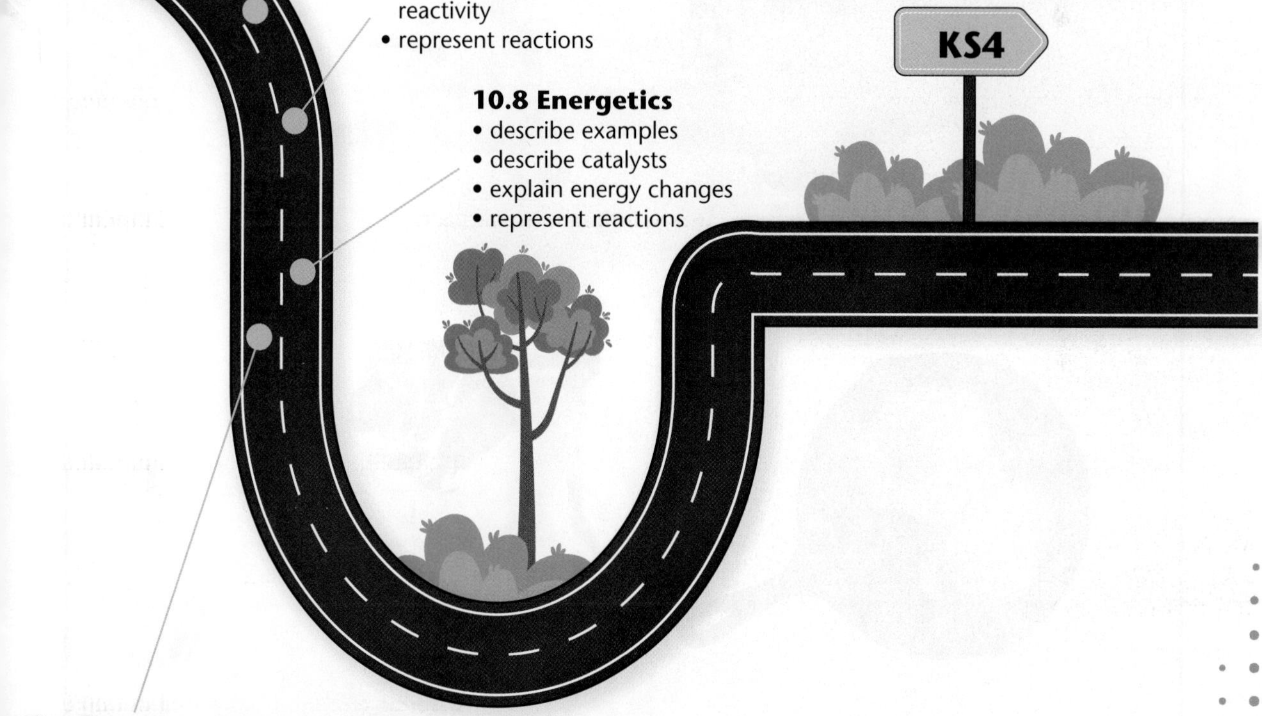

Maths and practical skills

- planning an investigation, identifying and managing the variables
- presenting data using tables and graphs
- interpreting observations and data
- analysing data and identifying anomalous results
- presenting reasoned explanations
- using SI units and chemical names and symbols
- making scientific predictions

Chemical reactions

When substances are mixed together, chemical changes can happen. During a chemical reaction, atoms are rearranged to form new chemicals. A chemical equation can be used to show this rearrangement.

Chemical reactions and physical changes

Identify which of the following photographs show chemical reactions. How do you know it is a chemical reaction and not a physical change?

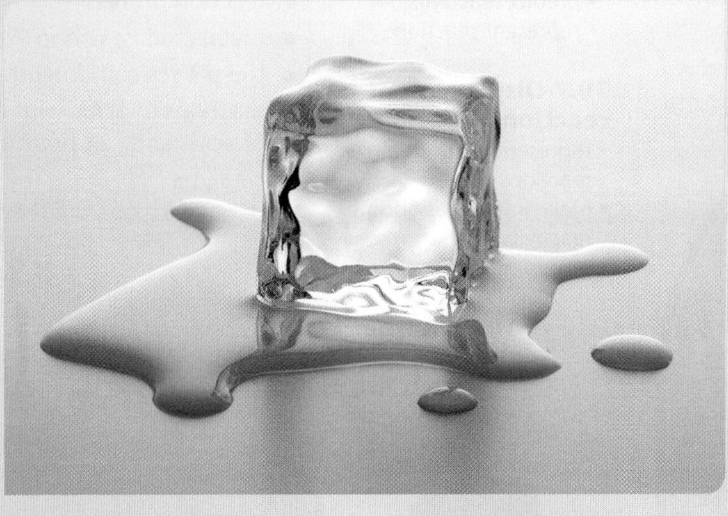

Using your science skills

Could you be a chef?

As a chef, you could be responsible for cooking food for people in places like pubs, restaurants and hotels. You might learn how to cook lots of different types of food from all over the world. There are many different types of chef, but it is common to start as a 'commis' or junior chef.

You use chemical reactions to cook food and improve its flavour. For example, without a chemical reaction your cakes would not rise! Baking powder contains two chemicals that react together to form carbon dioxide. It is this carbon dioxide gas, released during the reaction, which causes cakes to rise.

You use the Maillard reaction when cooking. It causes browning and gives the food lots of flavour. It is a reaction between sugars and amino acids in the food and was discovered by a French chemist called Louis-Camille Maillard. This reaction is responsible for the flavours in cooked meat, fried onions, roasted coffee and toasted bread.

Soil scientists gather information about the structure and properties of soil, and the organisms which live there. Good soil is important for healthy crop growth to sustain food production. Some soils may not have enough nutrients to grow crops. They may also be too acidic, or too alkaline. Soil scientists can recommend adding substances to improve the soil.

Marine biologists monitor and protect vulnerable ecosystems, such as coral reefs. The sea is becoming more acidic as more carbon dioxide dissolves in it. This has an effect on organisms like coral, which use calcium carbonate to build their skeletons. The more acidic sea water becomes, the less calcium carbonate it can hold. Marine biologists help us to understand the effect this is having on coral reefs.

Railway engineers use a chemical reaction called the thermite reaction to weld railway tracks together. The thermite reaction releases a lot of heat. Iron is usually produced in the reaction, and so much heat is released that the iron is molten. The molten iron welds the rail tracks together.

Builders work with many different materials to make buildings and other structures. They commonly use cement. Cement is a powdery substance that is mixed with water, sand and gravel to make concrete. A chemical reaction occurs in the cement when it is mixed with water. This gives out a lot of heat and produces a strong material that is very useful in the construction of buildings.

Industrial cleaners use very strong chemicals to clean. Chemicals known as bases or alkalis react with oils and fats, and so can degrease surfaces. Drain cleaners and oven cleaners normally contain sodium hydroxide, which is a strong base.

Knowledge organiser

A **chemical reaction** is a change in which new substances are made. During a chemical reaction you may see:

- bubbles of gas
- a change in temperature
- a colour change
- a change in mass.

In any chemical reaction, the total mass of the reactants is the same as the total mass of the products. This is called the law of conservation of mass. Sometimes it may appear that the mass has changed. When this happens, there is normally a gas, either as a reactant or as a product, which accounts for the 'missing' mass.

Burning is an example of a chemical reaction. The scientific name for burning is **combustion**. During combustion, a **fuel** reacts with oxygen to make carbon dioxide and water. The reaction releases useful energy. We can summarise combustion using an equation:

fuel + oxygen → carbon dioxide + water

If there is not enough oxygen available to react with all of the fuel, **incomplete combustion** takes place. The reaction has different products.

fuel + oxygen → carbon monoxide + carbon + water

During a chemical reaction, atoms rearrange and join together in a different way. New **products** are formed from the **reactants**. For example, hydrogen and oxygen react together to form water. Hydrogen and oxygen are the reactants and water is the product. One molecule of oxygen reacts with two molecules of hydrogen to form two molecules of water.

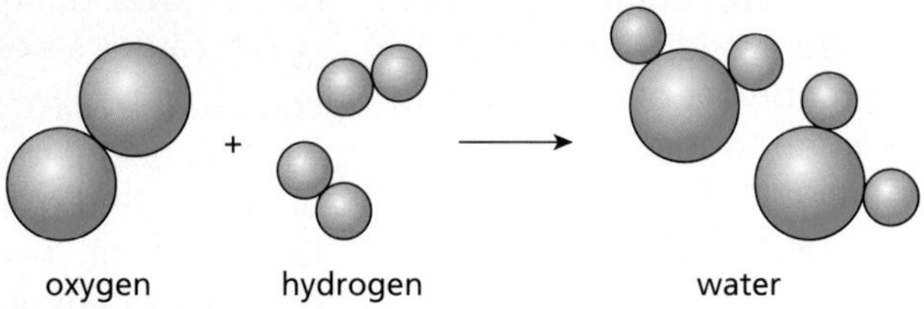

Notice that there are the same numbers of oxygen and hydrogen atoms at the start of the reaction as there are at the end of the reaction. They have been rearranged to form a new substance, water.

Some of the substances we use at home or in the laboratory are **acids**. Vinegar and lemon juice contain acids. Acids are substances with a **pH** less than 7. Concentrated acids are **corrosive**; dilute acids may be **irritants**. All acids contain the element hydrogen.

'Corrosive' hazard sign

'Harmful' hazard sign, which is used for substances that are not corrosive but are irritants.

Some other substances are **alkalis**. Soap and detergents contain alkalis. Alkalis are substances with a pH greater than 7. Like acids, concentrated alkalis can be corrosive and dilute alkalis may be irritants. All alkalis contain hydroxide particles (**chemical formula** OH).

An **indicator** is a substance that is a different colour in an acid and in an alkali. One example of an indicator is litmus. Litmus solution turns *red in acid* and *blue in alkali.* If a solution is neither an acid nor an alkali, we say it is **neutral.**

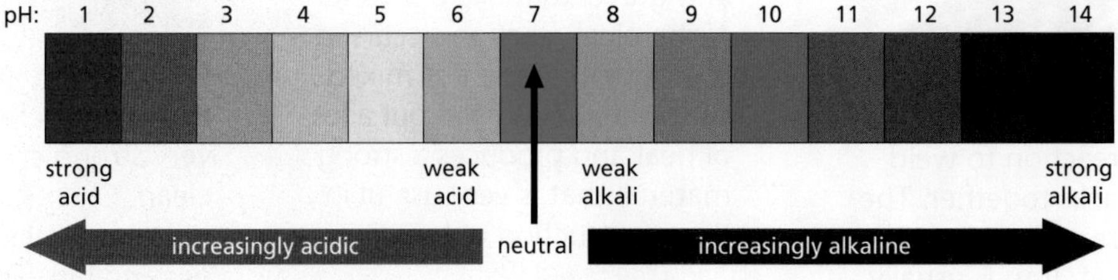

Universal indicator turns a range of different colours. The colour depends on whether the substance is an acid or an alkali *and* on how strong or weak it is. Each colour is given a **pH number**. The pH scale is a measure of the acidity or alkalinity of a substance.

Hydrochloric acid is an example of a strong acid, with a pH of 1. Vinegar is an example of a weak acid, with a pH of 3.

Oxidation reactions involve oxygen being added to another substance. This reaction forms compounds called oxides. During the combustion of a metal, oxygen is added to the metal:

metal + oxygen → metal oxide

The mass of the metal oxide is greater than the mass of the metal because oxygen has been added.

When oxygen is removed from a metal oxide, the reaction is called **reduction**. This is the opposite of oxidation.
Carbon can be used to remove oxygen from iron oxide.

Thermal decomposition reactions happen when some substances are heated and break down into simpler products. No new substances are added. When carbonates decompose, they produce a metal oxide and carbon dioxide:

metal carbonate → metal oxide + carbon dioxide

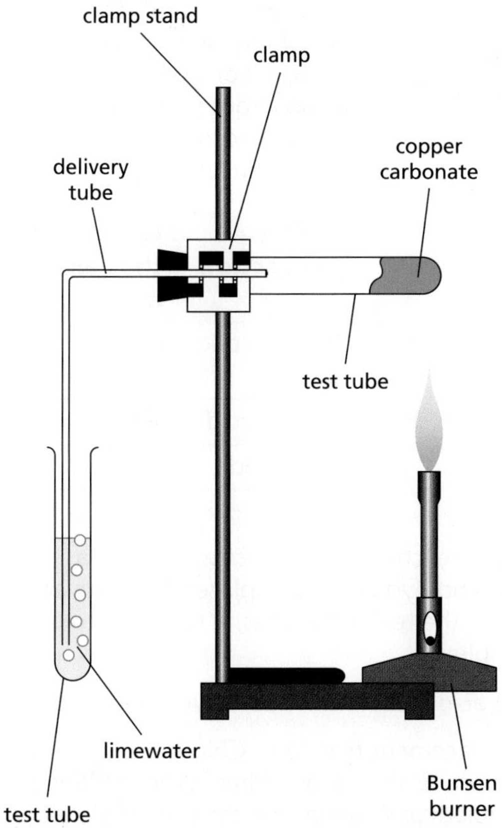

Key vocabulary	
acid	a substance that will neutralise a base; has a pH lower than 7
alkali	a base that is soluble in water; has a pH above 7
chemical formula	chemical symbols and numbers that show how many atoms of which elements are contained in a molecule of an element or compound
chemical reaction	a process in which one or more substances are changed into others, by the rearrangement of their atoms
combustion	the reaction of a fuel with oxygen that transfers thermal energy to the surroundings
conserved	when the quantity of something does not change after a process takes place
corrosive	can destroy skin and attack metal if spilled
fuel	any material that can be burned to release energy
incomplete combustion	when there is not enough oxygen available to react with all of a fuel during combustion
indicator	chemical that is a different colour in an alkali and an acid; used to identify whether an unknown solution is acidic or alkaline
irritant	a substance that causes the skin to become red, blistered and itchy
neutral	has a pH of 7
oxidation	a reaction in which a substance combines with oxygen
pH	a number from 1 to 14 on the pH scale of acidity and alkalinity
product	(of a chemical reaction) a substance made in a chemical reaction
reactant	a starting substance in a chemical reaction
reduction	a reaction in which oxygen is removed from a compound
thermal decomposition	a chemical change caused by heating, when one substance is changed into at least two new substances
universal indicator	an indicator that turns a range of different colours; each colour indicates a different pH value

A neutral substance has pH 7. It is made when an acid and alkali exactly neutralise one another. This is called **neutralisation**. Neutralisation is a chemical reaction; new products are formed.

acid + alkali → salt + water

Water is a product of the neutralisation reaction between acids and alkalis. The hydrogen from the acid combines with the hydroxide from the alkali to form water.

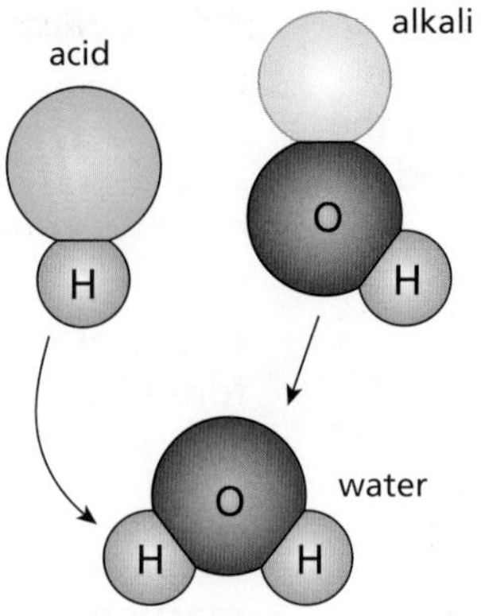

A **base** is any substance that neutralises an acid to produce a salt and water. An alkali is a soluble base – one that dissolves in water. Therefore, all alkalis are bases, but not all bases are alkalis. Metal oxides, metal hydroxides and metal carbonates are all examples of bases.

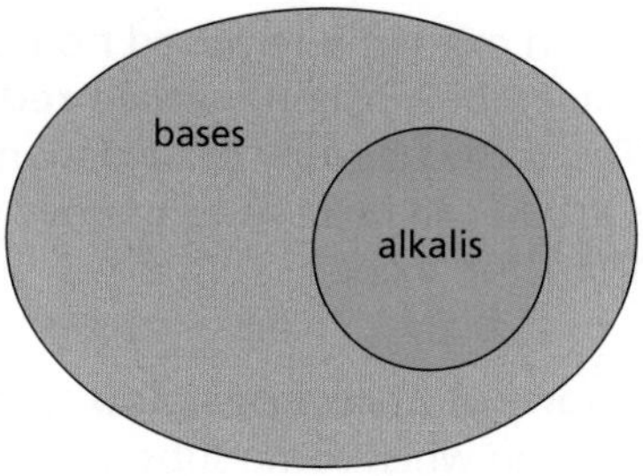

Acids react with bases to produce a **salt** and water. This is similar to the reaction you saw above between an acid and an alkali.

acid + base → salt + water

Salts are also formed in other reactions that involve acids. Acids react with metals to form a salt and hydrogen gas.

acid + metal → salt + hydrogen

Acids react with metal carbonates to form a salt, water and carbon dioxide.

acid + metal carbonate → salt + water + carbon dioxide

The name of a salt has two parts. The first part comes from the reactant that is not the acid; it is often a metal. For example, the alkali sodium hydroxide forms salts that start with 'sodium'. The end part of the name comes from the acid. For example, a salt formed from sulfuric acid and sodium hydroxide is called 'sodium sulfate'.

Acid used in reaction	Forms salts that end in...
hydrochloric acid	chloride
sulfuric acid	sulfate
nitric acid	nitrate

The reactivity series of metals places metals in order of their reactivity. It also includes two non-metals: hydrogen and carbon.

Most reactive

K	potassium
Na	sodium
Ca	calcium
Mg	magnesium
Al	aluminium
C	carbon
Zn	zinc
Fe	iron
Sn	tin
Pb	lead
H	hydrogen
Cu	copper
Ag	silver
Au	gold
Pt	platinum

Least reactive

In a **displacement reaction** a more **reactive** substance displaces (pushes out) a less reactive substance from a compound. An example is when iron is added to a copper sulfate solution. Iron is more reactive than copper. A chemical change occurs – iron displaces the copper to make iron sulfate:

iron + copper sulfate → iron sulfate + copper

Acids contain hydrogen. When reactive metals react with acids, a displacement reaction occurs and hydrogen is displaced from the acid. If a metal is above hydrogen in the reactivity series, it will react to displace hydrogen. For example:

zinc + hydrochloric acid → zinc chloride + hydrogen

Non-metals also undergo displacement reactions. Chlorine and iodine are non-metals. Chlorine is more reactive than iodine. When chlorine gas is passed through sodium iodide solution, the chlorine displaces the iodine:

chlorine + sodium iodide → sodium chloride + iodine

In a chemical reaction, existing **chemical bonds** are broken and new ones are made. Energy is needed to break chemical bonds; energy is released when new chemical bonds are made. The balance between these two processes explains why some reactions are endothermic and others are exothermic. If more energy is needed for **bond breaking** than is released in **bond making**, the reaction is endothermic. If less energy is needed for bond-breaking than is released in bond-making, the reaction is exothermic.

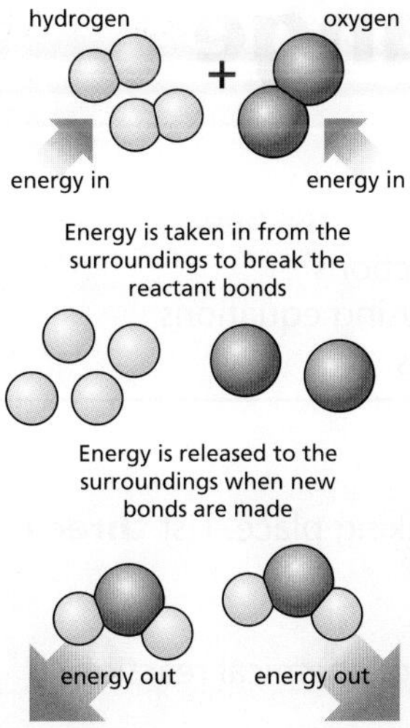

In some reactions, like combustion, there is an **energy transfer** to the surroundings – these are known as **exothermic reactions**, which cause the temperature of the surroundings to increase. Other reactions, like thermal decomposition, take energy from their surroundings – these are known as **endothermic reactions**, which cause the temperature of the surroundings to decrease. An energy profile diagram shows the energy changes taking place during exothermic and endothermic reactions.

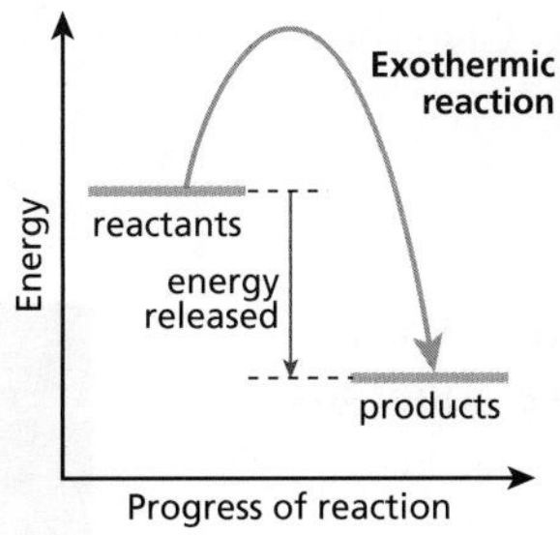

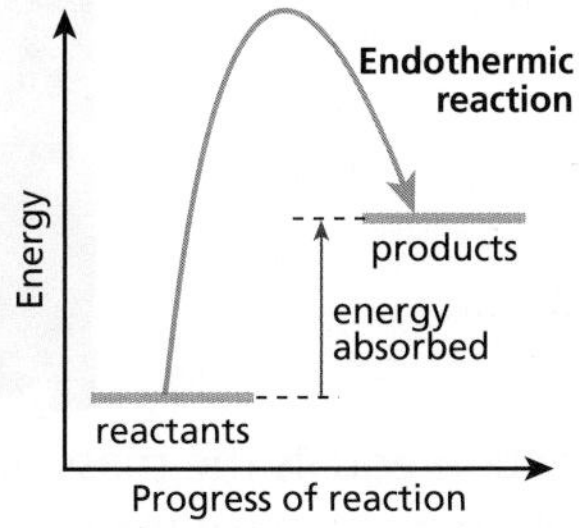

A **catalyst** is a substance that is added to a chemical reaction to make the reaction faster. Catalysts are not changed by the reaction – they alter the **rate of reaction**. Most catalysts provide an alternative 'pathway' for the reaction that lowers the amount of energy needed for the reaction to proceed.

Key vocabulary	
base	a substance that will neutralise an acid
bond breaking	when a chemical bond is broken by overcoming the force of attraction between particles; energy is transferred in from the surroundings
bond making	when a chemical bond is made by the force of attraction between particles; energy is transferred out to the surroundings
catalyst	substance that speeds up a chemical reaction
chemical bond	the force of attraction between two atoms
displacement reaction	a chemical reaction in which one substance takes the place of another in a compound
endothermic reaction	a chemical reaction in which energy is taken in, causing a cooling of the surroundings
energy transfer	the passing on of energy from one energy store to another energy store
exothermic reaction	a chemical reaction in which energy is given out, causing a warming of the surroundings
neutralisation	to make a substance neutral (pH 7) by adding an acid or a base
rate	the number of times something happens in a unit of time, such as a second
rate of reaction	a measure of the speed of a reaction; for example, the number of molecules of product produced over a set time
reactive	inclined to react in a chemical reaction; some substances are more reactive than others
salt	a substance formed when an acid reacts with a base, a metal or a metal carbonate

10.1 Chemical change

You are learning to:

- describe chemical reactions in terms of atoms
- recognise that mass is conserved in chemical reactions
- describe complete and incomplete combustion using equations
- represent reactions using formulae and equations.

1. A student observed a chemical reaction taking place. List **three** clues that we can look for to spot a chemical reaction.

2. Combustion is an example of which type of chemical reaction?
   - **a** thermal decomposition
   - **b** oxidation
   - **c** neutralisation
   - **d** displacement

3. The chemical formula for oxygen gas is O_2. Give the chemical formula for:
   - **a** carbon dioxide
   - **b** water.

4. A fuel is burnt during a combustion reaction. Which statement correctly completes this sentence about fuels?

   A fuel is a substance that…
   - **a** takes oxygen away from another substance.
   - **b** can be burned to release energy.
   - **c** has a pH lower than 7.
   - **d** causes skin to become red, blistered and itchy.

5. The mass of the reactants in a chemical reaction equals the mass of the products of the reaction. Explain why mass is conserved during a chemical reaction.

6. Methane is a gas which can be used as a fuel. Write the word equation for complete combustion of the fuel methane.

7. When the hole in the neck of a Bunsen burner is closed, the flame is orange. This is the 'safety flame'. Incomplete combustion of the fuel occurs. State the differences between complete and incomplete combustion.

Worked example

A student investigates thermal decomposition reactions. They heat 13.5 g of calcium carbonate until it decomposes completely. Carbon dioxide and 7.6 g of calcium oxide are produced. Use the law of conservation of mass to find the mass of carbon dioxide produced.

calcium carbonate → calcium oxide + carbon dioxide

The law of conservation of mass states that matter cannot be created or destroyed during a chemical reaction. This means that the mass of the reactants must equal the mass of the products.

The mass of the reactant in this reaction is 13.5 g. You have been given the mass of one of the products, 7.6 g of calcium oxide.

calcium carbonate →	calcium oxide +	carbon dioxide
13.5 g	7.6 g	? g

You can use this information to find the mass of the other product, carbon dioxide. The mass of carbon dioxide and calcium oxide added together must equal 13.5 g. You can subtract the mass of calcium oxide from 13.5 g to find the mass of carbon dioxide.

13.5 − 7.6 = 5.9 g of carbon dioxide

8 15.6 g of sodium reacted with chlorine to produce 39.7 g of sodium chloride. Use the law of conservation of mass to find the mass of chlorine used in the reaction.

sodium + chlorine → sodium chloride

9 Nitric acid reacts with zinc to form hydrogen gas and the salt zinc nitrate. How does this equation show that mass is conserved during the reaction?

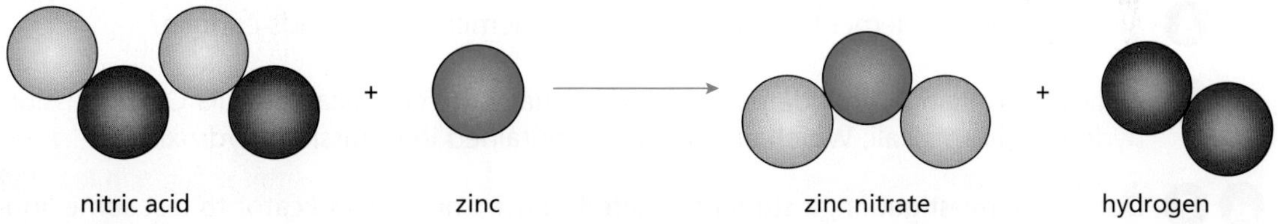

10 A student heated a strip of magnesium in a Bunsen burner flame. The magnesium reacted with oxygen in the air. The student measured the mass of the magnesium before the reaction and the mass of the product. Suggest what happened to the mass and why.

11 Hydrocarbons are substances that can be used as fuels. Suggest which **two** chemical elements can be found in all hydrocarbons.

10.2 Acids and alkalis

You are learning to:
- describe acids and alkalis in terms of what they have in common
- describe what the pH scale measures
- understand how to use indicators to identify acids and alkalis

1. Bottles of acids and alkalis used in the laboratory are labelled with hazard symbols. A hazard is something that could cause harm. What does the hazard symbol shown on the right mean?

2. Indicators change colour when they are added to solutions that are acidic or alkaline. Litmus is an example of an indicator. What colour does litmus turn in acid?

3. A student added universal indicator to an unknown solution. The results showed that the solution had a pH of 7.
   a What colour would the universal indictor turn to show the solution was pH 7?
   b What does this tell you about the solution?

4. A soluble substance dissolves in a solvent. An example of a solvent is water. What is the name given to a soluble base?
   a alkali
   b acid
   c hydroxide

5. All acids have an element in common. Which element do all acids contain?

6. All alkalis contain hydroxide particles, which have the chemical formula OH. Potassium hydroxide is an alkali. Which elements are contained in potassium hydroxide?

7. During an investigation, a student decided to use universal indicator to test some liquids. Explain the advantages of using universal indicator rather than litmus paper to test the acidity and alkalinity of liquids.

Worked example

A student tested several different substances using universal indicator solution. They recorded their findings in the following table.

Substance	pH
soap	10.0
bleach	12.1
ammonia	11.0
milk	6.8
baking soda	8.2
sodium hydroxide	14.0

Which substance is the least alkaline?

Alkaline substances have a pH greater than 7. A pH of 7 is considered neutral. The closer the pH of an alkaline substance is to 7, the less alkaline it is.

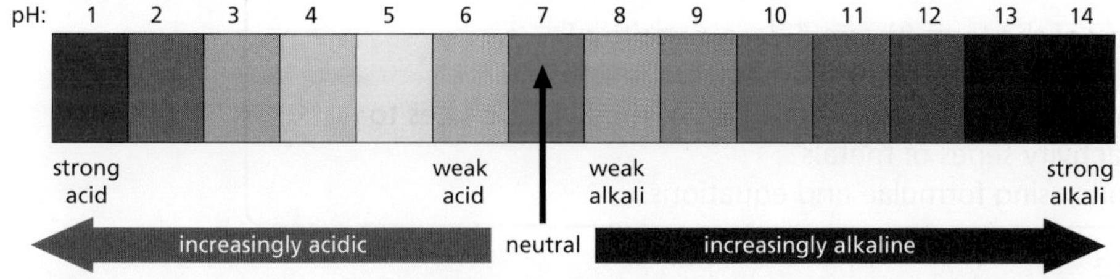

Therefore, the least alkaline substance will be an alkaline substance with a pH closest to 7. Looking at the table we can see that milk has the pH closest to 7, but it is an acidic substance, as its pH is less than 7. The question asks for the least **alkaline** substance. Baking soda is an alkaline substance with a pH closest to 7 of those in the table.

baking soda

8 The table shows the pH of some liquids. Which liquid is the least acidic?

Liquid	pH
lemon juice	2.2
milk	6.8
black coffee	5.0
beer	4.0

9 Sulfuric acid is a strong acid. Universal indicator turns red when added to sulfuric acid. Suggest the pH of sulfuric acid.

10 Vinegar is acidic. A student added a strip of magnesium to vinegar, and a strip of magnesium to hydrochloric acid. What would the student observe during the experiment? Explain your answer.

11 A student wrote: 'all alkalis are bases but not all bases are alkalis'. Explain what they meant by this sentence.

12 A solution was tested with universal indicator solution. The pH of the solution was 0. Suggest what a pH of 0 tells you about the solution.

10.3 Thermal decomposition

You are learning to:
- state the meaning of the term 'thermal decomposition'
- describe the thermal decomposition of metal carbonates
- use evidence from the thermal decomposition of metal carbonates to construct the reactivity series of metals
- represent reactions using formulae and equations.

1 Complete the following sentences about thermal decomposition. Use the words to help you.

heating **cooling** **oxidation** **reduction** **one** **two or more** **three**

Thermal decomposition is a chemical change caused by __**i**__.

In thermal decomposition, __**ii**__ compound breaks down into __**iii**__ substances.

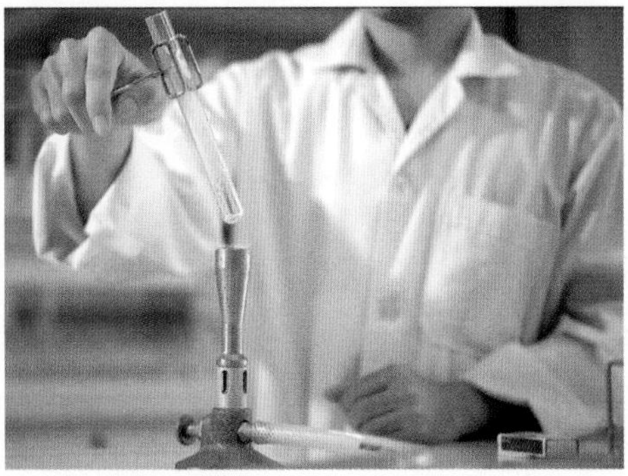

2 Which of these gases is produced when calcium carbonate, $CaCO_3$, is heated to a high temperature?

a oxygen

b hydrogen

c carbon dioxide

d water vapour

3 How would you test for the gas produced during the thermal decomposition of calcium carbonate?

4 Which one of these is the correct general equation for the thermal decomposition of a metal carbonate?

a metal carbonate + metal oxide → carbon dioxide

b metal carbonate → metal oxide + carbon dioxide

c metal oxide + carbon dioxide → metal carbonate

5 Why does the total mass of substances appear to decrease when calcium carbonate is heated?

6 Lead is a more reactive metal than copper. Both metals can form carbonates. Which statement about lead carbonate and copper carbonate is true?

a Lead carbonate needs more energy to decompose it than copper carbonate.

b Lead carbonate needs less energy to decompose it than copper carbonate.

7 A student heated white calcium carbonate during an experiment on thermal decomposition. After 5 minutes, the boiling tube still contained a white powder. The student's observation read: 'a reaction did not take place'.

a Is the student correct?

b Why do you think the student thought no reaction had occurred?

c Write a word equation for the thermal decomposition of calcium carbonate.

8 A student investigated the amount of energy needed to decompose different metal carbonates. Here are their results:

Metal carbonate	Energy for thermal decomposition (kJ/mol)
magnesium carbonate	101
barium carbonate	269
calcium carbonate	178

Use the data in the table to put the metals magnesium, barium and calcium in order of reactivity, from the most to least reactive. Explain your choice.

Worked example

When calcium hydrogen carbonate, $Ca(HCO_3)_2$, is heated it produces calcium carbonate, $CaCO_3$, water and carbon dioxide gas. Write a symbol equation for the thermal decomposition of calcium hydrogen carbonate.

This question looks complicated when you first read through, but it gives you most of the information you need. The reactant in the reaction is calcium hydrogen carbonate, the formula for this is given in the question: $Ca(HCO_3)_2$. There are no other reactants. You can write the formula for the reactant at the start of your equation:

$$Ca(HCO_3)_2 \rightarrow$$

Now you need to consider the products of the reaction: calcium carbonate, water and carbon dioxide. The formula for calcium carbonate is given in the question: $CaCO_3$. This can be added to the equation:

$$Ca(HCO_3)2 \rightarrow CaCO_3 +$$

You know that the formula for water is H_2O and for carbon dioxide it is CO_2. You can now add these to the equation to give your final answer.

$Ca(HCO_3)_2 \rightarrow CaCO_3 + H_2O + CO_2$

9 A student heated copper carbonate, $CuCO_3$ (a green powder), in a test tube.

A black powder (copper oxide, CuO) and a gas were produced during the reaction. The diagram below represents the reaction that occurred.

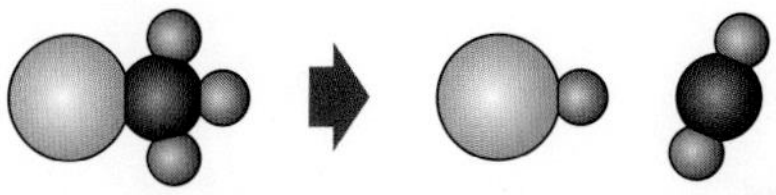

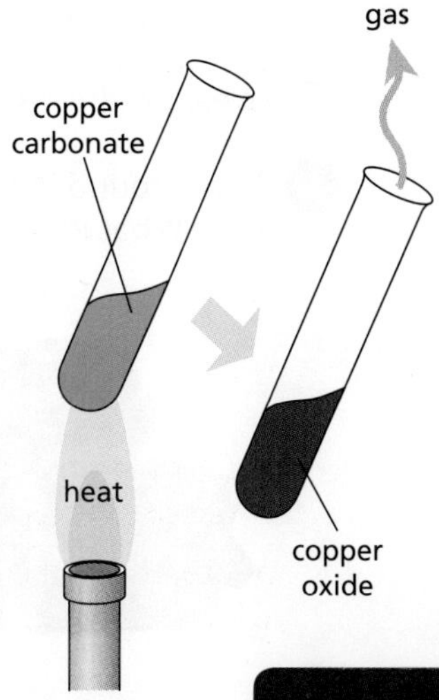

Write a symbol equation for the thermal decomposition of copper carbonate.

10.4 Oxidation

You are learning to:
- state the meaning of the term 'oxidation'
- describe the oxidation of metals
- describe the reduction of metal oxides
- represent reactions using formulae and equations.

1. Rust can form on the outside of iron objects. Rust is a form of iron oxide. Is iron oxide an element or a compound?

2. Complete the sentence about oxidation.

   Oxidation is a chemical reaction that involves …

3. Which **one** of the following reactions is an example of oxidation?

   a iron + oxygen → iron oxide

   b iron oxide → iron + oxygen

4. A student investigated the rusting of iron nails under different conditions. The table shows the results of their experiment.

Condition	Did the nail rust?
no oxygen	no
oxygen and water	yes
oxygen and no water	no
control (iron nail left in the air)	no

   What do the results tell you about the conditions needed for the oxidation of iron?

5. Iron is found in the Earth's crust as iron oxide, Fe_2O_3. Iron oxide can be reduced to produce iron. What is meant by the term 'reduced'?

6 Choose **two** similarities between rusting and combustion.

a they involve the production of gases

b they involve reduction

c they are chemical reactions

d they involve oxidation

e they are physical changes

f they can be reversed easily

g they need heating

Worked example

Which substance is being reduced in this reaction?

copper(II) oxide + hydrogen → copper + water

Reduction involves the removal of oxygen. You need to identify which substance has lost oxygen. The word 'oxide' in copper(II) oxide means oxygen is present in the compound. During the reaction, the copper(II) oxide is reduced by hydrogen, removing the oxygen to form copper and water.

copper(II) oxide

7 Iron oxide reacts with carbon to produce iron and carbon dioxide gas.

iron oxide + carbon → iron + carbon dioxide

a Which substance is being reduced in this reaction?

b Describe what is happening in this reaction using the terms 'oxidised' and 'reduced'.

8 A student investigated the oxidation of magnesium. They heated the magnesium in a small crucible with a lid. While heating, they used tongs to lift the lid to allow air into the crucible.

They measured the mass of the magnesium before the reaction and the mass of the product.

Explain why the mass of the product is greater than the mass of the original magnesium. Use ideas about the conservation of mass in your answer.

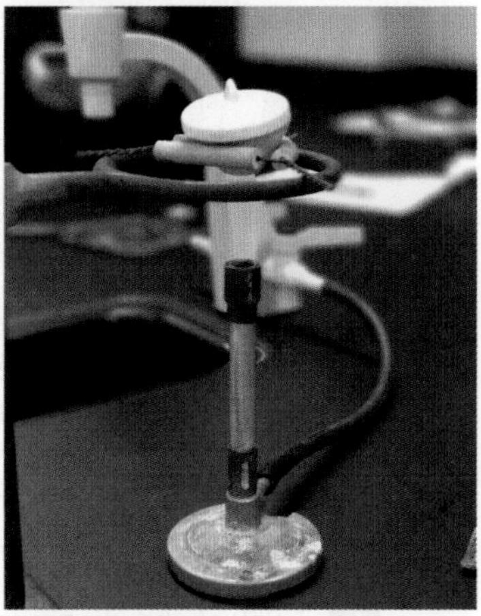

9 A teacher folded a piece of copper in half. They heated the copper in a hot flame for a few minutes. The outside surface turned black. After heating they opened the folded copper; inside it was still shiny and copper-coloured. Suggest why the copper turned black on the outside, but not on the inside.

10 Aluminium reacts quickly with oxygen in the air to make aluminium oxide. The surface of aluminium structures is protected by a layer of aluminium oxide. Iron also reacts with oxygen to make iron oxide (rust). This can flake off the surface of iron structures. Aluminium structures are less likely to corrode than iron structures.

a Write a word equation for the oxidation of aluminium.

b Suggest why aluminium structures are less likely to corrode than iron structures.

10.5 Neutralisation

You are learning to:

- recall the equation for a neutralisation reaction
- explain how water is made during a neutralisation reaction
- apply a model to explain neutralisation
- represent reactions using formulae and equations.

1 Complete the following general equation for the reaction between an acid and an alkali.

acid + alkali → __________ + ____________

2 What pH does a neutral solution have?

3 The stomach contains strong acid to help digestion. Indigestion tablets neutralise stomach acid. What does this tell you about the indigestion tablets?

4 A student tested a substance using universal indicator solution. The substance has a pH of 12. What would you add to the substance to neutralise it?

Worked example

The diagram below shows a model for the reaction between hydrochloric acid, HCl, and sodium hydroxide, NaOH. What are the two products of this neutralisation reaction? In your answer you should give the chemical formulae of the products.

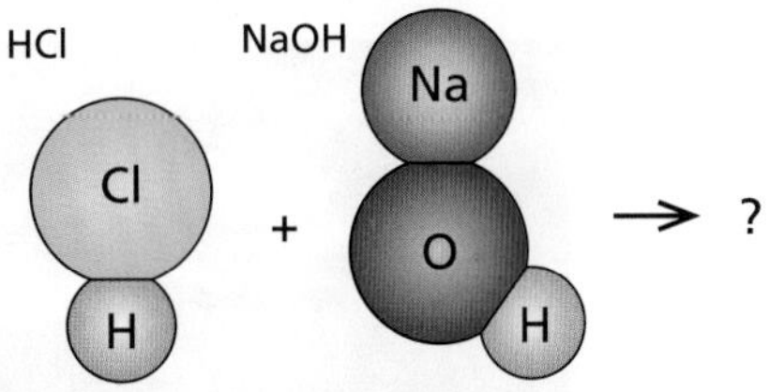

The model shows the structure of hydrochloric acid, HCl, and sodium hydroxide, NaOH, an alkali. You know that when the neutralisation happens a salt and water, H_2O, are produced. To work out the formula of the salt you need to look at the atoms that have been left behind once water is formed: Na and Cl. These two elements form the salt.

H_2O and NaCl

5 Look at the diagram. It shows a model of the reaction between an acid and an alkali.

Water is one of the products. Which of the following shows the other product? Choose the **one** correct statement.

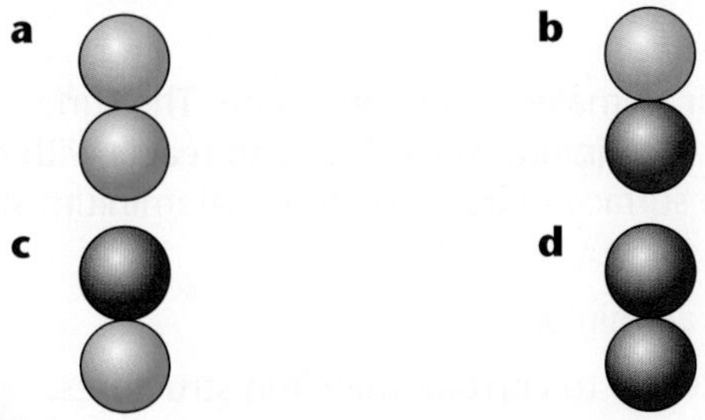

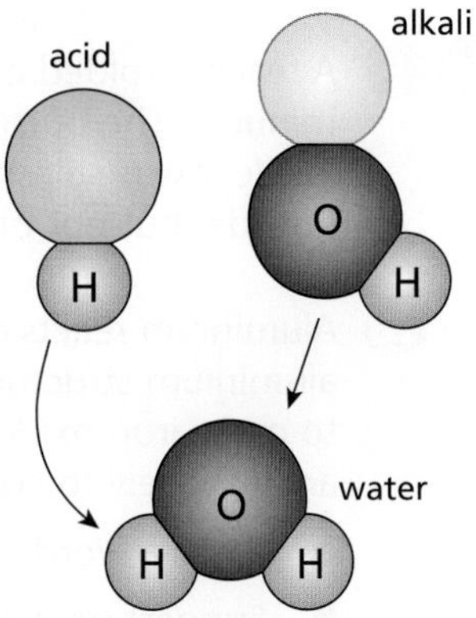

6 Give the chemical formulae of the two products formed in this neutralisation reaction.

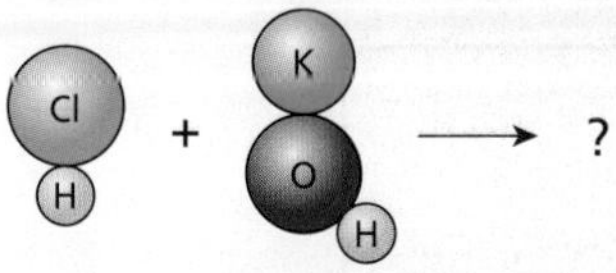

7 Ammonium phosphate is used as a fertiliser, which helps farmers to grow healthy crops. It can be made by reacting a substance called ammonium hydroxide with an acid.

Suggest which acid reacts with ammonium hydroxide to make ammonium phosphate.

a sulfuric acid

b hydrochloric acid

c phosphoric acid

d nitric acid

8 Complete the paragraph below about the formation of water in neutralisation reactions.

In a neutralisation reaction between an acid and an alkali, the ____**i**____ from the acid combines with the ____**ii**____ from the ____**iii**____. This forms water, H_2O.

9 A student investigated the neutralisation of hydrochloric acid. They put two drops of universal indicator into the acid and then added sodium hydroxide. The indicator turned blue. What does this result tell you about the reaction?

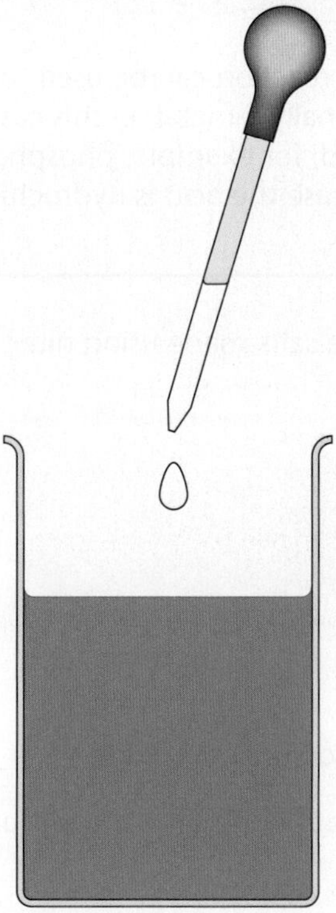

10.6 Reactions of acids and alkalis

You are learning to:

- describe the reaction between acids and metals
- describe the reaction between acids and carbonates
- predict the reactants used and the salt made by different neutralisation reactions
- represent reactions using formulae and equations.

1 Which statement completes the sentence about salts?

In science, a salt is a substance formed when…

a an acid is heated strongly.

b a soluble base dissolves in water.

c an acid reacts with a base.

d an alkali reacts with a base.

2 A student placed a piece of iron into a beaker containing hydrochloric acid. A gas was produced.

a How did the student know a gas was produced?

b Which gas is made when a metal reacts with hydrochloric acid?

Worked example

A student reacts hydrochloric acid with sodium hydroxide. Name the salt produced during this reaction.

The names of the acid and base in the reaction can be used to name the salt. The first half of the name comes from the base and is normally a metal; in this case, **sodium**. The second half of the name comes from the name of the acid; for example, phosphoric acid produces phosphates and sulfuric acid produces sulfates. In this case the acid is hydrochloric acid, which produces **chlorides**.

sodium chloride

3 Which **two** of the following are salts made using nitric acid?

a sodium chloride

b calcium sulfate

c sodium nitrate

d copper carbonate

e copper nitrate

4 Look at the following equation:

sulfuric acid + sodium hydroxide → ________ + water

Use the information in the equation to name the salt produced during the reaction.

5 Calcium hydroxide is an alkali. When calcium hydroxide reacts with hydrochloric acid, calcium chloride is formed.

Which **two** words best describe calcium chloride?

a element

b compound

c mixture

d base

e salt

6 A student added an indigestion tablet to some hydrochloric acid in a beaker. The student wrote down their observation as 'fizzing'.

The equation for the reaction is:

magnesium carbonate + hydrochloric acid → magnesium chloride + water + carbon dioxide

Use the equation to explain the student's observation.

7 Complete the following reaction equations:

a sulfuric acid + magnesium → __________ + ___________

b hydrochloric acid + magnesium hydroxide → _________ + water

c nitric acid + calcium carbonate → _________ + water + carbon dioxide

Worked example

Suggest the name of an acid and a base that could have been used to produce the salt magnesium nitrate during a neutralisation reaction.

The two parts of the name of the salt give you a clue about the names of the acid and the base. It is easier to work out the name of the acid first and then suggest the name of a base. The second half of the name of the salt comes from the name of the acid. 'Nitrate' indicates that nitric acid was used in the neutralisation reaction. The first half of the name of the salt comes from the base, in this case 'magnesium'. Bases are normally metal oxides, metal hydroxides or metal carbonates. If you had been told that one of the products was carbon dioxide, you would know a metal carbonate had been used. But you only know the name of the salt. So, the base could have been **magnesium oxide**, **magnesium hydroxide** or **magnesium carbonate**, and you just need to choose one of them. For this answer we have chosen magnesium hydroxide.

nitric acid and magnesium hydroxide

8 A student carried out a neutralisation reaction using an acid and a base.

During the reaction, water was produced alongside the salt, potassium sulfate. A gas was not produced. Suggest the name of an acid and a base that could have been used by the student to produce this salt.

9 Which of the following statements is **not** true?

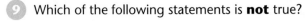

a When the acidity of a solution increases, the pH decreases.

b When an acid reacts with a base, a salt is produced.

c When an acid reacts with a metal, carbon dioxide is produced.

10.7 Displacement reactions

You are learning to:
- represent and explain displacement reactions using formulae and equations
- make inferences about reactivity from displacement reactions
- represent reactions using formulae and equations.

1. Complete the sentences about the reactivity series of metals.

   The reactivity series helps us to understand and predict displacement reactions that involve metals. In the reactivity series, metals are placed in order of reactivity, with _____**i**_____ metals at the top and _____**ii**_____ metals at the bottom.

2. Name the **two** non-metals found in the reactivity series of metals.

3. Chlorine and bromine are non-metals. Chlorine is more reactive than bromine. What will happen when chlorine is mixed with potassium bromide?

4. Give **one** observation that a student could make that shows there is a reaction between magnesium and copper sulfate.

Worked example

Use the reactivity series to explain what happens when iron is added to copper sulfate solution. Give an equation in your answer.

To answer this question you need to look at the reactivity series of metals and work out which is the more reactive metal: iron is more reactive than copper. This means the iron will displace the copper from the sulfate compound. You need to start your answer with the fact (what happens in the reaction) and then add the explanation.

Iron displaces the copper from the metal sulfate compound. This happens because iron is more reactive than copper.

The question also asks for an equation for the reaction, so you add that to your answer.

iron + copper sulfate → iron sulfate + copper

5. Use the reactivity series to explain what happens when potassium is added to magnesium nitrate solution. Give an equation in your answer.

6. A student carried out a series of displacement reactions. During their experiments they noticed that iron reacted with copper sulfate, but copper did not react with iron sulfate. Explain why.

7. Use the reactivity series to explain why carbon cannot be used to extract sodium from sodium oxide.

8 Describe the reaction between zinc and hydrochloric acid in terms of reactivity. Use an equation in your answer.

9 Use the reactivity series to complete the following equations.

a magnesium + potassium sulfate →

b potassium + magnesium nitrate →

c zinc sulfate + potassium →

d zinc + magnesium sulfate →

Most reactive	K	potassium
	Na	sodium
	Ca	calcium
	Mg	magnesium
	Al	aluminium
	C	carbon
	Zn	zinc
	Fe	iron
	Sn	tin
	Pb	lead
	H	hydrogen
	Cu	copper
	Ag	silver
	Au	gold
Least reactive	Pt	platinum

10 Chlorine, bromine and iodine are non-metals. Chlorine is a yellow gas, bromine is a brown/orange liquid and iodine is a purple solid. Chlorine is more reactive than bromine and bromine is more reactive than iodine. Match the reactants to the description of the reaction.

a chlorine + sodium iodide	**i** brown/orange solution is formed
b bromine + potassium chloride	**ii** purple precipitate is formed
c chlorine + sodium bromide	**iii** no change

11 A student predicted that metal **A** was more reactive than metal **B**. Plan an experiment to determine which metal is more reactive. You have samples of each metal and its metal sulfate.

You have the following equipment available:

- Beakers
- Pipettes
- Measuring cylinder
- Metal A
- Metal B
- Metal A sulfate solution
- Metal B sulfate solution
- Safety goggles

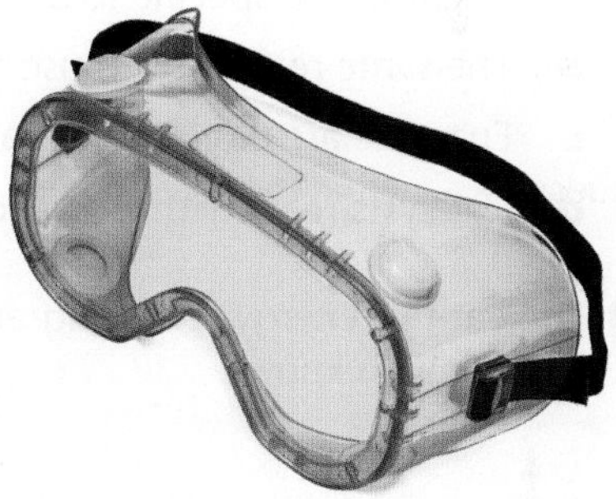

10.8 Energetics

You are learning to:
- describe examples of endothermic and exothermic reactions
- describe what a catalyst is and explain how they work
- explain the energy changes taking place during exothermic and endothermic reactions
- represent reactions using formulae and equations.

1 Name the piece of equipment used to measure differences in temperature.

2 What is a catalyst?

3 A student carried out an exothermic reaction.

a What would have happened to the temperature during this reaction?

b What happens to the energy released during an exothermic reaction?

4 Complete the table to show examples of endothermic and exothermic changes.

photosynthesis **thermal decomposition**
setting off fireworks **burning wood**

Endothermic changes	Exothermic changes

5 Which statement about catalysts is **false**?

a Catalysts are specific to a reaction.

b The same reaction can use many different catalysts.

c Enzymes are biological catalysts.

d Catalysts react with the reactants.

6 Look at this energy level diagram. Is it showing an exothermic or an endothermic reaction? How do you know?

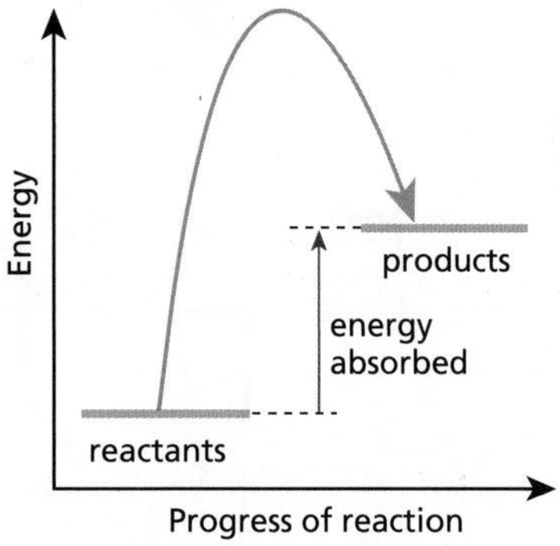

7 A teacher dissolved ammonium chloride in water. Ice formed on the outside of the conical flask, which stuck to a piece of wood.

Explain why ice formed on the outside of the flask.

8 A student investigated some reactions to see if they were exothermic or endothermic. They added reactant solutions to a test tube and measured the temperature change using a thermometer.

a Name **two** control variables for this investigation.

b Look at the photograph of the practical on the right. How could the student improve the method?

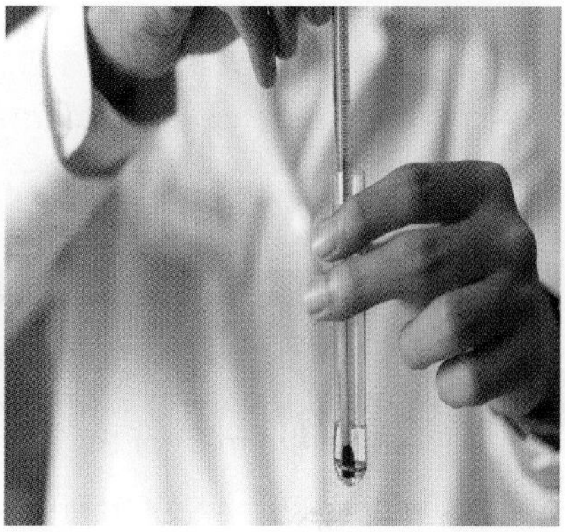

Worked example

Burning hydrogen is an example of an exothermic reaction.

hydrogen + oxygen → water

Explain why this is an exothermic reaction in terms of bond making and bond breaking.

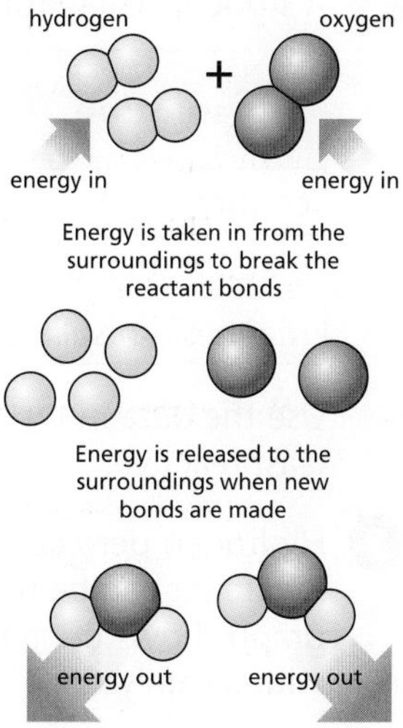

To answer this question you need to think about bond breaking and bond making. The hydrogen and oxygen molecules collide, putting energy into the molecules to break the reactant bonds. Bond breaking is endothermic, which means that energy is taken in from the surroundings. Bond making is exothermic. Energy is released to the surroundings when new bonds are made between the hydrogen and oxygen atoms to form water.

The difference between the amount of energy taken in to break the bonds and the amount of energy released when new bonds are formed determines if the overall reaction is exothermic or endothermic. Since you are told that this reaction is exothermic, it must be the case that more energy is released when the bonds are formed than is taken in when the bonds are broken.

The amount of energy released to the surroundings when the bonds are made in the water molecules is higher than the amount of energy taken in to break the bonds in the hydrogen and oxygen molecules. This means the overall reaction is exothermic.

9 Thermal decomposition of copper carbonate is an example of an endothermic reaction.

copper carbonate → copper oxide + carbon dioxide

Explain why this is an endothermic reaction in terms of bond breaking and bond making.

Maths and practical skills

1 Which of the following is the most appropriate unit to measure energy?

a centigrade **b** joules **c** seconds **d** amperes **e** degrees

2 A student tested a solution using universal indicator. The indicator turned yellow. What pH was the solution?

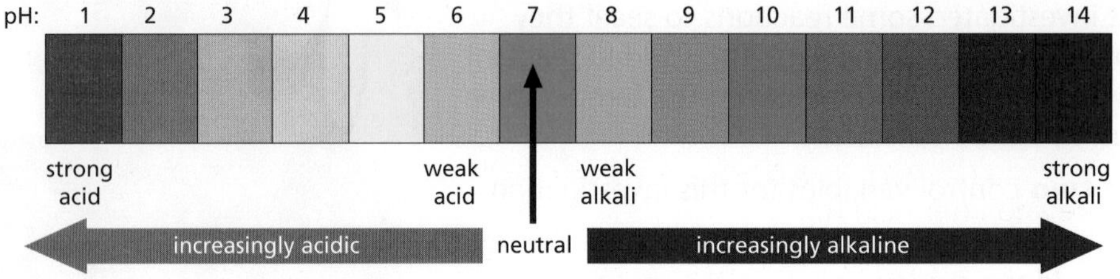

3 A student measures the mass of a strip of magnesium as 0.12 g. They heat the magnesium, then measure the mass of the magnesium oxide produced. The mass is 0.20 g.

magnesium + oxygen → magnesium oxide

a What is this type of reaction called?

b Calculate the mass of oxygen that reacted with the magnesium during the reaction. Show your working.

4 A student reacted three metals with different salt solutions. Here are their results.

Salt solution	Metal		
	Copper	**Magnesium**	**Metal X**
copper sulfate		reaction	reaction
metal X sulfate	no reaction	reaction	
magnesium sulfate	no reaction		no reaction

Use the data in the table to put the metals in order of reactivity, from the most reactive to the least reactive.

5 Hydrogen peroxide decomposes to make oxygen and water. A catalyst can be used to help the reaction take place. The graph shows the rate of decomposition of hydrogen peroxide with a catalyst.

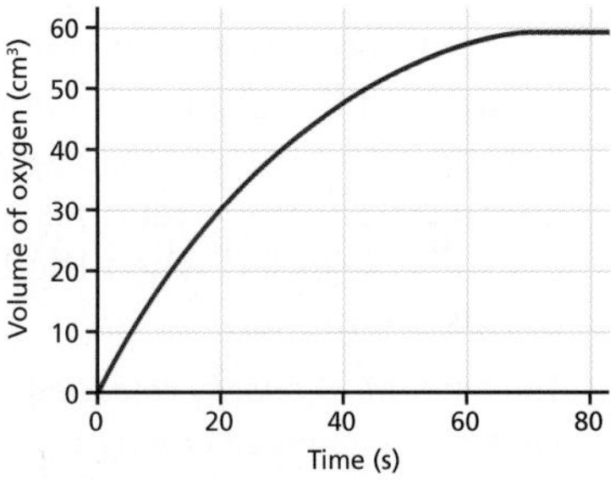

a What volume of oxygen has been produced after 20 seconds?

b At what time did the reaction stop?

6 A scientist had three solutions, labelled **Q**, **R** and **S**. Here is a table showing the pH of each solution.

Solution	pH
Q	7
R	1
S	5

Which of the following shows the correct universal indicator colour for each solution? Use the diagram in question 2 to help you.

a **Q** = red; **R** = yellow; **S** = green

b **Q** = green; **R** = red; **S** = yellow

c **Q** = green; **R** = yellow; **S** = red

d **Q** = yellow; **R** = red; **S** = green

7 A drop of alkali and a drop of acid are placed a few centimetres apart on a piece of filter paper. The acid and alkali spread through the paper. A neutralisation reaction takes place where the solutions meet in the middle. A few drops of universal indicator are placed on the middle of the filter paper. What colour is the universal indicator likely to be? Use the figure in question 2 to help you.

8 A teacher heated a crucible containing copper carbonate powder. They measured the mass of the crucible before and after heating.

copper carbonate → copper oxide + carbon dioxide

Mass of crucible (g)	Mass of crucible and copper carbonate (g)	Mass of crucible and copper oxide (g)
45.00	46.24	45.80

a What type of reaction is this?

b Use the results to find the mass of copper oxide and the mass of carbon dioxide produced during the reaction. Show your working.

9 A student placed a copper wire, a silver wire and a lead wire into dilute hydrochloric acid. Only one of the metals reacted.

a Which metal reacted and why? Use the reactivity series to explain your answer.

b Write a word equation for the reaction.

10 A student adds lumps of metal carbonate to an acid. The graph shows how the mass of metal carbonate changes during the reaction.

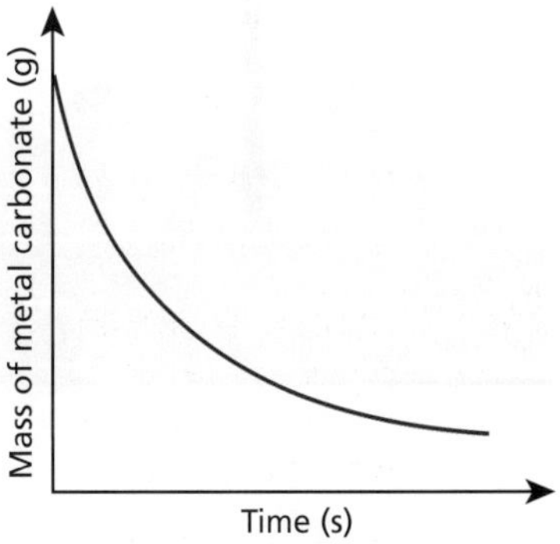

a Which reactant is used up in the reaction: the acid or the metal carbonate? How do you know?

b Use the information in the graph to describe the rate of reaction.

c Explain why the mass does not decrease at a constant rate.

d The experiment was repeated using the same mass of metal carbonate as a powder instead of lumps. The student drew a graph of their new results. Which **two** of these statements about the graph would be true?

i The mass of metal carbonate would fall more quickly.

ii The mass of metal carbonate would fall more slowly.

iii The mass of metal carbonate left at the end of the reaction would be the same.

iv The mass of metal carbonate left at the end of the reaction would be lower.

11 Materials road map

Where are you in your learning journey and where are you aiming to be?

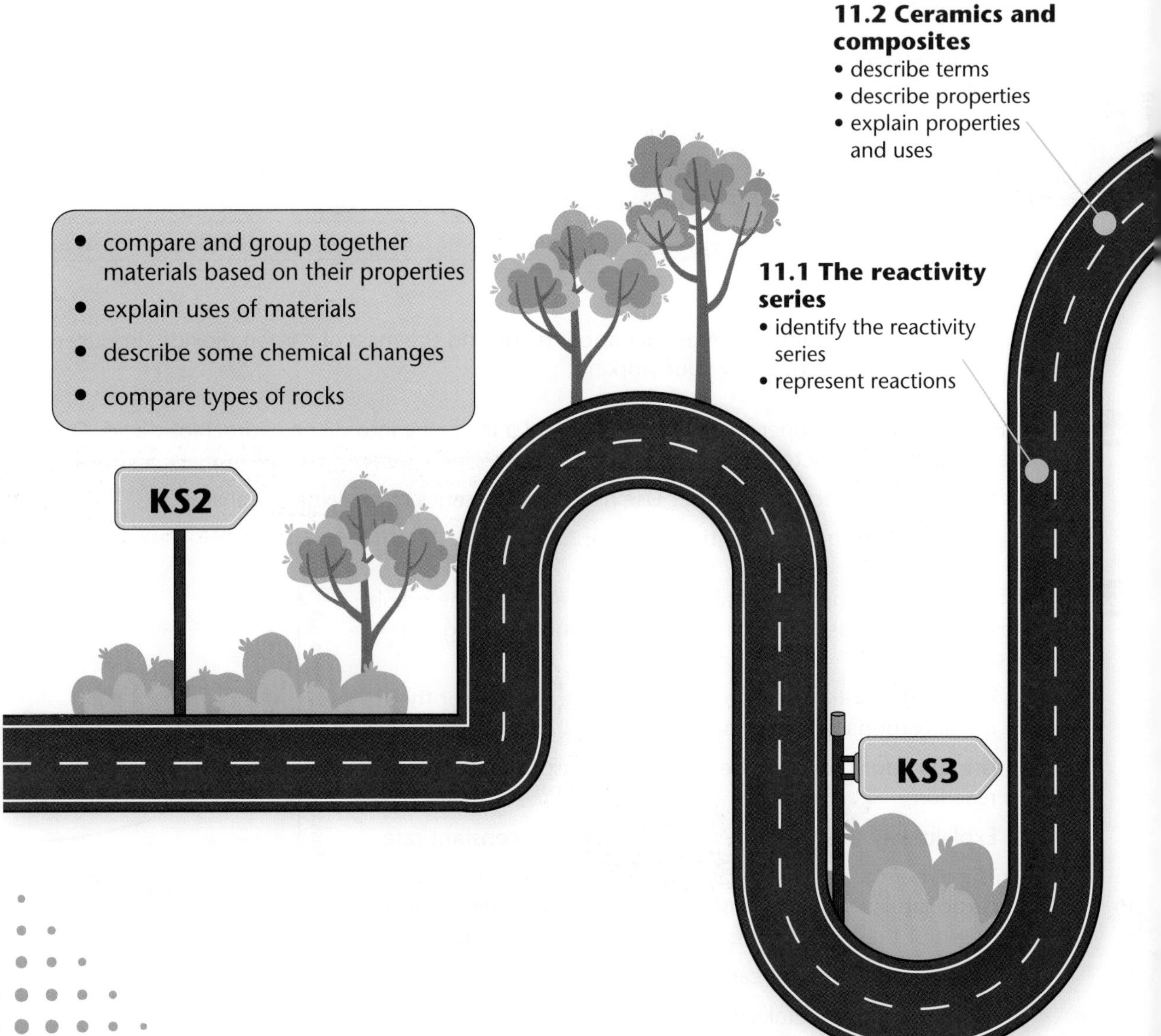

- the reactivity series
- extraction of metals and reduction
- alternative methods of extracting metals
- ways of reducing the use of resources
- polymers
- cracking and alkanes
- metal oxides
- oxidation and reduction in terms of electrons

11.3 Using the reactivity series
- describe extraction using carbon

11.4 Polymers
- present observations and data
- describe terms
- describe properties

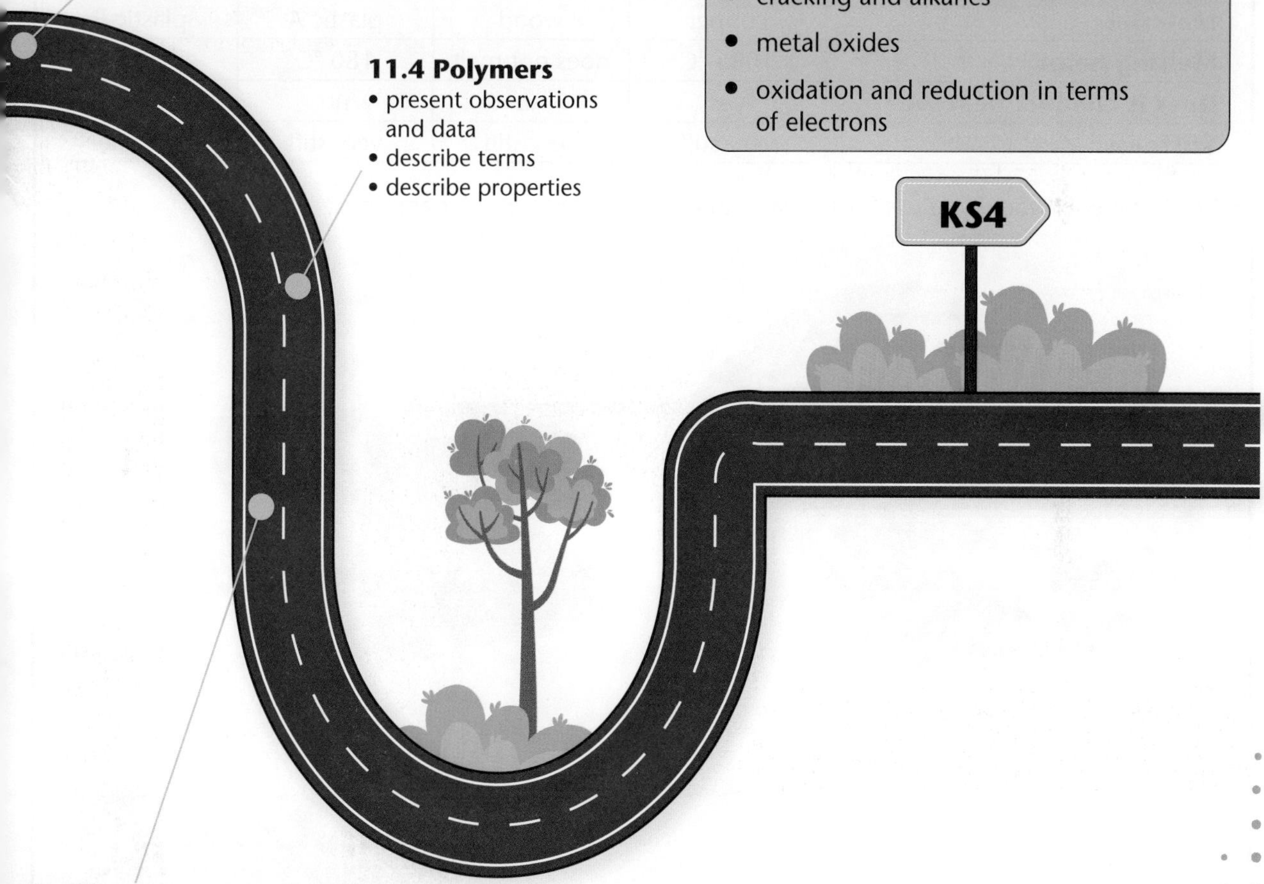

Maths and practical skills

- making scientific predictions
- presenting data using tables and graphs
- interpreting observations and data
- calculating results and converting between different units
- using equations to calculate answers
- using SI units and chemical names and symbols

11 Materials

Different materials are suitable for different jobs, depending on their properties. Ceramics, polymers, and composites are used for lots of different jobs, from bricks to bags, plates to false teeth. Metals are also useful materials. Some metals are more reactive than others, and we can put metals into a reactivity series to help us predict how they will react.

Which material is best for the job?

A company wants to make a saucepan and is deciding which material to use for the handle. Look at the following information, which shows the properties of some different materials. The melting point is the temperature at which a material melts.

Material	copper	wood	plastic A	plastic B
Melting point	1085 °C	does not melt	180 °C	220 °C
Does it conduct heat well?	yes	no	no	no
Stiffness	very stiff	very stiff	very stiff	flexible

Which material would you use for the saucepan handle? Explain your answer.

copper

wood

plastic A

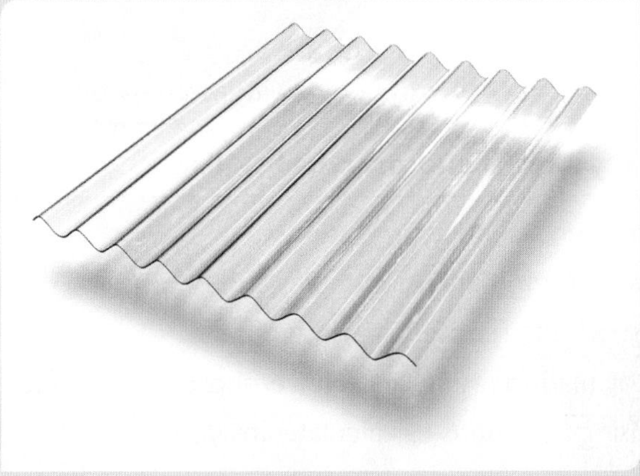
plastic B

Using your science skills

Could you be an aerospace engineer?

Could you be an aerospace engineer? Aerospace might sound daunting, but it actually just means anything above ground level, in the Earth's atmosphere or outer space. You would work with the materials, structures and machines used in the aerospace industry. You might work on aeroplanes, satellites or spacecraft. You would be discovering new ways to improve materials and processes for products used in the aerospace industry. To do this, you would need a good understanding of the manufacturing, processing and properties of relevant materials, including metals and composites.

You could be responsible for making the satellites and equipment that make weather forecasts, mobile phones, television broadcast and space flight possible. Or work with manufacturers to make aircraft safer, lighter and more efficient, reducing their environmental impact.

Natural and human-made materials are very important in lots of areas, including in medicine. A **polymer engineer** investigates possible uses of materials known as polymers, and develops new ones. Polymers have many uses in medicine, including in drug delivery and cancer therapy.

Materials engineers research the behaviour of materials used in industry to understand material failures and design them to be efficient and sustainable. They research new ways to combine materials by analysing test data to design and develop prototypes of new products and manufacturing processes.

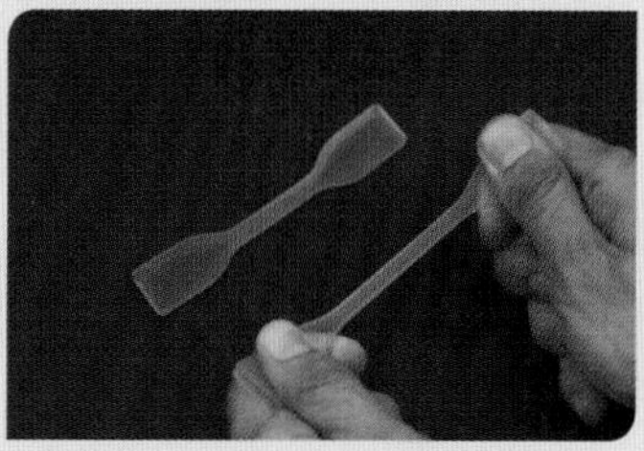

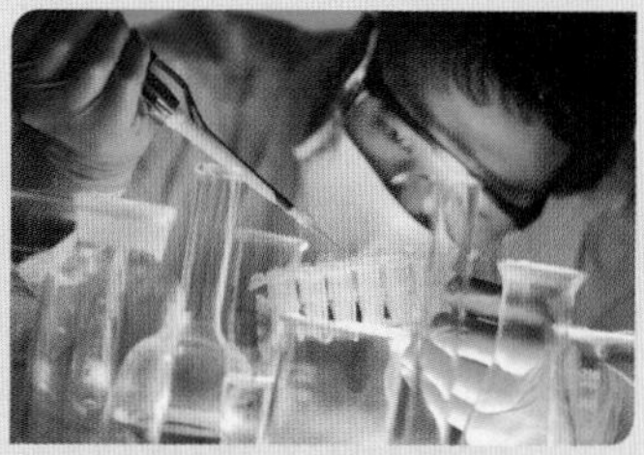

Chemical engineers turn raw materials into a range of useful substances. They need to understand how to make the large number of useful materials used in industries and homes. Chemical engineers focus on turning one chemical into something else, such as making plastic from oil.

Dental technicians work with a variety of different materials, including polymers and ceramics, to help improve and/or replace lost teeth. They work with information provided by dentists to make dentures, veneers, bridges, crowns and braces. Dental technicians need a good understanding of the science of dental materials, to ensure that the correct material is selected to benefit the required work.

Chemical metallurgists extract useful metals from their ores. They do this by testing the ore to see how easily the metal can be removed, and then design a process for removing the metal on a larger scale. These processes may require clever techniques or a lot of heat and energy in order to extract a useable metal. Chemical metallurgists can also be responsible for testing metals to make sure they are of a good quality. They also help to design cleaner, more efficient processes that produce less waste.

Knowledge organiser

Metals, ceramics, polymers and composites are useful materials with different properties. Understanding the properties of a material helps us to decide how best to use it. It also helps us to choose the most suitable material for a job. For example, a plate could be made from a ceramic (like pottery or glass), a metal or a polymer (like plastic). Each material has properties that make it useful for making plates, but they also have disadvantages. Evaluating the properties of each material helps us to select the most appropriate one.

A **ceramic** is an **inorganic** (not carbon-based), non-metallic solid. It is prepared by the action of heat on a substance, such as clay, followed by cooling. Ceramics have lots of uses, including for making tiles, glass, bricks, pottery, plates, vases and ornamental objects.

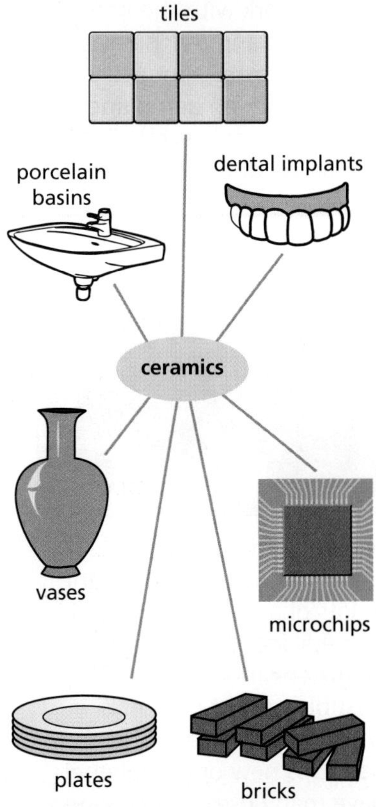

Some metals are more reactive than others. The reactivity of the different metals can be compared by observing their reactions – the more vigorous the reaction, the more reactive the metal.

Name of metal	Observations with acid
sodium	explosive reaction occurs; any hydrogen produced catches fire spontaneously
copper	no visible change occurs
magnesium	vigorous production of hydrogen bubbles; the test tube becomes hot quickly

This information on the reactivity of different metals can be used to form a **reactivity series** of metals. The non-metals carbon and hydrogen are also usually included in the reactivity series. This helps us to understand how the different metals will behave in some important chemical reactions.

Most reactive

K	potassium
Na	sodium
Ca	calcium
Mg	magnesium
Al	aluminium
C	carbon
Zn	zinc
Fe	iron
Sn	tin
Pb	lead
H	hydrogen
Cu	copper
Ag	silver
Au	gold
Pt	platinum

Least reactive

Ceramics are very useful because of their properties. Most are:

- hard and resistant to wear
- relatively light
- brittle – they can break easily if a force is applied
- **thermal insulators** – they keep heat in
- **electrical insulators** – they do not allow electric current to pass through
- non-magnetic
- chemically stable – they do not break down in air
- **non-toxic** – they can be used for food and drink
- non-**ductile** – they cannot be drawn out into wire.

Composites are formed when two or more materials, often with different properties, are combined. The composite is usually stronger, more **durable** or has other desirable properties compared to the materials it is made from.

Composites normally have two parts. One acts as the **matrix** or binder. The other is **reinforcement**, which is usually fibres, crystals or fragments.

Concrete is a composite made from natural materials, some of which have been processed. First, limestone and clay are heated to over 700 °C in a kiln to make cement. This is then added to sand, water and gravel to make concrete. The proportions of the ingredients determine the overall properties of the concrete.

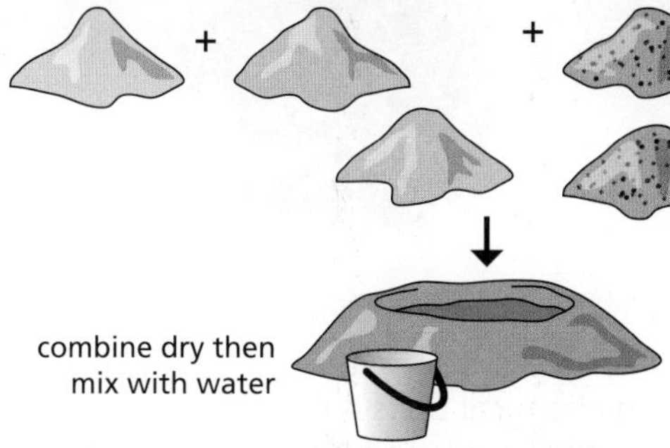

Wood and bone are natural composites. Wood is made of cellulose and lignin; the lignin acts as a glue, binding the fibres of cellulose together. Bone is made of a soft, flexible protein called collagen and a hard **brittle** mineral; the mineral reinforces the collagen, making it stronger.

Concrete can be reinforced with steel. Concrete and steel expand in a very similar way when heated. Concrete has a high **compressive strength**, making it strong when **compressed**. Steel has a high **tensile strength**; this means a lot of force can be applied before it will break.

Key vocabulary	
brittle	breaks easily if force is applied
ceramic	an inorganic, non-metallic solid prepared by heating and then cooling substances such as clay
composite	two or more materials combined together to improve their properties
compress	squash with a force
compressive strength	a measure of how well a material resists being squashed when a force is applied
ductile	can be stretched out into a thin wire
durable	hard-wearing; able to withstand wear
electrical insulator	a material that does not allow an electric current to pass through it
inorganic	not carbon-based
matrix	a substance in which other materials are embedded
non-toxic	not poisonous or toxic
reactive	inclined to react in a chemical reaction
reactivity series	a list of metals from the most reactive to the least reactive; also includes two non-metals (hydrogen and carbon)
reinforcement	a material included in a composite material to give it strength
tensile strength	the **tension** a material can withstand without breaking
tension	a force that stretches or elongates something
thermal insulator	a material that does not allow energy to pass through it quickly by the process of thermal conduction

Only a few metals are found in their **pure** form in the Earth's crust. Gold, silver and platinum are examples of these. The majority of other metals are found chemically combined with other elements in the form of an **ore**. Oxygen and sulfur are elements that metals are commonly combined with in ores.

Lead ore – galena, PbS

Iron ore – haematite, Fe_2O_3

Copper ore – malachite, $CuCO_3(OH)_2$

Lead metal, Pb

Iron metal, Fe

Copper metal, Cu

Carbon can be used to **extract** metals from their ores in a **displacement reaction**. This method can only be used to extract metals that are less reactive than carbon, such as copper or iron. The position of carbon in the reactivity series shows which metals are more reactive and which are less reactive than carbon.

Carbon is more reactive than iron; this means iron can be extracted from its ore using carbon. When iron ore is roasted with carbon, a displacement reaction happens. Carbon removes the oxygen or sulfur the iron is combined with and displaces the metal. If oxygen is removed, then **reduction** has occurred. Carbon is a **reducing agent** because it removes oxygen from the metal oxide:

iron oxide + carbon → carbon dioxide + iron

The more reactive a metal, the harder it is for the metal compound to decompose. This is because metals with a high reactivity make stronger bonds in compounds.

Polymers are chemicals made from long chains of repeating chemical units – the repeating molecule is called a **monomer**. Polymers have very large molecules. Their structure often has a shape that provides them with particular properties. The arrangement of molecules within a polymer defines this shape.

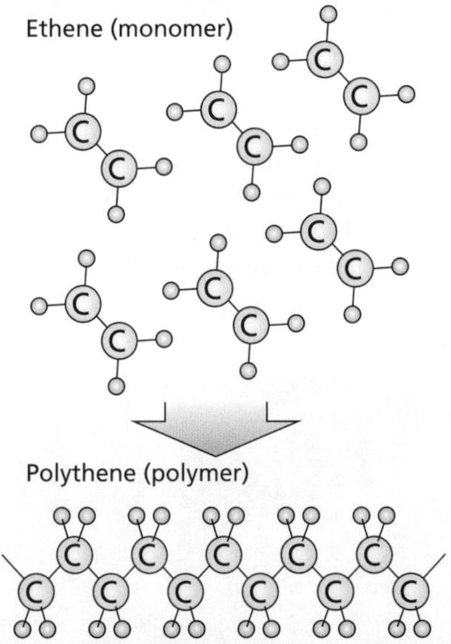

The type of monomer, the way it is bonded and the length of the polymer chain all determine the properties of a polymer. Many human-made (**synthetic**) polymers are strong and tough, but unlike ceramics, they tend to be flexible.

Many polymers are **strong** because of the number of chemical bonds within their structure. Some are **elastic**, for example, muscle fibre and rubber. In elastic polymers, the long chains are tangled up in their natural state and they straighten out into long lengths when a force is applied.

Human-made polymers include plastics. Polyethene is an example of a plastic. It is a polymer formed from a long chain of ethene monomers. The types of monomer, the way they are bonded and the length of the polymer chain all affect the properties of human-made polymers. The longer the polymer chain, for example, the higher the melting and boiling points. Many human-made polymers are not biodegradable. This means they will not break down completely in the environment.

In nature, starch, proteins and DNA are all examples of polymers. Like synthetic polymers, natural polymers can have very different properties. The way the monomers are arranged in the polymer gives it its shape. The shape of a natural polymer is often very important, because it can influence its behaviour and properties. Examples of this are starch and cellulose, which are both polymers made from glucose. They have different shapes and different properties. Starch is easy to break down, which makes it a useful way to store glucose inside cells. Cellulose is hard to break down and is very tough and strong, which makes it useful in plant cell walls.

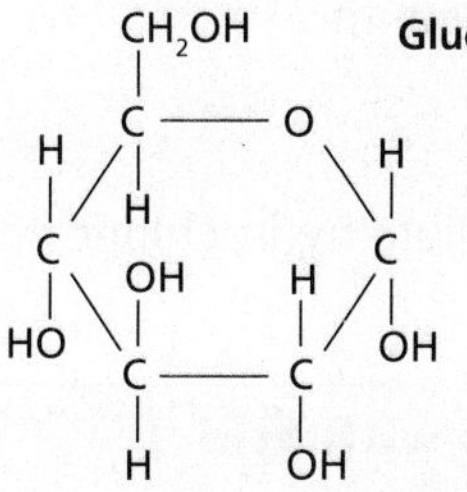

Glucose

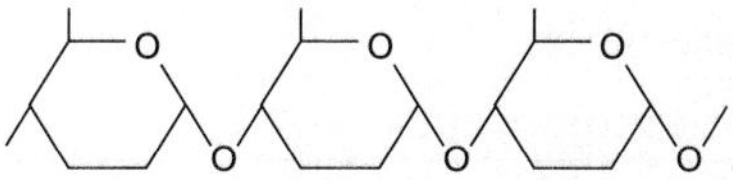

Starch

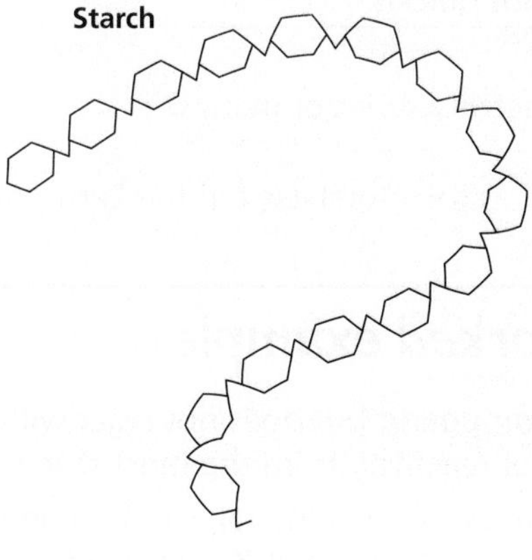

Key vocabulary

displacement reaction	a chemical reaction in which one substance takes the place of another in a compound
elastic	able to return to the original shape and size after a force is removed
extract	remove from
monomer	a small molecule that becomes chemically bonded to other monomers to form a polymer
ore	a naturally occurring rock that a metal (or mineral) can be extracted from
polymer	a large molecule made up of a very long chain of smaller molecules
pure	a substance containing only one type of element or compound
reducing agent	a chemical that removes oxygen from a compound
reduction	a chemical reaction in which oxygen is removed from a compound
strong	able to resist a force
synthetic	made by a chemical process, not naturally occurring

11.1 The reactivity series

You are learning to:
- use evidence to identify the reactivity series of metals
- represent reactions using formulae and equations.

1 Which **one** of these metals is found in the Earth's crust as a pure substance, not combined with any other element?

a iron **b** copper **c** sodium **d** gold **e** magnesium

2 Metals can be placed in order of reactivity in a reactivity series. What happens to the reactivity of the metals as you go down the reactivity series?

3 Magnesium is a metal. Metal **A** displaces magnesium from its compound. What does this tell you about metal **A**?

a metal **A** is calcium

b metal **A** is more reactive than magnesium

c metal **A** is less reactive than magnesium

d metal **A** is copper

4 A student reacted some metals with dilute hydrochloric acid. Compare the reactivity of the three metals.

Name of metal	Observations with acid
sodium	explosive reaction occurs; any hydrogen produced catches fire spontaneously
copper	no visible change occurs
magnesium	vigorous production of hydrogen bubbles; the test tube becomes hot quickly

5 Why is carbon included in the reactivity series of metals?

6 Explain why silver is mainly found as the metal itself in the Earth, rather than as a compound.

Worked example

Metal **X** displaces copper from its compound but does not react with zinc chloride. Put the metals **X**, copper and zinc in order of reactivity from the most reactive to the least reactive.

A more reactive metal will displace a less reactive metal from its compound. Metal **X** displaces copper from its compound. This tells you that metal **X** is more reactive than copper.

Metal X does not react with zinc chloride. This tells you that metal **X** is less reactive than zinc because it cannot displace zinc from its compound.

zinc (most reactive), metal X, copper (least reactive)

7 Students wanted to work out where an unknown metal **Z** is located in the reactivity series. They attempted to react the metal with iron oxide, magnesium oxide and tin oxide. Metal **Z** displaced tin and iron from their compounds but did not react with magnesium oxide. Iron is more reactive than tin.

a Place the metals in order of reactivity, from the most reactive to the least reactive.

b Write a word equation for the reaction between metal **Z** and iron oxide.

8 When aluminium was discovered, it cost more than gold. It was displayed next to the French crown jewels at an exhibition in 1855. Explain why aluminium was discovered so much later than gold.

the French crown jewels

aluminium spoon

9 A displacement reaction occurred when a student mixed iron filings with copper sulfate solution.

a What is meant by the term 'displacement'?

b Describe the observations you would expect to see in this reaction.

c Write a word equation for this reaction.

10 A student reacted three metals, **A**, **B** and **C**, with dilute hydrochloric acid. They also tested to see if compounds of the metals could be reduced by carbon.

Metal	Does the metal react with hydrochloric acid?	Is a compound of the metal reduced by carbon?
A	no	yes
B	yes	yes
C	yes	no

a What does the term 'reduced' mean?

b The compound of metal **C** was not reduced by carbon. What does this tell you about metal **C**?

c Place the metals in order of reactivity, with the most reactive metal first. Explain your answer.

11.2 Ceramics and composites

You are learning to:
- describe what is meant by the terms 'ceramic' and 'composite'
- describe the properties of ceramics and composites
- explain how the properties of ceramics and composites determine their uses.

1 Which of the following are examples of ceramics?

a pottery **b** plastic **c** wood **d** glass

2 What is a composite? Choose from the sentences below.

a Two or more materials combined together to improve their properties.
b A large molecule made up of a very long chain of smaller molecules.
c An inorganic, non-metallic solid.
d A substance into which other materials are embedded.

3 Bricks are made of clay that has been heated and then cooled. What type of material is brick?

4 State **two** properties of ceramics.

5 Which **one** of the following is a property of ceramics but **not** of metals?

a high melting point **b** hard **c** brittle **d** ductile

Worked example

Explain why wood is an example of a natural composite.

This question requires you to explain. Start with the relevant fact.

A composite contains a matrix (or binder) and a reinforcement, which is usually fibres, crystals or fragments.

Then explain why that fact means that wood is a composite.

Wood contains lignin and fibres of cellulose. The lignin acts like a glue, binding the fibres of cellulose together.

6 Explain why composites can be more useful than the individual materials they are made from.

7 What property of ceramics means that they are **not** used in electrical wires?

8 A student investigated the strength of concrete made from different mixtures of cement, sand and aggregate (small pieces of rock). They added the same amount of water to each mixture to make four concrete bars.

Concrete mixture	Aggregate (g)	Sand (g)	Cement (g)
A	150	100	50
B	200	100	50
C	250	100	50
D	300	100	50

a What is the independent variable for the investigation? Explain your answer.

b Name a control variable for the investigation.

c What is the ratio of cement to sand in mixture **A**?

d What is the ratio of cement to aggregate in mixture **C**?

9 Which of these processes could be used to make ceramics?

a thermal decomposition

b heating in a furnace

c melting sand

d shaping clay

e reducing metal oxide

10 Most composites contain a matrix (or binder) and a reinforcement. Explain how these two components work together in the composite.

11 Complete the paragraph about concrete that contains steel. Use the words below.

reinforcement **compressive** **tensile** **matrix** **brittle**

Concrete is a composite material. Steel rods can be added to concrete to make structures like buildings and bridges. The steel acts as a ____**i**____ in the concrete, making it stronger.

The steel helps the concrete to resist squashing forces, which gives it a high ____**ii**____ strength. It also helps to resist stretching forces, which means reinforced concrete also has a high ____**iii**____ strength.

11.3 Using the reactivity series

You are learning to:
- describe how carbon can be used to extract metals from metal oxides.

1 What is an ore?

2 Which statement correctly describes 'reduction'?

a the removal of oxygen from a compound

b the removal of any element from a compound

c a reaction in which one substance takes the place of another in a compound

d a reaction in which a larger molecule is broken into several smaller molecules

Worked example

Carbon can be used to extract lead from the compound lead oxide. Use the reactivity series to explain why.

This question requires you to explain. Start with the relevant fact: in this case, we need to look at the positions of lead and carbon in the reactivity series.

Carbon is above lead in the reactivity series, which means that carbon is more reactive than lead. Now explain the fact: why can carbon be used to extract lead? Explain the answer in terms of displacement: the more reactive element can displace the less reactive element from its compound.

Carbon is more reactive than lead. This means carbon can displace lead from lead oxide, to obtain lead.

Most reactive	K	potassium
	Na	sodium
	Ca	calcium
	Mg	magnesium
	Al	aluminium
	C	carbon
	Zn	zinc
	Fe	iron
	Sn	tin
	Pb	lead
	H	hydrogen
	Cu	copper
	Ag	silver
	Au	gold
Least reactive	Pt	platinum

3 Use the reactivity series to work out which of these metals **cannot** be extracted using carbon. Explain your answer.

a tin **b** potassium **c** copper

4 Complete the paragraph using the words below.

reduced **oxygen** **ores** **oxidised** **acids**

Metals react with ___**i**___ to form metal oxides. Many metal ___**ii**___ contain metal oxides. Iron oxide can be ___**iii**___ to remove the oxygen and form iron.

5 Which **two** of these words describe the extraction of metal from a metal oxide using carbon?

a displacement **b** oxidation **c** neutralisation **d** reduction

e thermal decomposition

6 Carbon can be used to extract lead from its ore, lead oxide, by reduction.

Write a word equation for the reduction of lead oxide by carbon.

7 Zinc oxide reacts with carbon to form zinc. Explain what happens to the zinc oxide and carbon in terms of oxidation and reduction.

8 Describe how carbon can be used to extract metals from their ores. Use these words in your answer:

reduce/reduction **reactivity series** **displacement reaction** **reducing agent**

9 Which of these metal oxides is easiest to reduce? Explain your answer.

a copper oxide **b** lead oxide **c** iron oxide

10 Iron can be extracted from its ore in a blast furnace. Inside the ore, the iron is found in compounds such as iron oxide, Fe_2O_3.

Carbon is a reducing agent used to extract iron from its ore.

a What does 'reducing agent' mean?

b Write a word equation for the reaction between carbon and iron oxide.

c Here is the symbol equation for the reaction:

$3C + 2Fe_2O_3 \rightarrow 3CO_2 + 4Fe$

Which substance has been oxidised in the reaction? Explain your answer.

11 A student attempted to extract the metals below by heating the metal oxides with carbon in a crucible.

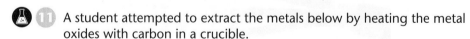

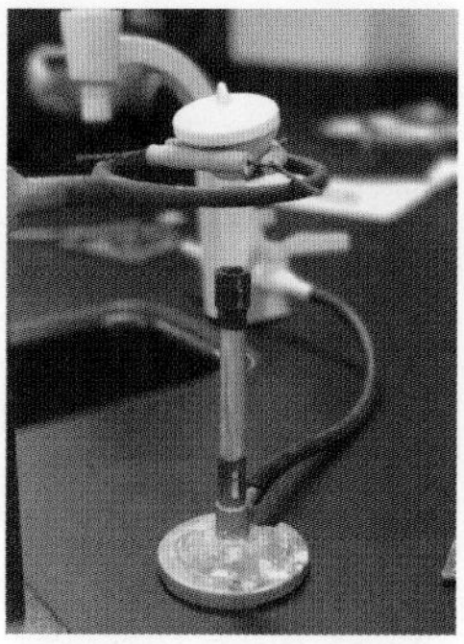

a zinc **b** aluminium

Describe and explain the results you would expect from the experiment. Include word equations where relevant.

12 Copper is extracted from copper oxide in a chemical reaction.

Copper oxide is formed from copper carbonate in a thermal decomposition reaction.

Compare these two chemical reactions. In your answer:

- Write a word equation for each reaction.
- Compare the products formed.
- Compare the types of reaction that happen.
- State whether heating is required for each reaction.

11.4 Polymers

You are learning to:
- present observations and data using appropriate methods, including tables and graphs
- describe what is meant by the term 'polymer'
- describe the properties and uses of human-made polymers.

1 What is a polymer? Choose from the statements below.

a A polymer is a large molecule made up of a very long chain of smaller molecules.

b A polymer is a small molecule that becomes chemically bonded to others to form a large molecule.

2 Which of the following is a polymer?

a nylon **b** aluminium **c** concrete

3 Starch is a natural polymer. Name **two** other natural polymers.

4 A type of human-made polymer is used to make plastic drinks bottles. Choose four properties from the table below that would make the polymer a good choice for drinks bottles. Explain your choices.

non-toxic	brittle	insoluble	lightweight
soluble	toxic	ductile	strong

5 A biodegradable substance can be broken down by microorganisms in the environment. Most human-made polymers are not biodegradable. Explain why this is a problem.

6 Both ceramics and polymers tend to be poor electrical conductors. Explain why polymers are used as insulation around electrical wires rather than ceramics.

Worked example

How many monomers are in the polymer chain shown below?

monomer

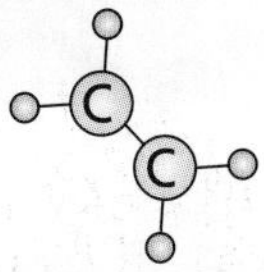

polymer

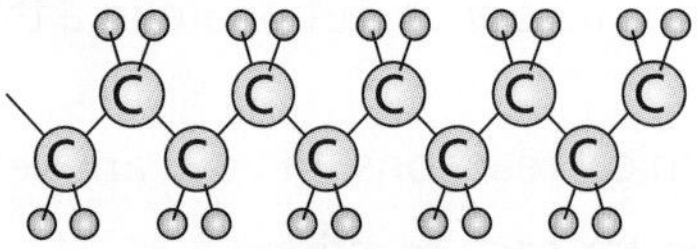

The easiest way to identify how many monomers are in this example is to look at the number of carbon atoms in the monomer and compare it to the number of carbon atoms in the polymer. There are ten carbon atoms in the polymer. As there are two carbon atoms in the monomer, this would suggest five monomers were needed to make this polymer.

5

7 Starch is a polymer of glucose molecules. Here is a simplified diagram of glucose and starch. How many monomers are in the polymer chain shown in the diagram?

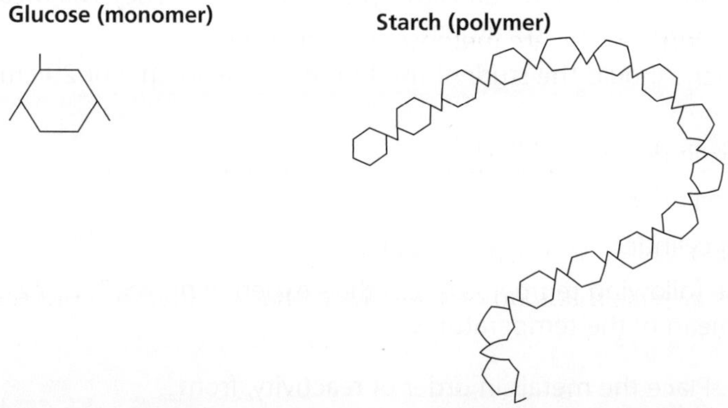

8 A group of students carried out an experiment to see how far a piece of plastic could be stretched before it broke. Their results are shown below.

Mass added to the plastic (g)	Distance the plastic stretched (mm)			
	Trial 1	Trial 2	Trial 3	Mean
0	0	0	0	0
100	17	19	18	18
200	42	41	41	?
300	73	74	73	73
400	112	113	112	112
500	147	149	148	148

a Calculate the mean extension for a mass of 200 g. Give your answer to 2 s.f.

b Explain why the students carried out repeats in their experiment.

c Plot a graph of the mass added to the plastic against the mean distance the plastic stretched.

9 The diagram below shows two types of plastic. The long polymer strands inside the plastic are shown by blue lines.

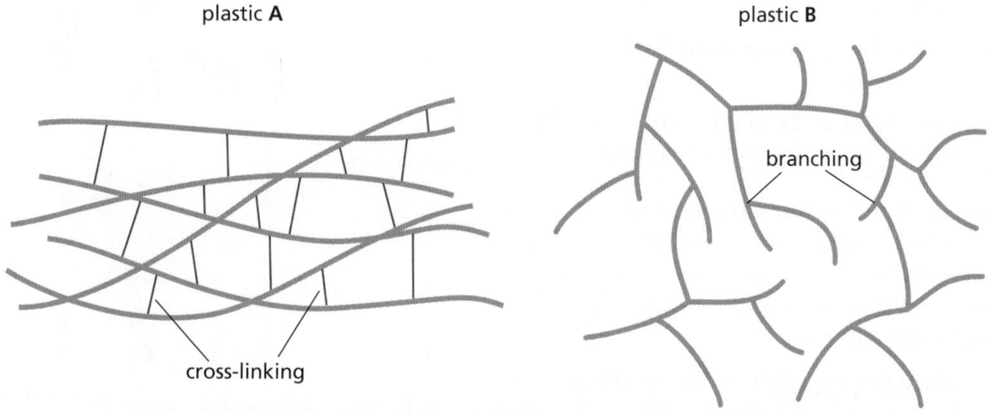

a Plastic **B** can easily be stretched. Why do you think this is the case? Use information in the diagrams to explain your answer.

b Suggest why plastic **A** has a high melting point.

c Suggest why plastic **B** has a lower density.

Maths and practical skills

1 A student plans an experiment to react a metal with hydrochloric acid. They will measure the temperature of the reaction during the experiment.

a Which piece of equipment should the student use to measure a volume of 20 cm^3 of hydrochloric acid?

i 10 cm^3 measuring cylinder

ii 25 cm^3 measuring cylinder

iii 100 cm^3 measuring cylinder

b The student records the following temperatures in their experiment: 65.7 °C, 72.1 °C, 65.2 °C and 73.4 °C. Find the mean of the temperatures.

2 Look at the following data. Place the metals in order of reactivity, from the most reactive to the least reactive.

Metal	Reaction with dilute acid observations
A	rapid bubbling, metal reacts quickly
B	very slow bubbling
C	lots of bubbles appearing on the surface of the metal

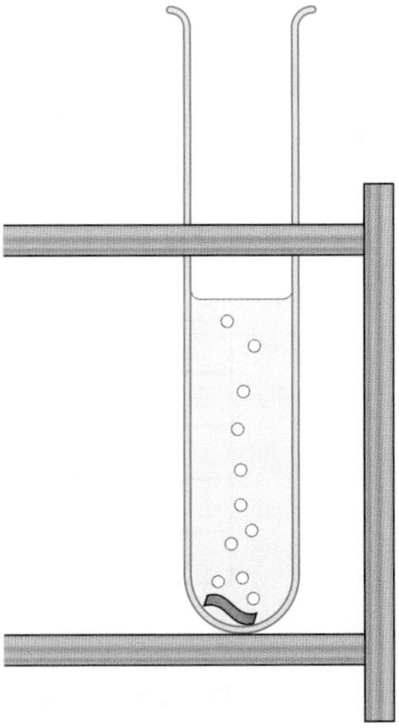

3 A student added small pieces of iron to dilute hydrochloric acid and measured the temperature change. They repeated the experiment using copper, lead and magnesium.

a What is the independent variable for this investigation?

b Name **two** control variables for this investigation.

c Name the piece of equipment used to measure the dependent variable.

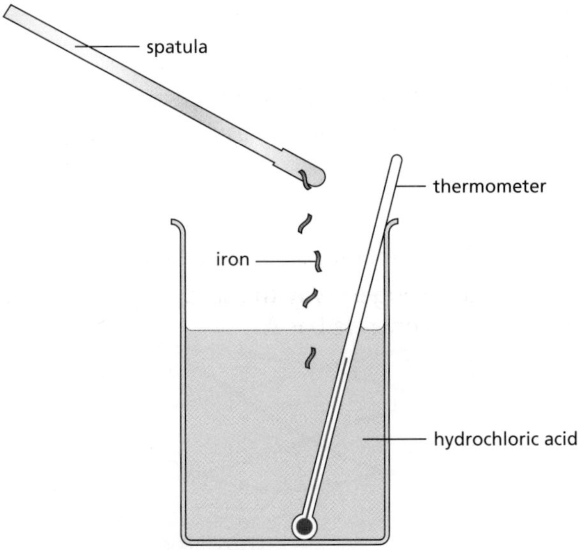

4 A teacher demonstrated the extraction of iron from its ore using carbon. They heated iron oxide and carbon in a crucible. The teacher repeated the demonstration with magnesium oxide and carbon.

a Describe the reaction taking place between iron oxide and carbon in terms of oxidation, reduction and displacement.

b Write a word equation for the reaction between iron oxide and carbon.

c Describe what would happen when the teacher heated aluminium oxide with carbon. Explain your answer.

5 A group of students investigated the change in temperature when different metals were used to displace copper from copper sulfate. They carried out four reactions, **A–D**.

Reaction	Metal used in reaction with copper sulfate	Temperature at the start of the reaction (°C)	Temperature at the end of the reaction (°C)	Difference in temperature (°C)
A	zinc	20.0	28.0	8.0
B	magnesium	20.0	30.5	?
C	silver	20.0	20.0	0.0
D	iron	20.0	23.5	3.5

a Calculate the difference in temperature for reaction **B**.

b Write a word equation for the reaction between copper sulfate and zinc.

c What does the result for reaction **C** tell you?

d The larger the temperature difference, the more reactive the metal. Use the results in the table to place the metals in order of reactivity. Include copper in your answer.

6 A student was given three unnamed metals: **X**, **Y** and **Z**. They were told that metal **X** was found in the ground as an element rather than a compound. The student investigated the reactivity of metals **Y** and **Z**. Here are their results.

Metal	Reaction observations
Y	Reacts violently with water. The oxide cannot be reduced by carbon.
Z	Does not react with water. The oxide can be reduced by carbon.

a Place the metals **X**, **Y** and **Z** in order of reactivity. Explain your answer.

b What does the observation about metal **Z** tell you about its position in the reactivity series? Explain your answer.

c Give two possible elements that metal **X** could be.

7 A student made three concrete bars using small stones, cement, sand and water. The mass of each ingredient stayed the same. All the bars were the same size: 10 cm × 2 cm × 2 cm. The student added different reinforcements to each bar:

- concrete bar **A** – no reinforcement
- concrete bar **B** – an iron rod
- concrete bar **C** – a wooden rod

They investigated the mass needed to break to the bar.

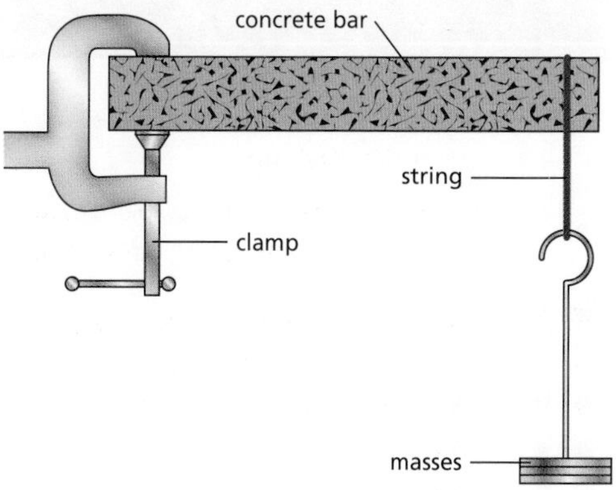

a Suggest why the student put no reinforcement into concrete bar **A**.

b What is the independent variable for this investigation?

c Calculate the volume of a concrete bar.

d Which bar do you think would need the largest mass to break it? Explain your answer.

12 Earth and atmosphere road map

Where are you in your learning journey and where are you aiming to be?

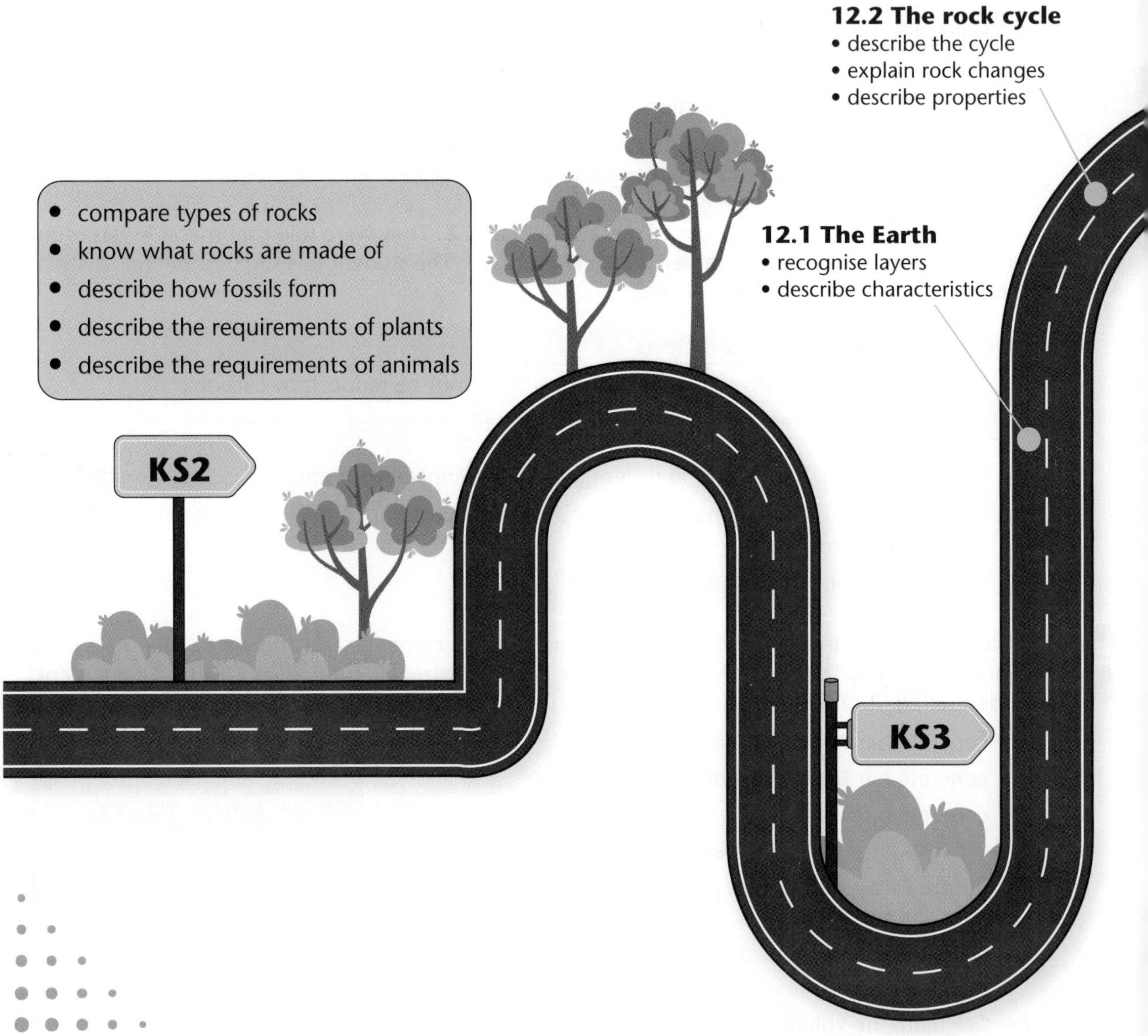

The atmosphere
te what the atmosphere is
cribe composition
ognise changes over time

12.4 The carbon cycle
- describe the carbon cycle
- describe impact of human activity
- understand the role of decomposers

- using the Earth's resources and obtaining potable water
- carbon dioxide and methane as greenhouse gases
- life cycle assessment and recycling
- the composition and evolution of the Earth's atmosphere
- common atmospheric pollutants and their sources

12.5 Climate change
- describe human activity
- describe the greenhouse effect
- describe global warming effects
- explain consequences

12.6 Sustainable development
- describe Earth's resources
- explain human activity
- describe benefits and limitations

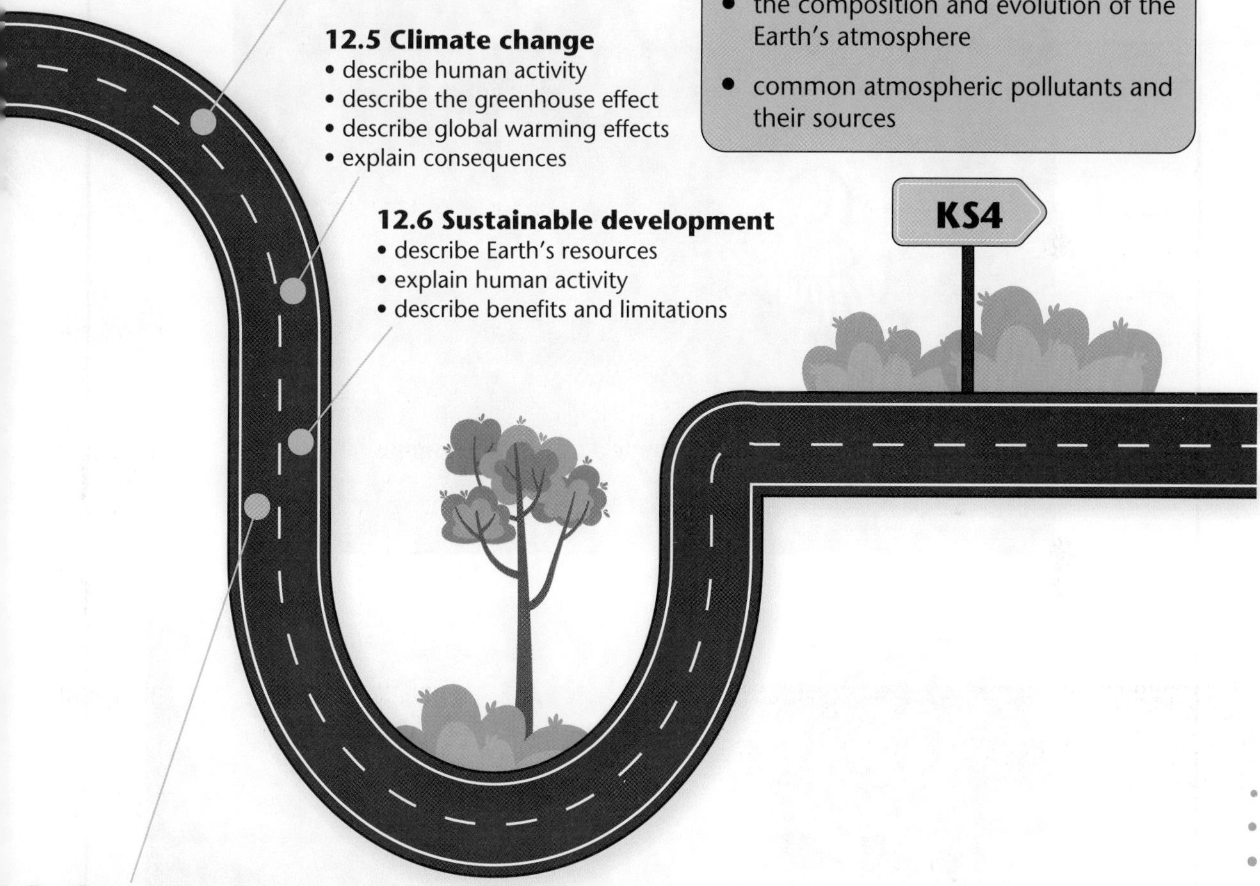

Maths and practical skills

- describing the development of scientific methods and theories over time, including publishing results and peer review
- making scientific predictions
- planning an investigation, identifying and managing the variables
- calculating results and converting between different units
- presenting reasoned explanations
- analysing data

12 Earth and atmosphere

The Earth is about 4.6 billion years old. It is made of different layers, some of which are constantly moving. The thin, rocky crust is where we live.

The Earth

These rock samples were found in different places across the world. One came from a mountain, one from a beach and one from a forest. What do these rocks have in common? What evidence can these rocks provide?

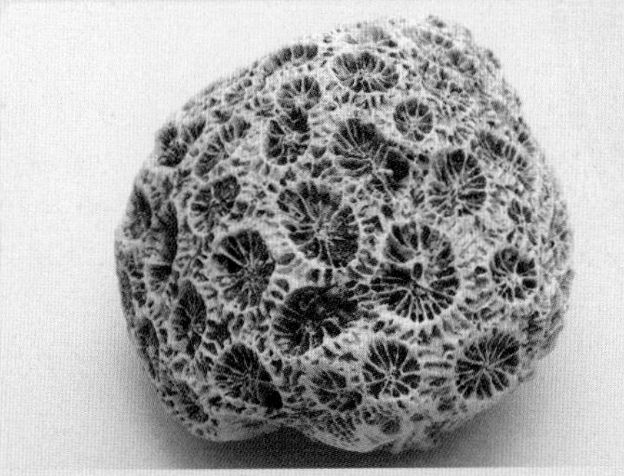

Using your science skills

Could you be a climate scientist?

As a **climate scientist,** you study the influences that humans are having on the Earth's climate. You monitor parts of the Earth that are changing, such as air, sea temperatures and the rate of ice melting. You predict how these changes might affect the planet in the future. The image shows scientists monitoring the health of a coral reef. Corals are living organisms and they become stressed by changes in ocean temperature. It is estimated that over 90% of coral reefs may be lost by 2050. Climate scientists may also design and build the equipment used to gather data, or write computer programmes to predict the future effects of climate change. Policy makers such as government advisors rely on the advice provided by climate scientists.

Farm managers ensure high-quality produce is farmed in a safe and environmentally sustainable way. Farmers require natural resources such as healthy and fertile soil, plenty of water and biodiversity to produce a successful crop yield. Crop production is levelling off in parts of the world due to factors such as increased temperatures, weather variability, weeds and pests. Farmers are at the forefront of changing methods to ensure that crops are less vulnerable to drought and more resilient to pests and diseases, and to improve the capacity to grow crops in shortened seasons with more erratic weather.

Palaeontologists study the history of life on Earth through the investigation of fossils. Their work helps us to understand how living things have changed over the 3.5 billion years that life has existed on Earth.

Environmental managers support organisations to continually improve their efforts to reduce their impact on the environment. Using renewable energy sources, increasing recycling, reducing the carbon footprint of products and monitoring any possible sources of pollution are important considerations for today.

Geotechnical engineers carry out testing and analyse risk for the design and construction industry. They use their specialist knowledge of rock, water and soil structure to assess the risk to humans and the environment from earthquakes, rock falls, sink-holes and landslides.

Knowledge organiser

The Earth is made of different layers:

- crust
- mantle
- outer core
- inner core.

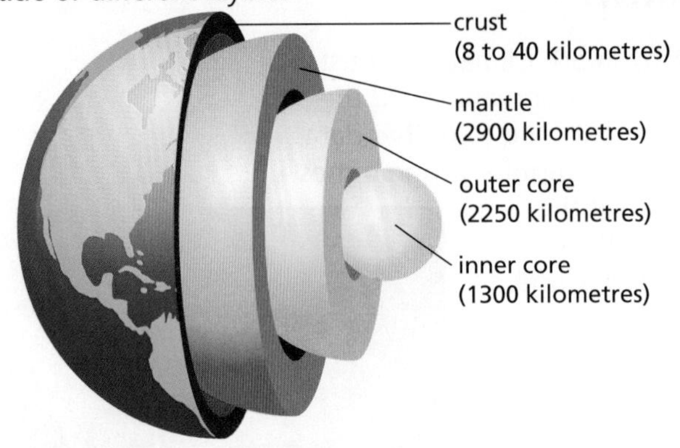

The Earth's **crust** is a thin, solid layer on the outer surface; humans live on this layer. The **mantle** is a very thick layer underneath the crust. It contains oxides of silicon, magnesium and iron. It is solid but can flow very slowly, transferring heat from Earth's **core** towards the surface. The Earth's core is very hot. It contains the elements nickel and iron. The **outer core** is liquid and the **inner core** is solid.

There are three different types of rock:

Type of rock	**igneous**	**sedimentary**	**metamorphic**
Examples	granite, basalt, pumice, obsidian	sandstone, limestone, shale, mudstone	marble, slate, gneiss
Features	• no layers • no fossils • randomly arranged crystals • usually hard to break	• often crumbly • contain **grains** • can contain fossils • found in layers	• hard wearing • no fossils • crystals are often aligned in one direction

The **rock cycle** shows how the Earth's rocks are slowly recycled into other types of rock over millions of years.

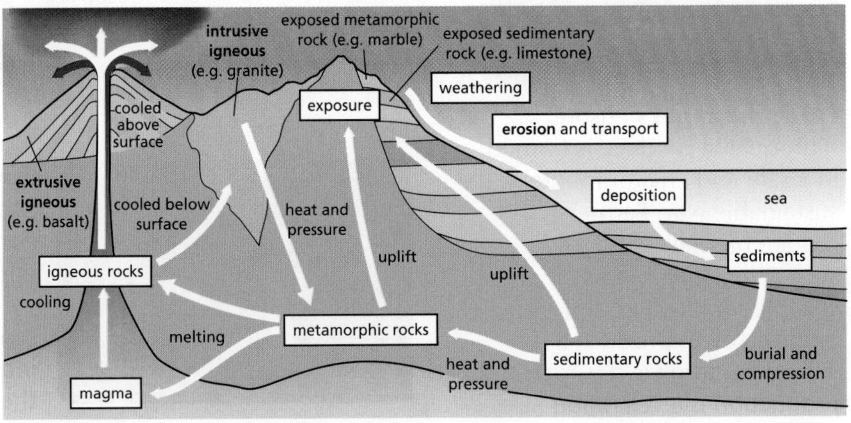

Exposed rocks are **weathered** over time – pieces break off and are transported by wind or water. Biological weathering can be caused by animals, including humans, wearing away the rock, or by plant roots growing down into cracks in the rock. As the roots get bigger, the rock cracks open. Chemical weathering can be caused by acid rain reacting with limestone and chalk rocks. Physical weathering can be caused by waves pounding the cliffs and hurling rocks around, or by repeated freezing and thawing of water that has seeped into cracks in the rock. Water expands as it freezes. The heat from the sun and the cool nights in deserts can cause expansion and contraction of the rock.

When wind, river or sea currents slow down they **deposit** weathered rock fragments. Over millions of years, they are buried under more sediments and **cemented** to form sedimentary rocks.

The movement of tectonic plates can cause rocks to be pushed below Earth's surface. Here, heat and pressure can change the rocks to form metamorphic rocks. They can also be melted to form **magma**, which cools to form igneous rock.

The Earth's crust and the upper part of the mantle are known as the **lithosphere**. The lithosphere is broken into about 20 different pieces called **tectonic plates**.

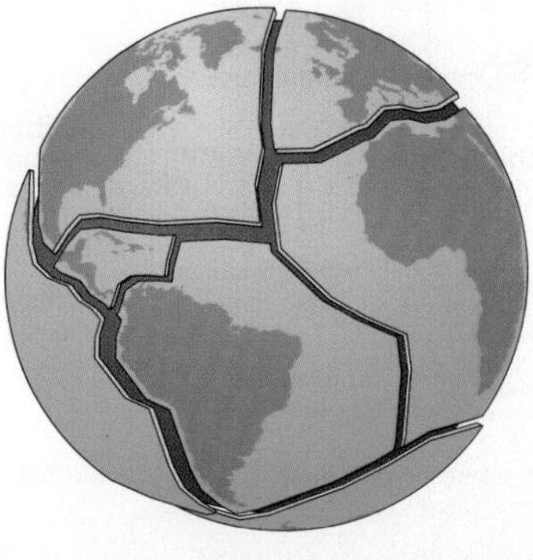

These move about slowly, causing the Earth's surface to change over time. When tectonic plates meet, they can push or move under or over each other. Earthquakes and volcanic eruptions can happen at these points, and the crust may crumple to form mountain ranges.

Earth is surrounded by a layer of gases called the **atmosphere**. The Earth's atmosphere consists mainly of nitrogen (78%) and oxygen (21%). There is also a small amount of argon (1%) and even smaller amounts of other gases, e.g. carbon dioxide (0.04%).

The Earth's atmosphere has remained about the same for the past 200 million years. Before then, it was very different. Around 4 billion years ago, the atmosphere is believed to have contained around 95% carbon dioxide, with water vapour and small amounts of ammonia and methane. The oceans formed when the Earth cooled to below 100 °C, allowing the water vapour to condense, around 3.8 billion years ago. When life forms first appeared about 3 billion years ago, they used up carbon dioxide to make food and transfer energy, and started to release oxygen into the atmosphere.

Key vocabulary

atmosphere	the mixture of gases around the Earth
cement	to stick together sediments in the process of making sedimentary rock
compact	to press together sediments in the process of making sedimentary rock
core	the hot inner layer of the Earth; it is divided into the inner core and outer core
crust	the rocky outer layer of the Earth; it is the surface on which humans live
crystal	a solid with a tightly ordered structure, usually with a characteristic shape
deposition	the laying down of sediment grains that are being carried by wind or water, for example when river water slows down
erosion	the wearing away of rocks or other surfaces such as soil
extrusive igneous	igneous rock formed from magma that cooled at the Earth's surface; it cooled quickly to form small crystals
grain	a small particle in sedimentary rocks
igneous rock	a type of rock made from cooled magma
inner core	the very hot, solid, innermost layer of the Earth
intrusive igneous	igneous rock formed from magma that cooled inside the Earth's crust; it cooled more slowly and has bigger crystals than extrusive igneous rock
lava	molten rock that has reached the surface of the Earth
lithosphere	the rocky outer section of the Earth, consisting of the crust and the upper part of the mantle; it is broken into tectonic plates
magma	molten rock found within the Earth
mantle	the thickest layer of the Earth; it sits between the hot outer core and the crust
metamorphic rock	a type of rock formed when other rocks are heated and put under a lot of pressure
outer core	a very hot liquid layer inside the Earth; it sits between the inner core and the mantle
rock cycle	the cycle in which rocks are changed into other types of rock
sedimentary rock	a type of rock made from layers of sediment grains that have been compacted and cemented together; often contains fossils
tectonic plate	a section of the Earth's crust that moves slowly relative to other plates
uplift	the upwards movement of Earth's surface in response to natural processes such as earthquakes; it can form mountains from rocks that were previously buried beneath the surface
weathering	the breaking down of rocks, soil and minerals by physical, biological or chemical processes

The carbon dioxide in the Earth's atmosphere is part of a cycle called the **carbon cycle**. Processes such as **combustion**, **respiration**, **photosynthesis** and decomposition cause carbon to move between the living and non-living parts of the Earth in a cycle that takes place over many years. Carbon dioxide from the air enters food chains through photosynthesis and is used by living organisms to make their body tissues. When these organisms die, **decomposers** such as bacteria and fungi help to return carbon to the atmosphere as carbon dioxide. If the conditions required for decomposition are not present, then carbon remains trapped in the dead body. Over millions of years, this trapped carbon is changed into **fossil fuels** (oil, coal and natural gas).

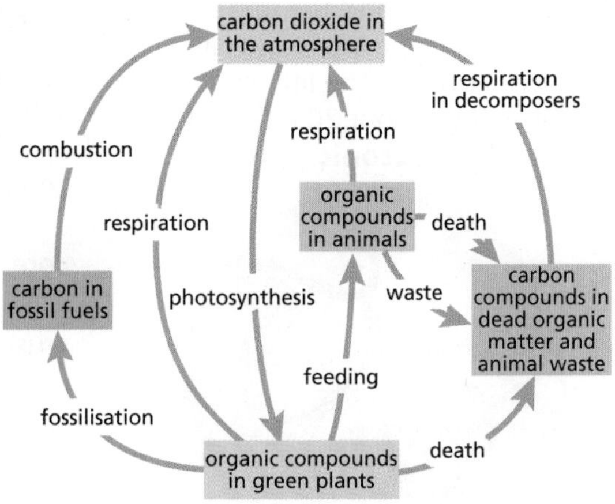

Combustion releases carbon in to the atmosphere as carbon dioxide. Many human activities currently rely on the combustion of fossil fuels because this process releases useful energy. When fossil fuels are burned, they release carbon that has been trapped underground for millions of years. Carbon dioxide stays in the Earth's atmosphere for a long time. Since humans began using fossil fuels in the industrial revolution, which began around 1750, the levels of carbon dioxide in the Earth's atmosphere have increased.

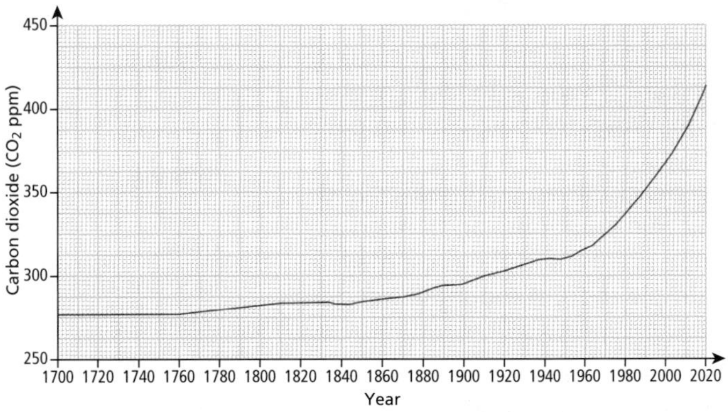

The impact of global warming on the Earth's climate is causing changes such as:

- the melting of polar ice sheets
- rising sea levels
- an increase in severe weather events
- reducing the availability of water in some areas
- longer growing seasons and faster crop growth in some regions
- an increase in pests and diseases such as malaria.

The Earth provides us with many resources, from the air we breathe and the wood and rocks used for building, to the minerals that we refine into metals. Life as we know it would not be possible without these precious resources, but as we process them, pollution is produced. Some of the resources that humans use cannot easily be replaced. They are non-renewable. Using resources in this way is not **sustainable**.

The **greenhouse effect** allows the Earth to be warm enough to support life. Without it, the Earth's air temperature would be around −18 °C. The greenhouse effect relies on **greenhouse gases**, which trap heat radiated from the Earth's surface. Only some of the gases in the Earth's atmosphere are greenhouse gases. Carbon dioxide and methane are examples of greenhouse gases. When more greenhouse gases are present in the atmosphere, the greenhouse effect is stronger and the Earth heats up.

Human activities have increased the levels of greenhouse gases in the atmosphere. This is causing a stronger greenhouse effect, which has caused the Earth's temperature to increase over the last century. This is known as **global warming**. The increase in temperature affects the Earth's weather systems, an effect known as **climate change**.

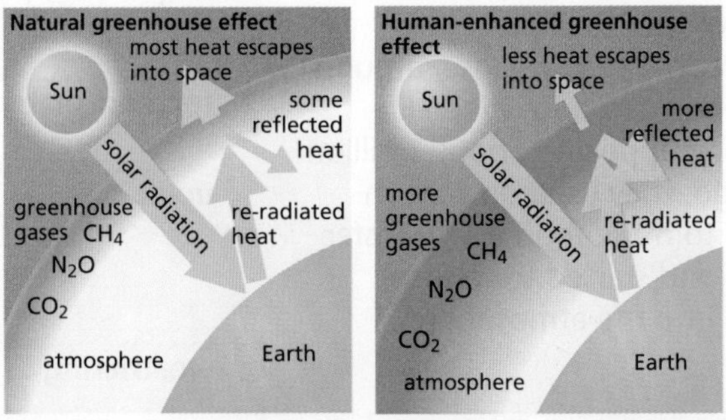

Examples of unsustainable activities include **deforestation**, overfishing and oil extraction. Deforestation is carried out to increase the amount of land for farming, to allow mining, to flood land to create hydroelectric power stations or to enable mining. It reduces **biodiversity** and increases carbon dioxide levels in the atmosphere.

Materials can be **recycled** to reduce the demand for natural resources. Recycling plastic can reduce the demand for fossil fuels. It can also reduce **pollution**, greenhouse gas **emissions** and the amount of waste sent to landfill. Less energy is needed to recycle some materials, such as metals, compared to mining and extracting raw materials from the Earth.

Some disadvantages of recycling are that recycling sites may cause pollution, be unsafe or be unhygienic. The costs of setting up recycling plants can be high, and some processes use a lot of energy. The separation of different materials can also be difficult. The quality of recycled material is not as good, so some materials have to be **down-cycled** into products that cannot themselves be recycled. For example, soft-drink bottles made from PET (a plastic) end up as polyester fibres in clothes or carpets.

Key vocabulary	
biodiversity	the range of different organisms within an ecosystem
carbon cycle	the way in which carbon atoms pass between living organisms and their environment
carbon footprint	total amount of greenhouse gases emitted by the actions of a person, group or company
climate change	a significant and lasting change in weather patterns over time
combustion	the reaction of a fuel with oxygen that transfers thermal energy to the surroundings
decomposer	an organism that breaks down dead animal or plant tissue
deforestation	the removal of large numbers of trees for use by humans, and/or to make space for human activities
down-cycling	the loss of viability or value in a product as it is recycled
emission	the release of something, for example, a greenhouse gas
finite	a resource that is not renewable; it will eventually run out
fossil fuel	a fuel formed from the compressed remains of plants and other organisms that died millions of years ago (coal, natural gas and crude oil)
fuel	any material that can be burned to release energy
global warming	the gradual increase in the average temperature of the Earth's atmosphere and oceans
greenhouse effect	the trapping of the Sun's infrared radiation by the Earth's atmosphere
greenhouse gas	any gas in the Earth's atmosphere, such as carbon dioxide, that reduces the transfer of heat away from the Earth
peer review	evaluation of scientific work by others working in the same field
photosynthesis	the process carried out by green plants and algae in which sunlight, carbon dioxide and water are used to produce glucose and oxygen
pollutant	a harmful substance in the environment
recycling	the process of changing waste materials into something useful
respiration	the process in living things that releases energy from food and carbon dioxide into the environment
sustainable	the use of a resource in such a way that it will be available to future generations

12.1 The Earth

You are learning to:

- recognise the layers that make up Earth
- describe the characteristics of the different layers.

1 The Earth is made of different layers. What are the names of these layers?

2 Complete the sentences using the words list.

atmosphere **lithosphere** **magnetic** **technical** **stratosphere** **tectonic**

The Earth's crust and upper part of the mantle are known as the ______**i**______, which is broken into slowly moving pieces. These pieces are called ______**ii**______ plates.

3 **a** Label the following sections through the Earth.

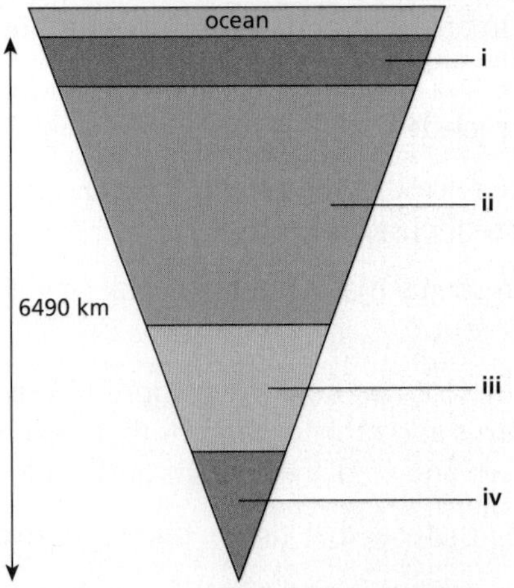

b Which of these layers is liquid?

c Which of these layers gives the Earth a magnetic field?

d In the diagram, the radius of the Earth is given as 6490 km. What is the diameter of Earth?

4 **a** Give a similarity between the Earth's inner and outer core.

b Give a difference between the Earth's inner and outer core.

c Why is it difficult for scientists to prove what the Earth's core is made of?

Worked example

Suppose a tectonic plate moves approximately 1.5 cm in a year. How far would the plate move in 80 years? Give your answer in metres.

Always check if the answer asks for a particular unit. You should also notice whether any units need to be converted so that they are in the same format as others. This question gives a distance in centimetres but asks for an answer in metres. You need to convert this value (1.5 cm) into metres. There are 100 cm in 1 m, so you will divide 1.5 by 100 to convert the value. This gives you the distance moved in 1 year. The question asks you to find the distance moved in 80 years, so you now need to multiply the value by 80. You need to remember to include the unit in your answer.

$1.5\,\text{cm} \div 100 = 0.015\,\text{m}$

$0.015 \times 80 = 1.2\,\text{m}$

5 Tectonic plates move approximately 3 cm a year. How far would a tectonic plate move in 70 years? Give your answer in millimetres.

6 **a** What is a tectonic plate made of?

i all of the crust

ii all of the crust and some of the mantle

iii all of the mantle

iv all of the outer core and some of the mantle

b Use your knowledge of the Earth's structure to match each of these parts to its thickness.

crust	125 km
mantle	35 km
tectonic plate	2900 km

7 Density is the mass of a material per unit volume. A dense material has a lot of mass in a given volume.

a Use the words below to complete the paragraph about the density of the different parts of Earth.

higher **lower**

The average density of rock in the Earth's crust is 2800 kg/m³. The overall density of the Earth is thought to be 5500 kg/m³. The Earth's crust has a ___**i**___ density than the overall density of Earth. This means that the mantle and the core must have a ___**ii**___ density than the crust.

b If the mantle has a density of 4500 kg/m³, which of the following figures would you predict to be the density of the core?

i 9200 kg/m³

ii 2700 kg/m³

iii 4300 kg/m³

8 The *Lystrosaurus* was a herbivore that lived 200 million years ago. Fossils of the *Lystrosaurus* have been found in the continents of India, Africa, Australia and Antarctica.

Which scientific theories does this piece of evidence help to support? Choose **two** statements.

a The crust is a thin, solid layer.

b The tectonic plates have moved apart over time.

c The inner core is a solid and the outer core is a liquid.

d The Earth's magnetic field comes from its outer core.

e The different continents were once attached.

12.2 The rock cycle

You are learning to:
- describe the rock cycle
- explain how rock can change from one type to another
- describe the properties of sedimentary, metamorphic and igneous rock.

1 Complete the table with the names of the three main types of rock **i** to **iii**, matching each description.

Rock type	Description
i	made of crystals which are randomly arranged; no layers or fossils
ii	made of grains which are cemented together; contains layers and sometimes fossils
iii	made of crystals which are often aligned in a particular direction; no fossils

2 A student is given a the rock shown in the photograph below. They draw a diagram of the rock and note down their observations. Which type of rock does the student have?

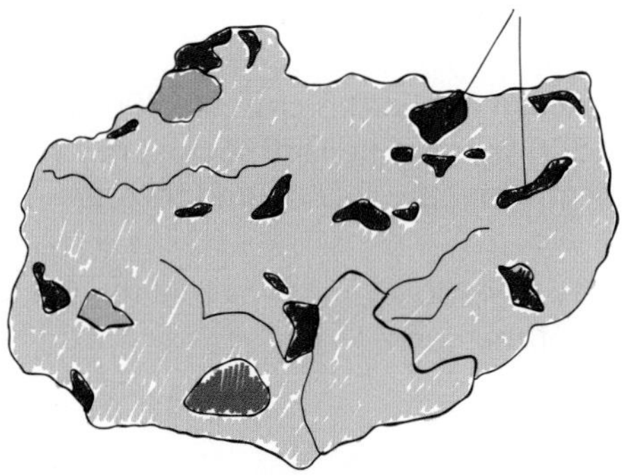

The rock is made of fragments of other rocks that have been stuck together.

3 Deposition is part of the rock cycle.

a Which sentence describes deposition?

i The laying down of sediment grains that are being carried by wind or water, for example when river water slows down.

ii The upwards movement of Earth's surface in response to natural processes such as earthquakes.

iii The transport of small rock pieces by wind, water or ice, away from the original rock.

b What type of rock does deposition help to form?

4 Weathering is part of the rock cycle.

a Name the **three** types of weathering that occur in the rock cycle.

b What type of rock does weathering help to form?

c Choose **one** type of weathering of rock and describe how it happens.

5 Match the key words from the box below to the correct number shown on the rock cycle diagram.

deposition	**magma**	**sedimentary**	**weathering**	**igneous**	**metamorphic**

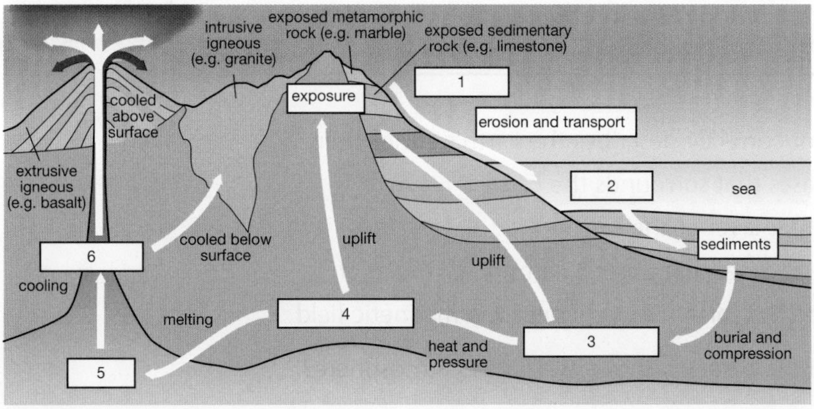

6 Processes in the rock cycle can change metamorphic rock into igneous rock, or into sedimentary rock.

a Describe how metamorphic rock can be changed into igneous rock.

b Describe how metamorphic rock can be changed into sedimentary rock.

7 Processes in the rock cycle can change igneous rock into sedimentary or metamorphic rock.

a Describe how igneous rock can be changed into sedimentary rock.

b Describe how igneous rock can be changed into metamorphic rock.

8 Which of the following keep the rock cycle going?

a climate change
b weathering and erosion
c heat from the inner core
d photosynthesis and respiration

9 The temperature on Mars is thought to range between 0 and −100 °C during a 12-hour time period.

a How might this affect rocks found on the surface of Mars?

b Why do these temperature fluctuations mean it would be difficult for green plants to survive on Mars?

c Images from the surface of Mars indicate the possible presence of dried-up rivers, extinct volcanoes and mountain ranges. Explain why it is possible that all three rock types may exist on Mars.

10 The rate at which lava or magma cools determines the size of the crystals in an igneous rock. If the rate of cooling is fast, the rock will have small crystals. If the rate of cooling is slow, the rock will have large crystals.

Obsidian is an igneous rock that has no or very few crystals. It looks like black glass.

a What does this information tell you about how quickly the molten rock cooled to form obsidian?

b In which of the environments below might obsidian have formed? Explain your answer.

i a volcano under the sea
ii a desert
iii deep underground below a mountain range
iv a temperate forest

12.3 The atmosphere

You are learning to:
- state what the Earth's atmosphere is
- describe the composition of today's atmosphere
- recognise that the Earth's atmosphere has changed over time.

1 Which statement correctly describes the Earth's atmosphere?

a a layer of gases that surrounds the Earth

b the rocky outer layer of the Earth

c a thin layer of gases that absorb harmful UV radiation

d a layer inside the Earth that generates the magnetic field

2 Which letter on the diagram shows the Earth's atmosphere?

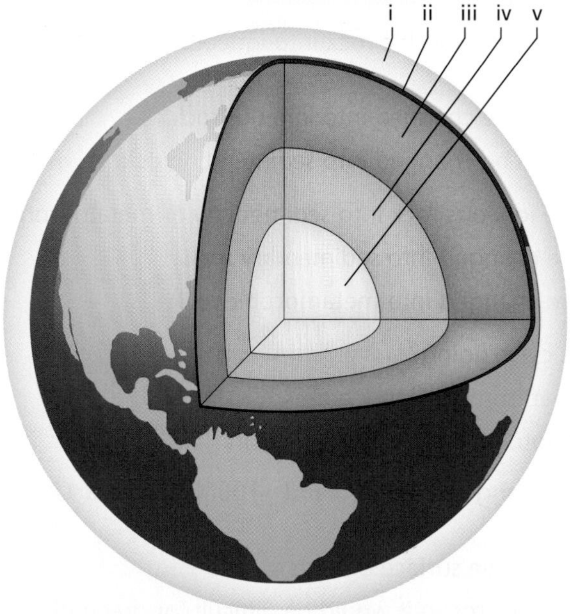

3 **a** Which of the following is the odd one out?

i carbon dioxide **ii** methane **iii** ammonia **iv** air

b Why was this one odd?

4 Name the **two** gases that account for approximately 99% of the Earth's atmosphere.

5 The pie chart shows the composition of the Earth's atmosphere.

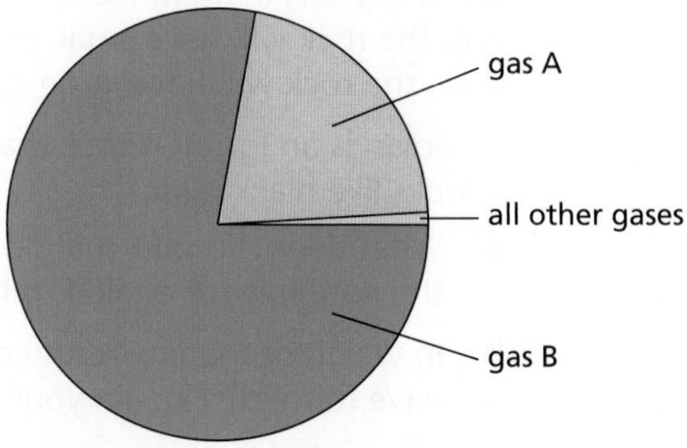

a What is the name of gas **A**?

b What percentage of the atmosphere does gas **A** make up?

c What is the name of gas **B**?

d What percentage of the atmosphere does gas **B** make up?

e Name a gas that would be present in the 1% 'all other gases' shown in the diagram.

6 The diagrams on the right show the different gases commonly found in the Earth's atmosphere. Match each one with its name in the table below.

Substance	Chemical formula	Diagram letter
oxygen	O_2	
carbon dioxide	CO_2	
water vapour	H_2O	
nitrogen	N_2	
argon	Ar	

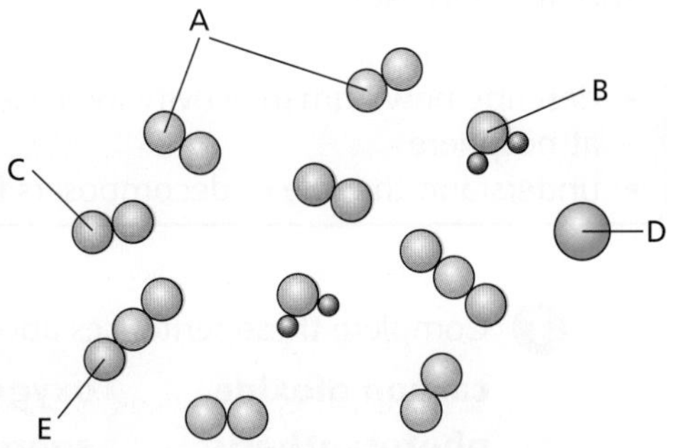

7 Read the passage below about the Earth's early atmosphere. Use the information to answer the questions that follow.

The Earth's early atmosphere was very different to today's atmosphere. Around 4 billion years ago, the atmosphere is believed to have mostly contained carbon dioxide, with water vapour and small amounts of ammonia and methane. The temperature of the Earth was also much higher than it is today. Over time, the Earth cooled to below 100 °C, and the levels of gases changed to those we would recognise today.

a The amount of which of the gases in the Earth's early atmosphere would have decreased when green plants evolved?

b Explain your answer to part **a**.

c Explain how the oceans formed on the Earth.

Worked example

The amount of water in the Earth's atmosphere changes because it is affected by factors such as temperature. If the amount of water vapour changed from 1.0% to 0.8%, what would be the percentage change?

In science, you often need to compare two sets of data, for example, before and after a chemical reaction, or before and after a period of time has passed. You can do this by calculating the percentage change, which allows values to be compared. A positive percentage change means there has been an increase and a negative percentage change means there has been a decrease.

To calculate the percentage change, you need to know the original figure and the final figure.

Use the equation: (new figure – initial figure) ÷ initial figure × 100 = percentage change

0.8 – 1.0 = –0.2

–0.2 ÷ 1.0 = –0.2

–0.2 × 100 = –20%

(This is a percentage decrease because the answer is a negative number).

8 The early atmosphere contained 95.00% carbon dioxide. Today's atmosphere contains 0.04% carbon dioxide. Calculate the percentage decrease in carbon dioxide levels.

12.4 The carbon cycle

You are learning to:
- describe the carbon cycle
- describe how human activity increases the amount of carbon in the atmosphere
- understand the role of decomposers in the carbon cycle.

1 Complete these sentences about carbon dioxide using the words below.

carbon dioxide **oxygen** **fossil fuels** **combustion**
photosynthesis **energy**

Human activities add ___**i**___ to the atmosphere. The main human activity that does this is burning ___**ii**___. This is known as ___**iii**___. Humans carry out this process because it releases useful ___**iv**___.

2 Select the correct statement from the list below:

a Carbon is a compound made by burning wood.

b Carbon is a non-metal element.

c Carbon is taken in by plants through their leaves for photosynthesis.

d Carbon is a gas found in the atmosphere.

3 Which statements about photosynthesis are true? Choose **two** answers.

a Photosynthesis happens in animals.

b Photosynthesis happens in plants.

c Photosynthesis makes carbon dioxide and water from glucose (sugar).

d Photosynthesis makes glucose (sugar) from water and carbon dioxide.

4 Which of these processes would **not** add carbon dioxide to the atmosphere?

a respiration **b** combustion **c** volcanic eruptions **d** photosynthesis

5 Name the process labelled **X** in the diagram of the carbon cycle below.

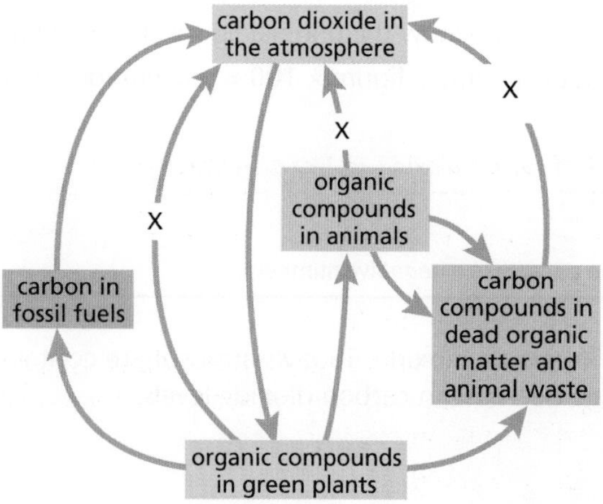

6 We can use the term hydrocarbons to describe fossil fuels. Hydrocarbons are substances that contain only carbon and hydrogen. Where did the carbon in fossil fuels come from?

7 a Name **one** process that removes carbon dioxide from the atmosphere.

b Name **two** processes that add carbon dioxide to the atmosphere.

c For thousands of years in the Earth's history, the level of carbon dioxide in the atmosphere did not change very much. Explain what must have been true about the processes you have named in parts **a** and **b** during this time.

8 Carbon is found in all living organisms. Fats, carbohydrates and proteins all contain carbon.

a How does our body obtain enough carbon for us to be able to grow?

b When a plant dies, what happens to the carbon contained in its tissues?

c What could occur if all the decomposers became extinct?

9 Human activities release carbon dioxide into the atmosphere. An example is burning fuels, such as fossil fuels and wood, to heat homes.

a Gas is a fossil fuel used to heat many homes in the UK. Which statements below are correct? Select all that apply.

i Fossil fuels are formed over millions of years.

ii Fossil fuels are renewable sources of energy.

iii Fossil fuels are limited resources.

iv Fossil fuels are made from fossils.

Homes can be heated by burning different fuels. The table shows the amount of carbon dioxide produced by burning 1 kg of common fuels. It also shows the amount of energy released by each fuel. The energy in fuel is measured in kilowatt-hours (kW h). The higher the value, the more energy is released when the fuel is burned.

Fuel	Amount of carbon dioxide released when 1 kg of fuel is burned (kg)	Energy contained in 1 kg of fuel (kW h)
wood	1.86	4.5
propane gas	2.99	13.8
heating oil	3.00	12.0
natural gas	2.75	15.4

Worked example

How much wood would be needed to produce the same amount of carbon dioxide as 1 kg of heating oil? Use the table above.

From the table you can see that 1 kg of wood produces 1.86 kg of carbon dioxide and 1 kg of heating oil produces 3.00 kg. To find how much wood would produce the same amount of carbon dioxide, you need to calculate the ratio of the amount produced by heating oil to the amount produced by wood.

$3.00 \div 1.86 = 1.61$ kg

1.61 kg of wood would produce the same amount of carbon dioxide as 1 kg of heating oil.

b Calculate how much wood would be needed to produce the same amount of carbon dioxide as 1 kg of natural gas.

c Which fuel releases the most energy when 1 kg of it is burned?

d A student states that using natural gas to heat a house to the same temperature produces more carbon dioxide that is released into the atmosphere than wood. Is the student correct? Use the data in the table to justify your answer.

e Is natural gas a renewable or non-renewable energy source?

f Is wood a renewable or a non-renewable energy source?

g Another student states that burning natural gas increases the total amount of carbon dioxide in the atmosphere over time, whereas burning wood does not. Explain why this statement is correct, using your knowledge of the carbon cycle.

12.5 Climate change

You are learning to:

- describe examples of human activity that produce carbon dioxide
- describe the greenhouse effect
- describe the effects of global warming
- explain the consequences of global warming for living things.

1 Which **two** statements about greenhouse gases are correct?

a Greenhouse gases keep the Earth warm enough to support life.

b All gases in the Earth's atmosphere are greenhouse gases.

c Greenhouse gases are concentrated in the ozone layer.

d Greenhouse gases reflect heat, which keeps the Earth cool.

e Greenhouse gases cause the greenhouse effect.

2 The Earth's atmosphere contains many different gases. Which of these gases in the Earth's atmosphere is **not** a greenhouse gas?

a water vapour **b** carbon dioxide **c** methane **d** nitrogen

3 Which sentence describes how the amount of carbon dioxide in the atmosphere affects the Earth's climate?

a As carbon dioxide levels decrease, the air temperature will increase.

b As carbon dioxide levels increase, the air temperature will increase.

c As carbon dioxide levels decrease, there will be more variability in the weather.

d Carbon dioxide levels do not affect the Earth's climate.

4 When a scientist collects data relating to global warming it will not initially be accepted by the scientific community. A different group of scientists must check the evidence first.

a What is this process called?

b Give **two** reasons why this process is needed.

5 This graph shows the amount of carbon dioxide in the Earth's atmosphere since 1700. The unit used for the amount of carbon dioxide is ppm, which stands for 'parts per million'.

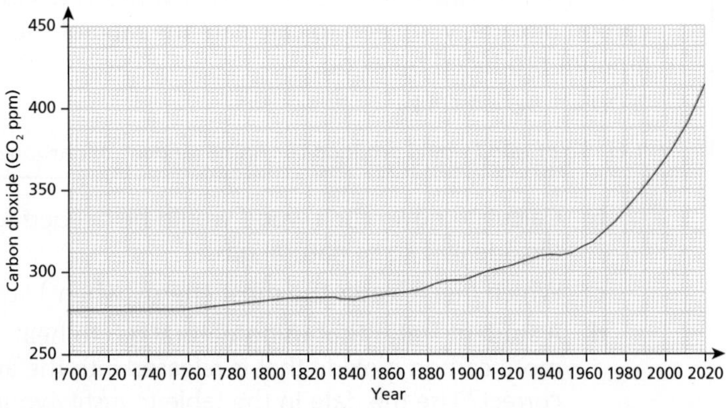

a About how much carbon dioxide was in the Earth's atmosphere in the year 1700?

b About how much carbon dioxide was in the Earth's atmosphere in the year 2020?

c Describe the trend shown in the graph.

d Carbon dioxide is a greenhouse gas that stays in the Earth's atmosphere for a long time. Describe how your answer to part **c** may affect the greenhouse effect.

6 Put these steps in the greenhouse effect into the correct order.

a The sun's radiation passes through the Earth's atmosphere.

b Heat is trapped in the atmosphere, causing it to warm up.

c The radiation is absorbed by the Earth's surface.

d The Earth radiates heat from its surface.

e The radiation is absorbed or reflected by greenhouse gases.

7 **a** What is climate change?

b How is climate change related to global warming?

8 Malaria is a disease that is spread by mosquitoes. It is currently found mainly in regions of the world with higher temperatures, for example, parts of Africa and Asia. Why is there a concern that global warming may increase the number of deaths from malaria across the world?

9 The amount of carbon dioxide in the Earth's atmosphere is measured by scientists at the Mauna Loa Observatory in Hawaii. Data from the observatory is shown in the graph. The amount of carbon dioxide follows a regular pattern. It is lowest in the summer of each year and highest in the winter.

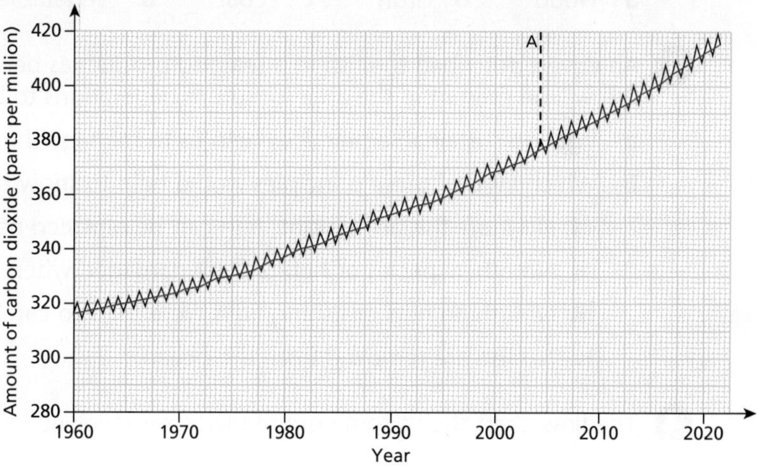

a What does the line labelled **A** represent on the graph?

b Use the line labelled **A** to describe the trend between 1960 and 2020.

c Green plants use carbon dioxide in photosynthesis. Suggest why the amount of carbon dioxide is lowest in the summer of each year and highest in the winter.

10 Solubility is the amount of a solute that dissolves in a solvent at a particular temperature. A group of students measured the solubility of carbon dioxide in water at different temperatures.

a What conclusion can the students make from the graph of their results?

b Calculate the change in carbon dioxide solubility when the water temperature changes from 10 °C to 15 °C.

c Global warming is causing the temperature of the oceans to increase. What effect might this have on the amount of carbon dioxide dissolved in the oceans? Explain your answer.

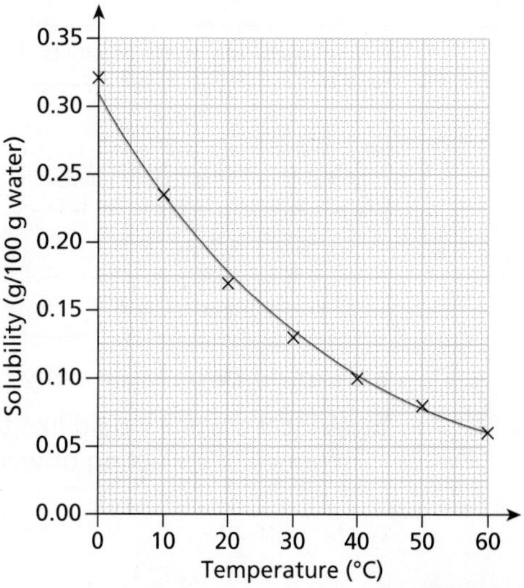

12.6 Sustainable development

You are learning to:
- describe some of the limited resources that the Earth provides
- explain how human activity threatens these resources
- describe the benefits and limitations of recycling.

1 Complete the sentences about the Earth's limited resources using the words below.

renewable **non-renewable** **replaced** **extracted**

A limited resource is a ___**i**___ resource. When it is used, it cannot be easily ___**ii**___.

2 Many human activities use resources that are limited.

Which of these resources are limited resources?

a wood **b** iron **c** coal **d** vegetables

3 An advert described the fish in a seafood product as being sustainable, which means that the fish will be present in the area for future generations to benefit from.

a Why do sustainable practices help us to manage the limited resources of the Earth?

b Which **two** of these principles would help to show that the fish was sustainably caught?

i No more fish are caught than can be replaced naturally by the population.

ii No other species or habitats are damaged when the fish are caught.

iii No fishing nets or fishing lines were used to catch the fish.

iv No fish are removed from the ocean.

4 The flow chart shows some of the processes involved in the life cycle of a metal.

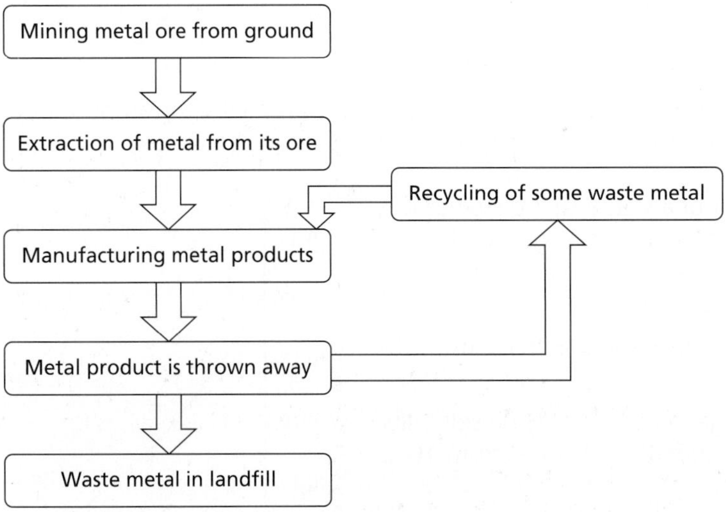

a Explain **two** reasons why recycling of metals is important. Use the flow chart to help you.

b A local council would like to recycle more metal. Suggest **two** disadvantages to the council of collecting unwanted metal items from householders along with their waste bins.

5 The photograph shows a solar farm that is used to generate electricity.

a Suggest **two** advantages of using solar energy to produce electricity compared to using fossil fuels such as coal, oil or gas.

b Suggest **two** disadvantages of using solar energy to produce electricity compared to fossil fuels in the UK.

6 A town council needs to replace a small bridge over a stream. It has decided to use a frame made from either aluminium or wood.

	Aluminium	**Wood**
Limited resource	yes	no
Possible lifespan (years)	45	20
Cost per kg	£0.92	£2.60
Mass of material required (kg)	20	78

Worked example

Calculate how much the bridge would cost per year if it was made from wood.

The table shows that wood will last for 20 years. The cost of the wood to build the bridge can be calculated using: mass required × cost for 1 kg. Then this figure is divided by the number of years to find the cost per year.

£2.60 × 78 kg = £202.80 for materials

£202.80 ÷ 20 years = £10.14 a year

a Calculate how much the bridge would cost per year if it was made from aluminium.

b Give **three** reasons why the council may choose to make the bridge from aluminium.

c Give **one** reason why the council may choose to make the bridge from wood.

Maths and practical skills

1 A student weighed four similar shaped pieces of rock, **A** to **D**, and noted down their masses. They placed the rocks in a bowl of water for 1 hour. They then reweighed the rocks.

Rock sample	Initial mass (g)	Final mass (g)	Observations
A	35.5	35.5	none
B	22.3	25.8	bubbles were seen rising from the rock
C	27.2	28.4	two bubbles were seen
D	27.1	27.1	none

a Explain why rocks **B** and **C** increased in mass after being soaked in water.

b What type of rock are **B** and **C**?

i igneous **ii** metamorphic **iii** sedimentary

c How much mass did rock **B** gain?

d How much mass did rock **C** gain?

e Calculate the percentage change in mass for rock **C** using the equation:

(final mass – initial mass) ÷ initial mass × 100

2 Scientists make observations and ask questions. A good scientific question is one that can be answered by carrying out further observations or experiments; we say it is testable.

a Is the following a scientific question?

Is a red car made of more recycled materials than a silver car?

b Explain your answer to part **a**.

c Complete the table.

Question	Is it a scientific question? yes/no
Is recycling good for us?	
What is the best gas in the atmosphere?	
Are metamorphic rocks harder than sedimentary rocks?	
Do decomposers break down plant material faster than animal material?	

3 Minerals are the chemicals that rocks are made from. Friedrich Mohs was a scientist who studied minerals. He developed a scale that ranked the hardness of different minerals. The larger the number on the scale, the harder the mineral. The table below shows some minerals and their hardness on the Mohs scale.

Mineral name	Mohs scale
diamond	10.0
corundum	9.0
topaz	8.0
quartz	7.0
orthoclase	6.0
apatite	5.0
fluorite	4.0
calcite	3.0
gypsum	2.0
talc	1.0

a Steel has a hardness of 6.5 on the Mohs scale. Which of these minerals are harder than steel?

i apatite **ii** orthoclase

iii diamond **iv** quartz

b Harder minerals can scratch softer minerals when they are rubbed together. Which minerals can scratch topaz?

c Suggest why scratching one mineral against another is not a very accurate way of measuring the hardness of a mineral.

d Some metamorphic rocks contain calcite and others contain quartz. If uplift brings these rocks to the surface, which will weather the quickest? Explain your answer.

4 A student wanted to view the formation of crystals underneath a microscope. They planned an experiment using salol, which is a chemical that cools to form crystals. Salol melts at 45 °C. Their method is shown below.

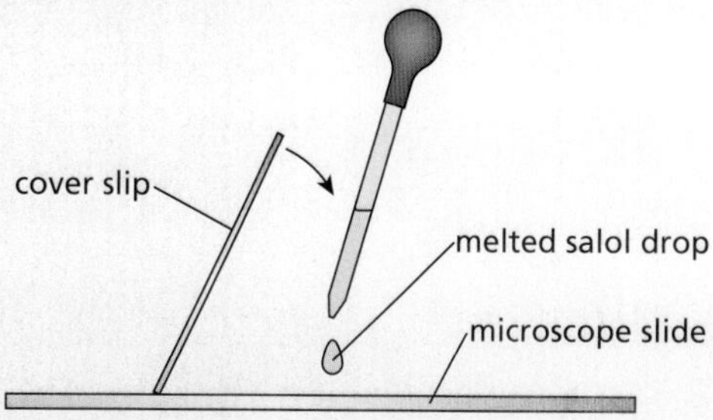

- 50 g of salol was warmed in a water bath at 50 °C.
- A clean microscope slide was placed in the freezer and a second slide was placed in hot water at 60 °C.
- One drop of warm salol was placed on the cold slide and a cover slip added
- A stopwatch was started when the slide was placed under the microscope.
- The time at which crystals began to form and the time at which no further changes were seen were recorded.
- The process was repeated using the heated microscope slide.

a Write a suggested equipment list for this experiment.

b Write a suitable scientific question that this method would test.

c Design a suitable table to record the results.

d Why do crystals form in the salol?

e Predict which microscope slide will produce the biggest crystals of salol.

f Predict which microscope slide will start to produce crystals first. Explain your answer.

g This experiment models part of the rock cycle. Which type of rock is represented by salol?

5 A scientist investigated the level of carbon dioxide in the air at different distances above the ground in a field of crops.

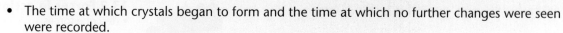

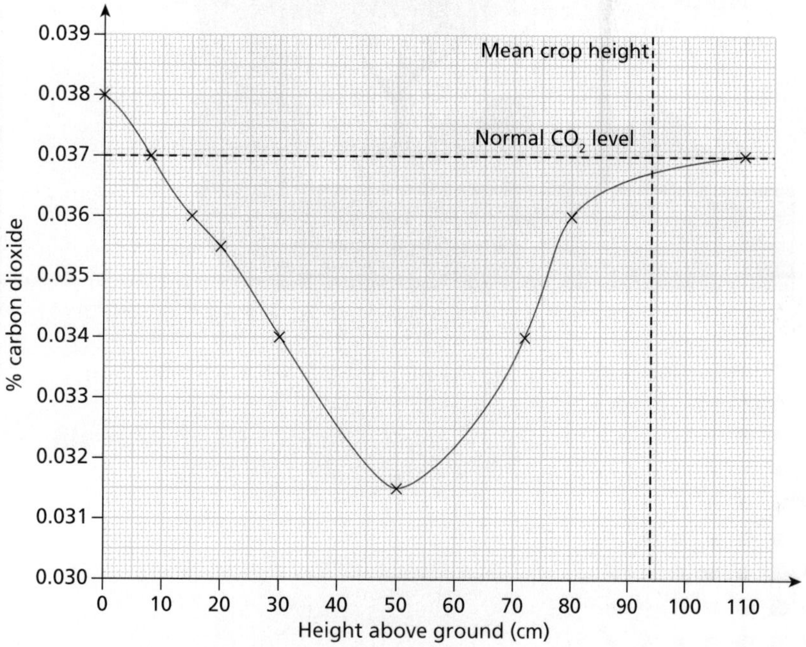

a At what height did the scientist record the lowest levels of carbon dioxide in the field?

b At what height did the maximum rate of photosynthesis occur?

c What did the scientist record as the normal level of carbon dioxide concentration in the air?

d Suggest a reason why the level of carbon dioxide was above the normal figure at ground level.

13 Forces road map

Where are you in your learning journey and where are you aiming to be?

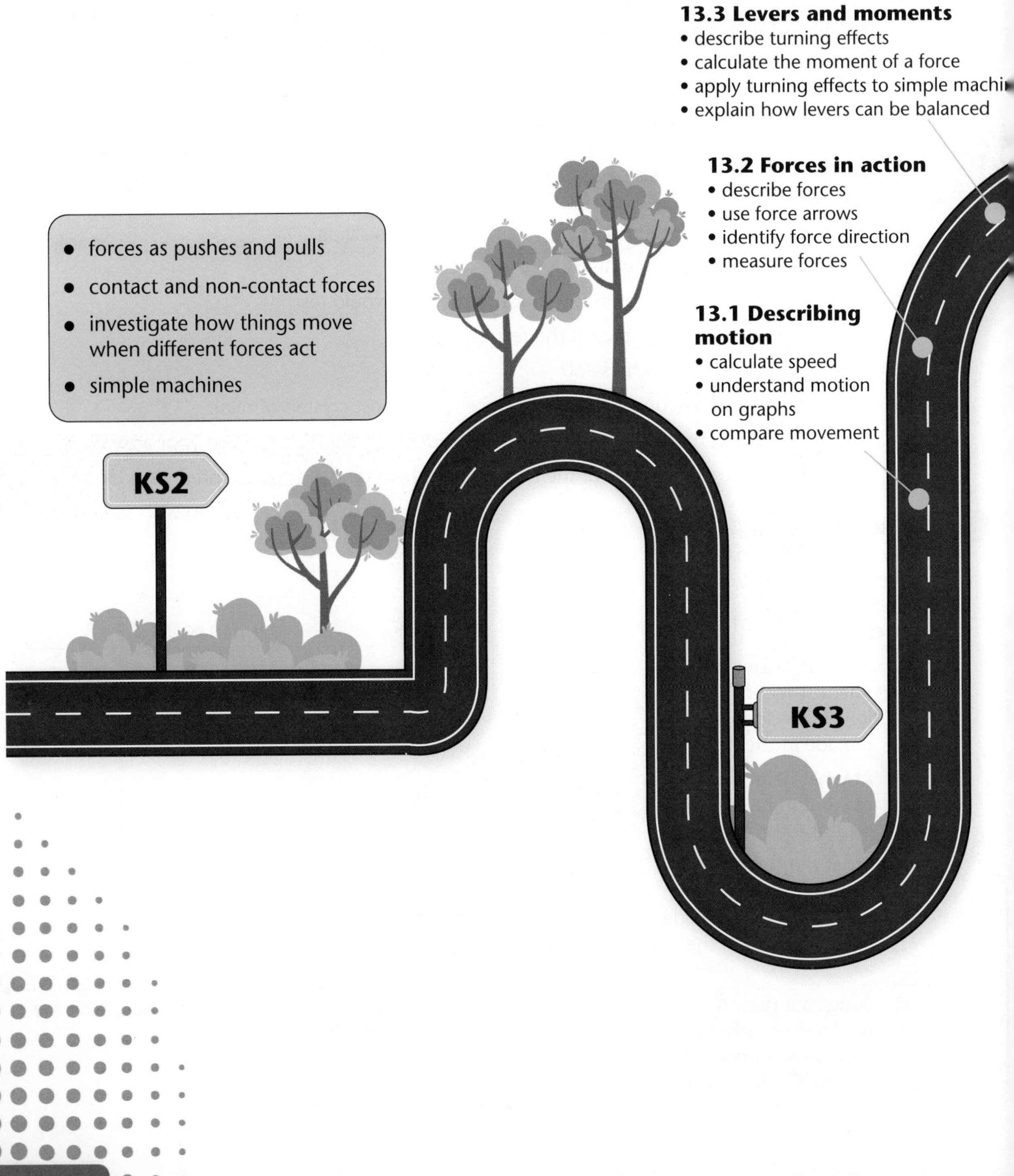

13.4 Stretch and compression
- describe how forces deform objects
- explain load and extension of a spring
- apply Hooke's Law
- describe energy changes

13.5 Pressure in solids
- understand pressure as a force
- calculate pressure
- explain how pressure can be altered

13.6 Pressure in fluids
- use the particle model
- explain pressure increases
- apply ideas about pressure

13.7 Using moments
- calculate work done
- explain bigger forces and smaller movement

13.8 Forces, motion and equilibrium
- describe balanced forces and equilibrium
- calculate the effect of several forces
- identify the effect of unbalanced forces

- forces and motion
- forces and elasticity
- momentum
- energy changes in a system
- work done and energy transfer
- forces and their interactions
- particle model and pressure

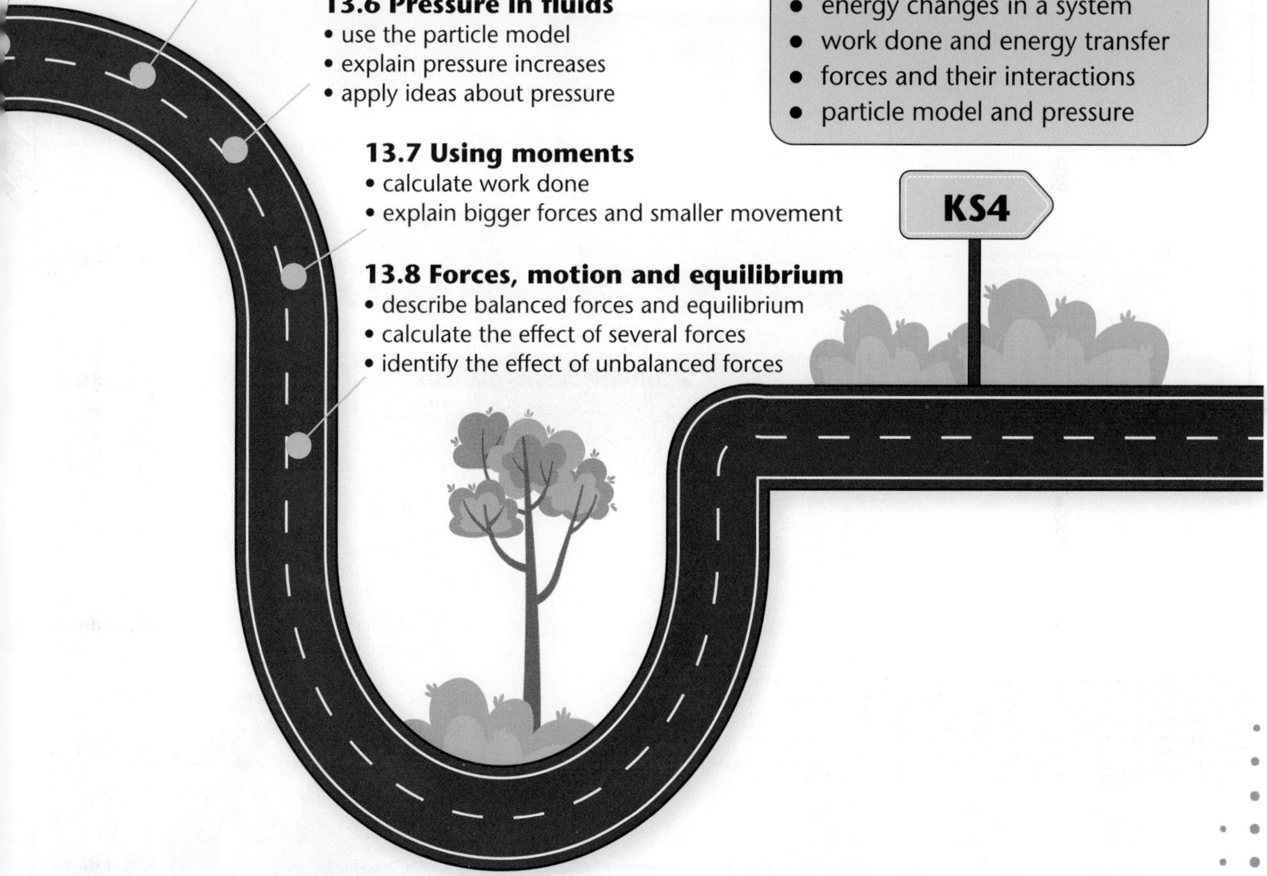

Maths and practical skills

- planning an investigation, identifying and managing the variables
- calculating results and converting between different units
- analysing data and identifying anomalous results
- using equations to calculate answers
- rearranging equations to change the subject

13 Forces

Forces are all around you, but you cannot see, touch or smell them. When forces cause movement you can see what they do, but when something is not moving there are still forces at work.

What can you see?

Describe or name the forces you can see in action in these images. Suggest what the effect of each of these forces is.

Using your science skills

Could you be an air traffic controller?

Being an air traffic controller is challenging, but exciting and fulfilling. You work under pressure and you have to make quick and accurate decisions to keep aircraft safely separated from each other. There's a lot of training but you need to be good at understanding distances and speeds, and at problem solving. Working as a team is crucial too – and you'll need good verbal communication skills to give clear instructions to pilots.

Lorry drivers need to understand relative motion to judge how to drive safely. Speeds are higher on motorways but the speed relative to other vehicles will be lower than on an ordinary main road.

Materials engineers help design cars to improve performance whilst maintaining the safety aspect. This includes reducing the weight to reduce the energy needed to run the car, absorbing the impact energy during accidents, and increasing the recyclability of car components.

Mechanics use their knowledge of how different forces work together to understand how machines work. They can then make and fix things that people rely on every day to make their lives easier.

This excavator forces fluid through pipes to move the arm and bucket. **Design** and **maintenance engineers** need a good understanding of forces, machines and systems.

Bus timetablers use lots of information about distance and time to schedule bus services and make the best use of vehicles.

Aircraft maintenance staff have to service the engine so it can provide enough thrust to overcome the friction of the aircraft moving through the air.

Knowledge organiser

A force applied to an object can stretch, **compress**, twist or try to snap it, or cause it to speed up, slow down or change its direction of motion.

Forces can be **contact** forces, such as water or **air resistance**, or **non-contact forces**, such as gravity.

Forces can be shown by arrows. The direction of the arrow shows the direction of the force and the length of the arrow indicates the size of the force.

Hooke's Law says that if an object is loaded then the **extension** will be proportional to the **load** as long as the **elastic limit** is not exceeded.

The **moment** of a force is its turning effect. Its size is the force multiplied by the distance from the turning point.

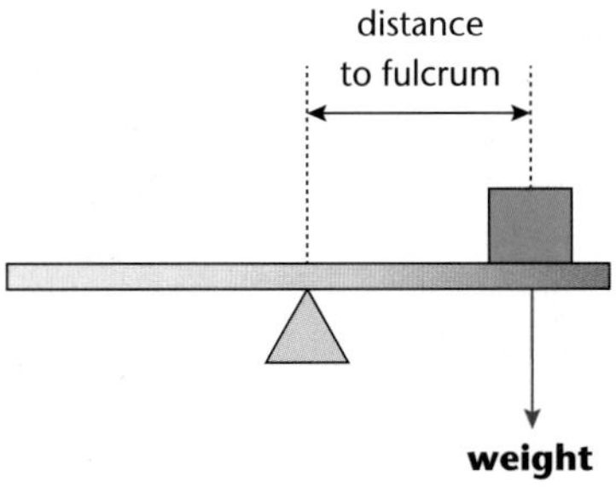

Speed is calculated using the equation:

speed = distance ÷ time

The average (mean) speed for a journey is the total distance divided by the total time.

A journey can be displayed on a **distance–time graph**, with distance on the vertical axis and time on the horizontal axis. The gradient of the line shows the speed.

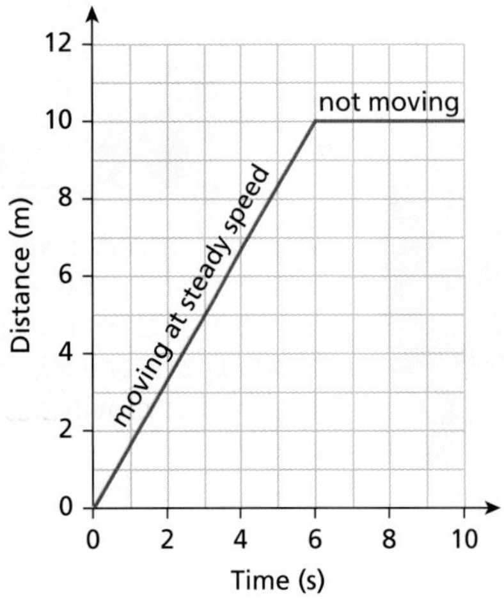

Key vocabulary

air resistance	frictional resistance when something moves through the air
elastic behaviour	when a material returns to its original shape and size after a stretching or compressing force is removed
effort	the force applied when using a machine
elastic limit	the maximum force that can be applied for a material to remain elastic; if this limit is exceeded the extension will no longer be proportional to the force
extension	the amount by which an elastic material has got longer
friction	a force that opposes movement
fulcrum	the point about which something turns; also called a pivot
lever	a machine that either increases the size of a force or the distance over which the force acts; this is done by using the turning effect of a force around a fulcrum (pivot)
moment	size of turning effect of a force around a fulcrum (pivot) – the direction of the moment can be clockwise or anticlockwise
newtonmeter	a device that uses the stretching of a spring to measure force
normal contact force	the force that acts when an object touches a surface; it is at right angles (90°) to the surface
relative speed	movement of one moving object in relation to another object
speed	how fast something travels; measured in metres per second (m/s)
weight	the force of gravity acting on an object

An **unbalanced force** is needed to get an object to move, to stop it from moving, to change its speed or alter its direction. This change will depend on the size and direction of the different forces.

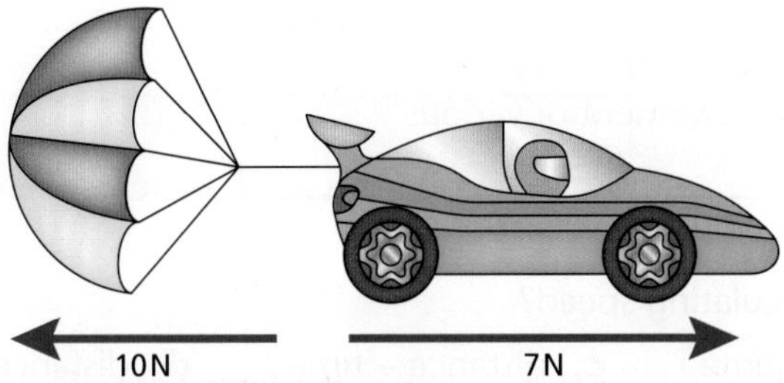

If all the forces are **balanced**, a moving object will continue at the same speed and in the same direction.

Objects float because of balanced forces. The weight of the object is balanced by the **upthrust** provided by the water.

If opposing forces act on an object they may hold it in **equilibrium**. An example of this is a weight suspended on a spring.

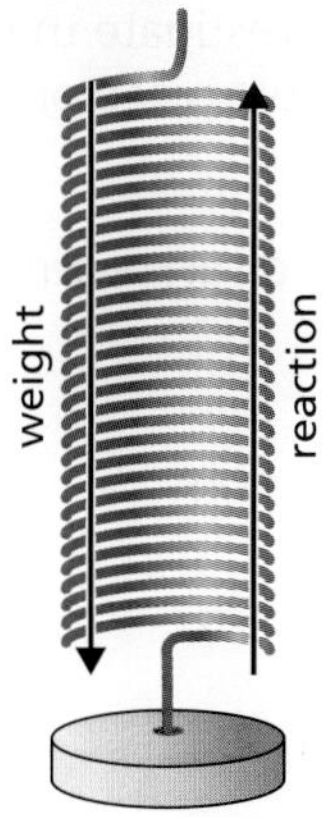

Pressure is calculated using the equation

pressure = force ÷ area

If the force is measured in **newtons** and the area in square metres the pressure will be in newtons per square metre (N/m^2).

The higher in the atmosphere, the lower the **atmospheric pressure** on a surface. This is because the pressure is caused by the weight of the air above that surface.

The deeper down in a liquid, the greater the pressure becomes, because there is more liquid above that point.

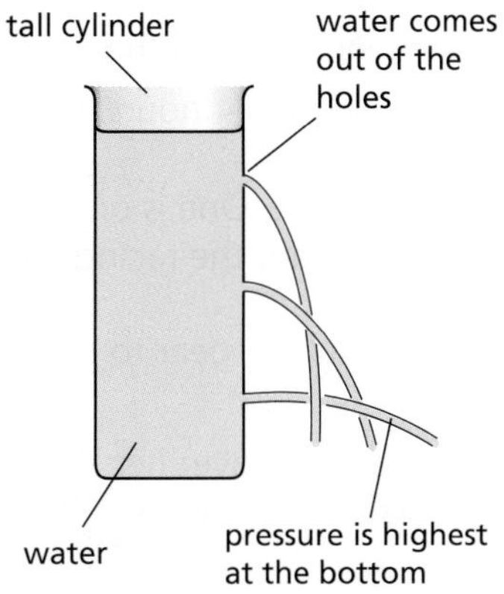

Key vocabulary	
atmospheric pressure	the pressure on a surface exerted by the weight of air above that point
balanced forces	forces on an object that act in opposite directions and where the total force in one direction is equal in size to the total force in the opposite direction
equilibrium	a state of rest or balance due to opposite forces being equal
gravitational force	the force that pulls masses towards one another
newton (N)	the standard unit of force
pressure	the force acting divided by the area over which the force acts; measured in N/m^2
unbalanced forces	forces acting on an object where the total force acting in one direction is not equal in size to the total force acting in the opposite direction
upthrust	the upward force that a fluid exerts on an object in it
work done	energy transferred by a force moving a load, measured in joules (J)

13.1 Describing motion

You are learning to:

- calculate speed from distance and time
- understand how motion is represented on a distance–time graph
- use the idea of relative motion to compare the movement of various moving objects.

1 Which of these is the correct way of calculating speed?

a distance × time **b** distance + time **c** distance ÷ time **d** distance – time

2 Motorcycles **A** and **B** both travel 50 km. Motorcycle **A** takes 1 hour and motorcycle **B** takes 75 minutes. Which has the lower average speed?

3 Car **C** travels 25 km in half an hour and car **D** travels 30 km in one hour. Which has the higher average speed?

4 On a distance–time graph a straight line sloping upwards indicates:

a no movement **b** steady speed **c** speed increasing **d** speed decreasing.

5 A group of students is going to investigate the motion of a trolley down a ramp and calculate its average speed. Suggest a suitable piece of equipment to measure:

a the length of the ramp

b the time taken for the trolley to run down the ramp

c the angle of the ramp.

6 Calculate the average speed in m/s of:

a a dog running 70 m in 10 s

b a car traveling 300 m in 15 s

c an aircraft travelling 3600 m in 15 s.

7 Calculate the average speed in m/s of:

a a train travelling 60 km in 40 minutes

b a racing car completing a 5.4 km lap in 3 minutes

c a long-distance runner covering 30 km in 4 hours. Give this answer to 2 decimal places.

8 Two cyclists are waiting at a red traffic light. One is on an ordinary bicycle and the other is on a racing bicycle. When the cyclists move off, the racing bicycle builds up speed quicker and pulls away from the ordinary bicycle.

a Describe how the racing bicycle would appear to move to the person on the ordinary bicycle.

b The cyclist on the racing bicycle glances over her shoulder at the ordinary bicycle. Describe how the ordinary bicycle appears to be moving to her.

Worked example

This distance–time graph shows a journey in two stages. The first stage is shown by the line from point A to point B and the second stage by the line from point B to point C.

a Calculate the speed during the section AB.

b Describe the speed during the section BC.

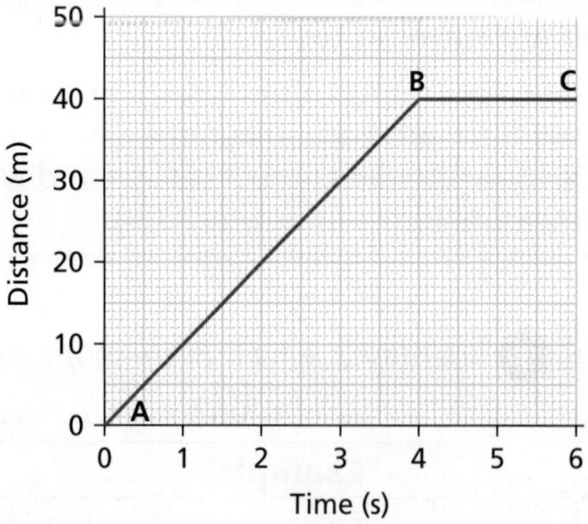

For part **a**, read the values and units from the graph axes. You can see that the distance increases from 0 to 40 m so the object has travelled 40 m. You can also see that this happened as the time increased from 0 to 4 s, so the time taken was 4 s.

a speed $= \frac{\text{distance}}{\text{time}}$

$= \frac{40\text{ m}}{4\text{ s}} = 10\text{ m/s}$

b **In section BC the graph is a horizontal straight line, which means that the distance is not changing, and therefore the object is stationary (not moving).**

9 On a distance–time graph a horizontal straight line indicates:

a no movement **b** steady speed **c** speed increasing **d** speed decreasing

10 Look at this distance–time graph:

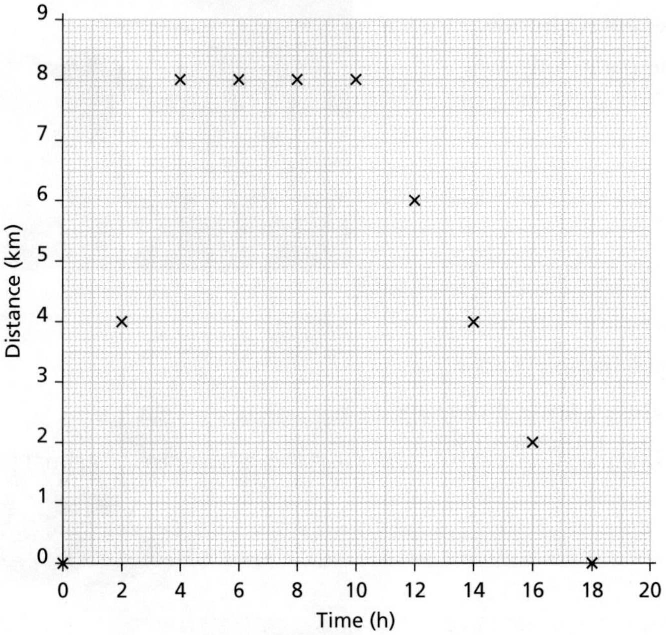

a The first part of the journey lasts for 4 hours. Calculate the speed of the object in km/h during this section.

b During the first part of the journey is the speed increasing, constant or decreasing?

c Describe the motion of the object during the second section, starting at $t = 4$ hours.

d Compare the third part of the journey (after $t = 10$ hours) with the first part of the journey. Refer to both the speed and direction of travel.

11 Khalid's group is going to investigate how changing the gradient of a ramp will affect the speed of toy cars travelling down the ramp. They have a 1 m long wooden ramp, a selection of supports to hold up one end of the ramp, various toy cars and a stopwatch.

a Describe a procedure they could use to determine the speed of a toy car down the ramp.

b This procedure will give them a value for the average speed of the journey. Explain why this is.

c Explain why it would be a good idea to take repeat readings in this experiment.

13.2 Forces in action

You are learning to:

- describe examples of contact and non-contact forces
- use force arrows in diagrams
- identify the direction of friction and air resistance forces
- measure forces in newtons (N).

1 Identify ✓ which of these are examples of contact forces and which are examples of non-contact forces.

	Example	Contact?	Non-contact?
i	finger rubbed on bench surface		
ii	pencil case pulled downwards when allowed to fall		
iii	magnet picking up paper clips		
iv	stool pushed across floor		
v	pieces of tissue paper being attracted to a balloon that has been charged by rubbing it on a jumper		

2 This parachutist is jumping out of an aircraft. They are being pulled downwards by a force.

a What is the name given to this force?

b Is this a contact or a non-contact force?

c Suggest another force the parachutist will experience as soon as they start to fall.

3 This person is travelling downhill on a toboggan.

a State the direction in which friction is acting.

b Suggest why the person travels faster if they are lying down on the toboggan rather than sitting upright on it.

Worked example

A boy holds a bucket of water. Draw a diagram of the bucket and show the forces that are acting on it by adding arrows and labelling them.

The direction of each arrow shows the direction of the force. The force of weight acts downwards and the force applied by the boy acts in the opposite direction. Make sure the force arrows touch the object that the force acts on.

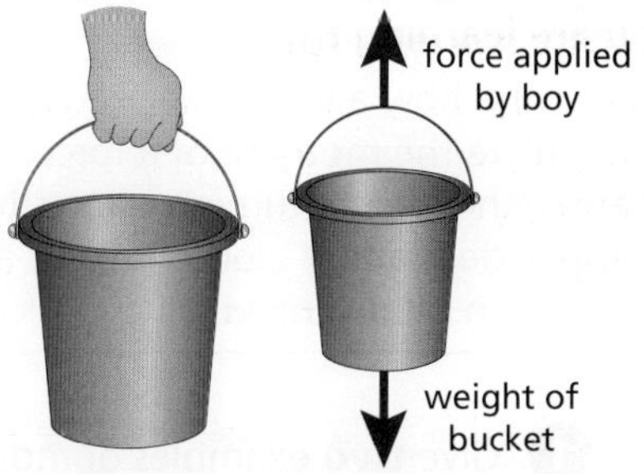

4 This apple is falling through the air. Draw an outline of the apple, then add and label **two** arrows to show the forces acting on it as it falls.

5 Draw and label force diagrams to show:

a the horizontal forces acting on a supermarket trolley being pushed along

b the vertical forces acting on a firework rocket shooting upwards.

6 A girl kicks a football. Identify what forces act horizontally on the football after it is kicked.

7 Sharks have a shape that reduces friction and makes movement through water easy.

a In what direction do drag forces act on a shark that is swimming forwards?

b Use the photo to identify what features the shark has that reduce the drag forces acting on it as it swims.

8 A group of students is investigating how friction varies for different types of trainers. They use three different designs of trainer, each the same size. Each trainer is placed in turn on a carpet tile. Weights are placed inside the trainer and a newtonmeter is used to measure the force needed to drag the shoe across the carpet.

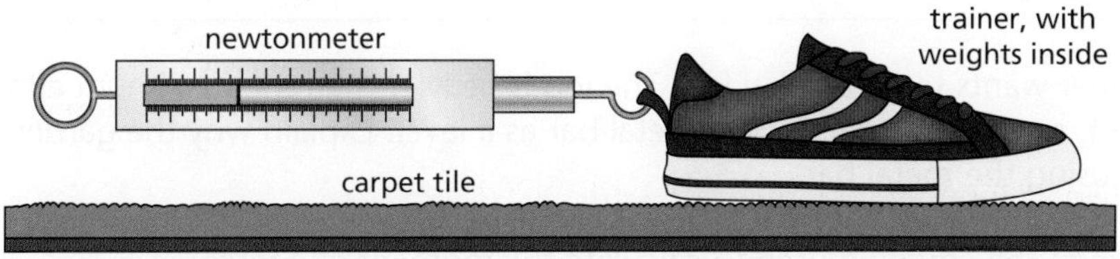

a Make a simple copy of the diagram and add arrows to show the pulling force applied to the trainer by the newtonmeter and the force of friction.

b Describe how the students made the experiment a fair comparison between the trainers.

c Explain how the readings obtained would indicate which trainer has the best grip.

9 A group of students is investigating the drag force on objects moving through water. They have a large clear plastic bottle filled with water. They also have some modelling clay, a top pan balance, a stopwatch and a ruler. The idea they are exploring is how the shape of a piece of clay will affect the time it will take to reach the bottom of the bottle.

a Describe how the students could use the equipment to see if the shape of the clay affects how quickly it reaches the bottom of the bottle.

b Explain how the shape of a piece of clay could affect how quickly it falls through the water.

c Explain why it is important that each piece of clay has the same weight.

13.3 Levers and moments

You are learning to:

- describe how a force can produce a turning effect
- calculate the moment of a force
- apply the idea of turning effects to explain the actions of simple machines
- apply ideas about clockwise and anticlockwise moments to explain how a lever can be balanced.

1. Give **two** examples of moments in action in a kitchen.
2. Identify what acts as the fulcrum when a cupboard door is opened.
3. State the **two** ways of increasing the turning effect of a force.

Worked example

The devices shown in the picture, called tap turners, are attached to the tops of ordinary taps to make them easier to turn on and off. They are often used by people who have less strength in their hands.

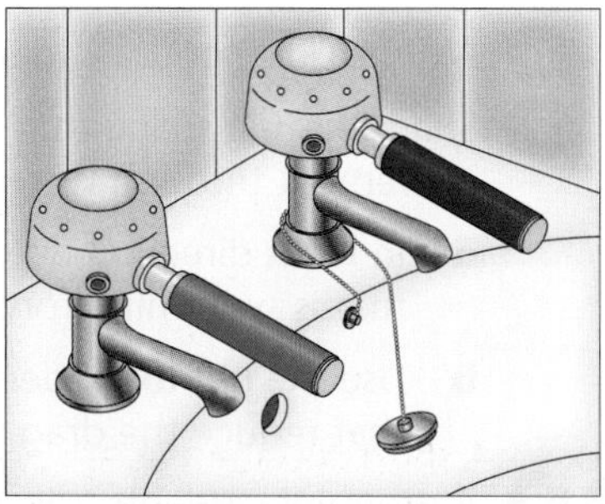

Explain how tap turners reduce the force needed to turn a tap on or off.

When asked for an explanation, make sure you include a reason for what is suggested. It's a good idea to use connectives such as 'because' or 'therefore'.

The force that turns the tap is applied by twisting the handle. This produces a turning force or moment. The size of the moment depends upon the size of the force and the distance between the force and the fulcrum (the centre of the tap). People with weaker hands can't apply a large force but the longer handle of the tap turner increases the size of the moment, so less effort is needed.

4. A gardener wants to lift a fallen log. The log is heavier than the maximum effort the gardener can exert, so they decide to use a metal bar as a lever. Explain why the gardener is able to lift the log using the metal bar.
5. Write down the equation used to calculate the moment of a force.
6. Agnes is trying to use a spanner to undo a wheel nut on her car. The nut has been done up very tightly and is difficult to turn. She wonders if using a longer spanner might make the job easier but then thinks that she can't push down on a long spanner any harder than on a short one. Explain whether you think using a longer spanner would help.
7. Explain how a pair of scissors can be used to cut a piece of string. Explain why it is easier to cut the string if it is placed close to where the blades are joined together. Use the words **pivot**, **effort** and **force** in your answer.
8. Explain in each of these situations where the effort is being applied, where the fulcrum is and where the lever applies the force:

   a a person levering open the lid on a paint tin with a screwdriver blade

   b a crowbar being used to force open a door.

9 Look at the balanced see-saw in the diagram. Explain why, in order to get the see-saw to balance, the heavier child has to sit nearer to the fulcrum.

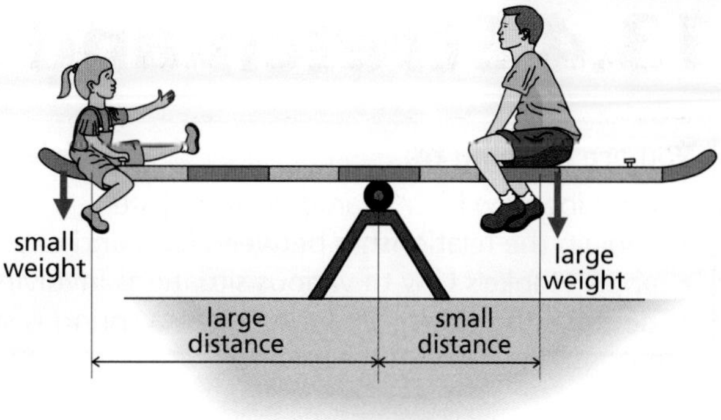

Worked example

A 30 cm long spanner is being used to apply a force of 20 N to turn a nut. Calculate the size of the moment being applied to the nut.

moment = force applied × distance from turning point

distance = 30 cm = 0.3 m

moment = 20 N × 0.3 m

= 6 N m

10 Calculate the turning effect of a 50 N force applied to a bolt using a 30 cm long spanner. Use the equation:

turning effect of a force = force applied × distance

11 A shop counter has a hinged flap that can be raised to allow staff through and then lowered to form part of the counter. The flap is 600 mm from its hinge to the edge. Lifting the flap at its end needs a force of 15 N. Calculate the turning effect of this force at the hinge.

12 The door between the dining area of a restaurant and the kitchen is sprung so that it can be pushed open and then swing back into place. It takes a force of 28 N to open the door if it is pushed at the edge opposite to the hinges.

a Calculate the force needed to open the door if it is pushed at a point halfway across the door instead of at the edge.

b Explain your reasoning.

13 Tower cranes have a counterweight to balance the effect of the load. The counterweight can be moved towards the tower or away from it in order to balance the structure. More counterweights can also be added.

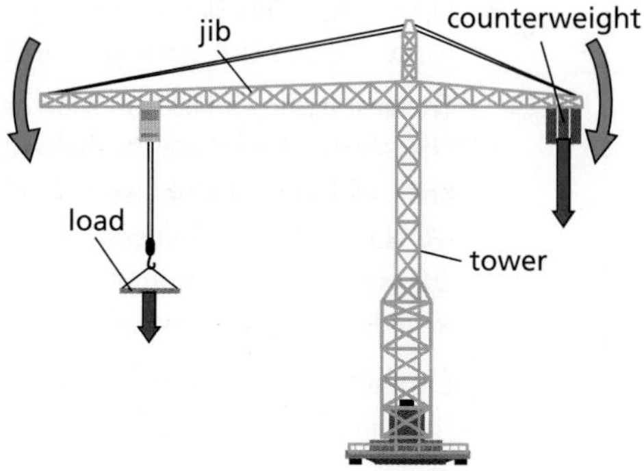

a Explain why a tower crane needs a counterweight.

b The counterweight weighs 5000 N and the right-hand side of the jib is 10 m long. Calculate the maximum possible clockwise moment.

c The counterweight is moved so that it is 6 m from the tower and the load is 24 m from the tower. Calculate the maximum load that the crane can lift.

d If the crane was going to be used to lift lighter loads, suggest **two** ways of adjusting the counterweight to balance the structure.

e The load is suspended from a small trolley which can be moved along the jib. If the load is moved towards the tower, which way would the counterweight have to be moved to continue balancing the crane?

13.4 Stretch and compression

You are learning to:

- describe how forces can deform objects
- explain the relationship between load and extension of a spring
- apply Hooke's Law to various situations involving springs
- describe the energy changes when a spring is stretched or compressed.

1 **a** Name a material that will stretch when a force is applied to it.

b Suggest what would happen eventually if you kept on loading it.

c Name a material which, if loaded, wouldn't seem to stretch but would break.

2 A group of students is going to compare how different elastic bands stretch when the weight attached to the bands is increased.

a State the **two** values they will need to measure each time a different weight is added.

b The students decide they need to calculate the extension of the elastic band. Explain how they could do this.

c State **two** possible hazards if the elastic band suddenly snapped.

d Describe **two** safety precautions that the students should take to reduce the risk of harm to themselves if this happened.

3 A wildlife keeper uses an elastic catapult to fire food high into the air to feed birds of prey. Describe the changes in energy when the stretched catapult is released.

Worked example

A group of students hung a spring from a hook and measured its length. They then hung a load from the spring and measured its length again. They repeated this process for more loads. They calculated the extension for each force applied and plotted a graph of force against extension.

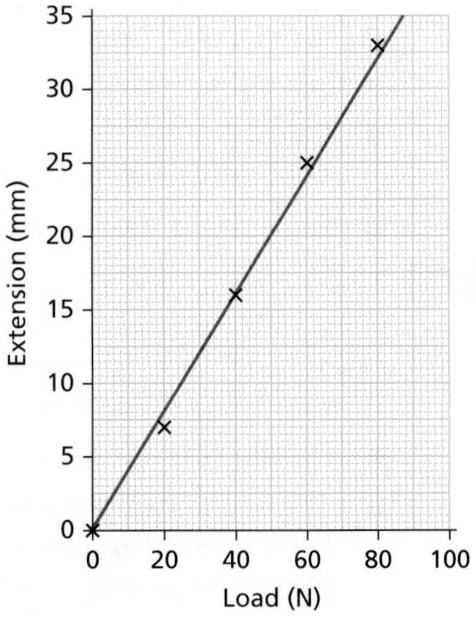

a Describe what the graph shows about the way that the force causes the spring to extend.

The graph shows that if twice as much force is applied to the spring then the extension is twice as much. For example, the line of best fit shows that if the load is doubled from 40 N to 80 N, the extension doubles from 16 mm to 32 mm. The extension is directly proportional to the force, as indicated by the straight line through the origin.

b Explain what would happen if the students exceeded the elastic limit of the spring.

The graph shows that the students have not exceeded the elastic limit of the spring because the line is straight. Exceeding the limit would cause the line to curve after a certain load.

4 A spring stretches by 3 cm when a force of 10 N is applied to it. If it behaves according to Hooke's Law and its elastic limit is not exceeded, how far would you expect it to extend when the following loads are attached to it?

a 20 N **b** 70 N **c** 2 N

5 Look at this graph showing how the weight added to a spring produces an extension.

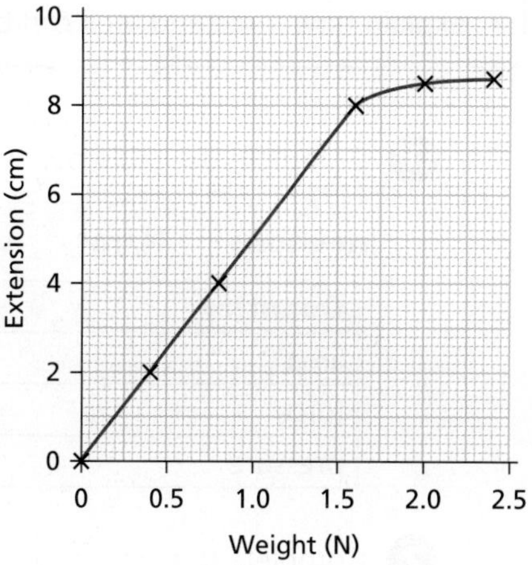

a Describe the relationship between weight and extension up to a weight of 1.5 N.

b Use the graph to find how much force is needed to extend the spring by 7 cm.

c How much will the spring extend by if a force of 1 N is applied to it?

d Suggest approximately what size of force is needed to exceed the elastic limit of this spring.

e Suggest how the spring's length would compare to its original length if it was loaded to the largest value shown and then unloaded.

6 Explain in your own words what is meant by the phrase 'exceeding the elastic limit of a material'.

7 A group of students was investigating how loads added to a spring caused it to be extended. Their results are shown in the table below.

Load (N)	0	5	10	15	20	25	30	35	40
Extension of spring (mm)	0	6	11	17	22	28	35	44	55

a Plot a line graph to display the data. Plot the load on the *x*-axis and the extension on the *y*-axis. Include a line of best fit.

b State what can be concluded from the graph about the relationship between extension and force for this spring.

c Suggest the load that was the elastic limit of the spring.

8 A group of students is investigating the relationship between the load being carried by a plastic carrier bag and the amount the bag stretches. They decide to compare a cheap, thin carrier bag with a higher priced long-life bag. They will gather data and plot graphs to find out how the bags compare.

a Suggest how the students could design the investigation to produce a valid comparison between the two bags.

b The students decide to plot the data for both carrier bags on one graph instead of drawing two different graphs. Suggest **one** advantage and **one** disadvantage of doing this.

c One of the students suggests that they should test not just one bag of each sort but, say, ten bags of each sort, and then take the average (mean) of the readings. Comment on whether this would improve the experiment.

13.5 Pressure in solids

You are learning to:
- understand pressure as the force applied per unit area
- calculate pressure from force and area
- explain how force and area can be changed to alter the pressure applied.

1 Complete the table below using the units and abbreviations listed.

newtons **N/m²** **square metres** **N** **newtons per square metre** **m²**

Quantity	Unit	Abbreviation
area		
force		
pressure		

2 Complete this sentence: The smaller the area that a force acts over, the ______________ the pressure will be.

3 Explain how snow shoes enable people to walk on soft snow. Use the words **area**, **force** and **pressure** in your answer.

4 Which of the following is the correct equation for calculating pressure?

a pressure = force × area

b pressure = force ÷ area

c pressure = force + area

d pressure = force – area

5 If a pressure is calculated using force in newtons and area in square millimetres, state the unit the answer should be in.

6 Calculate the pressure exerted on soft ground by a piece of wood with a base area of 5 m^2 and weighing 40 N.

7 A group of students is finding out how the pressure exerted by a block of stone on the ground underneath it will vary. The block can be turned so that different faces are in contact with the ground. The block has dimensions of 40 cm × 10 cm × 5 cm. It has a weight of 40 N.

a Calculate the pressure (in N/cm^2) the block exerts on the ground if the face in contact with the ground measures:

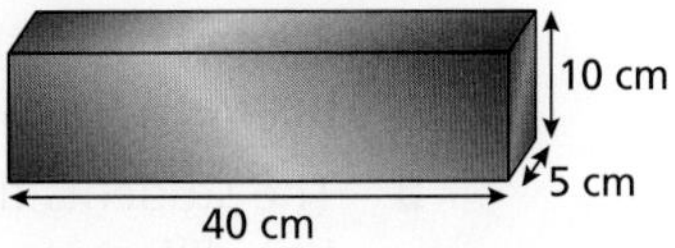

i 40 cm × 5 cm

ii 40 cm × 10 cm

iii 10 cm × 5 cm

b The ground the block is stood on is rather soft and muddy. When stood on one of its faces the block starts to sink into the ground. Suggest which of the faces was in contact with the ground for this to happen.

8 A concrete base for a child's swing has a weight of 2500 N and an area of 20 m^2. Calculate the pressure it exerts on the ground.

9 Which exerts the least pressure – a crate weighing 600 N acting on a surface of 8 m^2 or one weighing 420 N acting on a surface of 6 m^2? Give a reason for your answer.

Worked example

A bridge needs to take loads up to 45 000 N. The pressure on the ground must not be greater than 5000 Pa or the bridge will sink into the ground. Calculate the total area needed for the bridge supports.

Remember that pressure = force ÷ area. If you know what the values of two of the quantities in the pressure equation are, you can calculate the third quantity by rearranging the equation.

area = force ÷ pressure or force = pressure × area

If the force is in newtons, N, and the pressure is in pascals, Pa, the area will be in square metres, m^2.

area = force ÷ pressure

= 45 000 ÷ 5000 = 9 m^2

10 A hide is going to be constructed in a wetland area to enable people to watch birds without disturbing them. The ground is soft so the structure will have a wide wooden base to stop it from sinking. The structure has a weight of 6000 N and the engineer estimates that the maximum pressure the ground can take is 80 N/m^2. Calculate the area that the base of the hide should be.

11 Mio wants to lay paving slabs in her garden. Each slab is 600 mm by 600 mm. She doesn't want the slabs to sink into the liquid cement while it is setting. If the wet cement can support a pressure up to 50 N/m^2, calculate the maximum weight of each slab.

12 Different designs of skis are used for different purposes. The skier on the left is going over deep powder snow, which is loose. Their skis are 160 cm long and 12.5 cm wide. The skier on the right is racing down a slope of firm, tightly packed snow. Their downhill skis are 200 cm long and 8 cm wide. Both skiers have a weight of 720 N.

a Calculate the surface area in metes squared of a pair of deep powder snow skis.

b Calculate the surface area in metes squared of a pair of downhill skis.

c Suggest why the skis designed for use on powdered snow have a larger surface area than those used on tightly packed snow.

d Calculate the pressure applied by each skier on the snow in Newtons per square metre.

13.6 Pressure in fluids

You are learning to:

- use the particle model to explain what causes pressure in fluids
- explain why pressure increases with depth in fluids
- apply ideas about pressure to various situations.

1 A person blows air into a balloon to inflate it and ties a knot in the neck of the balloon to keep the air in.

a Draw a simple diagram of the balloon and add arrows to show how atmospheric pressure is acting on the outer surface of the balloon.

b Now add more arrows to show the pressure acting on the inside surface of the balloon, caused by the air trapped in the balloon.

2 A child is playing with a plastic ball in the bath. They hold the ball under the surface of the water and then release it. Name the force that makes the ball rise to the surface.

Worked example

A mountaineer climbs to the top of a high mountain and measures the pressure of the atmosphere. They find the pressure is less than it was at the foot of the mountain. Explain why this is so.

At the top of a mountain there is less air above the mountaineer and so the weight of the gases pressing down on a surface is less.

3 When a submarine dives deeper in the ocean there is more pressure upon it. Explain why this is.

4 This diagram shows a model of the arrangement of particles of water in a tall container.

a Suggest **two** ways in which this is a good model of the water particles.

b Suggest **two** ways it is not a good model of the water particles.

c If you measured the pressure at point A and compared it with the pressure at point B how would the two values compare?

d Explain your answer to part **c**.

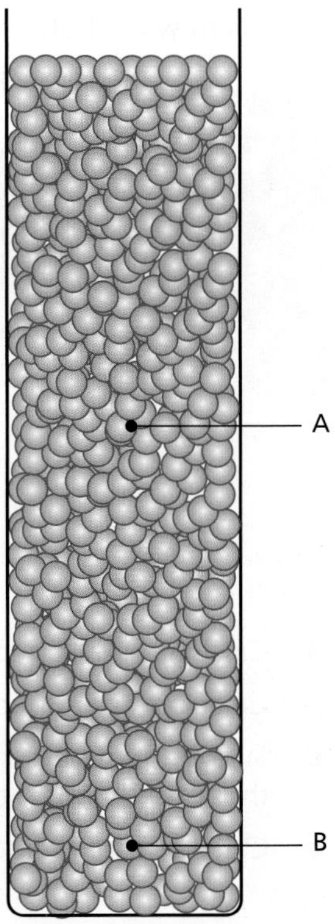

5 The diagram shows a metal block suspended above a container of water.

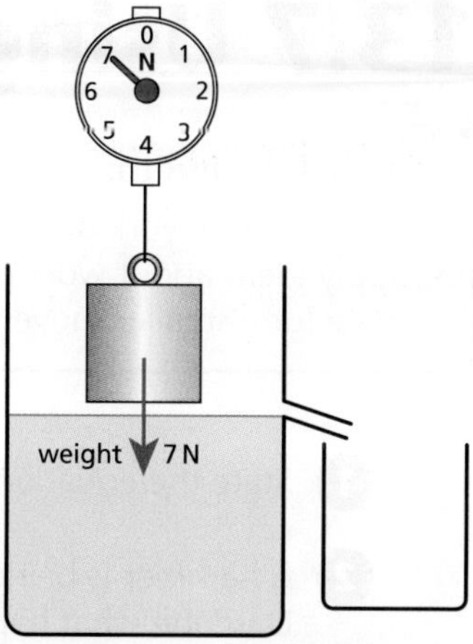

a The block is now lowered into the water so that it is completely immersed. Which of these statements about the reading on the newtonmeter will be true?

A The reading will now be zero.

B The reading will be more than zero but less than 7 N.

C The reading will be 7 N.

D The reading will be more than 7 N.

b Explain your answer to part **a**.

6 A scientist on a TV programme is explaining how pressure under water increases with depth.

a First, the scientist inflates a balloon by blowing air into it and then tying the neck. She says that it is air pressure that keeps the balloon inflated. Using ideas about particles, explain what the air is doing to keep the balloon inflated.

b The scientist then gets into a swimming pool with the balloon and dives down, holding the balloon deep under the water. The balloon is now smaller and she explains that if she could dive deeper and push the balloon lower its volume would decrease even more. Using ideas about particles, explain why the balloon is now smaller.

7 A teacher carries out a demonstration to show the force on a surface due to atmospheric pressure. They connect a vacuum pump to a metal can and pump the air out of it. As they do so, the sides of the can collapse inwards. The diagram shows the can before and after the air is pumped out.

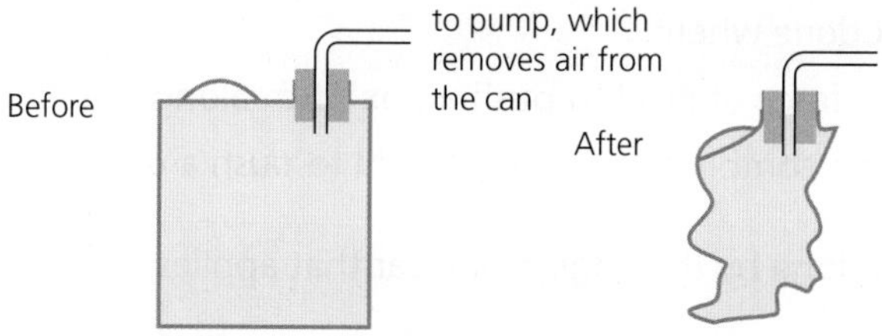

a Copy the diagram and add arrows to show how the atmosphere applies pressure to the sides of the can:

i before the air is removed

ii after the air is removed.

b Explain why the can was crushed.

c One of the students said that the sides of the can had been sucked in. Explain why this is not a very scientific explanation.

8 This is a weather balloon. It is being released so that it can take and transmit measurements of conditions in the upper atmosphere. The balloon is filled with helium, which is lighter than air. The balloon is closed so the gas is trapped inside. The balloon will rise up to a height of around 30 000 m and then explode, and the transmitter will return to Earth attached to a small parachute.

a Explain why the volume of the balloon will increase as it rises through the atmosphere.

b Explain why the balloon will explode at a high altitude.

13.7 Using moments

You are learning to:
- calculate the work done by a force
- apply ideas about work to explain how a simple machine produces a bigger force for a smaller movement.

1 State the equation used to calculate the moment, or turning effect, of a force.

2 A hammer is being used to pull a nail out of a piece of wood. Describe what happens to the size of the force that needs to be applied if the hammer has a longer handle.

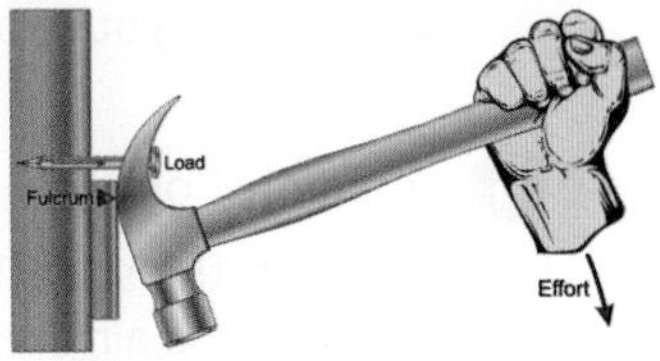

Worked example

A conveyor belt at an airport uses a force of 5 N to move a suitcase 50 m. Calculate the work done. Give your answer in joules (J).

work done = force × distance moved

= 5 N × 50 m = 250 N m

1 N m equals 1 J, so work done = 250 J

3 Calculate the work done when:

a a woman uses a force of 60 N to push a box 10 m along the floor

b four people use a combined force of 5000 N to push a car a distance of 50 m.

4 How much work is done by the engine of a car that applies a force of 25 000 N to move the vehicle 2 km?

Worked example

A pair of scissors is a simple machine. It can produce a bigger force on the object being cut (the load), than the force applied on the handles (the effort).

Use the idea of work done to explain how a pair of scissors increases the force being applied.

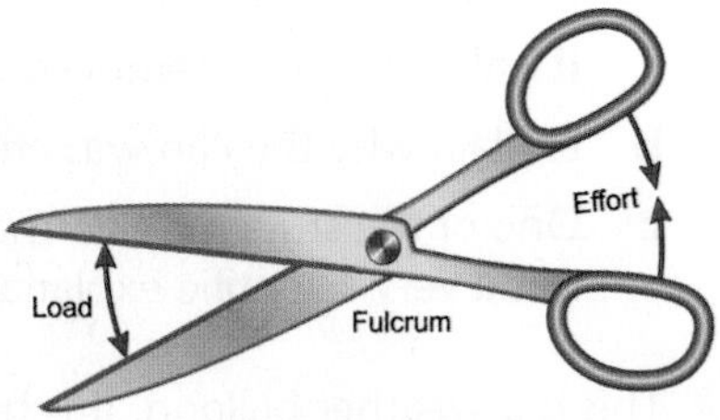

When scissors are used to increase the size of the force, the object being cut is placed close to the fulcrum. The force exerted on the object is greater than the effort force. However the effort is applied further from the fulcrum so the effort has to move through a greater distance. As the amount of work done is the same for each force, the value of force × distance moved must be the same. The small force moves a greater distance and the bigger force moves a smaller distance.

5 A student says that if a machine can turn a small force into a larger one we are 'getting something for nothing'. Use what you know about the distances that each force moves to explain why the student is wrong.

6. In Josh's kitchen there is a pedal bin. It has a lid which is opened by pressing on the pedal. Josh notices that he only has to push the pedal a short distance and the lid moves a long way.

   Compare the force Josh applies to the pedal with the force this applies to the lid and explain your answer. Use the idea of work done.

7. The man in the diagram is using a lever to move a crate. He is pushing down on the lever to apply an upwards force on the crate.

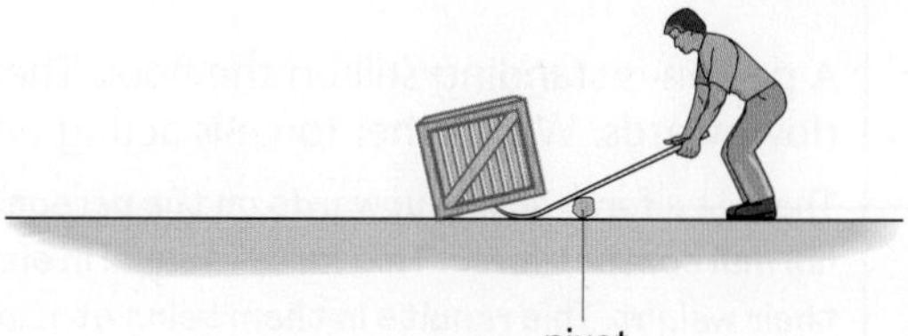

   a He is pushing down with a force of 250 N at a distance of 1 m from the fulcrum. Calculate the moment he is producing.

   b State the size of the moment being applied to the crate.

   c The distance from the fulcrum to the contact point with the crate is 10 cm. Calculate the size of the force on the crate.

   d Consider your answer to part **c** and explain why the man is using a lever rather than just lifting the crate.

   e Compare the work done by the man and the work done by the lever.

8. This diagram shows two people using a revolving door. The view is from above. They are both pushing on the door. As the door turns they can pass into or out of the building. The man on the left is pushing with a force of 40 N at a place on the door 60 cm from the turning point. The woman on the right is pushing with a force of 60 N at 40 cm from the turning point.

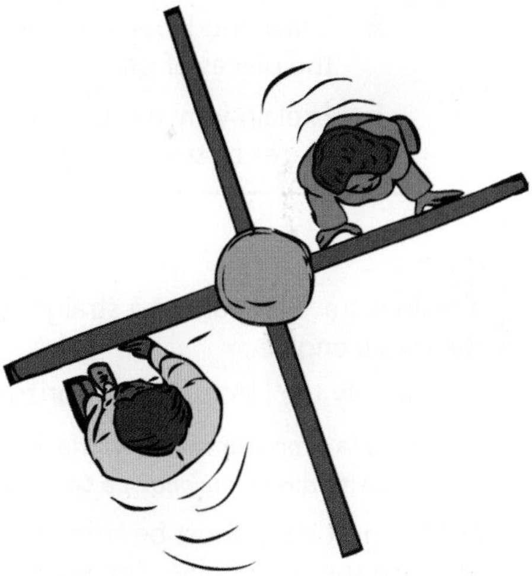

   a Calculate the moment of the force the woman applies to the door. State the direction of the moment.

   b Calculate the moment of the force the man applies to the door. State the direction of the moment.

   c Calculate the total moment being applied to the door, and its direction.

   d Explain what would happen if one person was trying to push the door in the opposite direction. Assume they apply the same force at the same distance from the turning point.

9. Khalim and Misbah are sitting on either side of a see-saw and trying to make it balance. Khalim weighs 200 N and Misbah weighs 150 N. The see-saw is 4 m long and the fulcrum is in the centre. Misbah sits right at the end on one side. Calculate the position Khalim must sit at to balance the see-saw.

13.8 Forces, motion and equilibrium

You are learning to:
- describe how balanced forces can hold an object in equilibrium
- calculate the effect of several forces acting in opposing directions
- identify the effect of unbalanced forces that don't cancel each other out.

Worked example

A person is standing still on the floor. There is a force on them due to their weight. This force acts downwards. What other force is acting on the person? Explain why the person is stationary.

There is a force acting upwards on the person as they are in contact with the floor; this force is called the normal contact force. This force is equal in size to the person's weight and acts in the opposite direction to their weight. This results in them being stationary (not moving).

1 An apple is resting on a table. Explain why the apple is not moving.

2 Explain why a coat hanging on a peg is an example of forces in equilibrium.

3 A teacher is demonstrating static charge. They have combed their hair with a plastic comb to charge the comb. The comb then attracts some pieces of tissue paper.

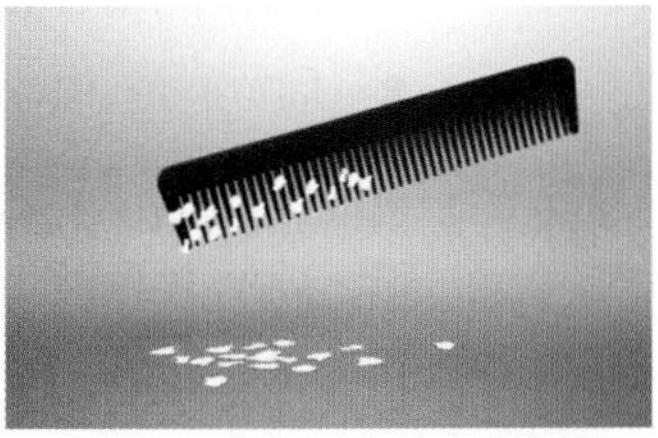

a Draw and label a diagram to show the forces acting on one of the pieces of paper as it rises up to the comb.

b Explain why the teacher has to tear the tissue paper into small pieces to see any effect.

Worked example

A train is travelling along a straight section of track. It is accelerating due to the power generated by the diesel engine.

a Identify the forces acting horizontally on the train.

There is a force in the forwards direction due to the power of the engine. There are two forces in the opposite direction: one due to friction and another due to air resistance.

b Suggest what must be true about the size of the force being applied by the engine compared with the size of any opposing forces.

The train is travelling forwards, so the force due to the engine must be greater than the total of the forces due to air resistance and friction.

4 This cyclist is pedalling along a straight, level road at a constant speed.

a Describe the various forces acting on a bicycle being pedalled at a steady speed.

b Explain why the bicycle is not accelerating.

c The cyclist now stops pedalling and his speed decreases. Explain why this happens by referring to the forces acting.

5 This boat is accelerating forwards.

a Describe the forces acting on the boat.

b Explain how the force due to the engine compares in size and direction with the forces opposing the motion.

6 Draw force diagrams to show the forces acting on:

a a plastic bowl floating in a bath of water

b the same bowl now carrying some marbles and floating in a bath of water

c a rubber duck which usually floats but is being held under water.

7 Look at the diagram on the right. In each case the object is already moving towards the left when the pushing force shown is applied. Suggest what the motion of the object will be in each case.

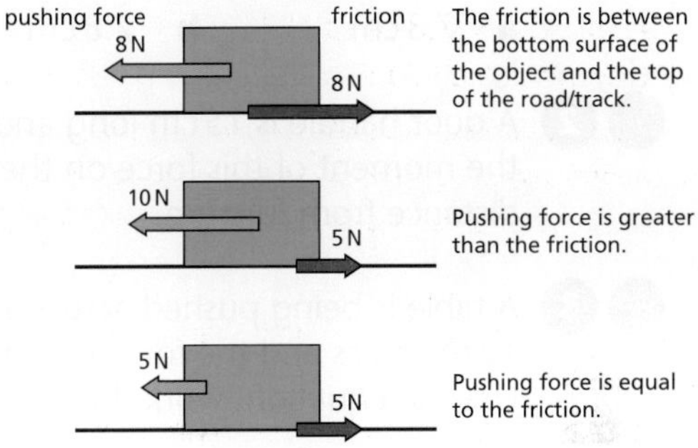

8 A parachutist has his parachute open and is descending at steady speed.

a Describe the forces acting on the man and the parachute, indicating the direction of each one.

b Suggest what is true about the size of the forces if the parachutist's speed and direction are not changing.

Worked example

Sahid is cycling along a level road at a steady speed. The force he is applying to the pedals to cause the forwards motion is 100 N and the motion of the bicycle is opposed by frictional forces of 20 N. He is also having to work against air resistance. Calculate the size of the air resistance. Include your reasoning.

If his speed is constant, the forces in the forward and opposite directions are equal – they are balanced. The forwards force is 100 N so there must be a total force in the opposite direction of 100 N. Therefore, the air resistance is 100 N.

9 A freight train consists of a diesel engine pulling a number of wagons. The engine can provide a force of 50 000 N to move the train along the track, but this force is opposed by 4000 N of air resistance and 6000 N of friction acting on the engine. Every wagon adds a further force due to air resistance of 1000 N and a friction force of 4200 N. Calculate the number of wagons the engine can pull.

10 Think about an archer, firing an arrow from a bow.

a When an arrow is fired straight ahead (horizontally), what effect will the downward force of weight have?

b What effect will air resistance have on the flight of the arrow?

c An arrow is fired vertically upwards. Describe the force(s) that act after the arrow is fired.

d Why does pulling the string back further on the bow affect how far the arrow flies?

Maths and practical skills

1 The picture shows a 10 cm ruler.

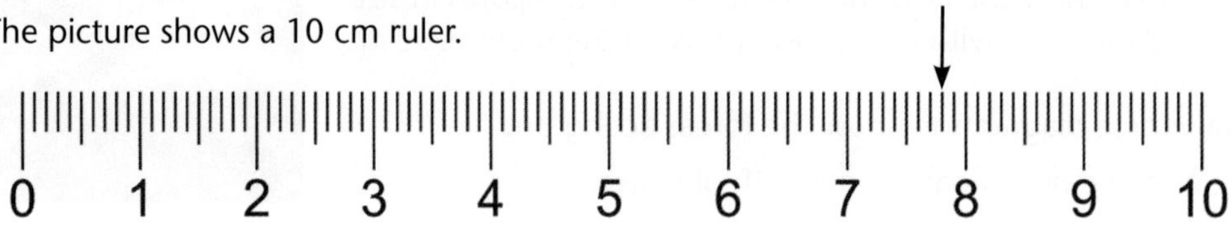

Which of the following is the reading indicated by the arrow on the scale?

a 7.3 cm **b** 7.8 cm **c** 8.2 cm **d** 8.7 cm

2 A door handle is 15 cm long and a force of 25 N is applied at the end of the handle. Calculate the moment of this force on the pivot in newtonmetres. Use the equation: moment = force × distance from fulcrum.

3 A table is being pushed across a floor from one side of the room to the other. The room is 12 m across and the force being applied to the table is 40 N. Calculate the work being done. Use the equation: work done = force × distance moved.

4 Fatima is plotting a graph and knows that she needs to get the dependent and independent variables the right way round. Copy and complete this sentence to remind her:

The ______**i**______ variable goes on the *x*-axis and the ______**ii**______ variable goes on the *y*-axis.

5 Salim's group is investigating the extension of a spring and are adding 10 g masses to increase the load. Salim's job is to measure the length of the spring each time the load is increased. These are the lengths he writes down. He makes a mistake with one measurement. Identify which measurement is incorrect.

10.4 cm, 12.2 cm, 12.0 cm, 12.8 cm, 13.6 cm, 14.4 cm

6 A concrete block with a weight of 160 000 N is standing on the ground. The block is a cube with sides of length 2 m. Calculate the pressure applied on the ground.

7 A door measures 70 cm from the handle to the hinges. A force of 8 N is needed to open the door. Calculate the moment of the force at the hinge in newtonmetres.

8 A teacher has shown a class of students that a newtonmeter has a spring inside it. She shows them that when a force is applied to the instrument the spring is stretched and the pointer moves along a scale.

She then asks the students to test different springs to see which would be the most suitable for a newtonmeter used to measure forces between 0 and 10 N. The students have a selection of springs, slotted masses (100 g), a ruler and a stand for supporting the springs. The weight of a 100 g mass is 1 N.

a Describe how the students could collect data to compare the springs.

b They find that all the springs they test are extended by a 10 N load. Suggest how they should select the most suitable spring for use in the newtonmeter.

c They have now selected a spring they think is suitable. How could they find the resolution of their newtonmeter?

Worked example

A truck is driving along a motorway at 70 km/h and is being overtaken by a car doing 80 km/h. In the other carriageway a motorcycle is travelling at 90 km/h in the opposite direction.

a Calculate the speed of the car relative to the truck.

The car and the truck are travelling in the same direction, so the speeds are subtracted.

$80 - 70 = 10$ km/h

b Calculate the speed of the motorcycle relative to the truck.

The motorcycle and the truck are travelling in the opposite direction, so the speeds are added.

$70 + 90 = 160$ km/h

9 A person sets off jogging along a cycle path at 4 km/h at the same time as a cyclist sets off from the same place and travels in the same direction at 10 km/h.

a Calculate how far each one will travel in a quarter of an hour.

b Calculate their relative speed.

c Suggest how the cyclist would appear to be moving to the jogger as they both travel along.

Worked example

A group of students is investigating the motion of a toy car down a ramp. They are going to explore how altering the gradient of the ramp will affect how far the car travels across the floor when it leaves the bottom of the ramp. Identify the independent variable, the dependent variable and any control variables.

The independent variable is the one the students will change and select values for. The dependent variable is the one that will change as a result of the independent variable. The control variables are things that could change but which the students should keep the same so that only one variable is allowed to affect the dependent variable.

Independent variable: gradient of ramp

Dependent variable: the distance the car travels across the floor from the bottom of the ramp

Control variables: could include the material of the surface of the ramp, the mass of the vehicle, the vehicle itself

10 The diagram shows an experiment that a group of students is carrying out. They are exploring how a force acting on a trolley will affect its final speed. They are going to vary the force by adding masses to the hanger on the right-hand side. The trolley is stationary at first but will start to move as the mass drops.

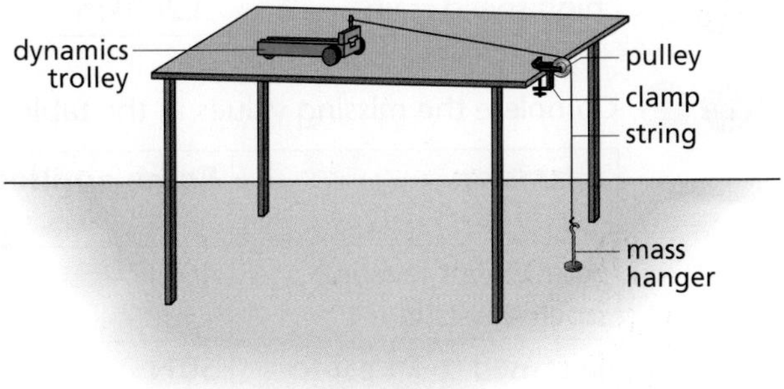

a Identify the independent variable, the dependent variable and any control variables.

b Suggest what precautions the students should take to reduce the risk of equipment falling on their feet.

c Explain why altering the number of masses on the hanger will affect the motion of the trolley.

11 The gas tap in a school science lab is 45 mm long. The maximum force that can be applied to the lever on the tap is 50 N. Calculate the moment of this force.

12 Calculate the speed in metres per second of a motorcycle that travels 1.25 km in 1 minute. Give your answer to one decimal place.

13 Calculate the average speed in m/s of the following objects:

a a snail covering 6 cm in one minute

b a runner travelling 1.2 km in 10 minutes

c a rocket travelling 27 000 km in an hour.

Worked example

a A train is travelling between Bristol and Exeter, a distance of 144 km, at an average speed of 120 km/h. Calculate the time taken for the journey.

If you know the distance and the speed you can calculate the time by rearranging the equation speed = distance ÷ time to give time = distance ÷ speed.

time = distance ÷ speed

144 km ÷ 120 km/h = 1.2 h

b The train then travels on to Plymouth at the same average speed, in 42 minutes. Calculate the distance between Exeter and Plymouth.

If you know the time and the speed you can calculate the distance by rearranging the equation: distance = speed × time.

time in hours = 42 ÷ 60 = 0.7 hours

distance = speed x time

= 120 km/h x 0.7 h = 84 km

14 Complete the missing values in the table.

Object	Distance travelled	Time taken	Speed
toy train on circuit of track	50 cm	4 s	______ **i** ______ m/s
car driving along road	450 m	1.5 minutes	______ **ii** ______ m/s
jogger	1 km	______ **iii** ______ s	2 m/s
space rocket	______ **iv** ______ m	0.2 s	300 m/s
high speed train	200 km	______ **v** ______ s	50 m/s

15 Complete the missing values in the table.

Situation	Force applied	Distance from force to turning point	Turning effect of the force
screwdriver levering open paint tin	40 N	25 cm	______ **i** ______ Nm
jack used to lift car to change wheel	50 N	30 cm	______ **ii** ______ Nm
spanner used to tighten wing nuts	______ **iii** ______ N	50 cm	40 N m
crowbar prising apart pieces of wood	60 N	______ **iv** ______ cm	30 N m

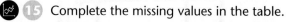

16 A group of students is investigating the friction between a rectangular block and the ramp it is placed on. The apparatus they use is shown in the diagram. A rectangular block is placed on the slope and the angle of slope increased until the block starts to slide down. The covering of the slope can also be altered.

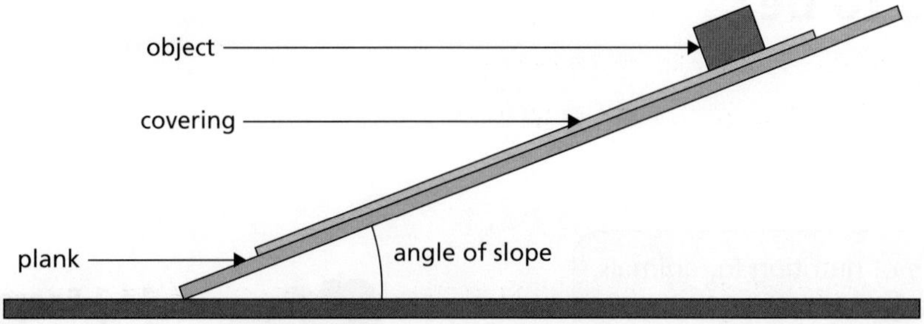

a Suggest what kind of coverings could be investigated using this equipment.

b Suggest how the type of covering will affect the angle at which the block starts to slide.

c Identify the independent and dependent variables and a control variable.

d Describe how the students should carry out the investigation to make it a fair test.

e The block was placed on the ramp. Starting with the ramp at an angle of 0° the angle is increased until the block starts to slide. The experiment was then repeated with a different covering and the block started to slide at a smaller angle. Suggest what conclusion can be drawn from these results.

f The students tested six different coverings and recorded the angles at which the block started to slide. Explain why it would be appropriate to display the results as a bar chart rather than as a line graph.

17 Sam is investigating moments and see-saws. He is using a metre rule that has been balanced on a fulcrum at its midpoint.

On one side of the see-saw he places a 1 N load, 20 cm from the fulcrum.

a Suggest the size of the load that would have to be placed 10 cm the other side of the fulcrum to balance the see-saw and explain your answer.

b Suggest the size of the load that would have to be placed 40 cm the other side of the fulcrum to balance the see-saw and explain your answer.

c Sam decides to find out if the 1 N load can be balanced by two loads on the other side of the see-saw but in different positions. He puts a 2 N load 5 cm from the fulcrum and a 0.5 N load 20 cm from the fulcrum. Predict whether these loads will balance the 1 N load. Explain your answer.

18 Jess is measuring the time it takes for a marble to roll down a short slope. She measures the length of the slope using a 30 cm ruler and the time using a stopwatch. The teacher asks her to think about sources of error in her readings, and which errors might be random and which systematic. Jess's ruler is a plastic one and is getting a bit twisted. She knows that her reaction time affects starting and stopping the stopwatch at exactly the right times.

Which of the rows in the table below correctly identifies the types of error Jess may be making.

	Use of ruler	Use of stopwatch
a	random	random
b	systematic	random
c	random	systematic
d	systematic	systematic

14 Energy road map

Where are you in your learning journey and where are you aiming to be?

14.2 Heating and cooling

- compare transfer of energy
- apply ideas to redeunwanted transfe

- light travelling from a source, such as a bulb, to our eyes
- sound being made from vibrations and detected by a microphone or our ears
- objects being pushed, pulled, stretched or twisted

KS2

materials being heated

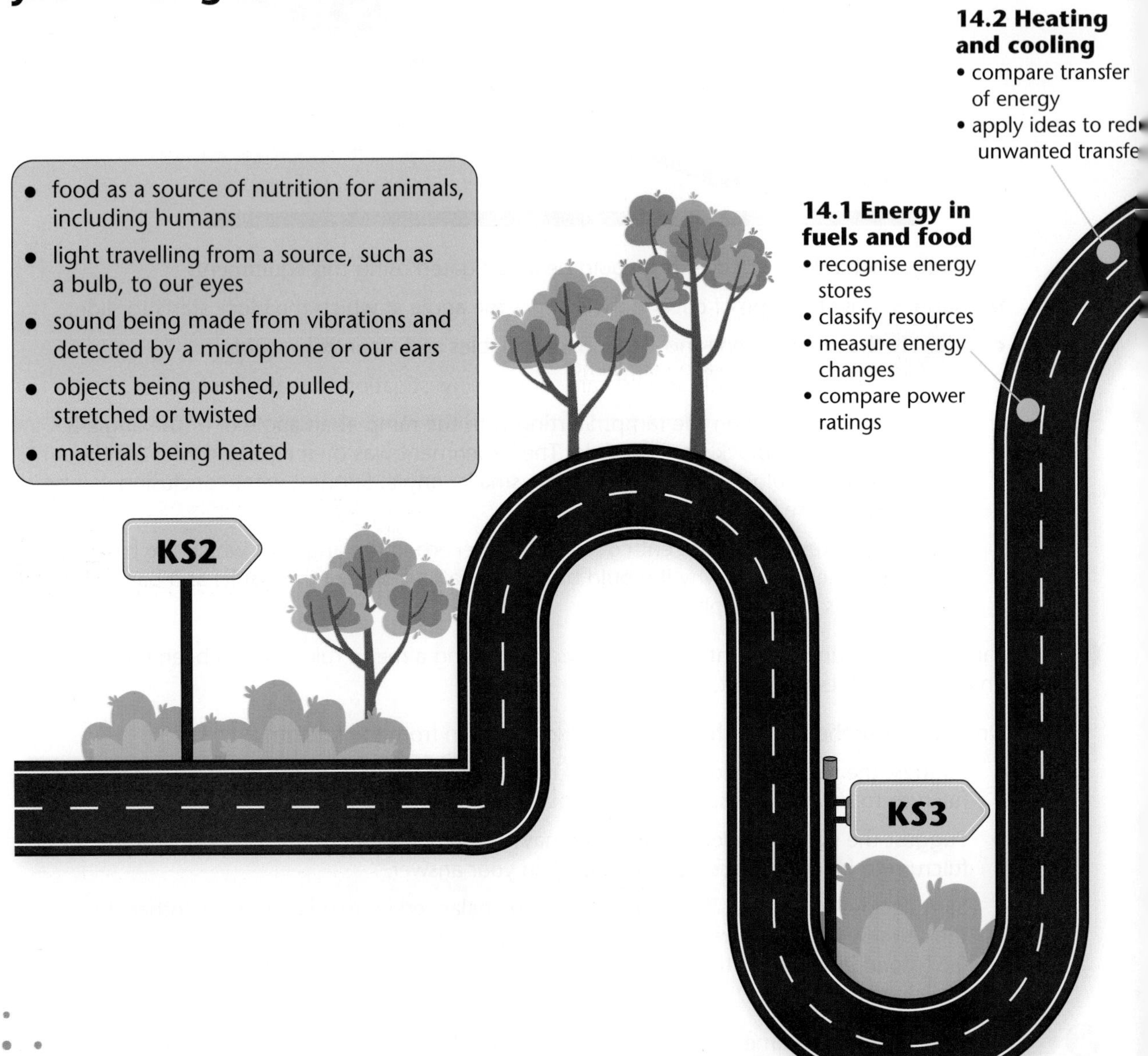

14.3 Processes involving energy transfer
- identify start and end stores
- identify processes
- calculate costs

14.4 Conservation of energy
- use Sankey diagrams
- apply the law of conservation of energy

- energy changes in a system, and the ways energy is stored before and after such changes
- conservation and dissipation of energy
- national and global energy resources
- energy transfers
- internal energy and energy transfers

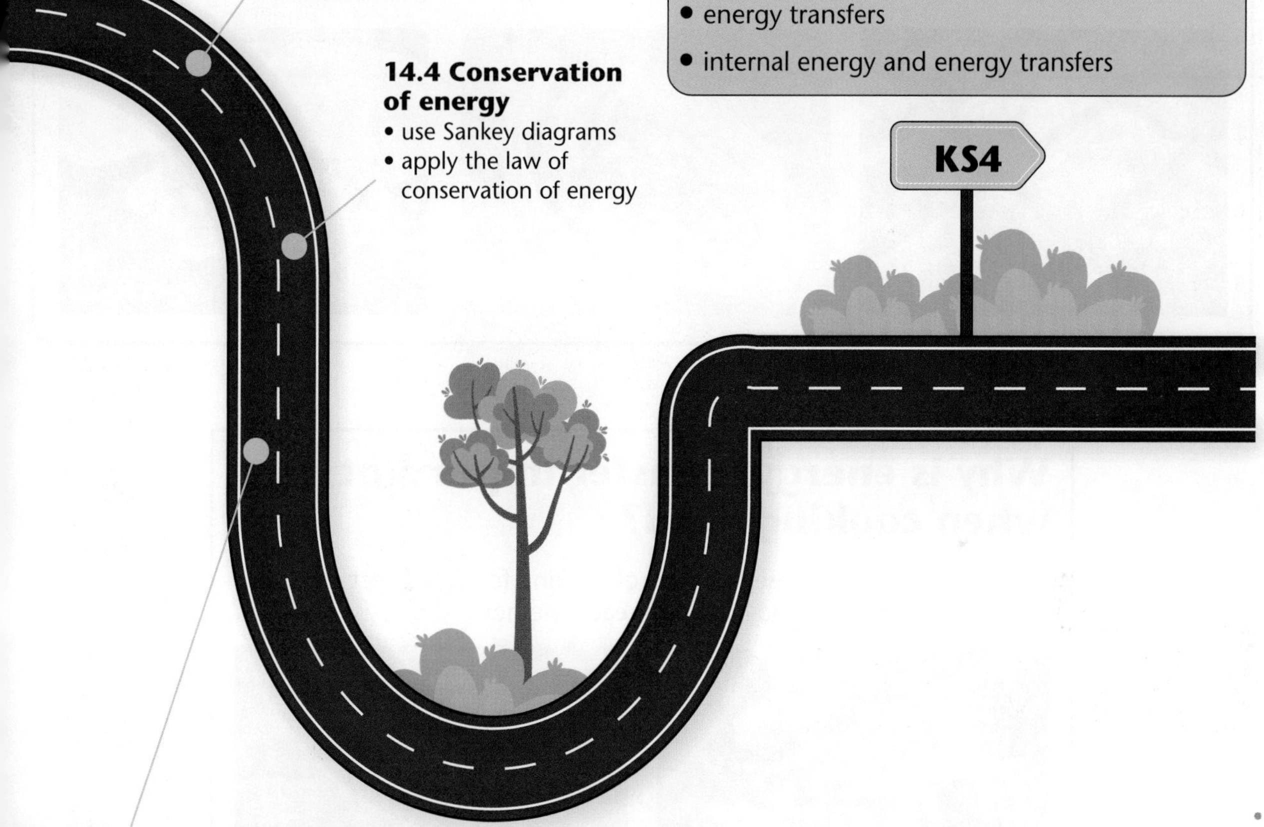

Maths and practical skills

- presenting data using tables and graphs
- interpreting observations and data
- carrying out practical work safely
- observing and measuring
- presenting reasoned explanations
- evaluating data, including being aware of possible errors

14 Energy

Energy can be stored in fuels or food, in something that's moving, in something that's been raised up or in other ways. When anything happens there is always an energy change and energy is transferred from a source to another place. When energy is transferred, useful things can happen.

What links food storage and energy?

Look at these food containers. They are all designed to keep food hot. For each container, suggest **one** advantage and **one** disadvantage.

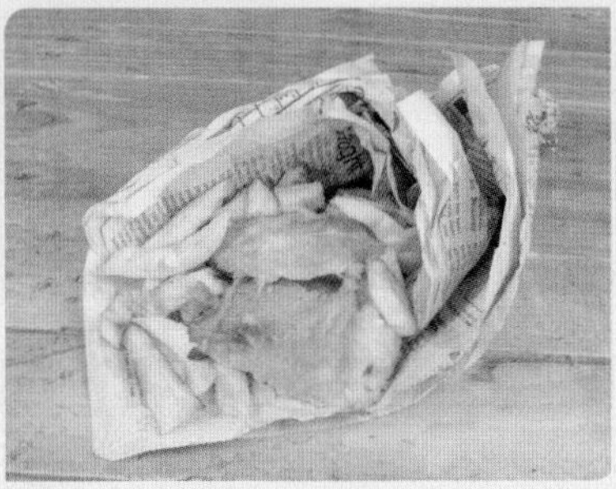

Why is energy transfer important when cooking food?

Think about each of these methods of cooking food. Suggest **one** advantage and **one** disadvantage of each method.

gas cooker

microwave

wood-fuelled oven

spirit burner

Using your science skills

Could you be a renewable energy engineer?

You research how renewable energy technologies can be used in different locations. An example of a project would be exploring the use of wind turbines in a desert in a Middle Eastern country. You have to analyse the climate of the area, suggest a suitable location for a wind farm and then identify how the turbines might fail. You need to identify the main risks of each location, such as increased wear of the mechanical parts and the impact of extreme temperatures on the lubrication.

Another example is to investigate replacing fossil fuel power stations in a city in Central America with renewable energy sources to improve the air quality. In this job, you use maths to model situations to predict problems. You have to work in a team and be able to explain your ideas to non-scientists.

Thermal insulation engineers survey buildings using thermal imaging cameras to plan where to install insulation or how to remove draughts, based on how energy is radiated and absorbed. This can cut fuel bills and keep people warm.

Solar panel installers design and fit photovoltaic panels to buildings that will generate electricity from energy transferred by sunlight. They need to work out how to place the panels to maximise the energy gathered.

Nutritionists know about the energy content of different foods and how they contribute to a healthy diet. They can advise a person to change their eating habits according to their energy requirements.

Sales managers and mechanics for electric vehicles need to understand the improvements that are being made to battery technology so that the cars can travel further on each charge.

Data analysts work for the National Grid, using past patterns of demand for electricity but also monitoring usage by the minute. They have to know which power stations they can call on to start generating electricity quickly if there is more demand.

Knowledge organiser

Stored **energy** is called **potential energy**. Energy can be stored in several different ways:

- **chemical potential energy** (for example, in **fuels** and food)
- **elastic potential energy** (for example, in a stretched or compressed spring)
- **gravitational potential energy** (for example, an apple on a tree)
- **kinetic energy** (for example, a moving car)
- **thermal energy** (for example, a hot cup of tea) – it is responsible for the temperature of an object.

Energy transfer is the passing on of energy from one store to another. Energy can be transferred between stores in various ways including heating, doing mechanical work, by an electrical current or by waves.

We measure energy in **joules (J)** or **kilojoules (kJ)**.

Power is the rate at which energy is transferred. It is measured in **watts (W)** and **kilowatts (kW)**.

Different **foods** contain different amounts of energy per gram.

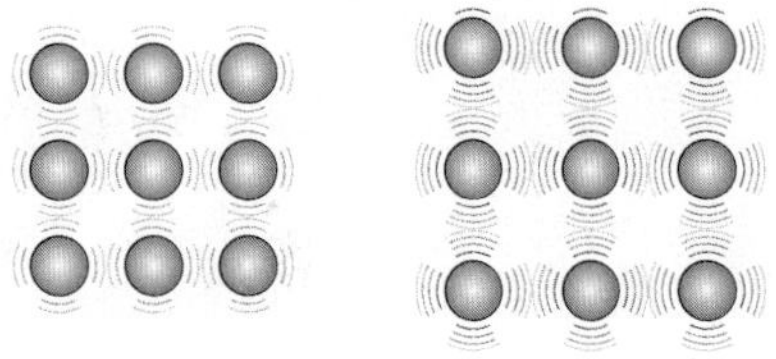

Thermal (heat) energy is transferred through a material by **conduction**. The vibrating particles within the material transfer energy by colliding with their neighbours. A material that conducts heat is called a **thermal conductor**, a material that does not is called a **thermal insulator**.

Electricity can be generated using **renewable energy** sources, such as the wind, or **non-renewable energy** sources, such as gas.

Gas and electricity companies calculate the cost of home energy use using the unit **kilowatt-hours (kW h)**.

The cost of using an electrical appliance can be calculated using the equation:

cost = power (kW) × time (hours) × price (per kW h)

Key vocabulary

conduction	the transfer of energy by passing on energy to nearby particles
energy	the potential to do work or produce heat
energy transfer	the passing on of energy from one energy store to another
food	a substance that provides living things with nutrients and energy
fuel	a material that is burned to release its stored energy
joule (J), kilojoule (kJ)	unit of energy; 1000 J = 1 kJ
kilowatt-hour (kW h)	the energy transferred in 1 h by an electrical appliance with a power rating of 1 kW
non-renewable energy	energy from a source, such as a fossil fuel, that will run out because it cannot be replaced quickly enough
power	amount of energy that something transfers each second; measured in watts (W)
radiation	energy given out in the form of a wave; it can pass through a vacuum
renewable energy	energy from a source that will not run out, such as the sun or wind
temperature	the measure of how hot or cold an object is; unit is degrees Celsius (°C)
thermal conductor	a material that allows energy to pass through it quickly by the process of thermal conduction
thermal insulator	a material that does not allow energy to pass through it quickly by the process of thermal conduction
watt (W), kilowatt (kW)	unit of power; 1000 W = 1 kW; 1 W is equal to a joule per second (1 J/s)

When energy is transferred, not all of the energy is useful for the intended purpose. We say that any energy transferred to a store where we cannot use it is **wasted energy**. This can happen, for example, when friction heats up two surfaces that rub together, or when a hot object heats up the air around it.

When energy is being transferred, we can keep track of the increase or decrease in the amounts of energy in each store by drawing an **energy transfer diagram**.

Whenever energy is transferred no energy is ever 'lost' or 'used up'. The quantity of energy stored before the change is the same as the quantity stored after the change. This is called the **law of conservation of energy**.

Thermal (heat) energy can be transferred from a hotter object to a cooler one by thermal **radiation**. The energy is transferred as a wave, and does not require the presence of particles to travel through.

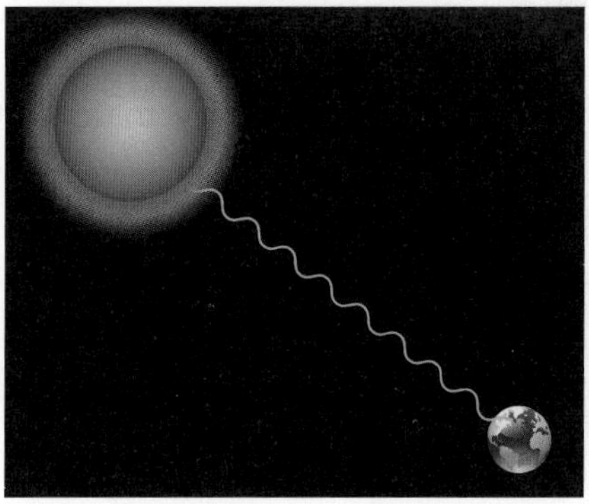

The energy supplied to and the energy outputs from a system can be represented on a **Sankey diagram**. This shows which of the outputs are useful. The width of each arrow represents how much energy is transferred, so the diagram also shows the proportion of the input energy that is useful and that the total amount of energy is conserved.

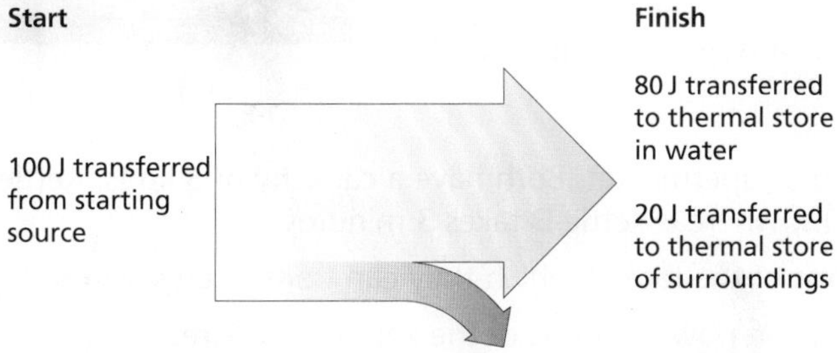

Key vocabulary

chemical potential energy	the energy store that is emptied during chemical reactions
elastic potential energy	the energy store of an elastic object when it is stretched or compressed
energy transfer diagram	a diagram with arrows showing how energy is transferred between energy stores
gravitational potential energy	the energy store of an object because of its height above the ground
kinetic energy	the energy stored in a moving object
law of conservation of energy	energy cannot be created or destroyed, only stored or transferred; this means that the total energy is the same before and after a change
Sankey diagram	an energy transfer diagram that shows what proportion of the input energy is transferred as useful or as wasted output
thermal energy	the energy store filled when an object is warmed up

14.1 Energy in fuels and food

You are learning to:
- recognise that energy is stored in fuels and as food
- classify energy resources as renewable or non-renewable
- measure energy changes in joules (J) and kilojoules (kJ)
- compare power ratings of appliances in watts (W) and kilowatts (kW).

1 Which row of the table correctly groups energy resources as renewable or non-renewable?

Response	Renewable	Non-renewable
a	solar, tidal, wind	coal, oil, gas
b	wind, oil, gas	coal, solar, tidal
c	coal, oil, gas	solar, wind, geothermal
d	coal, oil, tidal	gas, solar, wind

2 Which of these is the correct unit to measure energy?

a watts **b** joules **c** newtons **d** volts

3 Copy the table, but reorder the applications so each is matched to the correct fuel.

Fuel	Application
petrol	car
natural gas	lighting
wood	fireplace for heating
candle (paraffin wax)	cooking

4 The portable camping stove in the picture uses propane. When the propane is burned, the energy released is used to heat drinks or cook food.

a Where is the energy stored in this stove?

b Where is the energy transferred to when the stove is used?

c Suggest why this is a very practical way of cooking for people who are camping and hiking.

d Suggest why this is unlikely to be a way that people would cook in their home.

5 Two electric kettles are on display in a supermarket. Both have a capacity of 3 litres. Kettle **A** can boil this amount of water in 90 s, whereas kettle **B** takes 3 minutes.

a Compare the two kettles in terms of the rate at which they can transfer energy.

b Use your answer to suggest how the power ratings of the kettles compare.

6 What is the rate of energy transfer in joules per second (J/s) for a 10 W light bulb?

7 One light bulb is labelled 10 W and another is labelled 15 W. Explain the difference between these bulbs in terms of how quickly they transfer energy.

8 Which transfers energy at a greater rate, a 250 W television or a 2 kW electric kettle?

9 The table shows the energy content of three different fuels used to provide heating in homes.

Fuel	Energy (kJ/g)	Average cost (pence/MJ)
fuel oil	44	1.5
natural gas	37	1.4
wood	12	2.5

a The energy content is measured in kJ/g. Explain what this unit means.

b The table shows that the energy content of wood is relatively low. Suggest why some people still use wood to heat their homes.

c Which fuel releases the least energy per gram?

d Which would be the best fuel to keep costs down?

10 A solar panel on the roof of a family's campervan can provide a maximum power of 100 W. The table shows the power needed by each of the appliances the family has taken with them.

Appliance	Power needed to run (W)
mobile phone charger	5
laptop computer	50
TV	30
games console	45

a Calculate the power needed to run all the appliances at the same time.

b How many laptops can the family plug in at once, if no other devices are being used?

c Suggest **three** appliances that the family can run at the same time.

Worked example

A small packet of shortbread fingers has an energy content of 900 kJ and a mass of 40 g. Calculate the energy content of the shortbread per 100 g.

When doing a calculation, it is important to show your working. When a calculation has more than one step this can help avoid careless mistakes, such as dividing when a multiplication is required.

energy content per 100 g = energy in 1 g × 100 = (energy in 40 g ÷ 40) × 100

energy content of shortbread per 100 g = (900 kJ ÷ 40) × 100 = 2250 kJ

11 This food label shows the different nutrients in a food. Calculate how much energy (in kJ) there is in 100 g of the food.

Each serving (150g) contains

Energy	Fat	Saturates	Sugars	Salt
1046kJ 250kcal	3.0g LOW	1.3g LOW	34g HIGH	0.9g MED
13%	4%	7%	38%	15%

12 A student is researching foods that will supply her with energy to sustain her when running a marathon. She finds out that running a marathon will require an additional 12 000 kJ. The energy contents of three foods that she researches are shown in the table.

Food	Energy content per serving (kJ)	Mass of serving (g)
chocolate	1000	50
raisins	315	25
bananas	350	100

a Rank these foods in terms of the energy content per 100 g, from most to least.

b For the food with the greatest energy per 100 g, calculate how much Freya would need to eat to replace the additional energy transferred by running the marathon.

13 A student is doing some circuit training and his coach says that an exercise will use 1890 kJ. If a 25 g packet of raisins contains 315 kJ, how many packets will the student need to eat to replace this energy?

14.2 Heating and cooling

You are learning to:

- compare the transfer of energy by thermal conduction and by radiation
- apply ideas about radiation, conduction and insulation to reduce unwanted energy transfers.

1 How is energy being transferred to this boy from the fire?

2 Put the following objects in order of temperature, with the hottest first.

A – typical temperature for bath or shower

B – boiling water

C – body temperature of a healthy person

D – mixture of ice and water

E – typical temperature of a warm room

3 Describe, using examples of each, the difference between a thermal conductor and a thermal insulator.

Worked example

Two beakers are placed on the table in a room that is at 18 °C. Beaker A is filled with water at 40 °C and beaker B with water at 5 °C. Explain what will happen to the temperature of the water in both beakers over the next few minutes.

Beaker A is warmer than the surroundings so energy will be transferred out of it, causing its temperature to fall. This will continue until its temperature is the same as the temperature of the room. Beaker B is at a lower temperature than the surroundings so energy will be transferred into it until it reaches room temperature.

4 A blacksmith heats a piece of metal then plunges it into a bucket of water at room temperature.

a State the effect this will have on the temperature of the hot metal.

b State the effect this will have on the temperature of the water.

c At the end of the day, the water in the bucket is at the same temperature as it was at the start of the day. Suggest why this is.

5 A person buys a wrapped parcel of fish and chips and an open bag of chips from a takeaway on a cold evening. By the time they get home, the chips in the open bag are cold but the fish and chips wrapped in the parcel are still hot. Explain this difference in temperature using ideas about energy and insulation.

6 A group of students has carried out an experiment to compare different types of insulating material. The group is provided with a small hot water bottle, which they fill with hot water and try to keep hot for as long as possible by covering it in an insulating material. The temperature of the bottle was measured and recorded at the start and again after 20 minutes. The table shows their results.

Material	Starting temperature of bottle (°C)	Final temperature of bottle (°C)
expanded polystyrene beads	55	39
crumpled paper towels	46	32
cloth	51	36
wood shavings	61	43

a Calculate by how much the temperature fell in each case.

b Place the materials in order of the size of the temperature change, from largest to smallest.

c Suggest why it is not necessarily the case that the material that gives the largest temperature change is the worst insulator.

7 Describe how energy is transferred when a metal rod is heated at one end.

8 Twenty minutes after being made from boiling water, a cup of tea is lukewarm.

a Explain why the temperature has changed.

b A student says 'If you leave that tea for another 20 minutes it will have frozen over!' Explain why this is unlikely to be true.

9 The manager of a takeaway shop is thinking of changing the containers in which hot food is served. She is going to compare containers made of polystyrene, cardboard, aluminium and plastic to see which is most effective at keeping food hot.

a Suggest any other equipment the store manager might need.

b Describe a procedure she could use to make a fair comparison between the different containers.

c Suggest other reasons for selecting a particular container, apart from its insulating properties.

10 A mug of hot chocolate is at a temperature of 80 °C.

a Describe **two** different ways in which energy is transferred out of the drink.

b Suggest how the rate of energy transfer could be reduced.

11 Explain how a vacuum flask can keep a drink cold on a hot day. Refer to the diagram in your answer.

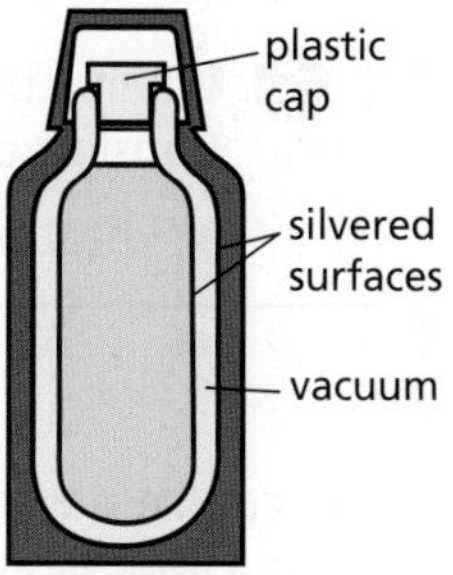

12 A double-glazed window has a layer of air trapped between two panes of glass. Explain why this reduces the amount of energy transferred through the window from the inside to the outside, compared to a single-glazed window.

14.3 Processes involving energy transfer

You are learning to:

- identify the start and end stores when energy is transferred
- identify processes that transfer energy between stores
- calculate the cost of using electrical appliances.

1 Match each of these systems with the store of energy it holds.

System	Store
hot water bottle full of hot water	gravitational potential
charged battery	thermal
lift at top of lift shaft	chemical potential

2 Match each of these systems to the transfer of energy stored in that system.

System	Transfer of energy
petrol in fuel tank as car travels along road	from thermal store to (different) thermal store
apple falling from tree towards ground	from chemical potential store to kinetic store
hot cup of tea standing on table	from gravitational potential store to kinetic store

3 Write the word or phrase that will correctly complete each of these sentences.

a As a mobile phone is charged up, its store of ________ energy is increased.

b As a lift rises to a higher floor in a building, its store of ________ energy is increased.

c As hot soup cools down, its store of ________ energy is decreased.

d As a worker on a building site shovels sand, their store of ________ energy is decreased.

4 Describe the energy transfers between stores when:

a a saucepan of water is heated on a gas flame

b a person dives off a diving board

c a toy airplane is launched by a stretched elastic band.

5 When a battery is recharged its store of chemical energy increases. Select the process that transfers energy to this store.

a heating **b** applying a force **c** using an electric current

Worked example

This candle is warming a water–oil mixture so that the scent diffuses more quickly into the room. Draw an energy transfer diagram to show how energy is being transferred between stores.

You draw the transfers between stores as arrows. Energy has been transferred from the store of chemical potential energy in the candle (the chemical store) to stores of thermal energy (thermal stores) in the water–oil mixture, and in the dish and the air that surrounds it. As there are transfers to two thermal stores, you draw two arrows.

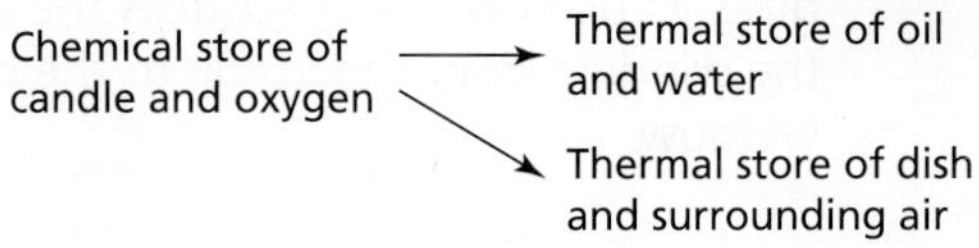

6 A girl is about to go down a slide.

Draw energy transfer diagrams to show how energy is being transferred between stores:

a as she starts to slide down

b as she gets to the end of the slide.

7 The immersion heater in a hot water tank has a power rating of 3 kW. If electricity costs 12 p per unit, calculate the cost of heating the water for 1.5 hours.

Use the equation: cost = power (kW) × time (hours) × price (per kW h)

8 **a** When a kettle boils, how is energy transferred to the surroundings?

b When a hairdryer is switched on, how is energy transferred:

i to its motor? **ii** to its heater?

9 Look at the toy in the photograph. Pulling this toy down stretches the spring. When the spring is released, the toy moves up and down several times and eventually comes to rest.

a Draw an energy transfer diagram for the process of stretching the spring.

b Draw an energy transfer diagram for when the toy starts moving.

c Explain where the energy has gone when the toy comes to a rest.

10 A child is on a swing.

Identify at which points on her journey she will:

a be at the greatest height

b be travelling at the highest speed

c have the most gravitational potential energy

d have the most kinetic energy.

11 A pendulum, shown in the diagram, is set swinging to and fro.

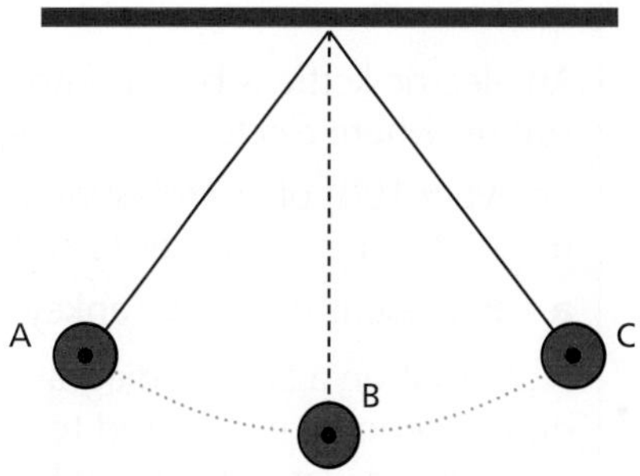

a Describe how the speed of the mass on the end of the string varies during one oscillation (the journey to and fro).

b Describe how energy is transferred between the gravitational potential and kinetic stores during an oscillation.

12 Calculate the cost of running a 50 W laptop for 2 hours if electricity costs 12 p per kW h.

13 Calculate the cost of using a 1.2 kW toaster for 3 minutes if electricity costs 12 p per kW h.

14 Darren wants to work out whether it is cheaper to heat a meal using a microwave oven or an electric oven. Heating the meal in a 1 kW microwave oven takes 6 minutes whereas in a 2 kW electric oven it would take 30 minutes. Electricity costs 12 p per kW h.

a Calculate the cost of cooking the meal in:

i the microwave oven **ii** the electric oven.

b Calculate the difference in the cost of electricity.

14.4 Conservation of energy

You are learning to:
- use Sankey diagrams to represent energy transfers, including useful and wasteful outputs
- apply the law of conservation of energy.

1 State the unit that kinetic energy is measured in.

2 A worker left his torch turned on and the battery is flat. Select the statement that is true.
- **a** The chemical potential store in the battery has increased.
- **b** There is now less energy overall.
- **c** The energy that was stored in the battery has all gone and no longer exists.
- **d** All the energy that was stored in the battery has been transferred to the surroundings.

3 Complete these sentences to explain what happens to energy when a lamp lights a room.

Energy is being transferred from one [**room** / **store**] to another.
[**All** / **Some**] of the energy exists afterwards.
You [**can** / **cannot**] end up with more energy than you had at the start.
This is the law of [**conservation** / **wasting**] of energy.

4 Which of these statements best explains what is meant by the law of conservation of energy?
- **a** People should use energy responsibly and not waste it.
- **b** Energy cannot be made or destroyed but only transferred from one store to another.
- **c** You can create new energy to replace lost energy, such as by recharging a battery.
- **d** Energy disappears unless you prevent all ways of wasting energy.

Worked example

An electric kettle is being used to heat water. The electricity supply is from a hydroelectric power station where electricity is generated by forcing falling water through turbines.

Of every 100 J of energy supplied, 80 J is transferred to the thermal store in the water and 20 J to the thermal stores of the kettle and the surroundings.

a Represent this on a Sankey diagram, showing the useful and wasted outputs.

Note that on a Sankey diagram the useful output (energy transferred to the thermal store of the water) is shown horizontally and the wasted output (energy transferred to the thermal stores of the kettle and the surroundings) is shown pointing downwards. To draw an accurate Sankey diagram on graph paper you need to make the width of each arrow proportional to how much energy is transferred.

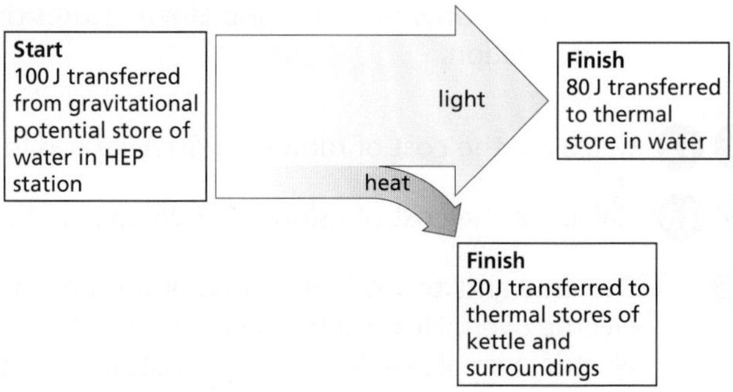

b Explain how your diagram shows that energy is conserved.

The diagram shows that energy is conserved because the two outputs add up to the input:

$80\,J + 20\,J = 100\,J$

5 An electric cement mixer is being used on a building site. Every second, the mains supply provides 1000 J and 650 J is transferred to the kinetic store of the cement mixer's motor. The remaining energy is transferred to the thermal store of the surrounding air.

a Identify which of the outputs are useful and which are wasted.

b Assuming that the electricity is generated from a gas power station, represent the energy transfers as a Sankey diagram.

c Explain how your diagram shows that energy has been conserved.

6 When the fan shown in the picture is used, only half of the energy from the battery goes into making the air move. The remaining energy is wasted, increasing the thermal store of the surroundings.

a Draw a Sankey diagram showing what happens to each 100 J of energy transferred from the battery.

b Explain how your diagram shows that energy is conserved.

7 The photograph shows a cliff railway used to transport people between two different levels. The two carriages are attached to each other by a long cable that goes around a pulley. As one carriage goes down, it pulls up the other carriage on the parallel track. Except for a brief initial acceleration, the two carriages move at a steady speed.

a Which carriage increases its store of gravitational potential energy?

b Which carriage decreases its store of gravitational potential energy?

c This railway uses a motor to supply additional energy to pull up the bottom carriage. If there was no friction in the railway, explain why no motor would be needed to lift a carriage of the same weight to the same level as the carriage that started at the top.

8 The diagram shows a roller coaster ride. At the start, the train is pulled up to the highest point on the track by an electric motor. From this point an unbalanced force acts on the train due to its weight. The train travels down the remainder of the track and brakes to a halt at the start point.

a At what point in the journey will the train's store of gravitational potential energy be at a maximum?

b Describe how energy is transferred between stores during the climb of the train to the highest point.

c By the end of the journey, the train is back at ground level and is stationary. Explain how energy has been conserved during the journey.

Maths and practical skills

1 Which **two** of these are units of energy?

a watts **b** joules **c** kilowatts **d** kilowatt-hours

2 One kilojoule (1 kJ) is a unit of energy. Select which of these is equivalent to 1 kJ.

a 0.001 J **b** 1 J **c** 1000 J **d** 1 000 000 J

3 Gavin is investigating how a rubber ball bounces. He tries dropping it from different heights and seeing how far back up it bounces. The table shows his results.

Height ball is dropped from (cm)	20	40	60	80	100
Height ball bounces back up to (cm)	12	24	36	48	60

a Describe what the results show about the height the ball bounces back to when dropped from a greater height.

b Describe what the results show about the height the ball bounces back to compared with its starting point.

c Suggest why the readings for the starting point will be more accurate than the readings for the height the ball bounced back to.

4 The equipment in the diagram is used to measure the amount of energy transferred by burning a peanut. The peanut is stuck on a needle, ignited and used to heat the water in the boiling tube.

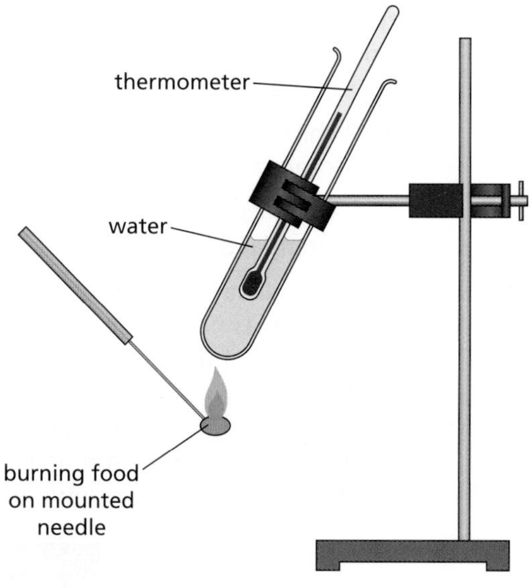

a What will happen to the thermometer reading during the experiment?

b What is the store of energy at the start of this experiment?

c Where is this energy transferred to during the experiment?

d Suggest two other foods that could be tested in this way.

e Suggest two foods that you couldn't test in this way.

f If a number of different foods were tested in this way, how would the data suggest which foods store the most energy?

g Suggest what you could do to make the experiment a fair comparison of different foods.

h The results from the investigation were much lower than the actual amount of energy stored in a peanut of this size. Suggest two possible reasons for this.

5 Energy is transferred into an electric food mixer at the rate of 2000 J/s. Calculate the power rating of the appliance in kW.

6 The graphs below both display data about the energy content of different fuels in kJ/g.

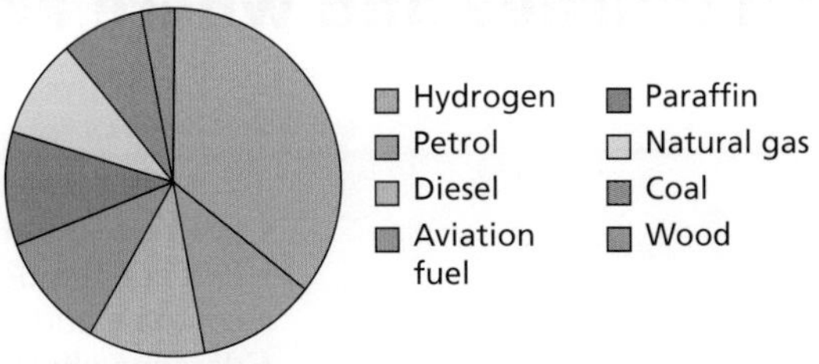

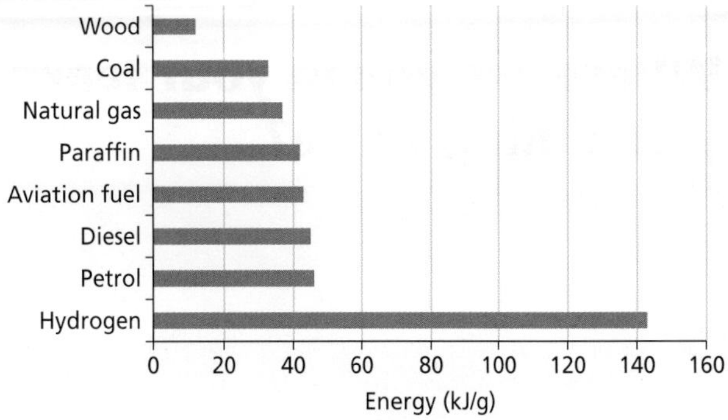

a Explain what is meant by the unit kJ/g.

b Use the data to estimate how many times greater the energy content of hydrogen is compared to petrol.

c These graphs show the same information but in different ways. Suggest which one is more useful and why.

7 A group of students is investigating the energy content of different fuels. They place a thermometer in a boiling tube that contains a measured amount of water and clamp the tube in a stand. Beneath the boiling tube they place a metal dish, into which 1 g of each fuel being tested can be placed in turn and ignited.

a Draw and label a diagram to show how the equipment should be set up.

b Describe how the students could collect data that would enable them to compare the energy content of the different fuels.

c Suggest **two** possible sources of error in this experiment.

d Suggest **three** types of fuel that could be tested using this equipment.

8 The figure shows the energy bill for a home. Home energy is measured in kilowatt-hours (kW h) rather than joules.

a How does the supply company know how many kilowatt-hours of energy from gas and electricity the customer has used?

b How much energy from electricity has been used?

c How much does 1 kW h of energy from electricity cost?

d How much energy from gas has been used?

e If gas is a cheaper supply of energy, why do you think this customer is obtaining more of their energy from electricity instead of gas?

Meter readings (E = estimate, C = customer, A = actual)

Electricity readings

Period	Meter no.	Previous	Present	Rate	kilowatt-hours
4 Sept 14 to 12 Nov 14	S08B 06654	12549 E	12757 C	Normal	208

Gas readings

Period	Meter no.	Previous	Present	Units	kilowatt-hours
30 Aug 14 to 12 Nov 14	674215	02938 A	02954 C	16 m^3	converts to 178

Charges

Electricity charges

4 Sept 14 to 12 Nov 14		£43.69
208 kilowatt-hours (kWh) used at 12.66p each	£26.33	
Standing charge – 69 days at 25.16p per day	£17.36	

Gas charges

30 Aug 14 to 12 Nov 14		£26.33
Gas 178 kilowatt-hours (kWh) used at 3.981p each	£7.09	
Standing charge – 69 days at 27.89p per day	£19.24	

Total charges

Total electricity and gas charges (excluding VAT)	£70.02

f There is a standing charge that has to be paid for each energy source. This is a fixed amount and is in addition to the charge for the amount of energy used. Is it true that if the customer had used twice the amount of electricity and twice the amount of gas in that period, their bill would be twice as high? Explain your answer.

15 Waves road map

Where are you in your learning journey and where are you aiming to be?

- sounds are made by something vibrating; the vibrations travel through a medium (such as air) to the ear
- the pitch and the volume of a sound relate to the vibrations that produced it
- we see objects because they give out or reflect light into the eye
- shadows are formed when the light is blocked by a solid object

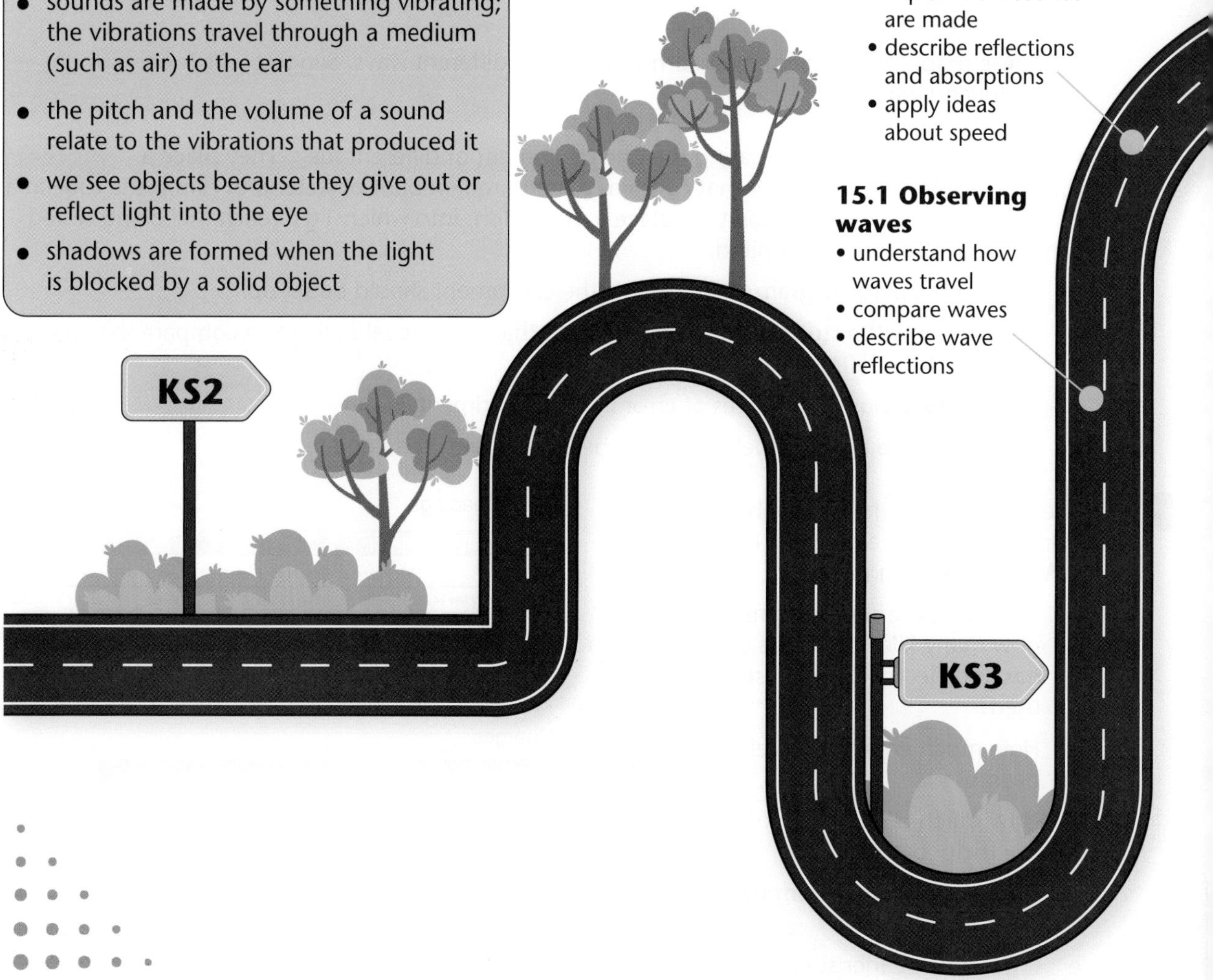

15.1 Observing waves
- understand how waves travel
- compare waves
- describe wave reflections

15.2 Making sound waves
- explain how sounds are made
- describe reflections and absorptions
- apply ideas about speed

15.3 Hearing and soun
- describe sound detection
- describe frequency
- compare audible ranges
- describe ultrasound

15.4 Energy and waves
- describe ultrasound
- give examples of waves transferring energy
- describe energy transfer

15.5 How light travels
- identify similarities and differences
- recognise light travelling through a vacuum
- use diagrams
- describe examples

15.6 Vision and images
- recognise light refraction
- use ray diagrams

15.7 Exploring coloured light
- describe lights of different colours
- describe spectrums
- explain white light on different objects

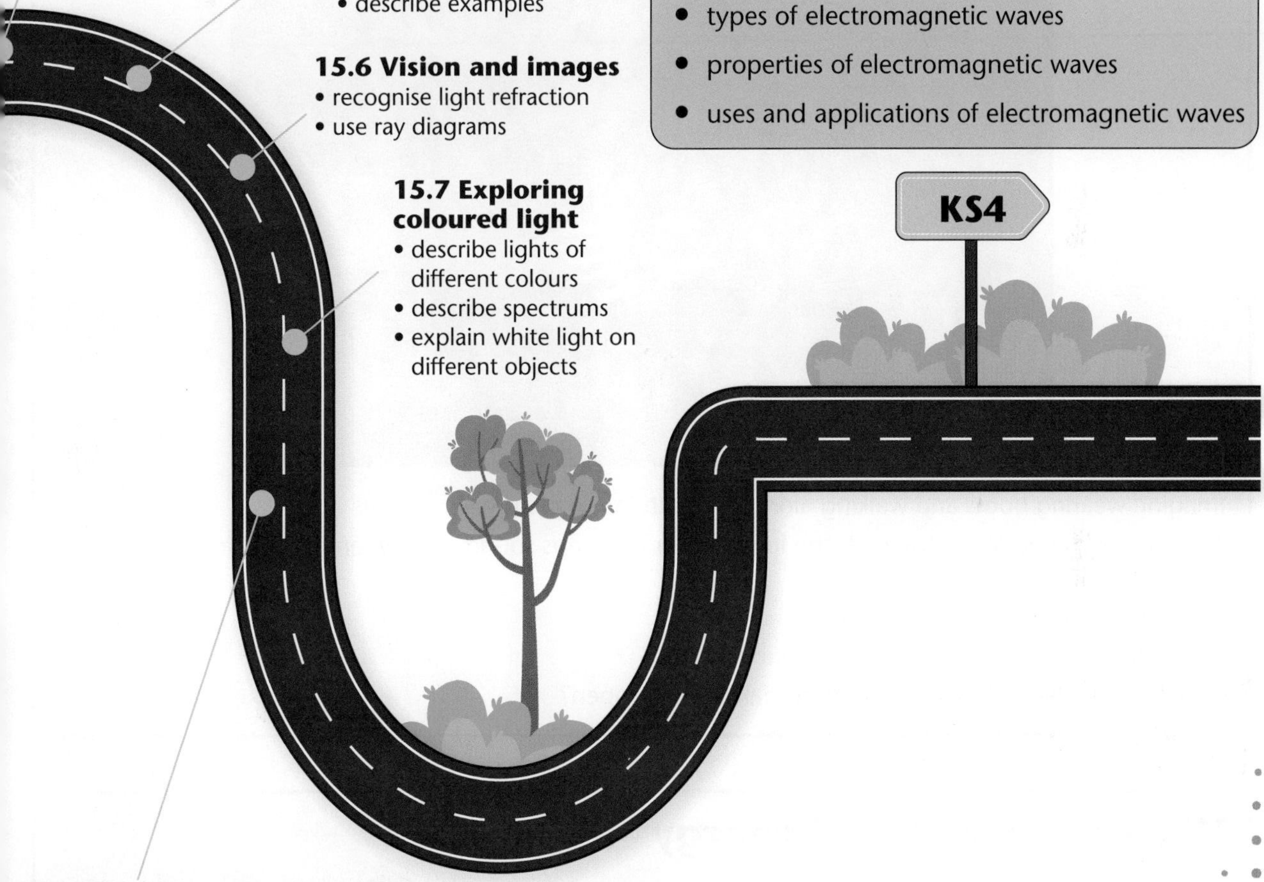

- transverse and longitudinal waves
- properties of waves
- types of electromagnetic waves
- properties of electromagnetic waves
- uses and applications of electromagnetic waves

Maths and practical skills
- carrying out scientific enquiries to test predictions
- planning an investigation, identifying and managing the variables
- suggesting improvements to practical work
- interpreting observations and data
- evaluating data, including being aware of possible errors

15 Waves

Waves cannot always be seen but they are extremely useful, carrying energy in many different ways. Microwave ovens, TV remote controls, mobile phones and being able to see are all only possible because of waves. Waves also carry sound and make many types of communication possible.

Waves as carriers of energy – sound waves

Imagine wearing boots and walking along the path in the picture.

The further you go along the path the louder your footsteps sound, and when you get into the tunnel it sounds really loud.

- Try to explain why this happens.
- Suggest what this tells you about sound.
- What is it about these surfaces that makes this happen?

Waves as carriers of energy – light waves

Look at these pictures of bright objects. Compare how light travels from these objects into your eyes.

Using your science skills

Could you be a sound engineer?

As a studio **sound engineer**, your job is to plan recording sessions with musicians. You have to set the equipment up so you can record each instrument separately. You then edit the recorded tracks. When the tracks are mixed the level of each input has to be adjusted so nothing gets lost. You sometimes modify sounds as well, such as adding some echo to an instrument.

Working in a recording studio is great but you also may work on live events. Those are great fun but very hard work; you have to try and ensure that every member of the audience can hear the show. Speakers have to be correctly positioned – you have to know how sound will be absorbed or reflected as this will change the effect. Some sounds may be pre-recorded, which needs organising. You also have to manage which sounds performers will hear through a stage monitor system. They have to be able to hear the other instruments – and themselves as well.

Lighting engineers work in theatres, concert halls, shops and factories to make sure that buildings and activities are well lit. You have to understand how light is reflected and absorbed but also know how to get particular effects by using different types of lights and coloured filters. Sometimes the light needs to be even across a space, but on other occasions it might be useful to use colour or shadow to achieve particular effects, such as highlighting an area.

Sound pollution can be dangerous as well as being unpleasant. **Health and safety officers** monitor sound levels in businesses to see if sound levels are dangerously high and whether regulations are being broken. Airports, busy roads and factories all need to be checked and made to comply. As well as recording data and drawing conclusions, they help businesses assess risks and manage the workplace so that employees are protected.

Photographers use cameras and lighting equipment to take pictures that tell stories. To take a great photograph, they have to understand how to capture light and create particular effects. In a studio they might use lights and reflectors to soften light for a portrait or they might want bright lights and shadows to create drama.

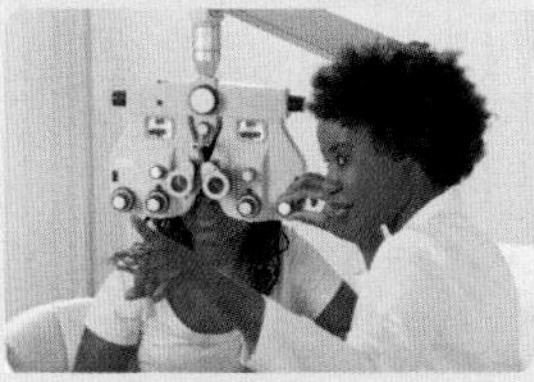

One of the most common uses of lenses is in spectacles and contact lenses. **Optometrists** help people to improve their eyesight by finding out what type of lens will work best for them.

Knowledge organiser

Waves can travel through water; the water rises and falls but the wave moves on. This is a **transverse wave**.

Water waves can be **reflected**.

If two sets of waves meet they can add to each other or cancel each other out.

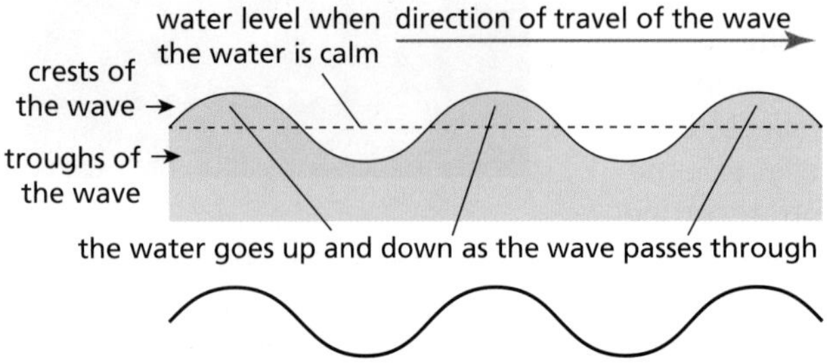

Sound waves are **longitudinal waves**. The wave travels in a direction parallel to the **vibrations** of the material that the wave is travelling through. Sound waves can vary in **frequency**, which is measured in **hertz** (Hz). Sound waves can be reflected (an **echo**) or **absorbed**.

Waves carry energy from one place to another. The energy transferred by **ultrasound** waves can be used to clean objects and for physiotherapy.

Sound waves need a medium to travel through so it cannot travel through a **vacuum**. Sound travels faster in solids than in liquids, and it travels slowest in gases.

The range of frequencies that humans or animals can hear is known as the **auditory range**. This range is different for different animals.

Sound is produced by objects vibrating, such as the flexible cone in a **loudspeaker**. Sound is detected as the effect on, for example, eardrums and **microphones**, of vibrations sent through the air. The energy transferred by sound waves is converted by a microphone to an electrical signal carrying information about the sound.

Key vocabulary

amplitude	the maximum displacement of a point on a wave from its undisturbed position
auditory range	the range of sound frequencies from the lowest to the highest that an animal or human can hear
echo	the reflection of a sound wave from a surface
frequency	number of waves that pass a point, or are emitted, in one second; unit hertz (Hz)
hertz (Hz)	unit of frequency; equal to one wave per second
longitudinal wave	a wave in which the vibrations are parallel to the direction of energy transfer
loudspeaker	apparatus that converts electrical impulses into sound waves
microphone	a device for changing effect of vibrations from sound waves into electrical signals
oscilloscope	a device that allows sound waves that have been turned into electrical signals to be viewed as waveforms
pitch	how high or low the frequency of a sound is
reflection	when a wave, such as a sound or light wave, bounces off a surface
superposition	when two waves meet each other at the same point
transverse wave	wave in which oscillations are at right angles to direction of energy transfer
ultrasound	sound with a frequency higher than 20000 Hz
wavelength	distance along a wave from one point to the next corresponding point where the wave motion begins to repeat itself – for example crest to crest
vacuum	a space where there are no particles of matter

Light can travel through some materials but it may also be absorbed, **scattered** or reflected.

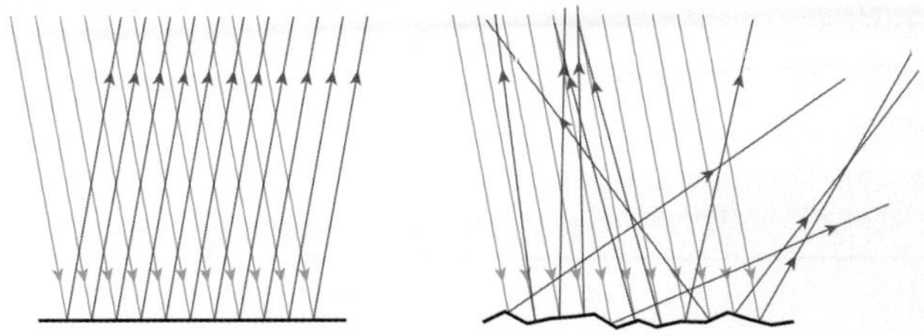

Each colour of light has its own range of frequencies. White light is a mixture of different colours, which can be separated by a **triangular prism**.

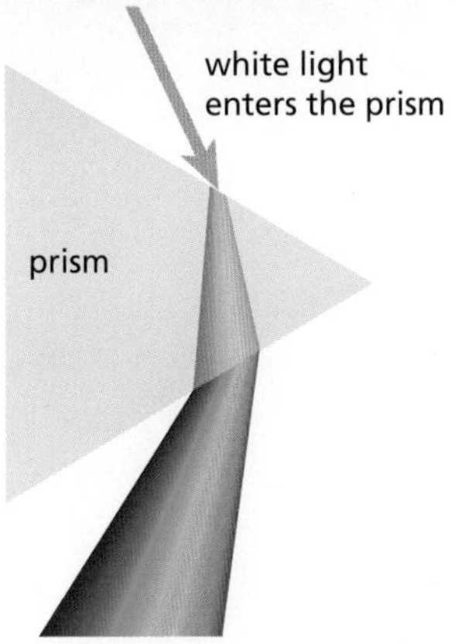

Objects look coloured because they reflect or absorb the different colours in white light.

The absorption of light as energy is how light is detected by a camera or by the light-sensitive cells on the **retina** of the eye.

Some electrical devices can detect light by producing an electrical current when energy from light is absorbed.

The speed of light is much higher than the speed of sound.

A key difference between light waves and sound waves is that light does not need a medium to travel through. Light waves can travel through a vacuum.

Ray diagrams show how light is reflected by a mirror, and how a pinhole camera forms an image.

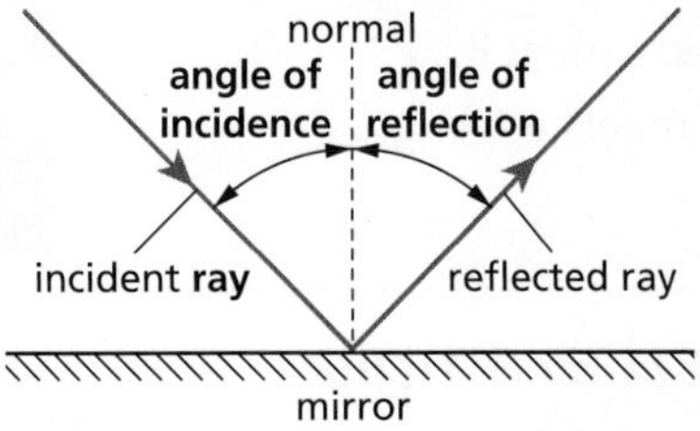

Light can be **refracted** through lenses and prisms. Ray diagrams show how light is refracted, including in the eye.

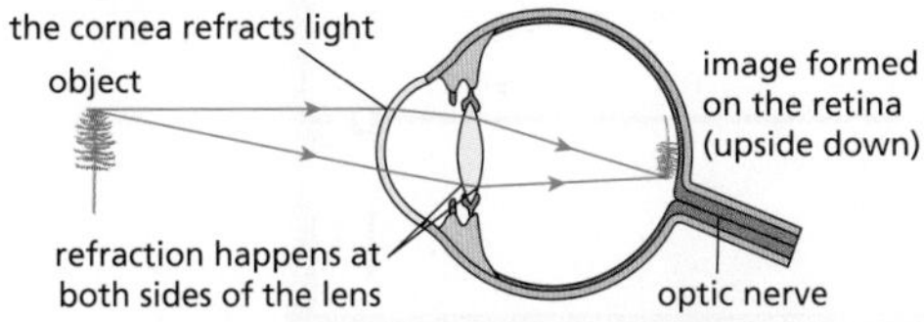

Key vocabulary

angle of incidence	the angle between the normal and the incident ray
angle of reflection	the angle between the normal and the reflected ray
convex lens	a lens that is thicker in the middle and bends light rays towards each other
concave lens	a lens that is thinner in the middle and spreads out light rays
image	the picture of an object that we see in a mirror or through a lens or system of lenses
lens	a specially shaped piece of transparent material that refracts light passing through it to form an image
normal	a line at right angles to a surface, from which angles of reflection or refraction are measured
opaque	material that allows no light to pass through
prism (triangular)	a three-dimensional shape with five flat faces, two of which are triangles and the other three of which are rectangles
ray	a line with an arrow to show how a light wave travels as it is reflected off a mirror or passes through a transparent material
refraction	a change in the direction of a wave such as light when it hits a boundary between two different media at an angle, for example, when a light ray passes from air into a glass block
retina	a layer at the back of the eye with light-detecting cells, where an image is formed
scattering	when light from a particular direction reflects from a rough surface in all directions
spectrum	a continuous range of values of frequencies or wavelengths, for example in the visible spectrum of light
translucent	a material that lets some but not all light pass through
transparent	a material that allows light to pass through

15.1 Observing waves

You are learning to:
- understand how waves travel on the surface of water
- compare transverse and longitudinal waves
- describe how waves are reflected.

1 Copy the diagram of a wave on water and mark on it:

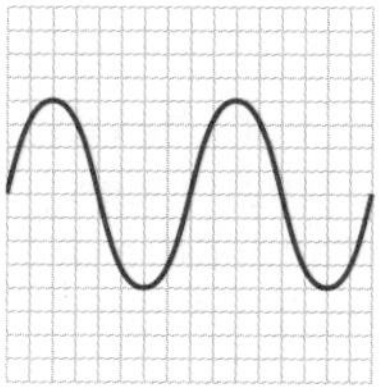

a the crests

b the troughs

c a straight line to show the undisturbed position of the water.

2 Look at the four diagrams of waves.

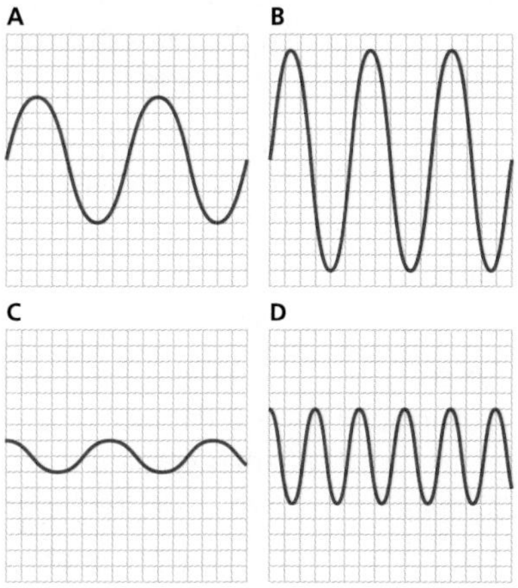

If the size of each square in the grid is 1 cm:

a measure the amplitude of each wave

b put the four waves in order, from greatest amplitude to least.

3 Two waves are travelling across the surface of water, starting from different places.

Describe what will happen where the waves meet if:

a a crest meets a crest **b** a crest meets a trough.

Worked example

A teacher ties one end of a length of rope to a door handle. They make a single wave travel along the rope by raising and lowering the free end.

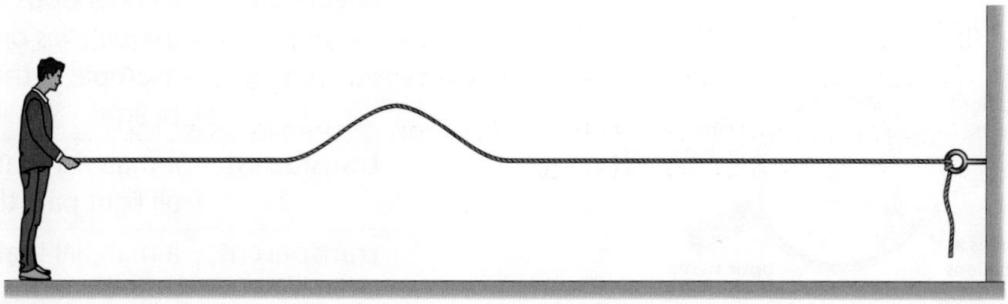

a Sketch the shape of the rope and mark an arrow on it to show:

i the direction that one part of the rope moves in as the wave travels along the rope

ii the direction in which the wave travels.

Imagine a ribbon tied to one part of the rope. Mark this spot with a dot. It will move only up and down without moving along the rope. The wave travels at right angles to this.

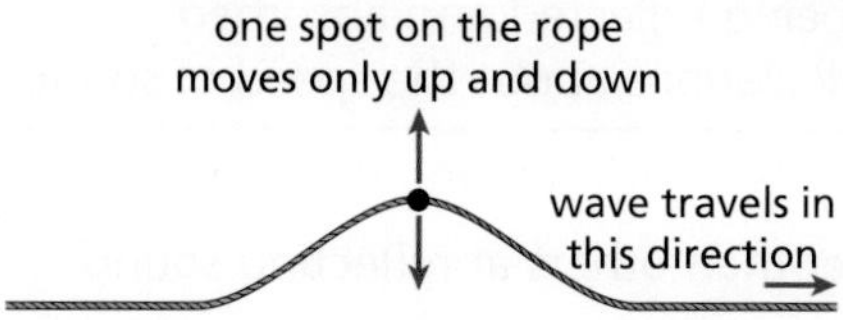

b State what type of wave this is.

Transverse wave

4 These diagrams show two different ways, **X** and **Y**, of making waves using a 'slinky' spring.

X

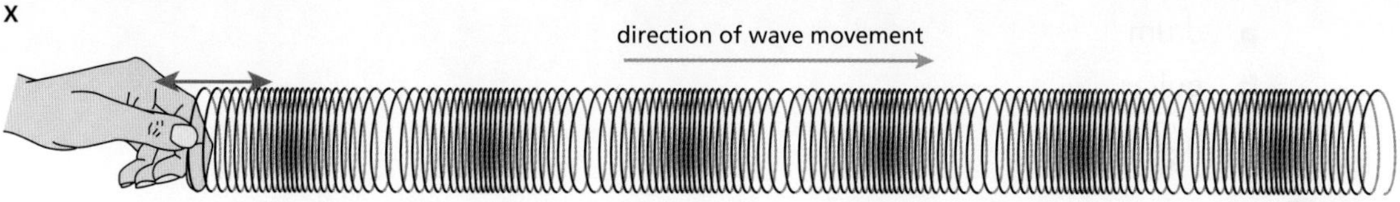

Y

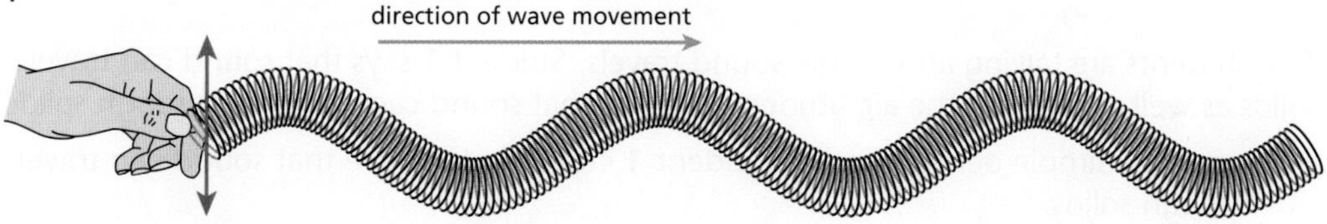

a Which diagram shows a transverse wave and which shows a longitudinal wave.

b Compare these two waves in terms of the direction in which energy is transferred to the wave.

5 A teacher is showing a class how water waves are reflected by a solid barrier. He sends a series of straight waves towards a barrier. This diagram shows the barrier and the first few waves.

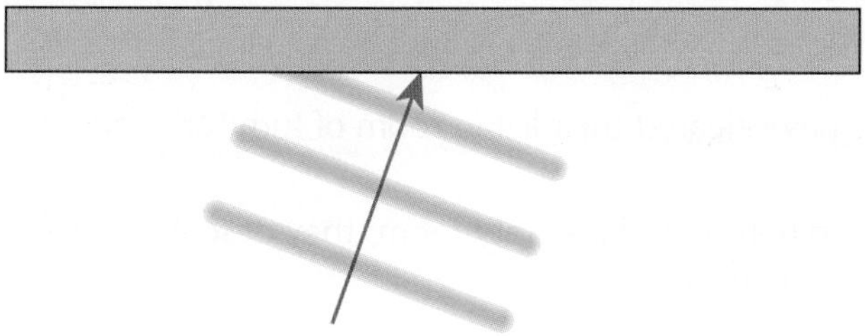

a Copy and complete the diagram to show more waves as they reach the barrier and are reflected.

b The diagram includes an arrow showing the direction of the waves. Complete this arrow on your diagram to show the direction of the waves as they are reflected.

c Describe the relationship between the direction of the waves as they approach the barrier and their direction after they are reflected.

15.2 Making sound waves

You are learning to:

- explain how sounds are made and how sound waves travel through a medium
- describe examples of sounds being reflected and absorbed
- apply ideas about speed to calculations about the speed of sound.

1 Some surfaces are better than others at reflecting sound.

a Give **two** examples of surfaces that are good at reflecting sound.

b Give **two** examples of surfaces that are poor at reflecting sound.

2 Sounds are made by something vibrating. Suggest what is vibrating when each of the following makes a sound:

a drum

b guitar

c trumpet.

3 A teacher tells the class that 'sound needs a medium to travel through'. One student is not quite sure what this means. How could you explain this?

4 Two students are talking about how sound travels. Student **1** says that sound can travel through solids as well as through the air. Student **2** thinks that sound cannot travel through solids.

a Suggest a simple demonstration Student **1** could do to prove that sound can travel through solids.

b The students then write a description of how sound travels through a solid. Choose the correct word from each pair to complete the sentences.

Sound travels as a wave, by passing on **i** [**a vacuum**/**vibrations**] from one place to another. This means that sound waves **ii** [**need**/**do not need**] a medium to travel through.

Sound travels well through a solid because the particles in a solid are **iii** [**close together**/**far apart**]. This means the particles can **iv** [**absorb**/**transmit**] energy quickly and easily when they are pushed together.

5 A family is moving house and they have cleared their living room of furniture and curtains. The room is now completely bare.

They notice that their voices sound different in the empty room; they describe it as being 'echoey'. Explain why you think this might be so.

Worked example

If sound travels at 340 m/s in air, how far will a sound wave travel in 30 s?
Use the equation distance = speed × time

distance = speed × time = 340 m/s × 30 s = 10 200 m or 10.2 km

6 Sound travels in air at 340 m/s. Using the equation distance = speed × time, calculate the distance that sound will travel in:

a one second **b** 10 seconds **c** one minute

7 A student is listening to someone playing drums on a stage. She notices that the sound is quieter on the other side of the thick stage curtain. Suggest what has happened to the energy of the sound wave.

8 The 1979 film *Alien* was advertised using posters that included the statement 'In space no one can hear you scream'.

a State whether this is true. **b** Explain your answer.

9 Explain why sounds get quieter the further away you are from the source.

10 The table shows the speed of sound in various different materials.

Material	Speed of sound (m/s)
air (at room temp)	343
aluminium	5100
diamond	1200
steel	5060
water (at room temp)	1430

a Identify the material in which sound travels the fastest.

b Identify the material in which sound travels the slowest.

c Using the examples given in the table, compare how fast sound travels through solids and gases.

d Suggest an explanation for your answer to **c**.

11 The starting pistol is fired for a 100 m race. If sound travels at 340 m/s and a spectator is sat 170 m from the starter, calculate the time interval between the pistol being fired and the spectator hearing it.

Worked example

Students are investigating echoes and how fast sound travels in air. They are standing on the school playing fields, opposite the end of the school hall. There are no other buildings around. One student bangs two cymbals together. Shortly afterwards they hear an echo.

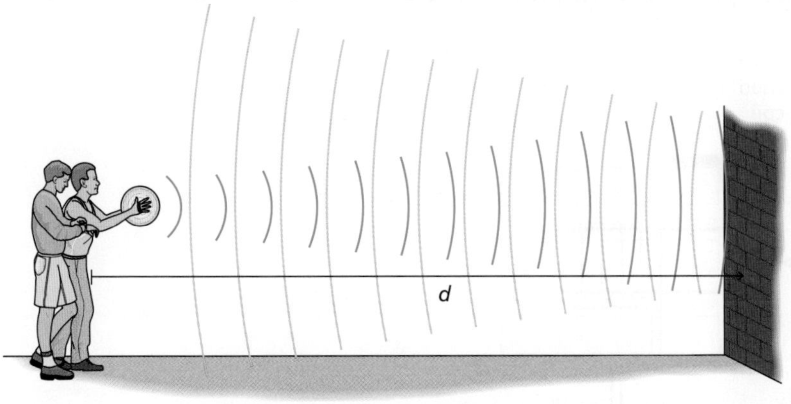

If sound travels at 340 m/s and they hear the echo 1.5 s after the student bangs the cymbals together, how far away are the students from the hall?

distance = speed × time = 340 m/s × 1.5 s = 510 m

The sound has travelled from the students to the wall and back again, so 510 m is the distance there and back. The distance to the hall is half of that, or 255 m.

12 Sonar is a system used on boats to detect objects in the water below by transmitting a pulse of sound waves into the water and measuring the time between when the pulse was sent and when a reflection is recorded.

A boat records a sonar echo from the seabed 0.4 s after sending the signal. How deep is the water? The speed of sound in water = 1500 m/s.

15.3 Hearing and sound

You are learning to:
- describe how sounds are detected by microphones and ears
- describe what is meant by the frequency of a sound wave and state the units
- compare the auditory range of humans and different animals
- describe what ultrasound is.

1 Which of these is the unit used to measure frequency of a wave?

a hertz **b** metres **c** metres per second **d** seconds

2 Which of these is the best definition of ultrasound?

a very loud sound **b** very quiet sound

c very high frequency sound **d** very fast travelling sound

3 Which of these is a typical value for the highest frequency that a human can hear?

a 20 Hz **b** 200 Hz **c** 2000 Hz **d** 20 000 Hz (20 kHz)

4 A person has their hearing tested and is told that the highest frequency of sound that they can hear is 12 kHz. Which of the following statements best describes what this means?

a They cannot hear very loud notes. **b** They cannot hear very low notes.

c They cannot hear very high notes. **d** They can only hear very high notes.

5 The diagram shows the inside of a microphone. Describe how the diaphragm would move for a high pitch sound compared to a low pitch sound.

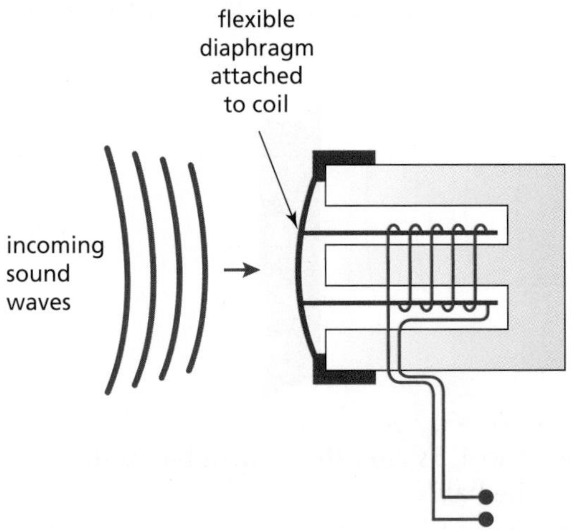

6 Write 28 kHz as a frequency in hertz (Hz).

7 A dog whistle emits a sound with a frequency of 28 kHz and is used to summon dogs. Explain why dogs can hear this whistle but humans can't.

8 A person standing in another part of the room is talking and you can hear what they are saying. Describe how:

a the sound is made **b** the sound travels to you **c** the sound is heard.

9 A musician is playing a guitar and singing.

a If they play a higher note on the guitar what does this mean about the frequency of vibration of the guitar string?

b She is using a sound system that consists of a microphone, an amplifier and a loudspeaker. Complete these sentences about the function of the microphone.

Sound waves are ___**i**___ waves. When sound waves enter the microphone, they make the diaphragm of the microphone ___**ii**___ . The higher the note she sings, the ___**iii**___ the diaphragm moves. The microphone converts the variations in the movement of the diaphragm into an ___**iv**___ signal for the amplifier. The amplifier amplifies this signal and makes the cone of the loudspeaker ___**v**___ .

10 If two different musical notes have different frequencies, describe the link between their frequencies and how they would sound.

11 The eardrum is part of the inner ear.

a Describe what happens to your eardrum when a sound reaches it.

b Explain why a hole in your eardrum would mean you would have difficulty hearing.

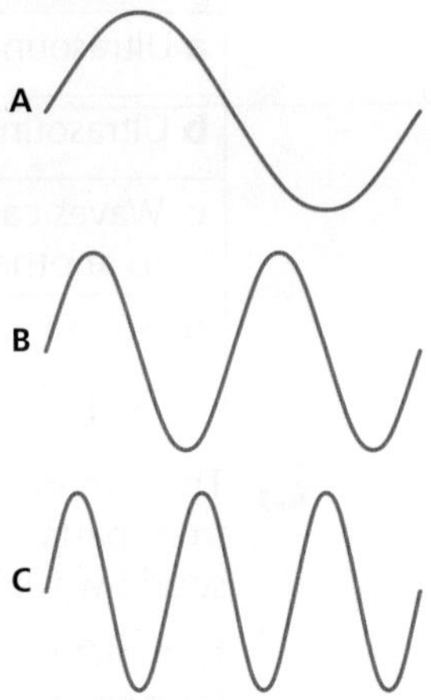

12 The diagram represents three different sound waves, **A**, **B** and **C**.

a State which of these sounds has the highest frequency.

b Suggest which of these sounds would sound the lowest.

13 If a person has an auditory range of 20 Hz to 20 kHz, which of these sounds could they hear?

a 10 Hz **b** 100 Hz **c** 1000 Hz **d** 10 000 Hz **e** 100 000 Hz

14 The table shows the audible range of ten different species of animal.

Species	Approximate hearing range (Hz)	Species	Approximate hearing range (Hz)
human	64–23 000	mouse	1000–91 000
dog	67–45 000	bat	2000–110 000
cat	45–64 000	elephant	16–12 000
cow	23–35 000	canary	250–8 000
rabbit	360–42 000	owl	200–12 000

a Which of these animals can detect the lowest frequency?

b Which of these animals can detect the highest frequency?

c Which of these animals has the greatest audible range?

d Which of these animals could hear a sound with a frequency of 80 kHz?

15 Bats use sound waves to find their way in the dark and to locate prey, such as moths. This is known as echolocation. The bat makes a high-pitched sound and listens for the reflected sound. The frequency of sound bats emit is typically in the range 20 kHz to 60 kHz.

a Why are these sounds not audible to humans?

b If a bat receives an echo 0.02 s after it transmits an ultrasound pulse, how far away is the moth? (Speed of sound in air = 330 m/s.)

c What else does the bat need to determine to be able to locate a moth?

d Cats typically have a hearing range of 45 000 Hz to 64 000 Hz. Suggest whether cats can hear the sounds the bats make.

15.4 Energy and waves

You are learning to:
- describe how ultrasound can be used for cleaning and physiotherapy
- give examples of how waves transfer energy from a source
- describe how energy transferred by sound waves is turned into an electrical signal.

1 Select which of the following statements are true.

Statement	True or false?
a Ultrasound is high frequency sound.	
b Ultrasound waves are transverse waves.	
c Waves can transfer energy from one location to another.	
d Sound waves carry particles of matter from one location to another.	

2 The picture shows an ultrasonic bath. It is used to remove dirt from parts of metal objects that are difficult to reach, using only sound waves transmitted though water.

Complete the sentences to explain how ultrasound is used for cleaning.

a All waves transfer ___**i**___ from a source. Ultrasound waves have a ___**ii**___ frequency. When ultrasound waves travel through water this makes the particles in the water ___**iii**___ at the same frequency as the ultrasound. The ultrasound waves transfer ___**iv**___ to the object, making it vibrate.

b Suggest why this is a good way of cleaning objects that have a complex shape, such as parts of machines or jewellery.

3 The diagram shows the inside of a microphone.

Select which **two** statements are true.

a The incoming sound waves make the diaphragm vibrate.

b The supply of electricity through the wires makes the diaphragm vibrate.

c The microphone converts information from sound waves to electrical signals.

d A microphone converts a smaller sound into a larger sound.

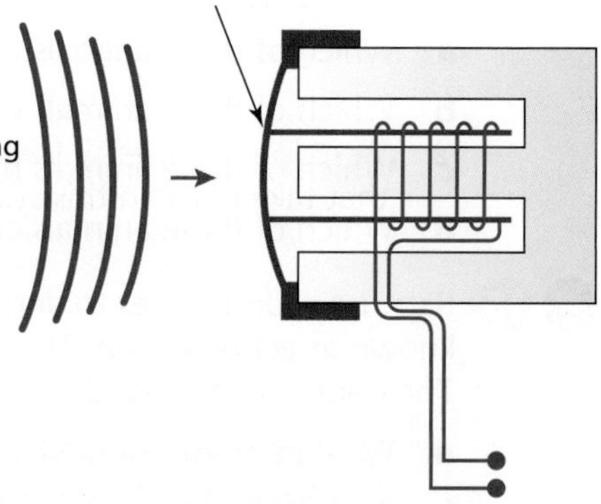

4 Ultrasound is sometimes used in physiotherapy to warm tissues in the body, such as muscles. The ultrasound device is held against the skin and produces high frequency sound waves. Use the idea of energy transfers to explain how the ultrasound warms muscles.

Worked example

The calculator in the picture has a small photovoltaic cell below the screen. Explain how the cell transfers energy to an electric current in the circuit.

Remember that 'explain' means you have to say what happens and also why it happens.

Light falling on the cell produces a current. This happens because energy is being transferred by waves from the sun (or another light source)

5 The house in the picture has been fitted with photovoltaic cells (also called solar or PV panels).

- **a** What is the light source for the current produced by these cells?
- **b** Suggest why the householder now has lower electricity bills.
- **c** Explain why it is useful for such systems to include a storage battery.

6 A group of students is investigating the output of photovoltaic cells. They are interested in finding out if the angle at which sunlight shines on a cell affects the transfer of energy from the sunlight to the production of electricity. They place a photovoltaic cell face up and flat on a bench, and connect it to a voltmeter. They are going to use a lamp clamped to a stand 50 cm from the cell. They begin their investigation with the light directly down onto the cell, and then gradually tilt the solar cell.

- **a** In this experiment, which is the dependent variable and which is the independent variable?
- **b** State the headings the students should use for their results table. Include the units.
- **c** Identify **two** variables which will be kept the same.
- **d** Explain why this investigation is relevant to an architect designing a new house.

7 The photo graph shows a solar water heater mounted on the roof of a house. The panels are made up of pipes filled with water. In sunlight the water gets hot and can be pumped indoors for uses such as washing clothes and dishes.

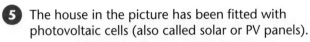

- **a** Describe the energy transfers that take place in this system.
- **b** Compare the energy transfers in this system with those in a photovoltaic cell system used to generate electricity.
- **c** Suggest why a south-facing roof is a good location for this system for a house in the UK.

15.5 How light travels

You are learning to:
- identify similarities and differences between light waves and other types of wave
- recognise that light can travel through a vacuum
- use diagrams to show what happens when light is reflected
- describe examples of how light can be scattered.

1 When a ray of light bounces off a mirror, what is the correct term for this?

a absorption **b** division **c** reflection **d** refraction

2 Why is it always important to include arrows on the light rays drawn in ray diagrams?

3 The picture shows a shadow being formed on a wall. The light source is low down and the person is between the light and the wall. The shadow is larger than the person.

State what has to be true about an object for it to form a shadow.

4 Give:

a **two** examples of transparent materials

b **two** examples of opaque materials.

5 Light travels as waves, and so does sound. Which **one** of these statements is **false**?

a Both light and sound waves can be reflected.

b Light and sound both travel as waves, but light travels much more quickly than sound.

c Light can travel through a vacuum but sound cannot.

d Light and sound are both examples of transverse waves.

6 The diagrams show light being reflected from two different surfaces.

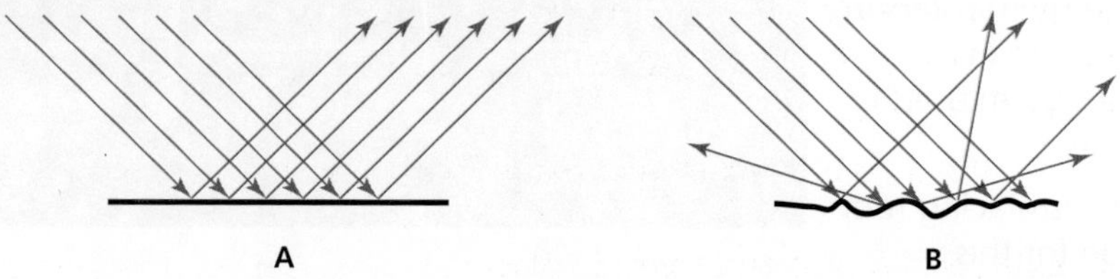

a Which diagram, **A** or **B**, shows how light is reflected by the surface of a mirror?

b Which diagram, **A** or **B**, shows scattering of light?

c Which diagram, **A** or **B**, explains why you can see your reflection in a shiny surface?

Worked example

A student wants to find out what happens if light is shone towards a mirror at different angles. Draw a diagram to show how the student should measure the angle of the ray approaching the mirror and the angle of the reflected ray.

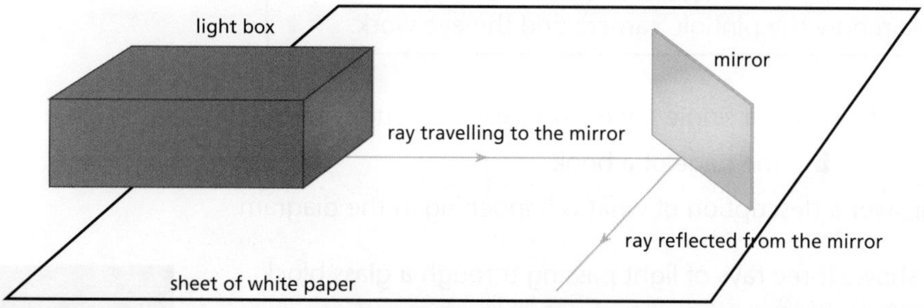

You should draw a dashed line at right angles to the surface of the mirror at the point where the incoming ray meets the mirror. This is called the normal. You should measure the angles of the rays from the normal.

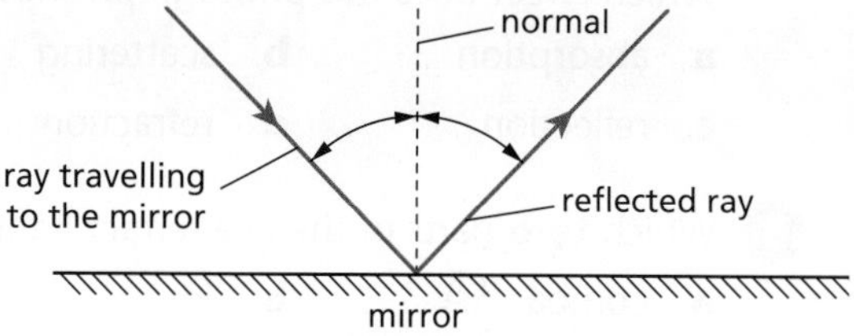

7 A group of students carried out an investigation into the reflection of light by a plane mirror. On a sheet of white paper, they set up a ray box with a slit to produce a single ray of light which they shone at the mirror. They used a pencil to draw a line along the mirror, a line along the incident ray of light and a line along the reflected ray of light. They measured the angle at which the ray approached the mirror and the angle at which it was reflected.

Angle of incidence (°)	Angle of reflection (°)
10	10
20	18
30	30
40	43
50	50

Their results are shown in the table.

a Draw a labelled diagram to show how they should measure the angles of incidence and reflection.

b The angles of reflection are not always the same as the angle of incidence. Assuming the students did not make a mistake, suggest **two** possible reasons for this.

c Describe the pattern in the results.

8 Which statement explains why no reflection of the trees can be seen on the water in the photograph?

a No light rays are travelling from the trees to the water's surface.

b No light rays from the trees are reflected by the water surface.

c Light rays from the sun travel to the water's surface and are reflected at many different angles.

d Light rays coming from the trees are reflected at many different angles by the water surface.

9 Optical fibres are long, extremely thin strands of solid glass or plastic that carry light from one place to another, no matter how curved the fibre is. The diagram shows how a ray of light travels along a single fibre.

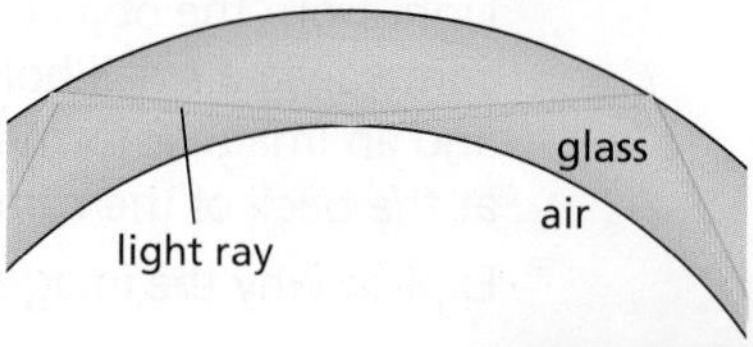

Use the diagram to describe and explain what happens each time the ray of light reaches the edge of the transparent fibre.

15.6 Vision and images

You are learning to:
- recognise when light is being refracted and how convex lenses form images
- use ray diagrams to show how light is reflected and refracted
- use ray diagrams to explain how the pinhole camera and the eye work.

1 Draw a diagram to show how a single ray of light reaches your eyes from:

a a light bulb **b** the page of a book

Include in your answer a description of what is happening in the diagram.

2 The photograph shows three rays of light passing through a glass block.

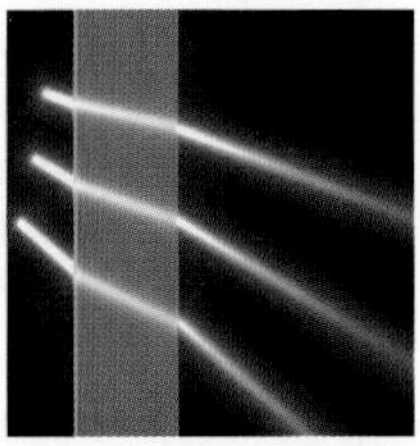

Which effect does this photograph show?

a absorption **b** scattering

c reflection **d** refraction

3 Which **two** parts of the eye refract light as it enters?

a cornea **b** iris **c** lens **d** retina

4 The picture shows a convex (converging) lens making an image.

Complete the following sentences to explain how the image is formed.

Rays of ___**i**___ from the lamp pass through the lens where they are made to converge on the ___**ii**___ . The rays are refracted by the ___**iii**___ .

The ___**iv**___ formed is smaller than the object and is upside down.

5 A teacher sets up a ray box with three slits so that it produces three rays of light. They then put a glass block shaped like a lens across the path of the rays. The picture shows a top-down view of the equipment.

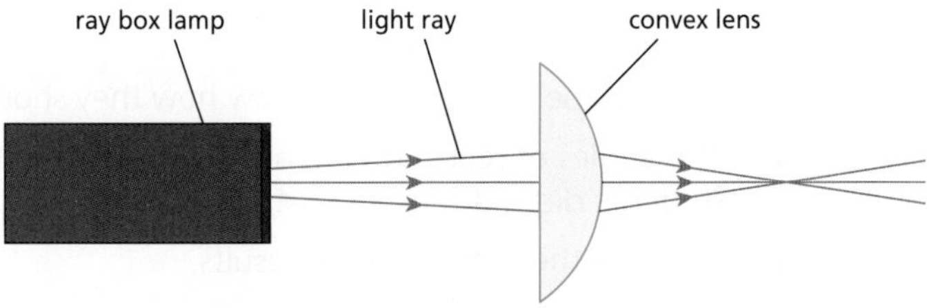

Complete the following sentences to describe how the lens affects the rays of light.

When the light rays from the lamp pass through the lens they cross over, showing they have changed ___**i**___ . This is called ___**ii**___ .

The lens brings the rays together to one point, called the ___**iii**___ point. This type of lens is a converging lens, also called a ___**iv**___ lens.

6 The diagram shows how a pinhole camera works.

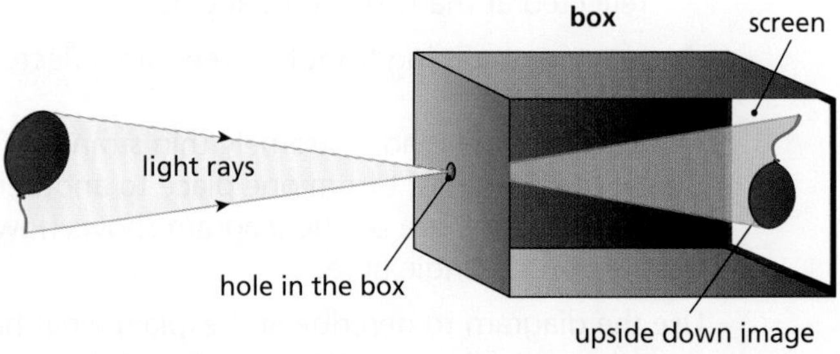

Light from the object enters the camera via a small hole in the box and an image is formed on the screen at the back of the camera.

Explain why the image is upside down.

7 A group of students is investigating how the direction of a ray of light is affected by passing through a rectangular glass block. They shine a single ray of light into a block as shown in the picture.

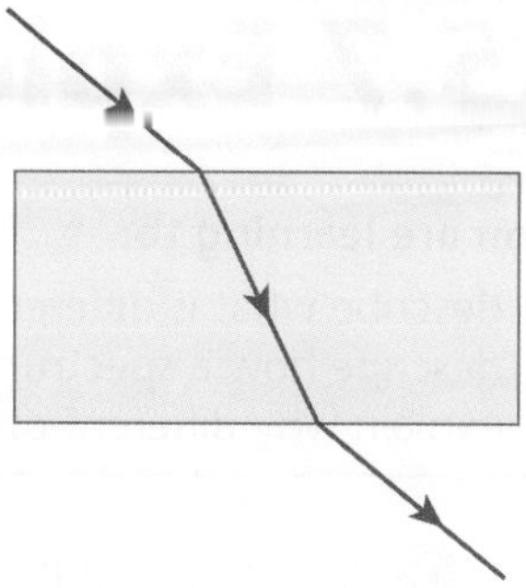

Select the row that is an accurate description of what happens when the light enters and leaves the block.

Response	As the light enters the block it:	As the light leaves the block it:
a	is refracted towards the normal.	is refracted towards the normal.
b	is refracted towards the normal.	is refracted away from the normal.
c	is refracted away from the normal.	is refracted towards the normal.
d	is refracted away from the normal.	is refracted away from the normal.

8 The diagram shows some of the parts of a human eye. Match the name of each part of the eye to its function.

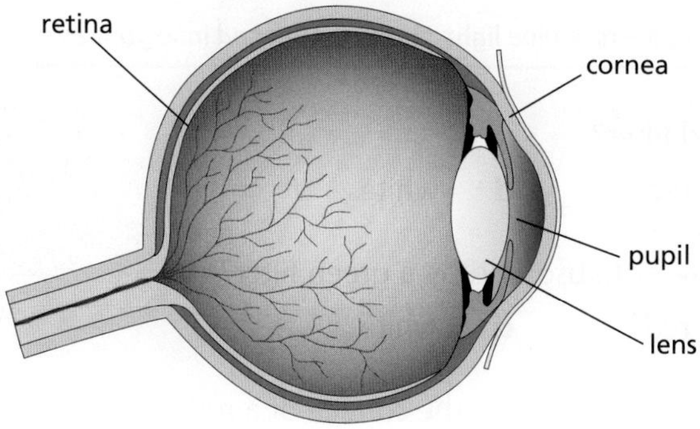

Part of eye	Function
pupil	**a** focuses light rays on the retina
cornea	**b** made of light-sensitive receptor cells to detect light and produce nervous impulses
lens	**c** hole in iris to let light through and control amount entering
retina	**d** transparent region of the front of the eye; protects eye and refracts light

9 The photo shows a pencil in a glass of water. The pencil is not broken or misshapen; the effect is due to refraction.

Select the statement that is **false**.

a Light is refracted when leaving the water.

b Light is refracted when leaving the glass.

c Light is refracted when entering the glass.

d Light is refracted when entering the pencil.

10 Both the eye and the pinhole camera produce images. There are similarities and differences in the way that they do this. Compare the eye and the pinhole camera.

15.7 Exploring coloured light

You are learning to:
- describe what is different about light of different colours
- describe how a spectrum can be produced from white light
- explain why different objects have colours when white light shines on them.

1 Which one of these colours is not one of the colours seen in the visible spectrum?

a blue **b** green **c** grey **d** orange

2 White light can be split into colours by using a triangular prism. What is the scientific term for this band of colours?

Worked example

a What colour or colours of light go through a blue filter?

A blue filter will remove every colour apart from blue – it is blue light that will go through.

b What colour or colours in white light will not be absorbed by a blue t-shirt?

The blue material will absorb everything except blue – it is blue light that is reflected into your eyes.

3 What colour light will pass through a red filter?

a blue **b** green **c** red **d** white

4 Which colour or colours in white light are not absorbed by a green filter?

a blue **b** green **c** red **d** white

5 What colour or colours in white light are reflected from the surface of a red t-shirt?

a blue **b** green **c** red **d** white

6 What colour does a blue shirt appear in red light?

a black **b** blue **c** green **d** red

7 Complete the sentence.

White light is a mixture of many different colours, each with a different ___________ .

8 The diagram shows light entering and leaving a triangular prism.

Which **one** of the following conclusions **cannot** be made from this diagram?

a White light can be split up into many different colours of light.

b A ray of light entering glass at an angle changes direction.

c Red light is refracted more than any of the other colours.

d Violet light is refracted more than any of the other colours.

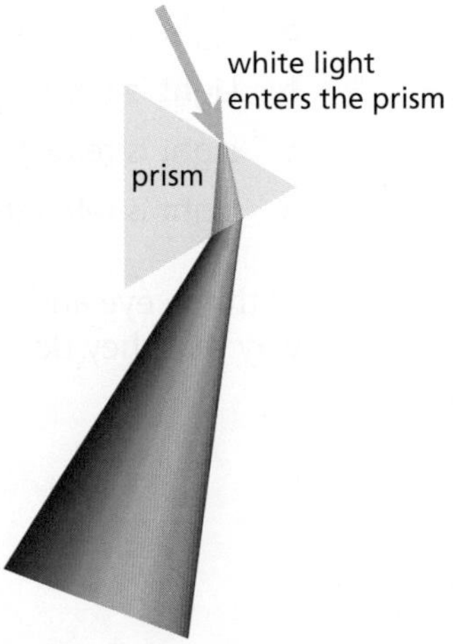

9 A student is controlling the lighting for the school play. He has learned how to put coloured filters in front of lights to produce different colours of light. He is adjusting the position of three spotlights – a red one, a green one and a blue one. The three lights are shining on the wall and their light overlaps. He notices that where all three colours overlap, the result is an area of white light, as in the picture.

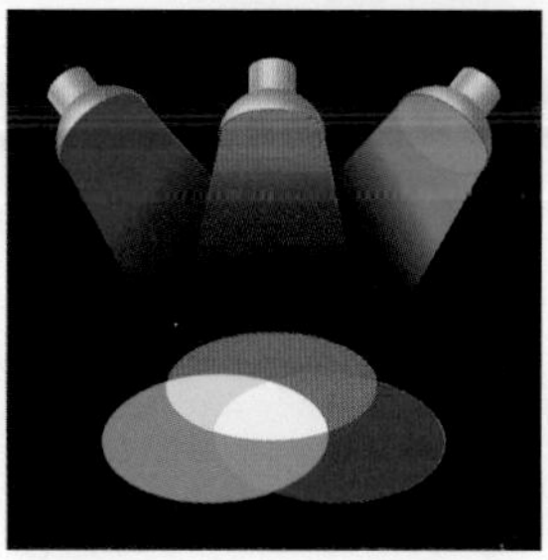

Which one of the following statements is **not** supported by this observation?

a White light can be made by mixing red, green and blue light.

b Mixing any two of the colours produces a different colour.

c The more colours of light you mix, the darker the product.

d Mixing red and green light produces yellow light.

10 On a sunny day, a teacher sets up the experiment shown in the diagram.

She positions a piece of black card with a small hole in it so that sunlight passing through the hole falls on a triangular prism. The light is split into a spectrum of colours. She then puts a thermometer in front of the screen, just beyond the red end of the spectrum. The reading on the thermometer rises above room temperature. When the thermometer is placed within the area of coloured light, the temperature does not rise above room temperature.

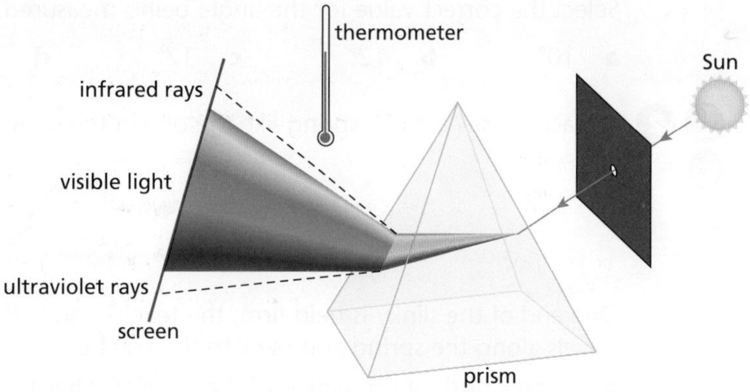

Which **one** of the following conclusions can be drawn from this experiment?

a Shining visible light on the thermometer makes it hot.

b Refracting light through a prism makes the glass hot.

c No energy is absorbed from light in the visible part of the sun's spectrum.

d More energy is absorbed from red light than from blue light.

11 Rainbows occur because of the way that raindrops affect light. The diagram shows how the path of a ray of light changes when it enters a drop of water.

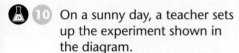

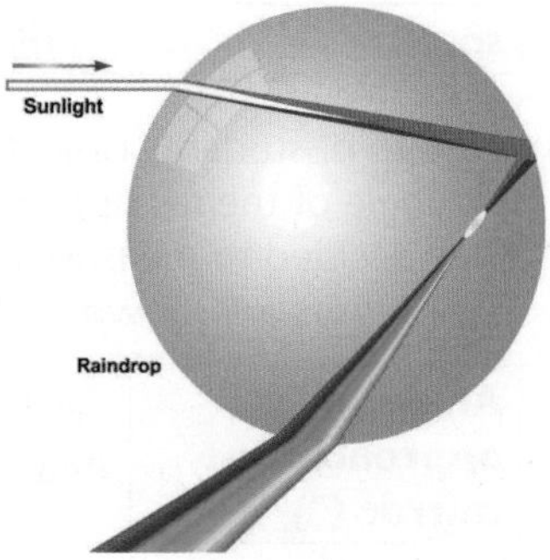

a Describe at what point or points the light is refracted.

b Describe at what point or points the light is reflected.

c As well as being changed in direction, what else happens to the white light entering the raindrop?

d Use the diagram to explain why a person looking in the direction of the sun has no chance of seeing a rainbow when it is raining.

Maths and practical skills

1 The protractor in the image is being used to measure the angle between a light ray and the normal. The normal is on the 0° line and the light ray is at the position marked by the arrow.

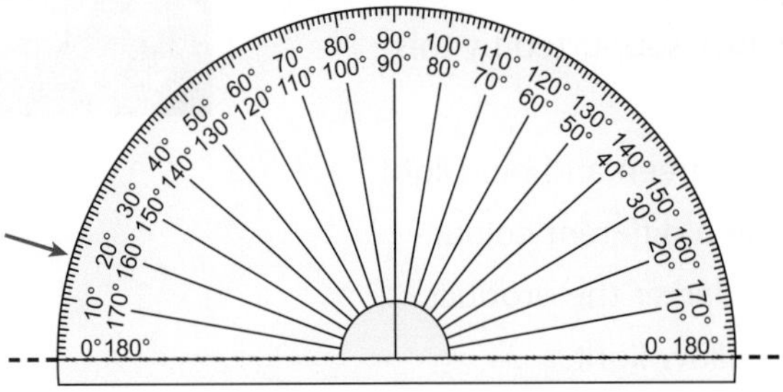

Select the correct value for the angle being measured.

a 10° **b** 12° **c** 17° **d** 22°

2 A teacher uses a slinky spring like the one in the diagram to produce transverse waves.

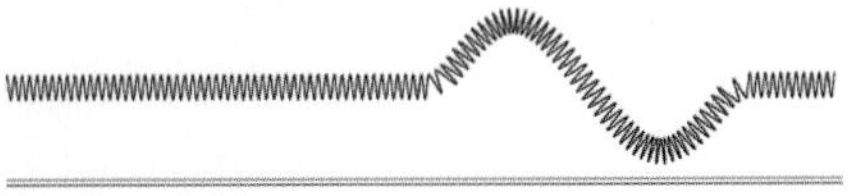

One end of the slinky is held firm; the teacher gives the other end a single shake. A wave travels along the spring and back to the teacher.

a If the length of the slinky is 2.5 m, how far has the wave travelled when it gets back to the teacher?

b The teacher asks a number of students to measure the time taken for the wave to complete this journey. Their results are: 2.4 s, 2.5 s, 3.9 s, 2.3 s and 2.4 s. Which of these results is anomalous?

3 Match up the units with the quantities being measured.

Quantity	Unit
frequency	metres per second
amplitude	hertz
speed	metres

4 A group of students is studying the reflection of a light ray by a mirror. They have measured the angle of the ray approaching the mirror and the angle of the ray reflected by the mirror. They decided to measure the angle of the reflected ray three times and calculate the mean. Their results are shown in the table.

Angle of ray approaching mirror (°)	Angle of the reflected ray (°)			Mean angle of the reflected ray (°)
	Reading 1	Reading 2	Reading 3	
10	11	9	10	
20	18	20	22	
30	21	29	31	

a Calculate the mean value of the angle of the reflected ray when the ray is approaching the mirror at:

i 10° **ii** 20°

b When the ray is approaching the mirror at 30°, one of the values for the angle of reflection is an anomaly. Give its value.

c Suggest what the students should do to get an accurate value for the angle of reflection when the light ray approaches the mirror at 30°.

5 How far away is a quarry if the sound of blasting is heard 3.5 s after the explosion? Use the equation: distance = speed × time; the speed of sound in air is 330 m/s.

6 A fishing boat is trying to locate a shoal of fish using sonar. The boat sends a signal directly downwards and an echo is received 0.6 s later. If the sonar waves are travelling at 1500 m/s, calculate the depth of the fish. Use the equation: distance = speed × time.

7 A group of students is exploring whether the distance between a photovoltaic cell and a lamp affects the potential difference produced by the cell.

a Describe a procedure they could use to investigate this.

b State what is the dependent variable and what is the independent variable.

c State the column headings the students should use in their results table, including the units.

d Suggest what else might affect the results and should be controlled.

8 A group of students is investigating which materials are suitable for reflective clothing. The materials should be good at reflecting light from cars so that at night the person wearing the clothing will be visible to motorists. The students are working in a small room with no windows, and have a torch, a selection of materials of different colours and surfaces, and a tablet device to take photographs.

a Write a plan to show how the students could use the equipment to select the best material. The plan should show how the experiment will be a fair test of the materials.

b The students test the following four materials: black velvet, grey cotton cloth, smooth white plastic and aluminium foil. Make and justify a prediction for:

i which of these materials will reflect the most light

ii which of these materials will reflect the least light.

9 A group of students is exploring how light is affected by passing through a triangular glass prism. They know that the white light entering the prism will be refracted and that the white light will be split into a spectrum of colours. They are trying to find out the angles at which the red and violet lights emerge.

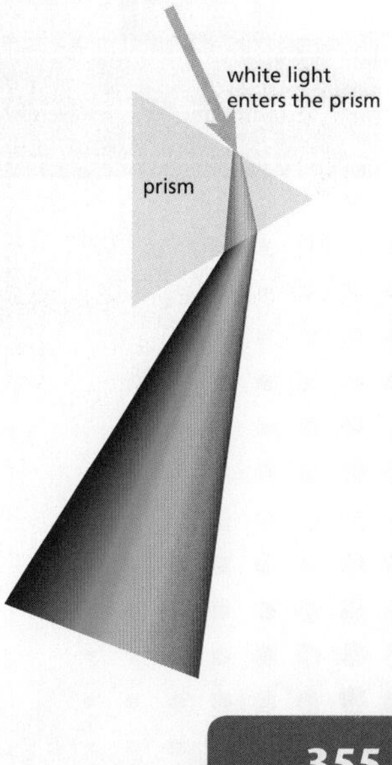

a Plan a procedure the students could use to find out, for a particular angle at which a ray of white light enters the prism:

i the angle at which the red light emerges

ii the angle at which the violet light emerges.

b Suggest the potential sources of error when measuring these angles.

16 Electricity and magnetism road map

Where are you in your learning journey and where are you aiming to be?

- describe magnets as having two poles
- know that magnetic forces can act at a distance
- know that magnets attract some materials and not others
- identify common appliances that run on electricity
- construct and analyse simple series electrical circuits
- compare how electrical components function

16.1 Static electricity
- recognise effects of charges
- understand electron transfer
- explain an electric field

16.2 Current electricity (1)
- describe a current as a flow of charge
- explain how electrons receive energy
- describe how current and potential difference are measured
- describe how good conductors have a low resistance

16.3 Current electricity (2)
- describe differences between series a
  parallel circuits
- explain what resistance is
- describe how current is shared in cir

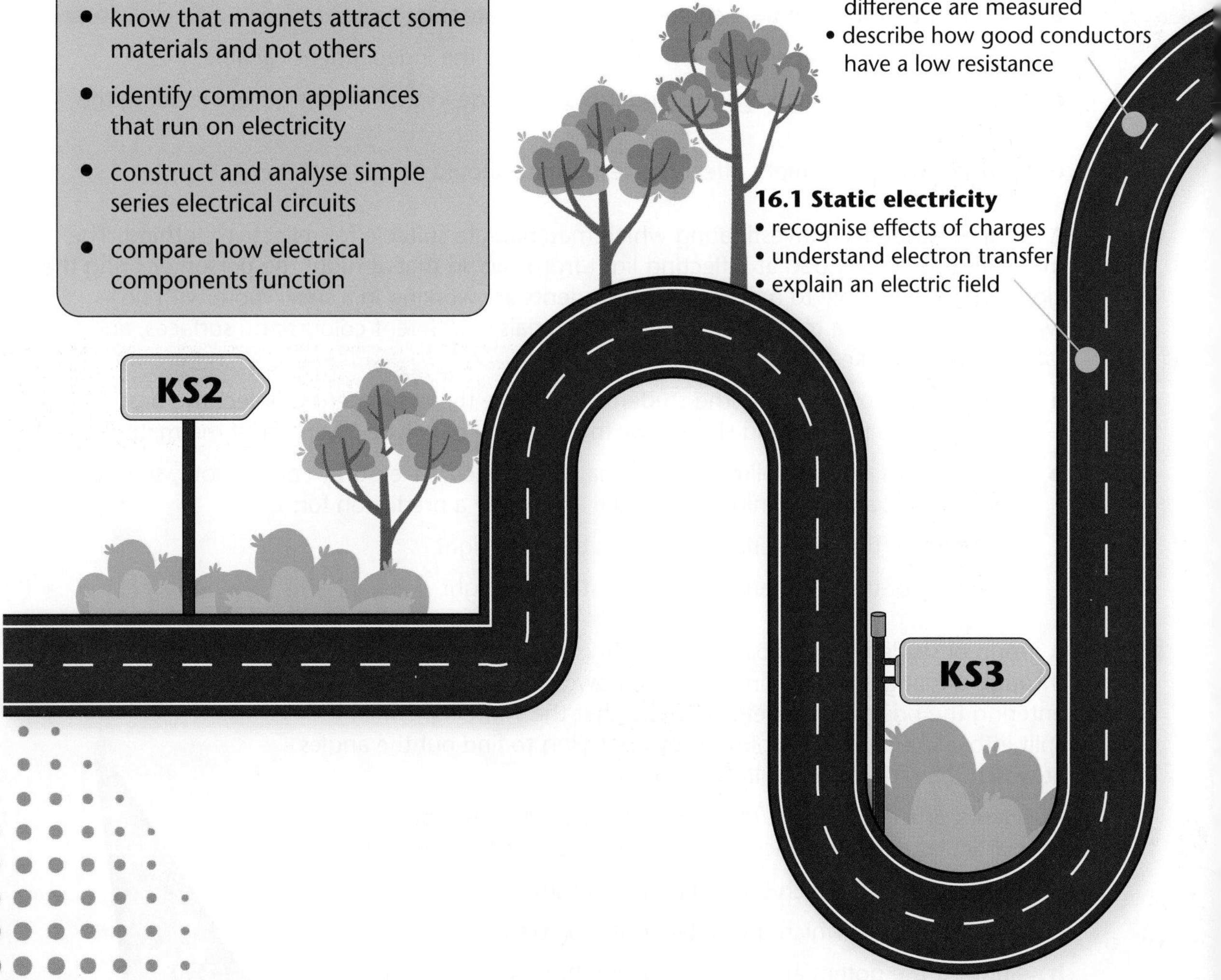

16.4 Magnetism
- describe attraction and repulsion
- describe plotting shape and direction
- describe the Earth's magnetic field

16.5 Magnetic effects of a current
- describe magnetic effects
- explain making electromagnets
- describe effects of a magnetic field

- current, potential difference and resistance
- series and parallel circuits
- domestic uses and safety
- energy transfers
- permanent and induced magnetism, magnetic forces and fields
- the motor effect

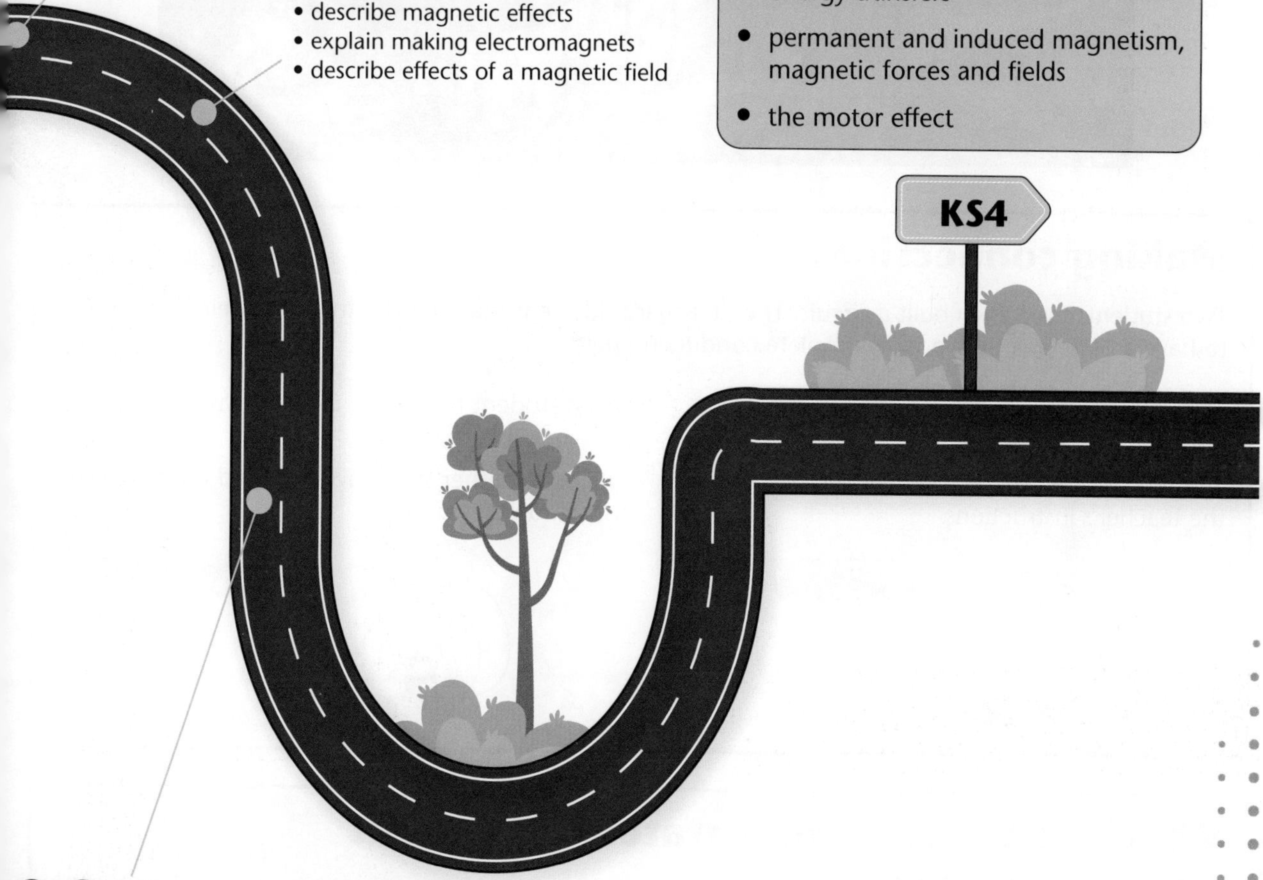

Maths and practical skills

- presenting data using tables and graphs
- interpreting observations and data
- carrying out practical work safely
- observing and measuring
- presenting reasoned explanations

16 Electricity and magnetism

Electricity affects how we communicate, travel, are entertained, cook our food and power our homes. Magnetism has a key role in this; homes have dozens of motors, including in the fridge, vacuum cleaner, computer, printer and washing machine.

Making connections

Two students have each built a circuit. Their teacher told them that in order to work, their circuit has to have a battery, a bulb and a complete conducting path.

This is student A's circuit. Explain why it does not work.

Suggest whether they have followed the teacher's instructions.

This is student B's circuit. Explain why it does not work.

Suggest whether they have followed the teacher's instructions.

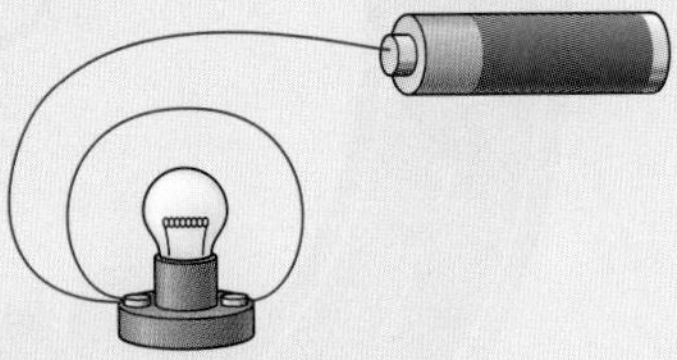

Which of the following statements about circuits are true?

- If the battery is flat, the circuit will not work.
- A circuit has to have a switch in it or it will not work.
- There has to be a complete circuit with a battery for the lamp to light.
- If the bulb is placed next to the battery in the circuit (instead of after the switch) it will be brighter.
- The battery has positive and negative terminals.
- The battery has to be the right way around in the circuit for the bulb to light.

Using your science skills

Could you be an electric vehicle mechanic?

There's going to be a huge change over the next few years as more people switch to electric vehicles. To be an electric vehicle mechanic it helps if you are good at understanding circuits and being able to find faults. Part of being a good mechanic is finding which component might need replacing or repairing. You start off by connecting a diagnostic system to the car and this may identify the fault but sometimes you have to figure things out yourself.

You need to qualify as a mechanic before going on a specialist training programme. You learn about the common faults of electric vehicles, how the motor works and how to use the diagnostic software programme. The course also covers the types of risk involved in working on electric vehicles, which use a 400 V battery to power the motor and a 12 V system for the lights, sound system and wipers.

Health and safety consultants monitor the hazards of equipment that companies use, and risks such as electric shock, fire or explosion due to static electricity charge and discharge. A consultant assesses the risks that people are exposed to and advises the business on how to take action. They need to understand the law, be prepared to be assertive about keeping people safe and be good at suggesting solutions.

Electronic repair technicians maintain and repair computers, which contain complex circuit boards made from millions of tiny components. They need to be good at problem solving and interpreting circuit diagrams. Circuit designs change as new processors are developed and specifications improve, so they have to be good at keeping up to date with changes.

Commercial electricians design, install and maintain wiring systems in buildings. They have to understand how devices such as motors are used in air-conditioning systems and automatic doors, and be able to measure current and voltage in circuits and test continuity of conductors. Teamwork is important as they need to liaise with other professionals about systems such as alarms, fire sprinklers and electronic sensors.

Electrical project managers oversee the design, installation and supply of electrical systems that supply electricity to homes and businesses, or key functions such as street lights and traffic lights. They also work on renewable energy projects or gas-fired power stations.

Paramedics use a defibrillator to send an electrical shock to restart someone's heart. They need to understand how this works and when it is needed, so they have to be good at interpreting data on the patient's cardiac rhythm and also know how to prevent the risk of electric shock to themselves and others.

Knowledge organiser

When some materials are rubbed together, the surfaces become electrically charged. This means that electrons have been transferred from one surface to the other. Objects with like charges repel each other and those with opposite charges attract each other.

An uncharged object has an equal number of positive and negative charges. Bringing a charged object near to an uncharged object attracts the opposite charges and repels the like charges. The charged object and the uncharged object will now attract.

The space around a charged object is called an **electric field**. Any charged objects in the field experience a force.

Electric current is measured using an **ammeter**. The unit of measurement is **amperes** (**A**). Current is a flow of charge.

Some materials allow a **current** to pass through easily; these are electrical **conductors**. Materials that do not allow a current to pass through easily are **insulators**.

Potential difference is measured using a **voltmeter**, in **volts** (**V**). Batteries and bulbs are rated in volts.

Resistance is measured in **ohms** (**Ω**); it is the ratio of the potential difference across a component to the current passing through it:

resistance = potential difference/current

Increasing the resistance in a circuit decreases the current.

A **series circuit** has the **components** connected in a single loop, one after the other.

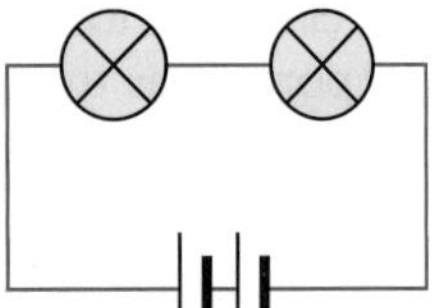

A **parallel circuit** has the components in separate branches; the current from the battery is divided between the loops.

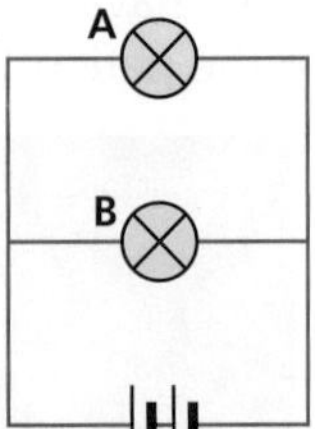

When charges move round a circuit there is an electric current. In a metal, the charged particles that flow are **electrons**, which have a negative charge.

When a circuit is switched on, energy is transferred from the battery or power supply to the charges to make them move. The moving charges transfer energy to the circuit components.

Key vocabulary	
electron	a tiny negatively charged particle in an atom
electrostatic force	the non-contact force between two charged objects
negatively charged	an object that has gained electrons as a result of a charging process
parallel circuit	an electric circuit in which each component is connected separately in its own loop
positively charged	an object that has lost electrons as a result of a charging process
resistance	the property of an electrical component that makes it difficult for charge to pass through; unit of measurement is the ohm (Ω)
series circuit	circuit in which all components are connected one after the other in a loop
static electricity	an imbalance between positive and negative charges on the surface of a material

The Earth has a magnetic field, which nearly lines up with the geographic north and south poles. The magnetic field can be detected using a compass which points in the direction of the field. Using a compass you can work out which compass direction you are facing.

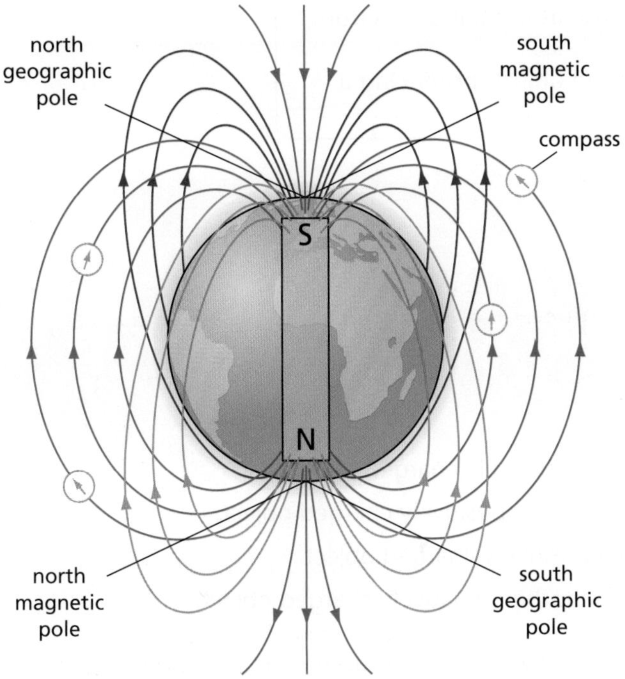

Every magnet has a north **pole** and a south pole. Like poles repel and opposite poles attract.

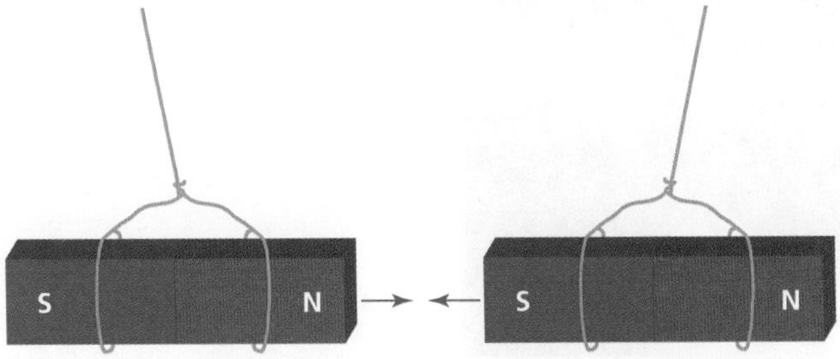

The area between magnetic poles is a **magnetic field**. Magnetic fields can be explored by moving a **compass** in the field. The shape and direction of the field can be represented by field lines.

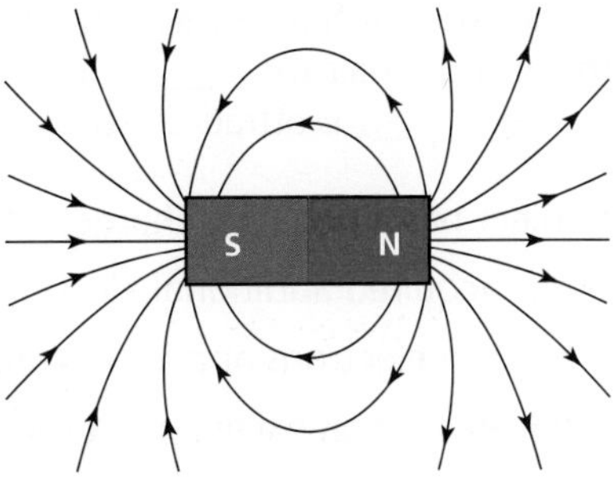

Key vocabulary

compass	an instrument that shows the direction of a magnetic field
electromagnet	a type of temporary magnet that is magnetic only when an electric current passes through it
magnetic	is attracted by a magnet
magnetic field	a region in which a magnetic material feels a force
pole	an end of a magnet; may be the north pole or the south pole
solenoid	a cylindrical coil of wire acting as a magnet when carrying electric current

A current through a wire produces a magnetic field around the wire.

This effect is used in **electromagnets** and in motors.

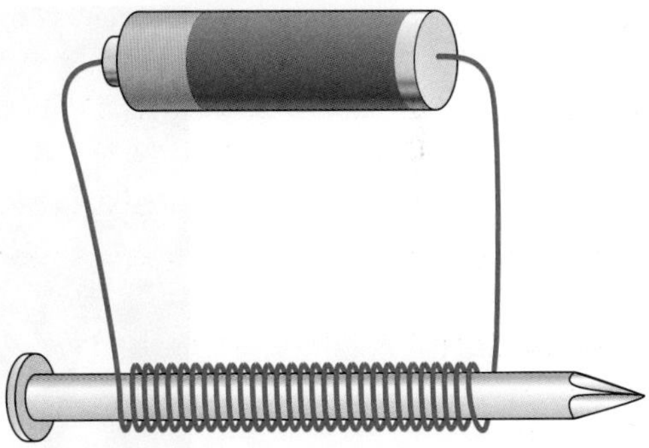

16.1 Static electricity

You are learning to:
- recognise how positive or negative charges affect each other
- understand how objects may acquire a static charge as a result of electron transfer
- explain that an electric field exists around a charged object, producing a force on other charged objects.

1 How many types of charge are there?

a one

b two

c four

d ten

2 Which one of these statements is true?

a A positively charged object will attract a negatively charged object.

b A positively charged object will attract another positively charged object.

c A negatively charged object will repel a positively charged object.

d A negatively charged object will attract another negatively charged object.

3 A student has long straight hair and notices that when they comb their hair vigorously and then hold the comb near to their hair, the hair is attracted to the comb.

Identify the words needed to complete this explanation.

Combing the hair has caused a transfer of ______**i**______ The comb has one kind of charge and the hair the ______**ii**______ kind. Opposite charges ______**iii**______ so the ______**iv**______ is attracted to the comb.

4 If an object has a negative charge, which of these statements is true?

a It has acquired additional electrons.

b It has lost electrons and is now short of them.

c It has neither an excess nor a shortage of electrons.

5 An object has been charged up and now has a negative static charge. Explain this in terms of electron transfer.

6 The photograph shows a piece of charged amber. Amber is fossilised tree resin and when it is rubbed against wool it becomes charged.

a If the amber becomes negatively charged when rubbed against wool, what kind of charge does the wool gain?

b State where electrons have been transferred from and to.

7 The painter in the photograph is using an electrostatic paint sprayer which sends out a spray of droplets of paint and gives each of them a positive charge. The piece of metal he is painting has a negative charge. The metal ends up with a very even covering of paint.

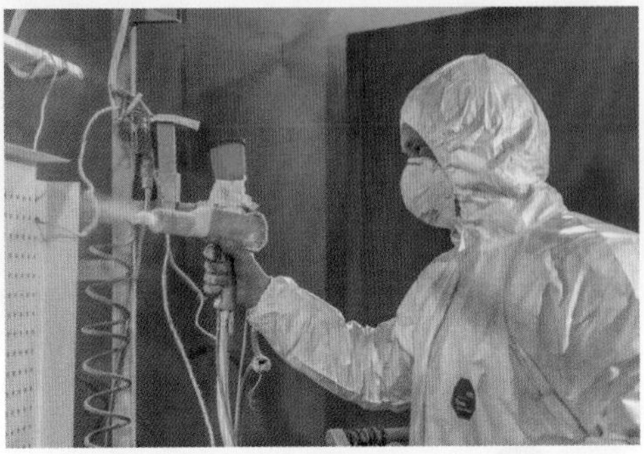

a Describe the direction of the force between a droplet of paint and the metal.

b Describe the direction of the force between the droplets of paint.

c Explain why very little paint ends up on the floor.

d Explain why the paint covering is very even.

8 If you walk across a nylon carpet and then touch a metal object you might experience a small electric shock. Explain why.

9 A student inflates a balloon and rubs it on his sweatshirt.

a Suggest how they could tell if the balloon has become charged.

b If the balloon has become negatively charged, where have electrons been transferred from and to?

c It is a damp day and the student notices that 10 minutes later the balloon no longer has a charge. Suggest what has happened.

10 A student tears some tissue paper into small pieces and puts them in a thin transparent plastic box. They put the lid on the box and rub it vigorously. Using the idea of an electric field, explain why the pieces of paper have been attracted to the lid.

11 State **two** similarities and **two** differences between magnetic forces and electrostatic forces.

12 A student has charged up the hair on their head by vigorously brushing it. The strands of hair have become positively charged.

a Explain why, if they then hold the hairbrush near some pieces of tissue paper, it will attract the paper.

b Explain why, after a few minutes, the strands of hair will gradually settle down again.

c The student finds that if they do this experiment on a dry day it takes longer for their hair to settle down again. Suggest why this might be.

16.2 Current electricity (1)

You are learning to:
- describe a current as a flow of charge (electrons in a wire)
- explain that a battery transfers energy to the electrons
- describe how current is measured in amps, using an ammeter, and how potential difference is measured in volts, using a voltmeter
- describe that good conductors have a low resistance to electric current.

1 What is the unit of current?

2 Pencil lead is made not of lead but of a material called graphite. If a piece of graphite is placed in a circuit with a battery and a bulb, the bulb will light up.

a What does this show about graphite?

b Graphite is a non-metal; why might this result be unexpected?

3 A student has constructed a circuit with a battery and a bulb. Her teacher has asked her to measure the current through the bulb and has provided her with an ammeter. Should she connect the meter in series with the bulb or in parallel with it?

4 Look at the circuit diagram.

Give the name of the component represented by each of these symbols:

a 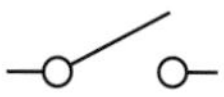 **b**  **c** 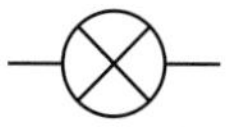

5 A student wants to measure the current through a bulb and the voltage across it. Which of these rows shows the correct way to connect an ammeter and a voltmeter?

	The ammeter should be connected:	**The voltmeter should be connected:**
a	in series with the bulb	in series with the bulb
b	in parallel with the bulb	in series with the bulb
c	in series with the bulb	in parallel with the bulb
d	in parallel with the bulb	in parallel with the bulb

6 A student's torch contains a simple circuit consisting of a battery, a switch and a bulb.

a Draw a circuit diagram to represent this circuit using the correct symbols.

b Draw a circuit diagram to show how to connect a voltmeter to measure the potential difference across the bulb.

7 AA batteries provide a potential difference of 1.5 V. They are to be used to light a 6 V bulb.

- **a** How many batteries should be used to make sure the bulb is brightly lit but not overheated (which might break the bulb)?
- **b** Should these batteries be connected in series or in parallel?
- **c** Explain how the terminals of each battery should be connected to the next battery, and why this is important.

8 Two light bulbs are part of a complete circuit with a battery. Which **two** statements are true?

- **a** Electrons in the wire move round the circuit when the battery is connected.
- **b** When electrons in the wire pass through the battery, energy is transferred to them.
- **c** When there is no current, there is no charge in the wires.
- **d** When the circuit is switched off, there is still energy being transferred to the electrons from the battery.

9 Some students are using a continuous loop of rope to model an electric circuit. One of the students plays the role of the battery and grips the rope, pulling it through their hands with their left hand and pushing it out with their right hand so that it travels through everybody else's hands. The other students hold the rope loosely, guiding it but not holding it. The movement of the rope represents an electric current. The diagram shows what this might look like, viewed from above.

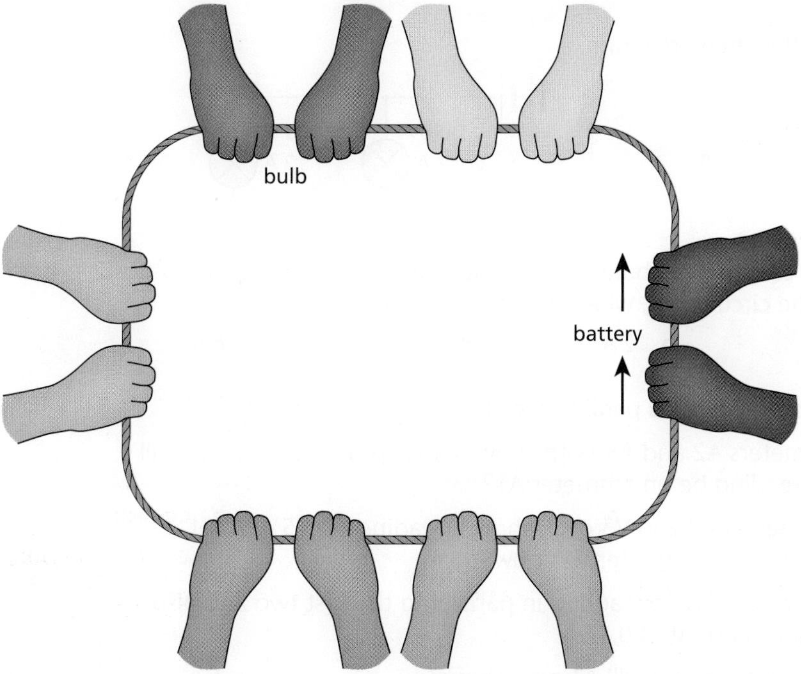

- **a** What does the push and pull of the person playing the part of the battery represent?
- **b** As the rope slips through the hands of each of the other students, their palms start to feel warm. What does this represent in a real circuit?
- **c** Describe how the model could be modified to represent a conductor with more resistance.
- **d** Describe how this would feel for the student playing the part of the battery.
- **e** Identify **one** strength and **one** weakness of the rope model as a representation of current in a circuit.

16.3 Current electricity (2)

You are learning to:

- describe the difference between series and parallel circuits
- describe the relationship between resistance, potential difference and current
- describe how current is shared between the loops in a parallel circuit.

1 Look at these two circuits:

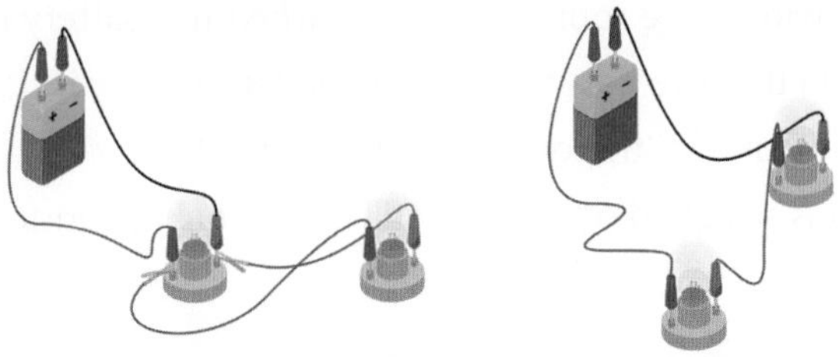

Decide which of these statements are true and which are false.

a The circuit on the left is a parallel circuit.

b If one of the bulbs in the circuit on the right breaks, the other bulb would go out.

c In both circuits the battery has to be connected the right way round to get the circuit to work.

2 Look at the circuit diagram.

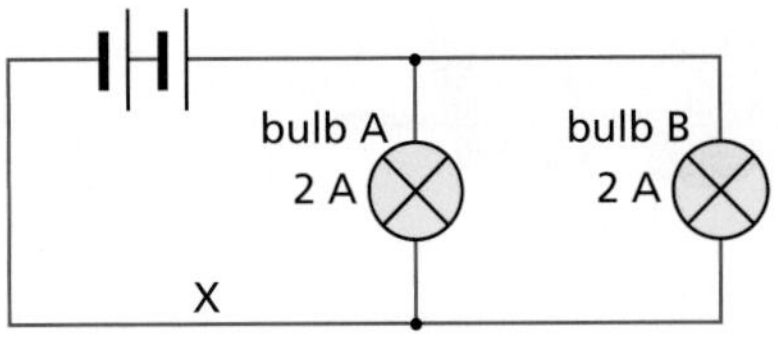

The current through bulb **A** is 2 A and the current through bulb **B** is 2 A. If an ammeter was put in the circuit at X, what would the reading be?

a 0 A **b** 2 A **c** 4 A **d** 6 A

3 The diagram shows a parallel circuit.

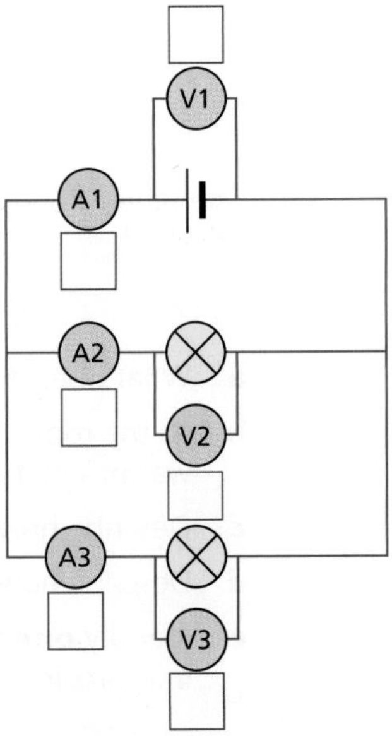

a Ammeters A2 and A3 both show readings of 0.15 A. What will the reading be on ammeter A1?

b Voltmeters V2 and V3 each show a reading of 1.5 V. What reading will voltmeter V1 show?

c A third bulb is now added in parallel to the first two and also draws a current of 0.15 A.

i What reading will A1 now show?

ii What reading will V1 now show?

4 Identify which **one** of these statements about a series circuit is false.

a There is the same current through all of the components in a series circuit.

b If there is a break anywhere in the circuit, the current stops everywhere in the circuit.

c If there are a number of identical bulbs connected in series to a battery, the bulb nearest to the battery will always be brighter.

d The potential differences across each of the components in a series circuit add up to the potential difference supplied by the battery.

Worked example

A teacher sets up the circuit shown in the diagram to demonstrate the relationship between potential difference, current and voltage.

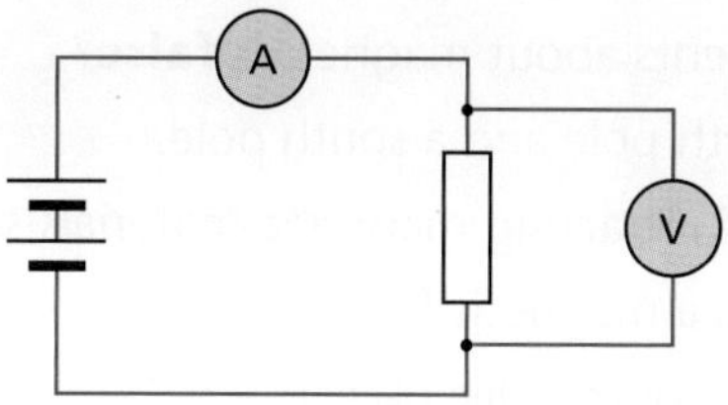

The voltmeter shows a reading of 0.5 V and the ammeter shows a reading of 0.1 A. Calculate the resistance of the resistor.

It is important to give a unit with your calculated answers. In this case, the potential difference is in volts and the current is in amps, so the resistance will be in ohms (Ω).

resistance = potential difference ÷ current = 0.5 V ÷ 0.1 A = 5 Ω

5 The circuit shown in the diagram is set up with a light bulb and a battery. There is a voltmeter across the bulb and an ammeter in series with the bulb. The variable resistor is included so that the potential difference across the bulb can be altered.

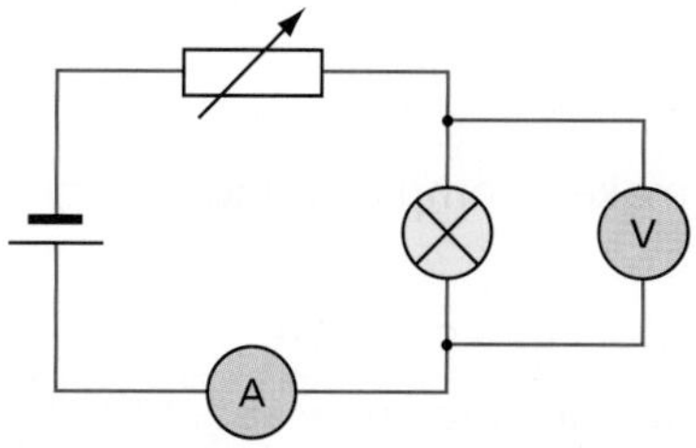

The table shows the readings of the potential difference and current as the variable resistor is adjusted.

Potential difference (V)	1.0	2.0	3.0	4.0	5.0	6.0
Current (A)	0.10	0.19	0.28	0.36	0.44	0.00

a Comment on the way that the current varies as the potential difference across the bulb increases.

b There is no current reading for a potential difference of 0 V. Suggest what it would have been.

c Calculate the resistance of the bulb when the potential difference across it is 1 V.

d Suggest why the current through the bulb was 0 A when the potential difference across it was 6 V.

16.4 Magnetism

You are learning to:
- describe how magnetic poles cause attraction and repulsion
- describe how to plot the shape and direction of a magnetic field
- describe the Earth's magnetic field and how it can be detected.

1 Which **one** of these statements is **true**?

a A north pole will attract another north pole.

b A north pole will attract a south pole.

c A south pole will repel a north pole.

d A south pole will attract another south pole.

2 Which **one** of these statements about magnets is **false**?

a Every magnet has a north pole and a south pole.

b Either pole is capable of attracting magnetic materials such as steel paper clips.

c Around every magnet is a magnetic field.

d Magnets attract all types of metallic objects.

3 The diagram shows the magnetic field pattern around a bar magnet. Select which **two** of these statements are **true**.

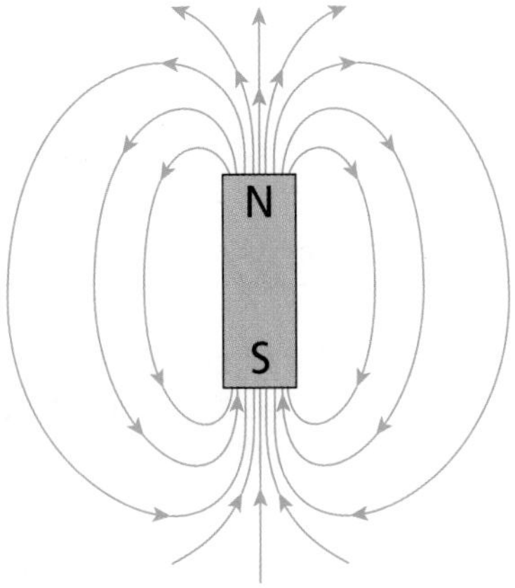

a The magnetic field is stronger where the field lines are closer together.

b The direction of the magnetic field lines is from south pole to north pole.

c The magnetic field lines never cross each other.

d The magnetic field lines are always drawn going from the top of the diagram to the bottom.

4 A class is exploring how to make a compass using a magnetised needle placed on a leaf floating on a bowl of water.

a Explain how this would work as a compass.

b State what else they would need to know about the needle to be able to use this equipment as a compass.

Worked example

A teacher is demonstrating how to plot the magnetic field around a magnet. They set up a bar magnet with a number of plotting compasses around it, as shown in the photograph on the right.

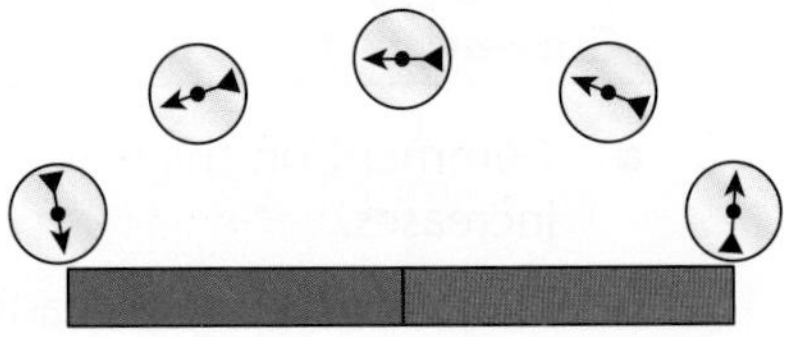

a Identify the north pole and the south pole of the magnet.

b Draw the magnetic field lines around the compasses.

The needle of a plotting compass points from the north pole to the south pole of the magnet. The compass needles show the direction of the line of force in that place; the tip of one needle points to the next needle, so continuous lines can be drawn as shown. Make sure the lines do not cross each other. You should put arrows on the field lines, pointing from the magnet's north pole to its south pole.

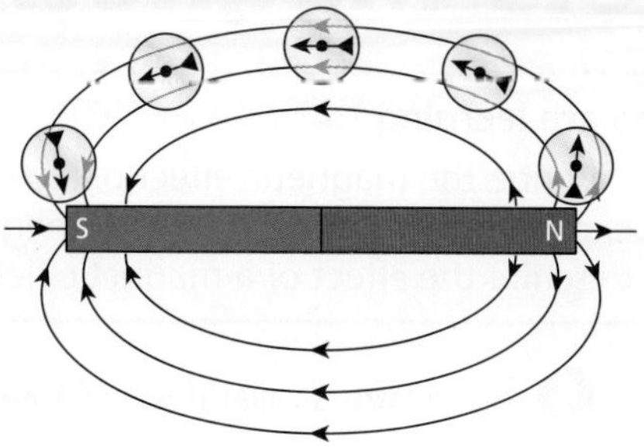

5 A student is exploring the magnetic field pattern around a horseshoe magnet. They put a number of plotting compasses near to the magnet and observe the directions in which the needles point. The arrangement of the magnet and compasses is shown in the diagram.

- **i** Copy the diagram and add lines to show the magnetic field lines in the area.
- **ii** Add arrows to show the direction of the field lines.

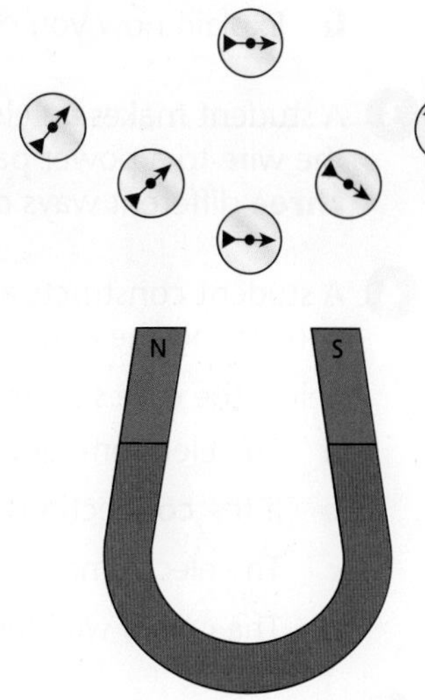

6 The diagram below is a representation of the Earth's magnetic field. It also shows the geographic North Pole and South Pole, which are found where the imaginary axis about which the Earth rotates meets the Earth's surface.

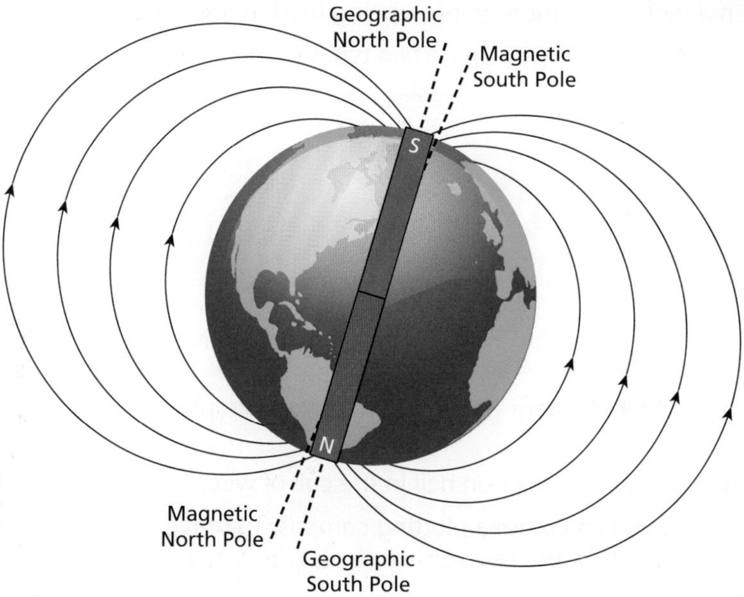

- **a** Describe what the diagram shows about the position of the magnetic poles compared with the geographic poles.
- **b** A compass is a small magnet and points north to south. A compass needle's north pole points north. Explain why this diagram is correct in showing the geographic North Pole as a magnetic south pole.
- **c** Compare the shape of the Earth's magnetic field with that of a bar magnet.

16.5 Magnetic effects of a current

You are learning to:
- describe the magnetic effect of an electric current
- explain how to make an electromagnet and vary its strength
- describe the effect of a magnetic field on a current-carrying wire or coil.

1. State **two** similarities and **two** differences between an electromagnet and a permanent magnet.

2. **a** State when a wire produces a magnetic field.
   b Explain how you could show that a magnetic field has been produced around a wire.

3. A student makes an electromagnet by coiling wire around a pencil and attaching the ends of the wire to a power pack. It works but does not produce a strong magnetic field. Suggest **three** different ways of making the electromagnet stronger.

4. A student constructs an electromagnet by wrapping a length of wire around a nail and connecting the ends of the wire to a power pack.
   Select the **one** statement below that is **false**.
   a The electromagnet has two poles, north and south.
   b If the connections to the power pack are reversed, the north and south poles are reversed.
   c The electromagnet will attract any metallic object.
   d The coil of wire feels warm after it has been on for a while.

5. The electromagnet in the photograph is being used in a scrapyard.
   a Explain why it can only pick up certain types of metal.
   b State what needs to be done to release the metal and explain your answer.

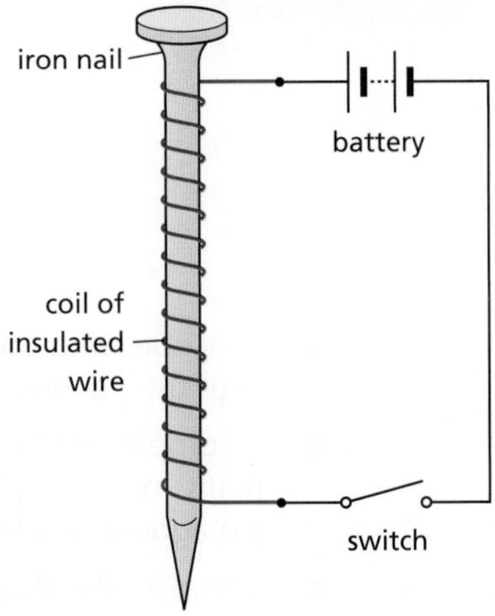

6. The equipment in the diagram was set up to make a simple electromagnet.
   a State **two** functions of the iron nail in the coil of wire.
   b Describe how you could use a plotting compass to prove that the north pole of the electromagnet was, in fact, a north pole.
   c If this equipment was set up as shown, explain why:
      i the coil of wire would get warm quickly
      ii the battery would quickly become flat.

7 A teacher set up the apparatus shown in the diagram to demonstrate what happens when a current-carrying wire is placed in a magnetic field.

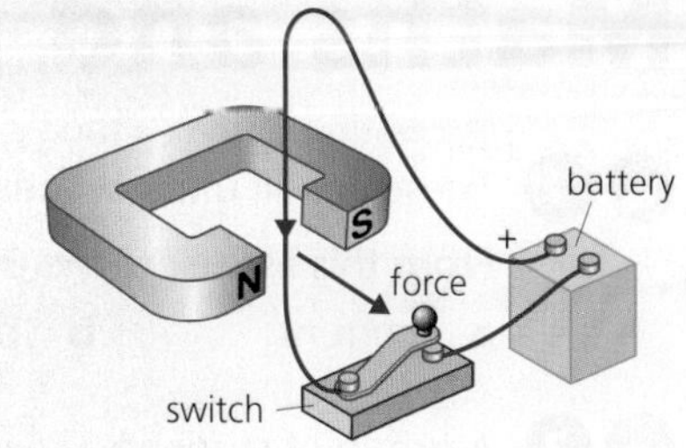

When the teacher closes the switch, the wire is forced away from the magnet.

Complete the following sentences:

a The current in the wire produces …

b The wire is in the field of a permanent …

c Where the two magnetic fields are in the same direction they add together to make …

d This makes the wire …

e The effect this causes is called …

f The direction the wire is pushed can be reversed in two ways: either by … or …

8 The diagram shows the design of an electromagnetic circuit breaker.

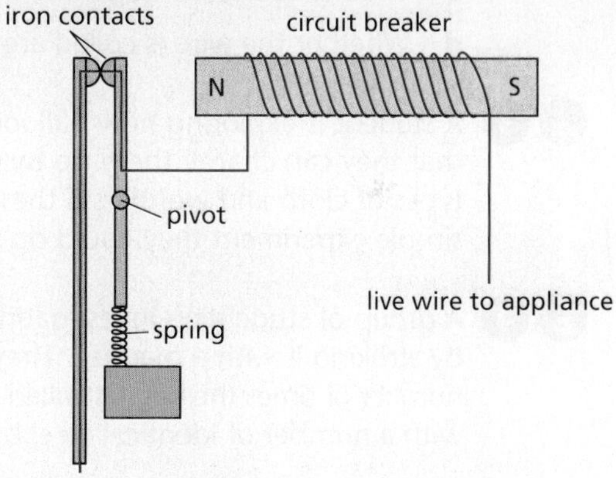

The device will cut off the power to an appliance if the current in the wire is larger than normal. The current passes through the coil and through the contacts. Normally the current is not large enough to produce a strong magnetic field.

a What will happen to the magnetic field if the current increases?

b The right-hand contact is made from steel. What will happen if a larger current passes through the coil?

9 The diagram shows the inside of an electric bell.

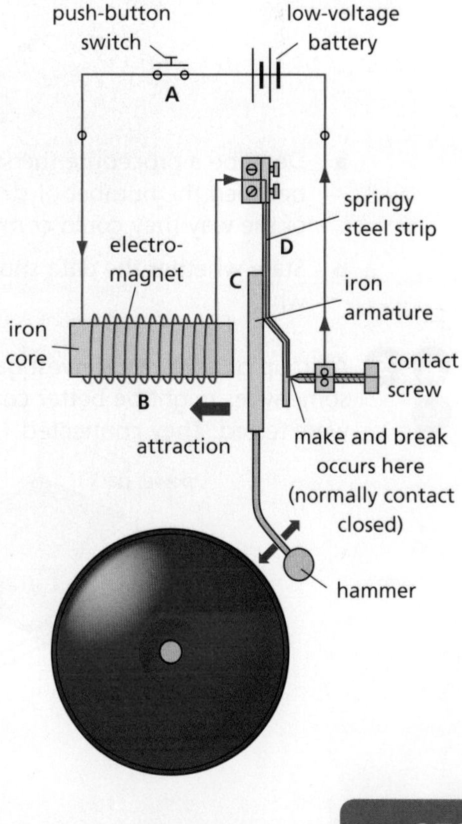

When the switch is pushed, the circuit is completed and an electric current passes through the coil. The electromagnet attracts the iron arm, which makes the hammer hit the gong. The movement of the iron arm breaks the contact between the strip and the screw, which breaks the circuit and the iron arm springs back.

a Explain step-by-step why, if the switch is kept pushed in, the hammer hits the gong repeatedly and not just once.

b Explain what would happen if the electromagnet was replaced with a permanent magnet.

Maths and practical skills

1 These are all units of measurement: amps, ohms, seconds, volts, watts.

From this list select the unit used to measure:

a current **b** potential difference **c** resistance.

2 A group of students is exploring how to make an electromagnet. They have been provided with a variable-voltage power supply, a length of insulated wire, a nail, a pencil and some paper clips. Which **one** of the following is **not** an example of an independent variable that could be investigated?

a Altering the voltage output on the power supply.

b The number of paper clips the electromagnet will attract.

c The number of turns on the coil.

d Whether the wire is coiled around the pencil or the nail.

3 A student is exploring how balloons behave when charged. They have two balloons and know that they can charge them up by rubbing them with cloth. The student has two different types of cloth and wonders if these will give the balloons different types of charge. Suggest a simple experiment they could do to find out.

4 A group of students is investigating the idea that it is possible to turn a steel bar into a magnet by stroking it with a magnet. They are exploring whether there is a relationship between the number of times the bar is stroked and the strength of the magnet it produces. They are supplied with a number of identical steel bars, a bar magnet, some paper clips and a 30 cm ruler.

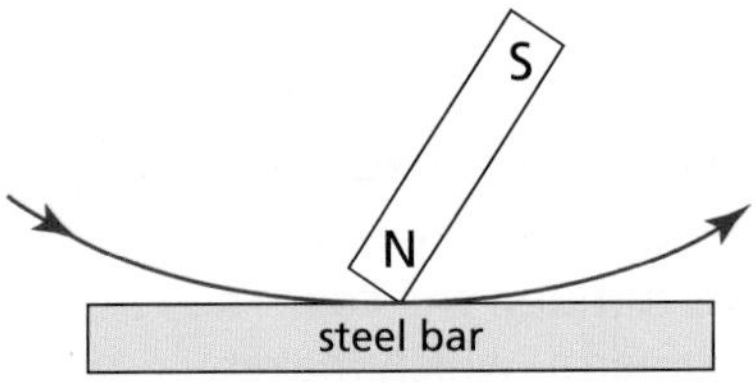

a Describe a procedure the students could use to see whether there is a relationship between the number of strokes and the strengths of the magnet produced. Include details of the way they could compare the strengths of the magnets produced.

b State whether the data should be displayed on a bar chart or scatter graph, and explain why.

5 A group of students is investigating the idea that, although all metal wires are conductors, some wires might be better conductors than others. Four different thicknesses of copper wire were tested. They connected 1 m of each wire in turn to the circuit shown in the diagram.

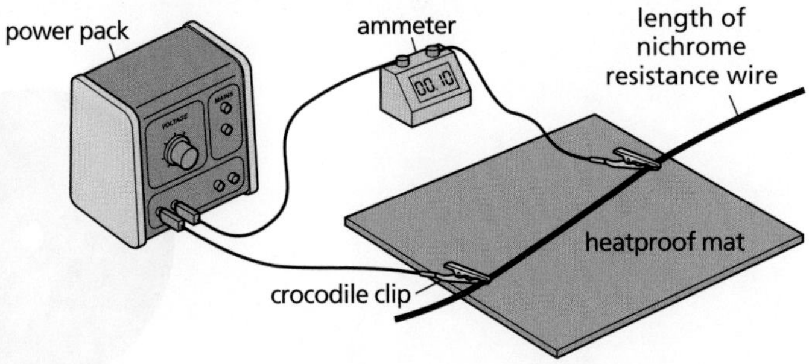

The table shows the results.

Wire	Potential difference across wire (V)	Current through wire (A)
A	0.2	2
B	0.12	1.6
C	0.16	0.8
D	0.1	2

a Explain why the wire is set up on a heatproof mat.

b Calculate the resistance of each of the wires.
Use the equation: potential difference ÷ current = resistance.

c Use the figures for the resistance to state which wire is the best conductor.

d Place the four wires in order of greatest resistance to least resistance.

e Suggest why it is often desirable to use connecting wires with a low resistance.

Worked example

A resistor is placed in a circuit with a power supply so that current flows through the resistor. The amount of current and also the potential difference across the resistor are measured.
If the potential difference is 6 V and the current is 15 mA, what is the resistance of the resistor?

resistance = potential difference ÷ current

The current needs to be in amps, so you need to convert 15 mA to amps.
1 mA = 0.001 A, so 15 mA = 0.015 A

resistance = 6 V ÷ 0.015 A = 400 Ω

6 A teacher has provided a group of students with a selection of resistors and asked them to determine the resistance of each of them. As well as the resistors, they have a 12 V power supply, connecting wires, a voltmeter and an ammeter. They test each resistor in turn, recording the potential difference across it and the current flowing through it. Their results are shown in the table.

Resistor	Potential difference across resistor (V)	Current flow through resistor (mA)
A	6	12
B	6	8
C	4	16
D	4	20

a Calculate the resistance of each of the resistors in ohms.

b Place the four resistors in order of resistance, starting with the greatest resistance.

17 Matter road map

Where are you in your learning journey and where are you aiming to be?

- compare and group materials together, according to their state of matter and their properties
- know that some materials change state when heated or cooled, and find out at what temperature
- know that some materials will dissolve to form a solution, and how to recover the material
- know that dissolving, mixing and changes of state are reversible changes.

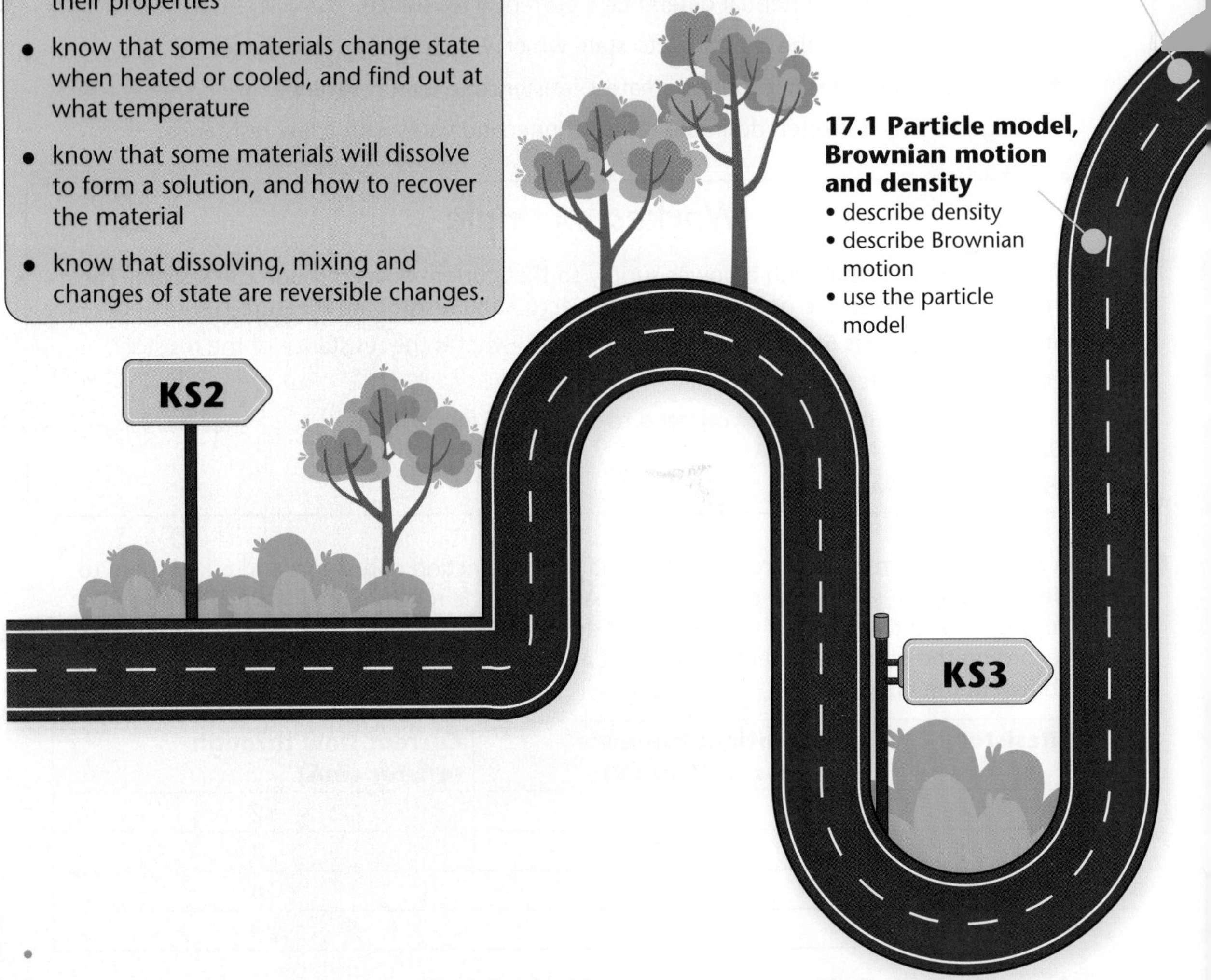

17.1 Particle model, Brownian motion and density
- describe density
- describe Brownian motion
- use the particle model

17.2 Particle model and physical changes
- use the particle model

17.3 Energy stored in matter

- describe thermal expansion
- explain temperature changes
- describe heating increases
- describe changes in temperature and state

- changes of state and the particle model
- internal energy and energy transfers
- particle model and pressure

Maths and practical skills

- select suitable apparatus and consider accuracy of measurements
- calculate results and convert between different units
- analyse data to draw conclusions
- use equations to calculate answers
- rearrange equations to change the subject

17 Matter

Scientists are really interested in what makes up the materials around us. It is useful to think about these in terms of particles and what these particles might be doing when the material changes state, for example when water changes to ice or steam. The particle model can also be used to explain why some materials are denser than others.

Living in a material world

Student A is making a cup of coffee. They have a cup of hot water and are dissolving instant coffee powder into it.

- Describe the change that is taking place.
- Would it be possible to reverse this change and separate the coffee powder and the water?

Student B likes sugar in their coffee.

- Suggest **three** ways in which they could get the sugar to dissolve quicker.
- Is there a limit to how much sugar they could dissolve in their coffee?

Using your science skills

Could you be a metallurgist?

Being a **metallurgist** is a highly skilled job and involves meeting the challenges set by the modern uses of metals. You need specialist knowledge about the properties of metals and recommending how they can be used for different purposes. There is variety to the job – you might be advising civil engineers investigating thermal expansion in bridges for one project and then selecting metals to withstand the high forces and high temperatures in an aircraft engine for another project. You have to be good at maths to do this job: there are a lot of data and graphs to analyse. Metallurgy is on the border between physics and chemistry, so you need an understanding of both these sciences. You also have to be good at teamwork – you're always working as part of a group of professionals, each with their own specialist knowledge, such as engineers, chemists and other materials scientists.

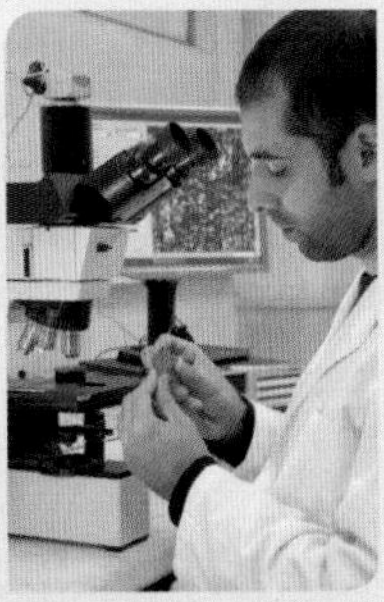

A ship's officer is responsible for organising how the load is distributed on a ship. Loading a ship is a skilled business – it's not only a case of the ship being balanced but the level at which it floats is crucial. Sea water varies around the world – the ship will float lower or higher in the water in different places. A fully loaded ship is more fuel efficient but it has to be safe.

Oceanographers study ocean currents and explain the effect of changes in the sea. They study data and draw conclusions: for example, they look at how the formation of sea ice affects the salinity of sea water; this then affects the movement of water in the ocean. They have a key role in reporting on changes in the global climate.

Metalsmiths need an artistic flair but also need to understand the materials they are working with. Some metals are more malleable and can be worked into different shapes more easily. Sometimes ductile metals are needed if they are to be drawn into a thin strand.

When a **brewer** makes beer or wine, they need to monitor how far the fermentation process has progressed and they do this by measuring the density of the brew. Brewers measure something called 'specific gravity', which is closely linked to density. Part of their job is to use changes in specific gravity to monitor the process. These measurements produce lots of data and this needs interpreting. Using the data well is crucial to getting a quality product for the right price.

Civil engineers turn plans into real structures – often really big ones, such as buildings, roads, bridges and tunnels. They have to understand the properties of materials and what makes structures work. They also have to understand and use ideas such as density when they deal with the soil in different places and thermal expansion in the case of large rigid structures. They are often out on site, seeing a large construction as it is being built and problem solving when difficulties arise.

Knowledge organiser

In a solid the **particles** are closely packed and arranged in a fixed pattern. In a liquid the particles are still close together but are not in a fixed arrangement. In a gas the particles are much further apart and move around freely in all directions, colliding with each other and the container.

gas liquid solid

Changes of **state** occur when a material goes from one state to another; for example, **melting** is when a solid changes to a liquid. The particles do not change apart from gaining or losing energy and the number of particles of the substance stays the same.

Metals change shape easily when a force is applied, because they have layers of **atoms** that slide over each other. This makes metals **malleable** and **ductile**.

When a substance **dissolves** in water, the solution that forms is a mixture of the solute particles and particles (**molecules**) of water. Dissolving is a physical change and can be reversed by **evaporation**.

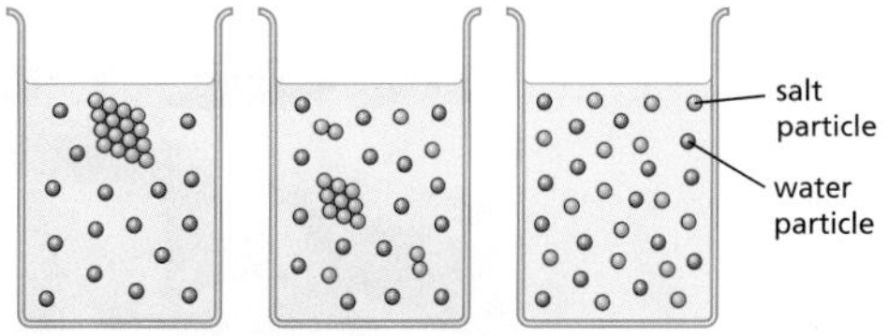

Physical changes such as melting and dissolving are reversible because no new substance is made. **Chemical changes** are irreversible because in a chemical reaction atoms are combined in new ways to produce one or more new substances. There is **conservation of mass** in both physical and chemical changes.

The term particles can refer to both atoms and molecules. This is because in some substances the atoms move or are arranged individually but in others two or more atoms have combined to form molecules.

The closeness of particles in solids, liquids and gases explains why solids are denser than liquids and gases are less dense than either.

Key vocabulary	
atom	the basic 'building block' of an element; an atom cannot be chemically broken down
boiling point	temperature at which a liquid changes state to a gas (or a gas condenses)
chemical change	an irreversible change caused when one substance combines with another to form a new substance or one substance breaks down to form two others
condensation	process that happens when a gas changes into a liquid
density	the mass per unit volume; unit kg/m^3
dissolve	the process in which particles of a solute mix with particles of a solvent to form a solution
evaporation	the process that happens when a liquid changes to a gas at the surface of the liquid
freezing	the process in which a liquid changes to a solid; it occurs when the liquid reaches its freezing point
melting point	the temperature at which a solid changes to a liquid (or a liquid substance freezes)
physical change	a reversible change, such as dissolving and changes of state
state (of matter)	solid, liquid or gas
sublimation	the process when a solid turns into a gas, without becoming a liquid first
thermal expansion	when particles in a solid or a liquid gain enough energy to occupy more space

As a result of energy being transferred by heating there may be a change in the temperature of a material, or a change in how close the particles in a material are to each other.

Changing the **internal energy** of a material will alter either its temperature or its state. Melting and boiling can take place without a change in temperature because the additional energy transferred by heating gives particles energy to move further apart and overcome forces of attraction.

When a substance is heated the internal energy of its particles increases. This means particles of the material have different amounts of internal energy when the material is a solid, liquid or gas.

As the temperature of a material is increased, its particles move faster.

Key vocabulary

Brownian motion	the movement of solid particles caused by collisions with gas particles
conservation of mass	matter cannot be destroyed or created, just transformed; this means the total mass does not change during physical or chemical reactions
internal energy	the sum of the kinetic energy and the chemical potential energy of all the particles in a material

Most solids expand when heated and contract when cooled. This is because increasing the temperature causes the particles to move faster and so take up slightly more space. Liquids also expand when heated.

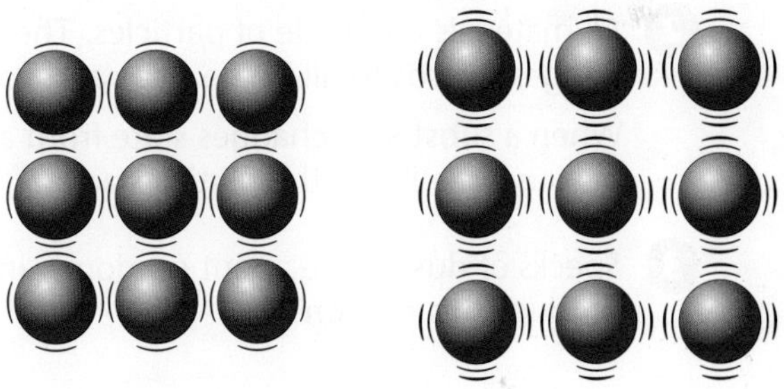

Both these effects cause an increase in the material's store of internal energy.

Most materials get less **dense** when going from a solid to a liquid, and more dense when going from a liquid to a solid.

The change from ice to water is different to other solids when they melt. Unlike other solids, water expands and becomes less dense when it is cooled close to its **freezing** point. This is why ice floats on water.

Particles of dust or smoke suspended in a gas move randomly in all directions. This is known as **Brownian motion** and is caused when the dust specks are hit by the moving particles that make up the gas.

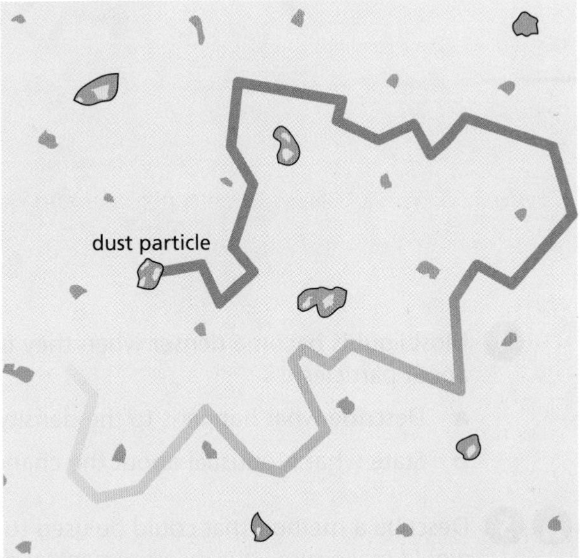

17.1 Particle model, Brownian motion and density

You are learning to:

- describe what density means and calculate the density of a material
- describe Brownian motion and explain what causes it
- use differences in the arrangements of particles in solids, liquids and gases to explain differences in density
- use the particle model to explain that the expansion of water when it freezes is unusual.

1 Select which **two** of these are not units of density.

a kg/m^3

b g/cm^3

c N/m^3

d N/m^2

2 All materials are made of particles. These are arranged differently in solids, liquids and gases. Suggest words to fill in the gaps and complete these sentences.

When a substance changes state from a gas into a liquid, its density _____**i**_____ . This is because in a liquid the particles are _____**ii**_____ than in a gas.

3 Specks of dust move about randomly in still air. What is colliding with the dust particles to produce this motion?

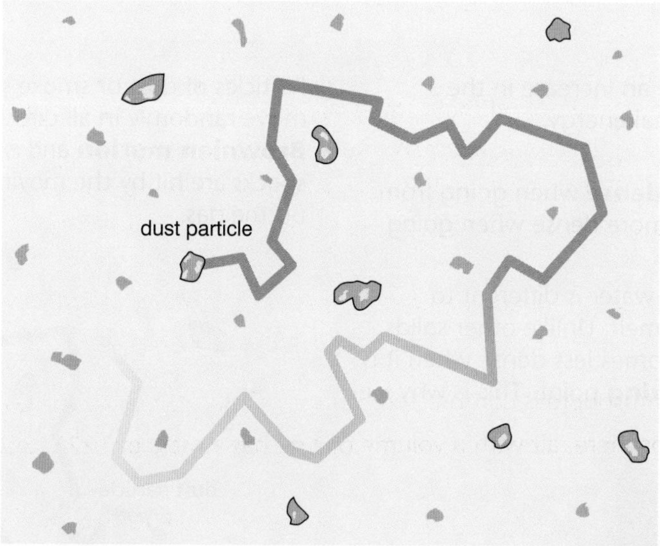

4 Most liquids become denser when they freeze, but water expands when it freezes. Using ideas about particles:

a Describe what happens to the density of water when it freezes

b State what is unusual about the change in density of water as it freezes.

5 Describe a method that could be used to determine the density of olive oil. Include how you would make sure your measurements were as accurate as possible.

Worked example

Carbon dioxide is used in fire extinguishers, as it prevents combustion. Carbon dioxide is stored in the extinguisher under pressure, as a liquid.

A fire extinguisher has a mass of 6.8 kg when fully loaded and 1.8 kg when empty.

a If the volume of liquid carbon dioxide is 5000 cm^3, calculate its density in g/cm^3.

Use the equation density = mass/volume

It is important to show each stage of your working. Write the equation down first and then show how you get the numbers you need to substitute into it. Remember to take care with the units; the mass has to be converted from kg to g.

density = mass/volume

Mass of carbon dioxide equals the mass of loaded container minus mass of empty container:

6.8 − 1.8 = 5.0 kg = 5000 g

Volume = 5000 cm^3

Density = 5000 g/5000 cm = 1 g/cm^3

b Explain why the density of the liquid carbon dioxide in the extinguisher is much greater than the density of the carbon dioxide when it is in the atmosphere as a gas.

When the carbon dioxide is a liquid the particles are much closer together so the density of the substance will be greater.

6 Ice and steam are water in different states of matter.

a An iceberg has a volume of 4500 m^3 and a mass of 4 050 000 kg. Calculate its density in kg/m^3. Use the equation density = mass/volume.

b 600 g of water is boiled and turns into steam, filling a 1 m^3 container. Calculate its density in kg/m^3.

c Explain why the two answers for density are very different, even though ice and steam are chemically identical.

7 Air from the atmosphere is compressed to form a liquid and stored in tanks for divers.

a In the atmosphere, air with a volume of 1 m^3 has a mass of 1225 g. Calculate its density in kg/m^3.

b A diving bottle has a volume of 0.01 m^3 and the air it contains has a mass of 8700 g. Calculate the density of the liquid air in kg/m^3.

c Calculate how many times greater the density of liquid air is than air at normal atmospheric pressure. Round your answer to the nearest whole number.

d Explain why the two states of the same material have different densities.

8 Brownian motion is named after Robert Brown, who noticed that grains of pollen mixed into water and observed through a microscope were moving around randomly. Explain why pollen grains move in still water, and why they change direction randomly.

17.2 Particle model and physical changes

You are learning to:
- use the particle model to explain the difference between chemical and physical changes
- use the particle model to explain conservation of mass in changes of state and dissolving
- use the particle model to explain why a solid metal can change shape when a force is applied.

1 When a piece of solid metal is heated and melts, the arrangement of particles changes. Which is the best description of the arrangement of particles in each state?

	Below melting point	Above melting point
a	fixed in place and vibrating	fixed in place and vibrating
b	in random motion and vibrating	fixed in place and vibrating
c	fixed in place and vibrating	in random motion and vibrating
d	in random motion and vibrating	in random motion and vibrating

2 Decide which of these statements are **true** and which are **false**.

a When a solid melts and becomes a liquid, its mass becomes less.

b When a material changes state, there are the same number of particles before and after the change.

c When a gas condenses to a liquid its mass increases.

d A change of state means the arrangement of particles changes but the mass of the material stays constant.

3 Evaporation, boiling, condensing and subliming are physical changes.

a Give **two** more examples of physical changes.

b State **two** differences between chemical changes and physical changes.

c Is combustion a chemical or a physical change?

4 A student measures the mass of a block of ice. They put it into an empty beaker and leave it to melt.

Which statement is **true**?

a The mass of the water after the ice has melted is greater than the mass of the ice.

b The mass of the water after the ice has melted is the same as the mass of the ice.

c The mass of the water after the ice has melted is less than the mass of the ice.

d We are not told the mass, so we do not know if it has changed.

5 A student knows that ice is less dense than water. They measure the volume of a block of ice, put it into an empty beaker and leave it to melt. Suggest, with a reason, whether the volume of water after the ice has melted will be greater than, the same as or less than the volume of the ice.

6 A student adds sugar to a cup of tea. They talk to their friends about how this affects the mass of the tea and the sugar.

Student **A** says that the mass of the sweetened tea will be less than the mass of the unsweetened tea plus the mass of the sugar. They say that when sugar dissolves the crystals disappear, and its mass is reduced.

Student **B** says that the mass of the sweetened tea will be the same as the mass of the unsweetened tea plus the mass of the sugar. They say that dissolving the sugar in the tea will not affect the mass of either the sugar or the tea.

Student **C** says that the mass of the sweetened tea will be more than the mass of the unsweetened tea plus the mass of the sugar. They say that when sugar crystals get wet, they swell up and their mass increases.

a State who has the correct explanation and explain why. Include ideas about particles.

b Respond to the other two ideas and suggest why their reasoning is incorrect.

7 A teacher is demonstrating ideas about the properties of metals. They put several pieces of thick cardboard in a pile. The teacher asks the class whether this is a good model for explaining why some metals are malleable and ductile.

Student **A** says that this is a good model as the layers of cardboard can slide over each other and this shows how layers of atoms in a metal can move past each other.

Student **B** says that it is not a good model as it is easy to push one sheet of cardboard over another whereas working with most types of metal takes a lot of effort.

Student **C** says that it is not a good model, as metals conduct both thermal energy and electricity and cardboard does not conduct either.

Discuss whether this model is a good one to explain the properties the teacher is talking about.

17.3 Energy stored in matter

You are learning to:
- describe what is meant by thermal expansion
- explain how temperature changes affect the motion and spacing of particles
- describe that heating increases the internal energy of a material
- describe that increased internal energy can cause a change in temperature, or a change of state.

1. Does the speed of particles increase, decrease or stay the same when the temperature of a material increases?

2. An ice cube melts in a dish. The internal energy of the ice increases as it melts. Choose the correct words to complete the sentences.
   - **a** The internal energy increases because the molecules of water in ice need to **gain/lose energy** to become liquid water.
   - **b** The energy is being used to move the particles **closer together/further apart**.
   - **c** This process requires energy because the molecules of water in ice are held together by **forces that attract/forces that repel**.

3. An iron bar is being heated. As it does so its length increases. Explain why.

4. State whether the following statements are **true** or **false**.
   - **a** Particles in a gas have weaker forces between them than particles in a liquid.
   - **b** Particles in a liquid have more internal energy than particles in a gas of the same material.
   - **c** Particles in a solid do not have any internal energy because they do not move.

5. A block of concrete is warming up in sunlight. Which **one** of these statements is **true**?
   - **a** The internal energy of the block is increasing because it is getting hotter.
   - **b** The internal energy of the block is not altering as the particles are held in a rigid pattern.
   - **c** The internal energy of the block is decreasing because more energy is being supplied externally.

6. The photograph shows a structure in a railway line called an expansion gap. The gap is designed to stop damage to the line on a hot day.

Describe what will happen to the gap on a hot day. Give a reason for your answer.

7 The apparatus in the diagram is designed to demonstrate thermal expansion. The horizontal metal bar is clamped tight on the left-hand side but is free to slide through the support at the right-hand side. As the bar slides it will push or pull on the lever. Any movement of the lever is displayed by the pointer moving on the scale.

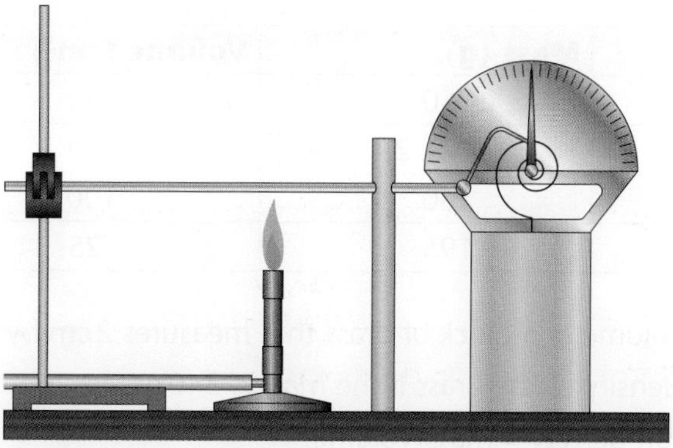

The bar is heated and the pointer moves towards the right.

a Describe what is happening to the particles in the bar as it is heated.

b State what is happening to the amount of internal energy in the bar as it is heated.

c After being heated for several minutes, the Bunsen burner is turned off. Describe what will happen in the next few minutes.

d The horizontal bar is then wrapped in a cloth that has been soaked in cold water. Explain what will happen now.

e Explain why it is important that the left-hand end of the bar is clamped tight.

8 This question is about a bimetallic strip. The strip consists of two pieces of metal, one iron and one copper, which are attached to each other along their lengths.

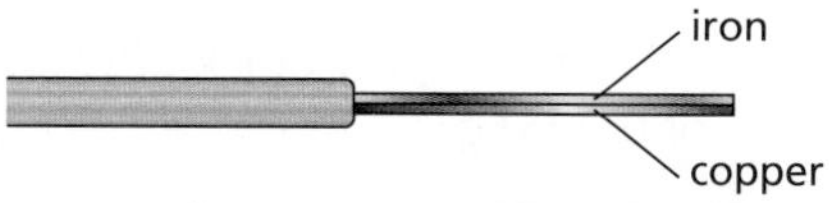

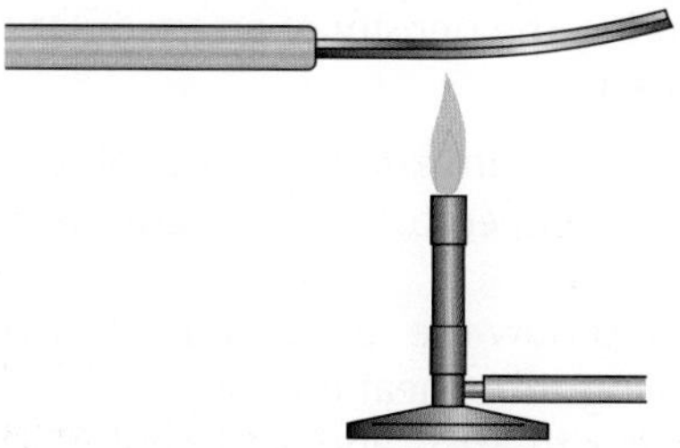

The strip is initially straight and horizontal, as shown in the upper picture.

a In the lower diagram, the strip is being heated with a flame and the strip is bending upwards. Select which of these statements is true.

i The copper is expanding and the iron is contracting.

ii Both the copper and the iron are contracting but the iron is contracting more.

iii Both the copper and the iron are expanding but the iron is expanding more.

iv Both the copper and the iron are expanding but the copper is expanding more.

b Predict what will happen to the strip if it is removed from the Bunsen flame and held under cold water from a tap. Explain your answer.

Maths and practical skills

1 Use the equation density = mass/volume to calculate the density of each of the materials in the table.

Material	Mass (g)	Volume (cm^3)	Density (g/cm^3)
a water	50	50	
b blood	21.2	20	
c granite	260	100	
d iron	195	25	

2 **a** Calculate the volume of a block of brass that measures 2 cm by 4 cm by 5 cm.

b Calculate the density of the brass if the mass is 340 g.

Use the equation density = mass/volume.

3 The table shows the densities of a number of common gases.

Gas	Density (kg/m^3)
air	1.27
carbon dioxide	1.94
hydrogen	0.09
oxygen	1.41

a Explain why, if this information is to be displayed graphically, a bar chart should be used rather than a scatter graph.

b Draw a graph to compare the densities of the gases in the table.

4 Calculate the density in g/cm^3 of a rectangular block of wood which has dimensions of 3 cm by 3 cm by 10 cm and a mass of 0.225 kg.

Use the equation density = mass/volume.

5 A group of students is measuring the density of an irregular solid. They use a displacement can to find the volume of the object.

They fill the can with water to the brim and lower the object into the can using a thread tied to the object. Describe what they need to do to determine the volume of the object.

6 A group of students is exploring how the temperature of candle wax changes as it solidifies. They place solid wax in a boiling tube, heat it gently and put a thermometer in the wax when it melts. They then heat the wax to 80 °C and let it cool. They measure and record the temperature every minute. The table shows their results.

Time (minutes)	0	1	2	3	4	5	6	7	8	9	10	11
Temperature (°C)	80	76	73	71	70	70	70	70	70	68	65	62

a Plot a graph of temperature against time.

b Draw a line of best fit.

c Use the graph to find the melting point of wax. Give a reason for your answer.

7 The graph shows the relationship between the temperature of water and its density.

a At what temperature does water have its maximum density?

b State the maximum density the water reaches, to two decimal places.

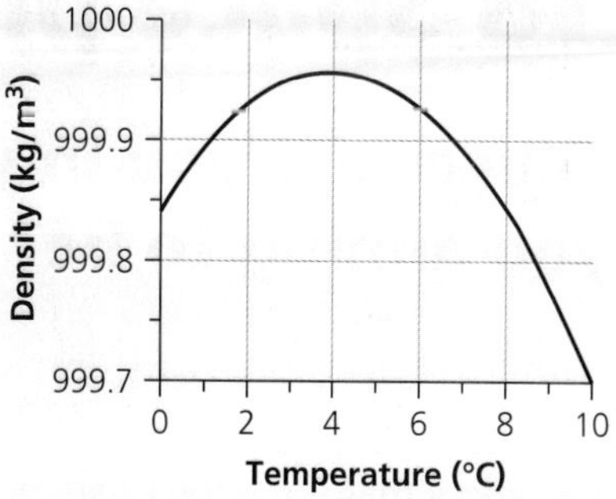

Worked example

Lead has a density of 11.3 g/cm³. Calculate the mass of a lead sample that has a volume of 150 cm³.

density = mass/volume

If you know what the values of two of the quantities in the density equation are, you can calculate the third quantity by rearranging the equation:

mass = density × volume or volume = mass/density

If the density is in g/cm³ and the volume is in cm³, the mass will be in g.

mass = density × volume

= 11.3 g/cm³ × 150 cm³

= 1695 g

8 Calculate the missing values in this table of data.

Material	Mass (g)	Volume (cm³)	Density (kg/m³)
a carbon dioxide (solid)	1600	1000	
b carbon dioxide (gas)	2000	1 000 000	
c ice	4600		920
d steam		1000	0.6

9 A group of students is trying to measure the density of a rectangular block of wood.

a State the relationship between density, mass and volume.

b State how the students could measure the mass of the wood.

c Describe a suitable method for determining the volume of the piece of wood.

d If the block of wood has a mass of 0.4 kg and a volume of 500 cm³, calculate its density in g/cm³.

10 Over 2000 years ago, a king asked Archimedes to find out whether a goldsmith was cheating him. The goldsmith had made the king a crown. The king suspected that the goldsmith had alloyed (mixed) the gold used to make the crown with a cheaper metal. This meant that the gold would not be pure. Archimedes knew what the mass of the crown was, and also the density of pure gold. He knew that he could find out whether the goldsmith had cheated if he could find the volume of the crown. He did this by immersing the crown in a container full of water and catching the overflow.

a Explain how Archimedes measured the volume of the crown.

b If the volume of the crown was 100 cm³ and the mass was 1800 g, what was the density of the crown?

c If Archimedes knew that the density of gold was 19.3 g/cm³, what did that mean about the purity of the gold in the crown?

18 Space physics road map

Where are you in your learning journey and where are you aiming to be?

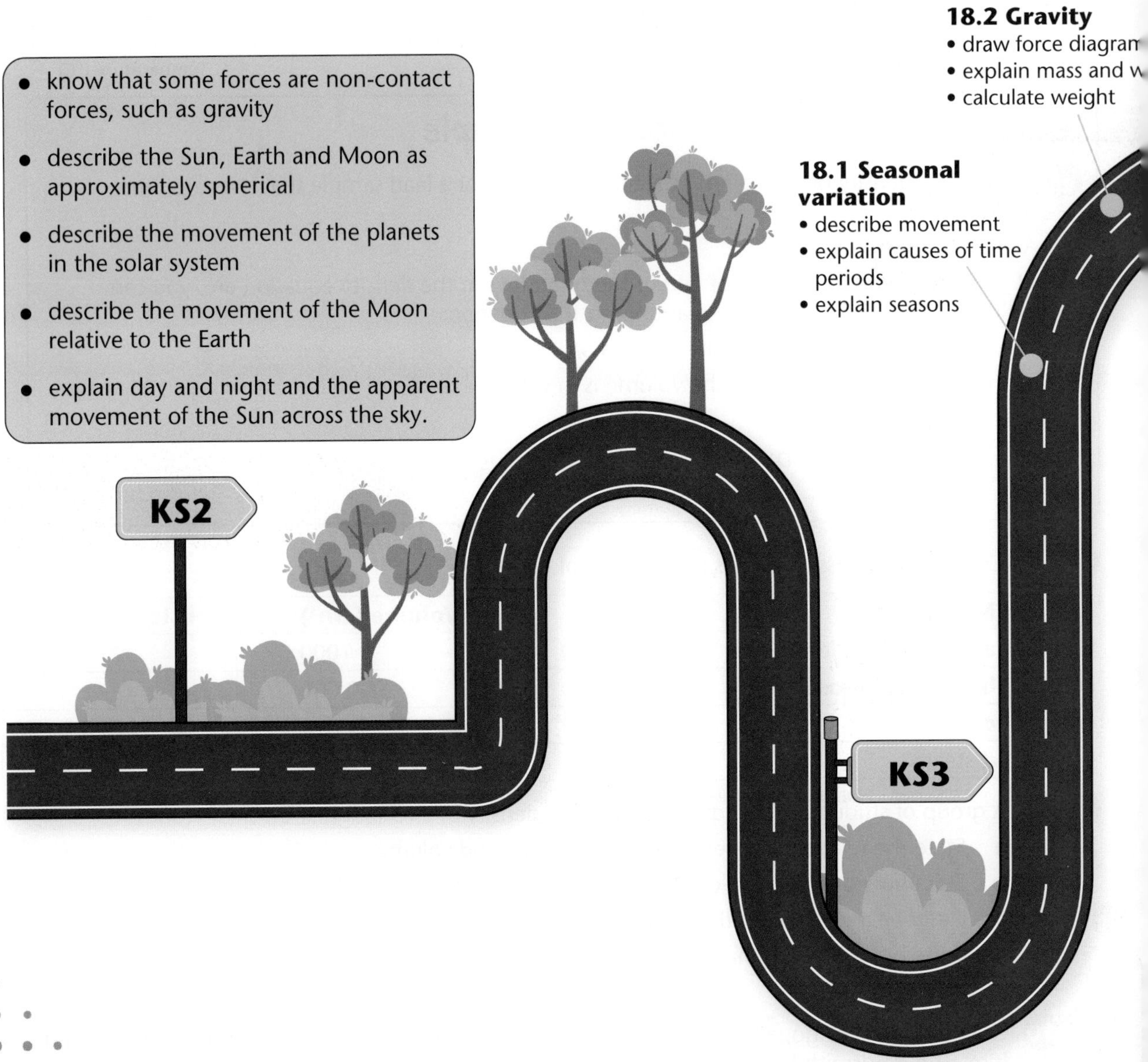

18.3 Stars and light-years
- recognise the Sun as a star
- describe relationships
- describe light-years

- gravity
- acceleration
- our solar system
- life cycle of a star
- orbital motion, natural and artificial satellites
- red shift

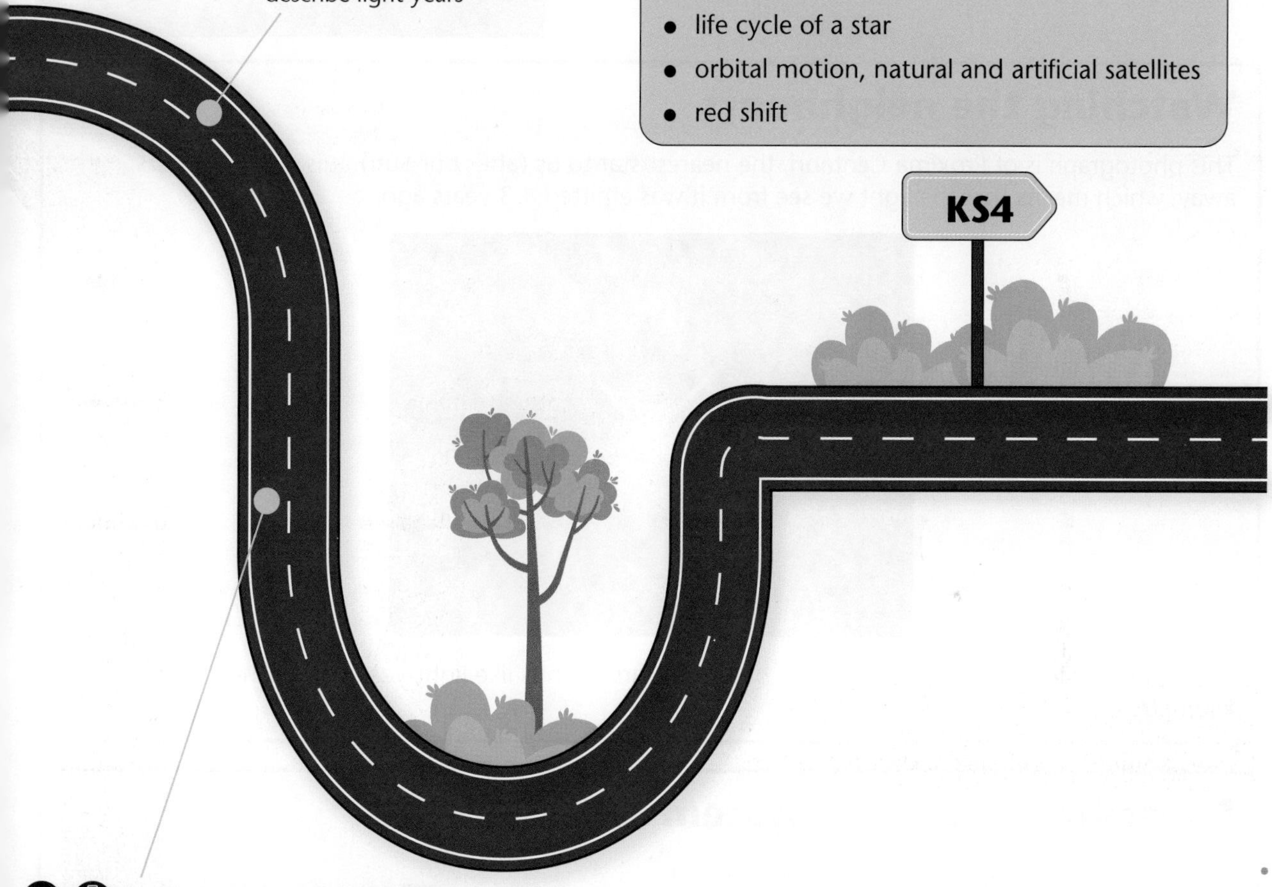

Maths and practical skills

- observing and measuring
- calculating results and converting between different units
- presenting data using tables and graphs
- interpreting observations and data
- presenting reasoned explanations
- using equations to calculate answers
- rearranging equations to change the subject

18 Space physics

Understanding gravitational forces is key to understanding the Solar System, our Sun and other stars. Our galaxy is one of many, but both the size of galaxies and the distances between them are enormous.

The photograph shows the Eagle Nebula, in which material collapses due to gravity to form new stars.

Watching the neighbours

This photograph is of Proxima Centauri, the nearest star to us (after our Sun). It is 4.3 light-years away, which means that the light we see from it was emitted 4.3 years ago.

Why do you think we measure distances between stars in units like light-years rather than, say, kilometres?

Modelling the Solar System

Look at this artist's impression of the Solar System.

- How could we use a diagram like this to explain:
  - what causes day and night on planets?
  - what causes the length of a year on planets?
- Suggest:
  - ways in which this picture is helpful in understanding the Solar System
  - how the picture is inaccurate and could lead to misunderstandings about the Solar System.

Using your science skills

Could you be an aerospace engineer?

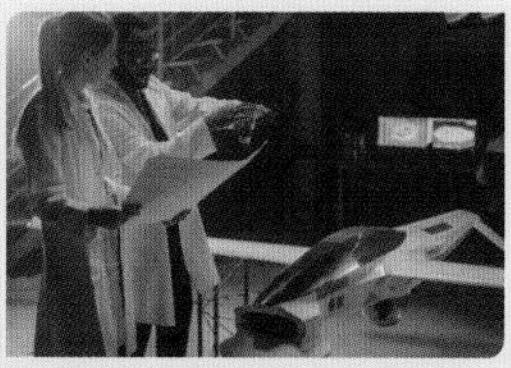

As an aerospace engineer you might be asked to design aeroplanes, helicopters, satellites, planetary rovers, missiles or rockets. Your job is to design, build and maintain the aircraft and the parts and instruments that go inside them. It is your responsibility to make them safe and fuel efficient. Weight is a crucial factor in aircraft design; it needs to be kept to a minimum and be distributed so that the craft is stable. The job also includes planning, testing and maintenance; aircraft have to be as safe and reliable at the end of their lives as at the start.

There is a lot of teamwork in this industry; you might work with specialists in materials, electronics, aerodynamics and also production and maintenance. You need to be good at maths and science, and be a good problem solver!

Data scientists deal with numbers and data. Everything in aerospace and space exploration, from experiments using models to flight tests with prototypes and missions to Mars, generates data, which needs to be managed and analysed. Data scientists might be using software to process gigabytes of data but then working out the best way of presenting this data to find patterns and explain these to other people.

Electronics technicians work on objects that fly, which all use electronics in their monitoring and control systems; these need installing and maintaining. Some of the systems, such as landing gear, communications systems and cockpit displays, are used under extreme conditions, and they are often crucial to the success of the mission. Being good at problem solving and being able to think clearly under pressure are important skills.

Software engineers produce the code for computerised systems such as instrumentation systems on board a spacecraft. Their job is to design the software and write code. They might be writing the program or getting someone else's program to work properly. Logical thinking and a systematic approach are crucial, as is attention to detail. They have to consider how different systems work and communicate with each other, and work in a team to meet the goals of the project.

Earth observation engineers use satellite technology to look down at the Earth and get a clear view of how the surface and the atmosphere are changing over time. An application of this is weather recording and forecasting. They need to be able to analyse data and images, interpret patterns and make predictions, and turn the information into something useful.

Astronomers work largely in a university, but often travel to observatories, and use images and data as well as physics knowledge in their research. They may be refining ideas about how the Universe was formed and how it is developing, or they may be studying exoplanets or supernovas. They need to be good with numbers, good at developing explanations and also good at communicating ideas to other people.

Knowledge organiser

The Earth rotates on its axis and makes a full rotation every 24 hours. This causes day and night.

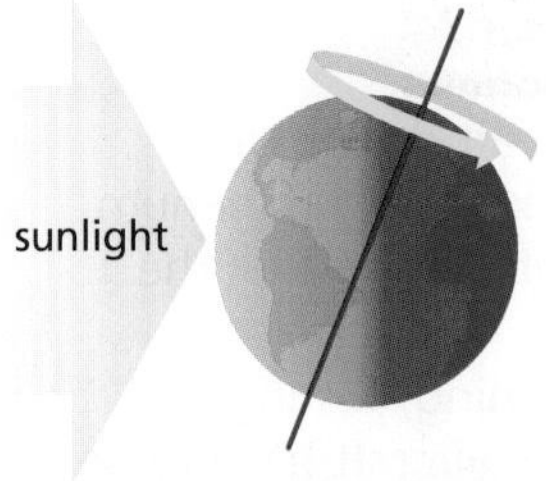

The Moon orbits the Earth; a complete orbit takes around 28 days.

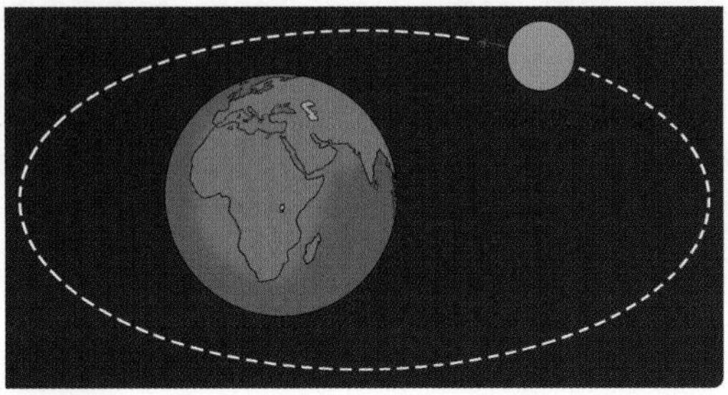

The Earth's **axis of rotation** is tilted relative to its **orbit** around the Sun. This causes seasonal variation in day length and temperature.

The **seasons** in the southern hemisphere are different from the seasons in the northern hemisphere, because when the northern hemisphere is tilted towards the Sun the southern hemisphere is tilted away from the Sun. When it is summer in a hemisphere the Sun's rays reach the land more directly, and in winter the rays are more spread out.

weight (N) = mass (kg) × gravitational field strength (N/kg)

This means that the **weight** of an object in a gravitational field is directly proportional to its mass

The Earth has a gravitational **field** that extends far out into space. Any **mass** in this field experiences a (non-contact) **gravitational force**. At the Earth's surface the **gravitational field strength** is 10 N/kg, which means there is a force of 10 newtons on every kilogram. Other planets have stronger or weaker gravitational fields.

The Earth is held in orbit around the Sun due to the gravitational attraction each has on the other. The Moon is held in orbit around the Earth due to the gravitational attraction each has on the other.

Key vocabulary

axis of rotation	the imaginary line around which something rotates; for Earth, this is the line joining its north and south poles
field	an area where an object feels a force, e.g. the region around a mass where another object feels a gravitational force
mass	the amount of matter (stuff) in an object, measured in kilograms (kg)
orbit	the path taken by a satellite, planet or star moving around a larger body
season	a division of the year, marked by changes in weather and hours of daylight: summer, autumn, winter and spring
weight	the force of gravity acting on an object, measured in newtons (N)

The Earth orbits the Sun, taking just over 365 days for one orbit. This determines the length of a year on Earth. Other planets in the Solar System also orbit the Sun.

Our Sun is a **star**, one of many in the Universe.

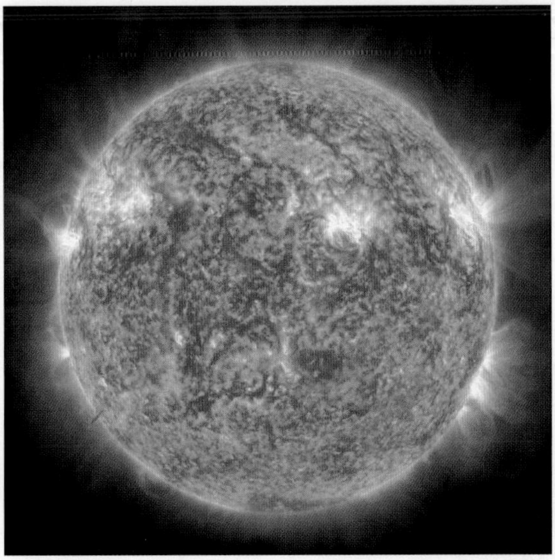

Key vocabulary	
galaxy	a group of billions of stars held together by gravity
light-year (ly)	the distance travelled by light in one year
Milky Way	the galaxy containing our Solar System
star	a body in space that emits large amounts of energy; for many stars some of this can be seen as light

There are millions of stars in our **galaxy**, which is called the Milky Way. There are billions of other galaxies in the Universe.

The **light-year** is used as a unit of astronomical distance. It is the distance that light travels in one year. It is used because the distances being measured are huge and a large unit is needed.

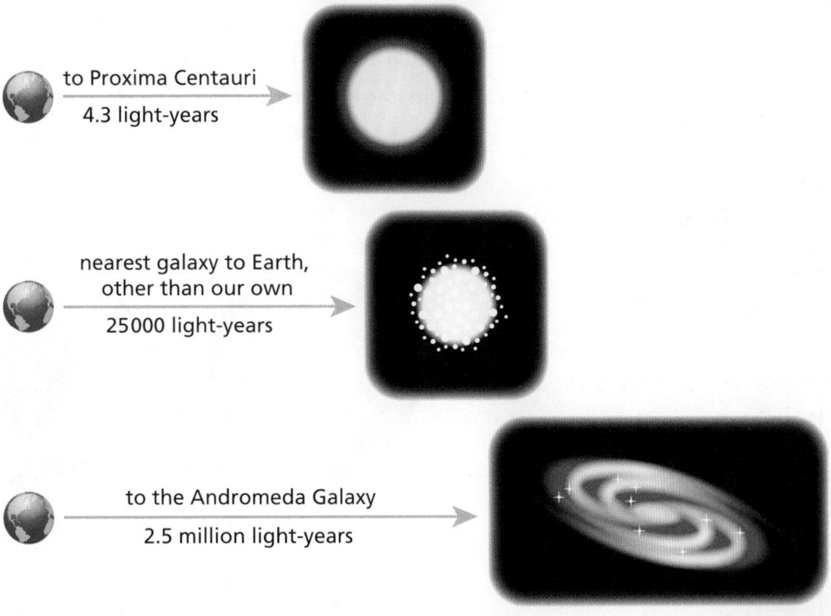

18.1 Seasonal variation

You are learning to:
- describe the movement of the Earth on its axis and relative to the Sun
- explain what causes day length, year length and seasonal variation, including temperature
- explain why seasons north of the equator are the opposite of seasons south of the equator.

1. List the four seasons of the year, in order, starting with spring.
2. Explain why the Sun appears to move across the sky during the day.
3. Describe how a winter's day differs from a summer's day in the UK in terms of:
   a the number of hours of sunlight
   b the average temperature
   c the height of the Sun in the sky at midday.
4. Select which **one** of these statements is true.
   a When days are getting longer in the northern hemisphere, they are getting shorter in the southern hemisphere.
   b When days are getting longer in the northern hemisphere, they are also getting longer in the southern hemisphere.
   c There is no connection between day length in the northern hemisphere and in the southern hemisphere.
   d When days are longest at the equator, both the North Pole and the South Pole will have 24 hours of darkness.

Worked example

Describe how the Sun, Earth and Moon move in relation to each other. Use a diagram to assist in your description.

When you are asked to use a diagram, make sure you label it with the same terms that you use in your answer. A label and its line must clearly point to part of the diagram.

The Earth is rotating upon its axis and it is orbiting the Sun. The Moon is orbiting around the Earth.

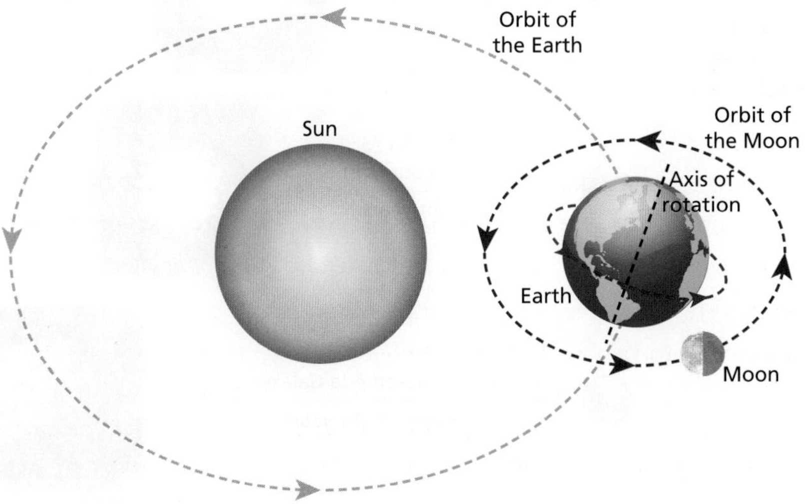

5 The picture shows the planet Mars.

Explain what determines the length of a day on Mars.

Include a labelled diagram, with arrows to show any movement that is relevant to your explanation.

6 Draw and label a diagram to explain what determines the length of year for a planet orbiting a star.

Include arrows to show any movement that is relevant to your explanation.

7 **a** Explain why we have seasons.

b At some times of the year, countries north of the equator will have more than 12 hours of sunlight per day. Describe at what points in the Earth's orbit around the Sun this happens.

c The day of the year with the fewest hours of daylight for the southern hemisphere is 21 June. This is also the day on which the northern hemisphere has the greatest number of hours of daylight. Explain why this is.

8 The Earth's axis is tilted at 23° to the Sun. If it was tilted by a smaller angle, suggest how this would affect the seasons and explain why.

9 The graph shows how the number of hours of daylight in a day varies throughout the year for two different towns in the UK.

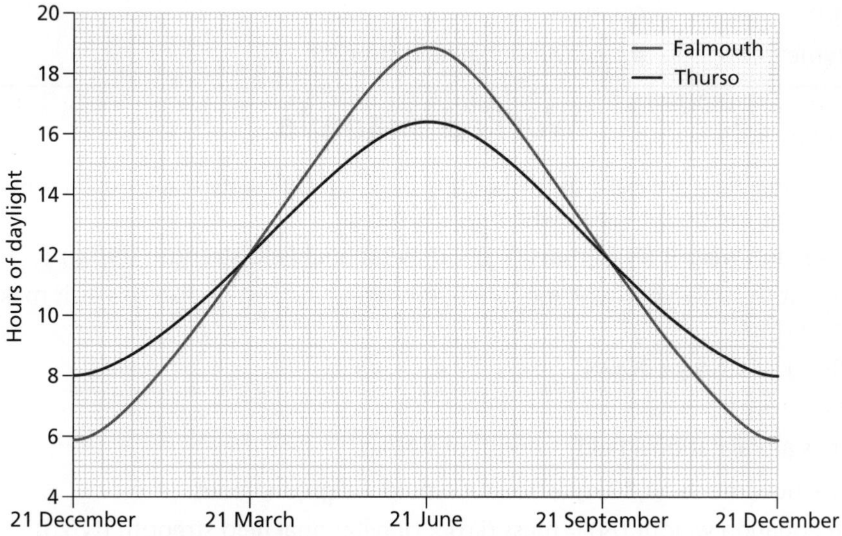

a How many hours of daylight are there in Thurso on 21 June?

b How many hours of daylight are there in Falmouth on 21 December?

c In which parts of the year does Thurso have fewer hours of daylight than Falmouth?

d In which parts of the year does Thurso have more hours of daylight than Falmouth?

e On which dates is the day length in the two towns the same?

f Thurso is much further north than Falmouth. Explain how this causes the difference in the number of hours of daylight each town gets at different times of the year.

g Both of these towns are in the northern hemisphere. What would the graph for a town in the southern hemisphere look like? Give a reason for your answer.

18.2 Gravity

You are learning to:
- draw force diagrams for weight on different planets and for gravitational forces between the Earth and the Sun or the Moon
- explain the difference between mass and weight
- calculate weight from mass and gravitational field strength.

1 Identify which of these are units of force and which are units of mass.

Unit	Unit of force?	Unit of mass?
newton, N		
gram, g		
kilonewton, kN		
kilogram, kg		

2 Choose the correct words to complete the sentences.

a Gravity is a **contact/non-contact** force.

b When gravity acts on an object it **always attracts/always repels** it.

c Gravity acting on an object causes that object to have **mass/weight**.

3 Select from the list the **two** factors that affect the weight of an object.

a shape

b volume

c mass

d gravitational field strength

Worked example

The gravitational field strength of the Earth is 10 N/kg. Calculate how much an 80 kg astronaut would weigh on Earth, where g = 10 N/kg.

Use the equation weight (N) = mass (kg) × gravitational field strength (N/kg)

It is important to show your working when answering a question like this as it makes it easier to spot any errors.

weight = 80 kg × 10 N/kg = 800 N

4 Venus has a gravitational field strength of 9 N/kg.

Calculate how much an 80 kg astronaut would weigh on Venus.

Use the equation weight (N) = mass (kg) × gravitational field strength (N/kg)

5 Which **one** of these statements is true about your weight and mass on a planet where the gravitational field strength is half that of Earth?

a Weight is the same, mass is half.

b Weight and mass are both the same.

c Weight and mass are both half.

d Weight is half, mass is the same.

6 The gravitational field strength on Mars is 3.7 N/kg, whereas on Earth it is 10 N/kg. Calculate the weight of a 2 kg rock on the surface of each of these planets.

7 The Lunar Roving Vehicle used on the Apollo 15 mission had a mass of 210 kg.

The Earth's gravitational field strength is 10 N/kg and the Moon's gravitational field strength is 1.7 N/kg. Calculate the weight of the Lunar Roving Vehicle:

a on the Earth **b** on the Moon.

8 The Earth is in the Sun's gravitational field. Explain what this means.

9 A spacecraft is exactly halfway between the Earth and the Moon. Select which **one** of the following statements is true.

a Neither the Earth nor the Moon will exert a gravitational attraction on the spacecraft.

b The Earth will exert a gravitational attraction on the spacecraft but the Moon will not.

c Both the Earth and the Moon will exert a gravitational attraction on it; the two forces will be opposite in direction.

d Both the Earth and the Moon will exert a gravitational attraction on it, in the same direction.

10 The gravitational field strength on Mars is 3.7 N/kg, whereas on Earth it is 10 N/kg. Describe how the weight of an astronaut would change if they travelled from the Earth, through space, to Mars.

11 A group of students is using an electronic balance. It is calibrated in grams. They have just been learning about mass and weight.

Student **A** says that the balance should not be calibrated in grams because it is actually measuring force. Putting an object on top means its weight pushes down and the balance should therefore be calibrated in newtons.

Student **B** says that the balance is correct as it is. If you put a 100 g mass on it, the reading is 100 g.

Student **C** says that it works because it is only ever going to be used where there is the same relationship between mass and weight. It measures weight but can show this as mass.

Comment on each of these ideas and explain whether the balance should be calibrated in grams.

18.3 Stars and light-years

You are learning to:
- recognise that our Sun is a star
- describe the relationship between stars, galaxies and the Universe
- describe how the light-year is used to measure astronomical distances.

1 Suggest words to complete the missing gaps in these sentences.

The Sun is a star and is at the ____**i**____ of our Solar ____**ii**____ .

It emits ____**iii**____, which is radiated outwards and travels throughout the ____**iv**____ System and beyond.

It is a source of light and thermal ____**v**____ .

2 Decide which of these statements are **true** and which are **false**.

a The Sun is at the centre of the Solar System.

b The Sun is at the centre of the Milky Way.

c Our Solar System is in the Milky Way.

d The Milky Way is another name for the Universe.

e Our Sun is the only star in our Solar System.

f Our Sun is the only star in the Milky Way.

3 This is a picture of Saturn's rings taken with a telescope on Earth.

Saturn can be seen from Earth because light travels from Saturn to Earth. Which **one** of these statements is true?

a Saturn produces its own light.

b Saturn reflects light from the Sun.

c Saturn reflects light from the Earth back to us.

d Saturn reflects light from many stars.

4 In space physics, the light-year is used as a unit of measurement. Which of these is the correct definition of one light-year?

a The amount of light that lands on a planet in a year.

b The distance that light will travel through space in a year.

c The time for which a source of light will last.

5 This is a picture of the Milky Way, which is a galaxy.

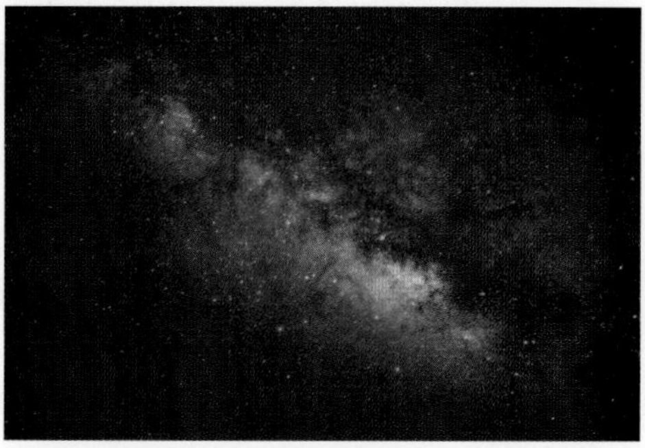

Which of these is the best description of a galaxy?

a A large number of stars.

b A large group of stars held together by gravity.

c All the stars in existence, apart from our own Sun.

d The remains of dead and dying stars.

6 The table shows some distances in space, measured in light-years. Match each description of the distances listed to the correct value.

Description of distance	Distance in light-years (ly)
a diameter of the Milky Way	**i** 323
b diameter of the Solar System	**ii** 2 520 000
c distance from Earth to Polaris (the Pole Star)	**iii** 100 000
d distance from the Earth to the Andromeda Galaxy	**iv** 1

7 The nearest star to the Earth (apart from the Sun) is called Proxima Centauri. It is 4.3 light-years away from us. Decide which of the following statements are **true** and which are **false**.

a It takes 4.3 years for light to travel from Proxima Centauri to us.

b When we look at Proxima Centauri, we are seeing it as it was 4.3 years ago.

c If we were to send a light beam towards Proxima Centauri, it would take 4.3 years to get there.

d If a spaceship could travel at the speed of light, it would take 4.3 years to travel from Earth to Proxima Centauri, but a light beam would get there instantly.

8 A group of students is looking at stars in the night sky. They know that all of the stars they see are many light-years away.

Student **A** says that, when we look at those stars, we are seeing light that set off many years ago and that if we received an alien signal from a star, the aliens may not be there anymore.

Student **B** says that they know the stars are a huge distance away but that light travels so quickly the light and also any alien signal will only have taken a few minutes to arrive.

Explain who you think is right.

9 Our Sun is approximately 8 light-minutes away, and Sirius, the brightest star in the night sky, is approximately 8 light-years away.

a Explain what is meant by a light-minute as a unit of distance.

b Explain the difference between light-minutes and light-years.

c Calculate how many times further away Sirius is from us than our Sun.

Maths and practical skills

1 Match these units to the quantities they measure.

Unit	Quantity
a light-year, ly	**i** mass
b newton, N	**ii** speed
c kilogram, kg	**iii** distance
d kilometres per second, km/s	**iv** force

2 Use the equation weight (N) = mass (kg) × gravitational field strength (N/kg) to calculate the weight of a 120 kg space suit in each of these locations:

a on Earth, where $g = 10$ N/kg

b on the Moon, where $g = 1.7$ N/kg

Worked example

A class is making a scale model of the Solar System. They use a beach ball to represent the Sun and a dried pea for the Earth. The teacher says that, to be to scale, the Earth will have to be 32 m from the Sun. The teacher then gives a student a rice grain, and tells the student that this represents Mars and it has to be a distance from the Sun 50% greater than that of the Earth. Calculate how far from the beach ball the student should place the rice.

The radius of the Mars orbit is 50% greater than the radius of the Earth orbit. The Earth orbit is 32 m so the Mars orbit will be 150% of that. The 32 m needs to be multiplied by 1.5.

$32 \times 1.5 = 48$ m

3 The class in the worked example above then continues with its model. Calculate how far from the model Sun each of these planets should be:

a Saturn, which orbits at 10 times the distance of the Earth from the Sun

b Uranus, which orbits at 20 times the distance of the Earth from the Sun

c Neptune, which orbits at 30 times the distance of the Earth from the Sun.

4 The Apollo Moon missions brought back to Earth a total of 380 kg of geological samples. On Earth, $g = 10$ N/kg and on the Moon, $g = 1.7$ N/kg.

a Calculate the weight of the samples when they were on the Moon.

b Calculate the weight of the samples when brought to the Earth.

c Calculate, to the nearest whole number, how many times heavier the samples are on Earth than they were on the Moon.

5 A class is looking at the Solar System and which planets have moons. A student has asked the teacher if it is true that the more mass a planet has, the more moons it has. The teacher has asked them to use data to evaluate the evidence for this statement. In the table below, the mass of each planet is compared to that of the Earth.

Planet	Mercury	Venus	Earth	Mars	Jupiter	Saturn	Uranus	Neptune
Mass compared to Earth	0.05	0.82	1	0.11	318	95	15	17
Number of moons	0	0	1	2	79	82	27	14

a Which planet has the least mass?

b How many moons does this planet have?

c Which planet has the greatest mass?

d How many moons does this planet have?

e Plot a scatter graph of mass (compared to Earth) against the number of moons for the four outer planets.

f Use your graph to suggest whether it is true that the more massive planets have more moons.

6 Some planets in the Solar System, such as Venus and Mars, have been known about for hundreds of years because they are bright enough to be seen with the naked eye in the night sky. Neptune is too dim to see without a telescope but was discovered in 1846 after astronomers studied anomalies in the observed position of Uranus. Compared to its predicted speed, Uranus seemed to speed up a bit in one part of its orbit and then slow down a bit.

The diagram shows the orbits of Uranus and Neptune around the Sun at two different times (marked as **a** and **b**) a few years apart.

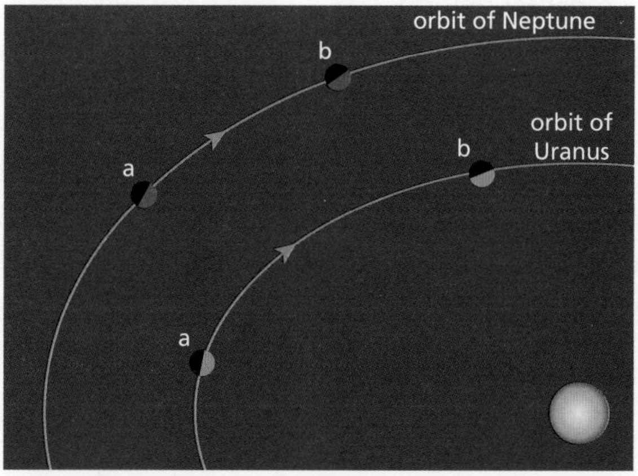

a Use your knowledge of gravitational forces to suggest why Uranus would speed up from its normal speed when Neptune is in position **a**.

b Use your knowledge of gravitational forces to suggest why Uranus would slow down from its normal speed when Neptune is in position **b**.

c Suggest how astronomers used the anomalies in Uranus's orbit to predict where Neptune might be found in the night sky.

Unit 1 Cells and organisation

1.1 Organisation of multicellular organisms

1 cells

2 a tissue

3 an organ

4 heart – circulatory system; brain – nervous system; stomach – digestive system; lungs – breathing (respiratory) system

5 heart – pumps blood around the body; brain – controls many functions of the body; kidneys – filter waste from blood; stomach – digests some foods; lungs – transfer gases between the blood and air

6 **a** made of one cell

b Any **two** of: amoebae, paramecia, yeasts, protozoa, algae

7 **a** heart muscle cell, **b** muscle tissue, **c** heart, **d** circulatory system, **e** human

8 They are able to reproduce rapidly, or other sensible suggestion.

9 Multicellular organisms have many different cells, adapted to different functions. Therefore, similar cells can work together to form tissues, tissues can work together to form organs and different organs can work together to form organ systems. This means that one organism can perform many different functions (for example, breathing, excreting, digesting).

10 Unicellular organisms grouped together (into colonies). Some of these unicellular organisms adapted in different ways, making them better suited to different functions. The cells began to vary more and formed groups of similar cells; these are what we call tissues. Tissues then worked together to form organs.

11 There are 120 minutes in 2 hours.

1 to 2 bacteria after 20 minutes

2 to 4 bacteria after 40 minutes (20 + 20)

4 to 8 bacteria after 60 minutes (20 + 20 + 20)

8 to 16 bacteria after 80 minutes (20 + 20 + 20 + 20)

16 to 32 bacteria after 100 minutes (20 + 20 + 20 + 20 + 20)

32 to 64 bacteria after 120 minutes (20 + 20 + 20 + 20 + 20 + 20)

Therefore, after 2 hours (120 minutes), there are 64 bacteria.

1.2 Comparing plant and animal cells

1 light microscope (allow microscope but do not allow electron microscope)

2 cell membrane, nucleus, cytoplasm

3 **a** cell membrane, **b** nucleus, **c** cytoplasm

4 **a** cell wall, **b** nucleus, **c** cytoplasm, **d** chloroplast, **e** cell membrane

5 **a** nucleus – contains the genetic material/controls the reactions inside the cell

b cell membrane – controls what passes in and out of the cell (examples, oxygen, water, glucose nutrients in, carbon dioxide out)

c chloroplast – contains chlorophyll, absorbs energy from the sun for photosynthesis

6 All chemical reactions take place in the cytoplasm. These reactions keep the cell alive and so all cells need to carry out these reactions and so need cytoplasm.

7 **a** **i** cytoplasm, **ii** cell membrane, **iii** nucleus

b mitochondria (or ribosomes, Golgi)

8 Red blood cells do not contain a nucleus.

9 Both Dev and Kristi are correct about what supports the plant cell: both the vacuole and the cell wall provide support and help to keep the shape of the plant cell. However, Kristi's idea about the cell wall controlling what moves in and out of the cell is incorrect because that is the function of the cell membrane (in both plant and animal cells).

10 **a** 2 million/microlitre

b 4 months

1.3 Studying cells

1 They magnify an object/make an image bigger than the object.

2 **c**

3 **a** stage, **b** eyepiece lens, **c** focusing wheel, **d** objective lens

4 Any **one** of: greater magnification/can see smaller objects or cells/can see smaller cell structures/therefore more detail.

5 The stain shows/enhances some of the features of the cell.

6 **a** provides a source of light to illuminate the sample

b to place the sample/slide on; to hold the sample for viewing

7 **a** ×40, **b** ×100, **c** ×400

8 **a** Repeat the experiment again or get someone else to carry out the same investigation; if the experiment is reliable, the same result will be seen.

b Carry out the same experiment but focus on temperatures between 40 °C and 50 °C/a smaller range of temperatures.

9 a Any **three** of: draw in pencil, not pen; do not include any air bubbles in the drawing; add a title (onion cells); include magnification; draw more cells; don't draw the circle.

b Any **three** of: cell wall, nucleus, cytoplasm, cell membrane.

10 a 1000 times smaller

b 0.01 mm

c i 1 μm

ii 0.001 mm

1.4 Unicellular organisms

1 they are made of only one cell

2 bacterium and yeast

3 prokaryotic

4 prokaryotes – genetic material floats in the cytoplasm; eukaryotes – stored within a nucleus

5 The organism in diagram **a** probably existed first because it does not have a nucleus, chloroplast or mitochondria.

6 The bacterium is adapted to live in conditions very unlike the conditions in the human body.

7 This organism feeds by absorbing nutrients rather than making its own food (as it has no chloroplasts for photosynthesis). Cilia beat to move the organism; this helps it to move towards nutrients.

8 a chloroplasts

b flagellum

9 a Some unicellular organisms are simple: prokaryotes are generally simple compared to eukaryotes and have no fixed nucleus and have few, or no, organelles. However, other unicellular organisms, such as protozoa, Euglena and yeasts, are eukaryotes and are complex: their single cell has similar parts to animal or plant cells. For example, Euglena contains chloroplasts, so can carry out photosynthesis, and contains mitochondria, so can carry out respiration. These eukaryotes are simple in that they are made of only one cell but are complex within, like animal and plant cells.

b Ben may think unicellular organisms are simple because they are made of only one cell.

10 Both have mitochondria so both carry out respiration. Both move but in different ways: **a** by cilia and **b** by its flagellum. However, **b** has chloroplasts, so makes its own food by photosynthesis; **a** has no chloroplasts and has a food store, so must absorb food from its surroundings.

1.5 Specialised cells

1 adapted

2 There are many different functions (jobs) within each living thing that keeps them alive; we need different specialised cells to perform different functions.

3 b

4

Name of cell	Image
red blood cell	**d**
nerve cell	**a**
muscle cell	**c**
leaf cell	**b**

5 a Plant cell because it has a cell wall, chloroplasts and vacuole.

b Plant cell because it has a cell wall and vacuole.

6

Name of cell	Function of cell	One way the cell is adapted to its function
red blood cell	carries oxygen to body cells	has no nucleus so there is more space to carry oxygen/ convex shape to increase surface area - more oxygen can be absorbed
nerve cell	carries/ transmits impulses	long extensions (of cytoplasm) to reach all parts of the body
muscle cell	creates movement	lots of mitochondria for energy for movement; protein fibres that move across each other for expansion/ contraction
leaf cell	carries out photo-synthesis	contains chloroplasts to absorb light energy for photosynthesis

7 **a** tail – allows movement to egg

b large head – carries genetic material in a large nucleus

c lots of mitochondria – for energy (from respiration) to move

8 **a** Red blood cells carry oxygen to the cells of the body. This oxygen is used in respiration to generate energy. In anaemia, there are fewer cells so less oxygen is carried to the cells, so less energy is transferred by respiration, leading to tiredness.

b The patient is likely to feel tired. Although the patient has a lot of red blood cells, the sickle cell shape means that they can't enter blood vessels, reducing blood flow. This means less oxygen is carried to body cells, so less energy is transferred by respiration, leading to tiredness. (The sickle cell shape also has a smaller surface than the regular red blood cells and so the cells carry less oxygen.)

9 **a** Similarities: both have cell membrane, cytoplasm, nucleus and mitochondria.

Differences: shape of cell and number of mitochondria, **i** has more per cell than **ii**.

b Cell membrane controls what moves in and out of the cell; cytoplasm allows reactions to take place in the cell; nucleus carries the genetic material of the cell, controls processes; and mitochondria allow respiration to take place, producing energy.

c **i** is heart muscle (**ii** is smooth muscle), shown by having more mitochondria as it needs to release more energy by respiration than other muscles.

10 **a** The elongated cytoplasm increases the surface area through which water can be absorbed; large vacuole for storage of water (and sugars); no chloroplasts as does not carry out photosynthesis.

b **i** A mean is calculated as each hair may vary, so this allows for fluctuations in measurements.

ii 1:1, 0.7:1, 0.5:1

iii plant 1

1.6 Movement in and out of cells: diffusion

1 particles, higher, lower

2 liquids and gases

3 Lydia

4 **a**

5 carbon dioxide – out, nutrients – in, urea – out, oxygen – in

6 **a** so that movement/diffusion of the liquid can be seen

b accuracy

7 **a** Tom, Monty, Anya, Ali

b The air freshener particles are moving as they have energy. As they move, they bump into each other and spread out. Straight from the can the particles are high in concentration; in the rest of the air in the room, the particles are in lower concentration. The air freshener particles move from higher to lower concentration and eventually reach the air near Ali.

c Similar – the oxygen molecules are spreading out as are the air freshener particles; particles move from higher concentration to lower concentration.

Different – the air freshener is not travelling across a (cell) membrane, whereas the oxygen does.

8 **a**

Length, breadth, height of cube (cm)	Surface area (cm^2)	Volume (cm^3)	Surface area-to-volume ratio
1, 1, 1	6	1	6
2, 2, 2	24	8	3
3, 3, 3	54	27	2

b The largest cube (3 × 3 × 3 cm) because although it has the largest surface area, it also has the largest volume and so has more cell to provide with oxygen and nutrients. Per unit, the smallest cube has the largest surface area to volume ratio.

9 **a** Organisms that take in nutrients do so by diffusion through their cell membrane. Organisms that make their food by photosynthesis rely on diffusion for the carbon dioxide to enter through the cell membrane. Unicellular organisms also rely on diffusion to take in oxygen for respiration and to remove waste products (e.g. carbon dioxide and urea).

b The bigger a unicellular organism (or cell), the smaller the surface area-to-volume ratio. A smaller surface area-to-volume ratio means that it is less likely that the rate at which diffusion happens will be high enough to support the entire cell with the substances it needs.

Small, unicellular organisms are more efficient at being able to get enough substances in and out to support the whole cell.

Multicellular organisms rely on transport systems, such as the circulatory system, to move substances and so are not solely reliant on diffusion.

Unit 1 maths and practical skills

1 c

2 μm, mm, m, km

3 **a** eyepiece lens, **b** objective lens, **c** stage, **d** light source

4 **a** Repeat using more cells of each type (to ensure the estimates are similar).

b Palisade cells are in the top layer of a leaf and so exposed to more sunlight and can carry out more photosynthesis than the other cell types.

5 **a** So that the cells and organelles can be seen.

b To stop the liquid on the slide getting onto the objective lens.

6 **a**

m	mm	μm
0.1	100	**100 000**
2.6	**2600**	2 600 000
24.0	24 000	24 000 000

b **i** 1 000 000 nm

ii 1 000 000 000 nm

7 **a** **i** temperature

ii distance travelled

b Does concentration affect diffusion?

8 Sample of cheek cells on a microscope slide, stained with dye, observe and record observations.

Add salt to the cells and observe under microscope/observe over time, record observations.

Produce fresh slide of cell and repeat with vinegar.

9 **a** ×100

b 0.2 mm

c 200 μm

10 **a** So that he could see the substance diffusing.

b **i** 4.0

ii 2.0

c 1.5 g/l

d As concentration increases, the rate of diffusion increases/time taken to travel through the agar decreases.

Unit 2 Reproduction

2.1 Plant reproduction

1 **A** filament; **B** anther; **C** stigma; **D** style; **E** ovary; **F** ovule

2 **a** pollination; **b** fertilisation; **c** dispersal

3 **a** pollen; **b** ovary

4 **a** anther; **b** stigma; **c** ovary; **d** petal; **e** filament

5 Some insects, such as bees, use the nectar as a food source. They come to collect the nectar and pollen sticks to them. When collecting nectar from another plant, they transfer the pollen.

6 Pollen travels from the stigma down the style by growing a pollen tube. This travels to the ovule where the pollen meets the egg cell. This is fertilisation.

7 So that it cannot fertilise itself (this supports variation).

8 Pollination is the process of transferring pollen from the anther of one flowering plant to the stigma of another flowering plant. Fertilisation is the joining of the nucleus of the pollen cell with the nucleus of the egg cell of another flowering plant. Pollination (Antonia) is one stage in plant reproduction and both pollination and fertilisation (Akeeb) are needed to produce new plants. Therefore, it is difficult to say one is more important than the other.

9 **i** **a** is insect-pollinated plant; **b** is wind-pollinated plant

ii Pollen is transferred to the stigma of another plant during pollination.

Insect-pollinated flower has long style/elevated stigma to increase chances of an insect rubbing pollen onto stigma as it visits the plant (e.g. to feed on nectar).

Wind-pollinated flower has long, feathery stigma to increase the chances of pollen blowing in the wind landing on it. Being feathery means low mass and easily blown.

iii Two features compared, for example: Insect-pollinated flower is coloured to attract insects; wind-pollinated flower is dull as does not need to attract insects.

Wind-pollinated flower has long filaments and elevated anthers to allow pollen to be blown off into the wind; insect-pollinated flower has shorter filaments as do not want the pollen to be blown in the wind.

10 **a** **i** sugar concentration

ii length of pollen tube

iii Any **two** of: time; temperature; volume of solution added; the type of plant that the pollen is taken from.

b **i** Thomas should repeat his investigation using a smaller range, focusing on concentrations between 10% and 20%. Intervals can then be smaller, e.g. 2%.

ii Thomas repeated his readings to check for precision and calculated an average. If any result does not fit with the repeats, a decision can be made to discount it. This allows for slight variation in results and helps to ensure data can be used to make conclusions.

iii 30 g glucose, 100 ml water

c **i** (×4) × (×40) = ×160

ii 32 mm = 32 000 μm

magnification = ×160

so, actual length = $\frac{20\,000}{160}$ = 200 μm

2.2 Seed dispersal

1 **a** becomes a seed; **b** becomes a fruit; **c** falls off; **d** falls off

2 Any **three** from: wind; water; animals excreting; on animal fur; exploding pods.

3 **a** 100; 4

b increase

4 nutrients; grow; temperature; germination

5 Plants need light, water and nutrients. Moving away from the parent plant means that it is more likely that there will be more light (as not in the shade of parent plant) and more water and nutrients available (as less taken from the soil by the parent plant).

6 Ovules containing the fertilised egg cell develop into seeds. Ovary develops into fruit. Fruit eaten by animal (but the seeds are not digestible). Animal carries the seeds inside them and then passes them out in their faeces. When conditions are suitable, seeds germinate and new tomato plants grow from the seeds.

7 **a** A fruit is what develops from the ovary of a plant after fertilisation. A fruit contains seeds, which develop from the ovules.

b Courgettes and pea pods contain seeds inside and so are classed as fruits.

8 Coconut – large to contain more nutrients for the seed. This is because it travels for long periods. Low mass for its size so that it floats on water.

Sycamore – small and low mass so it travels well in the wind. Has wings and aerodynamic shape to allow it to float and spin in the air.

9 **a** **A** 13–16 metres

b independent variable: wind speed

dependent variable: distance travelled

c As wind speed increases, the distance travelled by the seeds increases.

10 **a** germination of seeds requires water

b **A** $\frac{492}{3}$ = 164

B $\frac{552}{3}$ = 184

c **A** 82%; **B** 92%

d both

e Repeat the investigation but count the number of germinated seeds every day for 10 days and calculate the germination rate for each day. Identify the day on which the germination percentage reaches 80%.

2.3 Reproduction in humans

1 reproductive; sperm; eggs

2 The nucleus of the egg cell joining with the nucleus of sperm cell (combining the genetic material).

3 **A** uterus; **B** oviduct; **C** ovary; **D** cervix; **E** vagina

4 **A** sperm duct; **B** prostate gland; **C** urethra; **D** testis; **E** scrotal sac; **F** penis

5 **b**

6 **a** passing sperm to the prostate gland;

b producing sperm; **c** controlling the temperature of the testes; **d** passing sperm into the vagina

7 **a** passing eggs from the ovary to the uterus;

b producing eggs; **c** where sperm are released during sexual intercourse; **d** where the foetus develops

8 Because the sperm travels to the uterus and this is where fertilisation could happen.

9 **a** pollen; **b** ovule; **c** anther; **d** ovary

10 **a** microscope

b **A** 15 000; **B** 8000; **C** 200 000

c **i** 9.4 million per ml

ii Yes

d Sperm may not be formed properly (e.g. abnormal tail, small head) which means that they cannot travel to the egg.

11 **a** Ovulation is when the egg is released from the ovary.

b The egg travels from the ovary along the oviduct to the uterus (moved along by movement of tiny hairs in the oviduct).

During intercourse, the penis transfers millions of sperm to the vagina.

The sperm travel from the vagina through the cervix to the uterus.

One sperm penetrates the egg; chemicals are released to prevent any other sperm entering.

The nucleus of the sperm cell joins with the nucleus of the egg cell; this is fertilisation.

12 Both humans and flowering plants have male and female sex cells. Both have eggs as the female sex cells, but plants have pollen and humans have sperm as the male sex cells.

A flowering plant contains both the female and male parts whereas humans contain either male parts or female parts.

In flowering plants, male sex cells are made by anthers; in humans, male sex cells are made by testes.

In both flowering plants and humans the female sex cells are made by the ovary.

Fertilisation in both is the joining or fusing of the nuclei of the male sex cell and female sex cell to allow combining of genetic material.

Both flowering plants and male humans produce millions of male sex cells. However, flowering plants only produce pollen when the stigmas are ready for fertilisation, whereas in humans, sperm is produced continuously (after puberty).

In flowering plants, the male sex cell travels to the egg cell down the style. In humans, sperm also travels to the egg (in the uterus) but the egg also must travel (to the uterus).

The offspring of flowering plants develop away from the parent plant (following germination of the seed), whereas in humans, offspring develop inside the mother.

2.4 Puberty and the menstrual cycle

1 puberty; reproduce; hormones

2 **B**

3 **a** males; **b** females; **c** both; **d** females

4 **b** 24–35 days

5 uterus

6 **c**

7 **a** 15.5 years

b 14 years

8 **a** to prepare for childbirth; **b** to prepare for breastfeeding; **c** to prepare for transferring sperm to the vagina; **d** to fertilise eggs

9 Make males more attractive to females, therefore more likely to find a partner to reproduce with.

10 Day 1 – **c**; Day 5 – **a**; Day 14 – **b**; Day 21 – **d**

11 Karla is correct. The fertilised egg implants in the uterus lining. Menstruation is due to loss of the uterus lining. Therefore, menstruation stops as uterus lining remains thick.

12 **a** Egg begins ripening in the ovary at approximately day 5.

Egg matures and is released into the oviduct (ovulation); egg is fertilised in the oviduct at approximately day 14.

(Fertilised egg travels to uterus and implants into uterus lining.)

b The length of cycle varies from female to female but also in one female from month to month.

c 104 (Each cycle is 28 days, so in 1 year (365 days) there are 13.0 cycles. In 8 years = 13 × 8 = 104 cycles; one egg per cycle.)

13 **a** **i** Ovulation is the release of a mature egg from the ovary. If this does not happen, or does not happen every month, there is no egg that can be fertilised.

ii The oviduct is the tube that the egg is released into and is fertilised in. If it is blocked, eggs cannot travel down it and so no fertilisation will happen.

iii Eggs are released from the ovary. If cysts grow on the ovary, they can prevent the eggs moving out and into the oviduct, meaning there is no egg to fertilise in the oviduct.

b **i** Hormones

ii Just **i** – lack of ovulation. Even if more eggs are made, there will be no benefit if there is a blockage in the oviduct or if an egg cannot move out of the ovary due to cysts.

2.5 Development of a foetus and the effect of lifestyle

1 fertilised egg; embryo; foetus; baby

2 oxygen; glucose; vitamins

3 **b**

4 **i** umbilical cord; **ii** placenta; **iii** uterus wall; **iv** amniotic fluid; **v** vagina

5 **a** 16–20 weeks

b Foetuses develop at different rates and we do not always know the exact date of fertilisation.

c The mother's use of a drug such as alcohol, nicotine or marijuana; possibly genetics.

6 **a** – **ii**; **b** – **i**; **c** – **iv**; **d** – **iii**

7 Nicotine is taken into the lungs as the mother smokes. The nicotine passes from the lungs (across the alveoli) into the blood. The nicotine is carried in the blood to the placenta. At the placenta, the mother's blood runs alongside the foetus's blood. Nicotine passes from the mother's blood to the foetal blood.

8 Advantages – useful substances can pass from the mother to the foetus, such as oxygen and nutrients such as glucose, digested protein, vitamins and minerals. These allow the foetus to grow and be healthy. Waste substances pass from the foetus to the mother, which could be harmful if they build up.

Disadvantages – harmful substances can also pass across the placenta from the mother to the foetus, such as carbon monoxide, nicotine (from cigarettes), alcohol and other drugs such as cocaine or marijuana. These can increase the risk of stillbirth, premature birth or lower birth rate, as well as other issues such as asthma (nicotine and carbon monoxide), poor development and learning difficulties.

9 **a** The time taken for cell division can vary in length and so we use an average.

b 256 cells

6 days = (24 × 6) = 144 hours

number of divisions = $\frac{144}{18}$ = 8

10 **a** **i** true; **ii** true; **iii** false; **iv** needs more information; **v** false

b Medical advice is to avoid as smoking can cause lower birth weights. This data does support the advice.

c **i** Study a larger sample.

ii Collect and analyse data on how much the mother smoked rather than just 'smoker' or 'non-smoker'.

Unit 2 maths and practical skills

1 seconds

2 **a** prediction; **b** validity; **c** repeatability

3 27 cm = 270 mm

Magnification is ×3

Actual size = $\frac{270}{3}$ = 90 mm

4 Any **one** from:

Wind-pollinated plants produce a smaller volume of pollen grains than insect-pollinated plants.

Wind-pollinated plants produce more pollen grains than insect-pollinated plants.

5 $\frac{100\,\mu m}{5.1\,\mu m}$ = 19.6

6 **a** 'Does changing the concentration of sugar affect how long pollen tubes grow?'

b 0–25%

c As a control test/to show that sugar is causing the pollen tubes to grow.

7 **a** That the evidence collected can answer the question that has been asked.

b Number of sperm (per unit volume) for men covering a range of ages.

c **i** age; **ii** number of sperm (per unit volume)

8 **a** **i** mass; **ii** distance travelled

b add paperclips or sticky tack

c **i** g; **ii** mm/cm

d introduces another variable as the wind could affect how far the seeds travel

e

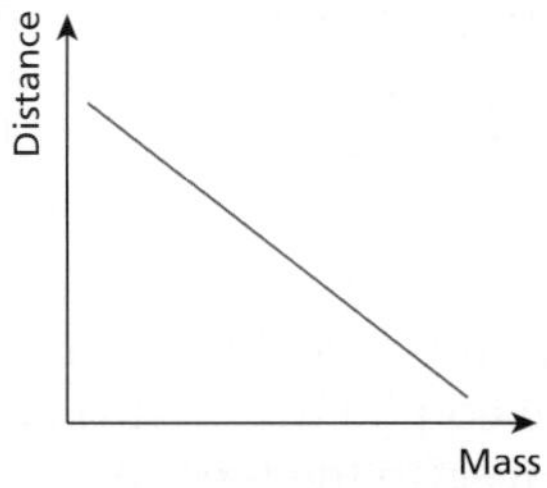

9 **a** **i** smoking/non-smoking; **ii** sperm concentration

b anything sensible such as age, race

c to increase repeatability, ensure evidence is consistent, spot anomalies

d **i** Group 4

ii ignore it/do not include

e Smoking decreases the concentration of sperm.

10 **a** **i** At higher birth weights such as 4000–4999 g, there are more babies of smokers than non-smokers; at 4500–4999 g there are more babies of smokers than non-smokers; at 3500–3999 g, there are more babies of smokers than non-smokers.

ii At low birthweights such as 1000–1499 g, there are more babies of smokers than non-smokers; at 1500–1999 g, there are more babies of smokers than non-smokers.

b Repeatability is the extent to which the same results are achieved in repeats/larger sample size and so increasing the sample size will improve repeatability.

c **i** In surveys and observations of living things, it is difficult to control all variables. The environment cannot be fully controlled as in a laboratory.

ii For example: genetics of the mother, diet of the mother, use of other drugs, etc.

Unit 3 Health and human systems

3.1 Healthy diet

1 **c**

2 **a** protein; **b** vitamins; **c** minerals; **d** fibre

3 **a** – **iii**; **b** – **iv**; **c** – **i**; **d** – **ii**

4 **a** – **iii**; **b** – **ii**; **c** – **iv**; **d** – **i**

5 **a** **i** anaemia; **ii** rickets; **iii** scurvy

b **i** e.g. deformities in bones.
ii e.g. tiredness, bleeding gums, fever.

c anaemia

6 **a** Sample **A** contains sugar but no starch. Sample **B** contains both starch and sugar.

b Sample **A** – honey; sample **B** – bread

7 **a** **i**

b We need fats to provide and store energy (and to help absorb vitamins). Misconceptions occur because fats are different and some are healthier for us than others. Too much of certain fats, for example butter or meat fat, can be unhealthy. Messages about removing or reducing fat intake usually refer to these less healthy fats.

8 **a** To help people to make healthy choices (for example, to lose or gain weight or to treat medical conditions) and to help people with allergies to avoid allergens.

b 540 calories

c 1.21 g

d 300 mg

9 **a** starchy products, fruits and vegetables (these first two could be accepted in either order); dairy products; proteins; foods high in fat and sugar

b $\frac{1}{6}$

c **i** dairy products and foods high in fat and sugar

ii dairy products and foods high in fat and sugar

iii carbohydrates and foods high in fat and sugar

d Not all meals will contain these proportions or all of these food types. For example, during a day, one meal may contain more carbohydrate and no fruit and vegetables (e.g. a meat sandwich), but the next meal may contain lots of fruits and vegetables and protein (e.g. chicken salad). But overall, the proportions will be as on the 'eat well plate'.

10 **a** Any **three** of: fewer joint problems; better mobility; less risk of heart disease; less risk of diabetes.

b Energy needs vary depending on size, age and level of activity and so needs will vary from man to man and from woman to woman.

c **i** 9 slices (one slice of buttered toast contains 435 kJ + 420 kJ = 855 kJ)

ii Toast and butter includes mainly carbohydrate, fat and some fibre. Butter is not the best type of fat for health. Any sensible suggestions such as: reducing this type of fat; introducing other food groups such as protein (fish, eggs, lean meat); dairy products such as milk, yoghurt; fruit and vegetables. Plus any reasons for including those food groups in her diet.

d i $\frac{10\,500\,\text{kJ}}{4.2} = 2500$ calories;

ii $\frac{8400\,\text{kJ}}{4.2} = 2000$ calories

3.2 Human digestive system

1 **b**

2 small intestine

3 chemical

4 pancreas

5 **i** – **a**; **ii** – **b**; **iii** – **c**; **iv** – **d**

6 These yoghurts contain bacteria (bacteria are microorganisms). Some bacteria help digestion (by producing enzymes), and so these yoghurts can be useful to add to the bacteria in our digestive system.

7 **a** pH

b Any **two** of: volume of protein solution (or concentration); volume of enzyme solution (or concentration); temperature.

c stomach, as the stomach is acidic

8 **a** **i** mechanical breakdown of food

ii digestion of food by enzymes

b **i** small intestine; **ii** mouth or stomach

c chemical digestion

9 **a** to move the food along the small intestine

b diffusion

c **i** shorter distance for molecules to move from the small intestine into the bloodstream

ii there is always blood near the wall for molecules to move into **or** maintains a concentration gradient between small intestine and bloodstream

iii provide a large surface area for the molecules to pass across

d **i** water is removed, making the waste (faeces) more solid

ii allows the waste (faeces) to leave the body

10 **a** carbohydrate (or starch)

b Digestion breaks down the larger food molecules to smaller food molecules. These smaller molecules are then used to release energy in the body.

c carbohydrase (or amylase)

d Enzymes carry out only one type of reaction (e.g. only break down carbohydrates, proteins or fats).

e Not enough carbohydrase enzyme means that not all of the starch/carbohydrate would be digested to glucose. As glucose is used to release energy (by respiration), a lack of glucose would lead to a lack of energy released and tiredness.

3.3 Effects of recreational drugs

1 **c**

2 **a** painkillers; **b** stimulants; **c** depressants; **d** hallucinogens

3 **a** – **iv**; **b** – **ii**; **c** – **i**; **d** – **iii**

4 **a** Drugs that are used for anything other than a medical purpose, for example for pleasure.

b They like the feeling it gives them, **or** it hides another feeling.

5 **a** – **iv**; **b** – **ii**; **c** – **i**; **d** – **iii**

e Relax the patient, anaesthetic and provide pain relief needed after the operation.

6 They are useful medically, for example to treat sleep problems or anxiety. Many patients do not experience serious side-effects if they use them as prescribed.

7 **a** any effect of a drug that is not its main purpose

b The benefits outweigh the side-effects for people who are experiencing constant serious pain and so for them it is worth the risk.

c **i** caffeine

ii Caffeine (stimulant) increases the heart rate, increasing the risk of heart attack. After the high may come a fatigue, leading to increased tiredness. It increases metabolism, could result in weight loss.

8 **a** Different people might experience different side-effects; helps to be sure that the side-effects observed are due to the energy drink if lots of people experience them.

b **i**

c This control group helps to show that the side-effects are caused by the energy drink; if the control group also experience the side-effects, it shows that they are not caused by the energy drink.

d Knowing whether or not you are drinking the new energy drink could affect what people notice and record; this could influence the conclusions or observations made.

9 a Depressant – depression in the long term; risk of death if overdose because it slows body systems down.

Hallucinogen – depression and anxiety because the drugs affect the balance of chemicals in the brain; weight loss.

b Advantage of cannabis: treatment of long-term pain.

Disadvantage of cannabis: side-effects, as it is both a depressant and a hallucinogen, such as those listed in part **a**.

Advantage of making cannabis use legal: people buying it, for example for treating pain, are not breaking the law and so cannot be arrested or fined.

Disadvantages of making cannabis use legal include: that it would become more freely available, meaning more people might use the drug and experience side-effects; that it is also addictive, so more people may become addicted.

Considering the evidence, I think … (any opinion, supported by evidence).

10 a i Use of depressants (e.g. heroin) can lead to long-term depression; risk of coma and death as the drug slows the nervous system and body systems; can cause vomiting which the user could choke on; injecting can damage the veins and reduce circulation.

ii As drug use is expensive, families may have less money available for essentials; family could be neglected as the addict spends time sourcing and taking drugs; families may need to care for the addict's medical needs.

iii Addict may steal from others or businesses to fund their habit as it is so difficult to stop using; addict may need lots of medical care, strain on health service; addict may go to prison, causing strain on prison service and cost to society to fund time in prison.

b Alcohol is legal, more widely available, cheaper and more acceptable to use, and so more people use alcohol than use heroin. As more people are exposed, there is more damage to the health of more people.

11 a Heroin causes the most deaths compared to cocaine and ecstasy (cocaine causes more than ecstasy), with 130 deaths from heroin, 17 from cocaine, and 6 from ecstasy.

b The risk of death is greater for all three drugs when taken with other drugs. The number of deaths for all three is more than doubled when taken with other drugs (for ecstasy the number is 20 with other drugs, compared to 6 on its own; for cocaine, 122 compared to 17; for heroin, 255 compared to 130).

c If the cost of the drugs decreases, people are more likely to be able to buy them, so drug use might increase and lead to an increased number of deaths.

3.4 Human skeleton, joints and muscles

1 a; c

2 c

3 a – iii; b – iv; c – i; d – ii

4 i – D; ii – B; iii – C; iv – A

5 d

6 a – iii; b – iv; c – i; d – ii

7 a protection

b i prevent the bones from breaking if they bend slightly on contact

ii makes it easier to move the bones

c blood cells

d The bones can have a lower mass (less dense), making it easier for birds to fly.

8 a where two bones meet

b **i** fixed; **ii** ball and socket; **iii** hinge; **iv** pivot

c i They protect what is underneath the bones.

ii The different joints allow different types of movement, so a combination gives us greater movement overall.

9 a i 114 cm; **ii** 1.14 m

b Teenage boys are still growing and so the body proportions cannot be accurately predicted.

10 a Pairs of muscles that work together to move bones at a joint; as one contracts, the other relaxes.

b i decreases in length, increases in breadth (shortens and fattens)

ii it relaxes (returns to its original size)

c Hamstring muscle contracts; it shortens and fattens. At the same time, quadriceps relaxes; it returns to original size, upper leg moves down.

11 a i Newtons (unit of force)

b i There will be variation between people and an average takes into consideration those variations. A number of repeat measurements also allows a check on repeatability.

ii If any results are anomalous, the tester can choose to repeat the measurement if there may have been an error, or choose to ignore that reading.

c i, **iv**

3.5 Human breathing system

1 a

2 b

3 C; **D**; **B**; **A**

4 a up and out; **b** down; **c** increases; **d** into

5 d

6 a i balloons; **ii** elastic membrane; **iii** glass tubing

b The bell jar cannot move whereas the ribcage can (or the bell jar does not have muscles, the ribcage does).

7 a i decreased
ii increased

b pascals, Pa

8 a A 5.8 l; **B** 5.7 l; **C** 6.3 l

b i 3.4 l

ii 6.1 l

c height, amount of exercise

9 a the volume of air breathed out following a big breath in

b so that you are measuring the full lung volume

c i Exercise does not have an instant effect, it takes regular exercise over time to change muscles or fitness.

ii to have a comparison at the end (as a baseline)

iii It allows a comparison to be made; helps to ensure any changes are due to exercise.

iv Regular exercise leads to an increase in lung volume.

v Exercise strengthens the muscles between the ribs, this means that the ribs move further up and out on a breath in, increasing the chest space.

10 a i more area for gases to pass across

ii shorter distance for the gases to pass across

iii the blood constantly moves the oxygen away allowing more oxygen to move into the blood (or keeps a concentration gradient)

b i

c i carbon dioxide

ii respiration

11 a i volume in the lungs increases

ii pressure inside lungs decreases

iii pressure inside lungs becomes less than atmospheric pressure

iv air moves into the lungs

b i 9.5 – 3.8 = 5.7 kPa = 5700 Pa

ii 3.8 kPa

c no overall movement (same movement into as out of the lungs)

Unit 3 maths and practical skills

1 d

2 127 × 3 = 381 kcal

3 d

4 b

5 a type of exercise; **b** breathing rate

6 a 4.8 l

b new result would be higher

7 a A starch only; **B** sugar only; **C** protein only

b i – **B**; **ii** – **C**; **iii** – **A**

c ii

8 a stimulant

b Stimulants cause temporary increase in energy and alertness but this may lead to a period of fatigue following the 'high'; risk of heart attack because of increased heart rate; weight loss.

c The public tend to trust and respect medical people and so are likely to be convinced that smoking is not bad for you/ may like to copy doctors.

d This could mean that the companies funding the research may look for any evidence to suggest that smoking is not bad for you, rather than being open about the evidence; idea that this is not impartial as the cigarette companies have something to gain from a specific finding of the research (smoking does not cause cancer).

9 **a** **i** agar gel; **ii** red food colouring; **iii** water

b The red food colouring would have spread further (or more of the water would be red).

c The food colouring diffuses from a higher concentration, in the gel, to a lower concentration, in the water.

10 **a** **i** small intestine; **ii** bloodstream

b **i** Starch was broken down into glucose by the amylase enzyme.

ii Glucose molecules moved through the Visking tubing into the water.

iii Starch molecules are too large to move through the holes in the tubing.

c **i** temperature; **ii** presence of glucose; **iii** any **two** of: concentration of enzyme, concentration of starch (or volumes of solutions), incubation time; **iv** 20–60 °C

Unit 4 Respiration and photosynthesis

4.1 Aerobic respiration

1 muscles; temperature; energy; oxygen

2 glucose; water

3 **b**, **d**

4 **d**

5 **a** – **iii**; **b** – **ii**; **c** – **i**; **d** – **iv**

6 **a**

7 **a** **A** – inner membrane; **B** – outer membrane; **C** – matrix; **D** – cristae

b **i** highly folded, increases the surface area for respiration

ii contains enzymes needed for respiration.

c Respiration takes place in cristae. More respiration is possible in the mitochondrion in part **c** because there are more cristae (larger surface area).

8 Breathing is the physical process that moves air in and out of the lungs. It involves oxygen because we use the oxygen from the air that we breathe in (and breathe out the carbon dioxide that we produce).

Respiration is a chemical reaction in cells that uses the oxygen we have breathed in. It is a reaction between oxygen and glucose to release water and energy.

9 Bread contains **starch**.

Digestion takes place and **enzymes** break down starch to **glucose**.

Honey contains glucose molecules and so digestion is not needed.

Glucose travels in the **bloodstream** to cells.

The **breathing** system brings air into the body.

Oxygen travels in the bloodstream to cells.

In the cells, glucose and oxygen move into the **mitochondria**.

Glucose and oxygen react in respiration, releasing energy.

10 **a** carbon dioxide

b to absorb carbon dioxide

c To show that there is no carbon dioxide in the air as it reaches the insects and seeds. This means any carbon dioxide is produced only by the insects and seeds.

d Limewater turns cloudy because the insects and seeds produce carbon dioxide.

e The limewater would stay colourless because the soda lime would absorb any carbon dioxide produced by the insects and seeds.

11 **a** We cannot count thousands of mitochondria accurately but we can count the number in a small area and then estimate the total number. Also cells will vary in the number of mitochondria they have.

b bar chart

c bar chart sketch similar to below, no actual numbers plotted

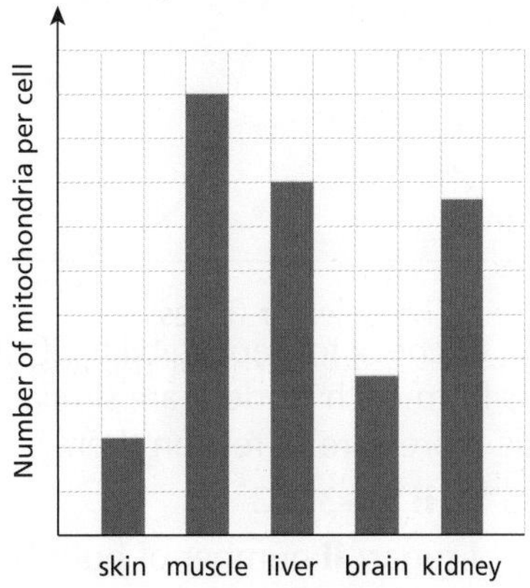

d muscle, liver, kidney, brain, skin

e $525\,\mu m^3 \left(\frac{15}{100}\right) \times 3500$

4.2 Anaerobic respiration

1 **a** true; **b** true; **c** false; **d** true

2 **b**, **c**

3 **a** – **iv**; **b** – **iii**; **c** – **ii**; **d** – **i**

4 **a**, **c**

5 **a** – **ii**; **b** – **i**; **c** – **iv**; **d** – **iii**

6 **a** to activate the yeast

b for respiration

c to collect and deliver all the gas to the beaker of water

d to enable students to see the bubbles of carbon dioxide released

7 **a** **ii**, **iii**

b **i** ethanol; **ii** carbon dioxide

c **i** carbon dioxide; **ii** carbon dioxide

8 **a** **1** aerobic; **2** aerobic; **3** anaerobic (or both aerobic and anaerobic); **4** aerobic

b **3** fast sprint (or at least part of it)

c muscles ache

d Lactic acid builds up during the sprint as the man respires anaerobically. This lactic acid can be broken down using oxygen. After the sprint, the man breathes heavily to get more oxygen into his body to break down the lactic acid (convert it to glucose). The oxygen needed to break down the lactic acid is the oxygen debt.

e Anaerobic respiration releases energy, not as much as aerobic respiration but the energy is useful to the man.

9 **a** As temperature increases up to 25 °C the number of bubbles increases, but after 25 °C the number of bubbles decreases.

b

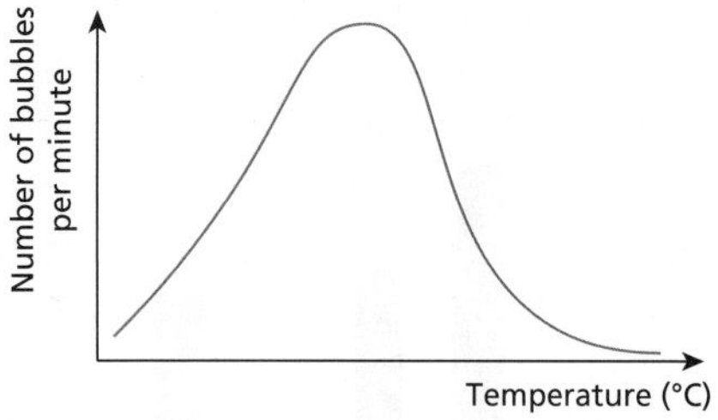

c Allows to check for repeatability. If the results from each student are similar, they can be more sure to rely on them.

d **i** 0–85 °C; **ii** 15–35 °C

10 **a** **i** type of sugar; **ii** number of bubbles; **iii** any **two** from: mass of sugar, temperature, mass of yeast, volume of warm water

b **i** sucrose, Trial 2

ii ignore the result when calculating averages

iii **A** – 22 bubbles; **B** – 13 bubbles; **C** – 7 bubbles

c bar chart, because the independent variable (type of sugar) has three distinct or discrete categories

4.3 The importance of respiration

1 digestive; breathing; circulatory; skeletal

2 **b**, **c**

3 **a** mitochondria; **b** cytoplasm

4 **a**, **c**

5 **a** **i** anaerobic; **ii** aerobic

b **i**, **iii**

6

	Reactants	Products	Amount of energy (more/less)
Aerobic respiration	glucose, oxygen	carbon dioxide, water	more
Anaerobic respiration	glucose	lactic acid	less

7 **a** – **iii**; **b** – **ii**; **c** – **i**

8 **a** speed reactions up

b carbohydrase (or amylase) enzyme

c aerobic as more energy is released (from glucose)

9 **a** Glucose can be broken down to release energy as and when it is needed.

b **i** muscles and liver; **ii** in fat reserves

10 **a** Respiration releases energy, without respiration we would not have the energy we need to move, grow, keep body temperature constant.

b **i** The digestive system digests carbohydrates to release glucose. Glucose is used in both aerobic and anaerobic respiration. Without digestion, glucose would not be available for respiration.

ii The breathing system brings oxygen into the body; oxygen is used in respiration. Without breathing in, oxygen would not be available for respiration. The breathing system removes carbon dioxide from the body. Without breathing out, we would not get rid of the carbon dioxide and it would stay in the body.

c Digestion uses muscles, for example, in the stomach and intestines. Breathing uses muscles, for example, between the ribs. Muscles need energy to contract. Without enough respiration, the muscles would not have enough energy to contract and so breathing and digestion would be impaired.

11 **a** **i** 13 400 (67 million/5000); **ii** the number of affected people will vary, 1 in 5000 is an average estimate.

b Muscles need the most energy (to contract); the heart is a muscle.

c **i** growth needs energy; **ii** digestion needs energy, for example, muscles contract in the stomach and intestines

4.4 Photosynthesis

1 water; oxygen

2 **c**

3 **c**

4 **a** – **iii**; **b** – **iv**; **c** – **i**; **d** – **ii**

5 light (the Sun)

6 **a** **i** both photosynthesis and respiration; **ii** only respiration

b Night time, because respiration produces carbon dioxide and there is no photosynthesis to remove the carbon dioxide.

7 **a** **i** temperature; **ii** number of bubbles or rate of photosynthesis; **iii** any **one** from: light intensity, carbon dioxide concentration, volume of water

b 60 °C

8 **a** No, because there is no carbon dioxide.

b Orange, because no starch would have been produced as there was no photosynthesis.

c Carbon dioxide allows photosynthesis to happen, this produces oxygen.

9 **a** **i** – **A**; **ii** – **D**; **iii** – **C**; **iv** – **B**

b **C**, because it allows the highest rate of photosynthesis. **D** would also allow the highest rate of photosynthesis but would cost more than **C**, because more carbon dioxide is needed to produce only a slightly higher rate of photosynthesis.

10 **a** **i** product; **ii** reactant

b Sunrise – there has been no photosynthesis overnight, so no oxygen produced overnight. But respiration has taken place and this uses oxygen. Therefore, by sunrise, oxygen concentration is low.

During the day, respiration uses oxygen and photosynthesis produces oxygen, so oxygen concentration increases.

c **i** sunset; **ii** sunrise

11 **a** **i** Increases the number of bubbles as rate of photosynthesis increases.

ii Decreases the number of bubbles as rate of photosynthesis decreases.

iii No effect on the number of bubbles as does not affect rate of photosynthesis.

b This is a control test; shows that any bubbles are due to the pondweed.

c **A**, because higher rate of photosynthesis at **A** (rate at **A** = 1.2 bubbles per second; rate at **B** = 0.5 bubbles per second).

4.5 Adaptations of plants for photosynthesis

1 **a** roots; **b** leaves; **c** leaves; **d** roots

2 **b**, **c**

3 **A** guard cell; **B** nucleus; **C** stoma

4 **a** – **iv**; **b** – **i**; **c** – **ii**; **d** – **iii**

5 **a**, **c**

6 **a** **i** take in water from the soil; **ii** form a pipeline to move water up the plant from the roots

b dry, windy, hot

7 **a** **i** 0.05 mm; **ii** 50 µm

b **i** it will decrease; **ii** it will decrease

8 **a** light may be limited in shady areas

b **i** allows light to reach the leaves underneath as well; **ii** the leaves underneath are not too shaded

9 **a** gas exchange – carbon dioxide moves in, oxygen moves out, water moves out

b **i** – **B**; **ii** – **A**; **iii** – **D**; **iv** – **C**

c 655 (10.4 × 63 = 655.2 but round down to whole stomata)

d Bar chart because there are distinct values for the variable 'environment' (low, high, etc.), rather than a range of values.

10 **a** **i** let light through so can reach the cells that absorb light for photosynthesis

ii long and narrow so can fit in more cells; chloroplasts contain chlorophyll to absorb light, so more chloroplasts at top where light does not have far to travel

iii chloroplasts contain chlorophyll to absorb light, air spaces allow gases to move within the leaf

iv open to allow carbon dioxide in and close to stop too much water being lost

b **i** contain lots of chloroplasts, absorb lots of sunlight

ii water evaporates from stomata, so being underneath guard cells can close stomata to reduce water loss

Unit 4 maths and practical skills

1 **c**

2 **a** 9000 μm (30 × 300); **b** 9 mm

3 **a** number of bubbles; **b** distance from lamp

4 **a**

5 **a** carbon dioxide; **b** turns cloudy (milky)

6 **a** 20% (3/15 min – sprint time divided by the total time)

b paying back the oxygen debt to break down the lactic acid built up during anaerobic respiration

7 **a** **B**

b **C**

c more of structure **B** in a muscle cell

8 **a** **i** to activate the yeast; **ii** so that yeast can respire; **iii** to deliver the gas to the water (so can count bubbles)

b carbon dioxide

c **i** mass of sugar; **ii** number of bubbles; **iii** any **two** from: mass of yeast, time bubbles counted for, volume of water added to yeast, type of sugar, temperature

9 **a** **i** removes chlorophyll (and waxy layer); **ii** test for starch

b **i** starch is present where the leaf is blue/black; **ii** photosynthesis has taken place where starch is present

10 **a** **i** number of bubbles per minute; **ii** temperature

b 40 °C

c **i** result at 50 °C; **ii** for example: counted bubbles incorrectly, incorrect temperature measurement

d **i** 60 °C, Trial 2; **ii** lower as from the graph a higher temperature was likely to produce fewer bubbles; **iii** ignore the anomaly, 51.7, 60.0, 45.0, 33.0 bubbles per minute

Unit 5 Ecosystems and interdependence

5.1 Food webs and interdependence

1 **a**

2 **c**

3 biomass; chain; web; energy

4 **a**

5 **a** – **iii**; **b** – **ii**; **c** – **i**

6 **a** parasitism; **b** mutualism; **c** commensalism

7 **a** **i** increase as more food available

ii increase as fewer trout eaten

iii decrease – if frogs decrease, fewer for kingfisher to eat and so kingfisher may eat more trout, trout decrease (*or* decrease in frogs means fewer dragonfly and pond fly eaten, so they increase; more waterweed eaten, waterweed decreases, less food for prawns and carp, they decrease; less food for trout, trout decrease)

b 5 (waterweed → pond fly → dragonfly → frog → snake/kingfisher)

8 **a** leaf litter → worm → shrew

b **i** decreases; **ii** organisms use some of the energy to move, grow, etc.

c light (photosynthesis)

d As the energy decreases at each level, there would not be enough energy for animals at higher trophic levels.

9 **a** **i** Predator population increasing as prey population increased just before, so more food for predator.

ii Prey population decreasing as predator population increased previously, so more prey eaten.

iii Predator population decreasing as prey population decreased just before, so less food for predator.

iv Prey population increasing as predator population decreased previously, so less prey eaten.

b **i** Prey will decrease as more being eaten.

ii Original predators will decrease as some prey will be eaten by other predators so fewer prey available.

c competition

10 **a** **i** star grass, red oat grass or acacia

ii pangolin or aardvark

iii termite, dung beetle, mouse

b **i** red oat grass

ii Pangolin feeds on harvester ant; if star grass and red oat grass decrease, harvester ant decreases; therefore, pangolin will decrease.

c If one food source decreases, organisms have other food sources in a food web; this increase chances of survival.

5.2 The importance of insects

1 **d**

2 **a**

3 **a** smaller; **b** lower; **c** more; **d** decreased

4 **c – a – d – b**

5 **a** **i** Asia and Middle East; **ii** Europe (only region to decrease)

b Europe (only region to decrease)

6 **a** Any suggestions that would lead to bee colony reduction, for example, weather, use of pesticides, disease, colony collapse disorder.

b apples 750 kg; pears 600 kg; tomatoes 11 kg; cucumbers 22 kg

c 70%

7 **a** **i** 18%

ii for example, if they are hungry regularly or can only afford non-nutritious food

b beverages

8 **a** Food security is the availability of sufficient food for all people at all times.

b Monoculture is growing only one crop over vast areas; the image shows rows of the same plant in a large field. Polyculture is growing more than one crop in the same area; the image shows a range of plants in the same field.

c **i** There is only food for bees when that one plant flowers, and no other food.

ii Lack of variety of plants might mean that not all nutrients that insects need are provided.

d It is a way of generating income because cocoa is a high-income crop.

9 **a** to feed on nectar inside the plants

b Different insects may pollinate different plants so a wider range of plants can exist; if numbers of one pollinator decrease, pollination can still continue by another insect.

c **i** type of insect

ii number of visits to the flowers

iii Not all visits to a flower will result in the insect picking up pollen and not all visits to another plant will result in pollen being transferred.

10 **a** 06:00–07:00

b 10:00–11:00

c Repeat the same observations another two times.

d 06:00–07:00

e any **two** of: temperature, light levels, weather (for example, raining or dry), wind speed, time of year, same location

5.3 Impact of organisms on their environment

1 **d**

2 **a**

3 **a – ii; b – iii; c – i**

4 **a – ii; b – i; c – iv; d – iii**

5 **c**

6 **b**

7 **a** Greenhouse gases (carbon dioxide and methane) trap heat within the Earth's atmosphere.

b **i** releases carbon dioxide; **ii** as waste decomposes, methane is released; **iii** fewer trees to take in carbon dioxide, so the level of carbon dioxide in the atmosphere increases

8 **a** **ii, iii**

b **A** – water weed; **B** – otter; **C** – small fish; **D** – large fish

c The toxin accumulates through the food chain and is more concentrated in the otter than in the water weed due to bioaccumulation. (*Or* Small fish eat more than one piece of water weed, big fish eat more than one small fish, otter eats more than one large fish and so the toxin becomes more concentrated.)

9 **a** the variety of animal and plant species

b the toucan

c Any **two** suggestions that would help survival, for example: create more habitats for the birds in the forest to allow more places for the birds to live, nest and feed; start a captive breeding programme to ensure that new offspring are born (and then reintroduce them back into the rainforest); ensure restrictions are in place to prevent capturing or hunting the birds.

10 **a** **i** 12.8; **ii** 4.0

b **i** amount of light; **ii** number of dandelions

c More dandelions are found where there is more sunlight (*or* fewer dandelions are found where there is less light).

d **i** $0.5 \times 0.5 = 0.25\,m^2$

ii *Either* 3080

(6 quadrats have area of $0.25 \times 6 = 1.5\,m^2$

total area of field = $10 \times 6 = 60\,m^2$

so, total field is $60 \div 1.5 = 40$ times bigger than quadrat area

total of 77 dandelions in 6 quadrats in full sunlight

so, total dandelions in field = $77 \times 40 = 3080$)

Or 3072

(area of field = $10 \times 6 = 60\,m^2$

number of quadrats in field = $60 \div 0.25 = 240$

one quadrat average = 12.8 dandelions

total dandelions in field = $12.8 \times 240 = 3072$)

11 **a** a chemical that causes harm

b mercury affects the nervous system

c **i** 50; **ii** 2500; **iii** 20 000; **iv** 200 000

d orca whale because it contains highest concentration of mercury

e **i** decrease; **ii** no effect

Unit 5 maths and practical skills

1 **c**

2 **b**

3 **b**

4 **a**

5 **b** – **c** – **a** – **d**

6 **a** **iv**; **b** 16 Mha; **c** tree cover loss has increased over time

7 **a** $9\,m^2$; **b** $0.0625\,m^2$; **c** 22% (220 ÷ 10)

8 **a** **i** albacore, sample 3 (0.02); **ii** ignore it/do not include it

b yellowfin – 0.21; albacore – 0.27; bigeye – 0.45

c bigeye, as it contains the highest concentration of methylmercury per kg

9 **a** **i** as length increases, mercury concentration increases; **ii** yes

b bigeye, because it contains the highest concentration of toxin

c 300 m

10 **a**

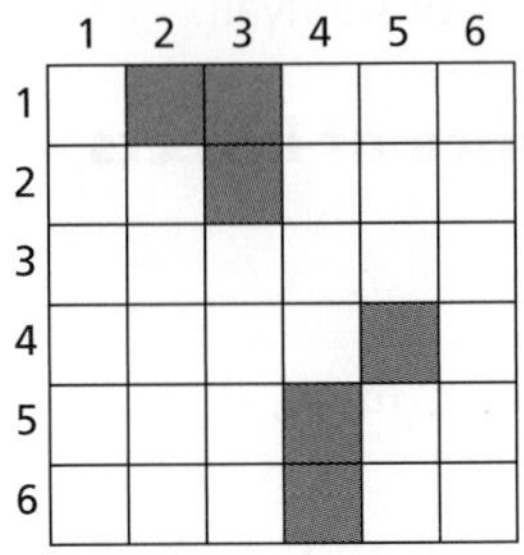

b it makes the areas sampled random, removes bias

c 0.5 m

d **i** 1/6; **ii** 108 (18 × 6)

e Repeat the sampling in the future at regular intervals over time. The data should then be analysed to look for changes in number over time.

Unit 6 Inheritance and evolution

6.1 Types and causes of variation

1 **a**, **c**

2 **b**, **c**

3 **a** continuous; **b** continuous; **c** discontinuous; **d** discontinuous

4 **a** – **iii**; **b** – **iv**; **c** – **i**; **d** – **ii**

5 **a** **i** examples such as: eye colour, hair colour, blood group, flower colour

ii examples such as: scars, dyed hair colour, tattoos

iii examples such as: weight, height, fitness, freckles, plant height, seed size, leaf patterns

b **iii**

6 **a** positive; **b** no correlation; **c** positive; **d** no correlation

7 **a** Discontinuous as there are discrete categories (only a limited number of values).

b

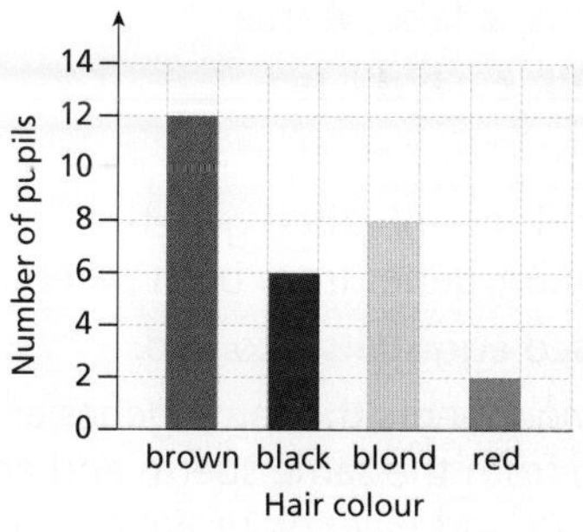

8 **a** 9

b **i** 80%; **ii** 15%

c The larger sample size means the results are likely to be more accurate.

9 **a** unlikely to get sick from the virus/their bodies have immunity to the virus

b Group **A** would survive but Group **B** could die.

c Group **B** would survive but Group **A** could die.

d Whichever virus they are exposed to, some rabbits are likely to survive. If there was no variation and no rabbits were resistant to the virus causing myxomatosis, for example, all rabbits could die.

10 **a** **i** independent; **ii** dependent; **iii** control

b As the height of the leaves increases, the number of spikes per leaf decreases.

c

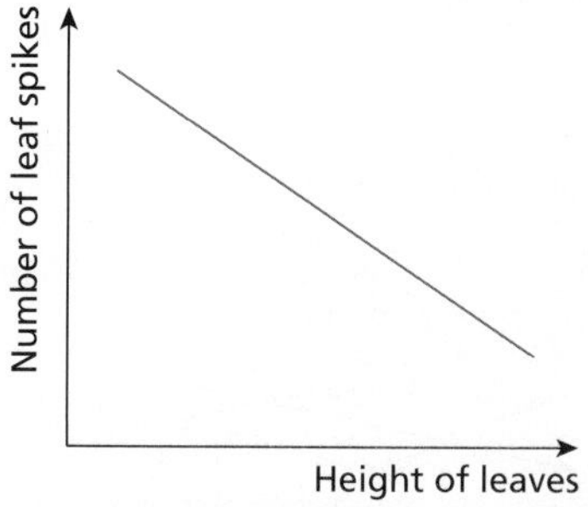

6.2 Natural selection and evolution

1 compete; variation; adapted; extinct

2 **d** – **b** – **a** – **c**

3 **a** – **iii**; **b** – **iv**; **c** – **i**; **d** – **ii**

4 **a** – **iii**; **b** – **iv**; **c** – **i**; **d** – **ii**

5 **a** – **iii**; **b** – **i**; **c** – **ii**

6 **b**, **c**

7 **a** when no individuals of that species are alive

b If a virus enters the population and no cheetahs have resistance to it, as there is little variation, all animals could be killed, species could become extinct.

c Mass extinction is the extinction of a large number of species; extinction can describe the extinction of just one species.

8 **a** **i** increased; **ii** decreased

b White mice are less well camouflaged, so more eaten; dark mice are better camouflaged, so fewer eaten.

c 2006 and 2008 as that is when the number of dark mice started to increase and the number of white mice decrease.

9 **a** **i** bird; **ii** moth

b **i** pale, peppered moth because it is better camouflaged/less likely to be eaten

ii dark, black moth because it is better camouflaged/less likely to be eaten

c Before: more light, peppered moths because they were better camouflaged and less likely to be eaten.

During: the number of light, peppered moths decreased and the number of dark, black moths increased, as the black moths were better camouflaged and less likely to be eaten. This meant that the black moths were more likely to reproduce and pass on their genetic material and more black moths were produced.

10 **a** To produce animals or plants with desirable features; could give examples such as produce lots of meat, lean meat, disease resistance, flower size.

b **i**, **ii**

c decreases variation

d Any two factual descriptions, such as: because variation is decreased the population may not be able to survive if the environment changes; can lead to deformities in the offspring.

e Select parent plants that produce large flowers. Of the offspring, choose those plants that produce large flowers and breed from those. Repeat over several generations.

11 Peacocks are in **competition** for mates. Coloured feathers are more attractive to peahens and so these peacocks have a **selective advantage**. Coloured feather peacocks are more likely to **reproduce** and pass on their genetic material. This is **natural selection**. This results in more offspring with coloured feathers. Repeating this over many generations leads to all having coloured feathers. This is **evolution**.

6.3 The role of chromosomes, genes and DNA in heredity

1 **b**, **c**

2 nucleus; chromosomes; DNA; genes; hair

3 **a**

4 **a** – **iii**; **b** – **iv**; **c** – **i**; **d** – **ii**

5 **b**, **c**

6 **a** true; **b** false; **c** false; **d** true

7 **a** nucleus

b Genes control characteristics; could give examples such as eye colour, blood group (made of sequences of bases, A, C, G and T).

c Red blood cells have no nucleus, and so have no chromosomes.

8 **a** Any **three** from: blood, saliva, semen, hair, skin.

b The DNA profile of the substance may be matched to the person under suspicion to show they have been at the scene, as DNA profiles are unique.

c Police can show that the DNA from the cow is similar to some cows from the farm from which it was stolen (as they are related).

d Objects such as pictures are non-living and do not contain DNA.

9 **a** **i** egg; **ii** sperm

b 24

c **i**, **iii**

10 **a** karyotype

b female, because have two X chromosomes (XX) (male would have XY)

c there would be half the chromosomes/only one of each pair

d because one of each pair comes from each parent

e 47

f 14

11 **a** bases

b TAAGAC

c mutation

d protein

e **i** yes; **ii** no; **iii** yes; **iv** yes

6.4 Explaining inheritance

1 **b**, **c**

2 **a**, **d**

3 **a** father's; **b** mother's; **c** parents'; **d** different

4 **a** true; **b** true; **c** false; **d** true

5 **a** – **ii**; **b** – **iii**; **c** – **i**; **d** – **iv**

6 **a** 4

b because it has inherited genetic information/genes from both parents

7 **a** A fertilised egg splits into two.

b Each twin inherits the same genes as they develop from the same sperm and egg. As eye colour and hair colour are controlled by genes, these will be the same in both twins.

c Yes, as blood group is genetic/inherited.

d Fingerprint development is also affected by the environment.

8 **a** **iii**

b the same probability: 1 in 4 or 25%

c 3

9 **a** **i** R; **ii** r; **iii** Rr; **iv** red

b Because one (dominant) allele controls the colour rather than the effects of the two alleles mixing.

10 **a** brown (as it is denoted by the capital letter)

b blue

c b, b

d bb, bb

e brown; brown; blue; blue

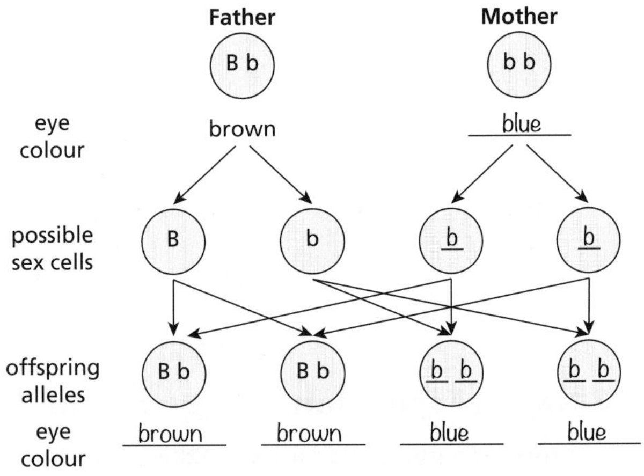

f 1 in 2 *or* 50% *or* 1:1

Unit 6 maths and practical skills

1 **d**

2 **a** – **ii**; **b** – **i**; **c** – **iii**

3 **b**

4 **a** – **iii**; **b** – **ii**; **c** – **i**

5 **a**, **d**

6 **b**

7 a continuous
b 177
c **i** as height increases, lung volume increases; **ii** positive

8 a continuous
b 3
c 22
d 16–19 m
e 0–31 m

9 a identical twins share the same genes;
b less
c **i** identical; **ii** yes

10 a **i** 1 in 2 *or* 50% *or* 1:1; **ii** 1 in 2 *or* 50% *or* 1:1
b **i** 1 in 2 *or* 50% *or* 1:1; **ii** 1 in 4 *or* 25% *or* 1:3
c 90

Unit 7 The particulate nature of matter

7.1 The properties of different states of matter

1 **a** – iii; **b** – i; **c** – ii

2 **b**

3 solids

4 no

5 The particles in a solid are in fixed positions, but the particles in a liquid can slide past each other. Solids have very strong forces between the particles which hold them in their positions. The forces between the particles in liquids are quite strong, but not strong enough to keep the particles in position.

6 a Air is a gas. There is nothing between the particles in a gas, the particles are spaced out, the particles can be pushed closer together.
b The pressure increases.
c The gas particles are closer together inside the syringe.
d There are still the same number of gas particles/atoms inside the syringe.

7 The forces between particles in liquids are stronger than in gases. Gases can be compressed, but liquids cannot. The space between particles in a gas is much bigger than in a liquid, where the particles are touching. Particles in a gas have higher energy than particles in a liquid. Liquid particles move/flow over and around each other, gas particles move quickly in all directions.

8 A sponge contains tiny holes full of air. When the sponge is compressed, the air escapes.

9 a More particles of air are pumped into the tyre so there are more collisions with the inside walls of the tyre.
b The pressure would increase, regardless of the temperature.
c The particles of gas will be moving more. They will hit the wall of the tyre more frequently *and* with more force.

10 If oil is more viscous than water, this suggests that the forces between particles in oil are stronger than those in water. This would make it more difficult for the particles in oil to slide past each other, which would mean that oil flows less easily than water.

11 a A and E
b B and F

7.2 Changes of state

1 **a** – ii; **b** – iv; **c** – i; **d** – iii

2 a boiling point
b Energy is transferred to the particles. The particles move around more quickly. The forces/attractions between the particles are broken/overcome.

3 0 °C

4 solid to a gas (without becoming a liquid)

5 a In the ice, the particles vibrate in fixed positions. As the ice is heated, the particles gain more energy and vibrate more in the fixed positions. As the solid melts, the particles are free to move and slide past one another.
b  to 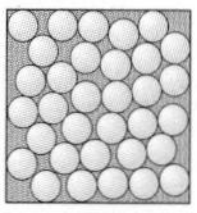
c Refreeze the water back into ice.

6 No the water is not boiling. For the water to be boiling its temperature would need to be 100 °C. Evaporation can happen at any temperature between the melting point of a liquid and its boiling point.

7 It would condense into a liquid.

8 Gas. –26 °C is higher than the boiling point of chlorine.

9 Metals with stronger forces between particles will have higher melting points.

7.3 Atoms, elements and compounds

1 element

2 **a**

3 **a** – ii; **b** – i; **c** – ii; **d** – i

4 **a** false; **b** true; **c** true; **d** false

5 carbon dioxide, ammonia

6 An atom is the smallest part of a substance. Elements are made of atoms. In an element, all the atoms are the same.

7 **b**

8 Student A – Water is a compound; it is made of two elements, hydrogen and oxygen, chemically bonded together.

Student B – Air is a mixture of different elements and compounds. The elements and compounds in air are not chemically bonded to each other, so air is not a compound. Rather, it is a mixture.

9 Atoms are too small to be seen. The model can help explain properties and observations of solids, liquids, gases and reactions.

10 3

11 **a** 4; **b** 2:1:4

12 2:1; H_2O

7.4 Conservation of mass

1 **c**

2 **b**

3 50 g

4 **c**

5 100 g

6 because a gas is formed, which escapes into the surrounding air

7 The mass would stay the same.

8 **c**

9 A gas is formed, which escapes into the surrounding air.

10 The magnesium reacts with a gas (oxygen) in the air and combines with it. The mass of the magnesium and the gas (oxygen) has a greater mass than the magnesium at the start.

7.5 Diffusion

1 **i** high; **ii** low; **iii** equal

2 false

3 The particles in a solid are in fixed positions and cannot move freely.

4 The bottle contains a high concentration of perfume particles and the classroom a low concentration. The perfume particles spread from the area of high concentration to the area of low concentration.

5 The particles in liquid move more slowly as they have less energy than those in a gas.

6 **b**

7 The higher the temperature, the faster the rate of diffusion. This is because the higher the temperature, the more energy the particles have and the faster they move.

8 **a** Any **two** from: temperature, wind, humidity.

b Any **two** from: size of material; volume of water soaked into the material; time on the washing line.

c Measure the mass of the material after it has been soaked in water and again after a set amount of time on the washing line.

9 Gas will diffuse out of the cell because the concentration of gas inside the cell is higher than outside. Gas will diffuse down the concentration gradient out of the cell.

10 Smaller particles diffuse faster than larger particles. Smaller particles will move faster than larger ones at any given temperature as they have more kinetic energy.

7.6 Energy changes

1 degrees Celsius, °C

2 **a**

3 **c**

4 As the particles are heated, they move around more quickly.

5 **a** mean $= \frac{(23.5 + 23.3 + 23.4)}{3} = 23.4$

b yes

c All the values are very similar to each other. Measurements are repeatable when the same person carries out the same experiment under the same conditions and gets similar results.

6 Accuracy describes how close something is to the true value. An accurate measurement is very close to the true value. Precision describes how close together, or spread out, repeated measurements are from each other. Precise measurements are close together.

7 The temperature remains constant/the same.

8 **a** A; **b** the water is boiling

9 **a** The ice was changing state. The energy was being used to overcome the forces between particles/attraction between the water molecules in the ice.

b After the ice has melted, the energy is increasing the kinetic energy/movement of the water particles (molecules), which increases the temperature.

c 50 g

10 **a, d**

11 70 °C. At this temperature the line on the graph is flat, the temperature is not changing, which means there is a change in state. Room temperature is about 20 °C and stearic acid is solid at room temperature. The stearic acid is changing from a liquid to a solid, so 70 °C represents its melting point.

Unit 7 maths and practical skills

1 **b**

2 diffusion

3 $\frac{(65 + 72 + 57)}{3} = 64.7 = 65$ seconds to 2 sf

(Remember, you normally give the answer to the same number of decimal places as the numbers in the question, unless the question asks for something different. In this case, the numbers in the question are given to 2 significant figures.)

4 **a** liquid to gas (boiling)

b to prevent burning of hands on hot can

c condenses back to a liquid

d Pressure decreases. The particles are moving around less, they are hitting the walls of the can less frequently and with less force.

e The gas pressure outside the can was greater than the gas pressure inside the can. The pressure outside the can was enough to crush the can.

5 **a** 883 °C; **b** gas; **c** aluminium;

d 660 to 883 °C

6 In the bowl of hot water, the air inside the bottle is heated. The hot air inside the bottle consists of air particles with high kinetic energy. When the bottle is placed in the cold water the air particles transfer energy to the bottle walls and their kinetic energy reduces. The collisions of air particles on the bottom of the egg are less frequent than those on the top, so the egg is pushed into the bottle.

Unit 8 Pure and impure substances

8.1 Working safely in the laboratory

1 **a – iv; b – i; c – ii; d – iii**

2 yellow

3 **a – ii; b – iii; c – i; d – iv**

4 These are some possible hazards and control measures. You may identify others.

Hazard	Steps to reduce risk
glass breakage	• Keep glassware away from edge of bench. • Use a dustpan and brush to remove broken glass and place in a glass bin. • Tell the teacher and do not pick it up with fingers. • Place the test tube in a test tube rack once finished.
hot liquid may leave the tube when heating	• Point the tube away from the body and face, and away from others. • Do not heat the tube strongly. • Do not heat the tube with a Bunsen burner directly; instead, place the tube in a water bath to heat it. • If hot liquid does spill on the skin, rinse the area under the cold tap for 10 minutes.
liquid spillage	• Tell the teacher. • Use a wet cloth to wipe away the spill. • Rinse the cloth and wipe again. • Dry with a paper towel and wash hands thoroughly.
hot equipment	• Do not touch the equipment until it has cooled down. • If hot equipment is touched, cool the burn for 10 minutes with cold running water.
paper by the Bunsen burner	• Remove all flammable materials from the workspace.

5 accurately

6

Time (s)	Water temperature (°C)
0	22
20	
40	
60	
80	
100	
120	

Time is on the left-hand side, as this is the independent variable.

Time is measured in seconds, so it is included in the heading but not the rows.

Time starts at 0 and we know that the starting water temperature is 22 °C.

Water temperature is measured in °C, so include this in the heading but not in the rows.

Time increases by 20 seconds up to 2 minutes (120 seconds).

7 a balance, measuring cylinder, stop watch/stop clock/timer, or any other sensible equipment

b thermometer/digital thermometer/temperature logger

c The amount of water and the amount of coffee powder. The student should carry out everything else in exactly the same way, such as the number of stirs and the timing method.

8 a The results were repeated four times but they are not all close to each other, so they are not very precise. The value 4.7 minutes appears to be an anomaly as it is not close to any of the other three readings. It should be discarded. The other readings are then within 0.5 minutes of each other, which is similar to the readings for 1.0 g of reactant. The mean is
(3.0 + 2.5 + 2.8) ÷ 3 = 2.8 minutes.

b It is likely to be a source of random error. This is because the time taken for the student to notice the amount of gas, and to stop the timer, may vary. This is difficult to predict and to control.

8.2 Mixtures

1 filter funnel, filter paper, conical flask/beaker/boiling tube

2 b

3 c, d

4 a the water was a clear blue colour/the copper sulfate crystals could not be seen

b i

c the student could warm the solution/the student could stir the solution

5 d filtration

6 a the water had evaporated

b The white substance would have been dissolved in the tap water. After the water evaporated the solid was left.

7 a Iron is magnetic and so it can be removed from the mixture using a magnet.

b Iron and sulfur have undergone a chemical reaction. They are now chemically joined to make iron sulfide. This compound has different properties to the separate elements.

8 The stain was soluble in ethanol but it was not soluble in water.

9 a 125 g; **b** 88 g (accept 86–89 g)

10 a 22 °C

b thermometer wrapped in dry cotton wool

c When the thermometer is wrapped in wet cotton wool, the water or ethanol evaporating from the cotton wool will lower the temperature because the process requires heat energy. Energy is transferred to the water or ethanol molecules, allowing them to make the transition from liquid to gas. This energy transfer makes the temperature of the thermometer drop.

8.3 Pure substances

1 b

2 a, c, d

3 a

4 No, they are not the same. Chemically pure substances are made from one type of element or one type of compound only. Naturally pure substances are made in nature and are free from artificial additives, but can contain many elements and/or compounds.

5 a

6 c

7 b

8 c The chemical formula of the substance. If the formula shows only one type of atom, the substance is an element. If the formula shows two or more types of atom, the substance is a compound. A compound contains two or more elements chemically bonded together.

9 impurities are present/the air pressure has increased

10 18 karat gold: (18 ÷ 24) × 100 = 75% gold
9 karat gold: (9 ÷ 24) × 100 = 37.5% gold

11 a No, it is not a pure substance. It contains 99.9% silver, which means it has some impurities (0.1%).
b Scandinavian silver contains 83% silver and 17% other metals (100 – 83 = 17). Scandinavian silver therefore contains less silver than sterling silver and is less pure.

8.4 Distillation

1 heating, cooling

2 condensed

3 a **A** heat/Bunsen burner; **B** thermometer; **C** distilled water/distillate
b The thermometer detects the temperature of the vapour as it enters the condenser. This will identify the substance being separated by its boiling point.
c **iii**

4 a colourless/no colour
b water
c Boil the distillate and check the boiling point, which should be 100 °C. (Also correct, but GCSE level answers: Use dry blue cobalt chloride paper and it will turn pink if water is present *or* Add some of the distillate to anhydrous white copper sulfate. It will turn blue if water is present.)
d For safety reasons: if all the liquid in the round-bottomed flask evaporates, the flask may shatter.

5 a by evaporation using warm air in the tumble dryer
b by condensing the vapour through cooling and then collecting the liquid

6 a ethanol has a lower boiling point than water and so will evaporate first
b distillation – the ethanol will condense and can be collected

7 a **A** evaporation; **B** condensation; **C** melting; **D** freezing
b **A**
c **B**

8 a to cool the vapour down so it condenses
b Sea water is heated. Water boils. Particles have enough kinetic energy to leave the liquid state and become water vapour. Vapour rises and passes down the condenser. Cold water around the condenser cools the vapour, so it condenses to a liquid and collects in the beaker.
c distillation (simple distillation)
d Less distillate would form as the vapour would not cool down and condense to be collected. The vapour will stay as a gas and be lost into the surrounding air.

9 a **A** – The condenser has an outer tube where cold water circulates and an inner tube that the vapour travels down.
b Less distillate will be collected. The condenser is unlikely to fill completely with cold water, so less condensation occurs.

8.5 Chromatography

1 soluble, solvent

2 two (blue, yellow)

3 a They each have only a single spot on the chromatogram.
b blue, yellow
c The chromatogram for the purple ink should show a spot at the same height as the pure blue spot and another spot at the same height as the pure red spot. This is because it is a mixture of red and blue dyes.

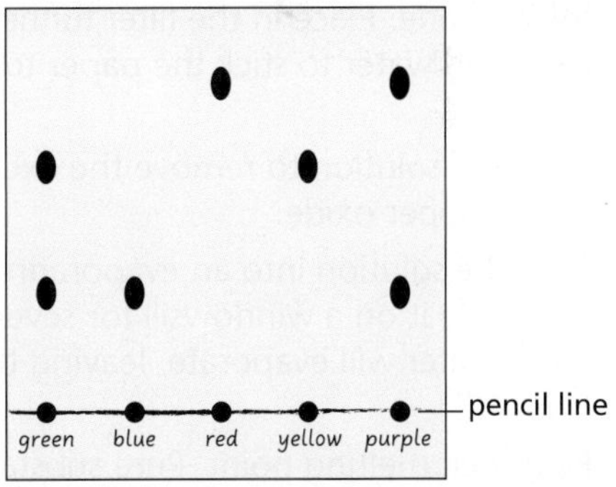

d The line must be drawn in pencil because it is not soluble in the solvent, and so will not move up the filter paper and interfere with the chromatogram.

4 a **B**, **D**
b 5
c Conditions are kept the same and the solvent is the same, the same piece of filter paper is used. The experiment is testing the sweets in the same controlled conditions, so comparisons can be made.

5 **i** green; **ii** pure; **iii** red

6 **a** 43 ÷ 53 = 0.81; **b** 26 ÷ 53 = 0.49

7 The pigments were not soluble in the solvent that the scientist used. They should use a different solvent.

8 To reduce the hazard from flammable substances there must be no naked flames present. To reduce the risk of inhaling solvents, we can:

- make sure the bottle top on the solvent is always replaced quickly after use
- keep windows/doors open to maintain good ventilation
- carry out the experiment in the fume cupboard
- keep the bung or lid on the chromatography experiment as much as possible
- wear breathing apparatus.

Unit 8 maths and practical skills

1 **c, b, a, d**

2 **a** – **iii**; **b** – **ii**; **c** – **i**; **d** – **iv**

3 **a** **A** filter paper; **B** residue; **C** filter funnel; **D** filtrate; **E** boiling tube

b Fold the filter paper in half, and then in half again. Open up one of the open edges to form a cone. Place in the filter funnel. Add a drop of water to stick the paper to the funnel.

4 **a** Filter the solution to remove the excess black copper oxide.

b Pour the solution into an evaporating basin and leave it on a windowsill for several days. Water will evaporate, leaving the solid crystals.

c Find their melting point. Pure substances have very clearly defined melting points, impure substances have a range of melting points.

5 **a** **iv**

b The cold tap water circulates around the outer layer of the condenser. Hot water vapour passes through the inner tube and warms up the water in the outer layer.

c 100 °C

d change of state from gas/vapour to a liquid; cooler when it leaves the condenser

6 **a** filtration

b **A**: 0.8 × 12.0 = 9.6

B: 0.75 × 9.2 = 6.9

C: 0.4 × 9.6 = 3.8

c No. Solutes (in this case, plant pigments) can be more or less soluble in different solvents. This means they may travel up the filter paper more easily or less easily with different solvents, which will affect the R_f values.

Unit 9 Periodic Table

9.1 The structure of the Periodic Table

1 **c**

2 **i** periods; **ii** groups

3 water is a compound; only elements are listed in the Periodic Table

4 **b**

5 **a** two (hydrogen, helium)

b false

6 **d**

7 **a** **ii** francium, Fr (helium is not in Group 1, but it is in Period 1)

b tellurium, Te

c similar chemical and physical properties

8 **a** **D, E, A, C, B**

b Each element is ordered from left to right in order of atomic number. Once the end of the period is finished, the next period starts on the left-hand side.

c **E**

9 Gold and silver are unreactive and exist naturally as elements (rather than within compounds) in the Earth's crust.

10 **a**

Element symbol	Atomic mass	Atomic number
Li	7	3
N	14	7
O	16	8
S	32	16

b Ne (neon)

c Mendeleev was able to use the atomic mass to order the elements.

d Any **three** from: the modern Periodic Table is arranged in order of increasing atomic number; Mendeleev knew of 64 elements, we now know of over 100 elements; the gaps he left are all filled in; some symbols have changed, for example, J to I; some atomic masses have been more accurately measured and so there are no uncertain values or duplications.

9.2 Properties of elements in the Periodic Table

1 Can be in any order in the correct column:

Metal	Non-metal
a	**c**
b	**d**
e	

2 group

3 **a** copper and iron; they are both metals

b iron

c neon; it is a noble gas

4 **a** **iii**

b physical properties

c **ii** – a flammable substance burns easily

5 **a** **A**, **B**, **C**, **D** – they are all metals

b **B** – this element is at the bottom of Group 1

c **E** – this element is in Group 7

6 **a**

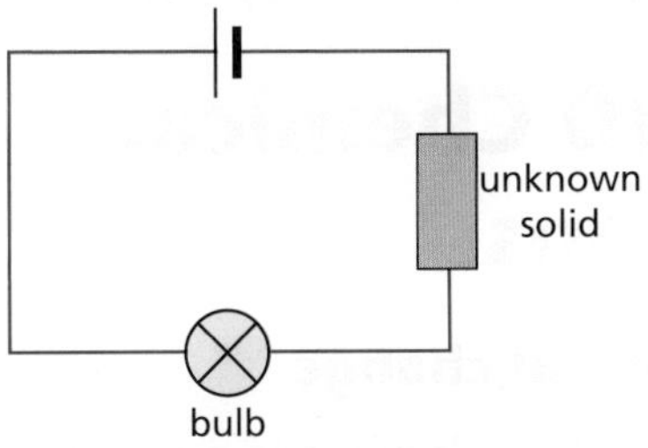

b If the bulb lights, the element is a metal. If it does not light, the element is a non-metal.

7 **a** gas

b **V** – it is denser than water

c **T** – its melting and boiling points are lower than those of element **S**

9.3 Reactions of elements and compounds

1 true

2 **a**

3 copper oxide

4 **a** potassium reacts with oxygen to form potassium oxide

b hydrochloric acid + calcium → calcium chloride + hydrogen

5 magnesium + oxygen → magnesium oxide

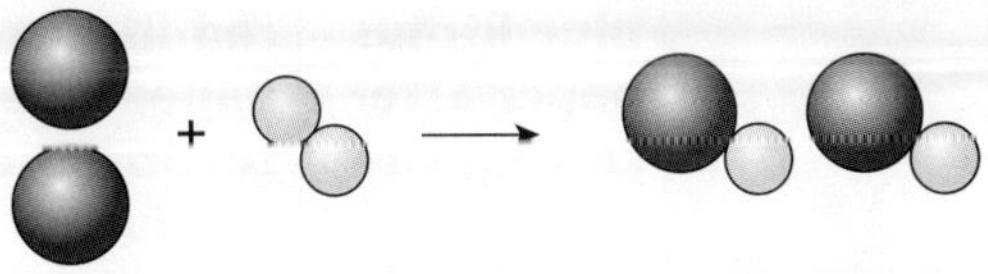

6 **a** The hydrogen gas was released into the atmosphere.

b Mass is never lost or gained during a chemical reaction.

c Put a lid or a balloon on the beaker after adding the metal. This would contain the gas and prevent it being lost to the atmosphere. (The gas could also be collected by displacing water, but this would be difficult to do on a balance.)

7 **a** **i** one; **ii** two; **iii** four

b

Element	Number of atoms on the left of the equation	Number of atoms on the right of the equation
iron (Fe)	3	1
oxygen (O)	5	8
carbon (C)	1	4

c **ii**

9.4 Using the Periodic Table

1 **i** oxygen; **ii** oxide

2 **a** Alkalis are bases that dissolve in water. Not all bases dissolve in water.

b yes

3 **a** titanium oxide

b basic

4 **a** magnesium oxide, MgO

b sulfur dioxide, SO_2

5 basic

6 aluminium, Al

7 **a** **B**, **C**

b metals form oxides that are bases; a base would have a pH from 8 to 12

8 **a** **D**, **E**, **G**

b **iv**

c **A**, **B**, **F**, **C**, **D**

d **G**, because it is a noble gas and these are unreactive elements

9

Oxide	Colour of blue litmus paper after testing the product	Colour of red litmus paper after testing the product
magnesium oxide, MgO	blue	blue
sulfur dioxide, SO_2	red	red
sodium oxide, Na_2O	blue	blue

Unit 9 maths and practical skills

1 27

2

Element	Did the bulb light?	Metal, non-metal or metalloid?
hydrogen, H	no	non-metal
sulfur, S	no	non-metal
scandium, Sc	yes, brightly	metal
tellurium, Te	yes, dimly	metalloid

3 a physical property

b it reacted with oxygen to form a metal oxide

c because they are very reactive with water and air

4 a i

b Fluorine, F, and neon, Ne, are both gases and so have already melted at room temperature. They must have a lower melting point than beryllium as it is a solid at room temperature.

c Elements in a period do not have the same physical properties as each other. There will be a trend in physical properties, but they will not be the same.

5 **i** 371.15 = (98 + 273.15)

ii 336.65 = (63.5 + 273.15)

6 a

Elements	Number of atoms in the reactants	Number of atoms in the products
carbon, C	3	3
hydrogen, H	8	8
oxygen, O	8	10

b No, because there are more atoms in the products than the reactants. There are more oxygen atoms present.

7 a fluorine, chlorine

b boiling point increases as you go down the group

c

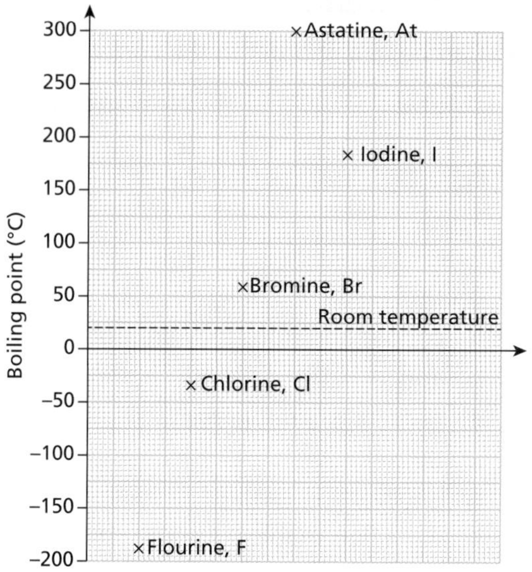

d iodine has a boiling point which fits the trend of Group 7/iodine has similar chemical properties to other Group 7 elements

Unit 10 Chemical reactions

10.1 Chemical change

1 Any **three** from: bubbles of gas; a change in temperature; a colour change; a change in mass.

2 **b**

3 a CO_2

b H_2O

4 **b**

5 Atoms/mass cannot be created or destroyed in a chemical reaction. This is the law of conservation of mass.

6 methane + oxygen → carbon dioxide + water

7 In incomplete combustion there is not enough oxygen available to react with all the fuel; in complete combustion there is enough oxygen and all the fuel is used up. The products of incomplete combustion are carbon monoxide, carbon (soot) and water; the products of complete combustion are carbon dioxide and water.

8 39.7 – 15.6 = 24.1 g

9 there is the same number of each type of atom on both sides of the equation

10 mass increased; magnesium reacted with oxygen to form magnesium oxide; mass of product includes mass of magnesium and mass of oxygen

11 hydrogen, carbon

10.2 Acids and alkalis

1 corrosive

2 red

3 **a** green

b it is neutral

4 **a**

5 hydrogen

6 potassium, oxygen, hydrogen

7 It turns a range of different colours rather than just two, and each colour gives the pH number on a scale; it can indicate how strong or weak the acid or alkali is.

8 milk

9 pH 1

10 A reaction would be observed in both cases because the metal will react with the acids to make bubbles of hydrogen (and a salt). There would be more bubbles of gas/a more vigorous reaction/more fizzing when the magnesium reacted with the hydrochloric acid than the vinegar. This is because the hydrochloric acid is a stronger acid than the vinegar.

11 A base neutralises an acid. Alkalis are a type of base that is soluble in water. Not all bases are soluble in water.

12 The solution is very acidic. It is more acidic than a solution with a pH of 1, because the pH number is lower.

10.3 Thermal decomposition

1 **i** heating; **ii** one; **iii** two or more

2 **c**

3 bubble the gas through limewater; limewater will turn milky/cloudy.

4 **b**

5 (carbon dioxide) gas released into atmosphere

6 **a**

7 **a** no

b reactant and solid product are both white

c calcium carbonate → calcium oxide + carbon dioxide

8 Barium is most reactive, followed by calcium, then magnesium. Barium needs the most energy to thermally decompose its carbonate. This suggests it has the strongest chemical bonds to break, so it must be the most reactive metal.

9 $CuCO_3 \rightarrow CuO + CO_2$

10.4 Oxidation

1 compound

2 the addition of oxygen to a substance

3 **a**

4 Both oxygen and water are needed for rusting to occur.

5 the removal of oxygen from a compound

6 **c**, **d**

7 **a** iron oxide

b The oxidised iron in the iron oxide is reduced by carbon. The carbon is oxidised to form carbon dioxide.

8 The magnesium reacted with oxygen in the air. The mass of the magnesium oxide is the same as the mass of the magnesium and oxygen at the start of the reaction. The student was only able to measure the mass of the magnesium at the start of the investigation.

9 On the outside of the folded copper, the copper has been oxidised by reacting with oxygen in the air. On the inside, the copper was protected and no oxygen was able to reach the surface to react with the copper.

10 **a** aluminium + oxygen → aluminium oxide

b Only the surface of the aluminium can react with oxygen in the air, the layer of aluminium oxide prevents the oxygen from reacting with any aluminium atoms inside the block of aluminium. When the rust flakes off the surface of the iron, it exposes the next layer to oxygen in the air so it can be oxidised.

10.5 Neutralisation

1 salt + water

2 pH 7

3 they contain bases

4 (strong) acid

5 **a**

6 H_2O, KCl

7 **c**

8 **i** hydrogen; **ii** hydroxide (or hydrogen and oxygen); **iii** alkali

9 The blue indicator tells us the final solution is alkaline. This means the student added more sodium hydroxide than was needed to neutralise the acid.

10.6 Reactions of acids and alkalis

1 **c**

2 **a** fizzing/production of bubbles

b hydrogen

3 **c**, **e**

4 sodium sulfate

5 **b**, **e**

6 The carbon dioxide formed during the reaction is a gas. This was observed as bubbles/fizzing.

7 **a** magnesium sulfate + hydrogen

b magnesium chloride

c calcium nitrate

8 sulfuric acid and either potassium oxide or potassium hydroxide (no carbon dioxide was produced during the reaction so the base could not have been potassium carbonate)

9 **c**

10.7 Displacement reactions

1 **i** more reactive; **ii** less reactive

2 carbon, hydrogen

3 Chlorine will displace the bromine, forming potassium chloride.

4 Any **one** from: temperature change, colour change, bubbles of gas (hydrogen)/fizzing.

5 Potassium displaces the magnesium from the magnesium nitrate because potassium is more reactive than magnesium.

potassium + magnesium nitrate → magnesium + potassium nitrate

6 Iron is more reactive than copper. This means that iron can displace copper from copper sulfate. As copper is less reactive than iron, it cannot displace iron from iron sulfate.

7 Carbon is less reactive than sodium, so it cannot displace sodium from its compound.

8 When metals react with acids a displacement reaction occurs, and hydrogen is displaced. Zinc is more reactive than hydrogen, so zinc displaces the hydrogen from the compound.

zinc + hydrochloric acid → zinc chloride + hydrogen

9 **a** magnesium + potassium sulfate (no reaction)

b potassium nitrate + magnesium

c potassium sulfate + zinc

d zinc + magnesium sulfate (no reaction)

10 **a** – **ii**; **b** – **iii**; **c** – **i**

11 Place metal **A** into a solution of metal **B** sulfate. If a reaction occurs, then metal **A** is more reactive than metal **B**. Check the result by placing metal **B** into a solution of metal **A** sulfate. There should be no reaction.

10.8 Energetics

1 thermometer (or a temperature probe with a datalogger)

2 a substance that speeds up the rate of reaction, without being used up in the reaction

3 **a** it would have increased

b it would have been transferred to the surroundings

4

Endothermic changes	Exothermic changes
photosynthesis	setting off fireworks
thermal decomposition	burning wood

5 **d**

6 Endothermic. The products contain more energy than the reactants; energy has been absorbed by the reaction.

7 There was a drop in temperature, cold enough for water in the atmosphere to condense and freeze on the surface of the flask. This is because the change in the flask is endothermic. Energy is being transferred from the surroundings to the reaction, causing the temperature to decrease.

8 **a** volume of solution; starting temperature

b use larger volumes of the reacting chemicals; use an insulating cup; use a test tube rack rather than holding the reaction vessel

9 The energy absorbed from the surroundings and used to break the bonds in copper carbonate is higher than the energy needed to make the bonds in copper oxide and carbon dioxide. This means the overall reaction is endothermic.

Unit 10 maths and practical skills

1 **b**

2 pH 5

3 a oxidation
  b mass of oxygen: 0.20 – 0.12 = 0.08 g
4 magnesium (most reactive), metal X, copper (least reactive)
5 a 30 cm^3
  b accept any time between 66 and 70 s
6 **b**
7 green
8 a thermal decomposition (endothermic)
  b mass of copper oxide = 45.80 – 45.00 = 0.80 g; mass of carbon dioxide = 46.24 – 45.80 = 0.44 g
9 a lead; copper and silver are both less reactive than hydrogen so cannot displace the hydrogen from the acid
  b lead + hydrochloric acid → lead chloride + hydrogen
10 a acid; when the reaction stops/levels off, there is still a mass of metal carbonate left
  b The reaction is fastest at the start and the mass of metal carbonate falls quite quickly. The reaction then slows down, eventually levelling off.
  c The reaction slows down over time as the reactants (metal carbonate and acid) are used up. When all the acid is used up, the reaction stops.
  d **i**, **iii**

Unit 11 Materials

11.1 The reactivity series

1 **d**
2 decreases
3 **b**
4 Sodium is the most reactive metal and copper the least reactive. Magnesium is more reactive than copper but less reactive than sodium.
5 It can be used to extract metals from their ores. Metals less reactive than carbon can be extracted in this way.
6 it is unreactive
7 a magnesium (most reactive), metal **Z**, iron, tin (least reactive)
  b metal **Z** + iron oxide → metal **Z** oxide + iron
8 Aluminium is more reactive than gold. Gold can be found as an element in the Earth's crust. Aluminium is found combined with other elements and needs to be extracted. The technology to extract aluminium from its ore took time to develop.
9 a one substance takes the place of another in a compound
  b temperature change, colour change, copper forming on the surface of the iron filings
  c iron + copper sulfate → iron sulfate + copper
10 a oxygen is removed
  b metal **C** is more reactive than carbon
  c metal **C** (most reactive), metal **B**, metal **A** (least reactive); metal **A** is the least reactive as it is the only one of the three metals that does not react with dilute hydrochloric acid; metal **C** is the most reactive as it is the only metal more reactive than carbon

11.2 Ceramics and composites

1 **a**, **d**
2 **a**
3 ceramic
4 Any **two** from: hard and resistant to wear; relatively light; brittle; thermal insulators; electrical insulators; non-magnetic; chemically stable; non-toxic; non-ductile.
5 **c**
6 Composites are made from two or more materials that usually have different properties. The composite combines the properties of these materials to make a substance that has more useful properties than any of the materials alone.
7 poor conductors of electricity; they are not ductile
8 a mass of aggregate; the masses of all other substances (cement, sand and water) in the mixture remain the same
  b Any **one** from: volume of water, mass of sand, mass of cement, size of concrete bar.
  c 1:2
  d 1:5
9 **b**, **c**, **d**
10 A matrix (or binder) binds together fibres or fragments, which act as reinforcement. The reinforcement adds strength to the composite material.
11 **i** reinforcement; **ii** compressive; **iii** tensile

11.3 Using the reactivity series

1 a naturally occurring rock from which a metal (or mineral) can be extracted

2 **a**

3 **b** potassium; it is more reactive than carbon, so carbon cannot displace potassium from its compound

4 **i** oxygen; **ii** ores; **iii** reduced

5 **a**, **d**

6 lead oxide + carbon → carbon dioxide + lead

7 zinc oxide is reduced to form zinc; carbon is oxidised to form carbon dioxide

8 Carbon will reduce any metal compound lower than carbon in the reactivity series. This happens in a displacement reaction, producing the metal and carbon dioxide. Carbon acts as a reducing agent.

9 **a** Copper oxide, because copper is the least reactive of the three metals. The more reactive the metal, the harder it is to reduce. This is because metals with a high reactivity make stronger bonds in their compounds.

10 **a** a chemical that removes oxygen from a substance

b carbon + iron oxide → carbon dioxide + iron

c carbon; it has gained oxygen during the reaction

11 **a** Zinc metal would be formed from zinc oxide. Carbon is more reactive than zinc, so would displace the zinc from zinc oxide; the zinc oxide would be reduced, and the carbon oxidised.

zinc oxide + carbon → zinc + carbon dioxide

b Aluminium would not be formed from aluminium oxide. Carbon is less reactive than aluminium, so would not displace aluminium from aluminium oxide.

12 **Extraction of copper from copper oxide**

copper oxide + carbon → copper + carbon dioxide

This is a displacement reaction. Carbon reduces the copper oxide to copper by removing the oxygen. Carbon dioxide is also formed. Copper oxide can be reduced with moderate heating.

Thermal decomposition of copper carbonate

copper carbonate → copper oxide + carbon dioxide

This is a thermal decomposition reaction which forms copper oxide and carbon dioxide. Both reactions form carbon dioxide. Copper carbonate must be heated to a high temperature for thermal decomposition to occur.

11.4 Polymers

1 **a**

2 **a**

3 Any **two** from: DNA; protein; RNA; cellulose; chitin; silk; rubber; examples of proteins (e.g. collagen and keratin). Allow any correct example.

4 non-toxic, so the contents are safe to drink; lightweight, so the bottle is not too heavy; insoluble in water, so the drink does not leak out; strong, so that it doesn't break easily

5 It means that most human-made polymers are difficult to dispose of. Plastics can remain in landfill sites for many years. Plastic that escapes into the environment can cause harmful pollution because it lasts for a long time. The partial breakdown of plastic produces microplastics; these are tiny plastic pieces that can end up inside animals and damage them.

6 Most polymers are flexible and can bend, ceramics are brittle and will break if bent.

7 14 (the last monomer is not complete)

8 **a** $(42 + 41 + 41) \div 3 = 41$ mm to 2 s.f.

b check for anomalies; check the range of the data; make sure the measurement is repeatable

c mass on x-axis and mean distance on the y-axis; points plotted in correct place; suitable curve of best fit drawn through all the points

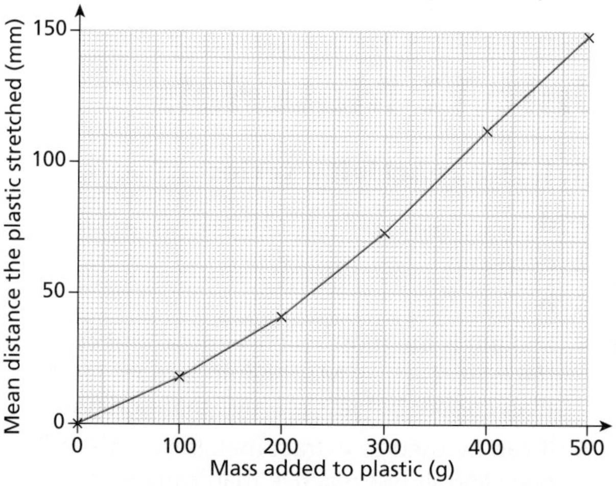

9 **a** The polymer molecules can slide over each other because there are no cross-links holding them in place.

b A high temperature is needed to break the cross-links between the strands of polymer.

c The branched structure of plastic **B** means that the polymer strands do not lie together as closely as the strands in plastic **A**, so there is more space between them.

Unit 11 maths and practical skills

1 a ii

b $(65.7 + 72.1 + 65.2 + 73.4) \div 4 = 69.1\,°C$

2 A > **C** > **B**

3 a type of metal

b Any **two** from: volume of acid; mass/size of piece of metal; concentration of acid.

c thermometer

4 a Carbon reduces the iron oxide to iron by removing the oxygen. Carbon is oxidised in this reaction, to carbon dioxide. The carbon is more reactive than the iron, so displaces it from the iron oxide.

b iron oxide + carbon → carbon dioxide + iron

c The aluminium oxide and carbon would not react. Aluminium is more reactive than carbon, so carbon cannot displace aluminium from the aluminium oxide.

5 a $(30.5 - 20.0) = 10.5\,°C$

b copper sulfate + zinc → zinc sulfate + copper

c no reaction occurred, so silver is less reactive than copper

d magnesium > zinc > iron > copper > silver

6 a Y > **Z** > **X**; metal **X** is the least reactive as it is found in the ground unreacted; metal **Y** is the most reactive as it reacts vigorously with water

b Carbon can displace metal **Z** from its compound, so metal **Z** is less reactive than carbon. Metal **Z** does not react with water, so it is less reactive than hydrogen. Therefore, metal **Z** is below hydrogen in the reactivity series.

c Gold, silver

7 a it acts as a control/to compare with the results of the other two rods

b the type of reinforcement

c $10 \times 2 \times 2 = 40\,cm^3$

d concrete bar **B**; because the concrete has been reinforced, and the iron is stronger than the wood

Unit 12 Earth and atmosphere

12.1 The Earth

1 crust, mantle, outer core, inner core

2 i lithosphere; **ii** tectonic

3 a i crust; **ii** mantle; **iii** outer core; **iv** inner core

b outer core

c outer core (accept core)

d $6490 \times 2 = 12\,980\,km$

4 a both are made of iron and nickel

b inner core is solid and outer core is liquid (accept inner core is more dense/hotter)

c it is too deep to drill down to/too hot

5 3 cm = 30 mm; in 70 years, $30 \times 70 = 2100\,mm$

6 a ii

b crust – 35 km; mantle – 2900 km; tectonic plate – 125 km

7 a i lower; **ii** higher

b i – The density of the Earth overall can be calculated by finding the mean of the densities of all the layers of the Earth. The density of the crust and mantle together is $2800 + 4500 = 7300\,kg/m^3$, which is divided by 2 to give a mean of $3650\,kg/m^3$. This shows that the density of the core must be much higher if an overall density of $5500\,kg/m^3$ is to be found. If the density of the core was $9200\,kg/m^3$ then the overall density for the Earth would be:
$2800 + 4500 + 9200 = 16\,500 \div 3 = 5500\,kg/m^3$.

8 b, e

12.2 The rock cycle

1 i igneous; **ii** sedimentary; **iii** metamorphic

2 sedimentary

3 a i

b sedimentary

4 a biological, chemical, physical

b sedimentary

c Any **one** from:

– Biological weathering is caused by animals scraping or wearing down the rock to small pieces or by plant roots growing into cracks and pushing the rock apart.

– Chemical weathering is caused by chemical reactions with the rock, e.g. acid rain reacts with limestone and chalk rock to create new products.

– Physical weathering can be caused by freezing and thawing of water which has seeped into cracks. Water expands as it freezes, causing small pieces to break away. In deserts the expansion and contraction of rock due to the heat from the sun causes pieces of rock to break off.

5 **1** weathering; **2** deposition; **3** sedimentary; **4** metamorphic; **5** magma; **6** igneous

6 **a** Metamorphic rock melts to form magma. When magma cools it forms igneous rock.

b Uplift causes metamorphic rock to reach the Earth's surface. Weathering and erosion cause rock fragments to break off and be carried away by water or wind. The fragments are eventually deposited, and over time they are compacted and cemented to form sedimentary rock.

7 **a** Uplift causes igneous rock to reach the Earth's surface. Weathering and erosion cause rock fragments to break off and be carried away by water or wind. The fragments are eventually deposited, and over time they are compacted and cemented to form sedimentary rock.

b Igneous rock is subjected to high heat and pressure. This causes changes in the structure of the rock, producing metamorphic rock.

8 **b**, **c**

9 **a** The rocks will expand and contract due to the extremes of heat and cold. This can cause weathering, which will make the rock split.

b Water would not exist as a liquid – it would be frozen all the time. Plants would not be able to take in water through their roots or move it around the plant for growth, transporting chemicals or carrying out photosynthesis.

c Sedimentary rock is likely because weathering of rock would produce sediments that could have been carried by the (now dried-up) rivers. Igneous rock is possible because there may be extinct volcanoes. Metamorphic rock is possible because uplift may have caused the formation of mountain ranges.

10 **a** the molten rock that formed obsidian cooled very quickly

b **i** – as the molten rock hit the cold sea there would not have been time for atoms to become arranged in a crystalline structure

12.3 The atmosphere

1 **a**

2 **i**

3 **a** **iv**

b air is a mixture and all the others are pure compounds

4 oxygen, nitrogen

5 **a** oxygen

b 21%

c nitrogen

d 78%

e Any **one** of: argon, water vapour, carbon dioxide, methane, ozone, CFCs.

6

Substance	Chemical formula	diagram letter
oxygen	O_2	**C**
carbon dioxide	CO_2	**E**
water vapour	H_2O	**B**
nitrogen	N_2	**A**
argon	Ar	**D**

7 **a** carbon dioxide

b Green plants carry out photosynthesis, which removes carbon dioxide from the atmosphere.

c When the Earth cooled to below 100 °C, water vapour in the atmosphere condensed to form liquid water, which made the oceans.

8 percentage decrease = (original figure – new figure) ÷ original × 100

95.00 – 0.04 = 94.96

94.96 ÷ 95.00 = 0.9996 × 100 = 99.96% decrease

12.4 The carbon cycle

1 **i** carbon dioxide; **ii** fossil fuels; **iii** combustion; **iv** energy

2 **b**

3 **b**, **d**

4 **d**

5 respiration

6 dead plants and animals

7 **a** photosynthesis (accept dissolving in the oceans)

b respiration, combustion (accept decomposition, volcanic eruptions)

c The rate of processes that added carbon dioxide to the atmosphere must have been balanced with the rate of processes that removed carbon dioxide from the atmosphere.

8 **a** from food

b it is released by decomposition back into the atmosphere as carbon dioxide c The carbon compounds in dead plants and animals and their waste would not be broken down to release carbon dioxide back into the atmosphere. Part of the carbon cycle would stop. Carbon sources are limited, and so the supply for photosynthesis and feeding would become less.

9 **a** **i**, **iii**

b 2.75 ÷ 1.86 = 1.48 kg (accept 1.478)

c (natural) gas

d No, the student is not correct. Wood releases less heat energy than natural gas. To release the same amount of energy as natural gas, more wood is needed and more carbon dioxide is produced overall. Compare the energy released by 1 kg of each fuel:

gas: 15.4 kW h

wood: 4.5 kW h

15.4 ÷ 4.5 = 3.42 kW h

So 1 kg of natural gas releases 3.42 times more energy than 1 kg wood. To release the same amount of energy as 1 kg of gas, 3.42 kg of wood is needed. The amount of carbon dioxide produced will therefore be 3.42 × 1.86 = 6.37 kg. This compares to 2.75 kg of carbon dioxide produced by burning 1 kg of natural gas.

e non-renewable

f renewable

g When natural gas is burned it produces carbon that has been stored underground for millions of years. This adds extra carbon dioxide to the atmosphere. When wood is burned it produces carbon dioxide that has recently been removed from the atmosphere by photosynthesis. The growth of new plants and trees can balance out the carbon dioxide that is produced when they are burned.

12.5 Climate change

1 **a**, **e**

2 **d**

3 **b**

4 **a** peer review

b Any **two** from: to ensure the experiment or observation is reproducible; to make sure accurate conclusions have been made without bias; to check for plagiarism (copying).

5 **a** about (just over) 275 ppm

b about 415 ppm

c the amount of carbon dioxide in the Earth's atmosphere has increased over the time period shown

d it is likely to make the greenhouse effect stronger, causing the Earth to get hotter – this is known as global warming

6 **a**, **c**, **d**, **e**, **b**

7 **a** Climate change is a significant and lasting change in the Earth's weather patterns over time. There have been many significant changes in the Earth's climate during its history.

b Global warming is causing climate change on Earth today. It is causing the average temperature of the Earth to increase, which is driving changes in the Earth's weather systems.

8 Global warming is causing the average temperature of the Earth to increase. Areas which previously had temperatures that were too cold for mosquitoes to live in may now become suitable for them to survive. The mosquitoes may increase in these areas, spreading malaria to the people who live there. People who were not used to taking precautions against catching malaria may die.

9 **a** the average (mean) amount of carbon dioxide

b the average (mean) amount of carbon dioxide in the Earth's atmosphere increased between 1960 and 2020

c the growth of plants means they can take in more carbon dioxide; in the winter plants/leaves die and carbon dioxide is released back into the atmosphere

10 **a** as temperature increases, the solubility of carbon dioxide in water decreases

b 0.04 g/100 g water

c There will be less carbon dioxide dissolved in the oceans. This is because carbon dioxide is less soluble in water at higher temperatures.

12.6 Sustainable development

1 **i** non-renewable; **ii** replaced

2 **b**, **c**

3 **a** Sustainable practices mean that a resource (for example, fish) is used in such a way it will be available to future generations to carry on using. This means that human activities are not limiting the supply of resources.

b **i**, **ii**

4 a Recycled metal can be used to make new metal products (shown in the flow chart). This means that less metal ore will be needed. Metal ores are a limited resource. They will be preserved for longer if recycled metal is used.

Recycling reduces the amount of metal that is thrown away (shown in the flow chart). This reduces the need for more landfill sites to be created.

(Other reasons include: less energy needed to recycle compared to mining raw materials and extraction; recycling is cheaper overall.)

b Additional steps are needed in the recycling process, for example, extra collection and transport, sorting of the different types of metals, removal of any impurities; the extra steps will need extra equipment, workers, time and energy.

Some metal products may not be recyclable and still have to be taken to landfill.

5 a Solar energy is a renewable energy resource so it will not run out.

Solar energy does not release carbon dioxide into the atmosphere.

b Any **two** from: the sun does not shine at night; less effective when it is cloudy; potential loss of land for crop farming.

6 a total cost of materials: $£0.92 \times 20 = £18.40$

cost per year: $£18.40 \div 45 = £0.41$ a year

b aluminium is cheaper (per kg and over the cost of the lifespan of the bridge); longer lifespan than a wooden bridge; mass of aluminium required is smaller than the mass of wood, so it will be easier to transport

c wood is not a limited resource/wood is a renewable resource

Unit 12 maths and practical skills

1 a Water soaked into gaps between the grains and displaced air.

b **iii**

c $25.8 - 22.3 = 3.5\,g$

d $28.4 - 27.2 = 1.2\,g$

e $(28.4 - 27.2) \div 27.2 \times 100 = 0.044 \times 100 = +4.4\%$

2 a no

b it is not easily tested, as red or silver cars can be different types and sizes and can be made of different materials

c

Question	Is it a scientific question? yes/no
Is recycling good for us?	no (this question depends on what 'good for us' means; recycling can be hazardous)
What is the best gas in the atmosphere?	no (this question depends on the person's preference)
Are metamorphic rocks harder than sedimentary rocks?	yes (this question can be tested)
Do decomposers break down plant material faster than animal material?	yes (this question can be tested, although it would depend on the decomposer as some only work on particular types of substance)

3 a **iii, iv**

b diamond, corundum

c The force used to scratch the minerals may not stay the same: for example, different people may apply different amounts of pressure. It might also be difficult to see the scratches.

d The rocks containing calcite will probably weather the quickest. This is because they are less hard than the rocks containing quartz, so they will probably be more easily broken down by weathering processes.

4 a microscope, two microscope slides and coverslips, salol, dropping pipette, water bath, kettle, thermometer, stopwatch, freezer

b Does environmental (air) temperature affect the size of crystals produced as salol cools? (The question must be specific so it can be tested.)

c

	Time crystals start to form (s)	Time no further change occurs (s)
cold slide		
warm slide		

(The independent variable usually goes in the left-hand column of a table.)

d because the salol molecules line up alongside each other in a regular pattern and bonds form between them

e largest crystals will form on the hot slide

f cool slide; the salol will take longer to cool on the hot slide and so molecules take longer to form into crystals

g igneous rock

5 a 50 cm

b 50 cm

c 0.037%

d carbon dioxide levels might be higher due to respiration of decomposers in the soil

Unit 13 Forces

13.1 Describing motion

1 c

2 A takes less time to cover the same distance so is travelling at a higher average speed

3 C has the higher average speed. **D** takes twice as long but only travels a small extra distance so therefore is travelling at a lower speed.

4 b

5 a metre rule/30 cm ruler

b stopwatch/timer

c protractor

6 a 70 m ÷ 10 s = 7 m/s

b 300 m ÷ 15 s = 20 m/s

c 3600 m ÷ 15 s = 240 m/s

7 a 40 minutes = 40 × 60 seconds = 2400 s
60 000 m ÷ 2400 s = 25 m/s

b 3 minutes = 3 × 60 seconds = 180 s
5400 m ÷ 180 s = 30 m/s

c 4 hours = 4 × 60 × 60 seconds = 14 400 s
30 000 m ÷ 14 400 s = 2.08 m/s

8 a The racing bicycle would appear to be moving away from the ordinary bicycle in a forward direction.

b The ordinary bicycle would appear to be moving away from the racing bicycle, in a backward direction.

9 a

10 a 8 km ÷ 4 h = 2 km/h

b The line is sloping upwards, so the speed is constant.

c The line is horizontal, so the object is stationary.

d First part of journey: travels 4 km from the starting point in 2 hours, i.e. travels at a a speed of 2 km/h.

Third part of journey: travels 8 km back to the starting point in 8 hours, i.e. at a speed of 1 km/h.

So it takes twice as long to return to the destination, and via a longer route.

The gradient of the third section is less than that of the first section, showing that the speed is less.

11 a Measure the distance, using a metre rule; measure the time taken from a marked/fixed point at the top of the ramp to a marked/fixed point at the bottom, using a stopwatch and then divide the distance by the measured time to obtain the speed of the car. The gradient is then altered by raising or lowering the start point of the ramp. The experiment is repeated and the new value of the speed related to the new height of the start point.

b Although the speed of the car will increase as it travels down the ramp, it is the total distance and total time that are measured. So the calculated speed will be an average value for the journey.

c The motion of the car may vary slightly during each journey, or there may be errors in measuring the time, or releasing the car correctly. Calculating the mean of several readings would give a more accurate result (closer to the true value).

13.2 Forces in action

1 i contact; **ii** non-contact; **iii** non-contact; **iv** contact; **v** non-contact

2 a force of gravity (or weight)

b non-contact

c air resistance

3 a Friction will act in the direction opposite to that of travel.

b When they are lying down there will be less air resistance because the shape is more streamlined, so their speed will be greater.

4

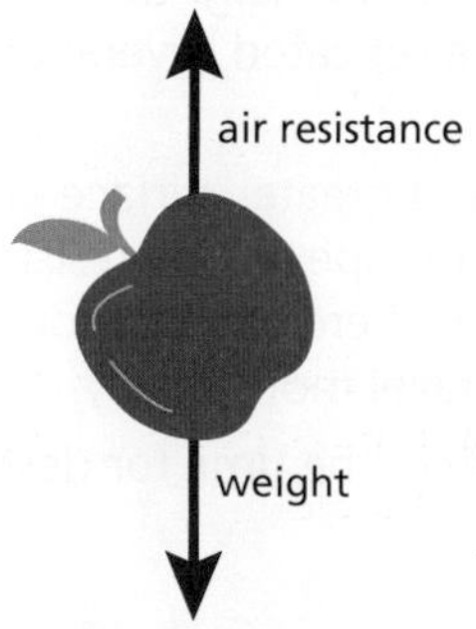

5 a

b

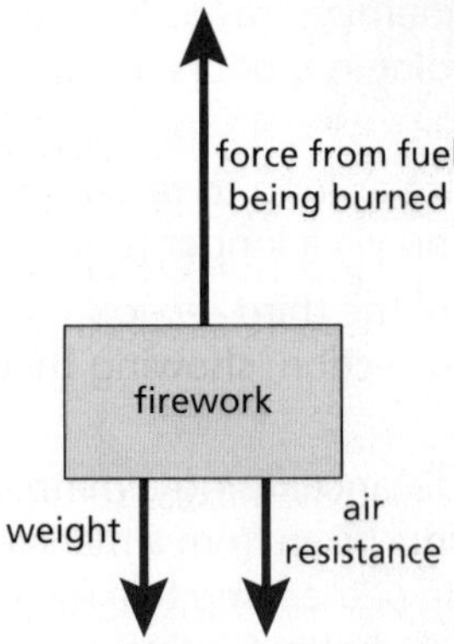

6 There is no force acting in the forwards direction after the ball has left the girl's foot. There is a force in the opposite direction, due to air resistance.

7 a It opposes the motion, acting in the opposite direction.

b streamlined shape: smooth curves, pointed nose, smooth curved fins

8 a

b same size shoe, same surface, same weights inside, pulled at similar speed

c the higher the reading on the newtonmeter, the greater the friction

9 a Shape the clay into a number of pieces, each with the same mass/weight, but each with a different shape. Measure the height of the water in the bottle. Release a clay piece and drop it into the bottle of water. Start the stopwatch when the clay shape is released and stop timing when the shape reaches the bottom of the bottle. Repeat the procedure for each of the clay pieces. The level of the water should be measured before each piece is released, and the level made up if required. Each clay piece should be released from the same height. The procedure should be repeated several times for each clay piece.

b A clay piece that has a greater surface area or a less streamlined shape will be resisted more by the water as there will be more drag and so it will travel more slowly.

c the weight could affect the time for descent

13.3 Levers and moments

1 Any two from: turning a tap, turning the control knobs on a cooker, turning the handle on a tin opener, twisting a pepper mill, pushing a door, etc.

2 the hinge

3 increasing the size of the applied force; increasing the distance from the fulcrum to where the force is applied

4 The log is closer to the fulcrum than the gardener, so the metal bar (lever) acts as a force multiplier. The output force (the upwards force exerted by the end of the bar on the log) is greater than the input force (the effort exerted by the gardener pushing down on the other end of the bar).

5 moment of a force = force applied × distance from the turning point

6 It will help because even though the force that Agnes can apply will be no greater, the longer distance to the fulcrum (the centre of the nut) will increase the moment of the force (so it will have a greater turning effect).

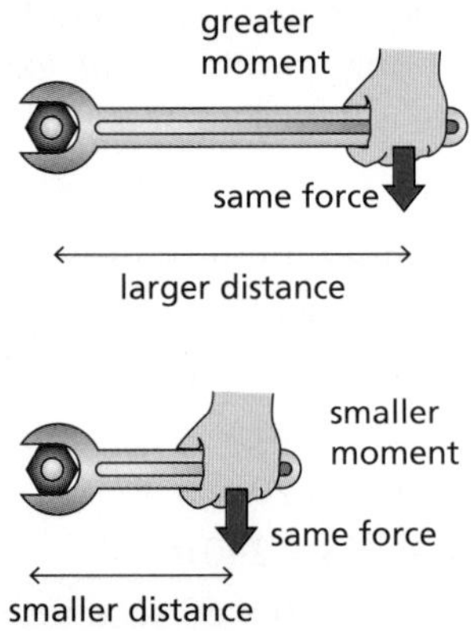

7 The scissors have a pivot (where the blades are joined together), a place where the effort is applied (the handles) and a place where the scissors apply the force to the object being cut (the blades). Placing the string closer to the pivot means that less effort is needed because the scissors act as a force multiplier. The output force (the force exerted on the string) is greater than the input force (the effort exerted by applying a force to the handles).

8 a effort – applied downwards on the end of the screwdriver handle; fulcrum – where the screwdriver rests on the edge of the tin; force – applied to the lid to push it upwards

b effort – applied by the person pushing or pulling on the end of the handle; fulcrum – where the crowbar rests on the doorframe; force – applied by the crowbar on the door

9 The smaller force is further from the fulcrum, so for the clockwise moment caused by the heavier child to be equal to the anticlockwise moment caused by the smaller child, the heavier child must sit nearer to the fulcrum.

10 30 cm = 0.3 m
turning effect = 50 N × 0.3 m = 15 N m

11 600 mm = 0.6 m
turning effect = 15 N × 0.6 m = 9 N m

12 **a** 2 × 28 = 56 N
b It will take the same turning effect or moment to open the door; if the distance to the hinge is halved, the force will need to be doubled to achieve the same moment.

13 **a** to balance the moment due to the load
b moment = 5000 N × 10 m = 50 000 N m
c Moment due to counterweight: 5000 × 6 = 30 000 N
To balance the jib, the maximum moment due to the load will be 30 000 N m.
Maximum load: 30 000 N m ÷ 24 m = 1250 N
d either move the counterweight towards the tower or use a lighter counterweight
e towards the tower.

13.4 Stretch and compression

1 **a** (might include) elastic, cotton, rubber, plastic, etc.
b it would break
c (might include) stone, slate, glass, etc.

2 **a** the weight/load/mass attached and the length of the elastic band
b subtract the original (unloaded) length of the elastic band from the length of the loaded band
c the weights would fall and land on the floor or a student's foot; the snapped elastic could fly out and hit someone in the face
d Any **two** from: limit the range of weights added, arrange the equipment so that the weights do not have far to fall, have a sand tray to catch the weights, wear goggles to protect their eyes.

3 Energy stored in the stretched elastic is transferred to the food, increasing its energy of movement (kinetic energy). As the food travels upwards, it gains in height but loses speed. Energy in the kinetic store of the food is transferred to the gravitational potential energy store.

4 **a** 6 cm **b** 21 cm **c** 0.6 cm

5 **a** As the weight increases from 0 N to 1.5 N the extension increases proportionately
b 1.4 N
c 5 cm
d 1.6 N
e It would be permanently stretched and wouldn't return to its original length.

6 When the load applied to a material has exceeded the value at which removing the load will cause the material to go back to its original length.

7 **a** line graph with labelled axes, suitable scale, accurately plotted points (crosses) and line of best fit (straight line from origin to 25 N and curving upwards beyond)
b The extension is proportional to the load up to a load of about 25 N, beyond which the extension increases for each additional 5VNs of load.
c Approximately 25 N

8 **a** carry out trial runs to find a suitable range of loads that produce a measurable extension for each bag; then using fresh bags (in case the bags had been damaged or permanently stretched by the trail runs), cut a strip from each bag that is the same width and same length; fix the strip so that the top end is supported and measure its length; add weights to the bottom end and, after each weight has been added, measure length again; subtract original length from each length with with load added to determine extension for that weight; draw graph of load against extension; draw line of best fit to show pattern
b Advantage: it is easier to compare the sets of data, e.g. what extension produced for the same force.
Disadvantage: there are two sets of data on the same graph and they could be confused.
c There is likely to be variation between bags (such as thickness of the plastic), so testing a number of bags would mean that the results were more representative.

13.5 Pressure in solids

1

Quantity	Unit	Abbreviation
area	square metres	m^2
force	newtons	N
pressure	newtons per square metre	N/m^2

2 greater

3 Snow shoes increase the area of snow over which the weight of the person pushes down, which reduces the pressure on the snow and stops the person sinking into the snow.

4 **b**

5 N/mm^2

6 $40\,N \div 5\,m^2 = 8\,N/m^2$

7 **a** **i** area: $40\,cm \times 5\,cm = 200\,cm^2$
pressure: $40\,N \div 200\,cm^2 = 0.2\,N/cm^2$

ii area: $40\,cm \times 10\,cm = 400\,cm^2$
pressure: $40\,N \div 400\,cm^2 = 0.1\,N/cm^2$

iii area: $10\,cm \times 5\,cm = 50\,cm^2$
pressure: $40\,N \div 50\,cm^2 = 0.8\,N/cm^2$

b The 10 cm × 5 cm face, as the pressure is greatest on this one.

8 $2500\,N \div 20\,m^2 = 125\,N/m^2$

9 first crate: $600\,N \div 8\,m^2 = 75\,N/m^2$
second crate: $420\,N \div 6\,m^2 = 70\,N/m^2$
The second crate exerts less pressure.

10 $6000\,N \div 80\,N/m^2 = 75\,m^2$

11 area: $0.6\,m \times 0.6\,m = 0.36\,m^2$
force: $50\,N/m^2 \times 0.36\,m^2 = 18\,N$

12 **a** $1.6\,m \times 0.125\,m \times 2 = 0.4\,m^2$

b $2\,m \times 0.08\,m \times 2 = 0.32\,m^2$

c The deep powder skis need to have a larger surface area so they spread the force due to the skier's weight over a larger area, reducing the pressure on the soft snow and stopping them from sinking in. The snow used by the downhill skier is firmer so sinking in is less of a problem; the area can be less for the same weight.

d deep powder skis: $720 \div 0.4 = 1800\,N/m^2$
downhill skis : $720 \div 0.32 = 2250\,N/m^2$

13.6 Pressure in fluids

1 **a**

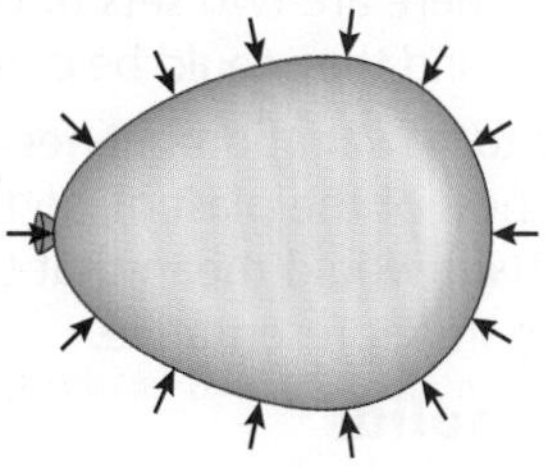

b

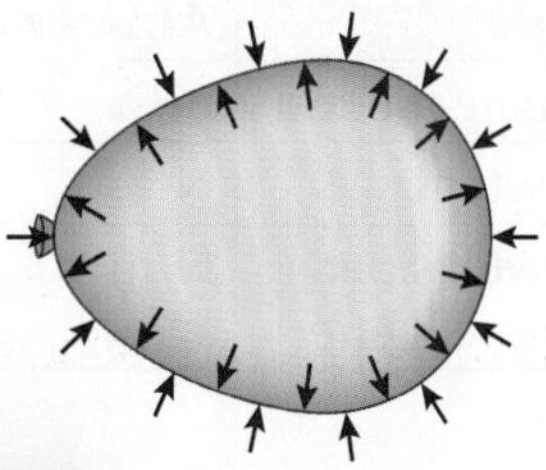

2 upthrust

3 The deeper the submarine goes, the more water there is above it. The pressure is greater because there is a greater weight of water above it, on the same area.

4 **a** particles are of a similar size to each other; they are in contact with each other

b actual particles are not that shape, colour or size and are always moving randomly

c pressure at **B** would be greater than at **A**

d There are more particles of water above point **B** so the weight of water above this point is greater than above point **A**, but the cross-sectional area is the same.

5 **a** **B**

b When the block is in the water, an upthrust force will act upwards on the block. This will reduce the overall downwards force.

6 **a** The particles of the gases in air are moving and colliding with the inside surface of the balloon. It is these collisions which keep the sides pushed out and the balloon inflated.

b Particles of water are colliding with the outside surface of the balloon and pushing it in; this water pressure is greater than the gas pressure inside the balloon, so the balloon contracts (gets smaller). It would get even smaller at greater depth in the water because water pressure increases with depth.

7 **a**

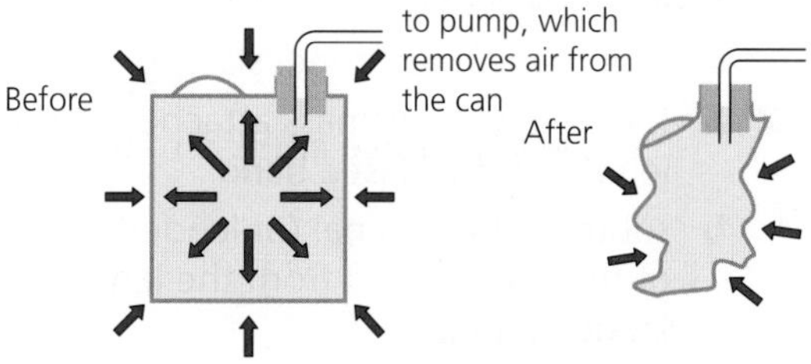

b Removing the air caused a partial vacuum inside the can; there was unequal air pressure between the inside and the outside of the can, so the greater air pressure on the outside of the can crushed it.

c 'Sucking in' suggests the sides had been pulled in from the inside whereas they have been pushed in from the outside.

8 **a** The gas pressure inside the balloon will stay the same because there is the same amount of helium gas inside but the atmospheric pressure on the outside will be less at higher altitudes; the difference in pressure causes the balloon to expand

b Eventually the difference in pressure between the inside and the outside of the balloon is too much for the balloon material to cope with and it will burst.

13.7 Using moments

1 moment = force applied × distance from force to fulcrum

2 If the hammer handle is longer, the size of the force needed to do the job decreases.

3 **a** 60 N × 10 m = 600 J

b 5000 N × 50 m = 250 000 J

4 25 000 N × 2000 m = 50 000 000 J or 50 MJ

5 Most machines turn a smaller force (the effort) into a larger force. However, the amount of work done, or energy transferred, is the same for each force. So the small force has to move through a much greater distance than the large one.

6 The force on the lid will be much smaller than the force Josh applies to the pedal. The work Josh does on the pedal will be the same as the work done on the lid. If the distance is much greater, then the force will be much less.

7 **a** 250 N × 1 m = 250 N m

b 250 N m

c 250 N m = force × 0.1 m, so force = 2500 N

d The lever is multiplying the force by 10, which makes the job easier.

e The work done by the man is the same as the work done by the lever, as the small force the man pushes down with has to move through a much greater distance than the large force applied to the rock.

8 **a** 60 N × 0.4 m = 24 N m clockwise

b 40 N × 0.6 m = 24 N m clockwise

c 48 N m clockwise.

d The anticlockwise moment would be subtracted from the clockwise moment: 24 N m – 24 N m = 0 N m. The moments would cancel each other out and the door wouldn't move.

9 Moment due to Misbah's weigh: 150 N × 2 m = 300 N m

Moment in the opposite direction due to Khalim's weight must also be 300 N m, so distance of Khalim from fulcrum is 300 N m ÷ 200 N = 1.5 m

13.8 Forces, motion and equilibrium

1 The weight of the apple is balanced by the upwards force (normal contact force) provided by the table. The apple does not move because the two forces are equal in size and opposite in direction, so they cancel out.

2 There is a downwards force on the coat due to the weight of the coat and an upwards force on the coat due to its contact with the peg. The two forces are equal in size and opposite in direction, so they balance out.

3 **a** Note that the arrow for the electrostatic force is longer. This is because, to make the paper move upwards, the electrostatic force on the paper must be bigger than its weight.

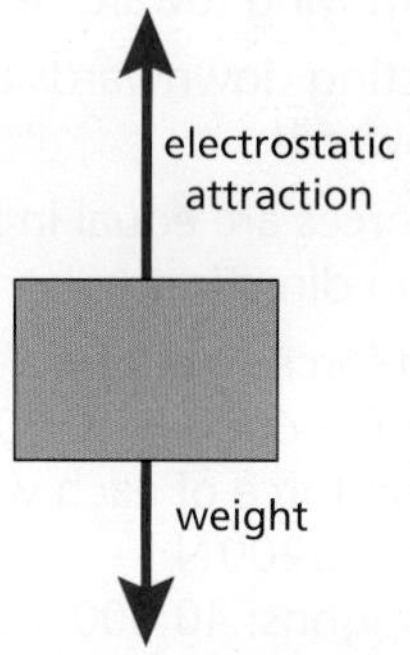

b Smaller pieces of paper are lighter. The weight of each piece of tissue paper must be less than the electrostatic force for the pieces to be lifted upwards.

4 **a** the force the cyclist applies to the pedals moves the bicycle forwards; the motion of the bicycle is opposed by friction and air resistance; the weight of the bicycle and rider acts downwards; the normal contact force from the ground acts upwards.

b The forwards force is exactly balanced by the combination of friction and air resistance.

c There is now no forwards force, but air resistance and friction are still acting to oppose the motion, so the bicycle slows down.

5 **a** force due to the engine acts forwards, air resistance and drag (the resistance to the boat's movement through the water) acts backwards; the boat's weight acts downwards, the upthrust of the water acts upwards

b The boat is accelerating, so the engine force must be greater than the total of the air resistance and drag.

6 **a** one arrow upwards from the bowl labelled 'upthrust' and one arrow downwards from the bowl labelled 'weight'; arrows both equal in length

b same as **a**, but both (equal length) arrows are longer

c two arrows downwards from the bowl, one labelled 'weight' and the other 'pushing force'; one arrow upwards marked 'upthrust' (or 'buoyancy'); the upwards arrow should be the same length as the total of the lengths of the two downwards arrows

7 a will keep moving towards left at steady speed

b will continue moving towards left but accelerating

c will keep moving towards left at steady speed

8 a weight acting downwards and air resistance acting upwards

b the two forces are equal in size and opposite in direction

9 total forward force of engine:
50 000 – 4000 – 6000 = 40 000 N
total opposing force of each wagon:
1000 + 4200 = 5200 N
number of wagons: 40 000 ÷ 5200 = 7.69, so the engine can pull a train of seven wagons

10 a it will pull the arrow towards the ground

b it will oppose the motion of the arrow and slow it down

c gravity and air resistance, both acting downwards

d Pulling the string back further increases the amount of energy supplied to the arrow, which will increase the distance the arrow can travel.

Unit 13 maths and practical skills

1 b

2 25 N × 0.15 m = 3.75 N m

3 40 N × 12 m = 480 J (or 480 N m)

4 **i** independent; **ii** dependent

5 12.2 cm; all the others are going up in steps of 0.8 cm

6 area of face: 2 m × 2 m = 4 m^2

pressure = 160 000 N ÷ 4 m^2 = 40 000 N/m^2

7 8 N × 0.7 m = 5.6 N m

8 a Set each spring up in turn on the stand, add weights up to 10 N and record how each spring extends over this range of weights.

b A suitable spring would be one which has a measurable extension for smaller weights so it can be used to measure a range of values; it would also be desirable for the spring not to extend too far, so that the newtonmeter it will be used in is of a practical size.

c They would need to try adding smaller and smaller weights (using 10 g masses), to find the smallest load that would result in a measurable movement by the end of the spring.

9 a jogger: 4 × 0.25 = 1 km

cyclist: 10 × 0.25 = 2.5 km

b 10 – 4 = 6 km/h

c The cyclist would be moving away from the jogger.

10 a independent variable: mass on hanger

dependent variable: speed/acceleration of trolley

control variables: mass of trolley, the nature of the surface of the table, etc.

b not stand too close to the falling weights and moving trolley, not let the trolley run out of control; place a tray on the floor to catch the weights

c Increasing the number of masses will increase the force acting on the trolley and make it accelerate more.

11 50 × 0.045 = 2.25 N m

12 1250 m ÷ 60 s = 20.8 m/s

13 a 0.06 m ÷ 60 s = 0.001 m/s

b 1200 m ÷ 600 s = 2 m/s

c 27 000 000 ÷ 3600 = 7500 m/s

14 **i** 0.125 m/s; **ii** 5 m/s; **iii** 500 s; **iv** 60 m; **v** 4000 s

15 **i** 10 N m; **ii** 15 N m; **iii** 80 N; **iv** 50 cm

16 a any solid surface over which the object could slide, e.g. wood, metal, plastic, felt, carpet, etc.

b The rougher the surface, the greater the friction and the greater the angle before the block starts to slide.

c independent variable – surface of the ramp; dependent variable – the angle of the slope at which the block starts to slide; possible control variables – the size and shape of the block and which face of the block is placed onto the ramp (the area in contact with the covering)

d Place the same face of the block on the ramp. Start the test with the ramp at the same small angle and increase the angle by the same small amounts until the object just starts to slide. Measure this angle. Replace the covering with a different one and repeat the test using the same procedure.

e The friction between the block and the second covering is less than that between the block and the first covering.

f The different types of covering vary by category rather than by numerical value, so they can't be represented by a numerical scale on the axis of a graph.

17 a A 1 N load placed 20 cm from the fulcrum will apply a moment of 20 N cm. To balance the see-saw there will need to be an equal moment acting in the opposite direction. The load will need to be: 20 N cm ÷ 10 cm = 2 N

b 20 N cm ÷ 40 cm = 0.5 N

c Moment due to 2 N load: 2 × 5 = 10 N cm. Moment due to 0.5 N load: 0.5 × 20 = 10 N cm. Total moment in this direction: 10 + 10 = 20 N cm. This is equal and opposite to the 20 N cm moment from the 1 N load on the other side of the fulcrum, so the see-saw balances.

18 b

Unit 14 Energy

14.1 Energy in fuels and food

1 a

2 b

3

Fuel	Application
petrol	car
natural gas	cooking
wood	fireplace for heating
candle (paraffin wax)	lighting

4 a in the chemical stores of the gas and the oxygen in the air

b into the food and also to the surroundings

c the fuel is portable and easily lit

d it would require changing the canisters regularly (inconvenient, also expensive)

5 a kettle **A** can transfer energy twice as quickly as it will get the water to boiling point in 90 s, whereas kettle **B** does this in 180 s (3 × 60 s)

b the power rating of kettle **A**, in watts (or kW), will be twice that of kettle **B**

6 10 J/s

7 A 10 W bulb transfers energy at the rate of 10 J/s and the 15 W bulb transfers 15 J/s. Therefore the 15 W bulb will transfer more energy in the same amount of time.

8 250 W is a transfer rate of 250 J/s and 2 kW is 2000 W or 2000 J/s, so the kettle transfers energy at a greater rate.

9 a the number of kilojoules (kJ, where 1 kJ = 1000 J) stored in 1 g of the fuel

b answers could include: it may have been collected for free; a wood fire is more attractive than several of the other options listed

c wood

d natural gas

10 a 5 + 50 + 30 + 45 = 130 W

b 100 ÷ 50 = 2 devices

c three possible answers:

phone charger + laptop + TV (85 W required)

phone charger + laptop + games console (100 W required)

phone charger + TV + games console (80 W required)

11 energy content per 100 g = energy content in 1 g × 100 = (energy in 150 g ÷ 150) × 100 so, energy content of food per 100 g = (1046 kJ ÷ 150) × 100 = 697 kJ

12 a For chocolate: 2 × 1000 kJ = 2000 kJ

For raisins: 4 × 315 kJ = 1260 kJ

For bananas: 350 kJ chocolate > raisins > bananas

b (12 000 ÷ 200) × 100 = 600 g

13 1890 ÷ 315 = 6 packets

14.2 Heating and cooling

1 by radiation

2 **B** > **A** > **C** > **E** > **D**

3 A thermal conductor is a material which will allow energy to pass through easily, such as a piece of copper or steel. A thermal insulator is a material which will not allow energy to pass through easily, such as wood or wool.

4 a it will decrease

b it will increase

c any energy transferred to water from the hot metal will have then been transferred to the bucket and the surrounding air

5 The food is hotter than the surroundings, so energy will be transferred from the food to the surroundings, cooling the food down. The paper is an effective insulator, so it slows down the loss of energy from the food to the surroundings. The open chips cool quickly but the wrapped food cools more slowly and stays hotter for longer.

6 **a** polystyrene beads 16 °C; paper towels 14 °C; cloth 15 °C; wood shavings 18 °C

b wood shavings > polystyrene beads > cloth > paper towels

c the students may not have used the same amount of each material; the different tests started off at different temperatures and this could make a difference (to the rate of cooling).

7 Heating the rod at one end transfers energy to the particles in the metal at that end. These particles start to vibrate more quickly. They collide with neighbouring particles and transfer energy to them. These particles now vibrate more quickly. This process continues up to the particles at the other end of the rod.

8 **a** Energy has been transferred from the boiling water to the surroundings (the cup and the air around it).

b The temperature of the tea will decrease until it reaches the temperature of the surroundings; when there is no temperature difference they will both stay the same temperature, so unless the surroundings are at 0 °C the tea will not cool to its freezing point.

9 **a** thermometer, timer

b Place an equal quantity of the same food in each container; record the starting temperature of the food (the food in each container should have approximately the same starting temperature); place a lid made of the same material as the container on each container; after a set amount of time open the containers and record the final temperatures of the food; calculate the temperature change for each container. The best container (insulator) will be the one in which there was the smallest change in the temperature of the food.

c Answers could include: cost; ease of recycling; appearance; reusable.

10 **a** from the hot chocolate to the mug by conduction and then to the surrounding air by radiation

b change the mug to one made of a material that is a better thermal insulator; add insulation around the mug; use a lid

11 Energy transfer by conduction from the warmer surroundings to the cold drink is prevented by the vacuum, as there are no particles to transfer energy. The plastic container and cap are poor thermal conductors, so help prevent the temperature of the drink in the flask increasing. The silvered surface is not relevant; the radiation from the sun does not reach it, so there is no reflection.

12 For a single-glazed window, energy is transferred by conduction through the glass (from the warm air inside to the colder outer surface of the window). The air trapped between the panes of a double-glazed window is a good insulator. This means that there is very little energy transfer by conduction to the outer surface of the window.

14.3 Processes involving energy transfer

1

System	Store
hot water bottle full of hot water	thermal
charged battery	chemical potential
lift at top of lift shaft	gravitational potential

2

System	Transfer of energy
petrol in fuel tank as car travels along road	from chemical potential store to kinetic store
apple falling from tree towards ground	from gravitational potential store to kinetic store
hot cup of tea standing on table	from thermal store to (different) thermal store

3 **a** chemical potential

b gravitational potential

c thermal

d chemical potential

4 **a** from a chemical potential store (of the fuel) to a thermal store (of the water)

b from the diver's gravitational potential to their kinetic store

c from an elastic potential store (of the band) to a kinetic store (of the toy)

5 **c**

6 **a** girl's gravitational potential store → girl's kinetic store

b girl's kinetic store → thermal store of slide and surrounding air

7 3 kW × 1.5 h × 12 p = 54 p

8 **a** heating and radiation

b **i** electric current; **ii** electric current

9 **a** chemical store in your muscles → elastic potential store of spring

b

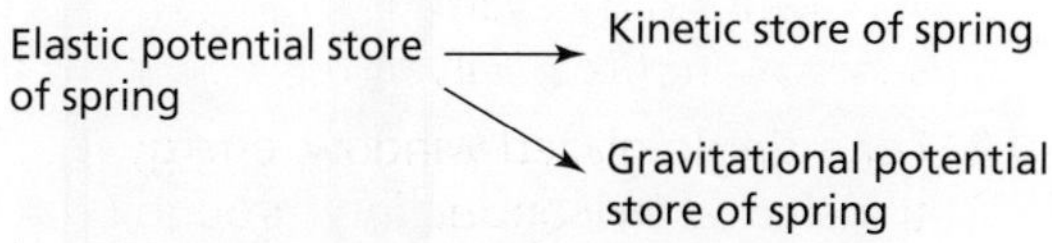

c The energy has been transferred to the thermal store of air surrounding the toy.

10 **a** at either end of the swing's journey when the swing is at its highest point

b at the centre point of the journey when the swing is at its lowest point

c at either end of the swing's journey, when the swing is at its highest point

d at the centre point of the journey, when the swing is at its lowest point and travelling at the highest speed

11 **a** The speed increases as it leaves one end of the oscillation and then decreases as it nears the other end of the oscillation, where it stops momentarily as it changes direction. This is repeated on the return oscillation.

b When the mass is raised up, the energy in the gravitational potential store increases. When the mass is released, the energy in the gravitational potential store is transferred to the kinetic store, so the energy in the gravitational potential store decreases and the energy in the kinetic store increases. As the mass swings up to the other end of the oscillation, the kinetic store becomes depleted and the energy in the gravitational potential store increases again. This is repeated on the return journey of the mass.

12 50 W = 0.05 kW
cost = 0.05 kW × 2 h × 12 p = 1.2 p

13 3 ÷ 60 = 0.05 h
cost = 1.2 kW × 0.05 h × 12 p = 0.72 p

14 cost = power (kW) × time (hours) × price (per kW h)

a **i** 6 min = 0.1 h
cost = 1 kW × 0.1 h × 12 p/kW h = 1.2 p

ii 30 min = 0.5 h
cost = 2 kW × 0.5 h × 12 p/kW h = 12 p

b using the microwave oven saves 10.8 p

14.4 Conservation of energy

1 joules (J) or kilojoules (kJ)

2 **d**

3 store; all; cannot; conservation.

4 **b**

5 **a** The kinetic energy (of the motor in the cement mixer) is useful; the thermal transfer to the surrounding air is wasted.

b

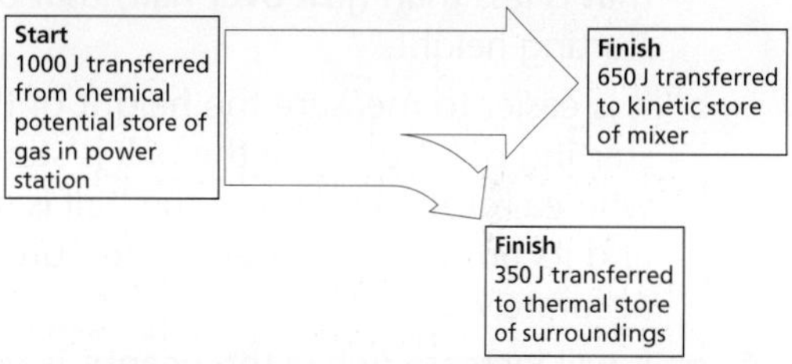

c energy has been conserved as total output is equal to the total input: 650 + 350 = 1000 J

6 **a**

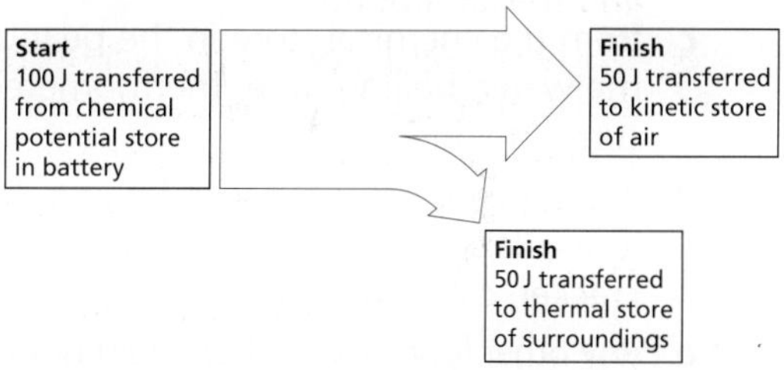

b The diagram shows that energy is conserved because the outputs add up to the energy supplied: 50 J + 50 J = 100 J

7 **a** the one that is raised up

b the one that goes down

c If there was no friction then there would be no transfer of energy to the thermal store of the environment. Energy would be conserved, so the decrease in the gravitational potential store of the descending carriage would be equal to the increase in the gravitational potential store of the ascending carriage. There would be no need to supply energy from the motor.

8 **a** at the top of the first slope, as this is the highest point

b the chemical store of fuel used to generate electricity → gravitational potential store of the train

c The train's stores of gravitational potential energy and kinetic energy are the same as they were at the start. The additional energy supplied by the motor has been transferred to the thermal store of the surroundings due to friction between the train and the track and heat from the electric motor.

Unit 14 maths and practical skills

1 **b**, **d**

2 **c**

3 **a** The greater the height the ball is dropped from, the greater the height it bounces back to.

b The ball always bounces back to a height that is less than (just over half) that of the starting height.

c It is easier to measure the height of the starting point because the ball is stationary, whereas at the end point the ball is moving and its position is harder to measure accurately.

4 **a** it will increase (while the peanut is being burned, and then decrease when it has finished burning)

b the chemical store of the peanut

c from the chemical store in the peanut to the water, boiling tube, thermometer and surroundings

d any other foods that could be impaled on a needle and ignited, e.g. bread, biscuit, cracker, cake, meat, etc.

e any other foods that either could not be mounted on a needle, e.g. soup, sauces, etc., or foods that would not ignite, e.g. soft fruit

f foods that store the most energy would cause a greater increase in the water temperature

g Answers to include: equal masses of food; water in tube at the same starting temperature; same mass/volume of water in tube; burning food held at same distance from tube.

h Some energy is transferred to the boiling tube and the thermometer; some energy is transferred to the surroundings; not all the peanut was burnt.

5 2000 J/s = 2000 W = 2 kW

6 **a** the number of kilojoules of energy stored in 1 g of fuel

b the energy content of hydrogen (142 kJ/g) is about three times that for petrol (45 kJ/g)

c The bar chart is the more useful one because it shows values for the energy content, this makes it easier to compare the different fuels using actual data rather than visually comparing angles on the pie chart.

7 **a**

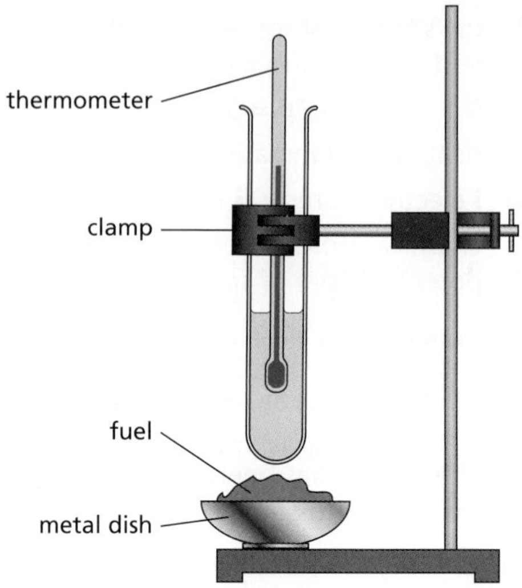

b Put a measured amount of water in the boiling tube and record its temperature. Measure out 1 g of a fuel and place it in the metal. Place the dish close to the bottom of the boiling tube. Ignite the fuel and record the maximum temperature the water reaches. Calculate the temperature increase of the water for each fuel; the greatest increase will indicate the fuel with the highest energy content.

c Any **two** from: some energy will be transferred to the surroundings instead of to the water; the glass of the tube and the metal of the dish will be heated as well; some energy will transfer to the water and out again; errors in measuring the temperature, the volume of water or the mass of fuel

d Any **three** from: wood, fire lighter, petrol, paraffin (allow coal, although it is hard to ignite)

8 **a** by the customer reading their gas and electricity meters and sending the readings to the supply company

b 208 kWh

c 12.66 p

d 178 kWh

e because some appliances can only work using electricity

f No, because the standing charge would be the same. Using twice as much energy would increase the bill but not double it.

Unit 15 Waves

15.1 Observing waves

1

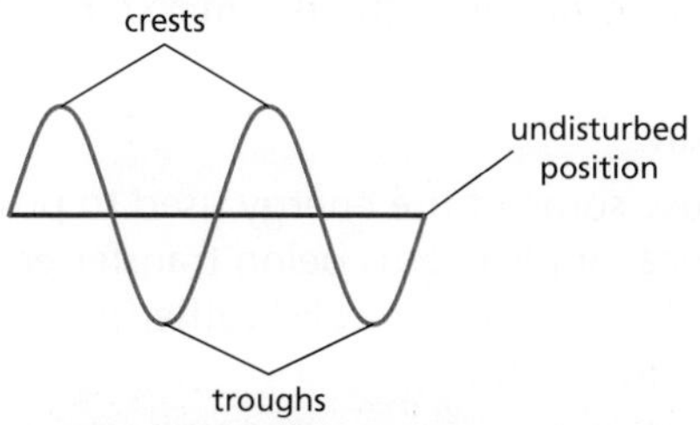

2 **a** **A** 4 cm; **B** 7 cm; **C** 1 cm; **D** 3 cm

b **B**, **A**, **D**, **C**

3 **a** waves combine to make a bigger wave

b waves cancel out – smooth water

4 **a** **X** – longitudinal wave and **Y** – transverse wave.

b Energy is transferred to the wave across, or at right angles to, the direction of wave travel in the transverse wave; in the longitudinal wave energy is transferred to the wave in the same direction as the wave travel.

5 **a, b**

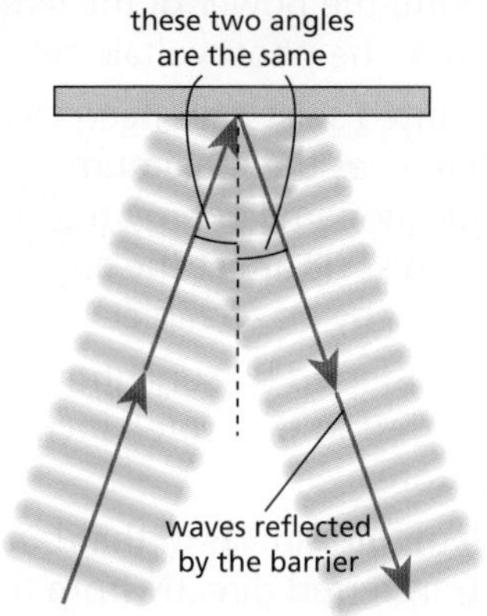

c The angle between the normal and the incident ray is equal to the angle between the normal and the reflected ray.

15.2 Making sound waves

1 **a** Any **two** surfaces that are hard and smooth, such as metal and concrete

b Any **two** surfaces that are soft, such as cloth, fabric or foam

2 **a** drum skin

b strings (and air in the sound box)

c air

3 Sound travels as the particles in the medium it is moving through vibrate and transfer energy/vibrations from one to another. This is why sound cannot travel through a vacuum – in a vacuum (empty space) there are no particles to vibrate.

4 **a** For example, sit with your ear against the surface of a wooden table and ask someone else to tap on the surface of the table. Answers could also include hearing loud TV through neighbour's wall, listening to a string telephone, etc.

b **i** vibrations; **ii** need; **iii** close together; **iv** transmit

5 The soft surfaces (such as sofas, carpets and curtains) that were previously in the room were good at absorbing the energy transferred by sound. In the empty room there are more hard surfaces such as bare floors and walls, which are better at reflecting sound and enabling echoes.

6 **a** distance = speed × time = 340 m/s × 1 s = 340 m

b distance = speed × time = 340 m/s × 10 s = 3400 m or 3.4 km

c distance = speed × time = 340 m/s × 60 s = 20 400 m or 20.4 km

7 It has been absorbed by the curtain material and transferred to the thermal store of the particles in the curtains.

8 **a** true

b Space is a vacuum so there is no medium (no particles of any material) to enable sound waves to be transmitted by passing on vibrations between nearby particles.

9 The further the sound wave travels, the greater the area it has spread out over, so the energy is spread out over a larger area and the sound will be fainter, as less energy is transferred to your eardrums so the sound is quieter.

10 **a** aluminium

b air

c it travels fastest through the solids shown and slowest in the gas shown

d In a solid the particles are close together/densely packed in a rigid framework with strong (attractive) forces between particles. This means that vibrations can pass from one particle to another quickly and easily.

11 170 m ÷ 340 m/s = 0.5 s

12 distance = speed × time = 1500 m/s × 0.4 s = 600 m

This is the distance there and back for the sound waves, so the water is 300 m deep.

15.3 Hearing and sound

1 **a**

2 **c**

3 **d**

4 **c**

5 It would vibrate more quickly for a high pitch sound than a low pitch one.

6 1 kHz = 1000 Hz, so 28 kHz = 28 000 Hz

7 28 kHz is above the audible range for humans but within that of dogs.

8 **a** the person's vocal cords vibrating

b the vibrations travelling from one particle (of gas in the air) to the next

c the vibrations of particles in the air/pressure waves passing through the air make the person's eardrums vibrate (these vibrations are converted into electrical signals which are interpreted by the brain)

9 **a** the frequency is higher than for a lower note

b **i** longitudinal; **ii** oscillate (or vibrate); **iii** faster; **iv** electrical; **v** oscillate (or vibrate)

10 The note that sounded higher, i.e. had a higher pitch, would have the higher frequency.

11 **a** sound waves in the air cause it to vibrate

b because of the hole the vibrations in the air would not cause as much movement of the eardrum, so there is likely to be a loss of hearing

12 **a** – **C**; **b** – **A**

13 **b**, **c** and **d**

14 **a** elephant; **b** bat; **c** bat; **d** mouse and bat

15 **a** above the auditory range for humans/ higher frequencies than humans can hear

b distance = speed × time = 330 m/s × 0.02 s = 6.6 m

distance to the prey is half this = 3.3 m.

c direction

d Yes, bat sounds are within a cat's auditory range.

15.4 Energy and waves

1 **a** true; **b** false; **c** true; **d** false

2 **a** **i** energy; **ii** high; **iii** vibrate; **iv** energy

b It removes dirt from parts that would be awkward to get to and it avoids the use of sharp tools which might damage the objects.

3 **a**, **c**

4 The ultrasound waves produced by the device transfer vibrations to particles in the skin, which pass on vibrations to particles deeper in the body (including muscle tissue). The waves spread into the body as a pressure wave (longitudinal wave). As the wave passes through the body, some of the energy it carries is transferred to the thermal store of the muscles, which get warmer.

5 **a** the sun

b because some of the energy used to power electrical appliances is being transferred from the sun (via the cells) rather than from the mains supply

c The cells only produce electricity when the sun is shining. If the electricity produced is used to charge up a storage battery, the energy in the battery's chemical store can be used when the sun is not shining.

6 **a** independent – angle of the solar cell; dependent – potential difference produced

b first column – angle of the solar cell (degrees); second column – potential difference produced (volts)

c Any **two** from: the distance between the lamp and the cell; the light level in the rest of the room; the power of the lamp; the type/area of the photovoltaic cell.

d Roof-mounted solar cells need to be at an angle that gives the maximum electrical output for the same energy transferred by sunlight. This will affect the angle of the roof selected by an architect.

7 **a** energy transferred by sunlight is absorbed by/transferred to the water, increasing its thermal store

b The systems are similar in that both use energy transferred directly from the sun. They are different because in PV cells the energy is transferred via an electric current to an appliance to do work (or to a battery to increase its chemical energy store), whereas in the solar water heater the energy is transferred to the thermal store of water in the hot water storage tank.

c In the UK (in the northern hemisphere) the sun rises in the south east and sets in the south west, so having the system on a south-facing roof means a greater proportion of the energy from the sunlight will be transferred to the water heater.

15.5 How light travels

1 **c**

2 to show the direction in which the light is travelling

3 it must be opaque

4 **a** any **two** from: glass, Perspex, water

b any **two** from: metal, wood, stone

5 **d**

6 **a** – **A**; **b** – **B**; **c** – **B**

7 **a**

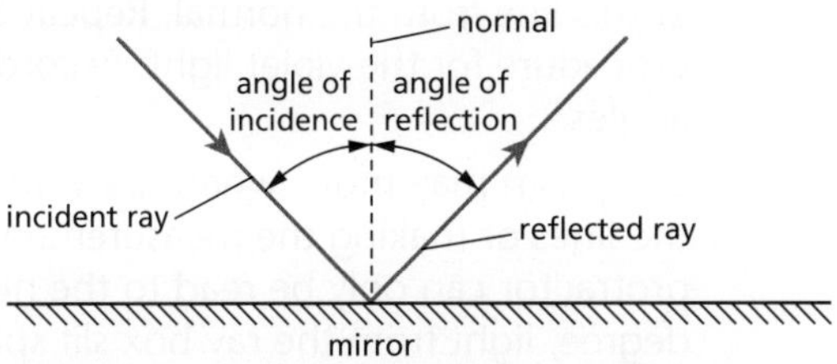

b mirror moved when drawing the line or making the measurement; can only read protractor to nearest degree, but the light from ray box slit spreads out and makes it difficult to decide where to draw the pencil line

c The angle of reflection is equal to the angle of incidence.

8 **d**

9 When the ray of light reaches the edge of the fibre, no light is transmitted into the air. Instead, all the light is reflected back into the fibre and travels onwards until it meets the edge again, where this process is repeated. Therefore light never escapes through the sides and all the light travels to the far end of the fibre.

15.6 Vision and images

1 **a**

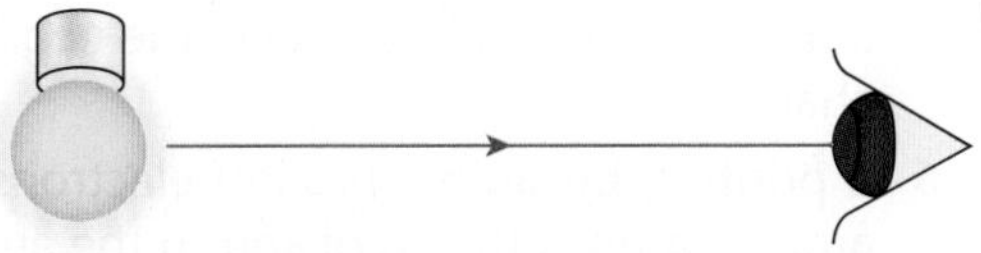

Light is travelling from the light bulb (the source) to the eye.

b

Light is travelling from the bulb (the source) to the book, where it is reflected and travels to the eye.

2 **d**

3 **a**, **c**

4 **i** light; **ii** screen/wall; **iii** lens; **iv** image

5 **i** direction; **ii** refraction; **iii** focal; **iv** convex

6 Light rays leaving the balloon and passing through the pinhole cross over. This means that rays from the top of the balloon end up lower down the screen and rays from the bottom of the balloon end up nearer the top of the screen.

7 **b**

8 **a** lens; **b** retina; **c** pupil; **d** cornea

9 **d**

10 Similarities include: they form upside down images; they form images that are smaller than the objects; they have a hole to allow some but not all rays of light from an object to enter. Differences include: only the eye refracts light (only the eye has a lens); only the eye can focus on objects that are different distances away.

15.7 Exploring coloured light

1 **c**

2 spectrum

3 **c**

4 **b**

5 **c**

6 **a**

7 frequency

8 **c**

9 **c**

10 **c**

11 **a** when it enters the droplet and when it leaves it

b at the back surface of the droplet (right-hand side of diagram)

c it is separated, or dispersed, into a spectrum of different colours

d the rays of light that enter the raindrops and are dispersed to form a spectrum of colours are reflected back towards the sun, so they do not travel through the raindrops towards the person. A person looking at the sun will see only sunlight and rain (only someone with the sun behind them has a chance of seeing a rainbow).

Unit 15 maths and practical skills

1 **c**

2 **a** 5 m (= 2 × 2.5 m)

b 3.9 s

3

Quantity	Unit
frequency	hertz
amplitude	metres
speed	metres per second

4 a **i** 10°; **ii** 20°

b 21°

c Either repeat the experiment or eliminate the anomalous value and calculate the mean using only the other two values.

5 330 m/s × 3.5 s = 1155 m (or 1.155 km)

6 1500 m/s × 0.6 s = 900 m

The sonar wave has travelled to the shoal and back again, so the shoal is 450 m away.

7 a Decide on the distances between the lamp and the cell that are going to be tested. Set up the cell and the lamp at one of these distances apart. Record the distance and the potential difference the cell produces at that distance. Repeat several times and evaluate to decide if any values should be eliminated or if further repeats are required. Repeat the procedure for each of the other selected lamp–cell distances.

b independent variable – distance; dependent variable – potential difference

c first column – distance (m); second column – potential difference (V)

d the angle the cell makes with the lamp should be kept the same such that the cell faces the lamp; other light in the room should be kept low in level and constant

8 a Place each of the materials in the darkened room, all at the same distance from the torch and facing it. Take a picture of the materials. The picture will show which of the materials is the brightest and therefore has reflected the most light. Other possible variables should be controlled by, for example, using the same area of each material, maintaining the same level of background light, and using the camera in the same way each time.

b **i** The aluminium foil will reflect the most light as it has a smooth reflective surface.

ii The black velvet will reflect the least light as both its rough surface (rough) and dark colour will make it good at absorbing light.

9 a Place a white sheet of paper underneath the experimental set-up. Draw a line to mark the edge of the prism where the light is emerging; draw a normal where the red light emerges; mark where the red light is emerging part way along the ray; draw a line back to the point where the red light leaves the prism and measure the angle of this line from the normal. Repeat the procedure for the violet light. Record both angles.

b The prism may move when drawing the lines or making the measurement; a protractor can only be read to the nearest degree, light from the ray box slit spreads out and makes it difficult to decide where to draw the pencil line for the incident ray; a judgment needs to be made about where the centre of the red (and the violet) light is.

Unit 16 Electricity and magnetism

16.1 Static electricity

1 two (positive and negative)

2 **a**

3 **i** charge (or electrons); **ii** opposite; **iii** attract; **iv** hair

4 **a**

5 It has gained additional electrons. Electrons have negative charges so more are needed by a neutral object if it is to become negatively charged.

6 **a** positive, because it has lost electrons to the amber; **b** from the wool and to the amber

7 **a** attraction; **b** repulsion; **c** because each droplet of paint is attracted towards the metal; **d** because the droplets of paint spread out due to repulsion

8 Walking across the carpet may have caused a static charge to build up on you. Touching a metal object such as a door handle provides a conducting path for electrons (negative charge) to move between you and the door until you are no longer electrostatically charged; the rapid movement of charge is felt as a shock (an electric current).

9 **a** hold the balloon close to small pieces of tissue paper, or strands of long hair, or a thin stream of water from a tap – if any of these are attracted to the balloon, the balloon is charged; alternatively hold the balloon close to another charged object and see if the balloon is attracted or repelled by it; **b** from the sweatshirt to the balloon; **c** because the air is slightly damp it was a conductor, allowing the excess negative charge on the balloon to move into the air (by electron transfer)

10 Rubbing the box lid has charged it up and there is now an electric field around it. The pieces of tissue paper become charged by induction and are attracted to the lid.

11 Similarities – any **two** of: they are non-contact forces; they are caused by a field (a region in which objects can be affected by the force without touching the object producing the field); they are caused by the interaction between two opposite properties of objects (two types of magnetic pole and two types of charge); they are less strong the further apart the objects are.

Differences – any **two** of: magnetic forces only affect magnetic materials whereas electrostatic forces affect objects made of many different materials (provided they are insulators and so can hold a static charge); magnetic forces are caused by the field around magnetic materials or electromagnets, electrostatic forces are caused by the field around charged objects; magnetic forces cannot be produced by friction/rubbing but electrostatic forces can.

12 **a** The brush and the hair gain opposite charges. The brush is negatively charged and repels electrons from the surface of the pieces of paper, leaving the pieces of paper more positively charged at the top and more negatively charged at the bottom. So the positive side of each bit of paper is attracted to the comb.

b The charge will gradually be conducted away from the student's hair, both through their body to the ground and through the air

c Dry air is a better insulator than humid air, so the charge won't be conducted by it as well.

16.2 Current electricity (1)

1 amps (amperes)

2 **a** it is an electrical conductor; **b** because generally non-metals are insulators

3 in series

4 **a** switch; **b** cell (battery); **c** bulb (lamp)

5 **c**

6 **a**

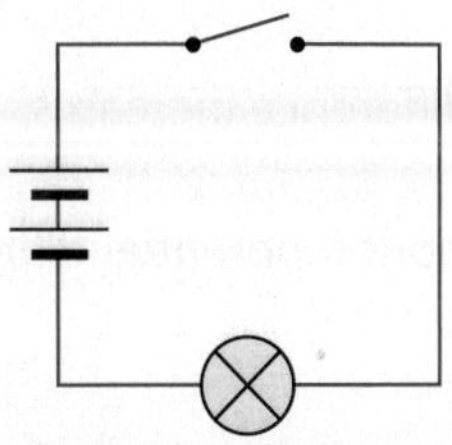

b

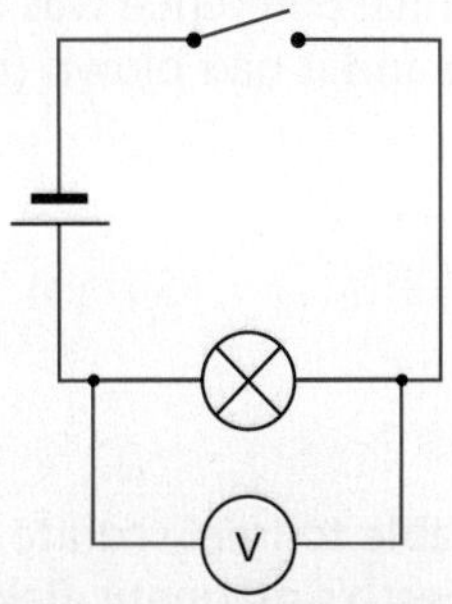

7 **a** 4 (6 divided by 1.5); **b** in series; **c** with the positive terminal of one battery connected to the negative terminal of the battery next to it, because otherwise its potential difference will be subtracted from that of the other batteries

8 **a**, **b**

9 **a** the voltage of the battery

b the resistance of the wire/energy being transferred to the wire by heating

c all the students could hold the rope a little more tightly

d be harder work/not so easy to move the rope

e Strengths – any **one** of: the loop shows a continuous circuit; the rope moves through each person's hands at the same speed, showing that current is the same everywhere in a series circuit; it models energy being transferred by heating of components; it models the effects of different resistances; it models the way that electrons are attracted to the battery's positive terminal and repelled from the negative terminal.

Weaknesses – any **one** of: it doesn't represent the current as individual electrons; it doesn't show the role of charge; the model is difficult to modify for parallel circuits

16.3 Current electricity (2)

1 **a** true; **b** true; **c** false

2 **c**

3 **a** 0.15 + 0.15 = 0.3 A

b 1.5 V

c **i** 0.15 + 0.15 + 0.15 = 0.45 A; **ii** 1.5 V

4 **c**

5 **a** as the potential difference increases, the current increases

b 0 A, because without a potential difference there can be no current

c $1\,\text{V} \div 0.1\,\text{A} = 10\,\Omega$

d because the potential difference was too great for the bulb and it had blown (broken)

16.4 Magnetism

1 **b**

2 **d**

3 **a**, **c**

4 **a** the needle, being able to freely rotate, will align itself with the Earth's magnetic field; **b** they would need to know which end of the needle was a north pole

5

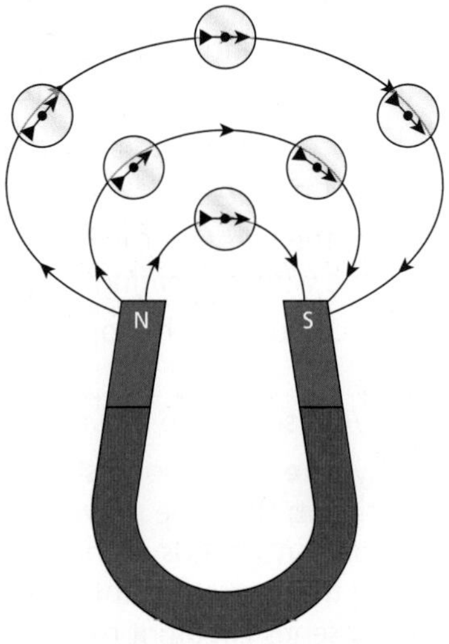

6 **a** they are close but not exactly aligned

b the north pole of a plotting compass is attracted by a south pole of a magnet, so the magnetic pole in the north must be a south pole

c it is the same shape, with field lines going from the (magnetic) north to the (magnetic) south; the field lines are concentrated at the poles

16.5 Magnetic effects of a current

1 Similarities – any **two** of: they both have two magnetic poles; they both produce a magnetic field; they both attract magnetic objects.

Differences – any **two** of: the electromagnet needs a current through its coils to produce the magnetic field; a bar magnet is a permanent magnet but the electromagnet can be turned on and off; the strength of an electromagnet can be varied easily but the strength of a permanent magnet cannot be changed; the field of an electromagnet can be reversed by reversing the current (turning the battery around).

2 **a** when there is a current through it

b a nearby compass needle will be deflected when the circuit is switched on

3 add more turns of wire; increase the current; use an iron core

4 **c**

5 **a** it will only attract magnetic metals

b turn the current off; when the current stops the magnetic field of the electromagnet ceases to exist

6 **a** to provide support and shape for the coil; to increase the strength of the magnetic field

b holding a plotting compass near the north pole of the electromagnet would result in the south pole of the compass being attracted towards it

c **i** as there is little resistance in the circuit, a large current will flow and this will cause the coil to get warm; **ii** as a large current will flow, the battery will soon run down

7 **a** a magnetic field around the wire; **b** magnet; **c** a stronger magnetic field; **d** move; **e** the motor effect; **f** either by reversing the direction of the current or by reversing the poles of the magnet.

8 **a** it will produce a stronger magnetic field

b the electromagnet will attract the right-hand contact and break the circuit (like opening a switch)

9 **a** When the hammer hits the gong and the contacts open; there is no longer a complete circuit so the current stops; this means the coil no longer produces a magnetic field and so the hammer falls back. This re-makes the complete circuit so current passes through the coil again. This cycle continues (as long as the switch is kept pushed in), meaning that the hammer repeatedly hits the gong.

b A permanent magnet will continuously attract the hammer which will then be held on the gong continuously, so the bell would only ring once.

Unit 16 maths and practical skills

1 **a** amps; **b** volts; **c** ohms

2 **b**

3 The student could charge the balloons by rubbing one balloon with one cloth and the other balloon with the other cloth. The student should then dangle the balloons from threads attached to a rod and carefully bring them near to each other. If the balloons have the same charge they will repel each other.

4 **a** The students could stroke each of the steel bars a different number of times (say, 20, 40, 60, 80, etc.) and then test the strength of the magnet produced using the paper clips. This can be done by: finding the maximum number of clips the steel bar will hold at once; or hanging paperclips from the magnet, one off the other in a chain until they fall off; or measuring the distance at which the magnet will just attract one paper clip. The students should always stroke the bar in the same direction and using the same pole of the magnet. They should use a different steel bar each time, so that it is not already magnetised when they start stroking it. They should check at the start that the steel bar has no magnetism and that the paperclips are not magnetised.

b a scatter graph as both of the variables are continuous.

5 **a** because the wire will get hot and the mat will prevent it from damaging the table surface

b **A** $0.2 \div 2 = 0.1\,\Omega$

B $0.12 \div 1.6 = 0.075\,\Omega$

C $0.16 \div 0.8 = 0.2\,\Omega$

D $0.1 \div 2 = 0.05\,\Omega$

c **D**

d **C**, **A**, **B**, **D**

e less energy will be transferred to the surroundings from the wires as heat

6 **a** **A**: $6 \div 0.012 = 500\,\Omega$
B: $6 \div 0.008 = 750\,\Omega$
C: $4 \div 0.016 = 250\,\Omega$
D: $4 \div 0.020 = 200\,\Omega$

b **B**, **A**, **C**, **D**

Unit 17 Matter

17.1 Particle model, Brownian motion and density

1 **c**, **d**

2 **i** increases; **ii** closer

3 molecules of gas (particles) in the air

4 **a** the density decreases as the particles move further apart

b it is the opposite to the change in most other materials, where particles move closer together upon freezing and the material becomes more dense

5 Choose a measuring cylinder with the smallest possible volume as this will enable more accurate readings to be made. Measure the mass of the empty cylinder. Add the sample of olive oil to the cylinder and measure the mass of the cylinder with the oil. Look to see if the top surface of the oil has a meniscus. Record the volume of the oil, reading from the bottom of the meniscus. Calculate the mass of the oil by subtracting the mass of the empty cylinder from the mass of the cylinder with the oil. Divide this mass by the volume of the oil to get the density.

6 **a** $4\,050\,000\,\text{kg}/4500\,\text{m}^3 = 900\,\text{kg/m}^3$

b $600\,\text{g} = 0.6\,\text{kg}$

$0.6\,\text{kg}/1\,\text{m}^3 = 0.6\,\text{kg/m}^3$

c The density of the steam is much lower than the density of ice because in steam the particles are much further apart.

7 **a** $1225\,\text{g} = 1.225\,\text{kg}$

$1.225\,\text{kg}/1\,\text{m}^3 = 1.225\,\text{kg/m}^3$

b $8700\,\text{g} = 8.7\,\text{kg}$

$8.7\,\text{kg}/0.01\,\text{m}^3 = 870\,\text{kg/m}^3$

c $870/1.225 = 710$

The liquid air is 710 times more dense than the air in the atmosphere.

d Liquid air has a much greater density than air in the atmosphere because the particles are packed together much more closely in the liquid state than in the gaseous state.

8 The pollen grains move because the water molecules are in constant motion and collide with the pollen grains. The pollen grains change direction randomly because the water molecules are moving in random directions and so the molecular collisions are random

– the grains are pushed first in one direction, then another, at random intervals of time.

17.2 Particle model and physical changes

1 **c**

2 **a** – false; **b** – true; **c** – false; **d** – true

3 **a** any **two** of: melting, freezing, dissolving

b Chemical changes cannot be reversed but physical changes can; chemical changes result in the formation of new products (due to the combination of particles/atoms in new ways) but in physical changes no new products are formed.

c a chemical change as the reactants cannot be recovered

4 b

5 The volume of the water will be less than the volume of the ice block, because water is denser than ice as the particles are closer together.

6 **a** Student **B** is correct because mass is conserved in dissolving; the sweetened tea will have the same total mass as the unsweetened tea and the sugar. This is because the same atoms which made up the unsweetened tea and the sugar are there in the sweetened tea (the solution).

b Student **A** is wrong because although the crystals disappear, the mass is still present; there are the same number of atoms in the sugar even though they are dissolved in the liquid. Student **C** is wrong because it is the tea that is getting the sugar wet and we are looking at the total mass, which is unchanged by the process of dissolving.

7 It is a good model for explaining malleability in that it shows how the sliding of layers past each other allow a metal to change shape. However, it does not represent the size of the force required to work a metal. In addition, the model does not explain ductility, as it cannot show how a metal can be drawn into a wire.

17.3 Energy stored in matter

1 increase

2 **a** gain; **b** closer together; **c** forces that attract

3 As the bar gets hotter, the particles of iron move around more vigorously and take up more space; this causes the bar to expand.

4 **a** – true; **b** – false; **c** – false

5 **a**

6 On a hot day the gap will reduce, because the metal on each side of the gap will expand to partly fill the gap.

7 **a** they are moving more in place (vibrating)

b it is increasing

c the bar will shrink back to its original size so the pointer will return to the central position

d the bar will shrink further and the pointer will move to the left

e if the bar was free to move at the left-hand end it could expand or contract without moving the pointer

8 **a** **iv**

b The strip will curve downwards (if it is still being held with the copper on the under side) because both metals will contract as they are cooled, but the copper will contract more than the iron.

Unit 17 maths and practical skills

1 **a** $50\,g/50\,cm^3 = 1\,g/cm^3$

b $21.6\,g/20\,cm^3 = 1.06\,g/cm^3$

c $260\,g/100\,cm^3 = 2.6\,g/cm^3$

d $195\,g/25\,cm^3 = 7.8\,g/cm^3$

2 **a** $2\,cm \times 4\,cm \times 5\,cm = 40\,cm^3$

b $340\,g/40\,cm^3 = 8.5\,g/cm^3$

3 **a** because the type of gas is not a continuous variable

b

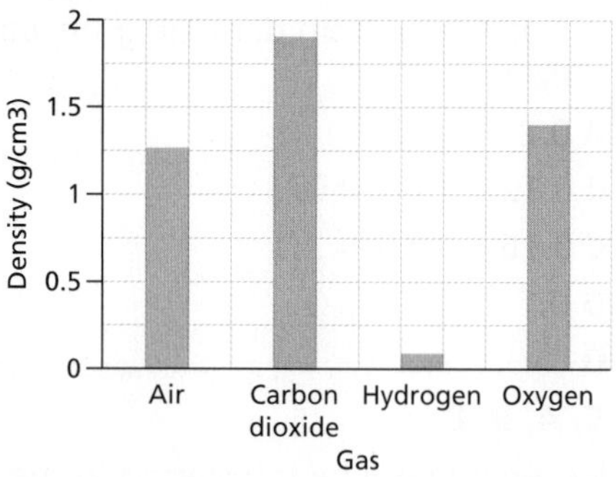

4 volume = $3\,cm \times 3\,cm \times 10\,cm = 90\,cm^3$

mass = $0.225\,kg = 225\,g$

density = $225\,g/90\,cm^3 = 2.5\,g/cm^3$

5 The volume of the water displaced by the object is equal to the volume of the solid. The students therefore need to collect all the water that overflows from the can and measure its volume using a measuring cylinder.

6 **a and b**

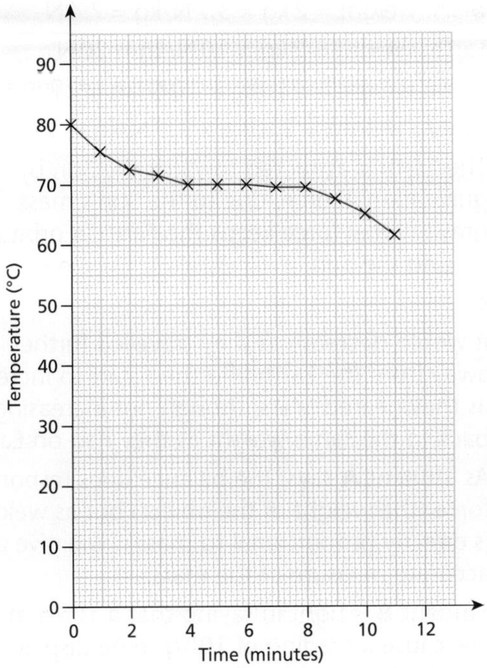

c 70 °C, because the temperature stays at this value for a period of time

7 **a** 4°C

b 999.95 °C

8 **a** 1600 g = 1.6 kg;
1000 cm^3 = 0.001 m^3
density = 1.6/0.001 = 1600 kg/m^3

b 2000 g = 2 kg;
1 000 000 cm^3 = 1 m^3
density = 2/1 = 2 kg/m^3

c 4600 g = 4.6 kg
volume = 4.6/920 = 0.005 m^3 = 5000 cm^3

d 1000 cm^3 = 0.001 m^3
mass = 0.6 × 0.001 = 0.0006 kg = 0.6 g

9 **a** density = mass/volume

b use a top pan balance

c measure the length, breadth and width of the wood (in the same units) and multiply them together

d 0.4 kg = 400 g
400 g/500 cm^3 = 0.8 g/cm^3

10 **a** when he immersed the crown in a full container of water, the volume of water overflowing (displaced by the crown) was equal to the volume of the crown

b 1800 g/100 cm^3 = 18 g/cm^3

c it means the crown was not made of pure gold

Unit 18 Space physics

18.1 Seasonal variation

1 spring, summer, autumn, winter

2 The Earth is rotating on its axis. As it does so, the Sun appears to travel across the sky.

3 **a** fewer; **b** lower; **c** lower

4 **a**

5 Drawing should show Mars rotating upon its axis and also the Sun or rays of light from the Sun; it should include labels for the Sun, Mars and the axis of rotation, like the diagram below. It should also include an arrow to show that Mars is spinning on its axis.

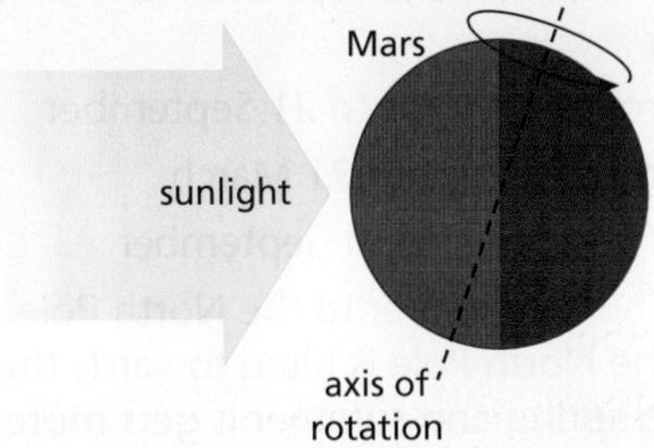

The side of Mars facing the Sun will be in daylight. The length of a day on Mars depends on its speed of rotation about its axis. The faster Mars rotates, the shorter a day will be. The time for one complete rotation is the length of one day.

6

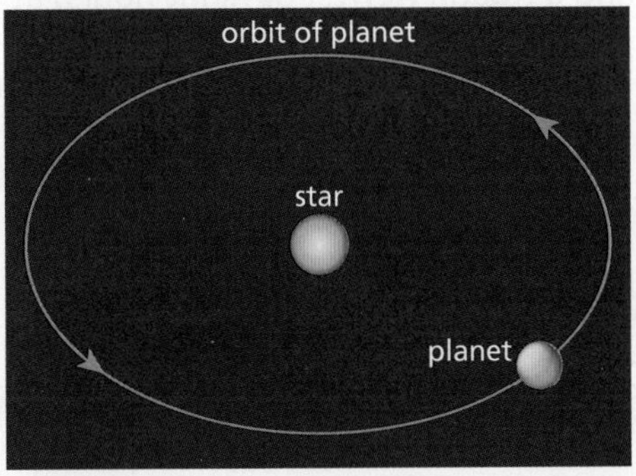

7 **a** We have seasons because the Earth's axis of rotation is tilted in relation to the Earth's orbit around the Sun. Sometimes the northern hemisphere is tilted towards the Sun and sometimes away from it.

b at points in the orbit when the northern hemisphere is tilted towards the Sun

c The Earth rotates on its axis and the axis is tilted in relation to the Earth's orbit around the Sun. This means that at some points in the Earth's orbit, the northern hemisphere is tilted towards the Sun and there will be more than 12 hours of sunlight per day.

Further round in the orbit, the northern hemisphere will be tilted away from the Sun and there will be fewer than 12 hours of sunlight per day. The situation in the southern hemisphere is the opposite; if one hemisphere is tilted towards the Sun, the other is tilted away from it.

8 There would be less seasonal variation, that is, there would be less difference between the seasons in the number of hours of daylight and the temperatures. This would mean that summers would be cooler than at present and winters warmer. This is because the Sun would not rise as high in the sky in the summer but would rise higher in the winter.

9 **a** 16

b 6

c from 21 March to 21 September

d from 21 Sept to 21 March

e 21 March and 21 September

f Thurso is nearer to the North Pole, so when the North Pole is tilted towards the Sun in spring and summer it gets more hours of sunlight in the day than Falmouth, but when the North Pole is tilted away from the Sun in autumn and winter it gets fewer hours of sunlight in the day.

g The shape would be reversed, with a peak (most daylight hours) at 21 December and a trough (fewest daylight hours) at 21 June. This is because when the northern hemisphere is tilted towards the Sun (and receiving more hours of daylight) the southern hemisphere is tilted away from the Sun and receiving fewer hours.

18.2 Gravity

1

Unit	Unit of force?	Unit of mass?
newton, N	✓	
gram, g		✓
kilonewton, kN	✓	
kilogram, kg		✓

2 **a** non-contact

b always attracts

c weight

3 **c**, **d**

4 weight = 80 kg × 9 N/kg = 720 N

5 **d**

6 Mars: weight = 2 kg × 3.7 N/kg = 7.4 N

Earth: weight = 2 kg × 10 N/kg = 20 N

7 Earth: weight = 210 kg × 10 N/kg = 2100 N

Moon: weight = 210 kg × 1.7 N/kg = 357 N

8 The Earth is attracted towards the Sun by a gravitational force, due to the Sun's mass. This gravitational force keeps the Earth in orbit around the Sun.

9 **c**

10 It would decrease as they travelled further away from the Earth and then start to increase as they neared Mars, though not increasing back to the same weight as they had on Earth.

11 As Student **A** says, the balance does respond to force (the weight of the object) but as weight is directly proportional to mass it will give an accurate measure of the mass.

Student **B** is right in saying that a 100 g mass will cause a reading of 100 g to be displayed, but this is only true when the balance is used on the surface of the Earth.

As Student **C** says, using the balance only on Earth means that the weight it responds to will be caused by something with a mass of 100 g. However, care should be taken to say that the reading (for example, 100 g) is the mass and not the weight of the object.

18.3 Stars and light-years

1 **i** centre; **ii** System; **iii** energy; **iv** Solar; **v** energy

2 **a** true; **b** false; **c** true; **d** false; **e** true; **f** false

3 **b**

4 **b**

5 **b**

6

Description of distance	Distance in light-years (ly)
a diameter of the Milky Way	**iii** 100 000
b diameter of the Solar System	**iv** 1
c distance from Earth to Polaris (the Pole Star)	**i** 323
d distance from Earth to the Andromeda Galaxy	**ii** 2 520 000

7 **a** true; **b** true; **c** true; **d** false

8 Student **A** is right. The light left those stars many years ago and anything we can see, such as the stars' brightness and the position, was determined by the stars as they were then.

9 **a** a light-minute is the distance light will travel in one minute

b a light-minute is the distance light will travel in one minute whereas a light-year is the distance light will travel in one year

c 60 (minutes in an hour) × 24 (hours in a day) × 365 (days in a year) = 525 600 times further away

Unit 18 maths and practical skills

1

Unit	Quantity
a light-year, ly	**iii** distance
b newton, N	**iv** force
c kilogram, kg	**i** mass
d kilometres per second, km/s	**ii** speed

2 **a** 120 × 10 = 1200 N

b 120 × 1.7 = 204 N

3 **a** 10 × 32 m = 320 m

b 20 × 32 m = 640 m

c 30 × 32 m = 960 m

4 **a** 380 kg × 1.7 N/kg = 646 N

b 380 kg × 10 N/kg = 3800 N

c 3800/646 = 5.88 (to 2 decimal places) so rounded to the nearest whole number is 6. The rocks are six times heavier on the Earth than they were on the Moon.

5 **a** Mercury

b 0

c Jupiter

d 79

e

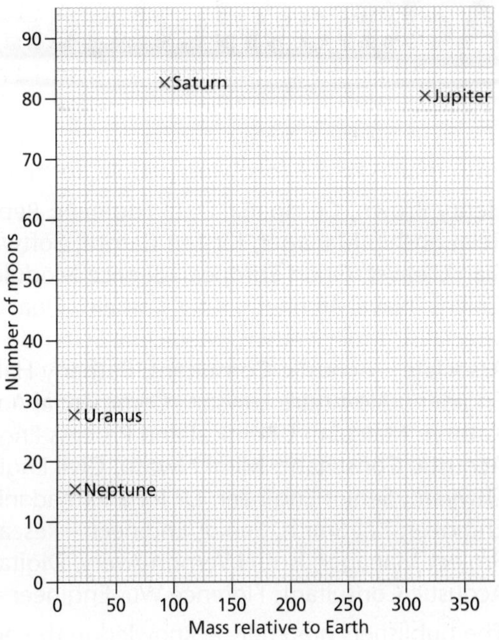

f It is partly true. The planets with a much greater mass have many moons and the planets with less mass tend to have fewer moons. However, it is not entirely true. Saturn has less mass than Jupiter but has more moons, and Uranus has less mass than Neptune but has more moons.

6 **a** As well as the gravitational force between Uranus and the Sun, there is a gravitational force between Uranus and Neptune and the direction of this force pulls Uranus forwards in its orbit.

b Neptune is being pulled backwards in its orbit by the gravitational force between Uranus and Neptune.

c They aimed a telescope to look beyond the orbit of Uranus and ahead of it (when it was being accelerated) or behind it (when it was being slowed down).

Acknowledgements

With thanks to the following people, for their input into the careers profiles, in partnership with WISE:

Henry Brown, Geospatial Data Engineer; Rebecca Brown, Specialist; Matthew Calveley, Industrial Relationship Manager; Kirsten Carotti, Software Developer; Beth Clarke, Advanced Consultant Engineer; Siân Cleaver, Orion European Service Module Industrial Manager; Alice Clutterbuck, GIS Analyst; Lucy Collins, Naval Architect; Katy Corfield, Quality Manager; Lucy Davies, Aerospace Engineer; Jesie Dyos, Field Specialist; Molly Francis, Medicinal Scientist; Ellie Gomes-Callus, Metals and Mining Analyst; Chris Hales, Associate – Acoustic Consultant; Bethany Hall, Electrical Systems Project Engineer; Junior Ishak, Electrical Engineer; Alexandra Lawson, Commercial Advisor – B2B Renewables Solutions; Dr Ronan GH Lee, Dentist; Kathryn Malcolm, Chemical and Process Engineer; Chris Marshall, Managing Director; James Meconi, Acoustic Consultant; Mimi Nwosu, Civil Engineer; Lilla Porkolab, Part 2 Architectural Assistant; Muneebah Quyyam, Senior Engineer; Dr Jona Ramadani, Lecturer in Forensic Science; Krystel Richards, Broadcast IT Engineer; Kat Smith, Senior Engineer – Research and Development; Natalie Staffurth, Energy Innovation Project Manager; Isobel Vernon-Avery, Digital and Circular Economy Strategy Consultant; Vicky Wills, Acoustic Consultant; Florence Wu, Engineer – Materials.

The publishers gratefully acknowledge the permission granted to reproduce the copyright material in this book. Every effort has been made to trace copyright holders and to obtain their permission for the use of copyright material. The publishers will gladly review any information enabling them to rectify any error or omission at the first opportunity.

P6tl Fusebulb/Shutterstock; p6tr Piotr Kuczek/Shutterstock; p6cl Hanahstocks/Shutterstock; p6cr Pixelheadphoto digitalskillet/Shutterstock; p6bl Aunt Spray/Shutterstock; p6br Phonlamai Photo/ Shutterstock; p7t Natee K Jindakum/Shutterstock; p7cl Angellodeco/Shutterstock; p7c Mila Supinskaya/ Shutterstock; p7cr Zolnierek/Shutterstock; p7bl Ravipat/Shutterstock; p7bc SciePro/Shutterstock; p7br Chomplearn/Shutterstock; p8 Kateryna Kessariiska/Shutterstock; p15t Choksawatdikorn/Shutterstock; p16t Kateryna Kessariiska/Shutterstock; p16b Creative Endeavors/Shutterstock; p20tr Phonlamai Photo/ Shutterstock; p22t Soleil Nordic/Shutterstock; p22c Ody_Stocker/Shutterstock; p26tl Gjermund/ Shutterstock; p26tcl Pixel-Shot/Shutterstock; p26tcr White Space Illustrations/Shutterstock; p26b Kateryna Kessariiska/Shutterstock; p28 Choksawatdikorn/Shutterstock; p32tl Anastasiya Abramava/Shutterstock; p32tc Mikhail Klyoshev/Shutterstock; p32tr Philip George Jones/Shutterstock; p32bl S_oleg/Shutterstock; 32bc Arina P Habich/Shutterstock; p32br FineShine/Shutterstock; p33t ESB Professional/Shutterstock; p33ctl Monkey Business Images/Shutterstock; p33ctr Popova Valeriya/Shutterstock; p33cbl Supermao/ Shutterstock; p33cbr Joshua Resnick/Shutterstock; p33bl Otsphoto/Shutterstock; p33br Monkey Business Images/Shutterstock; p34rt Anna_Huchak/Shutterstock; p34rc Kiorio/Shutterstock; p34rb Sai Tha/ Shutterstock; p39l Pavel Bredikhin/Shutterstock; p39r Wildlife GmbH/Alamy Stock Photo; p41l Emmy Liana/ Shutterstock; p41r Susumu Nishinaga/Science Photo Library; p43tl MasterQ/Shutterstock; p43tr Boonchuay 1970/Shutterstock; p43bl Ethan Daniels/Shutterstock; p43br Ray49/Shutterstock; p45 HelloSSTK/ Shutterstock; p58tl Sergey Nivens/Shutterstock; p58tc Imtmphoto/Shutterstock; p58tr Budimir Jevtic/ Shutterstock; p58bl Nopphon_1987/Shutterstock; p58bc Nugraha Defri/Shutterstock; p58br Africa Studio/ Shutterstock; p59t Juice Flair/Shutterstock; p59cl Bondart Photography/Shutterstock; p59c Aya Images/ Shutterstock; p59r Michaeljung/Shutterstock; p59bl Dmitry Markov152/Shutterstock; p59bc Imtmphoto/ Shutterstock; p59br Sutiwat Jutiamornloes/Shutterstock; p66 Tim Latham/Shutterstock; p67t Shah Rohani/ Shutterstock; p68 Martial Red/Shutterstock; p82 Granger – Historical Picture Archive/Alamy Stock Photo; p86tl Bigandt.com/Shutterstock; p86tc Maxisport/Shutterstock; p86tr Have a nice day Photo/Shutterstock; p86cl Rickshu/Shutterstock; p86cr Alexander Tolstykh/Shutterstock; p86bl Salvador Aznar/Shutterstock; p86br Gargonia/Shutterstock; p87t Studio Romantic/Shutterstock; p87cl GNT Studio/Shutterstock; p87c Vovidzha/Shutterstock; p87cr Dejan Dundjerski/Shutterstock; p87bl Cirkoglu/Shutterstock; p87br NassornSnitwong/Shutterstock; p97bl Uniqueton/Shutterstock; p97br Donot6_Studio/Shutterstock; p100bl Sportpoint/Shutterstock; p100br Milatas/Shutterstock; p107t Blackguitar1/Shutterstock; p107b Dew_gdragon/Shutterstock; p108 Maks Narodenko/Shutterstock; p110t Pissamai Boonkane/ Shutterstock; p111b LuckyStep/Shutterstock; p112c Gara pro/Shutterstock; p116tl EncikAn/Shutterstock; p116tr Jason Patrick Ross/Shutterstock; p116cl Creeping Things/Shutterstock; p116cr Traveller70/

Shutterstock; p116b Cktravels.com/Shutterstock; p117t Motortion Films/Shutterstock; p117cl Dejan Dundjerski/Shutterstock; p117cr Pressmaster/Shutterstock; p117bl Robert Kneschke/Shutterstock; p117bcl Salmonnegrostock/Shutterstock; p117bcr Gina Smith/Shutterstock; p117br Ground Picture/Shutterstock; p120t Desdemona72/Shutterstock; p120bl Samib123/Shutterstock; p121t Maratr/Shutterstock; p122 BlueRingMedia/Shutterstock; p125 BlueRingMedia/Shutterstock; p128tl Ningaloo.gg/Shutterstock; p128tr Pravruti/Shutterstock; p132tl Bryangww/Shutterstock; p132tr Ondrej Prosicky/Shutterstock; p134t Samib123/Shutterstock; p140tl Luscofusco/Shutterstock; p140tc Akkharat Jarusilawong/Shutterstock; 140tr Sfocato/Shutterstock; p140bl Sylv1rob1/Shutterstock; 140br Airdone/Shutterstock; p141t Zoka74/Shutterstock; p141cl SeventyFour/Shutterstock; p141ctr Photographee.eu/Shutterstock; p141cbr Cavan-Images/Shutterstock; p141bl DC Studio/Shutterstock; p141br Vlad Teodor/Shutterstock; p148 William Booth/Shutterstock; p149 Duncan Andison/Shutterstock; p151t Vaganundo_Che/Shutterstock; p152 IanRedding/Shutterstock; p153 Iprostocks/Shutterstock; p157t Bell Ka Pang/Shutterstock; p157ct Steve Buckley/Shutterstock; p157cb Vadim Zakharishchev/Shutterstock; p157b Dermatology11/Shutterstock; p160tl Richard Griffin/Shutterstock; p160tr Vilor/Shutterstock; p160bl Anne Punch/Shutterstock; p160br Srinivasan Clicks/Shutterstock; p165b Gala_Kan/Shutterstock; p168tl Evgeny Karandaev/Shutterstock; p168tc and p168tr New Africa/Shutterstock; p168b SJ Travel Photo and Video/Shutterstock; p169t Danae Abreu/Shutterstock; p169cl Rainer Lesniewski/Shutterstock; p169c Olena Yakobchuk/Shutterstock; p169cr Peterschreiber.media/Shutterstock; p169b Suwit Ngaokaew/Shutterstock; p173 Africa Studio/Shutterstock; p175b OB production/Shutterstock; p176t Petr Malyshev/Shutterstock; p176b V74/Shutterstock; p177 Jaromir Chalabala/Shutterstock; p179t RHJPhotos/Shutterstock; p179c Mia Garrett/Shutterstock; p180t Pukao/Shutterstock; 180c TakumiRL/Shutterstock; p180b Phetchanat Phonchan/Shutterstock; p181c HANA/Shutterstock; p181b Usk75/Shutterstock; p182 Studiovin/Shutterstock; p184 BlueRingMedia/Shutterstock; p186 Obielisa/Shutterstock; p187t Vins Contributor/Shutterstock; p187b Peter Hermes Furian/Shutterstock; p190t Olga Popova/Shutterstock; p190bl Shanti May/Shutterstock; p190br Nuu_jeed/Shutterstock; p191t Bits and Splits/Shutterstock; p191cl Aleksandar Malivuk/Shutterstock; p191cr Opsorman/Shutterstock; p191bl George Rudy/Shutterstock; p191br Gorodenkoff/Shutterstock; p194b Charles D. Winters/Science Photo Library; p196b Monkey Business Images/Shutterstock; p200 Lukas Jojda/Shutterstock; p201 VladKK/Shutterstock; p207 Flower Studio/Shutterstock; p210tl Dmitrii Kokorev/Shutterstock; p210tr Eszter Virt/Shutterstock; p210bl Lorena Fernandez/Shutterstock; p210br Phattipol/Shutterstock; p211t N_Sakarin/Shutterstock; p211cl Africa Studio/Shutterstock; p211cr Gorodenkoff/Shutterstock; p211c Friends Stock/Shutterstock; p211b Adwo/Shutterstock; p213t Elchin Javadov/Shutterstock; p213c Voyagerix/Shutterstock; p213b Harold Diaz Lara/Shutterstock; p214tl Charles D. Winters/Science Photo Library; p214tc Rvkamalovgmail.com/Shutterstock; p214tr Gayvoronskaya_Yana/Shutterstock; p219 Sergey Denisenko/Shutterstock; p221b Yes058 Montree Nanta/Shutterstock; p224 Charles D. Winters/Science Photo Library; p228t R.Classen/Shutterstock; p228c Moving Moment/Shutterstock; p228b Natalielme/Shutterstock; p229t Rido/Shutterstock; p229cl Singkham/Shutterstock; p229cr Magic Orb Studio/Shutterstock; p229bl Kapuska/Shutterstock; p229bc Unkas Photo/Shutterstock; p229br Lopolo/Shutterstock; p234t Benevolente82/Shutterstock; p234b Ggw/Shutterstock; p237 Leslie Garland Picture Library/Alamy Stock Photo; p238 Rabbitmindphoto/Shutterstock; p240t Mr Doomits/Shutterstock; p240b Levent Konuk/Shutterstock; p241 J_hphotography/Shutterstock; p243t Pavlo Lys/Shutterstock; p245t Ihor Matsiievskyi/Shutterstock; p245c Ihor Matsiievskyi/Shutterstock; p245b Rabbitmindphoto/Shutterstock; p246 Sciencephotos/Alamy Stock Photo; p247l Oleksandr Kostiuchenko/Shutterstock; p247r Pukach/Shutterstock; p248t Barbara Eads/Shutterstock; p249t Science Photo Library; p249b Rattiya Thongdumhyu/Shutterstock; p254tl Roy Palmer/Shutterstock; p254tr Elena Elisseeva/Shutterstock; p254bl Marco Lazzarini/Shutterstock; p254br Peter Sobolev/Shutterstock; p255t Gorodenkoff/Shutterstock; p255cl zWavebreakmedia/Shutterstock; p255c Bartu/Shutterstock; p255cr Fotohunter/Shutterstock; p255bl MarinaGrigorivna/Shutterstock; p255br Gorodenkoff/Shutterstock; p257b Aisyaqilumaranas/Shutterstock; p258tl Para1266/Shutterstock; p258tc Jiri Vaclavek/Shutterstock; p258tr Jiri Vaclavek/Shutterstock; p258bl Dorling Kindersley/UIG/Science Photo Library; p258bc Dorling Kindersley/UIG/Science Photo Library; p258br Dorling Kindersley/UIG/Science Photo Library; p261l Alexious Pappas/Shutterstock; p261r PhotoWin1/Shutterstock; p262 VladaKela/Shutterstock; p263 Aisyaqilumaranas/Shutterstock; p265t Panayot Savov/Shutterstock; p265c Nordroden/Shutterstock; p265b J_hphotography/Shutterstock; p266 Choze-KL/Shutterstock; p272t Liga_sveta/Shutterstock; p272c Henry Sudarman/Shutterstock; p272b Asia_K/Shutterstock; p273t Zaferkizilkaya/Shutterstock; p273cl M_Agency/

Shutterstock; p273cr Paleontologist natural/Shutterstock; p273c Volodmoyr Maksymchuk/Shutterstock; p273b Artur_Sarkisyan/Shutterstock; p277 Guentermanaus/Shutterstock; p279 Warpaint/Shutterstock; p281b TR_Studio/Shutterstock; p289 Soonthorn Wongsaita/Shutterstock; p294t Soumen82hazra/ Shutterstock; p294b ESB Professional/Shutterstock; p295t Gorodenkoff/Shutterstock; p295cl Jarek Kilian/ Shutterstock; p295c Benoist/Shutterstock; p295cr Evkaz/Shutterstock; p295bl Terryjking/Shutterstock; p295bc Jgolby/Shutterstock; p295br Prasit Rodphan/Alamy Stock Photo; p297ct Alina Reynbakh/ Shutterstock; p300t Mauricio Graiki/Shutterstock; p300b Photoschmidt/Shutterstock; p301ct Art Studio G/ Shutterstock; p301c Nerthuz/Shutterstock; p302b Tuaindeed/Shutterstock; p307tl Salomon; p307bl IM_ photo/Shutterstock; p307tr B.Stefanov/Shutterstock; p307br Salomon; p309b Edward Haylan/Shutterstock; p310 Fouad A. Saad/Shutterstock; p311t Jenson/Shutterstock; p311b TheBlackRhino/Shutterstock; p312t Haryigit/Shutterstock; p312b Ramon Espelt Photography/Shutterstock; p313t Freevideophotoagency/ Shutterstock; p314 Minigirov Yuriy/Shutterstock; p320tl Romeovip_md/Shutterstock; p320tc Olaf Speier/Shutterstock; p320tr ThamKC/Shutterstock; p320cl Goodbishop/Shutterstock; p320cr Goffkein .pro/Shutterstock; p320bl Andrewshots/Shutterstock; p320br Richard Schramm/Shutterstock; p321t BBStudioPhoto/Shutterstock; p321cl Dario Sabljak/Shutterstock; p321cr MontonTiemrak/ Shutterstock; p321bl Bangkok Click Studio/Shutterstock; p321bc NDAB Creativity/Shutterstock; p321br Bloomberg/Contributor/Getty Images; p322b Mteamorworks/Shutterstock; p323t Jordan Tan/ Shutterstock; p324 Lolostock/Shutterstock; p325 Tim Latham/Shutterstock; p326t Soloviova Liudmyla/ Shutterstock; p326b Zyabich/Shutterstock; p327b Vector street/Shutterstock; p328 Fertas/Shutterstock; p329t Dory/Alamy Stock Photo; p331t Honeybee49/Shutterstock; p331c Oleg Totskyi/Shutterstock; p331b Vertyr/Shutterstock; p336t Kelly VanDellen/Shutterstock; p336bl Yaraslau Mikheyeu/Shutterstock; p336bc Patchamol Jensatienwong/Shutterstock; p336br Kdshutterman/Shutterstock; p337t Gorodenkoff/ Shutterstock; p337ctr Oleksandr Nagaiets/Shutterstock; p337c Simon Turner/Alamy Stock Photo; p337cbr Rawpixel.com/Shutterstock; p337b Andrey_Popov/Shutterstock; p340c Sruilk/Shutterstock; p346t Wsf-s/Shutterstock; p347t Los_jan/Shutterstock; p347c Slavun/Shutterstock; p347b Robert Nyholm/ Shutterstock; p348t Udaix/Shutterstock; p349c DMG Vision/Shutterstock; p350t Russell Kightley/Science Photo Library; p350c Kim Christensen/Alamy Stock Photo; p351b Kuki Ladron de Guevara/Shutterstock; p353t Peter Hermes Furian/Shutterstock; p353b Fouad A. Saad/Shutterstock; p354b Fouad A. Saad/ Shutterstock; p358t Slavun/Shutterstock; p359t Roman Zaiets/Shutterstock; p359cl Aleksandar Karanov/ Shutterstock; p359ctr ALPA Prod/Shutterstock; p359cbr Phovoir/Shutterstock; p359bl Valery Zotev/ Shutterstock; p359br Gorodenkoff/Shutterstock; p360 Jasmina Andonova/Shutterstock; p362 Jasmina Andonova/Shutterstock; p363t Ntv/Shutterstock; p363b Nordroden/Shutterstock; p366t Patricia F. Carvalho/ Shutterstock; p370t Peter An/Shutterstock; p376t Tuomo V/Shutterstock; p376bl Kabachki.photo/ Shutterstock; p376br Pixel-Shot/Shutterstock; p377t Agefotostock/Alamy Stock Photo; p377cl Corepics VOF/Shutterstock; p377c Sabena Jane Blackbird/Alamy Stock Photo; p377cr Dmytro Sidelnikov/Alamy Stock Photo; p377bl Howard Sayer/Alamy Stock Photo; p377br ESB Professional/Shutterstock; p379bl Itechno/Shutterstock; p381 Evgenii mitroshin/Shutterstock; p382 R.classen/Shutterstock; p383 Barbara Rus/Shutterstock; p384 Maximillian cabinet/Shutterstock; p390t NASA/ESA/Hubble; p390c NASA/ESA/Hubble; p390b Walnut Bird/Shutterstock; p391t Gorodenkoff/Shutterstock; p391ctr Gorodenkoff/Shutterstock; p391ctl NDAB Creativity/Shutterstock; p391cbr REDPIXEL.PL/ Shutterstock; p391cbl Leo Morgan/Shutterstock; p391b Rido/Shutterstock; p392c Renklerin Kafasi/ Shutterstock; p392b Withan Tor/Shutterstock; p393t Triff/Shutterstock; p393c NASA; p395t Joshimerbin/ Shutterstock; p396 GrandeDuc/Shutterstock; p397t Tishomir/Shutterstock; p397b BlueRingMedia/ Shutterstock; p398t Abriendomundo/Shutterstock; p398b Chainfoto24/Shutterstock; p399 NASA/Bill Dunford.